OT 35
Operator Theory: Advances and Applications
Vol. 35

Birkhäuser Verlag
Basel · Boston · Berlin

Contributions to Operator Theory and its Applications

Proceedings of the Conference on Operator Theory and Functional Analysis,
Mesa, Arizona, June 11–14, 1987

Edited by

I. Gohberg
J.W. Helton
L. Rodman

1988

Birkhäuser Verlag
Basel · Boston · Berlin

Editors' addresses:

I. Gohberg
School of Math. Sciences
Raymond and Beverly Sackler
Faculty of Exact Sciences
Tel Aviv University
Ramat Aviv, Israel

J.W. Helton
Department of Mathematics
University of California
San Diego
La Jolla, CA 92093 USA

L. Rodman
Department of Mathematics
Arizona State University
Tempe, AZ 85287 USA

CIP-Titelaufnahme der Deutschen Bibliothek

Contributions to operator theory and its applications :
proceedings of the Conference on Operator Theory and
Functional Analysis, Mesa, Arizona, June 11 – 14, 1987 / ed. by
I. Gohberg ... – Basel ; Boston ; Berlin : Birkhäuser, 1988
(Operator theory ; Vol. 35)
ISBN 3–7643–2221–7 (Basel ...) Pb.
ISBN 0–8176–2221–7 (Boston) Pb.
NE: Gochberg, Izrail' [Hrsg.]; Conference on Operator Theory and
Functional Analysis <1987, Mesa, Ariz.> ; GT

Printed in Germany
ISBN 3-7643-2221-7
ISBN 0-8176-2221-7

CB-SHK SCIMON

Table of Contents

EDITORIAL INTRODUCTION

This volume contains the proceedings of the conference on Operator Theory and Functional Analysis held at the Hilton Pavilion, Mesa, Arizona, June 11 - 14, 1987. The conference, which preceded the international symposium on Mathematical Theory of Networks and Systems (Phoenix, Arizona, June 15 - 19, 1987) was the fourth of its kind; the previous three were held at Santa Monica, California (1981), Rehovot, Israel (1983) and Amsterdam, the Netherlands (1985). The next conference in this series is planned for June 26 - 29, 1989, to be held in Rotterdam.

The lectures presented at the conference reviewed recent advances in operator theory and its applications, with some emphasis on systems theory. They gave a cross-section of the theoretical developments in abstract operator theory as well as in the studies of different concrete classes of operators. Besides systems theory, applications included Toeplitz and Hankel operators, integral and differential equations, function theory, stationary processes, various factorization and interpolation problems and matrix theory.

We gratefully acknowledge the financial support of the National Science Foundation and of the Arizona State University. Special thanks are due to the College of Engineering and Applied Sciences, Graduate College, the Office of Vice-President for Research, and the Department of Mathematics, all of Arizona State University, for providing support. The Department of Mathematics and the Conference Services of Arizona State University provided most valuable administrative assistance.

Operator Theory:
Advances and Applications, Vol. 35

HYPONORMAL PAIRS OF COMMUTING OPERATORS*

Raúl E. Curto, Paul S. Muhly and Jingbo Xia

We analyze the notions of weak and strong joint hyponormality for commuting pairs of operators, with an aim at understanding the gap between hyponormality and subnormality for single operators. We exhibit a commuting pair $\mathbf{T} = (T_1, T_2)$ such that:

(i) $\mathbf{T}$ is weakly hyponormal;
(ii) $\mathbf{T}$ is not strongly hyponormal;
(iii) $T_1^{\ell_1} T_2^{\ell_2}$ is subnormal (all $\ell_1, \ell_2 \geq 0$);
(iv) $T_1 + T_2$ is not subnormal;
(v) $T_1 + T_2$ is power hyponormal; and
(vi) T_1 is unitarily equivalent to T_2.

§1. INTRODUCTION

Let $\mathscr{H}$ be a Hilbert space and let $\mathscr{L}(\mathscr{H})$ be the algebra of bounded operators on $\mathscr{H}$. For $S, T \in \mathscr{L}(\mathscr{H})$ we let $[S,T] := ST - TS$; $[S,T]$ is the *commutator* of S and T. For $n \geq 1$ we let $\mathscr{H}^{(n)}$ denote the orthogonal direct sum of $\mathscr{H}$ with itself n times. Given an n–tuple $\mathbf{T} = (T_1, \ldots, T_n)$ of operators on $\mathscr{H}$, we let $[\mathbf{T}^*, \mathbf{T}] \in \mathscr{L}(\mathscr{H}^{(n)})$ denote the *self–commutator* of $\mathbf{T}$, defined by $[\mathbf{T}^*, \mathbf{T}]_{ij} := [T_j^*, T_i]$ $(1 \leq i,j \leq n)$. For instance, if $n = 2$,

$$[\mathbf{T}^*, \mathbf{T}] = \begin{bmatrix} [T_1^*, T_1] & [T_2^*, T_1] \\ [T_1^*, T_2] & [T_2^*, T_2] \end{bmatrix}.$$

In analogy with the case $n = 1$, we shall say that $\mathbf{T}$ is *strongly hyponormal* (or simply *hyponormal*) if $([\mathbf{T}^*, \mathbf{T}]x, x) \geq 0$ for all $x \in \mathscr{H}^{(n)}$. $\mathbf{T}$ will be called *weakly hypornormal* if

$$LS(\mathbf{T}) := \left\{ \sum_{i=1}^{n} \alpha_i T_i : \alpha = (\alpha_1, \ldots, \alpha_n) \in \mathbb{C}^n \right\}$$

*Research partially supported by the National Science Foundation.

consists entirely of hyponormal operators. These notions (or variations thereof) have been considered by A. Athavale [At], J. Conway and W. Szymanski [CS], D. Xia [X2] and N. Salinas and P. Szeptycki [S]. First, we present a summary of basic facts about joint hyponormality.

Recall that an n–tuple $\mathbf{T} = (T_1,\dots,T_n)$ is said to be *normal* if $\mathbf{T}$ is commuting and each T_i is a normal operator. An n–tuple $\mathbf{S} = (S_1,\dots,S_n)$ is *subnormal* if $\mathbf{S}$ is the restriction of a normal n–tuple to a common invariant subspace; of course, a commuting n–tuple of subnormal operators need not be subnormal.

LEMMA 1.1. ([*At, Proposition 1 and Proposition 2*]) *Consider the following four statements about a commuting n–tuple:*

(i) $\mathbf{T}$ *is normal*

(ii) $\mathbf{T}$ *is subnormal*

(iii) $\mathbf{T}$ *is hyponormal*

(iv) $\mathbf{T}$ *is weakly hyponormal.*

Then (i) $\Rightarrow$ (ii) $\Rightarrow$ (iii) $\Rightarrow$ (iv).

LEMMA 1.2. ([*At, Remark 1*]) *Let* $\mathbf{T}$ *be a n–tuple of operators on* $\mathcal{H}$. *Then* $\mathbf{T}$ *is hyponormal if and only if*

$$\sum_{i=1}^{n} \|T_i x_i\|^2 + 2\mathrm{Re} \sum_{i<j} (T_i x_j, T_j x_i) \geq \left\| \sum_{i=1}^{n} T_i^* x_i \right\|^2$$

(*for all* $x_1,\dots,x_n \in \mathcal{H}$).

LEMMA 1.3. ([*CS, Proposition 2.5*]) *Let* $\mathbf{T} = (T_1,T_2)$ *be a pair of operators on* $\mathcal{H}$. *Then* $\mathbf{T}$ *is weakly hyponormal if and only if*

(i) T_1 *is hyponormal,*

(ii) T_2 is *hyponormal,*

and

(iii) $|([T_2^*,T_1]x,x)|^2 \leq ([T_1^*,T_1]x,x)([T_2^*,T_2]x,x)$

(*for all* $x \in \mathcal{H}$).

LEMMA 1.4. *Let* $\mathbf{T} = (T_1,T_2)$ *be a pair of operators on* $\mathcal{H}$. *Then* $\mathbf{T}$ *is hyponormal if and only if*

(i) T_1 *is hyponormal,*

(ii) T_2 *is hyponormal,*

and

(iii) $|([T_2^*,T_1]y,x|^2 \le ([T_1^*,T_1]x,x)([T_2^*,T_2]y,y)$

(for all $x,y \in \mathcal{H}$*).*

Proof. $[T^*,T] \ge 0 \Longleftrightarrow ([T^*,T]\begin{bmatrix} x \\ ty \end{bmatrix},\begin{bmatrix} x \\ ty \end{bmatrix}) \ge 0$ for all $x,y \in \mathcal{H}$ and all $t \in \mathbb{R}$. Thus,

$$[T^*,T] \ge 0 \Longleftrightarrow ([T_1^*,T_1]x,x) + t^2([T_2^*,T_2]y,y) + 2t\mathrm{Re}([T_2^*,T_1]y,x) \ge 0$$

(for all $x,y \in \mathcal{H}$, $t \in \mathbb{R}$). The result now follows by analyzing the above quadratic function of t. ■

COROLLARY 1.5. *Let* $\mathbf{T} = (T_1,T_2)$ *be a pair of operators on* $\mathcal{H}$. *Then* $\mathbf{T}$ *is hyponormal if and only if* T_1 *and* T_2 *are hyponormal, and*

$$[T_2^*,T_1] = [T_1^*,T_1]^{1/2} D[T_2^*,T_2]^{1/2}$$

for some contraction D.

Proof. Straightforward from Lemma 1.4 (cf. [X1, Lemma 4.4 with its proof]). ■

The following well–known result will be used often in this note.

LEMMA 1.6. *Let* $\mathcal{H} = \mathcal{H}_1 \oplus \mathcal{H}_2$, *and let*

$$A = \begin{bmatrix} A_{11} & A_{12} \\ A_{12}^* & A_{22} \end{bmatrix},$$

with A_{11} *and* A_{22} *self–adjoint, and* A_{11} *invertible. Then*

$$A \ge 0 \Longleftrightarrow A_{12}^*A_{11}^{-1}A_{12} \le A_{22}$$

COROLLARY 1.7. *Let* $\mathbf{T} = (T_1,T_2)$ *be a pair of operators on* $\mathcal{H}$. *Then* $\mathbf{T}$ *is hyponormal if and only if*

$$\begin{bmatrix} I & T_1^* & T_2^* \\ T_1 & T_1^*T_1 & T_2^*T_1 \\ T_2 & T_1^*T_2 & T_2^*T_2 \end{bmatrix} \ge 0$$

Proof. Apply Lemma 1.6 with $A_1 = I$, $A_{12} = (T_1^* \ T_2^*)$ and $A_{22} = \begin{bmatrix} T_1^*T_1 & T_2^*T_1 \\ T_1^*T_2 & T_2^*T_2 \end{bmatrix}$. ■

REMARKS 1.8. (a) Lemmas 1.3 and 1.4 are quite useful when one wants to break weak hyponormality or hyponormality (see Section 2 below).

(b) The implication (hyponormal $\Rightarrow$ weak hyponormal) can be seen to follow easily from

Lemmas 1.3 and 1.4. At the same time, the subtle change in condition (iii) of these lemmas hints that the converse implication should be false. We'll use this circle of ideas to construct our example in the next section.

We can use Lemma 1.6 to give the following interpretation of the Halmos–Bram characterization of subnormality [Br].

PROPOSITION 1.9. *Let* $S \in \mathcal{L}(\mathcal{H})$. *The following are equivalent:*

(i) S *is subnormal*;

(ii) $$\begin{bmatrix} I & S^* & S^{*2} & \cdots & S^{*k} \\ S & S^*S & S^{*2}S & \cdots & S^{*k}S \\ S^2 & S^*S^2 & S^{*2}S^2 & \cdots & S^{*k}S^2 \\ \vdots & \vdots & \vdots & & \vdots \\ S^k & S^*S^k & S^{*2}S^k & \cdots & S^{*k}S^k \end{bmatrix} \geq 0$$

(*all* $k \geq 1$);

(iii) $(I,S,S^2,\dots,S^k)$ *is jointly hyponormal* (*all* $k \geq 1$).

Proposition 1.8 can be extended to several variables as follows.

PROPOSITION 1.10. ([*At, Proposition 4*]) *Let* $\mathbf{T} = (T_1,T_2)$ *be a commuting pair of operators on* $\mathcal{H}$. *Then* $\mathbf{T}$ *is subnormal if and only if* $(I,T_1,T_2,T_1^2,T_1T_2,T_2^2,\dots,T_2^k)$ *is jointly hyponormal for all* $k \geq 1$.

REMARKS 1.11. Proposition 1.9 is very instructive, since it gives a measure of the gap between hyponormality and subnormality. In fact, the latter notion requires all $(k+1)$ by $(k+1)$ matrices in (ii) to be positive, while hyponormality only requires

$\begin{bmatrix} I & S^* \\ S & S^*S \end{bmatrix} \geq 0$. Between those two extremes there lies a whole slew of increasingly stricter conditions, each expressible in terms of joint hyponormality. Rather than staying with n–tuples all of whose coordinates are functions of a single operator (as in Proposition 1.9), we prefer to venture into the more general case of n–tuples with commuting entries. As a first step one ought to be able to understand fully joint hyponormality for commuting pairs, and we pursue that matter in the next section.

To conclude this Introduction, we list some examples of joint hyponormal (weak or strong) pairs.

EXAMPLE 1.12. Let $T \in \mathcal{L}(\mathcal{H})$ be hyponormal. Then (T,T) is hyponormal. However, (T,T^2) need not be weakly hyponormal, even if T is power hyponormal (cf. [F], [Jo] or see our example in Section 2).

EXAMPLE 1.13. Let $\mathbf{T} = (T_1,T_2)$ be a *doubly commuting* pair of operators on $\mathscr{H}$, i.e., $\mathbf{T}$ is commuting and $[T_1^*,T_2] = 0$. Then $\mathbf{T}$ is hyponormal. These are the pairs considered by J. Janas [Ja], M. Chō and A. Dash [CD] and others (see [Cu, Corollary 3.3]).
Therefore, if T_1 and T_2 are hyponormal operators, then $(T_1 \otimes I, I \otimes T_2)$ is jointly hyponormal.
EXAMPLE 1.14.([CS, Proposition 2.5]) If $N,T \in \mathscr{L}(\mathscr{H})$ and N is normal, then (N,T) is hyponormal if and only if (N,T) is weakly hyponormal if and only if T is hyponormal and $NT = TN$.
EXAMPLE 1.15. Let T be a non–normal hyponormal operator on $\mathscr{H}$, and write $T = H + iK$. Consider $X_1 := H \otimes I$, $X_2 := I \otimes H$ and $Y := I \otimes iK$. Then $[X_1,X_2] = 0$, $i[X_1,Y] \geq 0$, $i[X_2,Y] \geq 0$ and $i[X_1,i[X_2,Y]] \geq 0$, so that Y is hyponormal with respect to the pair $\mathbf{X}:=(X_1,X_2)$ in the sense of D. Xia [X2, Section 6]. However, $\mathbf{X} + iY:=(X_1+iY,X_2+iY)$ is not weakly hyponormal: For, since X_1+iY is normal, the weak hyponormality of $\mathbf{X} + iY$ would force $[X_1+iY,X_2+iY] = 0$ (by Example 1.14), which is not the case.
EXAMPLE 1.16. Hyponormality and weak hyponormality are invariant under conjugation by a unitary, under permutation of coordinates, and under translation by scalars. Also, if $\mathbf{T} = (T_1,T_2)$ is hyponormal (resp. weakly hyponormal), and N is a normal operator commuting with T_1 and T_2, then (NT_1,NT_2) is again hyponormal (resp. weakly hyponormal) (cf. [At, Remark 2(f)]).
REMARK 1.17. Building on J. Stampfli's characterization of subnormality for weighted shifts [S], A. Joshi [Jo], after observing that hyponormal weighted shifts (which are automatically power hyponormal) are not necessarily even quadratically hyponormal, obtained sufficient conditions for a weighted shift to be polynomially hyponormal. It is quite interesting to note that his conditions on a weighted shift T in Chapter 1, Theorem 4 assert that $(I,T,T^2,\ldots,T^k)$ is jointly hyponormal (from which it follows that T is polynomially hyponormal of degree at least k). Joshi used those conditions to demonstrate that given k one can always find a wighted shift T such that T is not subnormal but T is polynomially hyponormal of degree at least k. Whether one can choose T independent of k is an open question. Despite considerable effort by many investigators, the following problem has remained unsolved for years.

PROBLEM 1.18. Does there exist an operator T such that T is not subnormal but $p(T)$ is hyponormal for all polynomials p?

We shall have more to say about Problem 1.18 in Section 3.

REMARK 1.19. J. Stampfli gives in [St, p. 178] an example of a non–subnormal hyponormal weighted shift T such that T^n is subnormal for all $n \geq 2$. For that weighted shift, one quickly checks that (T,T^2) is not hyponormal (using Lemma 1.4 with $x:=\varphi_1$ and $y:=\varphi_2$), which explains why T is not subnormal.

§2. THE EXAMPLE

We devote this section to the construction and analysis of our main example. Let $\mathbb{Z}_+^2 := \mathbb{Z}_+ \times \mathbb{Z}_+$ and let $\ell^2(\mathbb{Z}_+^2)$ be the Hilbert space of square summable complex sequences indexed by $\mathbb{Z}_+^2$. For $a > 0$ and $\mathbf{k} = (k_1,k_2) \in \mathbb{Z}_+^2$ we let

$$w_1(\mathbf{k}) := \begin{Bmatrix} 1 & k_1 \geq 1 \text{ or } k_2 = 0 \\ a & k_1 = 0 \text{ and } k_2 \geq 1 \end{Bmatrix}$$

and

$$w_2(\mathbf{k}) := \begin{Bmatrix} 1 & k_1 = 0 \text{ or } k_2 \geq 1 \\ a & k_1 \geq 1 \text{ and } k_2 = 0 \end{Bmatrix}.$$

We now let $\mathbf{T}(a) = (T_1(a),T_2(a))$ denote the pair of 2–variable weighted shifts on $\ell^2(\mathbb{Z}_+^2)$ defined by w_1 and w_2, i.e.,

$$T_i(a)e_{\mathbf{k}} = w_i(\mathbf{k})e_{\mathbf{k}+\epsilon_i}$$

$(i = 1,2; \mathbf{k} \in \mathbb{Z}_+^2)$, where $\{e_{\mathbf{k}}\}_{\mathbf{k}\in\mathbb{Z}_+^2}$ is the canonical orthonormal basis for $\ell^2(\mathbb{Z}_+^2)$ and $\epsilon_1 = (1,0)$, $\epsilon_2 = (0,1)$. $\mathbf{T}(a)$ can be represented by the following diagram

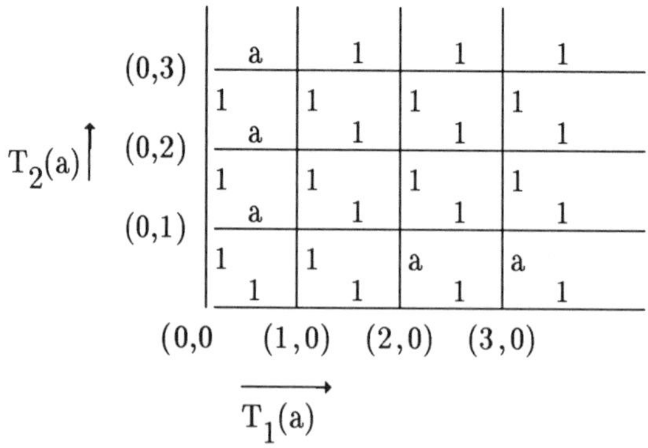

from which one gets at once that $T_1(a)T_2(a) = T_2(a)T_1(a)$. The diagram also allows us to read off the actions of $T_1(a)^*$ and $T_2(a)^*$. For instance, $T_2(a)^*e_{11} = ae_{10}$.

Hyponormality. If $\mathbf{T}(a)$ is hyponormal, we must have

$$|([T_2(a)^*,T_1(a)]e_{01},e_{10})|^2 \le ([T_1(a)^*,T_1(a)]e_{10},e_{10}) \cdot ([T_2(a)^*,T_2(a)]e_{01},e_{01}).$$

Since $[T_i(a)^*,T_i(a)]\epsilon_i = 0$ $(i = 1,2)$, we get

$$|((a^2-1)e_{10},e_{10})|^2 \le 0,$$

or $a = 1$. Thus, $\mathbf{T}(a)$ is hyponormal if and only if $a = 1$, i.e., if and only if $\mathbf{T}(a)$ is the pair of (unweighted) unilateral shifts on $\ell^2(\mathbb{Z}_+^2)$.

Weak Hyponormality. If $\mathbf{T}(a)$ is weakly hyponormal, then

$$|([T_2(a)^*,T_1(a)](e_{01} + e_{10}),\ e_{01} + e_{10})|^2$$
$$\le([T_1(a)^*,T_1(a)](e_{01} + e_{10}), e_{01} + e_{10}) \cdot ([T_2(a)^*,T_2(a)](e_{01} + e_{10}), e_{01} + e_{10}),$$

from which it follows at once that

$$(a^2 - 1)^2 \le a^4,$$

or $a \ge \frac{\sqrt{2}}{2}$. We shall see now that $\mathbf{T}(a)$ is indeed weakly hyponormal whenever $\frac{\sqrt{2}}{2} \le a \le 1$. Relative to the decomposition

$$\ell^2(\mathbb{Z}_+^2) = \ell^2(\mathbb{Z}_+ \times \{0\}) \oplus \ell^2(\mathbb{Z}_+ \times \{1\}) \oplus \ell^2(\mathbb{Z}_+ \times \{2\}) \oplus \dots,$$

we have

$$T_1 = S \oplus S_a \oplus S_a \oplus \dots$$

(where S is the unilateral shift on $\ell^2(\mathbb{Z}_+)$ and S_a is a weighted shift on $\ell^2(\mathbb{Z}_+)$ with weights $a,1,1,\ldots$), and

$$T_2 = \begin{bmatrix} 0 & 0 & 0 & 0 & \\ A & 0 & 0 & 0 & \\ 0 & I & 0 & 0 & \\ 0 & 0 & I & 0 & \ddots \\ & & & & \ddots \end{bmatrix}$$

(where A is the diagonal operator on $\ell^2(\mathbb{Z}_+)$ with diagonal entries $1,a,a,\ldots$). For $\alpha_1,\alpha_2 \in \mathbb{C}$, we thus get

$$\alpha_1 T_1(a) + \alpha_2 T_2(a) = \left[\begin{array}{c|cc} \alpha_1 S & 0 & 0 \\ \hline \alpha_2 A & \alpha_1 S_a & 0 \\ 0 & \alpha_2 & \alpha_1 S_a \\ & & & \ddots \end{array}\right] =: \left[\begin{array}{c|c} B & O \\ \hline C & D \end{array}\right].$$

Then

$$[(\alpha_1 T_1(a) + \alpha_2 T_2(a))^*, \alpha_1 T_1(a) + \alpha_2 T_2(a)]$$

$$= \begin{bmatrix} [B^*, B] + C^*C & C^*D - BC \\ D^*C - CB^* & [D^*, D] - CC^* \end{bmatrix},$$

and therefore, by using Lemma 1.6, it suffices to see that

(1) $[B^*,B] + C^*C$ is invertible

and

(2) $(D^*C - CB^*)([B^*,B] + C^*C)^{-1}(C^*D - BC^*) \le [D^*,D] - CC^*$.

We'll calculate explicitly the inverse of $[B^*,B] + C^*C$. Since $[B^*,B] = |\alpha_1|^2[S^*,S]$ and $C^*C = |\alpha_2|^2 A^*A$, we get

$$[B^*,B] + C^*C = \begin{bmatrix} |\alpha_1|^2 + |\alpha_2|^2 & & & \\ & |\alpha_2|^2 a^2 & & \\ & & |\alpha_2|^2 a^2 & \\ & & & \ddots \end{bmatrix}.$$

Observe now that S_a is subnormal (in fact, $\|S_a^k e_0\|^2 = a^2$ (all $k \ge 0$), so that the Berger measure associated to S_a is given by $\mu(\{0\}) = 1 - a^2$ and $\mu(\{1\}) = a^2$), and thus $T_1(a)$ is subnormal (all $a \in (0,1]$). Without loss of generality, we can therefore assume $\alpha_2 \ne 0$. Then

$$E = ([B^*,B] + C^*C)^{-1} = \begin{bmatrix} \frac{1}{|\alpha_1|^2 + |\alpha_2|^2} & & & \\ & \frac{1}{|\alpha_2|^2 a^2} & & \\ & & \frac{}{|\alpha_2|^2 a^2} & \\ & & & \ddots \end{bmatrix}.$$

Now,

$$D^*C - CB^* = \begin{bmatrix} \bar{\alpha}_1\alpha_2(S_a^*A - AS^*) \\ 0 \\ 0 \\ \vdots \end{bmatrix},$$

so that

$$(D^*C - CB^*)E(C^*D - BC^*) = |\alpha_1|^2|\alpha_2|^2(S_a^*A - AS^*)E(AS_a - SA) \oplus 0 \oplus 0 \oplus \ldots$$

On the other hand,

$$[D^*,D] - CC^* = (|\alpha_1|^2[S_a^*,S_a] + |\alpha_2|^2(I-A^2)) \oplus |\alpha_1|^2[S_a^*,S_a] \oplus |\alpha_1|^2[S_a^*,S_a] \oplus \ldots;$$

we must therefore show that

$$|\alpha_1|^2[S_a^*,S_a\} + |\alpha_2|^2(I-A^2) \geq |\alpha_1|^2|\alpha_2|^2(S_a^*A - AS^*)E(AS_a - SA)$$

for all $\alpha_1,\alpha_2 \in \mathbb{C}$ and all $\frac{\sqrt{2}}{2} \leq a \leq 1$. Note that

$AS_a = aS_a$ and $AS = aS$,

so that $S_a^*A - AS^* = \begin{bmatrix} 0 & a^2\text{-}1 & 0 & \\ 0 & 0 & 0 & \\ & & & \ddots \end{bmatrix}$.

Thus,

$$(S_a^*A - AS^*)E(S_a^*A - AS^*)^* = \begin{bmatrix} \frac{(a^2-1)^2}{|\alpha_2|^2a^2} & 0 & \\ 0 & 0 & \\ & & \ddots \end{bmatrix}.$$

(The last two matrices, as well as the matrix of E, are with respect to the canonical decomposition of $\ell^2(\mathbb{Z}_+)$.)

Since

$$|\alpha_1|^2[S_a^*,S_a] + |\alpha_2|^2(I-A^2)$$

$$= \begin{bmatrix} |\alpha_1|^2a^2 & & & \\ & |\alpha_1|^2(1-a^2) + |\alpha_2|^2(1-a^2) & & \\ & & |\alpha_2|^2(1-a^2) & \\ & & & \ddots \end{bmatrix},$$

we are left to prove that

$$|\alpha_1|^2 a^2 \ge \frac{|\alpha_1|^2 (a^2-1)^2}{a^2},$$

or
$$a^4 \ge (a^2-1)^2,$$

which certainly holds for $a \in \left[\frac{\sqrt{2}}{2}, 1\right]$.

PROPOSITION 2.1.

(i) $T(a)$ *is hypynormal iff* $a = 1$.

(ii) $T(a)$ *is weakly hyponormal iff* $\frac{\sqrt{2}}{2} \le a \le 1$.

REMARK 2.2. $T(a)$ is the first example of a weakly hyponormal pair which is not hyponormal (see [At, Remark 6]).

Subnormality. For $\boldsymbol{\ell} = (\ell_1, \ell_2) \in \mathbb{Z}_+^2$, we shall see now that $T(a)^{\boldsymbol{\ell}} := T_1(a)^{\ell_1} T_2(a)^{\ell_2}$ is subnormal for all $a \le 1$. First, we need some preliminaries.

LEMMA 2.3. (*Agler [Ag, Theorems 3.2 and 3.3]*) *Let* $T \in \mathcal{L}(\mathcal{H})$. *Then* T *is subnormal if and only if*

$$\sum_{k=0}^{M} (-1)^k \begin{bmatrix} M \\ k \end{bmatrix} T^{*k} T^k \ge 0$$

for all $M \ge 1$. *Equivalently,* T *is subnormal if and only if*

$$\sum_{k=0}^{M} (-1)^k \begin{bmatrix} M \\ k \end{bmatrix} ||T^k x||^2 \ge 0$$

for all $M \ge 1$ *and all* $x \in \mathcal{H}$.

For $\mathbf{m} \in \mathbb{Z}_+^2$ we shall let $\beta(\mathbf{m})$ denote the product of the weights when one follows a monotone path from $(0,0)$ to $\mathbf{m}$, e.g.,

$$\beta(\mathbf{m}) = w_1(0,0) \cdot \ldots \cdot w_1(m_1-1,0) w_2(m_1,0) \cdot \ldots \cdot w_2(m_1,m_2-1).$$

In our case, it is clear that

$$\beta(\mathbf{m}) = \begin{cases} a & m_1 \ge 1 \text{ and } m_2 \ge 1 \\ 1 & \text{otherwise} \end{cases}$$

PROPOSITION 2.4. *For* $\boldsymbol{\ell} \in \mathbb{Z}_+^2$, $T(a)^{\boldsymbol{\ell}}$ *is subnormal* (*all* $a \le 1$).

Proof. Since $T_1(a)$ is subnormal and $T_2(a)$ is clearly unitarily equivalent to $T_1(a)$, we may assume $\ell_1 \ge 1$, $\ell_2 \ge 1$. Let $x = \sum_{\mathbf{m}} x_{\mathbf{m}} e_{\mathbf{m}} \in \ell^2(\mathbb{Z}_+^2)$. For $k \in \mathbb{Z}_+$,

$$(T(a)^{\ell})^k x = \sum_m x_m \frac{\beta(m+k\ell)}{\beta(m)} e_{m+k\ell}.$$

Therefore,

$$\|(T(a)^{\ell})^k x\|^2 = \sum_m |x_m|^2 \frac{\beta(m+k\ell)^2}{\beta(m)^2},$$

and

$$\sum_{k=0}^{M} (-1)^k \begin{bmatrix} M \\ k \end{bmatrix} \|T(a)^{\ell})^k x\|^2 = \sum_m \frac{|x_m|^2}{\beta(m)^2} \sum_{k=0}^{M} (-1)^k \begin{bmatrix} M \\ k \end{bmatrix} \beta(m+k\ell\zeta)^2$$

$$= \sum_m \frac{|x_m|^2}{\beta(m)^2} \left[\beta(m^2) + \sum_{k=1}^{M} (-1)^k \begin{bmatrix} M \\ k \end{bmatrix} \beta(m+k\ell)^2\right]$$

$$= \sum_m \frac{|x_m|^2}{\beta(m)^2} \left[\beta(m)^2 + a^2(-1)\right]$$

$$= \sum_m |x_m|^2 - a^2 \sum_m \frac{|x_m|^2}{\beta(m)^2} = (1-a^2) \sum_{\{m:m_1=0 \text{ or } m_2=0\}} |x_m|^2$$

$\geq 0.$ ∎

Our next goal is to show that $T_1(a) + T_2(a)$ is not subnormal. We shall use Agler's criterion again. Since $\|T_1(a) + T_2(a)\| = 2$, we shall look at $\frac{T_1(a) + T_2(a)}{2}$.

PROPOSITION 2.5. $\frac{T_1(a) + T_2(a)}{2}$ *is* <u>*not*</u> *subnormal, unless* $a = 1$.

<u>Proof</u>. Consider

$$P_M := \sum_{k=0}^{M} (-1)^k \begin{bmatrix} M \\ k \end{bmatrix} \left\|\left[\frac{T_1(a) + T_2(a)}{2}\right]^k e_{00}\right\|^2.$$

A straightforward calculation reveals that for $k \geq 1$

$$(T_1(a) + T_2(a))^k e_{00} = e_{k0} + e_{0k} + a \sum_{j=1}^{k-1} \begin{bmatrix} k \\ j \end{bmatrix} e_{j,k-j},$$

so that

$$\|(T_1(a) + T_2(a))^k e_{00}\|^2 = 2 + a^2 \sum_{j=1}^{k-1} \binom{k}{j}^2$$

$$= 2 + a^2 \left[\binom{2k}{k} - 2\right], \ (k \geq 1).$$

(For later reference, note that $\|(T_1(1) + T_2(1)^k e_{00}\|^2 = \binom{2k}{k}$.)

Therefore,

$$P_M = 1 + \sum_{k=0}^{M} (-1)^k \binom{M}{k} \left[\frac{2(1-a^2)}{2^{2k}} + \frac{a^2}{2^{2k}} \binom{2k}{k}\right].$$

Now,

$$\sum_{k=1}^{M} (-1)^k \binom{M}{k} 2^{-2k} = \left(\frac{3}{4}\right)^M - 1 \longrightarrow -1 (M \longrightarrow \infty),$$

and

$$\sum_{k=1}^{M} (-1)^k \binom{M}{k} \binom{2k}{k} 2^{-2k} = -1 + \int_0^2 \left[1 - \frac{t^2}{4}\right]^M d\mu(t)$$

$$\longrightarrow -1 + \mu(\{0\}) = -1,$$

where μ is the Berger measure associated to $T_1(1) + T_2(1)$ (this is the operator of multiplication by $z_1 + z_2$ on $H^2(\mathbb{T} \times \mathbb{T})$).

(Observe that

$$\int_0^2 \left[1 - \frac{t^2}{4}\right]^M d\mu(t) = \sum_{k=0}^{M} (-1)^k \binom{M}{k} 2^{-2k} \int_0^2 t^{2k} d\mu(t)$$

and $\int_0^2 t^{2k} d\mu(t) = \|(T_1(1) + T_2(1))^k e_{00}\|^2 = \binom{2k}{k}$.)

Thus,

$$P_M \longrightarrow 1 - 2(1-a^2) - a^2 = a^2-1, \ (M \longrightarrow \infty).$$

Since P_M must be nonnegative (all M) if $T_1(a) + T_2(a)$ is subnormal, we conclude that $T_1(a) + T_2(a)$ is not subnormal unless $a = 1$. ■

Power Hyponormality. Our final task in this section is to prove that

$T(a) := T_1(a) + T_2(a)$ is power hyponormal $\left(\frac{\sqrt{2}}{2} \leq a \leq 1\right)$.

PROPOSITION 2.6. *For* $\frac{\sqrt{2}}{2} \le a \le 1$ *and* $\ell \ge 1$, $T(a)^\ell$ *is hyponormal.*

Proof. For $k \ge 0$ let

$$\ell^2(\mathbb{Z}_+^2)_k := \vee\{e_{0,k}, e_{1,k-1}, \dots, e_{k,0}\}$$

($\ell^2(\mathbb{Z}_+^2)_k$ is the homogeneous subspace of degree k); then $\ell^2(\mathbb{Z}_+^2) = \bigoplus_{k=0}^{\infty} \ell^2(\mathbb{Z}_+^2)_k$. Observe that $T(a)^\ell$ maps $\ell^2(\mathbb{Z}_+^2)_k$ into $\ell^2(\mathbb{Z}_+^2)_{k+\ell}$ (all $k,\ell \ge 0$) and that, for $k \ge \ell$, $T(a)^{*\ell}$ maps $\ell^2(\mathbb{Z}_+^2)_k$ into $\ell^2(\mathbb{Z}_+^2)_{k-\ell}$. It is obvious, therefore, that in order to prove the Proposition, it suffices to establish that

$$\|T(a)^\ell x\| \ge \|T(a)^{*\ell} x\|$$

for all $x \in \ell^2(\mathbb{Z}_+^2)_k$ $(k \ge \ell)$.

Given $x \in \ell^2(\mathbb{Z}_+^2)_k$, write $x = \sum_{i=0}^{k} x_i e_{i,k-i}$.

Assume first $k > \ell$. Then

$$\begin{aligned}
\|T(a)^\ell x\|^2 \ge\ & |T(a)^\ell x, e_{0,k+\ell})|^2 + |(T(a)^\ell x, e_{\ell,k})|^2 \\
& + \sum_{h=1}^{k-\ell-1} |(T(a)^\ell x, e_{\ell+h,k-h})|^2 \\
& + |(T(a)^\ell x, e_{k,\ell})|^2 + |(T(a)^\ell x, e_{k+\ell,0}|^2 \\
=\ & |x_0|^2 + |a x_0 + \sum_{j=1}^{\ell} \begin{bmatrix}\ell\\ j\end{bmatrix} x_j|^2 \\
& + \sum_{h=1}^{k-\ell-1} \left| \sum_{i=0}^{\ell} \begin{bmatrix}\ell\\ i\end{bmatrix} x_{h+i} \right|^2 \\
& + \left| \sum_{j=0}^{\ell-1} \begin{bmatrix}\ell\\ j\end{bmatrix} x_{k-\ell+j} + a x_k \right| + |x_k|^2,
\end{aligned}$$

while

$$\|(T(a)^{*\ell}x\|^2 = \sum_{i=0}^{k-\ell} |T(a)^{*\ell}x, e_{i,k-\ell-i}|^2$$

$$= |x_0 + a \sum_{j=1}^{\ell} \binom{\ell}{j} x_j|^2$$

$$+ \sum_{h=1}^{k-\ell-1} |\sum_{i=0}^{\ell} \binom{\ell}{i} x_{h+i}|^2$$

$$+ \left|a \sum_{j=0}^{\ell-1} \binom{\ell}{j} x_{k-\ell+j} + x_k\right|^2.$$

It follows that for $k > \ell$ we have

$$\|T(a)^{\ell}x\|^2 - \|T(a)^{*\ell}x\|^2 \geq \left[|x_0|^2 + |ax_0 + \sum_{j=1}^{\ell} \binom{\ell}{j} x_j|^2\right.$$

$$\left. - |x_0 + a \sum_{j=1}^{\ell} \binom{\ell}{j} x_j|^2\right]$$

$$+ \left[|x_k|^2 + \left|ax_k + \sum_{j=0}^{\ell-1} \binom{\ell}{j} x_{k-\ell+j}\right|^2\right.$$

$$\left. - \left|x_k + a \sum_{j=0}^{\ell-1} \binom{\ell}{j} x_{k-\ell+j}\right|^2\right].$$

Let $y_0 := \sum_{j=1}^{\ell} \binom{\ell}{j} x_j$ and $y_k := \sum_{j=0}^{\ell-1} \binom{\ell}{j} x_{k-\ell+j}$.

Therefore, for $k > \ell$,

$$\|T(a)^{\ell}x\|^2 - \|T(a)^{*\ell}x\|^2 \geq \left[|x_0|^2 + |ax_0 + y_0|^2 - |x_0 + ay_0|^2\right]$$

$$+ \left[|x_k|^2 + |ax_k + y_k|^2 - |x_k + ay_k|^2\right].$$

Now consider the case $k = \ell$.

$$\|T(a)^{\ell}x\|^2 \geq |(T(a)^{\ell}x,e_{0,2\ell}|^2 + |(T(a)^{\ell}x,e_{\ell,\ell})|^2$$

$$+ |(T(a)^{\ell}x,e_{2\ell,0})|^2$$

$$= |x_0|^2 + |ax_0 + \sum_{j=1}^{\ell-1} \begin{bmatrix}\ell\\j\end{bmatrix} x_j + ax_\ell|^2 + |x_\ell|^2,$$

while

$$|(T(a)^{*\ell}x\|^2 = |(T(a)^{*\ell}x,e_{00})|^2$$

$$= |x_0 + a \sum_{j=1}^{\ell-1} \begin{bmatrix}\ell\\j\end{bmatrix} x_j + x_\ell|^2.$$

Thus, for $k = \ell$ we get

$$\|T(a)^{\ell}x\|^2 - \|T(a)^{*\ell}x\|^2 \geq |x_0|^2 + |ax_0 + z + ax_\ell|^2$$

$$+ |x_\ell|^2 - |x_0 + az + x_\ell|^2,$$

where $z := \sum_{j=1}^{\ell-1} \begin{bmatrix}\ell\\j\end{bmatrix} x_j$.

The proof of the Proposition can now be completed by applying the next lemma. ∎

<u>LEMMA 2.7</u>. *Let* $x,y,z,t, \in \mathbb{C}$ *and let* $\frac{\sqrt{2}}{2} \leq a \leq 1$. *Then*

i) $|x|^2 + |ax + y|^2 \geq |x + ay|^2$

and

(ii) $|x|^2 + |t|^2 + |x + z + at|^2 \geq |x + az + t|^2.$

<u>Proof</u>. (i) $|x|^2 + |ax + y|^2 = \left\|\begin{bmatrix}1 & 0\\a & 1\end{bmatrix}\begin{bmatrix}x\\y\end{bmatrix}\right\|^2$

and

$$|x + ay|^2 = \left\|(1 \quad a)\begin{bmatrix}x\\y\end{bmatrix}\right\|^2,$$

so we must check that

$$\begin{bmatrix}1 & a\\0 & 1\end{bmatrix}\begin{bmatrix}1 & 0\\a & 1\end{bmatrix} \geq \begin{bmatrix}1\\a\end{bmatrix}(1 \quad a),$$

or

$$\begin{bmatrix} 1+a^2 & a \\ a & 1 \end{bmatrix} \geq \begin{bmatrix} 1 & a \\ a & a^2 \end{bmatrix},$$

which is true if $a \leq 1$.

(ii) $|x|^2 + |t|^2 + |ax + z + at|^2 = \left\| \begin{bmatrix} 1 & 0 & 0 \\ a & 1 & a \\ 0 & 0 & 1 \end{bmatrix} \begin{bmatrix} x \\ z \\ t \end{bmatrix} \right\|^2$

and

$$|x + az + t|^2 = \|(1 \;\; a \;\; 1) \begin{bmatrix} x \\ z \\ t \end{bmatrix}\|^2,$$

so we must check that

$$\begin{bmatrix} 1 & a & 0 \\ 0 & 1 & 0 \\ 0 & a & 1 \end{bmatrix} \begin{bmatrix} 1 & 0 & 0 \\ a & 1 & a \\ 0 & 0 & 1 \end{bmatrix} \geq \begin{bmatrix} 1 \\ a \\ 1 \end{bmatrix} (1 \;\; a \;\; 1),$$

or $$\begin{bmatrix} 1+a^2 & a & a^2 \\ a & 1 & a \\ a^2 & a & 1+a^2 \end{bmatrix} \geq \begin{bmatrix} 1 & a & 1 \\ a & a^2 & a \\ 1 & a & 1 \end{bmatrix},$$

or $$\begin{bmatrix} a^2 & 0 & a^2-1 \\ 0 & 1-a^2 & 0 \\ a^2-1 & 0 & a^2 \end{bmatrix} \geq 0.$$

Using Lemma 1.6, we must then verify that

$$\begin{bmatrix} 1-a^2 & 0 \\ 0 & a^2 \end{bmatrix} \geq \frac{1}{a^2} \begin{bmatrix} 0 & 0 \\ 0 & (a^2-1)^2 \end{bmatrix},$$

or $a^4 \geq (a^2-1)^2$,

which is true if $a \geq \frac{\sqrt{2}}{2}$. ∎

§3. CONCLUDING REMARKS AND OPEN PROBLEMS

Polynomial Hyponormality of $T(a)$

A. Lubin, M. Abrahamse and others have given examples of commuting pairs of subnormal operators which do not lift, i.e., which are not subnormal (see [Lu1], [Lu2], [Lu3], [Lu4], [Ab]. The typical proof of non–subnormality goes as follows: Once the pair $\mathbf{T} = (T_1, T_2)$ has been constructed, one proceeds to verify that $T_1 + T_2$ is not hyponormal, and therefore $\mathbf{T}$ is not subnormal (if $\mathbf{T}$ had a normal extension then $p(T)$ would be subnormal for all $p \in \mathbb{C}[z]$). Our example in Section 2 goes a bit beyond those previous examples, in that $T_1 + T_2$ is indeed power hyponormal. Although our $T(a)$ is clearly not subnormal (it is not even jointly hyponormal), additional work was required to show that $T_1(a) + T_2(a)$ is not subnormal.

CONJECTURE 3.1. There exists $r < 1$ such that $p(T(a))$ is hyponormal for all $r \leq a \leq 1$ and all $p \in \mathbb{C}[z]$.

There is some evidence that supports the conjecture:

1) Using the argument in the proof of the power hyponormality of $T(a)$ for $\frac{\sqrt{2}}{2} \leq a \leq 1$, we can establish without difficulty that $\|p(T(a))x\| \geq \|p(T(a))^*x\|$ for all $x \in \ell^2(\mathbb{Z}_+^2)_k$ (all $k \geq 0$ and $\frac{\sqrt{2}}{2} \leq a \leq 1$).

2) Since $T(a)\big|_{\ell^2(\mathbb{Z}_+^2) \ominus (\ell^2(\mathbb{Z}_+) \times \{0\})}$ is unitarily equivalent to $S_a \otimes I + I \otimes S$ and $(S_a \otimes I, I \otimes S)$ is a doubly commuting pair of subnormal operators, we see that the restriction of $p(T(a))$ to $\ell^2(\mathbb{Z}_+^2) \ominus (\ell^2(\mathbb{Z}_+) \times \{0\})$ is actually subnormal, for every $p \in \mathbb{C}[z]$ and all $a: 0 < a \leq 1$. Also, the compression of $p(T(a))$ to $\ell^2(\mathbb{Z}_+) \times \{0\}$ is subnormal (all $a: 0 < a \leq 1$ and all $p \in \mathbb{C}[z]$). When considered separately, neither 1) or 2) is very surprising or indicative of the hyponormality of $p(T(a))$. (After all, an ordinary hyponormal weighted shift T satisfies $\|p(T)e_k\| \geq \|p(T)^*e_k\|$ for all $p \in \mathbb{C}[z]$ and all k, where $\{e_k\}$ is the basis that T shifts.) However, the fact that the orthogonal decompositions $\ell^2(\mathbb{Z}_+^2) = \bigoplus_{k=0}^{\infty} \ell^2(\mathbb{Z}_+^2)_k$ and $\ell^2(\mathbb{Z}_+^2) = (\ell^2(\mathbb{Z}_+) \times \{0\}) \oplus (\ell^2(\mathbb{Z}_+) \times \{0\})^\perp$ are "linearly independent" (in a certain sense) is a strong sign that $p(T(a))$ may be hyponormal.

3) The proof of weak hyponormality for $T(a)$ actually shows that

$$T(a) \text{ is weakly hyponormal}$$
$$\Longleftrightarrow T(a) \text{ is hyponormal}$$

(notice how the dependence of $\alpha_1 T_1(a) + \alpha_2 T_2(a)$ on α_1 and α_2 gets washed away in the last few steps of that proof). Our preliminary calculations with polynomials of degree 2 indicate that a similar phenomenon takes place there, i.e., that

$(T_1(a), T_2(a), T_1(a)^2, T_1(a)T_2(a), T_2(a)^2)$ is weakly hyponormal if and only if $T_1(a) + T_2(a) + T_1(a)^2 + T_1(a)T_2(a) + T_2(a)^2$ is hyponormal. For our purposes, however, a weaker statement is of interest, namely, we would like to know if $(T(a), T(a)^2)$ is weakly hyponormal when $T(a) + T(a)^2$ is. If such a statement could be proven for arbitrary powers of $T(a)$, the proof of the conjecture would be reduced to establishing that $T(a) + ... + T(a)^{\ell}$ is hyponormal for all ℓ and for a in $[r,1]$, where $r < 1$ is independent of ℓ.

Restricting oneself to one polynomial per degree is of great importance when making calculations. There is another way to eliminate the consideration of all polynomials. First, one establishes that for each ℓ there exists a number $R(\ell) < 1$ such that $(T(a), ..., T(a)^{\ell})$ is jointly hyponormal for $a \in [R(\ell),1]$, thereby concluding that $p(T(a))$ is hyponormal for all $p \in \mathbb{C}[z]$ with $\deg(p) \leq \ell$ and $a \in [r(\ell),1]$, with $r(\ell) \leq R(\ell)$. Although probably true, this fact would not, in all likelihood, help. Already for $\ell=2$, we have been able to establish that $R(2) \geq \sqrt{\frac{5}{6}}$. Since it's clear that $R(\ell) \longrightarrow 1$ as $\ell \longrightarrow \infty$ (otherwise $T(a)$ would be subnormal for some $a < 1$, by Proposition 1.9), we would need a tight control on $r(\ell)$ in terms of $R(\ell)$ to be able to claim $\sup_{\ell} r(\ell) < 1$.

4) Following a suggestion by W. Wogen we have studied the restriction of $T(a)$ to some cyclic subspaces. For $\mathcal{M} := \bigvee\{T(a)^{\ell}e_{00}:\ell \geq 0\}$, for p of degree 5 or less, and for $a = \frac{\sqrt{2}}{2}$, we can show that $p(T(a))|_{\mathcal{M}}$ is hyponormal. (Observe that $T(a)|_{\mathcal{M}}$ is a weighted shift, so verifying the hyponormality of $p(T(a))|_{\mathcal{M}}$ is non–trivial.) Of course, to check hyponormality of $p(T(a))$ by subspaces one needs to consider all 2–cyclic ones (cyclic subspaces generated by two linearly independent vectors), but the verification above is a step in the right direction. Finally, let us mention, in support of Conjecture 3.1, that at present the major obstacle towards a proof is of a technological nature. A powerful symbolic manipulator, unavailable to us at present, would allow us to carry out a very difficult calculation which is the key to obtain an inductive proof.

<u>Lifting of Commuting Subnormals</u>

Various versions of the following problem have appeared in the literature (see, for instance, [Lu2], [Lu4] and [Ab]).

PROBLEM 3.2. Given a pair $\mathbf{T} = (T_1,T_2)$ of commuting subnormal operators on $\mathcal{H}$, when is it possible to lift $\mathbf{T}$ to a pair $\mathbf{N} = (N_1,N_2)$ of commuting normal operators, i.e., when does there exist a Hilbert space $\mathcal{K} \supset \mathcal{H}$ and two commuting normal operators $N_1,N_2 \in \mathcal{L}(\mathcal{K})$ such that $N_i|_{\mathcal{H}} = T_i$ $(i = 1,2)$. Bram [Br, Theorem 7], Slocinski [Sℓ], Mlak[M] and others have given sufficient conditions for such a lifting to take place. On the other hand, examples have been given of cases where the lifting cannot exist. Based upon the available evidence and the results in those works, it seems plausible to formulate the following conjecture.

CONJECTURE 3.3. Let $\mathbf{T} = (T_1,T_2)$ be a pair of commuting subnormal operators. Then $\mathbf{T}$ lifts to a normal pair if and only if $\mathbf{T}$ is jointly hyponormal.

We claim that joint hyponormality provides the necessary "rigidity" to force the lifting to exist.

Joint Hyponormality à la Putinar

In light of M. Putinar's characterization of hypnormality ([Pu]), one might want to define joint hyponormality as follows:

Let $\mathbf{T} = (T_1,T_2)$ be a commuting pair of operators on $\mathcal{H}$. Assume that there exists an invertible map $V:\mathcal{H} \to \mathcal{K}$ such that $V\mathbf{T}V^{-1} := (VT_1V^{-1},VT_2V^{-1})$ is the restriction of the pair $M_{\mathbf{z}} = (M_{z_1},M_{z_2})$ of multiplication by the coordinate functions on a certain $\mathcal{H}$–valued Sobolev space $W^2(\mathbf{T}) \supseteq \mathcal{K}$.

Obviously, defining a class through its model is awkward; moreover, unraveling commutator properties from such a model seems very hard. However, we have begun work in the opposite direction: using the definition of hyponormality in Section 1, we have obtained partial results towards constructing a model. In a similar vein, we have also studied possible singular integral models (where the Hilbert transform gets replaced by Riesz transforms in several variables) along the lines of the ones found by the second author, J. Pincus and D. Xia (see [X1] for a thorough description). We hope to be able to report on these developments in the near future. Finally, let us mention that is is of interest to analyze the joint spectral properties of hyponormal and weak hyponormal n–tuples. (For existing work in case the n–tuples are doubly commuting, see [CD], [Ja] and [Cu]; for other n–tuples, we refer to [X2].)

Other Notions of Hyponormality

In light of the relations between subnormality, hyponormality, and polynomial hyponormality for single operators, it is natural to consider the corresponding notions for n–tuples and to study their hierarchical status. One is led to the consideration of the following diagram:

		subnormal		
completely weakly subnormal	$\Longrightarrow$	completely weakly hyponormal	$\Longleftarrow$	completely hyponormal
ℓ–weakly subnormal	$\Longrightarrow$	ℓ–weakly hyponormal	$\Longleftarrow$	ℓ–hyponormal
weakly subnormal	$\Longrightarrow$	weakly hyponormal	$\Longleftarrow$	hyponormal

[completely: property holds for every $\ell \geq 0$;
ℓ –: property holds for degree ℓ or less;
weakly: property holds for linear combinations
Example: completely weakly subnormal means polynomially subnormal.]

A good start towards Conjecture 3.3 would be a proof of the following.

CONJECTURE 3.4. Let $T = (T_1, T_2)$ be a completely weakly subnormal pair. Then T is subnormal if and only if T is hyponormal.

ACKNOWLEDGEMENTS. We are grateful to V. Paulsen, W. Szymanski and W. Wogen for helpful discussions and correspondence on the results of this paper.

REFERENCES

[Ab] M.B. Abrahamse, Commuting subnormal operators, Illinois Math. J. 22(1978), 171–176.

[Ag] J. Agler, Hypercontractions and subnormality, J. Operator Th. 13(1985), 203–217.

[At] A. Athavale, On joint hyponormality of operators, Proc. Amer. Math. Soc., to appear.

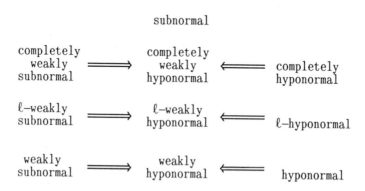

[Br] J. Bram, Subnormal operators, Duke Math. J. 22(1955), 75–94.

[CD] M. Chō and A.T. Dash, On the joint spectrum of doubly commuting seminormal operators, Glasgow Math. J. 26(1985), 47–50.

[CS] J. Conway and W. Szymanski, Linear combinations of hyponormal operators, Rocky Mountain J. Math., to appear.

[Cu] R.E. Curto, On the connectedness of invertible n–tuples, Indiana Univ. Math. J. 29(1980), 393–406.

[F] P. Fan, A note on hyponormal weighted shifts, Proc. Amer. Math. Soc. 92(1984), 271–272.

[Ja] J. Janas, Spectral properties of doubly commuting hyponormal operators, Ann. Pol. Math. 44(1984), 185–195.

[Jo] A. Joshi, Hyponormal polynomials of monotone shifts, Ph.D. dissertation, Purdue University, 1971.

[Lu1] A. Lubin, Weighted shifts and products of subnormal operators, Indiana Univ. Math. J. 26(1977).

[Lu2] A. Lubin, Extensions of commuting subnormal operators, Lecture Notes in Math. 693(1978), 115–120.

[Lu3] A. Lubin, A subnormal semigroup without normal extension, Proc. Amer. math. Soc. 68(1978), 176–178.

[Lu4] A. Lubin, Spectral inclusion and c.n.e., Canad. J. Math. 34(1982), 883–887.

[M] W. Mlak,Commutants of subnormal operators, Bull. Acad. Pol. Sci. 19(1970), 837–842.

[Pu] M. Putinar, Hyponormal operators are subscalar, J. Operator Th. 12(1984), 385–395.

[S] N. Salinas, private communication.

[Sℓ] Slocinski, Normal extensions of commuting subnormal operators, Studia Math. 54(1976), 259–266.

[St] J. Stampfli, Which weighted shifts are subnormal, Pacific J. Math.,

[X1] D. Xia, Spectral Theory of Hyponormal Operators, Operator Th.: Adv. Appl., vol. 10, Birkhäuser Verlag, Basel–Boston–Stuttgart, 1983.

[X2] D. Xia, On the semi–hyponormal n–tuple of operators, Int. Eq. Op. Th. 6(1983), 879–898.

R. Curto and P. Muhly
Department of Mathematics
University of Iowa
Iowa City, Iowa 52242
U.S.A.

J. Xia
Department of Mathematics
SUNY at Buffalo
Buffalo, New York 14214
U.S.A.

Operator Theory:
Advances and Applications, Vol. 35

CONDITIONAL EXPECTATIONS AND INVARIANT SUBSPACES

John Daughtry

Let Φ be a conditional expectation operator defined on a selfadjoint algebra of operators on a Hilbert space H. Let A be an invertible operator on H, and let M be a subspace of H. A sufficient condition for M to be invariant for $\Phi(A^{-1})\cdot A$ is obtained. A generalization involving sequences of conditional expectations yields a simplified and conceptually different proof of a recent theorem about operator factorization with respect to commutative sets of projections. It also provides a step toward the solution of the difficult problem of operator factorization with respect to noncommutative sets of projections.

The motivation for this work was the desire to extend the operator factorization methods of [3] to apply to factorization with respect to noncommutative sets of projections. While the achievements in this direction (Theorem 4) are not so easy to apply as the results for commutative sets of projections, the latter results are obtained via simpler arguments in the present paper (Theorem 3 and its application).

Because some of the results of this paper may interest a wide range of operator theorists independently of the operator factorization problem, we begin with the more general results (Theorems 1 and 2) and introduce technical concepts related to operator factorization as they are needed.

H denotes a Hilbert space (with real or complex scalars) of any dimension. B(H) is the space of all bounded, linear operators on H. For any A in B(H), rp(A) denotes the projection of H on the closure of the range of A. R(A) is the range of A. We use || || for the norm in B(H). A *-algebra A of operators on H is a subalgebra of B(H) which is closed with respect to the adjoint operation, *. If A is closed with respect to the norm (weak operator) topology, then A is a C* (W* or von Neumann) algebra of operators on H. For a subset of S of B(H), W*(S) is the W* algebra generated by S. I is the identity operator on H. The word "projection" is always used to mean an orthogonal projection. For $A \varepsilon B(H)$, Re A denotes $\frac{1}{2}(A+A^*)$.

The superiority of the methods of the present paper over those of [3] derives from the use of the following familiar concept:

DEFINITION: Let A be a *-algebra of operators on H with I in A, and let Φ be a linear mapping from A into A satisfying

i. if $X \varepsilon \mathsf{A}$ and $X \geq 0$, then $\Phi(X) \geq 0$,

ii. $\Phi(X^*) = \Phi(X)^*$ for all $X \varepsilon \mathsf{A}$,

iii. $\Phi o \Phi = \Phi$ and

iv. $\Phi(X)\,\Phi(Y) = \Phi(X\Phi(Y))$ for all X and Y in A.

Then Φ is a <u>conditional</u> <u>expectation</u> from A onto $R(\Phi)$.

REMARKS: 1. The identity $\Phi(X)\,\Phi(Y) = \Phi(\Phi(X)Y)$ is easily derived from iv and ii.

2. $R(\Phi)$ is the set of fixed points of Φ.

3. ii is a consequence of i when the scalars are complex.

The cornerstone result of this investigation is the following:

THEOREM 1: *Let* A *be a *-algebra of operators on* H *with* Φ *a conditional expectation from* A *onto a subset* D *of* A. *Suppose that* $Q \varepsilon \mathsf{A}$ *is a projection and* $A \varepsilon \mathsf{A}$ *is invertible in* A *with* $rp(AQ) \varepsilon \mathsf{D}$. *If* $\Phi(Q)$ *is a projection, then* $\Phi(A^{-1})A$ *maps* $R(Q)$ *into* $R(\Phi(Q))$.

We begin the proof of Theorem 1 with a

LEMMA: *With* A *and* Φ *as in Theorem 1, let* X *and* E *belong to* $B(H)$. *Assume that* E *and* $\Phi(E)$ *are projections. If* $R(X) \subseteq R(E)$, *then* $R(\Phi(X)) \subseteq R(\Phi(E))$.

PROOF: $R(X) \subseteq R(E)$ if and only if $XX^* \leq \lambda EE^* = \lambda E$ for some $\lambda > 0$ [6]. In this case, $\Phi(XX^*) \leq \lambda\Phi(E)$, so $\Phi(X^*)^*\Phi(X^*) \leq \lambda\Phi(E)$ by the Schwartz inequality for conditional expectations [14;pp. 117-118]. Thus $\Phi(X)\Phi(X^*) \leq \lambda\Phi(E) = \Phi(E)\Phi(E^*)$, so $R(\Phi(X)) \subseteq R(\Phi(E))$.

$\square$

To complete the proof of Theorem 1, observe that $R(\Phi(A^{-1})AQ) = R(\Phi(A^{-1})\ rp(AQ)\ AQ) = R(\Phi(A^{-1}rp(AQ))AQ)$. Apply the preceding lemma with $X = A^{-1}rp(AQ)$ and $E=Q$ to obtain $R(\Phi(A^{-1}rp(AQ))) \subseteq R(\Phi(Q))$. These equations establish that $R(\Phi(A^{-1})AQ) \subseteq R(\Phi(Q))$. |⁻|

The most obvious consequence of Theorem 1 is

COROLLARY 1: *If the hypotheses of Theorem 1 are satisfied,* $\Phi(Q) \leq Q$, *and* $\Phi(A^{-1})$ *has a left inverse in* $B(H)$ *which leaves* $R(Q)$ *invariant, then* A *leaves* $R(Q)$ *invariant.*

It often happens that $\Phi(A) = \Phi(A^{-1})^{-1}$. For example, this is the case if A and A^{-1} belong to a "subdiagonal algebra of $\mathbf{A}$ with respect to Φ" as defined in [1]. Therefore, it is interesting to notice

COROLLARY 2: *If the hypotheses of Theorem 1 are satisfied,* $\Phi(Q) = Q$, *and* $\Phi(A) = \Phi(A^{-1})^{-1}$, *then* A *leaves* $R(Q)$ *invariant if and only if* $\Phi(A)$ *does.*

To prove the implication which does not follow from Corollary 1, notice that $Q\Phi(A)Q = \Phi(QAQ) = \Phi(AQ) = \Phi(A)Q$ because $Q \in R(\Phi)$ and $R(Q)$ is invariant for A. |⁻|

In contrast to the situation of the preceding corollary, we observe

COROLLARY 3: *Let* A *be an invertible operator on* H *and let* Q *be a projection whose range is invariant under* A^{-1} *but not under* A. *Then there exists a conditional expectation* Φ *from* $W^*\{A, A^{-1}, Q\}$ *(indeed from* $B(H)$*) onto* $\mathbf{B} = W^*\{Q, rp(AQ), I\}$, *but for any such* Φ, $\Phi(A^{-1})$ *does not have a left inverse in* $\mathbf{B}$.

PROOF: $R(AQ) \supseteq R(Q)$, so $rp(AQ)$ comutes with Q. The existence of a conditional expectation from $B(H)$ onto $\mathbf{B}$ follows from the commutativity of $\mathbf{B}$ [14; 10.16].

If Φ is any conditional expectation from $W^*\{A,A^{-1},Q\}$ onto $\mathbf{B}$ such that $\Phi(A^{-1})$ has left inverse in $\mathbf{B}$, then that left inverse commutes with Q. Thus from Corollary 1 we conclude that A leaves $R(Q)$ invariant, contrary to hypothesis. |⁻|

COROLLARY 4: *If the conditions of Theorem 1 are satisfied,* $\Phi(Q) \leq Q$, *and there exists* $\delta > 0$ *such that* $\text{Re}\ A \geq \delta I$

and $\text{Re } A^{-1} \geq \delta I$, *then* A *maps* $R(Q)$ *onto* $R(Q)$ *if and only if* $\Phi(A^{-1})$ *leaves* $R(Q)$ *invariant.*

PROOF: Assume that A maps $R(Q)$ onto itself. Then $A^{-1}(R(Q)) = R(Q)$, so $\Phi(A^{-1})$ leaves $R(Q)$ invariant by the proof of Corollary 2.

Assume now that $\Phi(A^{-1})$ leaves $R(Q)$ invariant. $\text{Re } \Phi(A^{-1}) = \Phi(\text{Re } A^{-1}) \geq \delta I$, so from [12; Cor. 2.13, p. 33] we see that $\Phi(A^{-1})^{-1}$ leaves $R(Q)$ invariant. Theorem 1 implies that A leaves $R(Q)$ invariant, and another application of Corollary 2.13 of [12] yields the fact that A maps $R(Q)$ onto itself.

$\square$

For the reader's convenience, we now state Theorem 1 of [5], because we shall use it several times below. Let S be a selfadjoint, positive-definite, bounded, linear operator on H. Let X and Y be elements of $B(H)$. There exists A in $B(H)$ such that $A^*A = S$ and $rp(AX)$ commutes with $rp(AY)$ if and only if $rp(AX)$ commutes with $rp(AY)$ for all A in $B(H)$ such that $A^*A = S$.

Now we require some more terminology. (In all cases the projections referred to are in $B(H)$ and the order and the lattice operations are the usual ones for projections.) A lattice L of projections is <u>complete</u> if each subset has its least upper bound and greatest lower bound in L. A <u>nest</u> is a linearly ordered, complete set of projections which contains 0 and I. A complete lattice L of projections which contains 0 and I and satisfies $PQ = QP$ for all P and Q in L is a <u>commutative subspace lattice</u> (CSL).

For any CSL L and P in L, we define $\Delta^P = P - P^{\leftarrow}$, where $P^{\leftarrow}$ is the projection on the closed span of $\{R(Q): Q \in \mathsf{L}, Q < P\}$. $P^{\leftarrow} \in \mathsf{L}$ by completeness. L is <u>continuous</u> if $\Delta^P = 0$ for all P in L. For $\mathsf{S} \subset B(H)$, S' denotes the commutant of S. For a CSL L, L'' is the <u>core</u> of L.

It follows from Theorem 2 of [4] that if L is a countable CSL, $\sum_{P \in \mathsf{L}} \Delta^P = I$. In particular, $P \neq Q$ implies $\Delta^P \Delta^Q = \Delta^Q \Delta^P = 0$.

COROLLARY 5: *Let* $A \in B(H)$ *satisfy* $\text{Re } A \geq \delta I$ *and*

Re $A^{-1} \geq \delta I$ *for some* $\delta > 0$. *Let* L *be a countable CSL of projections on subspaces of* H, *and let* Q *be a projection in the core of* L. *If* rp(AQ) *commutes with each element of* L, *then* rp(AQ) = Q.

PROOF: Define $\Phi(X) = \sum_{P \in \mathsf{L}} \Delta^P X \Delta^P$ for X in B(H). (The sum can easily be shown to converge in the strong operator topology because $\sum_{P \in \mathsf{L}} \Delta^P = I$.) Then Φ is a conditional expectation of B(H) onto L'. Q and rp(AQ) are fixed by Φ because they are in L'. Because $\Phi(A^{-1}) \in \mathsf{L}'$, it commutes with $Q \in \mathsf{L}''$. By Corollary 4, rp(AQ) = Q. |_|

COROLLARY 6: *Consider* S *in* B(H) *such that* $S = A^*A$ *with* rp(AP) = P *for all* P *in* L, *a countable CSL of projections in* B(H). *Assume that there exists* $\delta > 0$ *with* Re $A > \delta I$ *and* Re $A^{-1} > \delta I$. *Let* Q *be any projection in the core of* L *such that* $rp(S^{\frac{1}{2}}Q)$ *commutes with* $rp(S^{\frac{1}{2}}P)$ *for all* P *in* L. *Then* rp(AQ) = Q.

PROOF: By Theorem 1 of [5], rp(AQ) commutes with rp(AP) = P for all P in L. Thus rp(AQ) = Q by Corollary 5. |_|

COROLLARY 7: *Assume that* H *is a complex Hilbert space. Let* L *be a CSL in* B(H) *and consider* T *in* B(H) *such that* T = UA *for* U *unitary and* A *and* A^{-1} *leaving invariant the range of each projection in* L. *Let* Φ *be any expectation from* B(H) *onto* L', *and let* M *denote* $W^*(\mathsf{L} \cup \{T, T^*\})$. *If* $\Phi(A^{-1})$ *is one-to-one and belongs to* M, *then* A *and* U *belong to* M.

PROOF: For all projections Q in M' and P in L, the fact that Q commutes with rp(TP) = U rp(AP) U* implies that U*QU commutes with rp(AP) = P. Also, U*QU = U* rp(TQ)U (because Q commutes with T) = $rp(U^{-1}TQ)$ = rp(AQ). Thus rp(AQ) commutes with L.

By Theorem 1, $\Phi(A^{-1})A$ leaves R(Q) invariant. The same argument applies to I-Q in the place of Q, so $\Phi(A^{-1})A$ commutes with Q. From the fact that $\Phi(A^{-1})$ is one-to-one, it follows that Q commutes with A. Because Q was an arbitrary projection in M', $A \in \mathsf{M}'' = \mathsf{M}$. $U = TA^{-1}$ also belongs to M. |_|

Corollary 7 was inspired by [15].

By now the reader is no doubt ready for a new idea. As the proof of Corollary 5 suggests, Theorem 1 is useful for studying countable CSL's but an extension is required for uncountable lattices. (The Φ defined in Corollary 5 would be the zero map for a continuous CSL, for example). For this purpose, we have

THEOREM 2: *Let* A *be a *-algebra of operators on* H, *and let* $\{\Phi_n: n=1,2,\ldots\}$ *be a sequence of conditional expectations from* A *into* A. *Assume that* $Q\varepsilon\mathsf{A}$ *is a projection,* $\Phi_n(Q) \leq Q$, $\Phi_n(Q)$ *is a projection,* A *is invertible in* A, $rp(AQ)\varepsilon R(\Phi_n)$, *and* $\Phi_n(A^{-1})$ *has left inverse* L_n *in* B(H) *for* $n = 1,2,\ldots$. *If* $QL_nQ - L_nQ$ *converges in norm to* 0 *as* n *approaches infinity, then* A *leaves* R(Q) *invariant.*

PROOF: By Theorem 1, $\Phi_n(A^{-1})A$ leaves R(Q) invariant for each n. Therefore, $AQ = (L_n\Phi_n(A^{-1}))AQ = L_nQ\Phi_n(A^{-1})AQ$. Given $\varepsilon>0$, we can choose n so large that $||QL_nQ - L_nQ|| < \varepsilon/(||A^{-1}||\cdot||A||)$. $||\Phi_n(A^{-1})|| \leq ||A^{-1}||$ because $||\Phi_n|| = 1$ [14; p. 118]. Thus $||QAQ-AQ|| = ||QL_nQ\,\Phi_n(A^{-1})AQ - L_nQ\,\Phi_n(A^{-1})AQ|| \leq ||QL_nQ - L_nQ|| \cdot ||\Phi_n(A^{-1})\,AQ|| \leq \varepsilon$. Because $QAQ - AQ$ is independent of n, it is 0 as claimed. |_|

In order to examine applications of Theorem 2, more terminology is required. If S is any set of projections, alg $\mathsf{S} = \{A\varepsilon\ B(H): PAP = AP$ for all P in $\mathsf{S}\}$. An <u>interval</u> in a CSL L is P-Q where P and Q belong to L and $Q\leq P$. A <u>partition</u> of a CSL is a countable set of mutually orthogonal intervals whose sum is I. For a CSL L, the Larson radical of alg L is $\{A\varepsilon$ alg L: given $\varepsilon>0$, there exists a partition $\{E_n\}$ of L such that $\sup_n ||E_nAE_n|| < \varepsilon\}$.

We refer to [10] and [11] for information about the Larson radical (of a nest), but we will need only the definition and the fact that when L is a continuous nest and K is a compact operator in alg L, K belongs to the Larson radical of alg L. In fact K belongs to the (smaller) Jacobson radical ([13] or [7; Theorem 4.4]).

The following theorem is the same as the main result of [3] except that in [3] only $(B+V)^{-1}$ and V are assumed to be in alg $\mathcal{L}$, while here we also assume that B belongs to alg $\mathcal{L}$. However, in all the applications we envision B belongs to alg $\mathcal{L}$. (We are ignoring the fact that the results of [3] are stated only for nests rather than for CSL's because the arguments in [3] may be extended to CSL's with no difficulty.)

The proof of the following result via Theorem 2 seems to us simpler, more pleasing, and more revealing than our original proof in [3].

THEOREM 3: *Let* $\mathcal{L}$ *be a CSL in* $B(H)$ *with* Q *a projection in* $\mathcal{L}'$. *Let* V *be any element of the Larson radical of alg* $\mathcal{L}$. *Suppose there exists* B *in alg* $\mathcal{L}$ *such that* B *leaves* $R(Q)$ *invariant,* $B + V$ *is invertible,* $(B + V)^{-1}$ *belongs to alg* $\mathcal{L}$, *and* $rp((B + V)Q)$ *commutes with* $\mathcal{L}$. *Then* V *leaves* $R(Q)$ *invariant.*

Thus if the spectrum of V *is* $\{0\}$, $rp((\alpha I + V)Q) = Q$ *for all nonzero scalars* α *if there exists a nonzero scalar* λ *such that* $rp((\lambda I + V)Q)$ *commutes with* $\mathcal{L}$.

PROOF: Choose a partition P_n of $\mathcal{L}$ such that $\sup_{E\varepsilon P_n} ||EVE|| < 1/n$ for $n = 1,2,\ldots$. Define $\Phi_n(X) = \sum_{E\varepsilon P_n} EXE$ for all X in $B(H)$. Then Φ_n is a conditional expectation of $B(H)$ onto the commutant of P_n, and it fixes Q and $rp((B + V)Q)$. Let $A = B + V$.

Using the orthogonality of the intervals in P_n, it is easily seen that Φ_n is multiplicative on the operators which leave invariant the ranges of the endpoints of the intervals in P_n. Because A and A^{-1} belong to alg $\mathcal{L}$, it follows that $\Phi_n(A) = \Phi_n(A^{-1})^{-1}$. $||Q\Phi_n(A)Q - \Phi_n(A)Q|| = ||Q\Phi_n(V)Q - \Phi_n(V)Q||$ because $Q\Phi_n(B)Q = \Phi_n(QBQ) = \Phi_n(BQ) = \Phi_n(B)Q$. The norm above approaches 0 as n goes to infinity because $||\Phi_n(V)|| = \sup_{E\varepsilon P_n} ||EVE||$ by a standard argument (essentially the same as on p. 31 of [8]).

An application of Theorem 2 shows that A, and therefore V, leave $R(Q)$ invariant. Finally, take $B = \lambda I$ and observe that under the hypotheses of the second paragraph of Theorem 3 $\lambda I + V$ leaves $R(Q)$ invariant and $(\lambda I + V)^{-1}$ has the same invariant subspaces as $\lambda I + V$. The remainder is then obvious.

$\square$

Remark: One can also prove something of interest by applying the preceding argument with $A = (B + V)^{-1}$ if the condition $rp((B + V)^{-1}Q) \in \mathcal{L}'$ is substituted for $rp((B + V)Q) \in \mathcal{L}'$. However, for the case when B is a multiple of I that result will be a special case of Theorem 4 below.

One cannot appreciate Theorem 3 fully without seeing its application to the operator factorization problem which we now describe. Let $\mathcal{S}$ be a set of mutually commuting projections and S a selfadjoint operator satisfying $S \geq \delta I$ for some positive number δ. Assume that $S = I + K$ with K in Macaev's ideal [9;p. 81 and Section 4 of Chapter 3]. (In particular, the condition that K is Hilbert-Schmidt, which often arises in applications, implies that K is in Macaev's ideal.) The problem is to factor $S = A^*A$ where $rp(AP) = P$ for all P in $\mathcal{S}$.

Assume that H is separable. Let $\mathcal{L}$ be the CSL generated by $\mathcal{S}$. It is proved on p. 482 of [2] that $\mathcal{L}$ contains a nest $\mathcal{N}$ with $\mathcal{N}' = \mathcal{L}'$. The theory of [9] as summarized on pp. 101-102 of [8] yields a factorization $S = (I + V)^*D(I + V)$ with D in $\mathcal{N}'$ and V in the Larson radical (in fact, the Jacobson radical) of alg $\mathcal{N}$. An apparently very naive approach to obtaining an analogous factorization along $\mathcal{L}$ is to hope that the preceding factorization "happens to work". Of course, because $\mathcal{N}' = \mathcal{L}'$ the only question is whether $rp((I + V)P) = P$ for all P in $\mathcal{L}$. Theorem 3 applied to $\mathcal{N}$ implies that otherwise there exists P in $\mathcal{L}$ such that $rp((I + V)P)$ does not commute with some element of $\mathcal{N}$. In that case, it follows from Theorem 1 of [5] that the desired factorization for S along $\mathcal{L}$ (and therefore $\mathcal{S}$) does not exist. Thus $A = D^{\frac{1}{2}}(I + V)$ works if anything does!

Moreover, one can determine which case occurs by studying $S^{\frac{1}{2}}$: it is not necessary to calculate the Gohberg-Krein factorization along $\mathcal{N}$ to determine whether a factorization along $\mathcal{S}$ exists. By combining Theorem 1 of [5] (stated above) with the preceding arguments, we see that S has the desired factorization if and only if $\{rp(S^{\frac{1}{2}}P):P \in \mathcal{L}\}$ is commutative.

For another specialization of Theorem 3, consider a unitary operator U in alg $\mathcal{L}$ with U^* also in alg $\mathcal{L}$. (Here $\mathcal{L}$ and Q are as in Theorem 3.) $UPU^* = P$ for all P in $\mathcal{L}$, so $rp(UQ) = UQU^*$ commutes with the elements of $\mathcal{L}$. Suppose there exists an element V of the Larson radical of alg $\mathcal{L}$ such that $U - V$ leaves $R(Q)$ invariant. Then Theorem 3 implies that V and (therefore) U leave $R(Q)$ invariant. Thus if U does not leave $R(Q)$ invariant, neither does any perturbation of U by an element of the Larson radical of alg $\mathcal{L}$.

The preceding result seems to provide a useful limitation on the elements of the Larson radical of alg $\mathcal{L}$, and little information of this type appears in the literature, even when $\mathcal{L}$ is a nest. Larson [11] has shown that the Larson radical of a continuous nest contains an idempotent, which suggests the question of how much larger than the Jacobson radical the Larson radical can be. Therefore, we summarize the preceding fact in

COROLLARY 8: *Let* $\mathcal{L}$ *be a* CSL *in* B(H), *with* Q *a projection in* $\mathcal{L}'$. *Let* U *be a unitary operator in alg* $\mathcal{L}$ *which is invertible in alg* $\mathcal{L}$. *If* U *does not leave* $R(Q)$ *invariant, then neither does* $U - V$ *for any* V *in the Larson radical of alg* $\mathcal{L}$.

Now we prepare to study the case where Q does not commute with $\mathcal{L}$.

DEFINITION: If $\mathcal{L}$ is a CSL in B(H) and Q is a projection, then $V \in B(H)$ is <u>Q-$\mathcal{L}$ negligible</u> if for all $\varepsilon > 0$ there exists a partition P_ε of $\mathcal{L}$ such that

i. $\sup_{E \in P_\varepsilon} \|(E \wedge Q)V(E \wedge Q)\| < \varepsilon$,

ii. $\sup_{E \in P_\varepsilon} \|(E \wedge (I-Q))V(E \wedge (I-Q))\| < \varepsilon$, and

iii. $\|RVR\| < \varepsilon$ where $R = I - \sum_{E \in P_\varepsilon} ((E \wedge Q) + (E \wedge (I-Q)))$.

The reader should observe that if Q commutes with the elements of $\mathcal{L}$ and V belongs to alg $\mathcal{L}$, then the definition above reduces to the condition that V belong to the Larson radical of alg $\mathcal{L}$.

THEOREM 4: *Let* $\mathcal{L}$ *be a CSL in* B(H) *and* Q *any projection. Let* V *be any* $Q-\mathcal{L}$ *negligible operator on* H.

i. Consider a scalar λ *such that* $\lambda I + V$ *is invertible in* B(H). *Assume that for all partitions* $\mathcal{P}$ *of* $\mathcal{L}$ *and all* E *in* $\mathcal{P}$, $rp((\lambda I + V)^{-1}Q)$ *commutes with* $E \wedge Q$ *and* $E \wedge (I - Q)$. *Then* $(\lambda I + V)^{-1}$ *leaves* R(Q) *invariant.*

ii. If 0 *is the only element of the spectrum of* V, *then* $rp((\alpha I + V)Q) = Q$ *for all nonzero scalars* α *if and only if there exists a nonzero scalar* λ *such that for all partitions* $\mathcal{P}$ *of* $\mathcal{L}$ *and all* E *in* $\mathcal{P}$, $rp(\lambda I + V)^{-1}Q)$ *commutes with* $E \wedge Q$ *and* $E \wedge (I - Q)$.

PROOF: (i.) Choose a partition $\mathcal{P}_n$ of $\mathcal{L}$ such that the quantities on the left hand side of i-iii in the definition of $Q-\mathcal{L}$ negligibility are each less than $1/n$ for $n = 1,2\ldots$. For X in B(H), define $\Phi_n(X) = \sum_{E \in \mathcal{P}_n} [(E \wedge Q)X(E \wedge Q) + (E \wedge (I - Q))X(E \wedge (I - Q))] + R_n X R_n$ where R_n is the obvious analogue of the R in the definition of $Q-\mathcal{L}$ negligibility. (The series converges in the strong operator topology because of the orthogonality of the projections involved.) Φ_n is a conditional expectation operator which fixes Q.

Let $A = (\lambda I + V)^{-1}$. Φ_n fixes rp(AQ) by the commutativity hypothesis. $\Phi_n(A^{-1}) = \lambda I + \Phi_n(V)$. $||\Phi_n(V)||$ approaches 0 as n approaches infinity by the definition of $Q-\mathcal{L}$ negligibility and the same argument as in the proof of Theorem 3. $\lambda \neq 0$ because V is not bounded below. It follows that for n sufficiently large, $\Phi_n(A^{-1})$ is invertible in B(H). Without loss of generality we assume that $n = 1$ is "sufficiently large". Moreover, $||Q\Phi_n(A^{-1})^{-1}Q - \Phi_n(A^{-1})^{-1}Q||$ approaches 0.

From Theorem 2 we conclude that $(\lambda I + V)^{-1}$ leaves R(Q) invariant, which completes the proof of i. ii follows from i as in the proof of Theorem 3. |_|

The reader may find it interesting to examine why Theorem 4 does not have an obvious version with $rp((\lambda I + V)^{-1}Q)$ replaced by $rp((\lambda I + V)Q)$, in contrast with Theorem 3.

The theory of nonanticipative representations of Gaussian random fields provides motivation for studying the problem of factoring a positive definite operator in the form A^*A so that A leaves invariant the ranges of the projections in a (not necessarily commutative) subspace lattice. Theorem 4 was proved with that application in mind. However, one reason that Theorem 3 is so useful (in the case of a commutative subspace lattice) is that Theorem 1 of [5] allows us to translate a hypothesis on $rp(AP)$ to a hypothesis on $rp(S^{\frac{1}{2}}P)$ in the argument presented after Theorem 3. We have no such trick for the general case. Also, in the Gohberg-Krein factorization $S = (I+V)^*D(I+V)$, if Q is a projection which does not commute with the nest then V may not be Q-$\mathcal{L}$ negligible. The general operation factorization problem may well not have so neat a solution as that for the problem of operator factorization along commutative subspace lattices. Nevertheless, it seems clear that conditional expectation operators are useful tools for investigating operator factorization, even operator factorization along sets of non-commuting projections.

Finally, we call the reader's attention to an interesting extension of part of Theorem 4 to the situation with small perturbations of the operator V in the place of V. Notice that when Q commutes with $\mathcal{L}$, Q-$\mathcal{L}$ negligibility of V is the same as I-$\mathcal{L}$ negligibility. In this case, we say that V is <u>$\mathcal{L}$-negligible</u>.

THEOREM 5: *Let* $\mathcal{L}$ *be a CSL in* $B(H)$ *and* Q *any projection in the core of* $\mathcal{L}$. *Let* V *be an* $\mathcal{L}$*-negligible* *operator on* H *and consider a scalar* λ *such that* $\lambda I + V$ *is invertible in* B(H). *Then there exists a ball* $\mathcal{B}$ *centered at* V *such that for all* D *in* $\mathcal{B}$, $\lambda I + D$ *is invertible and if* $rp((\lambda I + D)^{-1}Q)$ *commutes with* $\mathcal{L}$, *then* $(\lambda I + D)^{-1}$ *leaves* R(Q) *invariant.*

PROOF: For X in B(H), define $\Phi_n(X)$ as in the proof of Theorem 3.

Φ_n is a conditional expectation operator from B(H) onto the commutant of $\mathcal{L}$.

Choose $\mathcal{B}$ to be an open ball centered at V with radius less than λ and sufficiently small that $\lambda I + D$ is invertible for all D in $\mathcal{B}$. Fix an arbitrary D in $\mathcal{B}$.

Φ_n fixes Q and $rp((\lambda I + D)^{-1})$ by the assumptions that they commute with $\mathcal{L}$. Apply Theorem 2 with $A = (\lambda I + V)^{-1}$. $\Phi_n(A^{-1}) = \lambda I + \Phi_n(D)$, which is invertible because $||\Phi_n(D)|| \leq ||\Phi_n(D - V)|| + ||\Phi_n(V)|| \leq ||D - V|| + ||\Phi_n(V)|| < \lambda$ when n is sufficiently large (by the $\mathcal{L}$ negligibility of V). Restrict attention to such "sufficiently large" n. Because $\Phi_n(A^{-1})$ commutes with $\mathcal{L}$, so does its inverse. It follows that $\Phi_n(A^{-1})^{-1}$ commutes with the core element Q. Thus all the hypotheses of Theorem 2 are satisfied, and we conclude that $(\lambda I + D)^{-1}$ leaves R(Q) invariant. $\square$

Perhaps we should give an example to illustrate the necessity of the invertibility of $\lambda I + V$ in Theorem 5. Let $V = \begin{pmatrix} 0 & 0 \\ C & 0 \end{pmatrix}$ with respect to the decomposition $H = R(Q) \oplus R(I - Q)$. If C maps onto $R(I - Q)$, then $rp\,(VQ) = I - Q$. Thus $rp(VQ)$ commutes with Q, and it is obvious that V is $\mathcal{L}$ negligible for $L = \{0,Q,I\}$. Nevertheless, $R(Q)$ is not invariant for V.

ACKNOWLEDGEMENT: The author is grateful to Alan Hopenwasser for assistance in keeping the terminology and notation consistent with that of the nest algebra literature. David R. Larson showed the author how to extend the discussion following Theorem 3 from CSLs containing continuous nests to arbitrary CSLs.

REFERENCES

1. Arveson, W.B., Analyticity in operator algebras, Amer. J. Math. 89 (1967), 578-642.

2. Arveson, W.B., Operator algebras and invariant subspaces, Ann. of Math. (2) (1974), 433-532.

3. Daughtry, J., Invariance of projections in the diagonal of a nest algebra, Proc. A.M.S., to appear.

4. Daughtry, J., Factorizations along commutative subspace lattices, Integral Equations Operator Theory, V. 10, 290-296.

5. Daughtry, J. and Dearden, B., A test for the existence of Gohberg-Krein representations in terms of multiparameter Wiener processes, J. Funct. Anal. 63 (1985), 403-411.

6. Douglas, R., On majorization, factorization, and range inclusion of operators on Hilbert space, Proc. A.M.S. 17 (1966), 413-415.

7. Erdos, J.A. and Longstaff, W.E., The convergence of triangular integrals of operators on Hilbert space, Indiana U. Math. J., v. 22 #10 (1973).

8. Feintuch, A. and Saeks, R., System Theory: A Hilbert Space Approach, Academic Press, New York (1982).

9. Gohberg, I. and Krein, M.G., Theory and Application of Volterra Operators in Hilbert Space, A.M.S. Translations of Mathematical Monographs, v. 24 (1970).

10. Hopenwasser, A., Hypercausal linear operators, SIAM J. Control Optim. v. 22 #6 (1984), 911-919.

11. Larson, D.R., Nest algebras and similarity transformations, Ann. of Math. 121 (1985), 409-427.

12. Radjavi, H. and Rosenthal, P., Invariant Subspaces, Springer-Verlag, New York (1973).

13. Ringrose, J.R., Superdiagonal forms for compact linear operators, Proc. London Math. Soc. 12 (1962), 385-399.

14. Serban, S., Modular Theory in Operator Algebras, Abacus Press, Tunbridge Wells, (1981).

15. Solel, B., Factorization in operator algebras, Proc. A.M.S., to appear.

Department of Mathematics
East Carolina University
Greenville, NC 27858-4353

Operator Theory:
Advances and Applications, Vol. 35

HAMILTONIAN SYSTEMS WITH EIGENVALUE DEPENDING BOUNDARY CONDITIONS

Aad Dijksma, Heinz Langer, Henk de Snoo[1]

1. Introduction

In earlier papers [DLS1–6] we have described the selfadjoint extensions, in indefinite inner product spaces and with nonempty resolvent sets of a symmetric closed relation S in a Hilbert space $\mathfrak{H}$ by means of generalized resolvents, characteristic functions and Štraus extensions. In this paper we show how these results can be applied when S comes from a $2n\times 2n$ Hamiltonian system of ordinary differential equations on an interval $[a,b)$,

(1.1) $$Jy'(t) = \big(\ell\Delta(t)+H(t)\big)\,y(t)+\Delta(t)f(t), \qquad t\in[a,b), \quad \ell\in\mathbb{C},$$

which is regular in a and in the limit point case in b; for further specifications see Section 5. We pay special attention to selfadjoint extensions beyond the given space $\mathfrak{H}$, as they give rise to eigenvalue and boundary value problems with boundary conditions of the form

(1.2) $$\mathcal{A}(\ell)y^1(a)+\mathcal{B}(\ell)y^2(a)=0,$$

in which the matrix coefficients $\mathcal{A}(\ell)$ and $\mathcal{B}(\ell)$ depend holomorphically on the eigenvalue parameter ℓ, see Theorem 7.1 below. The eigenvalue problem for such a selfadjoint extension in a larger space can be considered as a linearization of the corresponding boundary value problem (1.1) and (1.2).

Spectral problems related to canonical systems of ordinary differential equations were studied by M.G. Krein and L. de Branges (see [GK] and [dB5], and also [A], [KK], [Orl], [KR], [LT2,3], [K1,2], [I] and [HS1,2]). In some of the papers mentioned here, for instance in [KK], there

---

[1]This work was supported by the Netherlands Organization for the Advancement of Pure Research (Z.W.O.).

appear boundary conditions which correspond to extensions beyond the originally given space. In the present paper we first consider very general boundary conditions,. namely those which are in one to one correspondence with minimal selfadjoint extensions in Krein spaces with nonempty resolvent sets. Later we restrict ourselves to extensions in Pontryagin spaces; in particular, boundary conditions which are rational in the eigenvalue parameter ℓ give rise to such extensions, see for instance [D], [BP]. The special case of boundary conditions which are linear in ℓ and correspond to Hilbert space extensions has been considered in many papers, see for instance [F], [HS3], [R], [N], [SS1–3].

We briefly outline the contents of the paper. In Section 2 we recall from our earlier papers the description of generalized resolvents, characteristic functions and Štraus extensions of the given symmetric relation S. They are the objects in the originally given space which correspond to the selfadjoint extensions of S in larger spaces. We slightly weaken the hypotheses in the description of the generalized resolvents and give a shorter proof of the characterization of the Štraus extensions than the one in for example [DLS1]. After these preliminary results, we restrict ourselves in Section 3 to relations S which have finite defect numbers. This is the case of interest for ordinary differential equations. The Štraus extensions can now be described by a matrix $\mathcal{U}(\ell)$, which in the concrete situation of a Hamiltonian system immediately leads to boundary conditions containing the eigenvalue parameter ℓ. If the extending space is a Pontryagin space, we describe the Štraus extension of S in a real point by means of the limit of $\mathcal{U}(\ell)$ as ℓ in the upper half plane approaches this point nontangentially. As an example we consider in Section 4 in more detail the case, where $\mathcal{U}(\ell)$ is linear in ℓ; it corresponds to boundary conditions which are linear in the eigenvalue parameter. For this case we construct a concrete model of the selfadjoint extension determined by the matrix $\mathcal{U}(\ell)$. In Section 5 we collect the basic results concerning canonical systems of ordinary differential equations and the corresponding symmetric minimal, and maximal relations. Beginning in Section 6 we assume in the remainder of this paper that the canonical system is a definite Hamiltonian system under the assumptions mentioned in the first paragraph. In Section 6 we consider the Weyl coefficient M, an $n{\times}n$ matrix function of Nevanlinna class and list some of its properties. We show that the characteristic function of the symmetric closed minimal relation S associated with the system can be expressed in terms of $\mathcal{M}$. This function completely determines the simple part of S, which, as we prove in Section 7, coincides with the operator part S_s of S, $S_s = S \ominus S_\infty$ and $S_\infty = \{\{0,\varphi\} \in S\}$. We also show that the existence of real eigenvalues of S^* can be derived from the limit behavior of $\mathcal{M}(\ell)$ in these points.

The main results in Section 7 concern the description of the three families of operators or relations representing the selfadjoint extension, mentioned above in terms of the Weyl coefficient $\mathcal{M}$ and of the matrix $\mathcal{U}(\ell)$, which breaks down into the two $n \times n$ matrices $\mathcal{A}(\ell)$ and $\mathcal{B}(\ell)$, which appear in the boundary conditions (1.2). In particular, we mention here the characterization of the generalized resolvent. It can be calculated explicitly: it is an integral operator and in the kernel, expressed in terms of a fundamental solution Y of the system, there appears the matrix function Ω defined by

$$\Omega(\ell) = \begin{bmatrix} \Gamma(\ell)\mathcal{B}(\ell) & -\Gamma(\ell)\mathcal{A}(\ell) \\ \mathcal{M}(\ell)\Gamma(\ell)\mathcal{B}(\ell)+I & -\mathcal{M}(\ell)\Gamma(\ell)\mathcal{A}(\ell) \end{bmatrix},$$

where $\Gamma(\ell) = -\left(\mathcal{A}(\ell)+\mathcal{B}(\ell)\mathcal{M}(\ell)\right)^{-1}$. In the special case where $\mathcal{A}(\ell)=I$ and $\mathcal{B}(\ell)=O$, this matrix function essentially reduces to the Weyl coefficient $\mathcal{M}$; therefore, we call Ω the Weyl coefficient with respect to the Fourier transform related to Y and the matrices $\mathcal{A}(\ell)$ and $\mathcal{B}(\ell)$. We also show in Section 7 that $\mathcal{M}(\ell)$ is a socalled Q–function of S and that the description of the generalized resolvents can also be obtained from an extension of M.G. Krein's formula for generalized resolvents.

In the next sections we describe the extensions themselves, first in some particular cases, see Section 8, and then, in Section 9, in the general situation of extensions in Pontryagin spaces. As alluded to above the operator part S_s of the closed symmetric relation S and the minimal extensions A are characterized by $\mathcal{M}(\ell)$ and $\mathcal{A}(\ell)$, $\mathcal{B}(\ell)$, respectively. In Section 9 we consider π_κ–extensions only; therefore, the $2n \times 2n$ matrix function Ω belongs to the generalized Nevanlinna class $\mathbf{N}_\kappa^{2n\times 2n}$. (We say that an $n \times n$ matrix function Q belongs to the class $\mathbf{N}_\kappa^{n\times n}$ if Q is defined and meromorphic on $\mathbb{C}\backslash\mathbb{R}$, $Q(\bar{\ell})^* = Q(\ell)$ and the kernel $(\ell-\bar{\lambda})^{-1}\left(Q(\ell)-Q(\lambda)^*\right)$ has κ negative squares.) It follows that Ω admits a representation in terms of a selfadjoint relation $A(\Omega)$. We show that the extension $A \ominus S_\infty$ of S_s and $A(\Omega)$

are isomorphically equivalent. This implies that there is a close relation between the spectrum of the boundary value problem, i.e., the spectrum of the corresponding minimal extension A, and the analytic properties of Ω. For instance, the discrete spectrum of A corresponds to the poles of Ω and the continuous spectrum and embedded eigenvalues can also be obtained from the behaviour of Ω. We illustrate this in Section 10, where for the special case $n=1$, $\mathcal{A}(\ell)=I$ we characterize the real eigenvalues of nonpositive type of the boundary value problem. We hope to treat the general case, including chains corresponding to eigenvalues of nonpositive type, in another publication. A selfadjoint π_κ-extension gives rise to an expansion in eigenfunctions, which takes the form of a series, when the extension has a discrete spectrum. We intend to consider these problems elsewhere too.

2. Some preliminary results

In this section we briefly review the various notions and definitions concerning the characterization of selfadjoint extensions in (possibly indefinite) inner product spaces of a given symmetric relation. We refer to [DSL2,3,5], for the basic definitions of relations in definite and indefinite inner product spaces, their Cayley transforms and of colligations and their characteristic functions.

If $\mathfrak{F}$ and $\mathfrak{G}$ are inner product spaces we denote by $\mathbf{L}(\mathfrak{F},\mathfrak{G})$ the linear space of all bounded linear operators from $\mathfrak{F}$ to $\mathfrak{G}$; if $\mathfrak{F}=\mathfrak{G}$ we simply write $\mathbf{L}(\mathfrak{F})$ for this space. We use the notation $[\ ,\ ]$ for any inner product; it should be clear from the context to which space it refers. We make one exception: $(\ ,\ )$ denotes the usual inner product in $\mathbb{C}^k$, $k\in\mathbb{N}$. For a subset $\mathfrak{D}\subset\mathbb{C}$ we put $\mathfrak{D}^*=\{\,\ell\in\mathbb{C}\mid\bar{\ell}\in\mathfrak{D}\,\}$.

In what follows S stands for a closed symmetric linear relation in a Hilbert space $\mathfrak{H}$. The Von Neumann decomposition for the adjoint S^* of S reads as

$$S^*=S\dotplus M_\mu(S)\dotplus M_{\bar{\mu}}(S),\qquad \text{direct sums in } \mathfrak{H}^2,$$

where $\mu\in\mathbb{C}\backslash\mathbb{R}$ and for $\ell\in\mathbb{C}$ the defect subspace $M_\ell(S)$ of S is defined by

$$M_\ell(S)=\Big\{\ \{f,g\}\in S^*\mid g=\ell f\Big\}.$$

Let A be a selfadjoint extension of S in a Krein space $\mathfrak{K}$ with nonempty resolvent set $\rho(A)=\{\ell\in\mathbb{C}\mid(A-\ell)^{-1}\in\mathbf{L}(\mathfrak{K})\}$. By definition, $\mathfrak{H}\subset\mathfrak{K}$ and the definite and indefinite inner products on $\mathfrak{H}$ and $\mathfrak{K}$, respectively, coincide on $\mathfrak{H}$. By $P_{\mathfrak{H}}$ we denote the orthogonal projection of $\mathfrak{K}$ onto $\mathfrak{H}$. We say that $\mathfrak{K}$ is minimal if

$$\mathfrak{K} = \text{c.l.s.}\left\{ \{ (A-\ell)^{-1}\mathfrak{H} \mid \ell \in \rho(A) \} \cup \mathfrak{H} \right\}.$$

Here c.l.s. stands for closed linear span. The extension A of S induces in the Hilbert space $\mathfrak{H}$ the following families of operators or relations: the compressed resolvent, the characteristic function and the Štraus relation. We shall describe and characterize each of these families.

The compressed resolvent $R(\ell)$, $\ell \in \rho(A)$, associated with the extension A is defined by $R(\ell) = P_{\mathfrak{H}}(A-\ell)^{-1}|_{\mathfrak{H}}$. It is readily verified that

(a) $R(\ell)$ is a holomorphic mapping with values in $\mathbf{L}(\mathfrak{H})$ and with domain of holomorphy $\mathfrak{D}_R$, which is symmetric with respect to the real axis: $\mathfrak{D}_R = \mathfrak{D}_R^*$,

(b) $R(\ell)^* = R(\bar{\ell})$,

(c) $R(\ell)(S-\ell) \subset I$, the identity on $\mathfrak{H}$.

If $\mathfrak{K}$ is a Pontryagin space of index κ, then the kernel

$$\text{(2.1)} \qquad \mathsf{K}_R(\ell,\lambda) = \frac{R(\ell) - R(\lambda)^*}{\ell - \bar{\lambda}} - R(\lambda)^* R(\ell)$$

has at most κ negative squares; if, moreover, $\mathfrak{K}$ is minimal then it has exactly κ negative squares. Any operator family $R(\ell)$ satisfying (a)–(c) is called a generalized resolvent of S.

Proposition 2.1. *Let $R(\ell)$ be a generalized resolvent of S, $\mu \in \mathfrak{D}_R \cap \mathbb{C}^+$ and let $\mathfrak{D}$ be a simply connected open subset with smooth boundary $\partial\mathfrak{D}$ such that $\mu \in \mathfrak{D}$ and $\mathfrak{D} \cup \partial\mathfrak{D} \subset \mathfrak{D}_R \cap \mathbb{C}^+$. Then there exists a selfadjoint extension A of S in a Krein space $\mathfrak{K}$ with $\mu \in \rho(A)$, such that $R(\ell)$ is the compressed resolvent of A:*

$$\text{(2.2)} \qquad R(\ell) = P_{\mathfrak{H}}(A-\ell)^{-1}|_{\mathfrak{H}}$$

for all $\ell \in \mathfrak{D} \cup \mathfrak{D}^*$. The space $\mathfrak{K}$ can be chosen minimal, in which case A is uniquely determined up to weak isomorphisms. If the kernel $\mathsf{K}_R(\ell,\lambda)$ defined by (2.1) has κ negative squares on $\mathfrak{D}_R$, then (2.2) holds for all $\ell \in \mathfrak{D}_R$ and if, moreover, $\mathfrak{K}$ is minimal, then $\mathfrak{K}$ is a Pontryagin space of index κ and A is uniquely determined up to isomorphisms. In this last case the dimension of the Pontryagin space $\mathfrak{K} \ominus \mathfrak{H}$ is equal to the sum of the number of the positive and the negative squares of the kernel $\mathsf{K}_R(\ell,\lambda)$.

For the definition of a weak isomorphism we refer to [DLS5]. Under stronger assumptions Proposition 2.1 was proved in [DLS4] by different methods. As one may put $S=\{\{0,0\}\}$, it is actually valid for any holomorphic mapping $R(\ell)$ satisfying (a) and (b), i.e., without any reference to a symmetric relation, cf. the remarks following Theorem 2 in [DLS4].

Proof. To prove the first statement of the proposition we define the function $Q(\ell)$ by

$$Q(\ell)= (1/\mathrm{Im}\mu)\ \big(\ell-\mathrm{Re}\,\mu+(\ell-\mu)(\ell-\bar{\mu})R(\ell)\big).$$

Then $Q(\mu)=iI$ and Theorem 2 of [DLS4] implies that there exist a Krein space $\mathfrak{K}$, a mapping $\Gamma\in\mathbf{L}(\mathfrak{H},\mathfrak{K})$ and a unitary operator U in $\mathfrak{K}$ such that

$$Q(\ell)=i\Gamma^*\big(U+z(\ell)\big)\big(U-z(\ell)\big)^{-1}\Gamma,$$

where $z(\ell)=(\ell-\mu)/(\ell-\bar{\mu})$. Putting $\ell=\mu$ we find that $\Gamma^*\Gamma=I$. Also, $\Gamma\Gamma^*$ is a continuous orthogonal projection in the Krein space $\mathfrak{K}$ onto $\mathfrak{R}(\Gamma)$. Hence $\mathfrak{R}(\Gamma)$ is closed and a Krein space (see [B], Theorem V 3.4). As Γ is an isometry from $\mathfrak{H}$ onto $\mathfrak{R}(\Gamma)\subset\mathfrak{K}$, the space $\mathfrak{H}$ can be identified with the subspace $\mathfrak{R}(\Gamma)\subset\mathfrak{K}$, that is we can assume that $\mathfrak{K}$ contains $\mathfrak{H}$ as a Hilbert subspace, Γ is the restriction operator to $\mathfrak{H}$ and $\Gamma^*=P_{\mathfrak{H}}$. We define the selfadjoint relation A in $\mathfrak{K}$ as the inverse Cayley transform of U: $A=F_\mu(U)$. Then

$$Q(\ell)= (1/\mathrm{Im}\mu)\ \big(\ell-\mathrm{Re}\,\mu+(\ell-\mu)(\ell-\bar{\mu})P_{\mathfrak{H}}(A-\ell)^{-1}|_{\mathfrak{H}}\big)$$

and now (2.2) easily follows. For the remaining parts of the proposition we refer to [DLS1,4]. □

The characteristic function $\Theta(z)$, $z\in\mathbb{D}=\{z\in\mathbb{C}\mid |z|<1\}$, associated with the extension A is defined as follows. Choose $\mu\in\rho(A)\cap\mathbb{C}^+$ and put $\mathfrak{F}=\mathfrak{D}(M_{\bar{\mu}})$, $\mathfrak{G}=\mathfrak{D}(M_\mu)$. Then the Cayley transform $U=C_\mu(A)$ is a unitary extension of the isometry $V=C_\mu(S)$ and has the matrix representation

$$(2.3)\qquad U=\begin{bmatrix} T & F & O\\ G & H & O\\ O & O & V\end{bmatrix}:\begin{bmatrix}\hat{\mathfrak{K}}\\ \mathfrak{F}\\ \mathfrak{H}\ominus\mathfrak{F}\end{bmatrix}\to\begin{bmatrix}\hat{\mathfrak{K}}\\ \mathfrak{G}\\ \mathfrak{H}\ominus\mathfrak{G}\end{bmatrix},$$

where $\hat{\mathfrak{K}}=\mathfrak{K}\ominus\mathfrak{H}$ and T,F,G,H are bounded linear operators; in particular, T is a contraction. The function Θ is defined as the characteristic function Θ_Δ of the unitary colligation $\Delta=\big(\hat{\mathfrak{K}},\mathfrak{F},\mathfrak{G};T,F,G,H\big)$:

$$\Theta(z)=\Theta_{\Delta}(z)=H+zG(I-zT)^{-1}F,\ \ z=0\ \text{or}\ (1/z)\in\rho(T).$$

Clearly $\Theta\in\mathbf{S}(\mathfrak{F},\mathfrak{G})$, the class of holomorphic functions Θ with values in $\mathbf{L}(\mathfrak{F},\mathfrak{G})$ and with $0\in\mathfrak{D}_{\Theta}$, the domain of holomorphy of Θ in $\mathbb{D}$. We denote by $\mathbf{S}_{\kappa}(\mathfrak{F},\mathfrak{G})$ the (generalized) Schur class of functions $\Theta\in\mathbf{S}(\mathfrak{F},\mathfrak{G})$ for which the kernel

$$\text{(2.4)}\qquad \mathsf{S}_{\Theta}(z,w)=\frac{I-\Theta(w)^{*}\Theta(z)}{1-z\bar{w}}$$

has κ negative squares on $\mathfrak{D}_{\Theta}$. For $\kappa=0$ this class coincides with the Schur class of holomorphic contractions on $\mathbb{D}$. If the extending space $\hat{\mathfrak{K}}$ is a Pontryagin space of index κ, then the kernel S_{Θ} has at most κ negative squares; if, moreover, $\hat{\mathfrak{K}}$ is minimal in the sense that

$$\hat{\mathfrak{K}}=\text{c.l.s.}\Big\{\{\,T^{n}Ff\mid f\in\mathfrak{F},n\in\mathbb{N}\cup\{0\}\,\}\cup\{\,T^{*n}G^{*}g\mid g\in\mathfrak{G},n\in\mathbb{N}\cup\{0\}\,\}\Big\},$$

then it has exactly κ negative squares. Clearly, the steps taken to get from the extension A of S to Θ by means of a colligation Δ can be reversed. That is, given a unitary colligation $\Delta=\big(\hat{\mathfrak{K}},\mathfrak{F},\mathfrak{G};T,F,G,H\big)$, then $A=F_{\mu}(U)$, where U is defined by (2.3), is a selfadjoint extension of S with $\mu\in\rho(A)$. The following proposition (see [Az1,2] and [DLS3,5]) shows that any $\Theta\in\mathbf{S}(\mathfrak{F},\mathfrak{G})$ can be represented as a characteristic function of a unitary colligation.

PROPOSITION 2.2. *Let $\Theta\in\mathbf{S}(\mathfrak{F},\mathfrak{G})$ and $\mathfrak{D}$ be a simply connected open set with smooth boundary $\partial\mathfrak{D}$ such that $0\in\mathfrak{D}$ and $\mathfrak{D}\cup\partial\mathfrak{D}\subset\mathfrak{D}_{\Theta}$. Then there exists a unitary colligation $\Delta=\big(\hat{\mathfrak{K}},\mathfrak{F},\mathfrak{G};T,F,G,H\big)$ such that $\mathfrak{D}_{\Theta_{\Delta}}\supset\mathfrak{D}$ and*

$$\text{(2.5)}\qquad \Theta(z)=\Theta_{\Delta}(z)$$

for all $z\in\mathfrak{D}$. The colligation Δ can be constructed so that $\hat{\mathfrak{K}}$ is minimal in which case it is uniquely determined up to weak isomorphisms. If the kernel $\mathsf{S}_{\Theta}(z,w)$, defined by (2.4), has κ negative squares on $\mathfrak{D}_{\Theta}$, then (2.5) holds for all $z\in\mathfrak{D}_{\Theta}$ and if, moreover, $\hat{\mathfrak{K}}$ is minimal, then $\hat{\mathfrak{K}}$ is a Pontryagin space of index κ and Δ is uniquely determined up to isomorphisms. In this last case the dimension of the Pontryagin space $\hat{\mathfrak{K}}$ is equal to the sum of the number of the positive and the negative squares of the kernel $\mathsf{S}_{\Theta}(z,w)$.

The Štraus relation $T(\ell)$, $\ell\in\mathbb{C}\cup\{\infty\}$, associated with the extension A is defined in a purely algebraic fashion by the following:

$$T(\ell)=\Big\{ \{P_{\mathfrak{H}}f,\ P_{\mathfrak{H}}g\} \mid \{f,g\}\in A,\ g-\ell f\in\mathfrak{H} \Big\},$$

$$T(\infty)=\Big\{ \{f,\ P_{\mathfrak{H}}g\} \mid \{f,g\}\in A,\ f\in\mathfrak{H} \Big\},$$

see [DLS1,2]. Clearly, $S\subset T(\ell)\subset S^*$, and we have $T(\bar{\ell})\subset T(\ell)^*$, with equality if $\ell\in\rho(A)$. Moreover, we have

$$P_{\mathfrak{H}}\nu(A-\ell)=\nu(T(\ell)-\ell).$$

The connection between the generalized resolvent $R(\ell)$, the characteristic function $\Theta(z)$ and the Štraus relation $T(\ell)$ is given by

$$R(\ell)=(T(\ell)-\ell)^{-1} \quad\text{or}\quad T(\ell)=R(\ell)^{-1}+\ell, \qquad \ell\in\rho(A),$$

and with $\mu\in\rho(A)\cap\mathbb{C}^+$ fixed, $\mathfrak{F}=\mathfrak{D}(M_{\bar{\mu}}(S))$, $\mathfrak{G}=\mathfrak{D}(M_{\mu}(S))$, $z(\ell)=(\ell-\mu)/(\ell-\bar{\mu})$,

$$\Theta(z(\ell))=C_{\mu}(T(\ell))|_{\mathfrak{F}}\ ,\quad \Theta(z(\ell))^*=C_{\bar{\mu}}(T(\bar{\ell}))|_{\mathfrak{G}}\ ,$$

or

$$(2.6)\qquad \begin{cases} T(\ell)=S\dotplus\{\ \{\psi-\Theta(z(\ell))\psi,\bar{\mu}\psi-\mu\Theta(z(\ell))\psi\}\mid\psi\in\mathfrak{F}\ \},\\ \\ T(\bar{\ell})=S\dotplus\{\ \{\varphi-\Theta(z(\ell)^*\varphi,\mu\varphi-\bar{\mu}\Theta(z(\ell))^*\varphi\}\mid\varphi\in\mathfrak{G}\ \},\end{cases}$$

direct sums in $\mathfrak{H}^2$, $\ell\in\mathbb{C}^+$ such that $z(\ell)\in\mathfrak{D}_{\Theta}$.

A family of relations $T(\ell)$ in $\mathfrak{H}^2$ defined for ℓ in some open set $\mathfrak{D}=\mathfrak{D}^*\subset\mathbb{C}\backslash\mathbb{R}$ is called a Štraus extension of S if for some $\mu\in\mathfrak{D}\cap\mathbb{C}^+$

$$\begin{cases} S\subset T(\ell)\subset S^*,\\ T(\bar{\ell})=T(\ell)^*,\ \ \ell\in\mathfrak{D}\cap\mathbb{C}^+,\\ \Theta\in\mathbf{S}(\mathfrak{F},\mathfrak{G}),\ \text{ where } \Theta(z)=C_{\mu}(\ T(\ \dfrac{\bar{\mu}z-\mu}{z-1}\ )\ )|_{\mathfrak{F}}\ ,\end{cases}$$

with $\mathfrak{F}=\mathfrak{D}(M_{\bar{\mu}}(S)),\mathfrak{G}=\mathfrak{D}(M_{\mu}(S))$. It is called a Štraus extension of index κ if $\Theta\in\mathbf{S}_{\kappa}(\mathfrak{F},\mathfrak{G})$. Proposition 2.2 easily yields that Štraus extensions of S restriced to "smooth" domains are Štraus relations induced by selfadjoint extensions of S, and that Štraus extensions of S of index κ correspond to minimal selfadjoint extensions in Pontryagin spaces. We leave the further details to the reader.

3. Symmetric relations with finite defect numbers

In this section we concentrate on the case of interest for ordinary differential equations, namely the case where the defect subspaces of S have finite dimensions

$$\omega_+ = \dim M_\ell(S) < \infty, \quad \omega_- = \dim M_{\bar{\ell}}(S) < \infty, \quad \ell \in \mathbb{C}^+.$$

Recall that these numbers are independent of $\ell \in \mathbb{C}^+$. We put $p = \omega_+ + \omega_-$. For $\{f,g\}$, $\{h,k\} \in \mathfrak{H}^2$ we define

$$<\{f,g\},\{h,k\}> = [g,h] - [f,k]$$

and in what follows we fix a boundary map b connected with S, i.e., a linear map $b: S^* \to \mathbb{C}^p$ with $b(S) = 0$ and $b(S^*) = \mathbb{C}^p$. Furthermore, we implicitly define the associated operator Q in $\mathbb{C}^p$ by

$$(3.1) \qquad (1/i) <\{f,g\},\{h,k\}> = b(h,k)^* Q b(f,g), \qquad \{f,g\},\ \{h,k\} \in S^*$$

and note that Q is invertible, hermitian and of signature (ω_+, ω_-).

When we apply the results of this section to ordinary differential equations, $b(f,g)$ is a vector formed by the boundary values of f and g, and the relation (3.1) is Lagrange's identity or Green's formula. Finally, let Ψ $(1\times\omega_-)$, Φ $(1\times\omega_+)$ be row vectors whose entries form bases for $\mathfrak{F} = \mathfrak{D}(M_{\bar{\mu}}(S))$, $\mathfrak{G} = \mathfrak{D}(M_\mu(S))$, respectively, with $\mu \in \rho(A) \cap \mathbb{C}^+$. Then (2.6) and the fact that $T(\bar{\ell}) = T(\ell)^*$ for $\ell \in \rho(A)$ imply that for $\ell \in \mathbb{C}^+$ such that $z(\ell) \in \mathfrak{D}_\Theta$

$$T(\ell) = \left\{ \{f,g\} \in S^* \mid \mathcal{U}(\ell) b(f,g) = 0 \right\},$$

where for these ℓ's:

$$(3.2) \qquad \begin{cases} \mathcal{U}(\ell) = b\big(\Phi - \Theta(z(\ell))^*\Phi, \mu\Phi - \bar{\mu}\Theta(z(\ell))^*\Phi\big)^* Q, & (\omega_+ \times p), \\ \\ \mathcal{U}(\bar{\ell}) = b\big(\Psi - \Theta(z(\ell))\Psi, \bar{\mu}\Psi - \mu\Theta(z(\ell))\Psi\big)^* Q, & (\omega_- \times p). \end{cases}$$

It is not difficult to verify that $\mathcal{U}$ is a matrix function which is locally holomorphic with domain of holomorphy $\mathfrak{D}_{\mathcal{U}} = \mathfrak{D}_{\mathcal{U}}^* \subset \mathbb{C}\backslash\mathbb{R}$, such that for all $\ell \in \mathfrak{D}_{\mathcal{U}} \cap \mathbb{C}^+$

$$(3.3) \qquad \begin{cases} \mathcal{U}(\ell) \text{ is } (\omega_+ \times p), \quad \operatorname{rank} \mathcal{U}(\ell) = \omega_+, \\ \\ \mathcal{U}(\bar{\ell}) \text{ is } (\omega_- \times p), \quad \operatorname{rank} \mathcal{U}(\bar{\ell}) = \omega_-, \end{cases}$$

$$(3.4) \qquad \begin{cases} \nu(\mathcal{U}(\ell)|_{b(M_\mu(S))}) = \{0\}, \\ \\ \nu(\mathcal{U}(\bar{\ell})|_{b(M_{\bar{\mu}}(S))}) = \{0\}, \end{cases}$$

$$(3.5) \qquad \mathcal{U}(\bar{\ell}) Q^{-1} \mathcal{U}(\ell)^* = 0$$

and if the extending space is a Pontryagin space of index κ, then the kernel

$$(3.6)\qquad \mathsf{K}_{\mathcal{U}}(\ell,\lambda) = (1/i)\,\frac{\mathcal{U}(\bar\lambda)Q^{-1}\mathcal{U}(\bar\ell)^*}{\ell-\bar\lambda}, \qquad \ell,\lambda\in\mathfrak{D}_{\mathcal{U}}\cap\mathbb{C}^+,$$

has at most κ negative squares and exactly κ negative squares if this space is minimal.

Proposition 3.1. *Let $\mathcal{U}(\ell)$ be a matrix function which is locally holomorphic on $\mathfrak{D}_{\mathcal{U}}=\mathfrak{D}_{\mathcal{U}}^*\subset\mathbb{C}\backslash\mathbb{R}$, $\mu\in\mathfrak{D}_{\mathcal{U}}\cap\mathbb{C}^+$ and let $\mathfrak{D}$ be a simply connected open subset with smooth boundary $\partial\mathfrak{D}$ such that $\mu\in\mathfrak{D}$ and $\mathfrak{D}\cup\partial\mathfrak{D}\subset\mathfrak{D}_{\mathcal{U}}\cap\mathbb{C}^+$. Assume that $\mathcal{U}$ satisfies (3.3)–(3.5) for all $\ell\in\mathfrak{D}\cup\partial\mathfrak{D}$. Then on $\mathfrak{D}\cup\mathfrak{D}^*$ the family of relations $T(\ell)$, defined by*

$$(3.7)\qquad T(\ell)=\Big\{\,\{f,g\}\in S^*\mid \mathcal{U}(\ell)b(f,g)=0\,\Big\},$$

coincides with a Štraus extension of S with corresponding characteristic function $\Theta(z(\ell))$, defined by

$$(3.8)\qquad \Theta(z(\ell))\Psi=\Phi\Pi(\ell)$$

with $\Pi(\ell)$ given by

$$\Pi(\ell)=\big(\,\mathcal{U}(\ell)b(\Phi,\mu\Phi)\,\big)^{-1}\big(\,\mathcal{U}(\ell)b(\Psi,\bar\mu\Psi)\,\big)$$

$$=[\Phi,\Phi]^{-1}\Big\{\big(\mathcal{U}(\bar\ell)b(\Psi,\bar\mu\Psi)\big)^{-1}\big(\mathcal{U}(\bar\ell)b(\Phi,\mu\Phi)\big)\Big\}^*[\Psi,\Psi]$$

for $\ell\in\mathfrak{D}_{\mathcal{U}}\cap\mathbb{C}^+$. The kernel $\mathsf{K}_{\mathcal{U}}(\ell,\lambda)$, defined by (3.6), is related to the kernel $S_\Theta(z,w)$, defined by (2.4), via

$$(3.9)\qquad \big[\,\mathsf{S}_\Theta(z(\ell),z(\lambda))\Psi,\Psi\,\big]=\big(\,\mathsf{K}_{\mathcal{U}}(\ell,\lambda)\,a(\ell),a(\lambda)\,\big),$$

where $a(\ell)$ is defined by

$$a(\ell)=(\ell-\bar\mu)\big(\,\big(\mathcal{U}(\bar\ell)b(\Psi,\bar\mu\Psi)\big)^{-1}\big)^*[\Psi,\Psi].$$

Hence, if the kernel $\mathsf{K}_{\mathcal{U}}(\ell,\lambda)$ has κ negative squares on $\mathfrak{D}$, the Štraus extension has index κ. In this case, if $\mathfrak{K}$ is the extending Pontryagin space, the dimension of $\mathfrak{K}\ominus\mathfrak{H}$ is equal to the sum of the number of the positive and the negative squares of the kernel $\mathsf{K}_{\mathcal{U}}(\ell,\lambda)$.

We shall give a proof of this proposition together with the proof of the following proposition. So far we have obtained an analytic description of the Štraus extension $T(\ell)$ of S only for nonreal values of ℓ. In the case where the extension is of index κ this can also be given for $\ell\in\mathbb{R}\cup\{\infty\}$. In this case we shall, and may without loss of generality, assume that $T(\ell)$ is given by (3.7) where $\mathcal{U}(\ell)$ has a domain of holomorphy $\mathfrak{D}_{\mathcal{U}}$ which coincides with $\mathbb{C}\backslash\mathbb{R}$ with the possible exception of at most finitely many points (satisfies (3.3)–(3.5) for $\ell\in\mathfrak{D}_{\mathcal{U}}\cap\mathbb{C}^+$ and has a kernel $K_{\mathcal{U}}(\ell,\lambda)$ with κ negative squares on $\mathfrak{D}_{\mathcal{U}}$). In the following proposition we denote by $\mathcal{L}_\lambda$, $\lambda\in\mathbb{R}\cup\{\infty\}$, the linear space

$$\mathcal{L}_\lambda=\Big\{ c\in\mathbb{C}^{\omega_-} \mid |\ell-\bar{\mu}|^2c^*\big(\mathcal{U}(\bar{\ell})b(\Psi,\bar{\mu}\Psi)\big)^{-1}K_{\mathcal{U}}(\ell,\ell)\big((\mathcal{U}(\bar{\ell})b(\Psi,\bar{\mu}\Psi))^{-1}\big)^*c \text{ has a finite limit in } \mathbb{C} \text{ as } \ell\hat{\to}\lambda\Big\}.$$

Here for $\lambda\in\mathbb{R}$, $\ell\hat{\to}\lambda$ denotes the limit as $\ell\in\mathbb{C}^+$ tends to λ nontangentially and for $\lambda=\infty$ it stands for the limit as $\ell\in\mathbb{C}^+$ tends to ∞ in a sector $\delta<\arg\ell<\pi-\delta$ for some $\delta\in(0,\frac{1}{2}\pi)$. We shall also denote such limits by the symbol $\widehat{\lim_{l\to\lambda}}$. In the proof of the proposition we shall show that if $c\in\mathcal{L}_\lambda$, then the expression

$$Q^{-1}\mathcal{U}(\bar{\ell})^*\big((\mathcal{U}(\bar{\ell})b(\Psi,\bar{\mu}\Psi))^{-1}\big)^*c$$

has a finite limit in $\mathbb{C}^p$ as $\ell\hat{\to}\lambda$.

PROPOSITION 3.2. *Let $T(\ell)$ be a Štraus extension of S of index κ, for nonreal values of ℓ described by*

$$T(\ell)=\Big\{ \{f,g\}\in S^* \mid \mathcal{U}(\ell)b(f,g)=0\Big\},$$

where $\mathcal{U}(\ell)$ satisfies the conditions mentioned above. Then for $\lambda\in\mathbb{R}\cup\{\infty\}$

$$T(\lambda)=\Big\{ \{f,g\}\in S^* \mid (\exists c\in\mathcal{L}_\lambda)\ b(f,g)=\widehat{\lim_{l\to\lambda}}\, Q^{-1}\mathcal{U}(\bar{\ell})^*\big((\mathcal{U}(\bar{\ell})b(\Psi,\bar{\mu}\Psi))^{-1}\big)^*c\Big\}.$$

Proof of Propositions 3.1 *and* 3.2. We define the mappings $\Theta(z):\mathfrak{F}\to\mathfrak{G}$ and $\Xi(z):\mathfrak{G}\to\mathfrak{F}$ for $z\in z(\mathfrak{D})$ by $\Theta(z(\ell))\Psi=\Phi\Pi(\ell)$ and $\Xi(z(\ell))\Phi=\Psi\Lambda(\ell)$, where

$$\Pi(\ell)=[\Phi,\Phi]^{-1}\Big\{\big(\mathcal{U}(\bar{\ell})b(\Psi,\bar{\mu}\Psi)\big)^{-1}\big(\mathcal{U}(\bar{\ell})b(\Phi,\mu\Phi)\big)\Big\}^*[\Psi,\Psi],$$

$$\Lambda(\ell)=[\Psi,\Psi]^{-1}\Big\{\big(\mathcal{U}(\ell)b(\Phi,\mu\Phi)\big)^{-1}\big(\mathcal{U}(\ell)b(\Psi,\mu\Psi)\big)\Big\}^*[\Phi,\Phi]$$

and denote by $\mathcal{B}$ the invertible $p\times p$ matrix $\mathcal{B}=\big(b(\Psi,\bar{\mu}\Psi):b(\Phi,\mu\Phi)\big)$. Then using (3.1) we see that $\mathcal{B}^*Q\mathcal{B}=2\mathrm{Im}\mu\,\mathrm{diag}\big(-[\Psi,\Psi]:[\Phi,\Phi]\big)$ and we obtain

$$\begin{bmatrix} b\big(\Phi-\Xi(z(\ell))\Phi,\mu\Phi-\bar{\mu}\Xi(z(\ell))\Phi\big)^* \\ b\big(\Psi-\Theta(z(\ell))\Psi,\bar{\mu}\Psi-\mu\Theta(z(\ell))\Psi\big)^* \end{bmatrix} Q=\begin{pmatrix} -\Lambda(\ell)^* & I_{\omega_+} \\ I_{\omega_-} & -\Pi(\ell)^* \end{pmatrix}\mathcal{B}^*Q\mathcal{B}\,\mathcal{B}^{-1}=$$

$$= 2\mathrm{Im}\mu \begin{bmatrix} O & [\Phi,\Phi]\left(\mathcal{U}(\ell)b(\Phi,\mu\Phi)\right)^{-1} \\ -[\Psi,\Psi]\left(\mathcal{U}(\bar{\ell})b(\Psi,\bar{\mu}\Psi)\right)^{-1} & O \end{bmatrix} \cdot$$

$$\cdot \begin{bmatrix} \mathcal{U}(\bar{\ell})b(\Psi,\bar{\mu}\Psi) & \mathcal{U}(\bar{\ell})b(\Phi,\mu\Phi) \\ \mathcal{U}(\ell)b(\Psi,\bar{\mu}\Psi) & \mathcal{U}(\ell)b(\Phi,\mu\Phi) \end{bmatrix} \mathcal{B}^{-1}$$

$$= 2\mathrm{Im}\mu \begin{bmatrix} [\Phi,\Phi]\left(\mathcal{U}(\ell)b(\Phi,\mu\Phi)\right)^{-1}\mathcal{U}(\ell) \\ -[\Psi,\Psi]\left(\mathcal{U}(\bar{\ell})b(\Psi,\bar{\mu}\Psi)\right)^{-1}\mathcal{U}(\bar{\ell}) \end{bmatrix}.$$

From (3.5) it now easily follows that $\Xi(z(\ell)) = \Theta(z(\ell))^*$ and we conclude that apart from invertible factors (3.2) holds. A simple dimension argument and (3.3) imply that (2.6) is valid and that $T(\bar{\ell}) = T(\ell)^*$ for all $\ell \in \mathfrak{D} \cup \partial\mathfrak{D}$. It is now easy to see that $T(\ell)$ is a Štraus extension of S. From the fact that

$$\{\Psi,\bar{\mu}\Psi\} - \{\Phi,\mu\Phi\}\Pi(\ell) \in T(\ell),$$

it follows that

$$\Pi(\ell) = \left(\mathcal{U}(\ell)b(\Phi,\mu\Phi) \right)^{-1} \left(\mathcal{U}(\ell)b(\Psi,\bar{\mu}\Psi) \right),$$

which proves (3.8). The proof of (3.9) is straightforward and is left to the reader. Concerning the description of $T(\lambda)$ for $\lambda \in \mathbb{R} \cup \{\infty\}$ in Proposition 3.2 we first note that the above calculations show that for $\tilde{c} \in \mathbb{C}^{\omega_-}$

$$Q^{-1}\mathcal{U}(\bar{\ell})^* \left(\left(\mathcal{U}(\bar{\ell})b(\Psi,\bar{\mu}\Psi)\right)^{-1} \right)^* (-2\mathrm{Im}\mu)[\Psi,\Psi]\tilde{c} =$$

$$= b(\Psi,\bar{\mu}\Psi)\tilde{c} - b(\Theta(z(\ell))\Psi, \mu\Theta(z(\ell))\Psi)\tilde{c}.$$

Now, by Von Neumann's formula, each $\{f,g\} \in S^*$ has the unique representation

$$\{f,g\} = \{f_0,g_0\} + \{\Psi,\bar{\mu}\Psi\}\tilde{c} - \{\Phi,\mu\Phi\}d$$

for some $\{f_0,g_0\} \in S$, $\tilde{c} \in \mathbb{C}^{\omega_-}$ and $d \in \mathbb{C}^{\omega_+}$, which implies that

$$b(f,g) = b(\Psi,\bar{\mu}\Psi)\tilde{c} - b(\Phi,\mu\Phi)d$$

and in [DLS2,3] it is shown that $\{f,g\} \in T(\lambda)$ if and only if $\tilde{c}$ and d are such that

(3.10) $|\ell - \bar{\mu}|^2 \left[S_\Theta(z(\ell), z(\ell))\Psi\tilde{c}, \Psi\tilde{c} \right]$ has a finite limit in $\mathbb{C}$ as $\ell \hat{\to} \lambda$

and

(3.11) $\Theta(z(\ell))\Psi\tilde{c}$ converges to Φd as $\ell \hat{\to} \lambda$.

Here the convergence in (3.11) follows from (3.10), see [DLS3], Theorem 9.1. Put $c=-2\mathrm{Im}\mu[\Psi,\Psi]\tilde{c}$. Then, on account of (3.9), (3.10) is valid if and only if $c\in\mathcal{L}_\lambda$ and the description of $T(\lambda)$, $\lambda\in\mathbb{R}\cup\{\infty\}$, now follows. □

In [DLS1] it was shown that if S is a densely defined symmetric operator then in the characterization of Štraus extensions of S of index κ condition (3.4) is superfluous. This is also the case, when we consider Hilbert space extensions, i.e., $\kappa=0$.

In the statements of the above propositions we described the characteristic operator function in just one half plane. Of course the complete statement would also involve a characterization of its adjoint in the other half plane. Here and in the rest of this paper we will be mostly concerned with just one half plane.

4. Štraus extensions in the linear case

As an example we consider the linear case, that is the case where $\omega_+=\omega_-=\omega$, say, and $\mathcal{U}(\ell)=\mathcal{V}+\ell\mathcal{W}$, where $\mathcal{V},\mathcal{W}\,(\omega\times 2\omega)$ are constant matrices such that (3.3)–(3.5) are satisfied. Then it follows from (3.5) that

$$\mathcal{V}\mathcal{Q}^{-1}\mathcal{V}^*=\mathcal{O},\ \ \mathcal{W}\mathcal{Q}^{-1}\mathcal{W}^*=\mathcal{O},\ \ \mathcal{W}\mathcal{Q}^{-1}\mathcal{V}^*=-\mathcal{V}\mathcal{Q}^{-1}\mathcal{W}^*.$$

Hence $\mathsf{K}_{\mathcal{U}}(\ell,\lambda)=i\mathcal{W}\mathcal{Q}^{-1}\mathcal{V}^*$ is hermitian, and there exists a unitary $\omega\times\omega$ matrix Γ such that

$$i\Gamma\mathcal{W}\mathcal{Q}^{-1}\mathcal{V}^*\Gamma^*=\begin{pmatrix}\mathcal{O}&\mathcal{O}\\ \mathcal{O}&\mathcal{D}\end{pmatrix},$$

where $\mathcal{D}$ is an invertible $k\times k$ diagonal matrix and $0\le k\le\omega$. The number of negative diagonal elements is equal to the number of negative squares of $\mathsf{K}_{\mathcal{U}}(\ell,\lambda)$. We have for $\ell,\lambda\in\mathbb{C}$ that

$$\Gamma(\mathcal{V}+\ell\mathcal{W})\mathcal{Q}^{-1}(\Gamma(\mathcal{V}+\lambda\mathcal{W}))^*=-i(\ell-\bar{\lambda})\begin{pmatrix}\mathcal{O}&\mathcal{O}\\ \mathcal{O}&\mathcal{D}\end{pmatrix}$$

which, together with (3.3) and (3.5), implies that for each pair $\ell,\lambda\in\mathbb{C}\backslash\mathbb{R}$ there exists an invertible $(\omega-k)\times(\omega-k)$ matrix Λ such that

$$(4.1)\qquad (I_{\omega-k}:\mathcal{O})\Gamma(\mathcal{V}+\lambda\mathcal{W})=(\Lambda:\mathcal{O})\Gamma(\mathcal{V}+\ell\mathcal{W}).$$

Introducing the matrices $\mathcal{F}$ $(k\times 2\omega)$, $\mathcal{G}$ $(k\times 2\omega)$ and $\mathcal{H}$ $((\omega-k)\times 2\omega)$ by

$$\Gamma(\mathcal{V}+\ell\mathcal{W})=\begin{pmatrix}\mathcal{H}\\ \mathcal{F}-\ell\mathcal{G}\end{pmatrix},$$

we may write $T(\ell)$ given by (3.7) as

(4.2) $T(\ell)=\left\{ \{f,g\}\in S^* \mid (\mathcal{F}-\ell\mathcal{G})b(f,g)=0,\ \mathcal{H}b(f,g)=0 \right\},\quad \ell\in\mathbb{C}\backslash\mathbb{R}.$

Note that on account of (4.1) the null space $\nu(\mathcal{H})$ is independent of $\ell\in\mathbb{C}\backslash\mathbb{R}$. It can easily be verified that $T(\ell)$ defined by (4.2) with given matrices $\mathcal{F}(k\times 2\omega)$, $\mathcal{G}(k\times 2\omega)$ and $\mathcal{H}((\omega-k)\times 2\omega)$ is a Štraus extension of S if and only if

$$(4.3)\quad \begin{cases} \mathcal{H}Q^{-1}\mathcal{H}^*=O,\ \mathcal{H}Q^{-1}\mathcal{F}^*=O,\ \mathcal{H}Q^{-1}\mathcal{G}^*=O,\ \mathcal{F}Q^{-1}\mathcal{F}^*=O,\ \mathcal{G}Q^{-1}\mathcal{G}^*=O, \\ \mathcal{D}:=i\mathcal{F}Q^{-1}\mathcal{G}^* \text{ is an invertible hermitian matrix,} \\ \operatorname{rank}\mathcal{H}=\omega-k \end{cases}$$

and

$$(4.4)\quad \nu\left(\begin{matrix}\mathcal{H}\\ \mathcal{F}-\ell\mathcal{G}\end{matrix} \Big|_{b(M_\ell(S))} \right)=\{0\} \text{ for some } \ell \text{ in } \mathbb{C}^+ \text{ and in } \mathbb{C}^-.$$

Moreover, it is a Štraus extension of index κ, where κ is the number of negative eigenvalues of $\mathcal{D}$. Now consider the Pontryagin space $\mathfrak{K}=\mathfrak{H}\oplus\mathbb{C}^k$ with inner product

$$[(\begin{smallmatrix} f\\ \alpha\end{smallmatrix}),(\begin{smallmatrix} g\\ \beta\end{smallmatrix})] = [f,g]+\beta^*\mathcal{D}^{-1}\alpha, \qquad f,g\in\mathfrak{H},\ \alpha,\beta\in\mathbb{C}^k,$$

and the relation A in $\mathfrak{K}$ defined by

$$(4.5)\quad A=\left\{ \left\{ \begin{bmatrix} f\\ \mathcal{G}b(f,g)\end{bmatrix}, \begin{bmatrix} g\\ \mathcal{F}b(f,g)\end{bmatrix} \right\} \,\middle|\, \{f,g\}\in S^*,\ \mathcal{H}b(f,g)=0 \right\}.$$

Then, on account of (4.3) and (4.4), A is a selfadjoint extension of S in $\mathfrak{K}$, $\rho(A)\neq\emptyset$, $\mathfrak{K}$ is minimal and hence a Pontryagin space of index κ and the Štraus relation induced by A equals $T(\ell)$ defined by (4.2). In fact, this model shows that

$$T(\ell)=\left\{ \{f,g\}\in S^* \mid (\mathcal{F}-\ell\mathcal{G})b(f,g)=0,\ \mathcal{H}b(f,g)=0 \right\},\qquad \ell\in\mathbb{C},$$

$$T(\infty)=\left\{ \{f,g\}\in S^* \mid \mathcal{G}b(f,g)=0,\ \mathcal{H}b(f,g)=0 \right\}.$$

For $\ell\in\mathbb{R}\cup\{\infty\}$ these equalities also follow from Proposition 3.2 and the fact that for these ℓ's the relations $T(\ell)$ are selfadjoint (see [DSL2], Theorem 3.3). Indeed, Proposition 3.2 implies that for $\lambda\in\mathbb{R}$

$$T(\lambda)\subset\left\{ \{f,g\}\in S^* \mid \mathcal{F}b(f,g)=\lambda\mathcal{G}b(f,g),\ \mathcal{H}b(f,g)=0 \right\}$$

and equality follows since both relations are selfadjoint. In a similar way we obtain the above equality for $\lambda=\infty$. An immediate consequence of the model is the property that

$$A \cap (\mathfrak{K} \ominus \mathfrak{H})^2 = \{0,0\}. \tag{4.6}$$

Conversely, if A is a selfadjoint extension of S in a Krein space $\mathfrak{K}$, with $\rho(A) \neq \emptyset$, such that (4.6) holds, then the corresponding Štraus relation $T(\ell)$ is defined by boundary conditions which are linear in ℓ, in the sense explained above. In order to see this, we repeat the arguments due to Röh [R]. We consider $\hat{S} = A \cap \mathfrak{H}^2$ and show first

$$\begin{cases} \omega_+ = \omega_- = \omega, \text{ say,} \\ 0 \leq k := \dim \mathfrak{K} \ominus \mathfrak{H} \leq \omega, \\ \dim S^*/\hat{S}^* = \dim \hat{S}/S = \omega - k. \end{cases} \tag{4.7}$$

Let $\mu \in \rho(A) \cap \mathbb{C}^+$ and $V = C_\mu(S)$, $\hat{V} = C_\mu(\hat{S})$ and $U = C_\mu(A)$. Then V and $\hat{V}$ are isometries in $\mathfrak{H}$, U is a unitary operator in $\mathfrak{K}$ and $V \subset \hat{V} \subset U$. It is easy to verify that

$$\begin{aligned}
&\omega_- = \dim \mathfrak{H} \ominus \mathfrak{D}(V) = \dim \mathfrak{H} \ominus \mathfrak{D}(\hat{V}) + \dim \mathfrak{D}(\hat{V}) \ominus \mathfrak{D}(V),\\
&\omega_+ = \dim \mathfrak{H} \ominus \mathfrak{R}(V) = \dim \mathfrak{H} \ominus \mathfrak{R}(\hat{V}) + \dim \mathfrak{R}(\hat{V}) \ominus \mathfrak{R}(V),\\
&\dim S^*/\hat{S}^* = \dim \hat{S}/S = \dim \mathfrak{D}(\hat{V}) \ominus \mathfrak{D}(V) = \dim \mathfrak{R}(\hat{V}) \ominus \mathfrak{R}(V),\\
&\omega_- + \dim \mathfrak{K} \ominus \mathfrak{H} = \omega_+ + \dim \mathfrak{K} \ominus \mathfrak{H},\\
&\dim \mathfrak{H} \ominus \mathfrak{D}(\hat{V}) + \dim \mathfrak{K} \ominus \mathfrak{H} = \dim \mathfrak{H} \ominus \mathfrak{R}(\hat{V}) + \dim \mathfrak{K} \ominus \mathfrak{H}.
\end{aligned}$$

Now, the mapping $P_{\mathfrak{K}\ominus\mathfrak{H}} U \mid_{\mathfrak{H}\ominus\mathfrak{D}(\hat{V})}$ is an injection from $\mathfrak{H} \ominus \mathfrak{D}(\hat{V})$ into $\mathfrak{K} \ominus \mathfrak{H}$. Hence

$$\dim \mathfrak{H} \ominus \mathfrak{D}(\hat{V}) \leq \dim \mathfrak{K} \ominus \mathfrak{H}.$$

On the other hand (4.6) implies that $U \cap (\mathfrak{K} \ominus \mathfrak{H})^2 = \{\{0,0\}\}$ which in turn implies that the mapping $P_{\mathfrak{H}} U \mid_{\mathfrak{K}\ominus\mathfrak{H}}$ is also an injection from $\mathfrak{K} \ominus \mathfrak{H}$ into $\mathfrak{H} \ominus \mathfrak{R}(\hat{V})$. Therefore

$$\dim \mathfrak{K} \ominus \mathfrak{H} \leq \dim \mathfrak{H} \ominus \mathfrak{R}(\hat{V}) \leq \omega_+ < \infty.$$

From these equalities and inequalities the equalities in (4.7) now easily follow. Those on the last line of (4.7) imply that there exists an $(\omega - k) \times 2\omega$ matrix $\mathcal{H}$ such that

$$\begin{aligned}
&\operatorname{rank} \mathcal{H} = \omega - k,\\
&\hat{S}^* = \left\{ \{f,g\} \in S^* \mid \mathcal{H} b(f,g) = 0 \right\}.
\end{aligned}$$

From the fact that $\hat{S}^* = P_{\mathfrak{H}}^{(2)} A$, where $P_{\mathfrak{H}}^{(2)}$ is the orthogonal projection from $\mathfrak{K}^2$ onto $\mathfrak{H}^2$, it follows that the elements of A are of the form

$$(4.8)\qquad \left\{ \begin{bmatrix} f \\ \alpha \end{bmatrix}, \begin{bmatrix} g \\ \beta \end{bmatrix} \right\}, \qquad \{f,g\} \in \hat{S}^*, \qquad \alpha,\beta \in \mathfrak{K} \ominus \mathfrak{H}.$$

On account of (4.6) the mappings $\{f,g\} \mapsto \alpha$ and $\{f,g\} \mapsto \beta$ defined from $\hat{S}^*$ to $\mathfrak{K} \ominus \mathfrak{H}$, such that the element given by (4.8) belongs to A, are well defined and surjective. Clearly, they coincide with the zero operator on S and now it is not difficult to see that there exist surjective linear mappings $\mathcal{G},\mathcal{F}:\mathbb{C}^p \to \mathfrak{K} \ominus \mathfrak{H}$ such that A is given by (4.5), which implies that the induced Štraus relation is linear in the eigenvalue parameter.

5. Canonical systems and corresponding relations

Let $(a,b) \subseteq \mathbb{R}$ be an open interval and consider in $\mathbb{C}^k$ the canonical system of differential equations

$$(5.1)\qquad Jy'(t) = \big(\ell\Delta(t) + H(t)\big)\, y(t) + \Delta(t)f(t), \qquad t \in (a,b), \quad \ell \in \mathbb{C},$$

where f is a $k\times 1$ vector function on (a,b), and also consider the corresponding homogeneous system

$$(5.2)\qquad Jy'(t) = \big(\ell\Delta(t) + H(t)\big)\, y(t).$$

Here J is a constant $k\times k$ matrix that satisfies

$$(5.3)\qquad J^* = J^{-1} = -J$$

and Δ and H are $k\times k$ matrix functions on (a,b), which are hermitian almost everywhere and locally integrable. The endpoint a (or b) is called regular if a (or b) is finite, and if the functions Δ and H are integrable on a right neighbourhood of a (or on a left neighbourhood of the point b). Let $Y(.,\ell)$ be a fundamental solution of (5.2), i.e., the $k\times k$ matrix function, which solves the initial value problem

$$JY'(t,\ell) = \big(\ell\Delta(t) + H(t)\big)\, Y(t,\ell), \qquad t \in (a,b),$$
$$Y(e,\ell) = I,$$

where $e \in (a,b)$, when both endpoints are singular, $e \in [a,b)$ when a is a regular endpoint, or $e \in (a,b]$ when b is a regular endpoint. Then it is easy to see that the identity

$$(5.4)\qquad Y(t,\lambda)^* JY(t,\ell) - J = (\ell - \bar{\lambda}) \int_e^t Y(s,\lambda)^* \Delta(s) Y(s,\ell)\; ds$$

holds for $t \in (a,b)$ and $\ell,\lambda \in \mathbb{C}$. Hence we obtain for $t \in (a,b)$ and $\ell \in \mathbb{C}$

(5.5) $\quad Y(t,\bar{\ell})^*JY(t,\ell)=J, \quad$ and $\quad Y(t,\ell)JY(t,\bar{\ell})^*=J.$

For each fixed $t\in(a,b)$ the matrizant $Y(t,\ell)$ is an entire function. From now on we assume

(5.6) $\quad \Delta(t)\geq 0,\quad$ for almost all $t\in(a,b)$.

Then it follows from (5.4) and (5.6) that for $t\in(a,b)$, $\ell\in\mathbb{C}\backslash\mathbb{R}$,

(5.7) $$\frac{Y(t,\ell)^*JY(t,\ell)-J}{\ell-\bar{\ell}}\geq 0,$$

but then from (5.7) and (5.5) it also follows that

$$\frac{Y(t,\ell)JY(t,\ell)^*-J}{\ell-\bar{\ell}}\geq 0.$$

We need one further condition: we require the system to be definite in the following sense:

(5.8) $\quad Jy'-Hy=0,\ \Delta y=0$ on $(a,b)\ \Rightarrow\ y=0$ on (a,b).

For the sake of completeness we include the following result, see [KR].

PROPOSITION 5.1. *The following assertions are each equivalent to the condition* (5.8):

(*i*) *For any* $\ell\in\mathbb{C}$ *and any nontrivial solution* $y(.,\ell)$ *of* $Jy'-Hy=\ell\Delta y$ *we have*

$$0<\int_a^b y(t,\ell)^*\Delta(t)y(t,\ell)\ dt\ \ (\leq\infty).$$

(*ii*) *There exists a compact interval* $[\alpha,\beta]\subseteq(a,b)$, *such that if* y *is a solution of* $Jy'-Hy=0$ *on* (a,b) *and* $\Delta y=0$ *a.e. on* $[\alpha,\beta]$, *then* $y=0$ *a.e. on the entire interval* (a,b).

Proof. It is easy to see that (5.8) is equivalent to the following condition:

(5.9) Let $\ell\in\mathbb{C}$. If $y(.,\ell)$ is a solution of $Jy'-Hy=\ell\Delta y$, $\Delta(.)y(.,\ell)=0$ on the interval (a,b), then $y(.,\ell)=0$ on (a,b).

We show that (5.9) implies (*i*). So let $y(.,\ell)$ be a nontrivial solution of $Jy'-Hy=\ell\Delta y$ with

(5.10) $$\int_a^b y(t,\ell)^*\Delta(t)y(t,\ell)\ dt=0.$$

Then by (5.6) $\Delta(.)y(.,\ell)=0$ on (a,b), and by (5.9) $y(.,\ell)$ must be trivial, contradiction. As to the converse, that is, (*i*) implies (5.9), let $y(.,\ell)$ be a solution of $Jy'-Hy=\ell\Delta y$, $\Delta(.)y(.,\ell)=0$ on (a,b). Then (5.10) is satisfied, and so $y(.,\ell)$ must be trivial. Now we show that (*ii*) implies (5.8). Let $y(.,\ell)$ be a solution of $Jy'-Hy=\ell\Delta y$, $\Delta(.)y(.,\ell)=0$ on (a,b), then certainly $\Delta y=0$ on $[\alpha,\beta]\subset(a,b)$, so that y must be trivial. As to the converse, i.e., (5.8) implies (*ii*), we introduce for every compact subinterval J of (a,b) the set

$$d(J)=\left\{ c\in\mathbb{C}^k \mid \|c\|=1,\quad \int_J c^*Y(t,0)^*\Delta(t)Y(t,0)c\ dt=0 \right\}.$$

It is clear that $d(J)$ is a compact subset of the unit ball in $\mathbb{C}^k$ and that $J_1\subseteq J_2$ implies $d(J_2)\subseteq d(J_1)$. Now we choose an increasing sequence of compact intervals J_n, $n\in\mathbb{N}$, of (a,b) with $\bigcup\{ J_n \mid n\in\mathbb{N}\}=(a,b)$. Then $\bigcap\{ d(J_n) \mid n\in\mathbb{N}\}=\emptyset$. For, if this is not true, there exists $c\in\mathbb{C}^k$, $\|c\|=1$ with

$$\int_{J_n} c^*Y(t,0)^*\Delta(t)Y(t,0)c\ dt=0$$

for all $n\in\mathbb{N}$, and hence

$$\int_a^b c^*Y(t,0)^*\Delta(t)Y(t,0)c\ dt=0.$$

But then by (5.8) $c=0$, a contradiction. Hence by the finite intersection property, there exists a compact interval $J=[\alpha,\beta]\subset(a,b)$, with $d(J)=\emptyset$. Let y be a solution of $Jy'-Hy=0$ on (a,b) and let $\Delta y=0$ on $[\alpha,\beta]$, then $y(.)=Y(.,0)c$ with

$$\int_\alpha^\beta c^*Y(t,0)^*\Delta(t)Y(t,0)c\ dt=0,$$

which implies $c=0$. This completes the proof. □

Now we review the linear relations corresponding to the equation (5.1), with Δ and H locally integrable and hermitian under the conditions (5.3), (5.6) and (5.8), see Orcutt [O]. We introduce in the space $\mathfrak{H}=L^2_\Delta(a,b)$ (equivalence classes!) with inner product defined by

$$[f,g]=\int_a^b g(t)^*\Delta(t)f(t)\ dt,$$

the maximal linear relation T_{max} by

$$T_{max}=\left\{ \{f,g\}\in\mathfrak{H}^2 \mid \text{there exist } \tilde{f}\in f,\ \tilde{g}\in g \text{ so that } J\tilde{f}'-H\tilde{f}=\Delta\tilde{g} \right\}.$$

If $\{f,g\}\in T_{max}$, then the equivalence class f contains precisely one locally absolutely continuous function $\tilde{f}$ such that $J\tilde{f}'-H\tilde{f}=\Delta\tilde{g}$. For, suppose that also $J\tilde{f}_1'-H\tilde{f}_1=\Delta\tilde{g}_1$, with $\Delta(\tilde{f}-\tilde{f}_1)=\Delta(\tilde{g}-\tilde{g}_1)=0$. Then $J(\tilde{f}-\tilde{f}_1)'-H(\tilde{f}-\tilde{f}_1)=0$, $\Delta(\tilde{f}-\tilde{f}_1)=0$ and, by condition (5.8), $\tilde{f}=\tilde{f}_1$. If no confusion arises we identify equivalence classes and representatives. For $\{f,g\}$, $\{h,k\}\in T_{max}$ and a compact interval $[p,q]\subset(a,b)$ integration by parts yields

$$\int_p^q h(t)^*\Delta(t)g(t)\ dt-\int_p^q k(t)^*\Delta(t)f(t)\ dt=h(q)^*Jf(q)-h(p)^*Jf(p)$$

and hence the Green's formula (cf. (3.1)) is given by

$$(5.11)\qquad <\{f,g\},\{h,k\}>=[g,h]-[f,k]=\lim_{q\to b}h(q)^*Jf(q)-\lim_{p\to a}h(p)^*Jf(p).$$

If a (or b) is a regular endpoint then the limit at a (or b) may be replaced by the value $h(a)^*Jf(a)$ (or $h(b)^*Jf(b)$, respectively). Next we introduce

$$T_0=\Big\{\ \{f,g\}\in T_{max}\mid f \text{ has compact support}\Big\}$$

and $S=(T_0)^c$, the closure of the relation T_0 in $\mathfrak{H}^2$.

PROPOSITION 5.2. *The relation S is symmetric and $S^*=T_{max}$. The defect spaces $\nu(S^*-\ell)$, $\ell\in\mathbb{C}\backslash\mathbb{R}$, are given by*

$$\nu(S^*-\ell)=\Big\{\ f\in L^2_\Delta(a,b)\mid Jf'=(\ell\Delta+H)f\ \Big\}$$

and hence $\dim\nu(S^*-\ell)\le k$.

If both a and b are regular endpoints, then the defect numbers are equal to (k,k), since all solutions of $Jf'=(\ell\Delta+H)f$ are continuous functions on the interval $[a,b]$ and hence belong to $\mathfrak{H}$.

In the rest of this paper we will assume throughout that the canonical differential equation (5.1) is a definite Hamiltonian system, i.e., we assume that the following conditions are satisfied:

(i) $H(t)$ hermitian for almost all $t\in(a,b)$,

(ii) $\Delta(t)\ge 0$, for almost all $t\in(a,b)$,

(iii) the system is definite,

(iv) $J=\begin{bmatrix}0 & -I_n\\ I_n & 0\end{bmatrix}$, $k=2n$.

For the fundamental solution $Y(.,\ell)$ we introduce a corresponding decomposition in block matrices

$$Y(.,\ell)=\begin{bmatrix}Y_{11}(.,\ell) & Y_{12}(.,\ell)\\ Y_{21}(.,\ell) & Y_{22}(.,\ell)\end{bmatrix}=\big(Y_1(.,\ell):Y_2(.,\ell)\big),$$

where each $Y_{ij}(.,\ell)$ is an $n\times n$ matrix function, $i,j=1,2$, and each $Y_i(.,\ell)$, $i=1,2$, is a $2n\times n$ matrix solution of the homogeneous differential equation.

For a vector $f \in \mathbb{C}^{2n}$ we use the notation

$$f = \binom{f^1}{f^2}.$$

The following result gives a lower bound on the defect numbers of the minimal relation S in a special case, see [KR], [O].

PROPOSITION 5.3. *Suppose that one of the endpoints is regular. Then the defect numbers satisfy the inequality* $n \le \dim \nu(S^* - \ell) \le 2n$, *with* $\ell \in \mathbb{C}\setminus\mathbb{R}$.

If the endpoint a is regular and the defect numbers are equal to (n,n), then the definite Hamiltonian system is said to be in the limit point case at the endpoint b. In this last case, which we shall consider in the rest of this paper, Green's formula (5.11) becomes

$$(5.12) \quad <\{f,g\},\{h,k\}> = h^1(a)^* f^2(a) - h^2(a)^* f^1(a)$$

and we have the following result.

PROPOSITION 5.4. *Suppose that the endpoint a is regular, and that the limit point case prevails at b, then*

$$S = \left\{ \{f,g\} \in T_{max} \mid f(a) = 0 \right\}.$$

6. THE SYMMETRIC RELATION IN THE LIMIT POINT CASE

In this section and often in the sequel we consider the definite Hamiltonian system with the assumption that the endpoint a is regular and that the limit point case holds at the endpoint b. We fix a fundamental solution $Y(.,\ell)$ of the homogeneous equation by $Y(a,\ell) = I_{2n}$. The socalled Weyl coefficient M is the $n \times n$ matrix function defined by

$$M(\ell) = -\lim_{t \to b} Y_{12}(t,\ell)^{-1} Y_{11}(t,\ell), \qquad \ell \in \mathbb{C}\setminus\mathbb{R}.$$

The limit point condition at b implies that this limit exists, cf. [HS1,2] and [Orl]. For $n \times n$ matrix functions Q we introduce the kernel N_Q:

$$\mathsf{N}_Q(\ell,\lambda) = \frac{Q(\ell) - Q(\lambda)^*}{\ell - \bar{\lambda}}, \qquad \ell,\lambda \in \mathbb{C}\setminus\mathbb{R}, \quad \ell \neq \bar{\lambda}.$$

Recall that the class $\mathbf{N}_\kappa^{n \times n}$ is the set of meromorphic $n \times n$ matrix functions Q with $Q(\bar{\ell})^* = Q(\ell)$ for which this kernel has κ negative squares; we refer to [KL5] for further details.

PROPOSITION 6.1. *The Weyl coefficient* $\mathcal{M}$ *has the properties:*

(*i*) $\mathcal{M}\in \mathbf{N}_0^{n\times n}$,

(*ii*) $\mathcal{M}(\ell)$ *is invertible for* $\ell\in\mathbb{C}\backslash\mathbb{R}$,

(*iii*) *The* n *columns of the* $2n\times n$ *matrix* $\Upsilon(.,\ell):=Y_1(.,\ell)+Y_2(.,\ell)\mathcal{M}(\ell)$ *form a basis for* $\nu(S^*-\ell)$, $\ell\in\mathbb{C}\backslash\mathbb{R}$.

In fact, we have for $\ell,\lambda\in\mathbb{C}\backslash\mathbb{R}$, $\ell\neq\bar{\lambda}$,

$$(6.1)\qquad \mathsf{N}_{\mathcal{M}}(\ell,\lambda) = [\Upsilon(.,\ell),\Upsilon(.,\lambda)] = \int_a^b \Upsilon(t,\lambda)^*\Delta(t)\Upsilon(t,\ell)\,dt$$

and $\operatorname{Im}\mathcal{M}(\ell)>0$ *for all* $\ell\in\mathbb{C}\backslash\mathbb{R}$.

The proof of this proposition is based upon a limiting procedure that is classical for Sturm–Liouville equations, and can be found in [HS1,2], a very general treatment can be found in [Orl]. We can express the characteristic function of the symmetric closed minimal relation S, given as in Proposition 5.4, in terms of this Weyl coefficient. For the definition of the characteristic function we refer to e.g. [DLS5].

PROPOSITION 6.2. *Let* $\mu\in\mathbb{C}^+$. *The characteristic function* X *of the symmetric closed minimal linear relation* S *is given by*

$$(6.2)\qquad X(z(\ell))\Upsilon(.,\mu)=\Upsilon(.,\bar{\mu})\big(\mathcal{M}(\ell)-\mathcal{M}(\bar{\mu})\big)^{-1}\big(\mathcal{M}(\ell)-\mathcal{M}(\mu)\big),\ \ell\in\mathbb{C}^+,$$

i.e., with respect to the bases $\Upsilon(.,\mu)$ *in* $\nu(S^*-\mu)$ *and* $\Upsilon(.,\bar{\mu})$ *in* $\nu(S^*-\bar{\mu})$ *the operator* $X(z(\ell))$ *has the matrix representation* $\big(\mathcal{M}(\ell)-\mathcal{M}(\bar{\mu})\big)^{-1}\big(\mathcal{M}(\ell)-\mathcal{M}(\mu)\big)$. *Furthermore, for* $\ell,\lambda\in\mathbb{C}^+$,

$$(6.3)\qquad \big[\,\mathsf{S}_X(z(\ell),z(\lambda))\Upsilon(.,\mu),\Upsilon(.,\mu)\,\big] = \big(\,\mathsf{N}_{\mathcal{M}}(\ell,\lambda)m(\ell),m(\lambda)\,\big),$$

with $m(\ell)=\mathsf{N}_{\mathcal{M}}(\ell,\mu)^{-1}\mathsf{N}_{\mathcal{M}}(\mu,\mu)$.

Proof. By definition $X(z(\ell))$ is the restiction of the Cayley transform $C_{\bar{\mu}}(S(\ell))$ to the space $\nu(S^*-\mu)$, where $S(\ell)$ is defined by $S(\ell)=S\dotplus\{\{\alpha,\ell\alpha\}|\alpha\in\nu(S^*-\ell)\}$. Let $\mathcal{A}(\ell)$ be the $n\times n$ matrix function such that $C_{\bar{\mu}}(S(\ell))\Upsilon(.,\mu)=\Upsilon(.,\bar{\mu})\mathcal{A}(\ell)$. As for all $\psi\in\nu(S^*-\mu)$,

$$C_{\bar{\mu}}(S(\ell))\psi\in\nu(S^*-\bar{\mu}),\qquad (\ell-\mu)\psi-(\ell-\bar{\mu})C_{\bar{\mu}}(S(\ell))\psi\in\Re(S-\ell)=\nu(S^*-\bar{\ell})^{\perp},$$

it follows that

$$(\ell-\mu)\Upsilon(.,\mu)-(\ell-\bar{\mu})\Upsilon(.,\bar{\mu})\mathcal{A}(\ell)\in\nu(S^*-\bar{\ell})^{\perp}$$

and thus, $(\ell-\mu)[\Upsilon(.,\mu),\Upsilon(.,\bar{\ell})]-(\ell-\bar{\mu})[\Upsilon(.,\bar{\mu}),\Upsilon(.,\bar{\ell})]\mathcal{A}(\ell)=0.$ Therefore, by

(6.1), $\left(M(\bar{\mu})-M(\bar{\ell})^*\right)A(\ell)=M(\mu)-M(\bar{\ell})^*$ and hence

$$A(\ell)=\left(M(\ell)-M(\bar{\mu})\right)^{-1}\left(M(\ell)-M(\mu)\right), \qquad \ell\in\mathbb{C}^+,$$

which proves (6.2). The equality (6.3) follows if we substitute

$$A(\ell)=I+\left(M(\ell)-M(\bar{\mu})\right)^{-1}\left(M(\bar{\mu})-M(\mu)\right), \qquad \ell\in\mathbb{C}^+,$$

into the lefthand side of (6.3), which is equal to

$$(6.4)\qquad \frac{(\ell-\bar{\mu})(\bar{\lambda}-\mu)}{4(\operatorname{Im}\mu)^2(\ell-\bar{\lambda})}\left[M(\mu)-M(\bar{\mu})-A(\lambda)^*\left(M(\mu)-M(\bar{\mu})\right)A(\ell)\right].$$

This completes the proof. □

Recall that the characteristic function $X(z(\ell))$ of S and therefore, according to Proposition 6.2, the function $M(\ell)$ characterizes the simple part of S, which coincides with the operator part S_s of S. The latter will be proved in the next section, see Proposition 7.4. Here we show how $M(\ell)$ contains information concerning the spectrum of S^*, cf. [Š3,4].

PROPOSITION 6.3. *The number $\lambda_0\in\mathbb{R}$ is an eigenvalue of the relation S^* if and only if there exists a function $c(\ell)$, defined and holomorphic in $\mathbb{C}^+$, such that*

(*i*) *$c(\ell)$ converges to some vector c_0,*

(*ii*) *$M(\ell)c(\ell)$ converges to some vector c_1,*

(*iii*) *$\left(\mathsf{N}_M(\ell,\ell)\,c(\ell),c(\ell)\right)$ is bounded,*

as $\ell\hat{\to}\lambda_0$ and c_0, c_1 are not equal to the null vector simultaneously.

Proof. Let $\lambda_0\in\mathbb{R}$ be an eigenvalue of S^*. Then it also is an eigenvalue of the adjoint of S_s in $(L^2_\Delta(a,b)\ominus S(0))^2$. As S_s is simple, we may apply Štraus' results in [Š1,Š4], see also [DLS3], Theorem 9.1 and [DLS2], Theorem 4.2, to conclude that there exists a nontrivial vector $e\in\mathbb{C}^n$ such that

$$\left(\mathsf{N}_M(\ell,\lambda)\,m(\ell)e,m(\lambda)e\right)=\left[\mathsf{S}_X(z(\ell),z(\lambda))\Upsilon(.,\mu)e,\Upsilon(.,\mu)e\right]$$

remains bounded as $\ell\hat{\to}\lambda_0$ and that then also

$$X(z(\ell))\Upsilon(.,\mu)e=\Upsilon(.,\bar{\mu})\left(M(\ell)-M(\bar{\mu})\right)^{-1}\left(M(\ell)-M(\mu)\right)e$$
$$=\Upsilon(.,\bar{\mu})e-((\mu-\bar{\mu})/(\ell-\bar{\mu}))\Upsilon(.,\bar{\mu})m(\ell)e$$

converges. Put $c(\ell)=((\mu-\bar{\mu})/(\ell-\bar{\mu}))m(\ell)e$. Then

$$\mathcal{M}(\ell)c(\ell) = \left(\mathcal{M}(\mu) - \mathcal{M}(\bar{\mu})\right)e + \mathcal{M}(\bar{\mu})c(\ell)$$

and (i)–(iii) now easily follow. For the converse we refer to Proposition 9.6 at the end of Section 9. □

7. Selfadjoint extensions

For $n\times n$ matrix functions $\mathcal{A}$ and $\mathcal{B}$ we define the kernel

$$\text{(7.1)} \qquad \mathsf{N}_{\mathcal{A},\mathcal{B}}(\ell,\lambda) = \frac{\mathcal{B}(\bar{\lambda})\mathcal{A}(\bar{\ell})^* - \mathcal{A}(\bar{\lambda})\mathcal{B}(\bar{\ell})^*}{\ell - \bar{\lambda}}.$$

Note that with the choice $\mathcal{A} = \mathcal{Q} \in \mathsf{N}_\kappa^{n\times n}$, $\mathcal{B} = I$ this kernel is equal to $\mathsf{N}_\mathcal{Q}(\ell,\lambda)$, as defined in Section 6.

Theorem 7.1. *The minimal selfadjoint extensions A in a Krein space with $\mu \in \rho(A) \neq \emptyset$, $\mu \in \mathbb{C}^+$, of the symmetric relation S are in one to one correspondence with the characteristic funtions Θ defined by*

$$\Theta(z(\ell))\Upsilon(.,\bar{\mu}) = \Upsilon(.,\mu)\left(\mathcal{A}(\ell) + \mathcal{B}(\ell)\mathcal{M}(\mu)\right)^{-1}\left(\mathcal{A}(\ell) + \mathcal{B}(\ell)\mathcal{M}(\bar{\mu})\right), \quad \ell \in \mathbb{C}^+,$$

interpreted as the equality (6.2), via pairs of holomorphic $n\times n$ matrix functions $\mathcal{A}$ and $\mathcal{B}$ which are defined in a symmetric neighbourhood of the points μ and $\bar{\mu}$, and satisfy

(i) rank $\left(\mathcal{A}(\ell)\ :\ \mathcal{B}(\ell)\right) = n$,

(ii) $\mathcal{A}(\ell)\mathcal{B}(\bar{\ell})^* - \mathcal{B}(\ell)\mathcal{A}(\bar{\ell})^* = 0$,

(iii) $\mathcal{A}(\ell) + \mathcal{B}(\ell)\mathcal{M}(\ell)$ *is invertible for* $\ell = \mu, \bar{\mu}$.

Furthermore, for $z(\ell), z(\lambda) \in \mathfrak{D}_\Theta$,

$$\left[\, \mathsf{S}_\Theta(z(\ell), z(\lambda))\Upsilon(.,\bar{\mu}), \Upsilon(.,\bar{\mu})\,\right] = \left(\, \mathsf{N}_{\mathcal{A},\mathcal{B}}(\ell,\lambda)\mathrm{c}(\ell), \mathrm{c}(\lambda)\,\right)$$

with $\mathrm{c}(\ell) = (\ell - \bar{\mu})\left(\left(\mathcal{A}(\bar{\ell}) + \mathcal{B}(\bar{\ell})\mathcal{M}(\bar{\mu})\right)^{-1}\right)^* \mathsf{N}_\mathcal{M}(\mu,\bar{\mu})$. *The Štraus relations corresponding to these minimal selfadjoint extensions are given by*

$$\text{(7.2)} \qquad T(\ell) = \left\{\, \{f,g\} \in T_{max} \mid \mathcal{A}(\ell)f^1(a) + \mathcal{B}(\ell)f^2(a) = 0 \,\right\},$$

for ℓ belonging to a symmetric neighbourhood of $\mu, \bar{\mu}$. The extension takes place in a Pontryagin space $\mathfrak{K}$ of index κ if and only if the kernel $\mathsf{N}_{\mathcal{A},\mathcal{B}}(\ell,\lambda)$ has κ negative squares, and then the dimension of $\mathfrak{K} \ominus \mathfrak{H}$ is equal to the sum of the number of positive and of negative squares of this kernel.

The proof of this theorem follows in a straightforward manner from the results in Sections 3 and 6, if we put

$$b(f,g)=\binom{f^1(a)}{f^2(a)} \quad \text{for } \{f,g\}\in S^*,$$

$$\mathcal{Q}=(1/i)\begin{bmatrix} O & -I_n \\ I_n & O \end{bmatrix}, \quad \mathcal{U}(\ell)=\left(\mathcal{A}(\ell):\mathcal{B}(\ell)\right)$$

and observe that

$$\Upsilon(.,\ell) = Y(.,\ell)\begin{bmatrix} I \\ \mathcal{M}(\ell) \end{bmatrix}, \qquad \Upsilon(.,\mu)=\Phi, \qquad \Upsilon(.,\bar{\mu})=\Psi.$$

We leave the details to the reader. With these substitutions Theorem 3.2 also yields a description of $T(\lambda)$ in terms of limits of $\mathcal{A}(\ell)$ and $\mathcal{B}(\ell)$ as $\ell \hat{\to} \lambda \in \mathbb{R}$, cf. [Š1,2,4].

As the defect numbers of S are equal, S has selfadjoint extensions within the Hilbert space $\mathfrak{H}$ itself. By means of Theorem 7.1 these socalled canonical extensions can be described in the following manner. Let $\mu\in\mathbb{C}^+$ be fixed. Then the canonical selfadjoint extensions of S are in one to one correspondence with the (constant) unitary mappings Θ from $\nu(S^*-\bar{\mu})$ onto $\nu(S^*-\mu)$ and these mappings have the matrix representations

$$\Theta\Upsilon(.,\bar{\mu})=\Upsilon(.,\mu)\left(A+\mathcal{B}\mathcal{M}(\mu)\right)^{-1}\left(A+\mathcal{B}\mathcal{M}(\bar{\mu})\right),$$

in which A and $\mathcal{B}$ are constant $n\mathrm{x}n$ matrices satisfying rank $\left(A \;:\; \mathcal{B}\right)=n$, $A\mathcal{B}^*-\mathcal{B}A^*=0$. (Note that now the matrix $A+\mathcal{B}\mathcal{M}(\ell)$is invertible.)

THEOREM 7.2. *Let $R(\ell)$ be the generalized resolvent corresponding to the Štraus relation* (7.2) *in Theorem* 7.1. *Then for $f\in\mathfrak{H}$ the function $R(\ell)f$ is the unique solution in $\mathfrak{H}$ of the boundary value problem*

$$(7.3) \qquad Jy'=(\ell\Delta+H)y+\Delta f, \quad \mathcal{A}(\ell)y^1(a)+\mathcal{B}(\ell)y^2(a)=0$$

and for $f\in\mathfrak{H}$ which vanishes near b it is given by

$$(7.4) \qquad R(\ell)f(x)=Y(x,\ell)\Omega(\ell)\int_a^b Y(t,\bar{\ell})^*\Delta(t)f(t)\,dt$$

$$-Y_2(x,\ell)\int_a^x Y_1(t,\bar{\ell})^*\Delta(t)f(t)\,dt-Y_1(x,\ell)\int_x^b Y_2(t,\bar{\ell})^*\Delta(t)f(t)\,dt.$$

Here the Weyl coefficient Ω is defined by

$$\Omega(\ell)=\begin{bmatrix} \Gamma(\ell)\mathcal{B}(\ell) & -\Gamma(\ell)\mathcal{A}(\ell) \\ \mathcal{M}(\ell)\Gamma(\ell)\mathcal{B}(\ell)+I & -\mathcal{M}(\ell)\Gamma(\ell)\mathcal{A}(\ell) \end{bmatrix}$$

with $\Gamma(\ell)=-\left(\mathcal{A}(\ell)+\mathcal{B}(\ell)\mathcal{M}(\ell)\right)^{-1}$.

Proof. The first statement follows from (7.2) and the fact that

$R(\ell)=(T(\ell)-\ell)^{-1}$. In order to obtain the expression (7.4) for the compressed resolvent $R(\ell)$ we solve the boundary value problem (7.3). We define

$$Y_a(t,\ell)=Y_1(t,\ell)\mathcal{B}(\bar{\ell})^*-Y_2(t,\ell)\mathcal{A}(\bar{\ell})^*.$$

Then Y_a is a solution of the homogeneous equation $Jy'-Hy=\ell\Delta y$, that satisfies the initial condition $\mathcal{A}(\ell)y^1(a)+\mathcal{B}(\ell)y^2(a)=0$. We consider for some matrices $\Gamma(\ell)$ and $\tilde{\Gamma}(\ell)$ the function

$$y(x,\ell)=\Upsilon(x,\ell)\Gamma(\ell)\int_a^x Y_a(t,\bar{\ell})^*\Delta(t)f(t)\,dt+ \\ +Y_a(x,\ell)\tilde{\Gamma}(\ell)\int_x^b \Upsilon(t,\bar{\ell})^*\Delta(t)f(t)\,dt.$$

It satisfies the boundary condition $\mathcal{A}(\ell)y^1(a)+\mathcal{B}(\ell)y^2(a)=0$, and we have

$$Jy'(x)=\ell\Delta(x)y(x)+H(x)y(x)+ \\ +J\left(\Upsilon(x,\ell)\Gamma(\ell)Y_a(x,\bar{\ell})^*-Y_a(x,\ell)\tilde{\Gamma}(\ell)\Upsilon(x,\bar{\ell})^*\right)\Delta(x)f(x).$$

Hence, if y is to be a solution of the boundary value problem (7.3) the matrices $\Gamma(\ell)$ and $\tilde{\Gamma}(\ell)$ must satisfy

$$\Upsilon(x,\ell)\Gamma(\ell)Y_a(x,\bar{\ell})^*-Y_a(x,\ell)\tilde{\Gamma}(\ell)\Upsilon(x,\bar{\ell})^*=-J,$$

and by using $Y(x,\ell)^{-1}J(Y(x,\bar{\ell})^*)^{-1}=J$ we get

$$\left(\begin{matrix} I \\ M(\ell)\end{matrix}\right)\Gamma(\ell)\left(\mathcal{B}(\ell)\ :\ -\mathcal{A}(\ell)\right)-\left(\begin{matrix}\mathcal{B}(\bar{\ell})^* \\ -\mathcal{A}(\bar{\ell})^*\end{matrix}\right)\tilde{\Gamma}(\ell)\left(I\ :\ M(\bar{\ell})^*\right)=-J. \tag{7.5}$$

Multiplying (7.5) from the left by the matrix $\left(\mathcal{A}(\ell)\ :\ \mathcal{B}(\ell)\right)$, and from the right by the matrix $\left(\mathcal{A}(\bar{\ell})\ :\ \mathcal{B}(\bar{\ell})\right)^*$ we obtain the identities

$$\left(\mathcal{A}(\ell)+\mathcal{B}(\ell)M(\ell)\right)\Gamma(\ell)\left(\mathcal{B}(\ell)\ :\ -\mathcal{A}(\ell)\right)=\left(-\mathcal{B}(\ell)\ :\ \mathcal{A}(\ell)\right),$$

$$-\left(\mathcal{B}(\bar{\ell})\ :\ \mathcal{A}(\bar{\ell})\right)^*\tilde{\Gamma}(\ell)\left(\mathcal{A}(\bar{\ell})^*+M(\bar{\ell})^*\mathcal{B}(\bar{\ell})^*\right)=-\left(-\mathcal{B}(\bar{\ell})\ :\ \mathcal{A}(\bar{\ell})\right)^*,$$

which leads to

$$\Gamma(\ell)=-\left(\mathcal{A}(\ell)+\mathcal{B}(\ell)M(\ell)\right)^{-1},\ \tilde{\Gamma}(\ell)=-\left(\mathcal{A}(\bar{\ell})^*+M(\bar{\ell})^*\mathcal{B}(\bar{\ell})^*\right)^{-1},$$

so that $\Gamma(\ell)=\tilde{\Gamma}(\bar{\ell})^*$. Now it is straightforward to show that these matrices $\Gamma(\ell)$ and $\tilde{\Gamma}(\ell)$ satisfy the conditions (7.5), i.e.,

$$\Gamma(\ell)\mathcal{B}(\ell)-\mathcal{B}(\bar{\ell})^*\tilde{\Gamma}(\ell)=O, \qquad -\Gamma(\ell)\mathcal{A}(\ell)-\mathcal{B}(\bar{\ell})^*\tilde{\Gamma}(\ell)M(\bar{\ell})^*=I,$$

$$M(\ell)\Gamma(\ell)\mathcal{B}(\ell)+\mathcal{A}(\bar{\ell})^*\tilde{\Gamma}(\ell)=-I, \qquad -M(\ell)\Gamma(\ell)\mathcal{A}(\ell)+\mathcal{A}(\bar{\ell})^*\tilde{\Gamma}(\ell)M(\bar{\ell})^*=O.$$

We define

$$N(\ell)=\left(\begin{matrix} I \\ M(\ell)\end{matrix}\right)\Gamma(\ell)\left(\mathcal{B}(\ell)\ :\ -\mathcal{A}(\ell)\right).$$

Then

$$\mathcal{N}(\ell)-\mathcal{N}(\bar{\ell})^{*}=-J=\begin{bmatrix} O & I \\ -I & O \end{bmatrix}$$

and the solution y can be written as

$$y(x,\ell)=Y(x,\ell)\mathcal{N}(\ell)\int_a^x Y(t,\bar{\ell})^{*}\Delta(t)f(t)dt+Y(x,\ell)\mathcal{N}(\bar{\ell})^{*}\int_x^b Y(t,\bar{\ell})^{*}\Delta(t)f(t)dt.$$

Finally, if we put

$$\Omega(\ell)=\mathcal{N}(\ell)-\begin{bmatrix} O & O \\ -I & O \end{bmatrix},$$

then $\Omega(\ell)=\Omega(\bar{\ell})^{*}$, and our expression for y leads to the desired expression for the compressed resolvent. □

In the special case $\mathcal{A}(\ell)=I, \mathcal{B}(\ell)=O$, i.e., when the boundary condition at a has the form $y^1(a)=0$ and the function $\Omega(\ell)$ has the form

$$\Omega(\ell)=\begin{bmatrix} O & I \\ I & \mathcal{M}(\ell) \end{bmatrix},$$

the formula (7.4) reduces to

$$R(\ell)f(x)=Y_2(x,\ell)\mathcal{M}(\ell)\int_a^b Y_2(t,\bar{\ell})^{*}\Delta(t)f(t)\,dt \tag{7.6}$$
$$+Y_2(x,\ell)\int_x^b Y_1(t,\bar{\ell})^{*}\Delta(t)f(t)\,dt+Y_1(x,\ell)\int_a^x Y_2(t,\bar{\ell})^{*}\Delta(t)f(t)\,dt.$$

An application of the Stieltjes–Livšic inversion formula shows that the spectral measure corresponding to the Fourier transform

$$f\mapsto\int_a^b Y_2(t,\bar{\ell})^{*}\Delta(t)f(t)\,dt$$

and the canonical extension determined by the boundary condition $y^1(a)=0$ is given by the spectral measure in the integral representation of the Weyl coefficient $\mathcal{M}$. More generally, the function Ω is called the Weyl coefficient with respect to the Fourier transform

$$f\mapsto\int_a^b Y(t,\bar{\ell})^{*}\Delta(t)f(t)\,dt \tag{7.7}$$

and the boundary conditions $\mathcal{A}(\ell)y^1(a)+\mathcal{B}(\ell)y^2(a)=0$. It can be shown that the Fourier transform (7.7) is a directing mapping in the sense of Langer and Textorius [LT2,3] with respect to the symmetric minimal relation S. In the case of Sturm–Liouville equations we have studied the corresponding Weyl coefficient in our recent paper [DLS6]. For the present Weyl coefficient Ω we will state similar results in the next sections.

Let $\mathring{A}$ be a canonical selfadjoint extension of S, $\mathring{\Theta}$ the corresponding (constant) unitary mapping from $\nu(S^*-\bar{\mu})$ onto $\nu(S^*-\mu)$ with $\mu\in\mathbb{C}^+$ fixed (see the remark after the proof of Theorem 7.1) and let $\mathring{R}(\ell)=(\mathring{A}-\ell)^{-1}$, $\ell\in\rho(\mathring{A})$. Let Γ_μ be a fixed bijection from $\mathbb{C}^n$ onto $\nu(S^*-\mu)\subset\mathfrak{H}$. The socalled Q–function of S associated with $\mathring{A}$ and Γ_μ, see [KL1,2] and also [LT1], [DLS1], is defined as the $n\times n$ matrix function $Q(\ell)$, $\ell\in\rho(\mathring{A})$, that satisfies

$$\frac{Q(\ell)-Q(\lambda)^*}{\ell-\bar{\lambda}}=\Gamma_\lambda{}^*\Gamma_\ell,$$

where $\Gamma_\ell=\left[I+(\ell-\mu)\mathring{R}(\ell)\right]\Gamma_\mu$ is a bijection from $\mathbb{C}^n$ onto $\nu(S^*-\ell)$. The function Q is uniquely determined up to a constant hermitian $n\times n$ matrix $\mathcal{S}$ and has the form

$$Q(\ell)=\mathcal{S}+\Gamma_\mu{}^*\left[\ell-\mathrm{Re}\mu+(\ell-\bar{\mu})(\ell-\mu)\mathring{R}(\ell)\right]\Gamma_\mu$$

(see also Section 9). It can be used to characterize all generalized resolvents of S via an extension of Krein's formula:

$$R(\ell)=\mathring{R}(\ell)-\Gamma_\ell\left[Q(\ell)+\mathcal{T}(\ell)\right]^{-1}\Gamma_{\bar{\ell}}{}^*.$$

This formula establishes a one to one correspondence between the generalized resolvents of S and the closed linear relations $\mathcal{T}(\ell)$ in $\mathbb{C}^n$ with the properties that the Cayley transform $C_{\bar{\mu}}(\mathcal{T}(\ell))$ is a holomorphic contraction and the inverse $(Q(\ell)+\mathcal{T}(\ell))^{-1}$ exists, i.e., is an operator, in a neighbourhood of μ and $\mathcal{T}(\bar{\ell})=\mathcal{T}(\ell)^*$.

Consider again the special canonical extension $\mathring{A}$ of S corresponding to the matrix functions $\mathcal{A}(\ell)=I,\mathcal{B}(\ell)=O$, see Theorem 7.1 and the remark following the proof of Theorem 7.2. Then the relation between the Weyl coefficient $\mathcal{M}(\ell)$ and $\mathring{A}$ together with the mapping Γ_μ: $\mathbb{C}^n\to\nu(S^*-\mu)$ defined by $\Gamma_\mu c=\Upsilon(.,\mu)c$ can be expressed as follows.

COROLLARY 7.3. *$\mathcal{M}(\ell)$ is the Q-function of S associated with $\mathring{A}$ and Γ_μ. Moreover, the formula*

(7.8) $$R(\ell)f=\mathring{R}(\ell)f-\Upsilon(.,\ell)\left[\mathcal{M}(\ell)+\mathcal{T}(\ell)\right]^{-1}[f,\Upsilon(.,\bar{\ell})],\qquad f\in\mathfrak{H},$$

establishes a one to one correspondence between the uniquely defined solution of the boundary value problem (7.3) and the relation

$$\mathcal{T}(\ell)=\left\{\{c,d\}\in\mathbb{C}^n\times\mathbb{C}^n\mid\mathcal{A}(\ell)c=\mathcal{B}(\ell)d\right\}=\left\{\{\mathcal{B}(\bar{\ell})^*e,\mathcal{A}(\bar{\ell})^*e\}\mid e\in\mathbb{C}^n\right\}$$

with $A(\ell)$, $\mathcal{B}(\ell)$ *as in Theorem* 7.1 (*i*)–(*iii*). *The relation* (7.8) *can also be written as*

$$R(\ell)f-\mathring{R}(\ell)f=\Upsilon(.,\ell)\Gamma(\ell)\mathcal{B}(\ell)\int_a^b \Upsilon(t,\bar{\ell})^*\Delta(t)f(t)\ dt.$$

Proof. First we note that by (7.6) the canonical resolvent $\mathring{R}(\ell)$ can be expressed as

$$\mathring{R}(\ell)f(x)=\Upsilon(x,\ell)\int_a^x Y_2(t,\bar{\ell})^*\Delta(t)f(t)\ dt+ +Y_2(x,\ell)\int_x^b \Upsilon(t,\bar{\ell})^*\Delta(t)f(t)\ dt.$$

As Γ_ℓ maps $\mathbb{C}^n$ onto $\nu(S^*-\ell)$ we have that for some $n{\times}n$ matrix function $\Lambda(\ell)$

$$\left(I+(\ell-\mu)\mathring{R}(\ell)\right)\Upsilon(.,\mu)=\Upsilon(.,\ell)\Lambda(\ell)$$

and evaluating both sides at the point a and using formula (6.1) we find that

$$\begin{bmatrix} I \\ M(\mu) \end{bmatrix}+(\ell-\mu)\begin{bmatrix} O \\ I \end{bmatrix} \mathsf{N}_M(\mu,\bar{\ell})=\begin{bmatrix} I \\ M(\ell) \end{bmatrix}\Lambda(\ell).$$

It follows that $\Lambda(\ell)=I$ and hence $\Gamma_\ell c=\Upsilon(.,\ell)c$, $c\in\mathbb{C}^n$. This implies that (6.1) can be rewritten as

$$\frac{M(\ell)-M(\lambda)^*}{\ell-\bar{\lambda}}=\Gamma_\lambda{}^*\Gamma_\ell,$$

which proves the first statement. The second one follows from a calculation of the difference $R(\ell)f-\mathring{R}(\ell)f$ via the representation (7.4), which leads to

$$R(\ell)f(x)-\mathring{R}(\ell)f(x)=\Upsilon(x,\ell)\Gamma(\ell)\mathcal{B}(\ell)\int_a^b \Upsilon(t,\bar{\ell})^*\Delta(t)f(t)\ dt,$$

since

$$\Omega(\ell)-\begin{bmatrix} O & I \\ I & M(\ell) \end{bmatrix}=\begin{bmatrix} I \\ M(\ell) \end{bmatrix}\Gamma(\ell)\mathcal{B}(\ell)\left[\ I\ :\ M(\bar{\ell})^*\ \right].$$

It is easy to check that $\mathcal{T}(\ell)=\{\{c,d\}\in\mathbb{C}^n{\times}\mathbb{C}^n\,|\,\mathcal{A}(\ell)c=\mathcal{B}(\ell)d\}$ if and only if $\Gamma(\ell)\mathcal{B}(\ell)=-\left(M(\ell)+\mathcal{T}(\ell)\right)^{-1}$. □

If $\mathcal{A}$ and $\mathcal{B}$ are as in Theorem 7.1 and the kernel $\mathsf{N}_{\mathcal{A},\mathcal{B}}(\ell,\lambda)$ in (7.1) has a finite number of negative squares, we define the spectrum of the boundary problem (7.3), as the spectrum $\sigma(A)$ of the minimal selfadjoint extension A of S corresponding to this problem as in Theorem 7.1. Moreover, $\lambda\in\mathbb{C}$ is said to be an eigenvalue of the boundary value problem (7.3) if it is an eigenvalue of A; if it is not, $\lambda\in\sigma(A)$ belongs by definition to the continuous spectrum of the problem. Recall that $\sigma(A)$ and hence the spectrum of the boundary problem (7.3) consists of the nonreal poles of $R(\ell)$ and of those points in $\mathbb{R}$ into which $R(\ell)$ cannot be continued analytically.

Using an argument due to Gilbert [G1] we obtain as a consequence of Theorem 7.2 the following result.

PROPOSITION 7.4. *The operator part $S_s = S \ominus S_\infty$ is simple in $\mathfrak{H} \ominus S(0)$.*

Proof. We choose a canonical selfadjoint extension A of S in $\mathfrak{H}$, obtained by the boundary conditions $\mathcal{A}y^1(a) + \mathcal{B}y^2(a) = 0$, where $\mathcal{A}$ and $\mathcal{B}$ are constant $n \times n$ matrices which satisfy rank $(\mathcal{A} : \mathcal{B}) = n$, $\mathcal{A}\mathcal{B}^* - \mathcal{B}\mathcal{A}^* = 0$. Let again Y_a denote the solution of $Jy' - Hy = \ell \Delta y$, which satisfies the initial condition $\mathcal{A}y^1(a) + \mathcal{B}y^2(a) = 0$, so that

$$Y_a(t,\ell) = Y_1(t,\ell)\mathcal{B}^* - Y_2(t,\ell)\mathcal{A}^*.$$

Now let $f \in \mathfrak{H} \ominus \nu(S^* - \ell)$, $\ell \in \mathbb{C} \backslash \mathbb{R}$. Then the argument in the proof of Theorem 7.2 shows that

$$R(\ell)f(x) = \Upsilon(x,\ell)\Gamma(\ell)\int_a^x Y_a(t,\bar{\ell})^* \Delta(t) f(t)\, dt + \\ + Y_a(x,\ell)\Gamma(\bar{\ell})^* \int_x^b \Upsilon(t,\bar{\ell})^* \Delta(t) f(t)\, dt$$

$$= \int_a^x \left(-Y_2(x,\ell)Y_1(t,\bar{\ell})^* + Y_1(x,\ell)Y_2(t,\bar{\ell})^* \right) \Delta(t) f(t)\, dt.$$

For any function $g \in \mathfrak{H}$ with compact support the function $[R(\ell)f, g]$ is entire in ℓ and hence by the Stieltjes–Livšic inversion formula we obtain $[E(J)f, g] = 0$ for any compact subinterval J of $\mathbb{R}$, whose endpoints are continuity points of E, the orthogonal spectral function of the canonical extension A of S. Since now $[E(\infty)f, g] = 0$ for all g with compact support, we conclude that $f \in A(0)$, the nonoperator part of A. Now note that $\nu(S^* - \ell) \subset \mathfrak{D}(S^*) \subset S(0)^\perp$. So if in the above we choose $f \in \mathfrak{H} \ominus S(0)$ and use a special extension A, namely one for which $A(0) = S(0)$, we obtain $f \in S(0)$ and we conclude $f = 0$. Hence by Krein's criterion, see [Kr] §1.3, we find that the operator part of S in $\mathfrak{H} \ominus S(0)$ is simple. □

8. SOME SPECIAL REPRESENTATIONS OF THE EXTENDING RELATION

We recall that if A is a selfadjoint extension in a Krein space $\mathfrak{K}$ with $\rho(A) \neq \emptyset$, of a symmetric relation S in a Hilbert space $\mathfrak{H}$, then the corresponding Štraus relation is given by

$$(8.1) \quad T(\ell) = \left\{ \{P_{\mathfrak{H}}\tilde{f}, P_{\mathfrak{H}}\tilde{g}\} \mid \{\tilde{f}, \tilde{g}\} \in A,\ \tilde{g} - \ell\tilde{f} \in \mathfrak{H} \right\}, \quad \ell \in \mathbb{C}.$$

In this section we consider several concrete examples concerning Hamiltonian systems, in which we describe $T(\ell)$ as the restriction of S^* by means of boundary conditions in terms of a pair of matrices $(\mathcal{A}(\ell):\mathcal{B}(\ell))$ as in (7.2). We call two pairs $(\mathcal{A}(\ell):\mathcal{B}(\ell))$ and $(\mathcal{A}_1(\ell):\mathcal{B}_1(\ell))$ of the kind considered in Theorem 7.1 equivalent, if

$$\mathcal{C}(\ell)\,(\mathcal{A}(\ell):\mathcal{B}(\ell)) = (\mathcal{A}_1(\ell):\mathcal{B}_1(\ell))$$

for some invertible, locally holomorphic matrix function $\mathcal{C}$.

Extensions with singular Hamiltonian systems in the limit point case. We consider on an interval $(\tilde{a},b)$ a Hamiltonian system $J\tilde{f}'-H\tilde{f}=\Delta\tilde{g}$ with the property that both endpoints $\tilde{a}$ and b are singular and in the limit point case. Then the corresponding symmetric closed minimal relation in the Hilbert space $\mathfrak{K}=L^2_\Delta(\tilde{a},b)$ turns out to be selfadjoint. We denote it by A. We choose an intermediate point a, $\tilde{a}<a<b$. If we restrict the above system to the interval $[a,b)$ (or $(\tilde{a},a]$) then the endpoint a is regular and the endpoint b (or $\tilde{a}$, respectively) remains singular and in the limit point case. Let $\mathfrak{H}=L^2_\Delta(a,b)$ and let S be the symmetric closed linear relation in $\mathfrak{H}$ which corresponds to the restriction of the system to the interval $[a,b)$. Clearly, $\mathfrak{H}\subset\mathfrak{K}$, the projection $P_{\mathfrak{H}}$ is given by $P_{\mathfrak{H}}\tilde{f}=\mathbb{1}_{[a,b)}\tilde{f}$ where $\mathbb{1}_{[a,b)}$ is the indicator function on $(\tilde{a},b)$ of the interval $[a,b)$ and A is a selfadjoint extension of S. In order to describe the Štraus extension (8.1) of S corresponding to A, we let $\tilde{Y}(.,\ell)$ be the fundamental solution of the equation $J\tilde{f}'-H\tilde{f}=\ell\Delta\tilde{f}$ with $\tilde{Y}(a,\ell)=I$ and $\tilde{M}\in\mathbf{N}_0^{n\times n}$ be the Weyl coefficient corresponding to the system restricted to the interval $(\tilde{a},a)$, compare Section 6. Then $J\tilde{f}'-H\tilde{f}=\ell\Delta\tilde{f}$ on $(\tilde{a},a]$ and $\tilde{f}\in L^2_\Delta(\tilde{a},a)$ if and only if, for some $c\in\mathbb{C}^n$, $\tilde{f}=(\tilde{Y}_1(.,\ell)-\tilde{Y}_2(.,\ell)\tilde{M}(\ell))\,c$. It is now not difficult to verify that

$$T(\ell)=\left\{\{f,g\}\in S^*\mid \mathcal{A}(\ell)f^1(a)+\mathcal{B}(\ell)f^2(a)=0\right\},$$

where the matrix functions $\mathcal{A}(\ell)$ and $\mathcal{B}(\ell)$ are defined by

$$(8.2)\qquad (\mathcal{A}(\ell)\,:\,\mathcal{B}(\ell)) = (\tilde{M}(\ell)\,:\,I),\quad \ell\in\mathbb{C}\backslash\mathbb{R}.$$

Extensions with regular Hamiltonian systems. We consider on an interval $[\tilde{a},b)$ a Hamiltonian system $J\tilde{f}'-H\tilde{f}=\Delta\tilde{g}$ and suppose that the endpoint $\tilde{a}$ is regular and the endpoint b is in the limit point case. Let T_{max} be the maximal relation associated with the system in the space $\mathfrak{K}=L^2_\Delta(\tilde{a},b)$ and let A be the selfadjoint relation

$$A=\left\{\{\tilde{f},\tilde{g}\}\in T_{max}\mid \tilde{A}\tilde{f}^1(\tilde{a})+\tilde{B}\tilde{f}^2(\tilde{a})=0\right\},$$

where the constant matrices $\tilde{A}$ and $\tilde{B}$ satisfy rank $(\tilde{A}\ :\ \tilde{B})=n$, $\tilde{A}\tilde{B}^*=\tilde{B}\tilde{A}^*$. As in the preceeding example we choose a point a, $\tilde{a}<a<b$, put $\mathfrak{H}=L^2_\Delta(a,b)$ and let S be the symmetric closed linear relation in $\mathfrak{H}$ associated with the system restricted to $[a,b)$. Again A is a selfadjoint extension of S and therefore $T(\ell)$ defined by (8.1) satisfies $T(\ell)\subset S^*$. In order to describe $T(\ell)$ we consider $\{\tilde{f},\tilde{g}\}\in A$ and assume that $\tilde{g}-\ell\tilde{f}\in\mathfrak{H}$. Then $\tilde{g}-\ell\tilde{f}=0$ on $[\tilde{a},a]$ and hence, for some $c\in\mathbb{C}^{2n}$, $\tilde{f}=\tilde{Y}(.,\ell)c$, where $\tilde{Y}(.,\ell)$ is the fundamental solution of the equation $J\tilde{f}'-H\tilde{f}=\ell\Delta\tilde{f}$ on $[\tilde{a},a]$ with $\tilde{Y}(a,\ell)=I$. Since $\tilde{f}$ satisfies the boundary condition at $\tilde{a}$ there must exist some $d\in\mathbb{C}^n$ such that

$$\tilde{Y}(\tilde{a},\ell)c=\begin{pmatrix}\tilde{B}^*\\ -\tilde{A}^*\end{pmatrix}d,\quad\text{or}\quad c=\left(\tilde{Y}(\tilde{a},\ell)\right)^{-1}\begin{pmatrix}\tilde{B}^*\\ -\tilde{A}^*\end{pmatrix}d$$

and hence,

$$\tilde{f}=\tilde{Y}(.,\ell)\tilde{Y}(\tilde{a},\ell)^{-1}\begin{pmatrix}\tilde{B}^*\\ -\tilde{A}^*\end{pmatrix}d\ \text{ and }\ \tilde{f}(a)=\tilde{Y}(\tilde{a},\ell)^{-1}\begin{pmatrix}\tilde{B}^*\\ -\tilde{A}^*\end{pmatrix}d.$$

Therefore, we see that

$$\tilde{f}(a)\in\Re\left(\tilde{Y}(\tilde{a},\ell)^{-1}\begin{pmatrix}\tilde{B}^*\\ -\tilde{A}^*\end{pmatrix}\right).$$

One can now easily prove that

$$T(\ell)=\left\{\{f,g\}\in S^*\mid \mathcal{A}(\ell)f^1(a)+\mathcal{B}(\ell)f^2(a)=0\right\},$$

where

$$(8.3)\qquad \left(\mathcal{A}(\ell)\ :\ \mathcal{B}(\ell)\right)=\left(\tilde{A}\ :\ \tilde{B}\right)\tilde{Y}(\tilde{a},\ell),\quad \ell\in\mathbb{C}.$$

In the cases where the pair $(\mathcal{A}(\ell):\mathcal{B}(\ell))$ in the Štraus relation (7.2) is equivalent to the one in (8.2) with $\tilde{M}$ as described above, or to the one in (8.3) with $\tilde{A},\tilde{B}$ and $\tilde{Y}(\tilde{a},\ell)$ as described above, the Hamiltonian system on the larger interval $(\tilde{a},b)$ can serve as a model for the selfadjoint extension A in the larger space $L^2_\Delta(\tilde{a},b)$ of the minimal relation S in the space $L^2_\Delta(a,b)$. To verify whether $(\mathcal{A}(\ell):\mathcal{B}(\ell))$ is equivalent to either of these pairs amounts to solving an inverse spectral problem: determine a Hamiltonian system from the Weyl coefficient $\tilde{M}$, or from the data $\tilde{A},\tilde{B}$ and $\tilde{Y}(\tilde{a},\ell)$. A very general result in the positive definite case of 2×2 systems is due to de Branges [dB1–5]. In some situations in the indefinite case results from [KL3,4] can be used. As an illustration we present the following simple special case. Consider on the interval $[0,1]$ the Hamiltonian system defined by

$$\Delta(t)=\begin{bmatrix} O & O \\ O & O \end{bmatrix},\quad t\in[0,\tfrac{1}{2}],\qquad \Delta(t)=\begin{bmatrix} 2\omega & O \\ O & O \end{bmatrix},\quad t\in[\tfrac{1}{2},1],$$

$$H(t)=\begin{bmatrix} O & O \\ O & 2\varepsilon \end{bmatrix},\quad t\in[0,\tfrac{1}{2}],\qquad H(t)=\begin{bmatrix} O & O \\ O & O \end{bmatrix},\quad t\in[\tfrac{1}{2},1],$$

where ω and ε are $k\times k$ matrices. Let $Z(.,\ell)$ be the fundamental matrix solution with $Z(0,\ell)=I$. Then

$$Z(1,\ell)=\begin{bmatrix} I & \varepsilon \\ -\ell\omega & I-\ell\omega\varepsilon \end{bmatrix}.$$

We will suppose that $\omega\geq 0$, which implies that on $[0,1]$ the Hamiltonian system satisfies (5.6), but condition (5.8) need not be satisfied. However, if the present system is pasted at one endpoint to a Hamiltonian system which satisfies (5.8), then the new Hamiltonian system will satisfy this condition by Proposition 5.1. For linear boundary conditions $\mathcal{A}(\ell)=\mathcal{A}_0+\mathcal{A}_1\ell$, $\mathcal{B}(\ell)=\mathcal{B}_0+\mathcal{B}_1\ell$, the matrices $\tilde{\mathcal{A}}$ and $\tilde{\mathcal{B}}$ such that

$$(\mathcal{A}_0+\mathcal{A}_1\ell : \mathcal{B}_0+\mathcal{B}_1\ell) = (\tilde{\mathcal{A}} : \tilde{\mathcal{B}})Z(1,\ell),\quad \ell\in\mathbb{C}.$$

are given by

$$\tilde{\mathcal{A}}=\mathcal{A}_0,\ \tilde{\mathcal{B}}=\mathcal{B}_0-\mathcal{A}_0\varepsilon,\ \varepsilon=\mathcal{A}_1^{-1}\mathcal{B}_1,\ \omega=-(\mathcal{B}_0-\mathcal{A}_0\mathcal{A}_1^{-1}\mathcal{B}_1)^{-1}\mathcal{A}_1,$$

provided the inverses $(\mathcal{A}_1)^{-1}$ and $(\mathcal{B}_0-\mathcal{A}_0\mathcal{A}_1^{-1}\mathcal{B}_1)^{-1}$ exist.

Linear boundary conditions. We consider a Hamiltonian system on an interval $[a,b)$, with regular endpoint a and endpoint b in the limit point case and the corresponding boundary value problem

$$Jf'=(\ell\Delta+H)f+\Delta g,\qquad (\mathcal{A}(\ell):\mathcal{B}(\ell))\binom{f^1(a)}{f^2(a)}=0,$$

where the pair $(\mathcal{A}(\ell):\mathcal{B}(\ell))$ is equivalent to $\binom{\mathcal{H}}{\mathcal{F}-\ell\mathcal{G}}$ for some constant matrices $\mathcal{H}$ $((n-k)\times 2n)$, $\mathcal{F}(k\times 2n)$, $\mathcal{G}$ $(k\times 2n)$ with $0\leq k\leq n$. According to the results in Section 4, this problem corresponds to a selfadjoint extension in a Pontryagin space $\mathfrak{K}$ if and only if rank $\mathcal{H}=n-k$ and

$$\begin{bmatrix} \mathcal{H} \\ \mathcal{F} \\ \mathcal{G} \end{bmatrix}\begin{bmatrix} O & I \\ -I & O \end{bmatrix}\begin{bmatrix} \mathcal{H} \\ \mathcal{F} \\ \mathcal{G} \end{bmatrix}^{*}=\begin{bmatrix} O & O & O \\ O & O & \mathcal{D} \\ O & -\mathcal{D} & O \end{bmatrix},$$

where $\mathcal{D}$ is an invertible, hermitian $k\times k$ matrix, cf. [D], Corollary 6.3. Under these conditions $\dim\mathfrak{K}\ominus\mathfrak{H}=k$ and the index of $\mathfrak{K}$ is equal to the number of negative eigenvalues of $\mathcal{D}$. In order to make the conditions more explicit we consider the matrices $\mathcal{H}_1$ through $\mathcal{G}_2$, each having n columns, such that

$$\mathcal{H} = (\mathcal{H}_1 : \mathcal{H}_2), \quad \mathcal{F} = (\mathcal{F}_1 : \mathcal{F}_2), \quad \mathcal{G} = (\mathcal{G}_1 : \mathcal{G}_2).$$

Then the boundary value problem

$$\begin{aligned} &Jf' = (\ell\Delta + H)f + \Delta g, \\ &\mathcal{H}_1 f^1(a) + \mathcal{H}_2 f^2(a) = 0, \\ &\mathcal{F}_1 f^1(a) + \mathcal{F}_2 f^2(a) = \ell\left(\mathcal{G}_1 f^1(a) + \mathcal{G}_2 f^2(a)\right) \end{aligned}$$

corresponds to a selfadjoint extension in a Pontryagin space $\mathfrak{K}$ if and only if

$$\begin{aligned} &\operatorname{rank}\,(\mathcal{H}_1 : \mathcal{H}_2) = n - k, \\ &\mathcal{H}_1\mathcal{H}_2^* - \mathcal{H}_2\mathcal{H}_1^* = O_{n-k}^{n-k}, \quad \mathcal{F}_1\mathcal{F}_2^* - \mathcal{F}_2\mathcal{F}_1^* = O_k^k, \quad \mathcal{G}_1\mathcal{G}_2^* - \mathcal{G}_2\mathcal{G}_1^* = O_k^k, \\ &\mathcal{H}_1\mathcal{G}_2^* - \mathcal{H}_2\mathcal{G}_1^* = O_{n-k}^k, \quad \mathcal{H}_1\mathcal{F}_2^* - \mathcal{H}_2\mathcal{F}_1^* = O_{n-k}^k, \\ &\mathcal{F}_1\mathcal{G}_2^* - \mathcal{F}_2\mathcal{G}_1^* = \mathcal{D}, \end{aligned}$$

where $\mathcal{D}$ is an invertible, hermitian $k\times k$ matrix. If for $\{f,g\}\in S^*$ we define

$$b(f,g) = \begin{pmatrix} f^1(a) \\ f^2(a) \end{pmatrix},$$

then in the Pontryagin space $\mathfrak{H}\oplus\mathbb{C}^k$ with inner product

$$\left[\begin{pmatrix} f \\ \alpha \end{pmatrix}, \begin{pmatrix} g \\ \beta \end{pmatrix}\right] = [f,g] + \beta^*\mathcal{D}^{-1}\alpha, \qquad f,g\in\mathfrak{H},\ \alpha,\beta\in\mathbb{C}^k,$$

the selfadjoint relation A given by (4.5) provides a model for our boundary value problem.

9. A GENERAL REPRESENTATION OF THE EXTENDING RELATION

In this section we show in the case of a Pontryagin space extension A of S, that the function Ω, introduced in Section 7 determines the pair S, A up to an isomorphism, in a sense to be explained below. To this end we consider an arbitrary $n\times n$ matrix function $\mathcal{M}\in\mathbf{N}_0^{n\times n}$ such that $\operatorname{Im}\mathcal{M}(\mu) > O$ (hence $\mathcal{M}(\ell)$ is invertible for all nonreal ℓ), and two matrix functions $\mathcal{A},\mathcal{B}$ satisfying the conditions of Theorem 7.1 and corresponding to π_κ-extensions, i.e.,

(9.1) $\mathcal{A}$ and $\mathcal{B}$ are $n\times n$ matrix functions, locally meromorphic in $\mathbb{C}\backslash\mathbb{R}$ with common domain of holomorphy $\mathfrak{D}_{\mathcal{A},\mathcal{B}} = \mathfrak{D}_{\mathcal{A},\mathcal{B}}^*$,

(9.2) $\operatorname{rank}\,(\mathcal{A}(\ell) : \mathcal{B}(\ell)) = n$,

(9.3) $\mathcal{A}(\ell)\mathcal{B}(\bar{\ell})^* - \mathcal{B}(\ell)\mathcal{A}(\bar{\ell})^* = 0$,

(9.4) $\mathcal{A}(\ell) + \mathcal{B}(\ell)\mathcal{M}(\ell)$ is invertible for at least one point ℓ in each of the half planes $\mathbb{C}^+$ and $\mathbb{C}^-$,

(9.5) the kernel $N_{A,B}(\ell,\lambda)$ defined by (7.1) has κ negative squares.

We define the $2n\times 2n$ matrix function Ω by

$$\Omega(\ell)=\begin{bmatrix} \Gamma(\ell)B(\ell) & -\Gamma(\ell)A(\ell) \\ M(\ell)\Gamma(\ell)B(\ell)+I & -M(\ell)\Gamma(\ell)A(\ell) \end{bmatrix}, \tag{9.6}$$

where $\Gamma(\ell)=-\left(A(\ell)+B(\ell)M(\ell)\right)^{-1}$, which exists for sufficiently many points according to assumption (9.4). It is not difficult to verify that $\Omega(\ell)^*=\Omega(\bar{\ell})$ and

$$\Omega(\ell)=\begin{bmatrix} -M(\ell) & I \\ A(\ell) & B(\ell) \end{bmatrix}^{-1}\begin{bmatrix} I & O \\ O & A(\ell) \end{bmatrix}=\begin{bmatrix} I & O \\ O & A(\bar{\ell})^* \end{bmatrix}\begin{bmatrix} -M(\ell) & A(\bar{\ell})^* \\ I & B(\bar{\ell})^* \end{bmatrix}^{-1}.$$

A straightforward calculation yields the following result.

PROPOSITION 9.1. *The $2n\times 2n$ matrix function Ω satisfies the following relation*

$$N_{\Omega}(\ell,\lambda)=\begin{bmatrix} -M(\bar{\lambda}) & I \\ A(\bar{\lambda}) & B(\bar{\lambda}) \end{bmatrix}^{-1}\operatorname{diag}\left(N_M(\ell,\lambda),N_{A,B}(\ell,\lambda)\right)\begin{bmatrix} -M(\ell) & A(\bar{\ell})^* \\ I & B(\bar{\ell})^* \end{bmatrix}^{-1}.$$

Hence it belongs to the class $\Omega\in\mathbf{N}_\kappa^{2n\times 2n}$.

In the following we use the fact that functions of the class $\mathbf{N}_\kappa^{m\times m}$ admit representations by means of unitary operators or selfadjoint relations in π_κ-spaces (see [KL5]). We shall formulate this representation and briefly describe the construction of the underlying spaces, operators and relations. Let $Q\in\mathbf{N}_\kappa^{m\times m}$. Then there exists a π_κ-space Π, a linear mapping $\Gamma\in\mathbf{L}(\mathbb{C}^m,\Pi)$, a hermitian $m\times m$ matrix S and a unitary operator U in Π such that

$$Q(\ell)=S+i(\operatorname{Im}\mu)\Gamma^*\left(I+z(\ell)U\right)\left(I-z(\ell)U\right)^{-1}\Gamma, \tag{9.7}$$

where $\mu\in\mathfrak{D}_Q\cap\mathbb{C}^+$ and $z(\ell)=(\ell-\mu)/(\ell-\bar{\mu})$. Clearly we have $S=\operatorname{Re}Q(\mu)$. The space Π can be chosen to be minimal:

$$\Pi=\text{c.l.s.}\left\{(I-zU)^{-1}\Gamma\mathbb{C}^m \mid z^{-1}\in\rho(U)\right\}, \tag{9.8}$$

and then U is uniquely determined up to isomorphisms. Conversely, if Q is defined by the righthand side of (9.7) with a given π_κ-space Π, a unitary operator U in Π, $\Gamma\in\mathbf{L}(\mathbb{C}^m,\Pi)$ and a hermitian $m\times m$ matrix S, then $Q\in\mathbf{N}_\tau^{m\times m}$ for some $\tau\leq\kappa$ and $\tau=\kappa$ if Π is minimal. Let the relation A be the inverse Cayley transform of U at μ: $A=F_\mu(U)$. Then A is selfadjoint, (9.7) becomes

$$Q(\ell)=S+\Gamma^*\left(\ell-\operatorname{Re}\mu+(\ell-\bar{\mu})(\ell-\mu)(A-\ell)^{-1}\right)\Gamma,\quad \ell\in\rho(A), \tag{9.9}$$

and (9.8) is equivalent to

$$\Pi = \text{c.l.s.}\left\{ (A-\ell)^{-1}\Gamma\mathbb{C}^m \cup \Gamma\mathbb{C}^m \mid \ell\in\rho(A)\right\}.$$

In order to find for a given function $Q\in\mathbf{N}_\kappa^{m\times m}$ the space Π, the operators Γ, U and the relation A, we consider the linear space $\mathfrak{L}$ of finite sums $\sum_\ell \varepsilon_\ell f_\ell$, where $\ell\in\mathfrak{D}_Q$, $f_\ell\in\mathbb{C}^m$ and ε_ℓ is a symbol associated with each $\ell\in\mathfrak{D}_Q$, provided with the (possibly degenerate, indefinite) inner product

$$[\ \textstyle\sum_\ell \varepsilon_\ell f_\ell,\ \sum_\lambda \varepsilon_\lambda g_\lambda\ ] \;=\; \sum_{\ell,\lambda}\ (\ \mathrm{N}_Q(\ell,\lambda) f_\ell, g_\lambda\ ).$$

Let the relation A_0 in $\mathfrak{L}$ and its Cayley transform $U_0 = C_\mu(A_0)$ with $\mu\in\mathbb{C}^+\cap\mathfrak{D}_Q$ be given by

$$A_0 = \left\{ \{\ \textstyle\sum_\ell \varepsilon_\ell f_\ell,\ \sum_\ell \varepsilon_\ell \ell f_\ell\ \} \mid \sum_\ell f_\ell = 0\right\},$$

$$U_0 = \left\{ \{\ \textstyle\sum_\ell \varepsilon_\ell(\ell-\mu) f_\ell,\ \sum_\ell \varepsilon_\ell(\ell-\bar\mu) f_\ell\ \} \mid \sum_\ell f_\ell = 0\right\}.$$

Then A_0 is a "symmetric" relation in $\mathfrak{L}$ and

$$(A_0-\lambda)^{-1}\varepsilon_\ell f = (\ell-\lambda)^{-1}(\varepsilon_\ell f - \varepsilon_\lambda f).$$

The operator U_0 with "dense" domain $\mathfrak{D}(U_0) = \{\sum_\ell \varepsilon_\ell f_\ell \mid f_\mu = 0\}$ and "dense" range $\mathfrak{R}(U_0)$ is "isometric" in $\mathfrak{L}$ and

$$U_0\varepsilon_\ell f = \frac{\ell-\bar\mu}{\ell-\mu}\varepsilon_\ell f - \frac{\mu-\bar\mu}{\ell-\mu}\varepsilon_\mu f, \qquad \ell\in\mathfrak{D}_Q,\ \ell\neq\mu,\ f\in\mathbb{C}^m.$$

Hence, in particular, $U_0\varepsilon_{\bar\mu} f = \varepsilon_\mu f$. Define $\Gamma_0 : \mathbb{C}^m \to \mathfrak{L}$ by $\Gamma_0 f = \varepsilon_\mu f$, $f\in\mathbb{C}^m$. Then a straightforward calculation shows that

$$(9.10)\quad Q(\ell)f = \operatorname{Re} Q(\mu) f + i(\operatorname{Im}\mu)\Gamma_0^{*}\left(I + z(\ell)U_0\right)\left(I - z(\ell)U_0\right)^{-1}\Gamma_0 f.$$

The completion of the quotient space $\mathfrak{L}/(\mathfrak{L}\cap\mathfrak{L}^\perp)$ with respect to the inner product defined above yields the π_κ-space Π, and A_0, U_0 and Γ_0 give rise to a selfadjoint relation A in Π, a unitary operator U with $U = \mathrm{C}_\mu(A)$ and a mapping $\Gamma\in\mathbf{L}(\mathbb{C}^m,\Pi)$. The representation (9.7) now follows from (9.10). Furthermore, it is not hard to check that

$$(A-\ell)^{-1}\varepsilon_\mu f = (A-\mu)^{-1}\varepsilon_\ell f.$$

Put $<\varepsilon_\ell> = \{\,\varepsilon_\ell f \mid f\in\mathbb{C}^m\,\}$, $\ell\in\mathfrak{D}_Q$, and let V_0 be the "isometry" in $\mathfrak{L}$ defined as the restriction of U_0 to $<\varepsilon_{\bar\mu}>^\perp$. It maps $<\varepsilon_{\bar\mu}>^\perp$ onto $<\varepsilon_\mu>^\perp$ and in Π it gives rise to an isometry $V\subset U$ with defect spaces $\mathfrak{D}(V)^\perp = U^{-1}\Gamma\mathbb{C}^m$ and $\mathfrak{R}(V)^\perp = \Gamma\mathbb{C}^m$. Finally, let $S = F_\mu(V)$, the inverse Cayley transform of V. In the following we shall use the notations $\mathcal{L}(Q)$, $\Pi(Q)$, $[\ ,\ ]_Q$, $U_0(Q)$, $U(Q)$ etc. to denote the dependence on Q of the spaces and operators we have just considered.

In terms of this model we now present a simple convergence criterion whose proof is similar to the proof of [IKL], Theorem 2.4, see also [DLS6], Lemma 5.2 (i).

LEMMA 9.2. *Let* $Q\in\mathbf{N}_\kappa^{m\times m}$ *and let* $\tilde{f}(\ell)$ *be an* $m\times 1$ *vector function, defined and holomorphic in* $\mathbb{C}^+$. *If, as* $\ell\hat{\to}\lambda_0\in\mathbb{R}$,

(i) $\tilde{f}(\ell)$ *converges in* $\mathbb{C}^m$,

(ii) $Q(\ell)\tilde{f}(\ell)$ *converges in* $\mathbb{C}^m$ *and*

(iii) $[\mathrm{N}_Q(\ell,\ell)\tilde{f}(\ell),\tilde{f}(\ell)]$ *is bounded in* $\mathbb{C}$,

then $\varepsilon_\ell\tilde{f}(\ell)$ *converges weakly in* $\Pi(Q)$ *as* $\ell\hat{\to}\lambda_0$. *Conversely, if* $\varepsilon_\ell\tilde{f}(\ell)$ *converges weakly in* $\Pi(Q)$ *as* $\ell\hat{\to}\lambda_0$, *then* (iii) *holds and if* $\operatorname{Im}Q(\mu)$ *is invertible for some* $\mu\in\mathbb{C}\backslash\mathbb{R}$, *then* (i) *and* (ii) *are also valid.*

Now let $M\in\mathbf{N}_0^{n\times n}$, then $\Pi(M)$ is a Hilbert space and the defect spaces of $V(M)$ in $\Pi(M)$, $\mathfrak{D}(V(M))^\perp$ and $\mathfrak{R}(V(M))^\perp$, are n dimensional. The characteristic function of the isometric operator $V(M)$ was defined in [DLS3].

PROPOSITION 9.3. *If* $M\in\mathbf{N}_0^{n\times n}$ *satisfies* $\operatorname{Im}M(\mu)>O$ *for some* $\mu\in\mathbb{C}^+$, *then the isometric operator* $V(M)$ *is simple and its characteristic function* X_M *is given by*

$$X_M(z(\ell)) = \left(M(\ell)-M(\bar{\mu})\right)^{-1}\left(M(\ell)-M(\mu)\right), \quad \ell\in\mathbb{C}^+.$$

Proof. As $\operatorname{Im}M(\bar{\mu})<O$ and $\operatorname{Im}M(\ell)>O$ for $\ell\in\mathbb{C}^+$, the inverse $(M(\ell)-M(\bar{\mu}))^{-1}$ exists. Since $\Pi(M)$ is minimal and $V(M)\subset U(M)$, the operator $V(M)$ is simple. To determine X_M it suffices to calculate $z(\ell)P_0\left(I-z(\ell)\tilde{V}_0\right)^{-1}\varepsilon_\mu x$ for $x\in\mathbb{C}^n$, where

$$\tilde{V}_0 x = \begin{cases} V_0(M)x, & \text{if } x\in\mathfrak{D}(V_0(M)), \\ O\ , & \text{if } x\in\mathfrak{D}(V_0(M))^\perp = \langle\varepsilon_{\bar{\mu}}\rangle \end{cases}$$

and P_0 is the projection in $\mathfrak{L}(M)$ onto $\langle\varepsilon_{\bar{\mu}}\rangle$. A straightforward calculation shows that for $\ell\neq\mu$:

$$P_0\varepsilon_\ell x = \varepsilon_{\bar{\mu}}C(\ell)x,\ C(\ell) = \frac{\mu-\bar{\mu}}{\ell-\mu}\left(M(\mu)-M(\bar{\mu})\right)^{-1}\left(M(\ell)-M(\mu)\right)$$

and

$$\tilde{V}_0\varepsilon_\ell x = U_0(M)(I-P_0)\varepsilon_\ell x = \frac{\ell-\bar{\mu}}{\ell-\mu}\varepsilon_\ell x - \frac{\mu-\bar{\mu}}{\ell-\mu}\varepsilon_\mu x - \varepsilon_\mu C(\ell)x.$$

This implies that

$$z(\ell)P_0\left(I-z(\ell)\widetilde{V}_0\right)^{-1}\varepsilon_\mu x=z(\ell)P_0\varepsilon_\ell\left(z(\ell)C(\ell)+(1-z(\ell))I\right)^{-1}x=$$

$$=\varepsilon_{\bar\mu}z(\ell)C(\ell)\left(z(\ell)C(\ell)+(1-z(\ell))I\right)^{-1}x=\varepsilon_{\bar\mu}\left(M(\ell)-M(\bar\mu)\right)^{-1}\left(M(\ell)-M(\mu)\right)x,$$

from which the proposition follows. □

With the pair $\mathcal{A},\mathcal{B}$ of $n\times n$ matrix functions satisfying (9.1)–(9.5) we associate in a similar way a π_κ–space $\Pi(\mathcal{A},\mathcal{B})$ starting from the linear set $\mathcal{L}(\mathcal{A},\mathcal{B})$ of all finite formal sums $\sum_\ell \delta_\ell f_\ell$, where $f_\ell\in\mathbb{C}^n$ and $\ell\in\mathfrak{D}_{\mathcal{A},\mathcal{B}}$, equipped with the inner product

$$[\textstyle\sum_\ell \delta_\ell f_\ell, \sum_\lambda \delta_\lambda g_\lambda]=\sum_{\ell,\lambda}\left(\mathrm{N}_{\mathcal{A},\mathcal{B}}(\ell,\lambda)f_\ell, g_\lambda\right),$$

cf. the construction given in [AD1–3].

THEOREM 9.4. *Let $M\in\mathbf{N}_0^{n\times n}$ satisfy $\operatorname{Im}M(\mu)>O$ for some $\mu\in\mathbb{C}^+$, $\mathcal{A}$, $\mathcal{B}$ be given by (9.1)–(9.5) and let Ω be defined by (9.6). Then the π_κ–space $\Pi(\Omega)$ of index κ can be identified with the orthogonal sum of the π_κ–space $\Pi(\mathcal{A},\mathcal{B})$ of index κ and the Hilbert space $\Pi(M)$: $\Pi(\Omega)=\Pi(\mathcal{A},\mathcal{B})\oplus\Pi(M)$. With this identification the operator $U(\Omega)$ is a unitary extension of the isometry $V(M)$ with characteristic function*

$$X_M(z(\ell))=\left(M(\ell)-M(\bar\mu)\right)^{-1}\left(M(\ell)-M(\mu)\right),$$

and, if $U(\Omega)$ has the matrix representation

$$U(\Omega)=\begin{pmatrix} T & F & O\\ G & H & O\\ O & O & V(M)\end{pmatrix}:\begin{pmatrix}\Pi(\mathcal{A},\mathcal{B})\\ \mathfrak{D}(V(M))^\perp\\ \mathfrak{D}(V(M))\end{pmatrix}\to\begin{pmatrix}\Pi(\mathcal{A},\mathcal{B})\\ \mathfrak{R}(V(M))^\perp\\ \mathfrak{R}(V(M))\end{pmatrix},$$

then $\Delta=\left(\Pi(\mathcal{A},\mathcal{B}),\mathfrak{D}(V(M))^\perp,\mathfrak{R}(V(M))^\perp;T,F,G,H\right)$ is a closely connected unitary colligation with characteristic function

$$\Theta_\Delta(z(\ell))=\left(\mathcal{A}(\ell)+\mathcal{B}(\ell)M(\mu)\right)^{-1}\left(\mathcal{A}(\ell)+\mathcal{B}(\ell)M(\bar\mu)\right),\qquad \ell\in\mathbb{C}^+.$$

Thus, for given M and $\mathcal{A},\mathcal{B}$ as above, the function M defines the isometric operator $V(M)$ (the symmetric relation $S(M)$) in $\Pi(\Omega)$, and the pair $\mathcal{A},\mathcal{B}$ essentially determines the unitary extension $U(\Omega)$ of $V(M)$ (the selfadjoint extension $A(\Omega)$ of $S(M)$, respectively).

Proof. We consider the construction of the space $\Pi(\Omega)$, using the special structure of the $2n\times 2n$ matrix function Ω. Let $\mathfrak{L}(\Omega)$ be the space spanned by elements of the form

$$\boldsymbol{\varepsilon}_\ell \begin{bmatrix} x \\ y \end{bmatrix}, \quad \ell \in \mathfrak{D}_\Omega, \quad x, y \in \mathbb{C}^n.$$

Then, as

$$\begin{bmatrix} -M(\ell) & A(\bar{\ell})^* \\ I & B(\bar{\ell})^* \end{bmatrix}^{-1} = \begin{bmatrix} \Gamma(\ell)B(\ell) & -\Gamma(\ell)A(\ell) \\ -\Gamma(\bar{\ell})^* & -\Gamma(\bar{\ell})^*M(\ell) \end{bmatrix},$$

each such element can be written as

$$\boldsymbol{\varepsilon}_\ell \begin{bmatrix} x \\ y \end{bmatrix} = \boldsymbol{\varepsilon}_\ell \begin{bmatrix} -M(\ell) & A(\bar{\ell})^* \\ I & B(\bar{\ell})^* \end{bmatrix} \begin{bmatrix} \Gamma(\ell)B(\ell)x - \Gamma(\ell)A(\ell)y \\ -\Gamma(\bar{\ell})^*x - \Gamma(\bar{\ell})^*M(\ell)y \end{bmatrix}$$

$$= \delta_\ell \Gamma(\bar{\ell})^*\left(-x - M(\ell)y\right) + \varepsilon_\ell \Gamma(\ell)\left(B(\ell)x - A(\ell)y\right),$$

where

$$\delta_\ell = \boldsymbol{\varepsilon}_\ell \begin{bmatrix} A(\bar{\ell})^* \\ B(\bar{\ell})^* \end{bmatrix}, \quad \varepsilon_\ell = \boldsymbol{\varepsilon}_\ell \begin{bmatrix} -M(\ell) \\ I \end{bmatrix}.$$

It is easy to check that for $x, y \in \mathbb{C}^n$ we have $[\varepsilon_\ell x, \delta_\lambda y]_\Omega = 0$ and

$$[\delta_\ell x, \delta_\lambda y]_\Omega = \left(\mathsf{N}_{A,B}(\ell,\lambda)x, y\right), \quad [\varepsilon_\ell x, \varepsilon_\lambda y]_\Omega = \left(\mathsf{N}_M(\ell,\lambda)x, y\right).$$

It follows that $\mathfrak{L}(A,B)$ ($\mathfrak{L}(M)$) can be identified with the linear subspaces spanned by the elements δ_ℓ (ε_ℓ, respectively) and that $\mathfrak{L}(\Omega) = \mathfrak{L}(M) \oplus \mathfrak{L}(A,B)$, the orthogonal sum of $\mathfrak{L}(A,B)$ and $\mathfrak{L}(M)$. Since

$$\begin{aligned} U_0(\Omega) &= \left\{ \{ \textstyle\sum_\ell \boldsymbol{\varepsilon}_\ell(\ell-\mu)f_\ell, \sum_\ell \boldsymbol{\varepsilon}_\ell(\ell-\bar{\mu})f_\ell \} \mid \sum_\ell f_\ell = 0 \right\} \\ &\supseteq \left\{ \{ \textstyle\sum_\ell \varepsilon_\ell(\ell-\mu)x_\ell, \sum_\ell \varepsilon_\ell(\ell-\bar{\mu})x_\ell \} \mid \sum_\ell \begin{pmatrix} -M(\ell) \\ I \end{pmatrix} x_\ell = 0 \right\} \\ &= \left\{ \{ \textstyle\sum_\ell \varepsilon_\ell x_\ell, \sum_\ell \varepsilon_\ell \frac{\ell-\bar{\mu}}{\ell-\mu} x_\ell \} \mid x_\mu = 0, \ [\sum_\ell \varepsilon_\ell x_\ell, \varepsilon_{\bar{\mu}} x] = 0, \ x \in \mathbb{C}^n \right\} \\ &= V_0(M), \end{aligned}$$

$U_0(\Omega)$ is an extension of $V_0(M)$. Now the first statements of the theorem easily follow. To prove the last statement recall that

$$(9.11) \quad U_0(\Omega)\boldsymbol{\varepsilon}_\ell f = \boldsymbol{\varepsilon}_\ell \frac{\ell-\bar{\mu}}{\ell-\mu} f - \boldsymbol{\varepsilon}_\mu \frac{\mu-\bar{\mu}}{\ell-\mu} f, \quad \ell \neq \mu, \quad f \in \mathbb{C}^{2n},$$

and this implies that for $\ell \neq \mu$ and $x, y \in \mathbb{C}^n$

$$(9.12) \quad U_0(\Omega) \begin{bmatrix} \delta_\ell x \\ \varepsilon_\ell y \end{bmatrix} = U_0(\Omega)\boldsymbol{\varepsilon}_\ell \begin{bmatrix} A(\bar{\ell})^*x - M(\ell)y \\ B(\bar{\ell})^*x + y \end{bmatrix} = \begin{bmatrix} \delta_\ell \frac{\ell-\bar{\mu}}{\ell-\mu} x - \delta_\mu \frac{\mu-\bar{\mu}}{\ell-\mu} u \\ \varepsilon_\ell \frac{\ell-\bar{\mu}}{\ell-\mu} y - \varepsilon_\mu \frac{\mu-\bar{\mu}}{\ell-\mu} v \end{bmatrix},$$

where u and v are given by

$$u=\Gamma(\bar{\mu})^*\big(-\big(\mathcal{A}(\bar{\ell})^*+\mathcal{M}(\mu)\mathcal{B}(\bar{\ell})^*\big)x+\big(\mathcal{M}(\ell)-\mathcal{M}(\mu)\big)y\big),$$

$$v=\Gamma(\mu)\big(\big(\mathcal{B}(\mu)\mathcal{A}(\bar{\ell})^*-\mathcal{A}(\mu)\mathcal{B}(\bar{\ell})^*\big)x-\big(\mathcal{A}(\mu)+\mathcal{B}(\mu)\mathcal{M}(\ell)\big)y\big).$$

The inclusion $V_0(\mathcal{M})\subset U_0(\Omega)$ yields the matrix representation

$$U_0(\Omega)\;=\;\begin{pmatrix} T_0 & F_0 & O\\ G_0 & H_0 & O\\ O & O & V_0(\mathcal{M})\end{pmatrix}:\begin{pmatrix}\mathfrak{L}(\mathcal{A},\mathcal{B})\\ <\varepsilon_{\bar{\mu}}>\\ <\varepsilon_{\bar{\mu}}>^{\perp}\end{pmatrix}\to\begin{pmatrix}\mathfrak{L}(\mathcal{A},\mathcal{B})\\ <\varepsilon_{\mu}>\\ <\varepsilon_{\mu}>^{\perp}\end{pmatrix},$$

where, on account of (9.12),

$$T_0\delta_\ell x=\delta_\ell\frac{\ell-\bar{\mu}}{\ell-\mu}x-\delta_\mu\frac{\mu-\bar{\mu}}{\ell-\mu}\Gamma(\bar{\mu})^*\big(-(\mathcal{A}(\bar{\ell})^*+\mathcal{M}(\mu)\mathcal{B}(\bar{\ell})^*)x\big),$$

$$G_0\delta_\ell x=-\varepsilon_\mu\frac{\mu-\bar{\mu}}{\ell-\mu}\Gamma(\mu)\big(\mathcal{B}(\mu)\mathcal{A}(\bar{\ell})^*-\mathcal{A}(\mu)\mathcal{B}(\bar{\ell})^*\big)x,$$

$$F_0\varepsilon_{\bar{\mu}}y=\delta_\mu\Gamma(\bar{\mu})^*\big(\mathcal{M}(\bar{\mu})-\mathcal{M}(\mu)\big)y,$$

$$H_0\varepsilon_{\bar{\mu}}y=-\varepsilon_\mu\Gamma(\mu)\big(\mathcal{A}(\mu)+\mathcal{B}(\mu)\mathcal{M}(\bar{\mu})\big)y.$$

A straightforward calculation shows that

$$\begin{aligned}\Theta_0(z(\ell))\varepsilon_{\bar{\mu}}x&=\big(H_0+z(\ell)G_0(I-z(\ell)T_0)^{-1}F_0\big)\varepsilon_{\bar{\mu}}x\\&=\varepsilon_\mu\big(\mathcal{A}(\ell)+\mathcal{B}(\ell)\mathcal{M}(\mu)\big)^{-1}\big(\mathcal{A}(\ell)+\mathcal{B}(\ell)\mathcal{M}(\bar{\mu})\big)x\end{aligned}$$

and this yields the formula for the characteristic function of the unitary colligation Δ. To prove that Δ is closely connected it suffices to show that $\Pi(\mathcal{A},\mathcal{B})$ does not contain a nonzero subspace invariant under $U(\Omega)$ (see [DLS3], Proposition 3.2). This follows from the fact that

(9.13) $$\Pi(\Omega)=\text{c.l.s.}\left\{U(\Omega)^n\big(\mathfrak{D}(V(\mathcal{M}))^{\perp}+\mathfrak{R}(V(\mathcal{M}))^{\perp}\big)\mid n\in\mathbb{Z}\right\}.$$

In order to see this relation we note that, by definition,

$$\Gamma_0(\Omega)\mathbb{C}^{2n}=<\boldsymbol{\varepsilon}_\mu>=\{\,\delta_\mu x+\varepsilon_\mu y\mid x,y\in\mathbb{C}^n\,\}$$

and that, on account of (9.12),

$$U_0(\Omega)\varepsilon_{\bar{\mu}}u=\delta_\mu\Gamma(\bar{\mu})^*\big(\mathcal{M}(\bar{\mu})-\mathcal{M}(\mu)\big)u-\varepsilon_\mu\Gamma(\mu)\big(\mathcal{A}(\mu)+\mathcal{B}(\mu)\mathcal{M}(\bar{\mu})\big)u.$$

As $\Gamma(\bar{\mu})^*\big(\mathcal{M}(\bar{\mu})-\mathcal{M}(\mu)\big)$ is invertible, this implies that

$$\Gamma_0(\Omega)\mathbb{C}^{2n}=\{\,U_0(\Omega)\varepsilon_{\bar{\mu}}x+\varepsilon_\mu y\mid x,y\in\mathbb{C}\,\},$$

cf. [G2], Theorem 3. Now (9.12) follows from the minimality of $\Pi(\Omega)$, see

(9.8), and the fact that $<\varepsilon_{\bar{\mu}}>$ and $<\varepsilon_{\mu}>$ give rise to the spaces $\mathfrak{D}(V(M))^{\perp}$ and $\mathfrak{R}(V(M))^{\perp}$, respectively. This completes the proof. □

Now we consider the Hamiltonian system (7.3) which is regular at a and in the limit point case at b and denote by S the associated symmetric closed minimal relation. Let $\mathcal{A}$ and $\mathcal{B}$ be functions which satisfy the conditions (9.1)–(9.5). Let A be the corresponding minimal selfadjoint extension of S in a Pontryagin space $\mathfrak{K}$ containing $\mathfrak{H}$. Then Theorems 7.1 and 9.3 imply that the simple operator part S_s of S in $\mathfrak{H}\ominus S(0)$, and the relation $A\ominus S_{\infty}$ in $\mathfrak{K}\ominus S(0)$ are basically described by the $2n\times 2n$ matrix function Ω as given by the expression in (9.6).

THEOREM 9.5. *Let S be the symmetric closed minimal relation in $\mathfrak{H}=L^2_{\Delta}(a,b)$ associated with the Hamiltonian system and let M be its Weyl coefficient, described in Section 6. Let $\mathcal{A},\mathcal{B}$ be $n\times n$ matrix functions satisfying (9.1)–(9.5) and let A in the π_{κ}–space $\mathfrak{K}$ be the corresponding minimal selfadjoint extension of S, see Theorem 7.1. Let Ω be given by (9.6). Then the following holds:*

(*i*) *The operator part S_s of S in $\mathfrak{H}\ominus S(0)$ is isomorphic to $S(M)=F_{\mu}(V(M))$, the inverse Cayley transform of $V(M)$ in $\Pi(M)$, and*

(*ii*) *The extension $A\ominus\{\{0,\varphi\}\,|\,\varphi\in S(0)\}$ of S_s in $\mathfrak{K}\ominus S(0)$ is isomorphic to $A(\Omega)=F_{\mu}(U(\Omega))$ in $\Pi(\Omega)$ in the representation (9.9) for the $2n\times 2n$ matrix function $Q=\Omega$.*

Proof. It follows from Propositions 6.2 and 9.3 that $C_{\mu}(S)$ and $V(M)$ have the same characteristic function. Hence their simple parts are isomorphic and the assertion (*i*) follows. Similarly the assertion (*ii*) follows from Propositions 7.1 and 9.4. □

PROPOSITION 9.6. *Let $M\in\mathbf{N}_0^{n\times n}$. Then $\lambda_0\in\mathbb{R}$ is an eigenvalue of $S(M)^*$ in $\Pi(M)$ if and only if there exists an $n\times 1$ vector function $c(\ell)$ defined and holomorphic on $\mathbb{C}^+$ such that as $\ell\hat{\to}\lambda_0$.*

$$
(9.14)\qquad \begin{aligned} &c(\ell)\to c_0,\ M(\ell)c(\ell)\to c_1,\ \textit{with}\ |c_0|^2+|c_1|^2\neq 0,\\ &\left(\mathsf{N}_M(\ell,\ell)\,c(\ell),c(\ell)\right)\ \textit{is bounded.}\end{aligned}
$$

Proof. If $\lambda_0\in\mathbb{R}$ is an eigenvalue of $S(M)^*$, then the existence of $c(\ell)$ with the stated properties can be shown as in the proof of Proposition 6.3. To prove the converse, we note that by Lemma 9.2, (9.14) implies that $\varepsilon_{\ell}c(\ell)$

converges weakly in $\Pi(M)$ to y_0, say. If in both sides of the equality

$$[\varepsilon_\ell c(\ell), \varepsilon_\ell x] = (\mathrm{N}_M(\ell,\lambda)\, c(\ell), x)$$

we let $\ell \hat{\to} \lambda_0$, we obtain for all $\lambda \in \mathfrak{D}_M$, $x \in \mathbb{C}^n$, that

$$[y_0, \varepsilon_\lambda x] = (\lambda_0 - \bar{\lambda})^{-1} (c_1 - M(\lambda)^* c_0, x).$$

As not both c_0 and c_1 are zero, it follows that $y_0 \neq 0$. Moreover, the last equality can also be written in the form

$$[\lambda_0 y_0, \varepsilon_\lambda x] - [y_0, \lambda\varepsilon_\lambda x] = (c_1, x) - (c_0, M(\lambda)x)$$

and thus for $\lambda_1, .., \lambda_k \in \mathfrak{D}_M$, $x_1, .., x_k \in \mathbb{C}^n$, we have

$$< \{y_0, \lambda_0 y_0\}, \{\sum_{i=1}^k \varepsilon_{\lambda_i} x_i, \sum_{i=1}^k \lambda_i \varepsilon_{\lambda_i} x_i\} > = (c_1, \sum_{i=1}^k x_i) - (c_0, \sum_{i=1}^k M(\lambda_i) x_i).$$

As the element $\{\sum_{i=1}^k \varepsilon_{\lambda_i} x_i, \sum_{i=1}^k \lambda_i \varepsilon_{\lambda_i} x_i\}$ belongs to $S(M)$ if and only if

$$\sum_{i=1}^k x_i = 0, \quad \sum_{i=1}^k M(\lambda_i) x_i = 0,$$

we find that $\{y_0, \lambda_0 y_0\} \in S(M)^*$. □

10. Some remarks on the spectrum

Recall that the function $\Omega \in \mathbf{N}_\kappa^{2n\times 2n}$ admits an integral representation (see [DL]):

$$(10.1) \quad \Omega(\ell) = \prod_{j=1}^q ((\ell - \alpha_j)(\ell - \bar{\alpha}_j))^{-\rho_j} \Big\{ (\ell^2 + y_0^2)^\rho \int_{\mathbb{R}} \frac{t\ell + y_0^2}{t - \ell} d\Sigma(t) + \sum_{r=0}^{2\rho+1} B_r \ell^r \Big\}$$

with some nondecreasing bounded $n\times n$ matrix function Σ on $\mathbb{R}$, nonnegative integers q, $\rho_1, \dots, \rho_q$, and ρ such that $\sum_{j=1}^q \rho_j \le \rho \le \kappa$, hermitian $n\times n$ matrices $B_0, .., B_{2\rho+1}$; $B_{2\rho+1} \ge O$, mutually different numbers $\alpha_j \in \mathbb{C}^+ \cup \mathbb{R}$ and $y_0 > 0$, $iy_0 \neq \alpha_j$, $j = 1, 2, .., q$.

As the selfadjoint relation $A \ominus S_\infty$ defined by the boundary value problem (7.3) is isomorphic to the relation $A(\Omega)$, well-known properties of the latter imply immediately the following result.

Corollary 10.1. *The finite eigenvalues of the boundary value problem (7.3) are the numbers α_j and $\bar{\alpha}_j$, $j = 1, 2, .., \rho$, and the points of discontinuity of the non-decreasing $2n\times 2n$ matrix function Σ in (10.1). The continuous spectrum of the boundary value problem consists of the points on $\mathbb{R}$ where Σ is continuous but not constant.*

The eigenvalues of the relation A can be characterized more explicitly in terms of the functions $\mathcal{M}$ and $\mathcal{A},\mathcal{B}$. To show this we observe that the eigenvalues of A are the zeros or generalized zeros (of positive, negative or neutral type) of the function Ω^{-1}, provided this inverse exists, and it remains to express the (generalized) zeros of Ω^{-1} in terms of $\mathcal{M}$ and $\mathcal{A},\mathcal{B}$. Here we shall consider only a real generalized zero of nonpositive type; real generalized zeros or generalized zeros of positive type and nonreal zeros can be characterized similarly.

In the remainder of this section we shall assume that $n=1$, $\mathcal{A}(\ell)=I$; thus, in particular, that Ω is invertible. This restriction not only simplifies the calculations and formulas, but it is also a technical one, as it is related to the method we use here. We intend to come back to the general case elsewhere.

According to [BL] a real generalized zero λ_0 of nonpositive type of the function

$$-\Omega(\ell)^{-1}=\begin{bmatrix} \mathcal{M}(\ell) & -I \\ -I & -\mathcal{B}(\ell) \end{bmatrix}$$

can be characterized as follows: There exists a 2×1 vector function $f(\ell)$, defined and holomorphic on $\mathbb{C}^+$, such that

$$\begin{aligned} &f(\ell)\to f_0\neq 0, \quad \Omega(\ell)^{-1}f(\ell)\to 0, \\ (10.2)\qquad &\left(\mathsf{N}_{-\Omega^{-1}}(\ell,\ell)f(\ell),f(\ell)\right) \text{ converges as } \ell\hat{\to}\lambda_0 \end{aligned}$$

and such that the limit of the last expression is nonpositive.. We write

$$f(\ell)=\begin{pmatrix} f^1(\ell) \\ f^2(\ell) \end{pmatrix}, \quad f_0=\begin{pmatrix} f_0^1 \\ f_0^2 \end{pmatrix},$$

where $f^i(\ell)$, f_0^i are scalars, $i=1,2$, and claim that (10.2) is equivalent to

$$\begin{aligned} &f^1(\ell)\to f_0^1, \qquad \mathcal{M}(\ell)f^1(\ell)\to f_0^2, \qquad f_0\neq 0, \\ (10.3)\qquad &\left(\mathsf{N}_{\mathcal{M}}(\ell,\ell)f^1(\ell),f^1(\ell)\right) \text{ converges as } \ell\hat{\to}\lambda_0 \end{aligned}$$

and

$$\begin{aligned} &f^2(\ell)\to f_0^2, \qquad \mathcal{B}(\ell)f^2(\ell)\to -f_0^1, \qquad f_0\neq 0, \\ (10.4)\qquad &\left(\mathsf{N}_{I,\mathcal{B}}(\ell,\ell)f^2(\ell),f^2(\ell)\right) \text{ converges as } \ell\hat{\to}\lambda_0. \end{aligned}$$

To prove the claim we note that Proposition 9.1 implies that

(10.5) $\quad N_{-\Omega^{-1}}(\ell,\ell)=\operatorname{diag}\left(N_{M}(\ell,\ell),N_{I,B}(\ell,\ell)\right)$

and therefore (10.2) follows from (10.3) together with (10.4). On the other hand, because of (10.5), (10.2) yields

(10.6) $\quad \left(N_{M}(\ell,\ell)f^{1}(\ell),f^{1}(\ell)\right)+\left(N_{I,B}(\ell,\ell)f^{2}(\ell),f^{2}(\ell)\right)$ converges as $\ell\hat{\to}\lambda_0$

and so to prove that (10.2) implies (10.3) and (10.4), it suffices to show that the first summand in (10.6) here converges as $\ell\hat{\to}\lambda_0$. To this end we go back to the construction of the space $\Pi(\Omega)$, Theorem 9.4 and its proof. It is easy to see that

(10.7) $\quad \varepsilon_{\ell}\Omega(\ell)^{-1}f(\ell)=\varepsilon_{\ell}f^{1}(\ell)+\delta_{\ell}f^{2}(\ell).$

On account of the first part of Lemma 9.2 with $Q=\Omega$ and $\tilde{f}(\ell)=\Omega^{-1}(\ell)f(\ell)$, (10.2) implies that the lefthand and hence the righthand side of (10.7) converges weakly in $\Pi(\Omega)$ as $\ell\hat{\to}\lambda_0$. It follows from Theorem 9.4 that $\varepsilon_{\ell}f^{1}(\ell)$ converges weakly in $\Pi(M)$. The second half of Lemma 9.2 with $Q=M$, $\tilde{f}(\ell)=f^{1}(\ell)$ yields that

(10.8) $\quad \left(N_{M}(\ell,\ell)f^{1}(\ell),f^{1}(\ell)\right)$ is bounded as $\ell\hat{\to}\lambda_0$.

As an $\mathbf{N}_0^{1\times1}$ function, M has the representation

$$M(\ell)=B_0+B_1\ell+\int_{\mathbb{R}}\left((t-\ell)^{-1}-t(t^2+1)^{-1}\right)d\sigma(t),\qquad \int_{\mathbb{R}}(t^2+1)^{-1}d\sigma(t)<\infty,$$

where B_0, $B_1\in\mathbb{R}$, $B_1\geq 0$ and σ is a nondecreasing function. If $f_0^1\neq 0$ then (10.8) implies that $\int_{\mathbb{R}}|t-\lambda_0|^{-2}d\sigma(t)<\infty$ and this in turn implies that the expression in (10.8) actually converges, cf. [L], Remark 3.2. Note that also $-M^{-1}\in\mathbf{N}_0^{1\times1}$ and

$$\left(N_{M}(\ell,\ell)f^{1}(\ell),f^{1}(\ell)\right)=\left(N_{-M^{-1}}(\ell,\ell)M(\ell)f^{1}(\ell),M(\ell)f^{1}(\ell)\right).$$

Therefore, if $f_0^1=0$, then $f_0^2\neq 0$ and the same argument but now with $-M^{-1}$ instead of M, again yields the convergence of the expression in (10.8). Thus, we have proved the first part of the following theorem.

THEOREM 10.2. *The point $\lambda_0\in\mathbb{R}$ is an eigenvalue of nonpositive type of the boundary value problem* (7.3) *with $n=1$, $A(\ell)=I$ if and only if there exists a* 2×1 *vector function f, defined and holomorphic on $\mathbb{C}^+$, such that* (10.3) *and* (10.4) *are valid and such that the limit in* (10.6) *is nonpositive. In this case also $T(\lambda_0)$, the Štraus extension at λ_0, has the eigenvalue λ_0 and an eigenfunction of $T(\lambda_0)$ is given by $y_1(.,\lambda_0)f_0^1+y_2(.,\lambda_0)f_0^2$.*

The last part follows from the fact that

$$[\varepsilon_\ell x, \varepsilon_\lambda y] = (\mathsf{N}_{\mathcal{M}}(\ell,\lambda)x, y) = [\Upsilon(.,\ell)x, \Upsilon(.,\lambda)y],$$

see (6.1). Hence the isomorphism between $\Pi(\mathcal{M})$ and $\mathfrak{H}\ominus S(0)$, see Theorem 9.5 (i), is given by the mapping

$$\varepsilon_\ell x \mapsto \Upsilon(.,\ell)x = y_1(.,\ell)x + y_2(.,\ell)M(\ell)x.$$

Now (9.11) implies that

$$\left(I - z(\ell)U(\Omega)\right)^{-1}\boldsymbol{\varepsilon}_\mu \Omega(\ell)^{-1} f(\ell) = ((\ell-\bar{\mu})/(\mu-\bar{\mu}))\boldsymbol{\varepsilon}_\ell \Omega(\ell)^{-1} f(\ell).$$

Applying Lemma 9.2 we find that, on account of (10.2), the element on the righthand side converges weakly to some nonzero element $((\lambda_0-\bar{\mu})/(\mu-\bar{\mu}))\boldsymbol{y}_0$ of $\Pi(\Omega)$, the element $\boldsymbol{\varepsilon}_\mu f(\ell)$ tends weakly to zero as $\ell \hat{\to} \lambda_0$. Hence, according to [BL], Lemma 2, $z(\lambda_0)^{-1}$ is an eigenvalue of $U(\Omega)$ and therefore, λ_0 is an eigenvalue of $A(\Omega)$, in both cases with eigenelement $\boldsymbol{y}_0$. The projection of $\boldsymbol{y}_0$ onto $\Pi(\mathcal{M})$ coincides up to some nonzero factor with the weak limit of $\varepsilon_\ell f^1(\ell)$. This limit according to the isomorphism mentioned above corresponds to the function $y_1(.,\lambda_0)f_0^1 + y_2(.,\lambda_0)f_0^2$ and belongs to $\nu(T(\lambda_0)-\lambda_0)$.

References

[AD1] D. Alpay, H. Dym, "Hilbert spaces of analytic functions, inverse scattering and operator models I", Integral Equations Operator Theory, 7 (1984), 589–641.

[AD2] D. Alpay, H. Dym, "Hilbert spaces of analytic functions, inverse scattering and operator models II", Integral Equations Operator Theory, 8 (1985), 145–180.

[AD3] D. Alpay, H. Dym, "On applications of reproducing kernel spaces to the Schur algorithm and rational J–unitary factorisation", Operator Theory: Adv. Appl, 18 I(1986), 89–159.

[A] F.V. Atkinson, *Discrete and Continuous Boundary Problems*, Academic Press, New York, 1968.

[Az1] T. Ya. Azizov, "On the theory of extensions of isometric and symmetric operators in spaces with an indefinite metric", Preprint Voronesh University, 1982; deposited paper no. 3420–82 (Russian).

[Az2] T.Ya. Azizov, "Extensions of J–isometric and J–symmetric operators", Funktsional. Anal. i Prilozhen, 18 (1984), 57–58 (Russian) (English translation: Functional Anal. Appl., 18 (1984), 46–48).

[BP] A.I. Benedek, R. Panzone, "On Sturm–Liouville problems with the square root of the eigenvalue parameter contained in the boundary conditions", Notas Algebra Anal., 10, Universidad Nacional del Sur, Bahia Blanca, 1981.

[B] J. Bognár, *Indefinite Inner Product Spaces*, Springer–Verlag, Berlin–Heidelberg–New York, 1974.

[BL] M. Borogovac, H. Langer, "A characterization of generalized zeros of negative type of matrix functions of the class $\mathbf{N}_\kappa^{n\times n}$", Operator Theory: Adv. Appl., to appear.

[dB1] L. de Branges, "Some Hilbert spaces of entire functions", Trans. Amer. Math. Soc., 96 (1960), 259–295.

[dB2] L. de Branges, "Some Hilbert spaces of entire functions II", Trans. Amer. Math. Soc., 99 (1961), 118–152.

[dB3] L. de Branges, "Some Hilbert spaces of entire functions III", Trans. Amer. Math. Soc., 100 (1961), 73–115.

[dB4] L. de Branges, "Some Hilbert spaces of entire functions IV", Trans. Amer. Math. Soc., 105 (1962), 43–83.

[dB5] L. de Branges, *Hilbert Spaces of Entire Functions*, Prentice Hall, Englewood Cliffs, N.J., 1968 (French translation: *Espaces Hilbertiens de Fonctions Entières*, Masson et Cie, Paris 1972).

[DL] K. Daho, H. Langer, "Matrix functions of the class $\mathbf{N}_\kappa$", Math. Nachr., 120 (1985), 275–294.

[D] A. Dijksma, "Eigenfunction expansions for a class of J-selfadjoint ordinary differential operators with boundary conditions containing the eigenvalue parameter", Proc. Roy. Soc. Edinburgh Sect. A, 86 (1980), 1–27.

[DLS1] A. Dijksma, H. Langer, H.S.V. de Snoo, "Selfadjoint Π_κ-extensions of symmetric subspaces: an abstract approach to boundary problems with spectral parameter in the boundary conditions", Integral Equations Operator Theory, 7 (1984), 459–515.

[DLS2] A. Dijksma, H. Langer, H.S.V. de Snoo, "Unitary colligations in Π_κ-spaces, characteristic functions and Štraus extensions", Pacific J. Math., 125 (1986), 347–362.

[DLS3] A. Dijksma, H. Langer, H.S.V. de Snoo, "Characteristic functions of unitary operator colligations in Π_κ-spaces", Operator Theory: Adv. Appl., 19 (1986), 125–194.

[DLS4] A. Dijksma, H. Langer, H.S.V. de Snoo, "Representations of holomorphic functions by means of resolvents of unitary or selfadjoint operators in Krein spaces", Operator Theory: Adv. Appl., 24 (1987), 123–143.

[DLS5] A. Dijksma, H. Langer, H.S.V. de Snoo, "Unitary colligations in Krein spaces and their role in the extension theory of isometries and symmetric linear relations in Hilbert spaces", Functional Analysis II, Proceedings Dubrovnik 1985, Lecture Notes in Mathematics, Vol. 1242 (1987), 1–42.

[DLS6] A. Dijksma, H. Langer, H.S.V. de Snoo, "Symmetric Sturm–Liouville operators with eigenvalue depending boundary conditions", Can. Math. Soc. Conference Proc. 8, (1987), 87–116.

[F] C.T. Fulton, "Singular eigenvalue problems with eigenvalue parameter contained in the boundary conditions", Proc. Roy. Soc. Edinburgh Sect. A, 87 (1980), 1–34.

[G1] R.C. Gilbert, "Simplicity of linear ordinary differential operators", J. Differential Equations, 11 (1972), 672–681.

[G2] R.C. Gilbert, "Spectral representation of selfadjoint extensions of a symmetric operator", Rocky Mountain J. Math., 2 (1972), 75–96.

[GK] I.C. Gohberg, M.G. Krein, *Theory of Volterra Operators in Hilbert Space and Its Applications*, Nauka, Moscow, 1967 (English translation: Amer. Math. Soc. Transl. Math. Monographs, 24 (1970)).

[HS1] D.B. Hinton, J.K. Shaw, "On Titchmarsh–Weyl $m(\lambda)$-functions for linear Hamiltonian systems", J. Differential Equations, 40 (1981), 316–342.

[HS2] D.B. Hinton, J.K. Shaw, "Hamiltonian systems of limit point or limit circle type with both endpoints singular", J. Differential Equations, 50 (1983), 444–464.

[HS3] D.B. Hinton, J.K. Shaw, "Spectrum of a Hamiltonian system with spectral parameter in a boundary condition", Can. Math. Soc. Conference Proc. 8, (1987), 171–186.

[I] A. Iacob, "On the spectral theory of a class of canonical systems of differential equations", Dissertation Weizman Institute of Science, Rehovot, 1986.

[IKL] I.S. Iohvidov, M.G. Krein, H. Langer, *Introduction to the Spectral Theory of Operators in Spaces with an Indefinite Metric*, Akademie–Verlag, Berlin, 1982 (Reihe: Mathematical Research, 9).

[K1] I.S. Kac, "Linear relations, which are generated by canonical differential equations on an interval with regular endpoints, and the expansibility in eigenfunctions", preprint, Odessa 1984.

[K2] I.S. Kac, "Expansibility in eigenfunctions of a canonical differential equation on an interval with singular endpoints and associated linear relations", preprint, Odessa 1986.

[KK] I.S. Kac, M.G. Krein, "On the spectral functions of a string", Supplement II to the Russian edition of F.V. Atkinson, *Discrete and Continuous Boundary Problems*, Mir, Moscow 1968 (Russian) (English translation: Amer. Math. Soc. Transl., (2) 103 (1974), 19–102).

[KR] V.I. Kogan, F.S. Rofe–Beketov, "On square–integrable solutions of symmetric systems of differential equations of arbitrary order", Proc. Roy. Soc. Edinburgh Sect. A, 74 (1976), 5–40.

[Kr] M.G. Krein, "Fundamental aspects of the representation theory of hermitian operators with deficiency index (m,m)", Ukrain. Math. Zh., 1 (1949), 3–66 (Russian) (English translation: Amer. Math. Soc. Transl., (2) 97 (1970), 75–143).

[KL1] M.G. Krein, H. Langer, "On defect subspaces and generalized resolvents of a Hermitian operator in the space Π_κ", Funktsional. Anal. i Prilozhen., 5 No. 2 (1971), 59–71; 5 No. 3 (1971) 54–69 (Russian) (English translation: Functional Anal. Appl., 5 (1971/1972), 136–146, 217–228).

[KL2] M.G. Krein, H. Langer, "Über die Q–Funktion eines π–hermiteschen Operators im Raume Π_κ", Acta Sci. Math. (Szeged), 34 (1973), 191–230.

[KL3] M.G. Krein, H. Langer, "On some extension problems which are closely connected with the theory of hermitian operators in a space Π_κ. III. Indefinite analogues of the Hamburger and Stieltjes moment problems, Part (I)", Beiträge Anal., 14 (1979), 25–40.

[KL4] M.G. Krein, H. Langer, "On some extension problems which are closely connected with the theory of hermitian operators in a space Π_κ. III. Indefinite analogues of the Hamburger and Stieltjes moment problems, Part (II)", Beiträge Anal., 15 (1981), 27–45.

[KL5] M.G. Krein, H. Langer, "Some propositions on analytic matrix functions related to the theory of operators in the space Π_κ", Acta Sci. Math. (Szeged), 43 (1981), 181–205.

[L] H. Langer, "A characterization of generalized zeros of negative type of functions of the class $\mathbf{N}_\kappa$", Operator Theory: Adv. Appl., 17 (1986), 201–212.

[LT1] H. Langer, B. Textorius, "On generalized resolvents and Q–functions of symmetric linear relations (subspaces) in Hilbert space", Pacific J. Math., 72 (1977), 135–165.

[LT2] H. Langer, B. Textorius, "Spectral functions of a symmetric linear relation with a directing mapping, I", Proc. Roy. Soc. Edinburgh Sect. A, 97 (1984), 165–176.

[LT3] H. Langer, B. Textorius, "Spectral functions of a symmetric linear relation with a directing mapping, II", Proc. Roy. Soc. Edinburgh Sect. A, 101 (1985), 11–24.

[N] H-.D. Niessen, "Singuläre S–hermitesche Rand–Eigenwertprobleme", Manuscripta Math., 3 (1970), 35–68.

[O] B.C Orcutt, *Canonical Differential Equations*, Dissertation, University of Virginia, 1969.

[Orl] S.A. Orlov, "Nested matrix disks depending analytically on a parameter, and the theorem on invariance of the ranks of the radii of limiting matrix disks", Izv. Akad. Nauk SSSR Ser. Mat., 40 (1976), 593–644 (Russian) (English translation: Math. USSR Izv. 10 (1976), 565–613).

[R] H. Röh, "Self–adjoint subspace extensions satisfying λ–linear boundary conditions", Proc. Roy. Soc. Edinburgh. Sect. A., 90 (1981), 107–124.

[SS1] F.W. Schäfke, A. Schneider, "S–hermitesche Rand–Eigenwertprobleme I", Math. Ann., 162 (1966), 9–26.

[SS2] F.W. Schäfke, A. Schneider, "S–hermitesche Rand–Eigenwertprobleme II", Math. Ann., 165 (1966), 236–260.

[SS3] F.W. Schäfke, A. Schneider, "S–hermitesche Rand–Eigenwertprobleme III", Math. Ann., 177 (1968), 67–94.

[Š1] A.V. Štraus, "On the extensions of symmetric operators depending on a parameter", Izv. Akad. Nauk SSSR Ser. Mat., 29 (1965),1389–1416 (Russian) (English translation: Amer. Math. Soc. Transl., (2) 61 (1967) 113–141).

[Š2] A.V. Štraus, "On one–parameter families of extensions of a symmetric operator", Izv. Akad. Nauk SSSR Ser. Mat., 30 (1966), 1325–1352 (Russian) (English translation: Amer. Math. Soc. Transl., (2) 90 (1970) 135–164).

[Š3] A.V. Štraus, "On the extensions and the characteristic function of a symmetric operator", Izv. Akad. Nauk SSSR Ser. Mat., 32 (1968), 186–207 (Russian) (English translation: Math. USSR–Izv., 2 (1968), 181–204).

[Š4] A.V. Štraus, "Extensions and generalized resolvents of a symmetric operator which is not densely defined", Izv. Akad. Nauk SSSR Ser. Mat., 34 (1970), 175–202 (Russian) (English translation: Math. USSR–Izv., 4 (1970), 179–208).

A. Dijksma and H.S.V. de Snoo
Wiskunde en Informatica
Rijksuniversiteit Groningen
Postbus 800
9700 AV Groningen
Nederland

H. Langer
Sektion Mathematik
Technische Universität
DDR–8027 Dresden
Mommsenstrasse 13
DDR

Operator Theory:
Advances and Applications, Vol. 35

ANALYTIC FUNCTIONS OF ELEMENTS OF THE CALKIN ALGEBRA, AND THEIR LIMITS

Domingo A. Herrero[1)]

Given an open subset Λ of the complex plane and an analytic function f defined on Λ, the norm-closure of $f[S_e(\Lambda)^\sim] := \{f(\tilde{A}): A$ is a linear bounded operator on the Hilbert space H, and $\sigma_e(A) \subset \Lambda\}$ is described in terms of f, Λ and the different parts of the spectra of the operators. (Here $\tilde{A}$ denotes the canonical projection of A in the Calkin algebra, and $\sigma_e(A)$ is the essential spectrum of A.) The results include spectral characterizations of interior $(f[S_e(\Lambda)^\sim]^-)$ and its closure, and formulas for the distance from a given element of the Calkin algebra to $f[S_e(\Lambda)^\sim]$, and to interior $(f[S_e(\Lambda)^\sim]^-)$.

1. INTRODUCTION

In a recent article, John B. Conway, Domingo A. Herrero and Bernard B. Morrel analyzed the following problems: let Λ be a nonempty open subset of the complex plane $\mathbb{C}$, and let f be an analytic function defined on Λ. If $S(\Lambda)$ is the set of all those (linear bounded) operators A, acting on a complex, separable, infinite dimensional Hilbert space H, such that the spectrum of A, $\sigma(A)$, is included in Λ, then it is possible to define f(A), via Functional Calculus, for all A in $S(\Lambda)$.

Find a simple characterization of the norm-closure of

$$f[S(\Lambda)] = \{f(A): \ A \in S(\Lambda)\}$$

in the algebra $L(H)$ of all operators acting on H. What is interior $f[S(\Lambda)]$? What is interior $(f[S(\Lambda)]^-]$, where the upper bar denotes norm-closure? Find the distance from a given operator to each of these sets, etc., etc. [7].

---

1) This article was written while the author was attending an Informal Seminar on Operator Theory (Summer, 1987) at the University of California at San Diego. The research was partially supported by a Grant of the National Science Foundation.

The purpose of this article is to solve the analogous problems when $L(H)$ is replaced by the quotient Calkin algebra

$$A(H) = L(H)/K(H),$$

where $K(H)$ denotes the ideal of all compact operators.

Let $\pi: L(H) \to A(H)$ be the canonical quotient mapping. If $A \in L(H)$, we shall write $\tilde{A} = \pi(A) = A + K(H)$ to indicate the projection of A in $A(H)$. The essential spectrum of A is the spectrum of $\tilde{A}$ in $A(H)$; that is, $\sigma_e(A) = \sigma(\tilde{A})$.

Let $S_e(\Lambda) = \{A \in L(H): \sigma_e(A) \subset \Lambda\}$, and let $f[S_e(\Lambda)^\sim] = \{f(\tilde{A}): \tilde{A} \in S_e(\Lambda)^\sim\}$, where $S_e(\Lambda)^\sim = \pi(S_e(\Lambda))$. As it was the case with $S(\Lambda)$ and $f[S(\Lambda)]$ in [7], we are dealing with classes that are *invariant under similarities*; that is, if $A \in S_e(\Lambda)$ and $\tilde{W} \in A(H)$ is invertible in the Calkin algebra, then

$$\sigma(\tilde{W}\tilde{A}\tilde{W}^{-1}) = \sigma(\tilde{A}) \subset \Lambda \text{ (and therefore } \tilde{W}\tilde{A}\tilde{W}^{-1} \in S_e(\Lambda)^\sim)$$

and

$$f(\tilde{W}\tilde{A}\tilde{W}^{-1}) = \tilde{W}f(\tilde{A})\tilde{W}^{-1} \in f[S_e(\Lambda)^\sim].$$

Therefore, we can apply (once again) the machinery for approximation developed in the monograph [3], [11].

The core of this article is the spectral characterization of the set $f[S_e(\Lambda)^\sim]^-$. The results also include spectral characterizations of interior $(f[S_e(\Lambda)^\sim]^-)$ and its closure, and formulas for the distance from a given element of the Calkin algebra to $f[S_e(\Lambda)^\sim]^-$ and to interior $(f[S_e(\Lambda)^\sim]^-)$.

2. PRELIMINARY RESULTS ON APPROXIMATION

Recall that $T \in L(H)$ is *semi-Fredholm* if ran $T = TH$ is closed, and at least one of the subspaces ker T and ker T^* $\simeq H \ominus$ ran T is finite dimensional. In this case, the *index* of T is defined by

$$\text{ind } T = \text{nul } T - \text{nul } T^*,$$

where nul T = dim ker T. The reader is referred to [5] for the properties of the semi-Fredholm operators. We shall define ind $\tilde{T}$ = ind T, whenever T is semi-Fredholm.

Let $\rho_{s-F}(T) = \{\lambda \in \mathbb{C}: \lambda - T \text{ is semi-Fredholm}\}$ denote the semi-Fredholm domain of T, and let $\sigma_{\ell re}(T) = \mathbb{C} \setminus \rho_{s-F}(T)$ (=the Wolf spectrum of T). If $\rho^{\pm}_{s-F}(T) = \{\lambda \in \rho_{s-F}(T): \text{ind}(\lambda - T) \neq 0\}$, then the Weyl spectrum of T, $\sigma_W(T)$, which is the largest part of $\sigma(T)$ that is invariant under compact perturbations, coincides with

$$\sigma_W(T) = \sigma_{\ell re}(T) \cup \rho^{\pm}_{s-F}(T) = \sigma_e(T) \cup \rho^{\pm}_{s-F}(T).$$

Furthermore, there exists $K \in K(H)$ such that $\sigma(T - K) = \sigma_W(T - K) = \sigma_W(T)$ [14]. Indeed, K can be chosen so that, in addition,

$$\min [\mathrm{nul}(\lambda - (T - K)), \mathrm{nul}(\lambda - (T - K))^*] = 0$$

for all $\lambda \in \rho_{s-F}(T - K) = \rho_{s-F}(T)$ [2], [11, Chapter 3].

For each $n \in \mathbb{Z}$, we define $\rho^n_{s-F}(T) = \{\lambda \in \rho_{s-F}(T):$ $\mathrm{ind}(\lambda - T) = n\}$; $\rho^{\infty}_{s-F}(T)$ and $\rho^{-\infty}_{s-F}(T)$ are defined in the obvious way.

If $\tilde{A} \in S_e(\Lambda)^{\sim}$, then $f(\tilde{A})$ is well-defined via Riesz-Dunford Functional Calculus. But it may happen that $\sigma_e(A) \subset \Lambda$, but $\sigma_W(A)$ is not included in Λ, and therefore there is no way to lift $\tilde{A}$ to some A in $L(H)$ for which f(A) is well-defined. If the components of Λ are *simply connected*, then $f[S_e(\Lambda)^{\sim}] = \pi(f[S(\Lambda)])$, and $f[S_e(\Lambda)^{\sim}]^{-} = \pi(f[S(\Lambda)]^{-})$ can be easily described with the help of Corollary 5.1 of [7]. (This is the case, for instance, when $\Lambda = \mathbb{C}$ and f is an entire function. Indeed, if the components of Λ are simply connected and $f(\tilde{A}) = \frac{1}{2\pi i}\int_\gamma f(\lambda)(\lambda - \tilde{A})^{-1}\,d\lambda$ for a suitably chosen finite family of rectifiable Jordan curves $\gamma \subset \Lambda$, then γ can be chosen so that the interiors of the curves are pairwise disjoint, and $\tilde{A}$ can be lifted to $A \in L(H)$ such that $\sigma(A) = \sigma_W(A) \subset$ interior γ. Clearly, f(A) is well-defined by $f(A) = \frac{1}{2\pi i}\int_\gamma f(\lambda)(\lambda - A)^{-1}\,d\lambda$, and $f(\tilde{A}) = \pi(f(A))$.)

But, if some component of Λ has a "hole" (= a bounded component of the complement), then we are facing a completely new phenomenon:

EXAMPLE 2.1. Let $\Lambda = \mathbb{C} \setminus \{0\}$, $f(\lambda) = 1/\lambda$ and S = the unilateral shift of multiplicity one; then $\sigma(S+K) \not\subset \Lambda$ for any K, but $\sigma_e(S) \subset \Lambda$, and therefore $f(\tilde{S})$ is well-defined. In fact, $f(\tilde{S}) = \tilde{S}^*$, and we have

$$\mathrm{ind}\ S = -1 = -\mathrm{ind}\ S^*;$$

that is, *by applying* f, *we have changed the sign of the index!*

EXAMPLE 2.2. (Douglas N. Clark's favorite "∞" curve) Let $\Lambda = \mathbb{C} \setminus \{1/2\}$, and let $f(\lambda) = \lambda + 1/(\lambda - 1/2)$. The function f maps the two points $\alpha_{\pm} = \frac{1}{4}(1 \pm i\sqrt{5})$ to 0. If $\lambda \in \partial\mathbb{D}$ (= the boundary of the open unit circle $\mathbb{D}$) moves *counterclockwise* from α_- to α_+, then its image describes a loop in the right half-plane, in the *clockwise direction* (first, from 0 to 3 in the first quadrant, then from 3 to 0 in the fourth quadrant). If $\lambda \in \partial\mathbb{D}$ moves *counterclockwise* from α_+ to α_-, then its image describes a loop in the left half-plane, in the *counterclockwise direction* (first, from 0 to -5/3 in the second quadrant, then from -5/3 to 0 in the third one).

Thus, f maps $\partial\mathbb{D}$ onto and "∞ - shaped curve", and (by continuity) a neighborhood of $\partial\mathbb{D}$ onto an "∞ - shaped open set" including this curve.

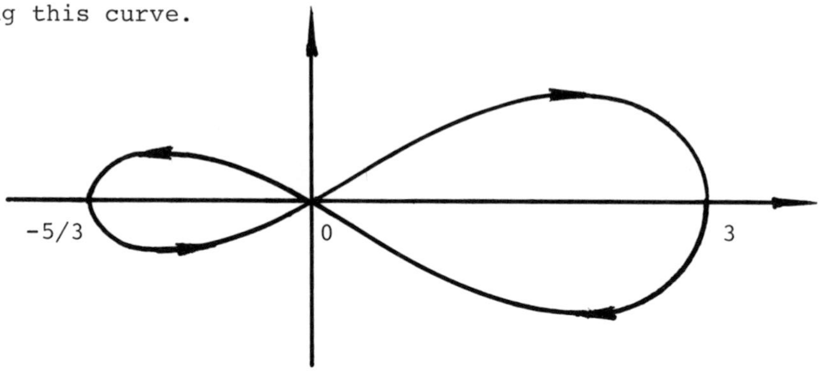

We have

$$f(\tilde{S}) = \tilde{T}_f,$$

where $T_f \in L(H^2(\partial\mathbb{D}))$ denotes the Toeplitz operator with symbol f; $\sigma(T_f)$ is the union of the two loops with their interiors, $\sigma_e(T_f) = \sigma_{\ell re}(T_f) = f(\partial\mathbb{D})$, and T_f satisfies

$$\operatorname{ind}(\lambda - T_f) = \begin{cases} 1 \text{ for all } \lambda \text{ inside the right loop,} \\ -1 \text{ for all } \lambda \text{ inside the left loop.} \end{cases}$$

Since $\tilde{S}$ is a normal element of the Calkin algebra, it readily follows that so is $f(\tilde{S})$, and

$$f(\tilde{S}) = \tilde{A}_+ \oplus \tilde{A}_-,$$

where $\sigma(A_+)$ ($\sigma(A_-)$) is the intersection of $\sigma(T_f)$ with the closed right (left, resp.) half-plane, and $\operatorname{ind}(\lambda - A_+) = 1$ ($\operatorname{ind}(\lambda - A_-) = -1$, resp.) for all λ inside the right (left, resp.) loop.

However, there is no $B = B_+ \oplus B_-$ in $L(H)$ such that $f(\tilde{B}_+) = \tilde{A}_+$ and $f(\tilde{B}_-) = \tilde{A}_-$ (see, e.g., [10]).

More generally, if γ is a regular analytic Jordan curve with interior $\gamma = \Omega$, and $g: \mathbb{D} \to \Omega$ is a conformal mapping from $\mathbb{D}$ onto Ω, then $g \in H^\infty(\partial\mathbb{D})$, and g can be analytically continued to a conformal mapping from a neighborhood of $\mathbb{D}^-$ onto a neighborhood of Ω^-. Clearly, g maps $\partial\mathbb{D}$ bijectively onto $\partial\Omega$; moreover, g is unique, up to a homographic transformation b from $\mathbb{D}$ onto itself. But $b(S)$ is unitarily equivalent to S. Thus, the analytic Toeplitz operator $T_+(\gamma) := T_g$ is uniquely determined by γ, up to unitary equivalence.

If $g(\lambda) = \sum_{n=0}^\infty a_n \lambda^n$, then we define $\tilde{g}(\lambda) = \sum_{n=0}^\infty \bar{a}_n \lambda^n$ and $T_-(\gamma) = T_{\tilde{g}}^*$. ($\tilde{g}$ is a conformal mapping from a neighborhood of $\mathbb{D}^-$ onto a neighborhood of $(\Omega^*)^-$), where $\Omega^* = \{\bar{\lambda}: \lambda \in \Omega\}$.) $T_+(\gamma)$ and $T_-(\gamma)$ are essentially normal operators, and we have

$$\sigma(T_+(\gamma)) = \sigma(T_-(\gamma)) = \Omega^-, \quad \sigma_e(T_+(\gamma)) = \sigma_e(T_-(\gamma)) = \partial\Omega$$
$$-\mathrm{ind}(\lambda - T_+(\gamma)) = \mathrm{ind}(\lambda - T_-(\gamma)) = \mathrm{nul}(\lambda - T_+(\gamma))^*$$
$$= \mathrm{nul}(\lambda - T_-(\gamma)) = 1$$

and $\mathrm{nul}(\lambda - T_+(\gamma)) = \mathrm{nul}(\lambda - T_-(\gamma))^* = 0$ for all $\lambda \in \Omega$.

Let $Z(f') = \{\lambda \in \Lambda: f'(\lambda) = 0\}$ (= the set of *critical points* of f in Λ). In every component of Λ, either f is constant and f' vanishes identically, or $Z(f')$ is a discrete set that can only accumulate on $\partial\Omega$. In either case, $f(Z(f'))$ is an at most denumerable set. Thus, given a Jordan curve γ_o, included in a component of Λ where f is not a constant, we can approximate γ_o (in the sense of Hausdorff distance) by regular analytic Jordan curves γ such that $\gamma \cap Z(f') = \emptyset$; moreover, we can also assume (if necessary) that $f(\gamma) \cap f(Z(f')) = \emptyset$.

If γ is a (positively oriented) regular analytic Jordan curve with the above described properties, then $f(\gamma)$ is, in general, a curve with finitely many self-intersecting points. The *winding number* of f on γ with respect to a point $\lambda \in \mathbb{C} \setminus f(\gamma)$ is defined, as usual, by

$$\nu(\lambda;\gamma) = \frac{1}{2\pi i} \int_\gamma \frac{f'(\zeta)}{f(\zeta) - \lambda}\, d\zeta.$$

(Roughly: the number of times that $f(\zeta)$ winds around λ as ζ runs over γ counterclockwise. This number is an integer, and only depends on the component of λ in $\mathbb{C} \setminus f(\gamma)$; moreover, $\nu(\lambda;\gamma) = 0$ for all λ in the unbounded component of this set.)

DEFINITION 2.3. Let $\gamma \subset \Lambda \setminus Z(f')$ be a regular analytic Jordan curve. The *string of sausges* (f,γ) is the set $f(\gamma)$ plus the winding numbers in the bounded components of $\mathbb{C} \setminus f(\gamma)$.

A typical string of sausages looks like this:

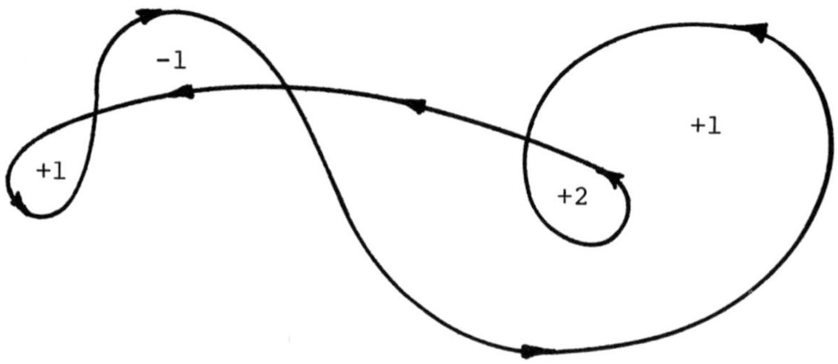

We shall need the following auxiliary result. The proof (as in the case of Example 2.2) can be found in [10].

LEMMA 2.4. *Let* $\gamma \subset \Lambda \setminus Z(f')$ *be a regular analytic Jordan curve; then* $f(\tilde{T}_-(\gamma))$ *and* $f(\tilde{T}_+(\gamma))$ *are normal elements of the Calkin algebra,* $\sigma[f(\tilde{T}_-(\gamma))] = \sigma[f(\tilde{T}_+(\gamma))] = f(\gamma)$, *and for each* λ *in* $\mathbb{C} \setminus f(\gamma)$

$$\operatorname{ind}[\lambda - f(\tilde{T}_-(\gamma))] = -\operatorname{ind}[\lambda - f(\tilde{T}_+(\gamma))] = \nu(\lambda;\gamma).$$

An *analytic Cauchy domain* Ω is a (not necessarily connected) nonempty bounded open subset of $\mathbb{C}$, whose boundary consists of finitely many pairwise disjoint regular analytic Jordan curves. For each such a domain, we define $H^2(\partial\Omega)$ as the closure of the rational functions with poles outside Ω^- in $L^2(\partial\Omega)$ (linear Lebesgue measure on $\partial\Omega$). $H^2(\partial\Omega)$ is invariant under $M(\partial\Omega)$ = "multiplication by λ" on $L^2(\partial\Omega)$. Thus, we have the matrix decomposition

$$M(\partial\Omega) = \begin{pmatrix} M_+(\partial\Omega) & Z(\partial\Omega) \\ 0 & M_-(\partial\Omega) \end{pmatrix} \begin{matrix} H^2(\partial\Omega) \\ L^2(\partial\Omega)\ominus H^2(\partial\Omega) \end{matrix}$$

where $M_+(\partial\Omega) = M(\partial\Omega)|H^2(\partial\Omega)$ and $M_-(\partial\Omega)$ are essentially normal operators, $Z(\partial\Omega)$ is a Hilbert-Schmidt operator,

$$\sigma(M_+(\partial\Omega)) = \sigma(M_-(\partial\Omega)) = \Omega^-,$$
$$\sigma_e(M_+(\partial\Omega)) = \sigma_e(M_-(\partial\Omega)) = \sigma(M(\partial\Omega)) = \sigma_e(M(\partial\Omega)) = \partial\Omega, \text{ and}$$
$$\text{ind}(\lambda - M_-(\partial\Omega)) = -\text{ind}(\lambda - M_+(\partial\Omega)) = \text{nul}(\lambda - M_-(\partial\Omega))$$
$$= \text{nul}(\lambda - M_+(\partial\Omega))^* = 1$$
and $\text{nul}(\lambda - M_-(\partial\Omega))^* = \text{nul}(\lambda - M_+(\partial\Omega)) = 0$ for all $\lambda \in \Omega$.

If $A \in L(H)$, $B \in L(H')$, we denote by $A\oplus B$ the direct sum of A and B acting in the usual fashion on the orthogonal direct sum $H\oplus H'$ of the underlying spaces. Similar notation will be used for finite or denumerable direct sums. For each α, $0 \leq \alpha \leq \infty$, $A^{(\alpha)}$ denotes the direct sum of α copies of A acting on $H^{(\alpha)}$, the orthogonal direct sum of α copies of H.

We shall use the symbols $\simeq$ and $\sim$ to indicate unitary equivalence and, respectively, similarity. (Both for operators in $L(H)$, and for elements of the Calkin algebra.)

The following results were taking from the monograph [3] [11]. As an important particular case of Theorem 9.3 of this reference, we have

COROLLARY 2.5. *Assume that* T, A $\in L(H)$ *and* $\sigma_e(T)$ *is a perfect set; then* $\tilde{A}$ *belongs to the norm-closure of the similarity orbit of* $\tilde{T}$,

$$S(\tilde{T}) = \{\tilde{W}\tilde{T}\tilde{W}^{-1}: \tilde{W} \in A(H) \textit{ is invertible}\},$$

if and only if the following conditions are satisfied:

(i) each component of $\sigma_{\ell re}(A)$ *intersects* $\sigma_e(T)$*; and*

(ii) $\rho_{s-F}(A) \subset \rho_{s-F}(T)$ *and* $\text{ind}(\lambda - A) = \text{ind}(\lambda - T)$ *for all* $\lambda \in \rho_{s-F}(A)$.

(We shall write $\tilde{T} \underset{sim}{\rightarrow} \tilde{A}$ to indicate that $\tilde{A} \in S(\tilde{T})^-$.)

PROPOSITION 2.6 ([3, Proposition 10.5]). $S_e(\Lambda)^-$ *is the set of all those* $\tilde{A} \in A(H)$ *such that*

(1_e) each component of $\sigma_e(A)$ *intersects* Λ^-,

(2_e) $\rho_{s-F}^{\pm\infty}(A) \subset \Lambda$*; and*

(3_e) if Ω *is a component of* $\rho_{s-F}^{\pm}(A)$, *then there exists a Cauchy sequence (in the Hausdorff metric) of compact sets* $\{\Sigma_n\}$ *such that* interior Σ_n *is connected,* $\Sigma_n = (\text{interior } \Sigma_n)^-$, *and* $\partial\Sigma_n \subset \Lambda$ *(for all* $n = 1,2,\ldots$*),* $\Omega \subset \Sigma := d_H\text{-lim}(n\to\infty)\Sigma_n$, *and* $\text{ind}(\lambda - A)$ *is constant for all* $\lambda \in \rho_{s-F}(A) \cap \Sigma$.

From [11, Chapter 4] and [3, Theorem 9.1], we have

LEMMA 2.7. *Let* $T \in L(H)$. *Given* $\varepsilon > 0$, *let* Ω *be an analytic Cauchy domain such that*

$$\sigma_{\ell re}(T) \subset \Omega \subset \sigma_{\ell re}(T)_\varepsilon := \{\lambda \in \mathbb{C}: \text{dist}[\lambda, \sigma_{\ell re}(T)] \le \varepsilon\}$$

and every component of Ω *intersects* $\sigma_{\ell re}(T)$. *If* N *is a normal operator such that* $\sigma(N) = \sigma_e(N) = \Omega^-$, *then there exists* T_ε *similar to* $T \oplus N$ *such that* $\|T - T_\varepsilon\| < 2\varepsilon$.

COROLLARY 2.8. *Given* $T \in L(H)$, $\varepsilon > 0$ *and* Ω *as in Lemma 2.7, there exists* $A \in L(H)$, *similar to*

$$M_-(\partial\Omega_\infty)^{(\infty)} \oplus M_+(\partial\Omega_{-\infty})^{(\infty)} \oplus [\oplus_{j=1}^{n} T_-(\gamma_j)^{(p_j)}]$$
$$\oplus [\oplus_{j=-1}^{-m} T_+(\gamma_{-j})^{(-p_{-j})}]$$

such that $\|\tilde{T} - \tilde{A}\| < 2\varepsilon$, *where*

(i) $(\Omega_\infty \cup \Omega_{-\infty}) \cap \Omega = \emptyset$,

(ii) Ω_∞ $(\Omega_{-\infty})$ *is an analytic Cauchy domain such that* $(\Omega_\infty)^- \subset \rho_{s-F}^{\infty}(T)$ $((\Omega_{-\infty})^- \subset \rho_{s-F}^{-\infty}(T)$, *resp.*),

(iii) $\partial\Omega = \cup_{j=-m, j\neq 0}^{n} \gamma_j$ (sign p_j = sign j *for all* j), *and*

(iv) $\rho_{s-F}(T) \setminus \Omega^- = \rho_{s-F}(A) \setminus \Omega^-$, *and* $\text{ind}(\lambda - T) = \text{ind}(\lambda - A)$ *for all* $\lambda \in \rho_{s-F}(T) \setminus \Omega^-$.

PROOF. Define $\Omega_\infty = \rho_{s-F}^{\infty}(T) \setminus \Omega^-$ and $\Omega_{-\infty} = \rho_{s-F}^{-\infty}(T) \setminus \Omega^-$.

Let Ω_1 be a component of Ω, and let $\tau_0, \tau_1, \ldots, \tau_s$ be the Jordan curves that form the boundary of Ω_1, where τ_0 is the boundary of the unbounded component of $\mathbb{C} \setminus \Omega_1$. Define

$$T(\Omega_1) = M_-(\tau_0) \oplus [\oplus_{j=1}^{s} M_+(\tau_j)].$$

Clearly, $\sigma_e(T(\Omega_1)) = \partial\Omega_1$ and $\text{ind}(\lambda - T(\Omega_1)) = 0$ for all $\lambda \in \mathbb{C} \setminus (\Omega_1)^-$. Let $T(\Omega_2), T(\Omega_3), \ldots, T(\Omega_t)$ be the operators similarly constructed with the other components of Ω.

Let Φ_1 be a component of $\rho_{s-F}^{\pm}(T) \setminus [\Omega \cup \Omega_\infty \cup \Omega_{-\infty}]^-$, and let $\kappa_0, \kappa_1, \ldots, \kappa_r$ be the Jordan curves that form the boundary of Φ_1. Let $n_1 \in \mathbb{Z} \setminus \{0\}$ denote the index of $\lambda - T$ for $\lambda \in \Phi_1$, and define

$$T(\Phi_1) = \begin{cases} \{T_-(\kappa_0) \oplus [\oplus_{j=1}^{r} T_+(\kappa_j)]\}^{(n_1)}, & \text{if } n_1 > 0, \\ \{T_+(\kappa_0) \oplus [\oplus_{j=1}^{r} T_-(\kappa_j)]\}^{(-n_1)}, & \text{if } n_1 < 0. \end{cases}$$

Clearly, $\sigma_e(T(\Phi_1)) = \partial\Phi_1$ and

$$\text{ind}(\lambda - T(\Phi_1)) = \begin{cases} n_1, & \text{if } \lambda \in \Phi_1, \\ 0, & \text{if } \lambda \in \mathbb{C} \setminus (\Phi_1)^-. \end{cases}$$

Let $T(\Phi_2), T(\Phi_3), \ldots, T(\Phi_q)$ be the operators similarly constructed with the other components of $\rho_{s-F}^{\pm}(T) \setminus [\Omega \cup \Omega_\infty \cup \Omega_{-\infty}]^-$.

Let

$$B = M_-(\partial\Omega_\infty)^{(\infty)} \oplus M_+(\partial\Omega_{-\infty})^{(\infty)} \oplus [\oplus_{i=1}^{s} T(\Omega_i)] \oplus [\oplus_{h=1}^{q} T(\Phi_h)].$$

It is not difficult to check that

$$[\oplus_{i=1}^{s} T(\Omega_i)] \oplus [\oplus_{h=1}^{q} T(\Phi_h)] = [\oplus_{j=1}^{n} T_-(\gamma_j)^{(p_j)}] \oplus [\oplus_{j=-1}^{-m} T_+(\gamma_{-j})^{(-p_j)}],$$

where $\{\gamma_j\}_{j=-m,j\neq 0}^{n}$ are the Jordan curves that form the boundary of Ω, enumerated in such a way that sign p_j = sign j for all j. (Beware! It may happens that some of the curves in the boundary of Ω is counted twice in this enumeration, because the curve is included both, in $\partial\Omega_i$ and in $\partial\Phi_h$ for some i and some h.)

Thus, B has the desired form, and it is straightforward to check that conditions (i) - (iv) are satisfied, provided we replace A by B in (iv).

By Corollary 2.5, $\tilde{B} \underset{\text{sim}}{\to} \tilde{T}_\varepsilon$, where $T_\varepsilon \sim T\oplus N$ is the operator defined in Lemma 2.7.

It readily follows that there exists $A \sim B$ (satisfying (i) - (iv)) such that $\|\tilde{T} - \tilde{A}\| < 2\varepsilon$. ∎

The proof of the following result is immediate (see [11, Chapter 1]).

LEMMA 2.9. *(i) Each of the sets* $f[S_e(\Lambda)^\sim]$, $f[S_e(\Lambda)^\sim]^-$, interior $f[S_e(\Lambda)^\sim]$, interior $f[S_e(\Lambda)^\sim]^-$, (interior $f[S_e(\Lambda)^\sim])^-$ *and* (interior $f[S_e(\Lambda)^\sim]^-)^-$ *is invariant under similarities.*

(ii) In particular, if $\tilde{A} \in$ interior $f[S_e(\Lambda)^\sim]$ *and* $\tilde{T} \underset{\text{sim}}{\to} \tilde{A}$, *then* $\tilde{T} \in$ interior $f[S_e(\Lambda)^\sim]$.

3. THE CLOSURE OF $f[S_e(\Lambda)^\sim]$

THEOREM 3.1. *Let* Λ *be a nonempty open subset of* $\mathbb{C}$ *and let* f *be an analytic function defined on* Λ *such that* interior $Z(f') = \emptyset$ *(that is,* f *is not constant on any component of* Λ*).*

The norm-closure of $f[S_e(\Lambda)^\sim]$ *is the set of all those* $\tilde{T}$ *in* $A(H)$ *satisfying the following conditions:*

(a) each component of $\sigma_e(T)$ *intersects* $f(\Lambda)^-$*;*

(b) $\rho_{s-F}^{\pm\infty}(T) \subset f(\Lambda)$*;*

(c) given an analytic Cauchy domain $\Omega \supset \sigma_{\ell re}(T)$, *there exist analytic Cauchy domains,* Ω_∞ *and* $\Omega_{-\infty}$, *finite families* $\{(f,\gamma_j)\}_{j=-m,j\neq 0}^{n}$ *of strings of sausages, and finite non-zero in-*

dices $\{p_j\}_{j=-m,j\neq 0}^{n}$ *(*sign p_j = sign j *for all* j*) such that*

(c₁) $(\Omega_\infty)^- \subset \rho_{s-F}^{\infty}(T)$, $(\Omega_{-\infty})^- \subset \rho_{s-F}^{-\infty}(T)$,

$$\partial(\Omega_\infty \cup \Omega_{-\infty}) \subset \Omega^- \setminus f(Z(f')),$$

(c₂) $[\cup_j f(\gamma_j)] \subset [\Omega \cap f(\Lambda)] \setminus (\Omega_\infty \cup \Omega_{-\infty})$, *and for each* $\lambda \in \rho_{s-F}(T) \setminus [\rho_{s-F}^{\pm\infty}(T) \cup \Omega]^-$,

$$\textstyle\sum_j p_j\, \nu(\lambda;\gamma_j) = \text{ind}(\lambda - T).$$

(Beware, λ *does not necessarily belong to* $f(\Lambda)^-$*!)*

PROOF. NECESSITY. Clearly,

$f[S_e(\Lambda)^\sim] \subset S_e(f(\Lambda))^\sim$ and $f[S_e(\Lambda)^\sim]^- \subset [S_e(f(\Lambda))^\sim]^-$.

Now (a) and (b) follow immediately from Proposition 2.6.

Let Ω be an analytic Cauchy domain including $\sigma_{\ell re}(T)$. By replacing (if necessary) Ω by a smaller subdomain, we can directly assume that every component of $\sigma_{\ell re}(T)$ intersects Ω and that $\partial\Omega \cap f(Z(f')) = \emptyset$.

Assume that $\|\tilde{T} - f(\tilde{A}_k)\| \to 0$ $(k \to \infty)$ for some sequence $\{A_k\}_{k=1}^{\infty} \subset S_e(\Lambda)$. If $\lambda \in \rho_{s-F}^{\infty}(T)$, then $\lambda \in \rho_{s-F}^{\infty}(f(\tilde{A}_k))$ (for all k large enough), and a simple analysis of the possible cases shows that $f^{-1}(\{\lambda\}) \cap \sigma_e(A)$ is necessarily a finite subset of $\rho_{s-F}^{\infty}(A_k)$, so that $\text{ind}(\alpha_k - A_k) = \infty$ for at least one $\alpha_k \in f^{-1}(\{\lambda\})$ (see, e.g., [5]). Thus, $\lambda = f(\alpha_k) \in f[\rho_{s-F}^{\infty}(A_k)] \subset f(\Lambda)$. By continuity, $f^{-1}(\rho_{s-F}^{\infty}(T))$ includes an analytic Cauchy domain $\Phi_\infty \subset \rho_{s-F}^{\infty}(A_k)$ such that $f(\Phi_\infty) = \rho_{s-F}^{\infty}(T) \setminus \Omega^-$ and $f(\partial\Phi_\infty) = \partial[\rho_{s-F}^{\infty}(T) \setminus \Omega^-]$.

Similarly, we can find an analytic Cauchy domain $\Phi_{-\infty} \subset \rho_{s-F}^{-\infty}(A_k)$ such that $f(\Phi_{-\infty}) = \rho_{s-F}^{-\infty}(T) \setminus \Omega^-$ and $f(\partial\Omega_{-\infty}) = \partial[\rho_{s-F}^{-\infty}(T) \setminus \Omega^-]$.

By Corollary 2.8 (since Λ is an open set) the A_k's can be chosen so that $\sigma_e(A_k)$ is a perfect set for all k. Since every component of Ω intersects $\sigma_{\ell re}(T)$, it follows from Corollary 2.5 that if M is a normal operator such that $\sigma(M) = \sigma_e(M) = \Omega^-$, then there exists operators A_k' such that $\tilde{A}_k'$ is similar to $\tilde{A}_k$, and $\|\widetilde{T\oplus M} - f(\tilde{A}_k')\| \to 0$ $(k \to \infty)$.

Hence, $\widetilde{T\oplus M} \in f[S_e(\Lambda)^\sim]^-$; furthermore, by combining Corollaries 2.5 and 2.8, we can replace A_k' by an operator B_k of the form described in the proof of Corollary 2.8, with Ω_∞ replaced by Φ_∞, $\Omega_{-\infty}$ replaced by $\Phi_{-\infty}$ (for all k = 1,2,...), and the $\gamma_j(k)$'s Jordan curves in $[\Lambda \setminus (\Phi_\infty \cup \Phi_{-\infty})] \cap f^{-1}(\Omega^-)$.

If B_k is similar to

$$M_-(\partial\Phi_\infty)^{(\infty)}\oplus M_+(\partial\Phi_{-\infty})^{(\infty)}\oplus[\oplus_{j=1}^{m(k)} T_-(\gamma_j(k))^{(p_j(k))}]$$
$$\oplus[\oplus_{j=-1}^{-n(k)} T_+(\gamma_j(k))^{(-p_j(k))}]$$

and $\|\widetilde{T\oplus M} - f(\tilde{B}_k)\|$ is small enough (that is, $k \geq k_1$ for some k_1 large enough), then for each $\lambda \in \rho_{s-F}(T) \setminus [\rho_{s-F}^{\pm\infty}(T) \cup \Omega]^-$, $\lambda - T\oplus M$ and $\lambda - f(\tilde{B}_k)$ will have the same index. By Lemma 2.4, we conclude that

$$\mathrm{ind}[\lambda - f(\tilde{B}_k)] = \textstyle\sum_j p_j(k)\ \nu(\lambda;\gamma_j(k)) = \mathrm{ind}(\lambda - T)$$

(for all $k \geq k_1$).

Hence, T satisfies (a), (b) and (c).

SUFFICIENCY. Now assume that T satisfies (a), (b) and (c). Given $\varepsilon > 0$, we can find T_ε (as in Lemma 2.7) similar to $T\oplus N$ such that $\|T - T_\varepsilon\| < 2\varepsilon$, where N is a normal operator such that $\sigma(N) = \sigma_e(N) = \Omega^-$ for some analytic Cauchy domain Ω with

$$\sigma_{\ell re}(T) \subset \Omega \subset \sigma_{\ell re}(T)_\varepsilon;$$

moreover, we can choose Ω so that every component of Ω intersects $\sigma_{\ell re}(T)$ and $\partial\Omega \cap f(Z(f')) = \emptyset$.

It is easily seen that T_ε also satisfies (a), (b) and (c). Clearly, it suffices to show that $\tilde{T}_\varepsilon \in f[S_e(\Lambda)^\sim]^-$; furthermore, by Lemma 2.9, it is enough to show that $\widetilde{T\oplus N} \in f[S_e(\Lambda)^\sim]^-$.

By using (c), we can find a finite union Φ_∞ ($\Phi_{-\infty}$) of components of $f^{-1}[\rho_{s-F}^{\infty}(T) \setminus \Omega^-]$ ($f^{-1}[\rho_{s-F}^{-\infty}(T) \setminus \Omega^-]$, resp.), such that $f(\Phi_\infty) = \rho_{s-F}^{\infty}(T) \setminus \Omega^-$ and $f(\partial\Phi_\infty) = \partial[\rho_{s-F}^{\infty}(T) \setminus \Omega^-]$ ($f(\Phi_{-\infty}) = \rho_{s-F}^{-\infty}(T) \setminus \Omega^-$ and $f(\partial\Phi_{-\infty}) = \partial[\rho_{s-F}^{-\infty}(T) \setminus \Omega^-]$, resp.). Since $\partial\Omega \cap f(Z(f')) = \emptyset$, Φ_∞ and $\Phi_{-\infty}$ are analytic Cauchy domains.

Moreover, we can also find finitely many regular analytic Jordan curves $\gamma_{-m},\gamma_{-m+1},\ldots,\gamma_{-1},\gamma_1,\gamma_2,\ldots,\gamma_n$ ($\gamma_j \subset \Lambda$ for all j) and non-zero finite indices $p_{-m},p_{-m+1},\ldots,p_{-1},p_1,p_2,\ldots,p_n$ (with sign p_j = sign j for all j) such that

$$\cup_j f(\gamma_j) \subset \Omega \setminus (\Omega_\infty \cup \Omega_{-\infty}) \text{ and } \textstyle\sum_j p_j\ \nu(\lambda;\gamma_j) = \mathrm{ind}(\lambda - T)$$

for all $\lambda \in \rho_{s-F}(T) \setminus [\rho_{s-F}^{\pm\infty}(T) \cup \Omega]^-$.

By proceeding as in the proof of Corollary 2.8, we can choose the γ_j's so that every component of Ω^- intersects $\cup_j f(\gamma_j)$.

Thus, if

$$A = M_-(\partial\Phi_\infty)^{(\infty)}\oplus M_+(\partial\Phi_{-\infty})^{(\infty)}\oplus[\oplus_{j=1}^{n} T_-(\gamma_j)^{(p_j)}]$$
$$\oplus[\oplus_{j=-1}^{-m} T_+(\gamma_j)^{(-p_j)}],$$

then $\sigma_e(A) \subset \Lambda$ is a perfect set and (by Corollary 2.5)

$$f(\tilde{A}) \underset{sim}{\to} \widetilde{T \oplus N}.$$

Hence, $\widetilde{T\oplus N} \in S(f(\tilde{A}))^- \subset f[S_e(\Lambda)^\sim]^-$.

The proof of Theorem 3.1 is now complete. ∎

REMARK 3.2. If Φ and Ω are analytic Cauchy domains such that $\Phi^- \subset \Lambda$, $\Omega^- \subset f(\Lambda)$, $f(\Phi) = \Omega$ and $f(\partial\Phi) = \partial\Omega$ (as in the proof of Theorem 3.1), then it is not difficult to check that the equation

$$f(\lambda) = \alpha$$

has exactly p roots (counted with multiplicity, for some $p \geq 1$) in Λ for each α in Ω. Following [7], we shall say that $f|\Phi$ is a *strictly* p-*valent mapping* from Φ onto Ω.

What happens when f' vanishes identically on an open subset of Λ? Observe that if Λ_o = interior Z(f') and $A \in S_e(\Lambda)$, then $\tilde{A}$ is similar to $\tilde{A}_o \oplus \tilde{A}_1$, where $\sigma_e(A_o) = \sigma_e(A) \cap \Lambda_o$ and $\sigma_e(A_1) = \sigma_e(A) \setminus \Lambda_o$. Clearly, $\sigma_e(A_o)$ can only intersect finitely many components, $\Lambda_1, \Lambda_2, \ldots, \Lambda_m$, of Λ_o. If $f|\Lambda_j \equiv \lambda_j$ $(j = 1,2,\ldots,m)$, then $\sigma_e(A_o) = \{\lambda_1, \lambda_2, \ldots, \lambda_m\}$ and $\Pi_{j=1}^m [f(\tilde{A}_o) - \lambda_j] = \tilde{0}$.

The proof of the general case follows by the same arguments as in the proof of Theorem 3.1. The details are left to the reader.

THEOREM 3.3. *Let* Λ *be a nonempty open subset of* $\mathbb{C}$ *and let* f *be an analytic function defined on* Λ. *Let* Λ_o = interior Z(f'). *The norm-closure of* $f[S_e(\Lambda)^\sim]$ *is the set of all those* $\tilde{T}$ *in* $A(H)$ *satisfying the conditions (a),*

(a$_1$) if a component σ *of* $\sigma_e(T)$ *does not intersect* $f(\Lambda \setminus \Lambda_o)^- \cup f(\Lambda_o)'$ *(where* $f(\Lambda_o)'$ *denotes the set of all limit points of* $\{f(\lambda): \lambda \in \Lambda_o\}$*), then* $\sigma = \{\mu\}$ *and* $\tilde{T} \sim \tilde{T}_\mu \oplus \mu\tilde{1}$ *for some isolated point* $\mu \in f(\Lambda)$, *where* $\mu \notin \sigma_e(T_\mu)$;

(b') $\rho_{s-F}^{\pm\infty}(T) \subset f(\Lambda \setminus \Lambda_o)$;

and (c).

4. THE CASES WHEN $f[S_e(\Lambda)^\sim]^- = \pi(f[S(\Lambda)])^-$

PROPOSITION 4.1. $f[S_e(\Lambda)^\sim]^-$ *coincides with* $\pi(f[S(\Lambda)])^-$ *if and only if the following condition is fulfilled:*

(o) Given a string of sausages (f,γ), *a component* Ω *of*

$\mathbb{C} \setminus f(\gamma)$ *such that* $\nu(\lambda;\gamma) = m \neq 0$ *(for all* $\lambda \in \Omega$*) and* $\varepsilon > 0$, *there exist a simply connected analytic Cauchy domain* Ω_ε, *analytic Cauchy domains* $\Phi_1, \Phi_2, \ldots, \Phi_r$, *and non-zero integers* $m_1, m_2, \ldots, m_r$, *such that* $(\Omega_\varepsilon)^- \subset \Omega \subset (\Omega_\varepsilon)_\varepsilon$, $f|\Phi_i$ *is a strictly* p_i*-valent mapping from* Φ_1 *onto* Ω_ε *(*$i = 1,2,\ldots,r$*), and*

$$\textstyle\sum_{i=1}^r m_i p_i = m.$$

PROOF. $\pi(f[S(\Lambda)])$ is a subset of $f[S_e(\Lambda)^\sim]$, and therefore $\pi(f[S(\Lambda)])^- \subset f[S_e(\Lambda)^\sim]^-$ in all cases.

Assume that $\pi(f[S(\Lambda)])^- = f[S_e(\Lambda)^\sim]^-$; then, in particular, $f(\tilde{T}_-(\gamma)) \in \pi(f[S(\Lambda)])^-$ for each analytic Jordan curve $\gamma \subset \Lambda \setminus Z(f')$. By Lemma 2.4, $\sigma[f(\tilde{T}_-(\gamma))] = f(\gamma)$ and $\operatorname{ind}[\lambda - f(\tilde{T}_-(\gamma))] = \nu(\lambda;\gamma)$ for each $\lambda \in \mathbb{C} \setminus f(\gamma)$.

Let $R \in L(H)$ be any operator such that $\sigma(R) = \sigma_W(R)$ and $\tilde{R} = f(\tilde{T}_-(\gamma))$; then $\tilde{R} \in \pi(f[S(\Lambda)])^-$. Observe that if Ω is a component of $\rho^{\pm}_{s-F}(R)$ $(\subset(\mathbb{C} \setminus f(\gamma)) \cap \sigma_W(R))$, then Ω is necessarily simply connected, because γ, and therefore $f(\gamma)$, are connected compact sets.) Now the necessity of condition (o) follows from [7,Theorem 2.2.].

Viceversa, if condition (o) is satisfied, then it follows from [7,Theorem 2.2] that for every string of sausages (f,γ), there exist $R_+(\gamma)$, $R_-(\gamma) \in f[S(\Lambda)]^-$ such that $\tilde{R}_+(\gamma) = f(\tilde{T}_+(\gamma))$ and $\tilde{R}_-(\gamma) = f(\tilde{T}_-(\gamma))$. But these are, precisely, part of the "construction blocks" of Theorems 3.1 and 3.3.

Since every $\tilde{T}$ in $f[S_e(\Lambda)^\sim]^-$ satisfies (a), (a_1) and (b') of Theorem 3.3, it is not difficult to deduce from [7,Theorems 2.2 and 2.3] that the other "construction blocks" also belong to $\pi(f[S(\Lambda)]^-)$, and therefore

$$f[S_e(\Lambda)^\sim]^- \subset \pi(f[S(\Lambda)]^-)^- = \pi(f[S(\Lambda)])^-. \blacksquare$$

REMARK 4.2. A slightly more elaborated analysis shows that $\pi(f[S(\Lambda)]^-) = \pi(f[S(\Lambda)])^-$ in all cases. (Use [7,corollary 5.1].)

Condition (o) of Proposition 4.1 is very subtle: the anaylitc Cauchy domain Ω_ε is simply connected, and $f|\Phi_i$ is a strictly p_i-valent mapping from Φ_i onto Ω_ε for all $i = 1,2,\ldots,r$, where $p_i \geq 1$. If $p_k = 1$ for some k, then $f|\Phi_k \to \Omega_\varepsilon$ is a conformal mapping. *But condition (o) can be satisfied even if there is no domain* $\Phi \subset \Lambda$ *such that* f *maps* Φ *conformally onto* Ω_ε*!*

EXAMPLE 4.3. Let $m,n \geq 2$ be two relatively prime natural numbers, and let Λ be the union of two analytic Cauchy domains, Φ_m and Φ_n, with disjoint closures, where Φ_m has m-1 holes and Φ_n has n-1 holes. In his well-known work on the Painlevé problem [1], L. V. Ahlfords proved that there exist analytic functions, f_m and f_n, defined on a neighborhood of $(\Phi_m)^-$ and, respectively, a neighborhood of $(\Phi_n)^-$, such that $f_m(\Phi_m) = f_n(\Phi_n) = \mathbb{D}$ and $f_m(\partial\Phi_m) = f_n(\partial\Phi_n) = \partial\mathbb{D}$; moreover, the equation

$$f_m(\lambda) = \alpha \quad (f_n(\lambda) = \alpha)$$

has exactly m (n, resp.) roots (counted with multiplicity) in $(\Phi_m)^-$ (in $(\Phi_n)^-$, resp.) for each $\alpha \in \mathbb{D}^-$.

Define $f|\Phi_m = f_m$ and $f|\Phi_n = f_n$.

Since $(m,n) = 1$, there exist integers p,q such that $pm + qn = 1$. Clearly, either $p > 0$ and $q < 0$, or $p < 0$ and $q > 0$. According to Proposition 4.1,

$$f[S_e(\Lambda)^\sim]^- = \pi(f[S(\Lambda)])^-.$$

Indeed, if Ω is an arbitrary analytic Cauchy domain such that $\Omega^- \subset \mathbb{D}$, then $f^{-1}(\Omega) = \Phi_m(\Omega) \cup \Phi_n(\Omega)$, where $\Phi_m(\Omega)$ and $\Phi_n(\Omega)$ are analytic Cauchy domains, $\Phi_m(\Omega)^- \subset \Phi_m$, $\Phi_n(\Omega)^- \subset \Phi_n$, $f|\Phi_m(\Omega)$ is a strictly m-valent map from $\Phi_m(\Omega)$ onto Ω, and $f|\Phi_n(\Omega)$ is a strictly n-valent map from $\Phi_n(\Omega)$ onto Ω. Since $pm + qn = 1$, it is immediate that (o) is satisfied in this case.

On the other hand, if $\mathbb{D}_r = \{\lambda \in \mathbb{C}: |\lambda| < r\}$ for some r, $0 < r < 1$, close enough to 1, then it is impossible to find a domain $\Phi_r \subset \Lambda$ such that f maps Φ_r conformally onto $\mathbb{D}_r$.

5. THE INTERIOR OF $f[S_e(\Lambda)^\sim]^-$

As in the case of $L(H)$, the set Λ_o = interior $Z(f')$ does not play any role in the characterization of the interiors of $f[S_e(\Lambda)^\sim]$ and its closure. The complete characterization of

$$\text{interior } f[S_e(\Lambda)^\sim]$$

is still an open problem, that we shall analyze in Section 7.

THEOREM 5.1. *Let* Λ *be a nonempty open subset of* $\mathbb{C}$ *and let* f *be an analytic function defined on* Λ. *Let* Λ_o = interior $Z(f')$; *then* interior $f[S_e(\Lambda)^\sim]^-$ *is the set of all those* $\tilde{T}$ *in* $A(H)$ *satis-*

fying the following conditions:

(a_{int}) $\sigma_e(T) \subset f(\Lambda \setminus \Lambda_o)$;

(b') $\rho^{\pm\infty}_{s-F}(T) \subset f(\Lambda \setminus \Lambda_o)$; *and*

(c_{int}) *given an analytic Cauchy domain* $\Omega \supset \sigma_{\ell re}(T)$, *there exist analytic Cauchy domains,* Ω_∞ *and* $\Omega_{-\infty}$, *a finite family* $\{\gamma_j\}^n_{j=-m,j\neq 0}$ *of regular analytic Jordan curves included in* $\Lambda \setminus Z(f')$ *and finite non-zero indices* $\{p_j\}^n_{j=-m,j\neq 0}$ *(*sign p_j = sign j *for all* j*) such that*

(c_1') $(\Omega_\infty)^- \subset \rho^\infty_{s-F}(T)$, $(\Omega_{-\infty})^- \subset \rho^{-\infty}_{s-F}(T)$,
$\partial(\Omega_\infty \cup \Omega_{-\infty}) \subset \Omega^- \setminus f(Z(f'))$,

($c_{2,int}$) *for each* j, $f(\gamma_j)$ *is an analytic Jordan curve included in* $f(\Lambda) \setminus f(Z(f'))$, $\cup_j f(\gamma_j) \subset \Omega^- \setminus (\Omega_\infty \cup \Omega_{-\infty})$, *and for each* $\lambda \in \rho_{s-F}(T) \setminus [\rho^{\pm\infty}_{s-F}(T) \cup \Omega]^-$,

$$\sum_j p_j \, \nu(\lambda;\gamma_j) = \text{ind}(\lambda - T).$$

(Beware, λ *does not necessarily belong to* $f(\Lambda)^-$*!)*

PROOF. NECESSITY. Suppose $\tilde{T}$ is an interior point of $f[S_e(\Lambda)^\sim]^-$; then there exists $\varepsilon > 0$ such that $\tilde{R} \in$ interior $f[S_e(\Lambda)^\sim]^-$ for all $\tilde{R}$ in $A(H)$ such that $\|\tilde{T} - \tilde{R}\| < \varepsilon$. If $\mu \in \sigma_e(T) \setminus f(\Lambda \setminus \Lambda_o)$, then $\mu \notin \rho_{s-F}(T)$ and (by standard arguments of approximation) we can find $\tilde{R}$ as above such that $\mu \in \rho^\infty_{s-F}(R)$ (see Section 2 and [3,Chapter 9]). By Theorems 3.1 and 3.3, $\tilde{R} \notin f[S_e(\Lambda)^\sim]^-$, a contradiction.

Hence, $\sigma_e(T)$ must be included in $f(\Lambda \setminus \Lambda_o)$; that is, $\tilde{T}$ satisfies (a_{int}). That $\tilde{T}$ satisfies (b') follows from Theorem 3.3.

Let Ω be an analytic Cauchy domain including $\sigma_{\ell re}(T)$. By replacing (if necessary) Ω by a smaller subdomain, we can directly assume that $\Omega \subset f(\Lambda \setminus \Lambda_o)$,

$\sigma_{\ell re}(T)_{\varepsilon/2} \subset \Omega \subset \sigma_{\ell re}(T)_{3\varepsilon/4}$ and $\partial\Omega \cap f(Z(f')) = \emptyset$.

Let Ω_∞ and $\Omega_{-\infty}$ be analytic Cauchy domains such that

$$\sigma_{\ell re}(T) \cup \rho^\infty_{s-F}(T) \subset \Omega_\infty \subset [\sigma_{\ell re}(T) \cup \rho^\infty_{s-F}(T)]_{\varepsilon/4}$$

and

$$[\rho^{-\infty}_{s-F}(T) \setminus \sigma_{\ell re}(T)_{\varepsilon/4}]^- \subset \Omega_{-\infty} \subset \rho^{-\infty}_{s-F}(T) \setminus \sigma_{\ell re}(T)_{\varepsilon/2}.$$

Let $\{\alpha_k\}^r_{k=1}$ be an enumeration of the components of $\partial\Omega \cap [\rho^{\pm}_{s-F}(T) \setminus \rho^{\pm\infty}_{s-F}(T)]$.

Define $T' = M_-(\partial\Omega_\infty)^{(\infty)} \oplus M_+(\partial\Omega_{-\infty})^{(\infty)} \oplus [\oplus^r_{k=1} \{M_-(\alpha_k)^{(p_k)} \oplus M_+(\alpha_k)^{(q_k)}\}] \oplus N'$, where N' is a normal operator with perfect spectrum $\sigma(N') \subset f(\Lambda \setminus \Lambda_o) \setminus \rho^{\pm}_{s-F}(T)$, and the p_k's and q_k's have been chosen so that $\min\{p_k, q_k\} = 0$ (for all $k = 1,2,\ldots,r$) and

$\mathrm{ind}(\lambda - T') = \mathrm{ind}(\lambda - T)$ for all $\lambda \in \rho^{\pm}_{s-F}(T) \setminus [\rho^{\pm\infty}_{s-F}(T) \cup \Omega]^-$.

Clearly, $\max\{p_k, q_k\} \geq 1$ for all $k = 1,2,\ldots,r$.

Let T" be defined exactly as T', with N' replaced by N" for some normal operator N" with $\sigma(N") = \sigma_{\ell re}(T)_{3\varepsilon/4}$. If N' is cleverly chosen, it follows from Theorem 3.3, Corollary 2.5 and Lemma 2.7 that there exist $\tilde{T}_1' \sim \tilde{T}'$ and $\tilde{T}_1" \sim \tilde{T}"$ such that $\tilde{T}' \underset{\text{sim}}{\rightarrow} \tilde{T}"$,

$$\max\{\|\tilde{T} - \tilde{T}_1'\|, \|\tilde{T} - \tilde{T}_1"\|, \|\tilde{T}_1' - \tilde{T}_1"\|\} < \varepsilon.$$

Thus, $\tilde{R} = \tilde{T}_1' \in$ interior $f[S_e(\Lambda)^{\sim}]$. Let $\tilde{R} = f(\tilde{B})$; then $\sigma_e(R) = f[\sigma_e(B)] = (\Omega_\infty \cup \Omega_{-\infty})^- \cup \{\cup_{k=1}^{r} \alpha_k\} \cup \sigma(N')$.

If $B \in L(H)$ is a lifting of $\tilde{B}$, then B is similar to $\{\oplus_{k=1}^{r} B_k\} \oplus B' + K$, where $K \in K(H)$, $f[\sigma_e(B_k)] = \alpha_k$ $(k = 1,2,\ldots,r)$ and $f[\sigma_e(B')] = \sigma_e(R) \setminus \cup_{k=1}^{r} \alpha_k$. Thus,

$$\sigma_e(B_k) = f^{-1}(\alpha_k) \cap \sigma_e(B) = \beta_k(0) \cup \{\cup_{i=1}^{s_k} \beta_k(i)\},$$

where $\{\beta_k(i)\}_{i=1}^{s_k}$ is a finite family of pairwise disjoint analytic Jordan curves included in $\Lambda \setminus Z(f')$ and $\beta_k(0)$ is a (possibly empty) subset of another union of analytic Jordan curves such that $\mathbb{C} \setminus \beta_k(0)$ is connected; moreover, there exist non-zero integers $\{m_k(i)\}_{i=1}^{s_k}$ such that $f|\beta_k(i)$ is an $|m_k(i)|$-to-1 mapping from $\beta_k(i)$ onto α_k $(i = 1,2,\ldots,s_k)$. (Since $\min\{p_k, q_k\} \geq 1$, we necessarily have $s_k \geq 1$ for all $k = 1,2,\ldots,r$. If $f|\beta_k(i)$ preserves orientation, then $m_k(i) > 0$; if $f|\beta_k(i)$ reverses orientation, then $m_k(i) < 0$.)

By using [13] and [14], we can write

$$B_k \sim B_k(0) \oplus \{\oplus_{i=1}^{s_k} B_k(i)\} + K_k,$$

where K_k is compact and $\sigma_e(B_k(i)) = \beta_k(i)$ $(i = 0,1,2,\ldots,s_k)$, $\sigma(B_k(0)) = \sigma_e(B_k(0))$, $\lambda_k(i) - B_k(i)$ is a Fredholm operator with $\mathrm{ind}(\lambda_k(i) - B_k(i)) = p_k(i)$ for all $\lambda_k(i) \in$ interior $\beta_k(i)$, and $p_k(i) \neq 0$ for at least one index i, $1 \leq i \leq s_k$.

The above construction shows that

$$\pi[M_-(\alpha_k)^{(p_k)} \oplus M_+(\alpha_k)^{(q_k)}] \sim f(\tilde{B}_k)$$

and, for each $\lambda \in$ interior α_k,

$$\sum_{i=1}^{s_k} p_k(i) m_k(i) = \sum_{i=1}^{s_k} p_k(i)\, \nu(\lambda; \beta_k(i))$$

$$= \mathrm{ind}[\lambda - M_-(\alpha_k)^{(p_k)} \oplus M_+(\alpha_k)^{(q_k)}]$$

$$= \begin{cases} p_k \geq 1, \text{ if } q_k = 0, \\ -q_k \leq -1, \text{ if } p_k = 0, \end{cases}$$

$(k = 1,2,\ldots,r)$.

Hence, if $\lambda \in \rho_{s-F}(T) \setminus [\rho_{s-F}^{\pm\infty}(T) \cup \Omega]^-$, we have

$$\text{ind}(\lambda - T) = \sum_{k=1}^{r} \sum_{i=1}^{s_k} p_k(i)\, \nu(\lambda;\beta_k(i)).$$

Therefore, $\tilde{T}$ also satisfies (c_{int}).

SUFFICIENCY. Now assume that $\tilde{T}$ satisfies (a_{int}), (b') and (c_{int}). By using the upper semicontinuity of separate parts of the essential spectrum, and the stability properties of the semi-Fredholm index, it is easily seen that $\tilde{T}'$ also satisfies those conditions for all $\tilde{T}' \in A(H)$ such that $\|\tilde{T} - \tilde{T}'\|$ is small enough. (Observe that $f(\Lambda \setminus \Lambda_o)$ is an open set.)

Thus, in order to complete the proof, it only remains to show that $\tilde{T} \in f[S_e(\Lambda)^\sim]^-$. But this follows immediately from (a_{int}), (b') and (c_{int}), and Theorems 3.1 and 3.3. (Each string of sausages (f,γ_j) has been reduced to a single analytic Jordan curve $f(\gamma_j)$ and a singly winding number, corresponding to a point in interior $f(\gamma_j)$.) ∎

From Theorem 5.1 and the proof of Theorem 3.1, we obtain the following consequence.

COROLLARY 5.2. *Let* Λ, f *and* Λ_o *be as in Theorem 5.1; then* $(\text{interior } f[S_e(\Lambda)^\sim]^-)^-$ *is the set of all those* $\tilde{T}$ *in* $A(H)$ *satisfying the following conditions:*

(a'_{int}) each component of $\sigma_e(T)$ intersects $f(\Lambda \setminus \Lambda_o)^-$;
(b') and (c_{int}).

6. THE DISTANCES TO $f[S_e(\Lambda)^\sim]$ AND TO $(\text{interior } f[S_e(\Lambda)^\sim]^-)$

Let $m_e(T) = \min\{r \in \sigma_e((T^*T)^{1/2})\}$ denote the minimum essential modulus of $T \in L(H)$, and let

$\Delta_\gamma(T) = \{\lambda \in \mathbb{C}:\ m_e(\lambda - T) \leq \gamma\}$ $(\gamma \geq 0)$.

For each $\Gamma \subset \mathbb{C}$, we write $\Gamma^* = \{\bar{\lambda}:\ \lambda \in \Gamma\}$.

By using the results of [3, Chapter 12], [12], we obtain

COROLLARY 6.1. *(i) Suppose* $\Lambda_o = \text{interior } f(Z(f')) = \emptyset$. *Given* $R \in L(H)$ *and* $\gamma > 0$, *let* $N_{\gamma,R}$ *be a normal operator such that* $\sigma(N_{\gamma,R}) = \sigma_e(N_{\gamma,R}) = \Delta_\gamma(R) \cup \Delta_\gamma(R^*)^*$; *then*

$$\operatorname{dist}[\tilde{R}, f[S_e(\Lambda)^{\sim}]] = \min\{\gamma \geq 0: \widetilde{R \oplus N_{\gamma,R}} \in f[S_e(\Lambda)^{\sim}]^{-}\}.$$

Furthermore, there exists $\tilde{T} \in f[S_e(\Lambda)^{\sim}]^{-}$ *such that* $\|\tilde{R} - \tilde{T}\| = \operatorname{dist}[\tilde{R}, f[S_e(\Lambda)^{\sim}]]$.

(ii) Moreover, the results of (i) remain valid for the case when $\Lambda_o \neq \emptyset$, *provided* $f(\Lambda)$ *has no isolated points.*

Similarly, we have

COROLLARY 6.2. *Given* $R \in L(H)$ *and* $\gamma \geq 0$, *let* $N_{\gamma,R}$ *be a normal operator such that* $\sigma(N_{\gamma,R}) = \sigma_e(N_{\gamma,R}) = \Delta_\gamma(R) \cup \Delta_\gamma(R^*)^*$ *; then*

$$\operatorname{dist}[\tilde{R}, (\text{interior } f[S_e(\Lambda)^{\sim}]^{-})]$$
$$= \min\{\gamma \geq 0: \widetilde{R \oplus N_{\gamma,R}} \in (\text{interior } f[S_e(\Lambda)^{\sim}]^{-})^{-}\}.$$

Furthermore, there exists $\tilde{T} \in (\text{interior } f[S_e(\Lambda)^{\sim}]^{-})^{-}$ *such that*

$$\|\tilde{R} - \tilde{T}\| = \operatorname{dist}[\tilde{R}, (\text{interior } f[S_e(\Lambda)^{\sim}]^{-})].$$

7. AN OPEN PROBLEM: interior $f[S_e(\Lambda)^{\sim}]$

The results obtained in [7] for $L(H)$ also include spectral characterizations of interior $f[S(\Lambda)]$ and $(\text{interior } f[S(\Lambda)])^{-}$.

What is interior $f[S_e(\Lambda)^{\sim}]$?

If $\tilde{T} \in A(H)$ and there exist analytic Cauchy domains $\Omega \subset f(\Lambda \setminus \Lambda_o)$ and $\Phi \subset \Lambda \setminus \Lambda_o$ such that $\Omega \supset \sigma_e(T)$ and f maps Φ conformally onto Ω, then we can define the inverse $g: \Omega \to \Phi$ of the mapping $f|\Phi: \Phi \to \Omega$. In this case, $\tilde{A} = g(\tilde{T})$ is well-defined via Functional Calculus, and

$$f(\tilde{A}) = f \circ g(\tilde{T}) = \tilde{T}.$$

Furthermore, the upper semicontinuity of the essential spectrum implies that Ω is a neighborhood of $\sigma_e(T')$ for all $\tilde{T}'$ in $A(H)$ such that $\|\tilde{T} - \tilde{T}'\|$ is small enough (see, e.g., [11, Chapter 1]). It readily follows that $\tilde{T} \in \text{interior } f[S_e(\Lambda)^{\sim}]$.

Comparison of this result with [7, Theorem 6.1] strongly suggests the following.

CONJECTURE 7.1. interior $f[S_e(\Lambda)^{\sim}]$ is the set of all those $\tilde{T}$ in $A(H)$ such that f maps some analytic Cauchy domain $\Phi \subset \Lambda \setminus \Lambda_o$ conformally onto a neighborhood of $\sigma_e(T)$.

Suppose $\tilde{T} \in \text{interior } f[S_e(\Lambda)^{\sim}]$, and let Ω be an analytic

Cauchy domain such that $\sigma_{\ell re}(T) \subset \Omega \subset \sigma_{\ell re}(T)_{\varepsilon}$ $(\varepsilon > 0)$ and $\partial\Omega \cap f(Z(f')) = \emptyset$. Let $\Omega_{\infty} = \rho_{s-F}^{\infty}(T) \cup \Omega$, and let $\Omega_{-\infty} = \rho_{s-F}^{-\infty}(T) \setminus \Omega^{-}$. By using Corollary 2.5 and Lemma 2.7, $\tilde{T}$ can be uniformly approximated by elements of the form $\tilde{T}_{\varepsilon}$, where T_{ε} is similar to

$$M_{-}(\partial\Omega_{\infty})^{(\infty)} \oplus M_{+}(\partial\Omega_{-\infty})^{(\infty)} \oplus L + K,$$

where L is some operator such that $\sigma_e(L) \subset \partial(\Omega_{\infty} \cup \Omega_{-\infty})_{\varepsilon} \setminus (\Omega_{\infty} \cup \Omega_{-\infty})^{-}$ and K is compact. Clearly, if $\|\tilde{T} - \tilde{T}_{\varepsilon}\|$ is small enough, then $\tilde{T}_{\varepsilon} \in$ interior $f[S_e(\Lambda)^{\sim}]$. By Lemma 2.9,

$$\pi[M_{-}(\partial\Omega_{\infty})^{(\infty)} \oplus M_{+}(\partial\Omega_{-\infty})^{(\infty)} \oplus L] \in \text{interior } f[S_e(\Lambda)^{\sim}];$$

furthermore,

$$R(X,Y,Z;L) = \begin{pmatrix} M_{-}(\partial\Omega_{\infty})^{(\infty)} & X & Y \\ 0 & M_{+}(\partial\Omega_{-\infty})^{(\infty)} & Z \\ 0 & 0 & L \end{pmatrix}$$

$$\sim \begin{pmatrix} M_{-}(\partial\Omega_{\infty})^{(\infty)} & \varepsilon X & \varepsilon^2 Y \\ 0 & M_{+}(\partial\Omega_{-\infty})^{(\infty)} & \varepsilon Z \\ 0 & 0 & L \end{pmatrix}$$

$$\underset{\varepsilon \downarrow 0}{\to} M_{-}(\partial\Omega_{\infty})^{(\infty)} \oplus M_{+}(\partial\Omega_{-\infty})^{(\infty)} \oplus L,$$

and therefore (by Lemma 2.9), $\tilde{R}(X,Y,Z;L) \in$ interior $f[S_e(\Lambda)^{\sim}]$ for all X,Y,Z.

Moreover, since $\sigma_e(L)$ is disjoint from $\sigma_e(M_{-}(\partial\Omega_{\infty})^{(\infty)} \oplus M_{+}(\partial\Omega_{-\infty})^{(\infty)}) = \sigma_{\ell re}(T) \cup \Omega^{-}$, by proceeding as in the proof of [7, Theorem 6.1], we deduce that if

$$S(X) = \begin{pmatrix} M_{-}(\partial\Omega_{\infty})^{(\infty)} & X \\ 0 & M_{+}(\partial\Omega_{-\infty})^{(\infty)} \end{pmatrix},$$

then $\tilde{S}(X) \in$ interior $f[S_e(\Lambda)^{\sim}]$ for all X.

By Theorem 3.1 and its proof, there exist analytic Cauchy domains Φ_{∞}, $\Phi_{-\infty} \subset \Lambda \setminus \Lambda_o$ such that $f|\Phi_{\infty}$ is a strictly p_+-valent mapping from Φ_{∞} onto Ω_{∞}, and $f|\Phi_{-\infty}$ is a strictly p_--valent mapping from $\Phi_{-\infty}$ onto $\Omega_{-\infty}$ (for some p_+, $p_- \geq 1$).

The proof of Theorem 6.1 in [7] suggests that if X,Y,Z (or just X) are cleverly chosen, then Φ_{∞} and $\Phi_{-\infty}$ can be chosen so that $p_+ = p_- = 1$, and f maps interior $(\Phi_{\infty} \cup \Phi_{-\infty})^{-}$ conformally onto interior $(\Omega_{\infty} \cup \Omega_{-\infty})^{-}$ (a neighborhood of $\sigma_e(T)$). An affirmative answer to this question would therefore provide an affirmative answer to Conjecture 7.1. But, unfortunately, the "translation" from the result for $L(H)$ to the Calkin algebra is not transparent at all!

If Conjecture 7.1 is correct, then the closure of interior $f[S_e(\Lambda)^{\sim}]$ can be easily obtained by using the results of Section 2. Indeed, we have

PROPOSITION 7.2. *The norm-closure of*

$Conf_e(f;\Lambda) := \{\tilde{A} \in A(H):$ f *maps an analytic Cauchy domain conformally onto a neighborhood of* $\sigma_e(A)\}$

is the set of all those $\tilde{T}$ *in* $A(H)$ *such that*

(a') *each component of* $\sigma_e(T)$ *intersects* $f(\Lambda \setminus \Lambda_o)^-$;

(b') $\rho_{s-F}^{\pm\infty}(T) \subset f(\Lambda \setminus \Lambda_o)$; *and*

(c_{conf}) given an analytic Cauchy domain $\Omega \supset \sigma_{\ell re}(T)$, *there exist analytic Cauchy domains* $\Omega_c \supset \rho_{s-F}^{\pm\infty}(T) \setminus \Omega$ *and* $\Phi_c \subset \Lambda \setminus \Lambda_o$ *such that each component of* $\sigma_e(T)$ *intersects* Ω_c, *for each component* Ψ *of* $\rho_{s-F}^{\pm}(T) \setminus \Omega$, *there exists an analytic Cauchy domain* $\Psi' \supset \Psi$ *such that* $\partial\Psi' \subset \partial\Omega_c$, *and* f *maps* Φ_c *conformally onto* Ω_c.

Furthermore, if $\tilde{R} \in A(H)$ *and* $\tilde{N}_{\gamma,R}$ *is a normal operator such that* $\sigma(N_{\gamma,R}) = \sigma_e(N_{\gamma,R}) = \Delta_\gamma(R) \cup \Delta_\gamma(R^*)^*$, *then*

$$\operatorname{dist}[\tilde{R}, Conf_e(f;\Lambda)] = \min\{\gamma \geq 0: \widetilde{R\oplus N}_{\gamma,R} \in Conf_e(f;\Lambda)^-\}.$$

Moreover, there exists $T \in Conf_e(f;\Lambda)^-$ *such that*

$$\operatorname{dist}[\tilde{R}, Conf_e(f;\Lambda)] = \|\tilde{R} - \tilde{T}\|.$$

REFERENCES

1. L. V. Ahlfords, Bounded analytic functions, Duke J. Math. 14 (1947), 1-11.

2. C. Apostol, The correction by compact perturbations of the singular behavior of operators, Rev. Roum. Math. Pures et Appl. 21 (1976), 155-175.

3. C. Apostol, L. A. Fialkow, D. A. Herrero and D. Voiculescu, Approximation of Hilbert space operators. Volume II, Research Notes in Math., vol. 102, Pitman Advanced Publ. Program, Boston-London-Melbourne, 1984.

4. L. G. Brown, R. G. Douglas and P. A. Fillmore, Unitary equivalence modulo the compact operators and extensions of C*-algebras, Proceedings of a conference on operator theory, Halifax, Nova Scotia 1973, Lect. Notes in Math., vol. 345, Springer-Verlag, Berlin-Heidelberg-New York, 1973, pp. 58-128.

5. S. Caradus, W. E. Pfaffenberger and B. Yood, Calkin algebras and algebras of operators on Banach spaces,

Lect. Notes Pure Appl. Math., vol. 9, Marcel Dekker, Inc., New York, 1974.

6. J. B. Conway, Subnormal operators, Research Notes in Math., vol. 51, Pitman Advanced Publ. Program, Boston-London-Melbourne, 1981.

7. J. B. Conway, D. A. Herrero and B. B. Morrel, The closure of $f[L(H)]$ for an entire function f, and related problems, Memoirs Amer. Math. Soc. (to appear).

8. J. B. Conway and B. B. Morrel, Roots and logarithms of bounded operators on Hilbert space, J. Funct. Anal. 70 (1987), 171-193.

9. C. Davis and P. Rosenthal, Solving linear operator equations, Can. J. Math. 26 (1974), 1384-1389.

10. R. G. Douglas, Banach algebras techniques in operator theory, Academic Press, New York and London, 1972.

11. D. A. Herrero, Approximation of Hilbert space operators. Volume I, Research Notes in Math., vol. 72, Pitman Advanced Publ. Program, Boston-London-Melbourne, 1982.

12. D. A. Herrero, The distance to a similarity invariant set of operators, Integral Equations and Operator Theory 5 (1982), 131-140.

13. M. Rosenblum, On the operator equation $BX - XA = Q$, Duke J. Math. 23 (1956), 263-269.

14. J. G. Stampfli, Compact perturbations, normal eigenvalues and a problem of Salinas, J. London Math. Soc. (2) 9 (1974), 165-175.

15. D. Voiculescu, A non-commutative Weyl-von Neumann theorem, Rev. Roum. Math. Pures et Appl. 21 (1976), 97-113.

Department of Mathematics,
Arizona State University,
Tempe, AZ 85287,
U.S.A.

Operator Theory:
Advances and Applications, Vol. 35

CHORDAL INHERITANCE PRINCIPLES AND POSITIVE DEFINITE COMPLETIONS OF PARTIAL MATRICES OVER FUNCTION RINGS

Charles R. Johnson[1] and Leiba Rodman[2]

Positive definite completions of partial matrices over function rings are considered. The basic problem is construction of completions of this form that, in addition, are in the same function ring. The main tools in solving this problem are inheritance principles which are developed as well.

INTRODUCTION

Positive definite completions of *scalar* partial Hermitian matrices are now fairly well understood, at least when the graph of the specified entries is chordal [DG, GJSW], and the importance of these results for electrical engineering systems theory is now being discovered. Thus far, the analogous situation in which the specified entries of a partial Hermitian matrix are from a class of complex-valued *functions* on some set has not been studied. If such a partial Hermitian matrix has a positive definite completion pointwise, it is natural to ask whether it has a function-valued completion, in which the functions providing the completion are from the same class. This is the primary question we address, and an answer is given in theorem 1.1.

---

1) The work of this author supported by National Science Foundation grant DMS-87 13762 and by Office of Naval Research contract N00014-87-K-0661.
2) The work of this author was partially supported by NSF grant DMS-87-00841 and was done while visiting The College of William and Mary.

As a tool in addressing this question we generalize the "permanence principle" of [EGL1] to chordal graphs. This is perhaps more naturally called an "inheritance principle" in our case and is perhaps of as great of interest as the completion results. Three versions of this principle are discussed in section 3.

As usual, contraction or norm preserving completions are closely related to positive definite completions and this connection is exploited in section 2. Positive semidefinite completions, which appear not as straightforwardly connected with positive definite completions as in the scalar case, are discussed in the function setting in section 5.

1. Main Result: Positive Definite Case.

Let G be an undirected graph without multiple edges and with a finite number of vertices (only such graphs will be considered in this paper). By V(G) we denote the set of vertices of G, and by $E(G) \subset V(G) \times V(G)$ the set of edges. Thus $(u,v) \in E(G)$ if an only if $(v,u) \in E(G)$. It will be assumed everywhere that $(v,v) \in E(G)$ for all $v \in V(G)$.

In this paper the class of graphs called *chordal* will be important. A graph G is called *chordal*, or *triangulated*, if every circuit (v_1,v_2), $(v_2,v_3), \ldots, (v_k,v_1) \in E(G)$ with $k \geq 4$ has a *chordal*, i.e., $(v_i,v_j) \in E(G)$ for some i,j such that $1 \leq i < j - 1 \leq k - 1$. The chordal graphs are a well-studied class that arises in consideration of many problems (see [G, GL, GJSW, AHMR, PP]), and we shall need some of their properties later on. An mxn array $A = [a_{ij}]_{i,j=1}^{m,n}$ will be called a *partial matrix* if its entries are either complex numbers or question marks. A *completion* of an m-by-n partial matrix $A = [a_{ij}]_{i,j=1}^{m,n}$ is, by definition, an ordinary ordinary mxn matrix $B = [b_{ij}]_{i,j=1}^{m,n}$ with complex entries such that $b_{ij} = a_{ij}$ whenever $a_{ij} \in \mathbf{C}$. Thus, one can view B as obtained from A by replacing all the question marks by complex numbers. A partial nxn matrix $A = [a_{ij}]_{i,j=1}^{n}$ is called *Hermitian* if all entries on the main diagonal are real numbers, and $a_{ij} \in \mathbf{C}$ implies $a_{ji} \in \mathbf{C}$ and $a_{ji} = \bar{a}_{ij}$. So a partial Hermitian matrix coincides with its conjugate transpose if we formally define the question mark to be its own transpose.

We will be interested in positive definite completions of partial Hermitian matrix. It is known (see [GJSW]) that among all positive definite completions (if they exist at all) of a given partial Hermitian matrix A there is precisely one completion B with the property that B is positive definite and $\det B \geq \det C$ for any other positive definite completion C of A. We call B the *maximal determinant* (shortly, *m.d.*) positive definite completion. The m.d. positive definite completion can be characterized in several other ways (see [GJSW], for example), some of them will be recalled later on in this paper.

Given a graph G, identify its vertices with the set $\{1, \dots, n\}$. A partial Hermitian matrix $A = [a_{ij}]_{i,j=1}^{n}$ is said to be *subordinate* to G if a_{ij} is a question mark precisely when $i \neq j$ and $(i,j) \notin E(G)$.

We state now one of the main results of this paper.

THEOREM 1.1. *Let* X *be a set, and let* K *be a ring of complex-valued functions* f(t) *on* X, *with the natural ring structure such that* $(f(t))^{-1} \in K$ *provided* $f(t) \in K$ *and* $f(t) > 0$ *for all* $t \in X$. *Let* G *be a chordal graph and let* $A(t) = [a_{ij}(t)]_{i,j=1}^{n}$ *be a partial Hermitian matrix subordinate to* G *such that* $a_{ij}(t) \in K$ *for every* $(i,j) \in E(G)$. *Then, assuming* A(t) *has a positive definite completion for each* $t \in X$, *the m.d. positive definite completion* $B(t) = [b_{ij}(t)]_{i,j=1}^{n}$ *of* A(t) *has the property that* $b_{ij}(t) \in K$ *for every pair of indices* (i,j).

Thus, the solution of the optimization problem max det C(t) subject to the conditions that C(t) is a positive definite completion of A(t), belongs (entrywise) to the same algebra K as the entries of A(t). This fact is notable because typically optimization problems do not have such properties (e.g., the pointwise maximum of a differentiable function depending on a parameter is not generally differentiable).

It should be noted that for a partial hermitian matrix A subordinate to a chordal graph G, a positive definite completion exists if and only if each maximal fully specified (i.e., without question marks) principal submatrix of A is positive definite (see [GJSW]). Thus, the hypothesis on existence of a positive definite completion in Theorem 1.1 can be replaced by an equivalent hypothesis that for each t every maximal fully specified principal submatrix of A(t) is positive definite.

An important particular case covered by theorem 1.1 is that in which A(t) is *block banded:* $A(t) = [A_{ij}(t)]_{i,j=1}^{r}$ where $A_{ij}(t)$ are matrices (not necessarily square) which for $|i-j| > k$ consist of question marks only and for $|i-j| \leq k$ consist of complex numbers only (of course being hermitian implies that $A_{ij}(t) = A_{ji}(t)^*$ for all $t \in X$ and that $A_{11}(t),\ldots, A_{rr}(t)$ are square hermitian matrices). Here $k \geq 1$ is a fixed integer.

For results concerning completion of block banded matrices see [DG, EGL1, EGL2]. Clearly, the graph G to which a block banded partial hermitian matrix is subordinate, is chordal. However, for many chordal graphs (e.g., trees which are not lines) there is no permutation of vertices that transforms the pattern of specified entries of G to a block banded pattern. See the appendix for additional information concerning graph - theoretical properties of block banded patterns.

2. Norm Preserving Completions.

We consider here the norm preserving completions of partial nxm matrices with entries in an algebra. The norm $\|A\|_2$ is the operator norm, i.e., the largest singular value of A.

A partial nxm matrix A is said to have a *norm preserving pattern* (see [JR]) if by permutations of rows and columns A can be brought to the following block "diagonal" form

$$\begin{bmatrix} B_1 & ? & \cdots & ? \\ ? & B_2 & & \cdot \\ \cdot & & & \cdot \\ \cdot & & & ? \\ ? & \cdots & ? & B_r \end{bmatrix},$$

possibly bordered by rows and/or columns of question marks, in which

$$B_j = \begin{bmatrix} B_{j11} & ? & ? \ \cdots & ? \\ B_{j21} & B_{j22} & & \vdots \\ \vdots & \vdots & & ? \\ B_{jp1} & B_{jp2} & \cdots & B_{jpp} \end{bmatrix}, \quad j=1, \ldots, r,$$

and the (possibly rectangular) blocks B_{jst}, $r \geq s \geq t \geq 1$, consist entirely of specified (i.e., number) entries. The terminology is justified by the fact (proved in [JR],[KL]) that the pattern of specified entries is norm preserving precisely when every partial nxm matrix A subordinate to this pattern admits a completion B with

$$\|B\|_2 = \max_{1 \leq j \leq p} \|A_j\|_2,$$

where $A_1, \ldots, A_p$ are all fully specified rectangular submatrices of A. (Actually, [JR] concerns contraction completions only, but a trivial scaling of A will give the result just quoted).

THEOREM 2.1. *Let* A *be a partial* nxm *matrix with a norm preserving pattern. Assume the specified entries of* A = A(t) *together with their complex conjugates belong to a ring* K *of (complex-valued) functions on a set* X *with the following properties: (a) if* $f(t) \in K$ *and* $f(t) > 0$ *for all* $t \in X$, *then* $(f(t))^{-1} \in K$; (b) *all constant positive functions belong to* K. *Then for every* $\varepsilon > 0$ *there is a completion* B = B(t) *of* A(t) *all of whose entries belong to* K *and such that*

$$\|B(t)\|_2 \leq \varepsilon + \sup_{t \in X} \max_{1 \leq j \leq r} \|A_j(t)\|_2, \tag{2.1}$$

where $A_1(t), \ldots, A_r(t)$ *are all fully specified (rectangular submatrices of* $A(t)$.

PROOF Let $M = \sup_{t \in X} \max_{1 \le j \le r} \|A_j(t)\|_2$. Consider the matrix

$$\hat{A} = \begin{bmatrix} (M + \varepsilon)I & A \\ A^* & (M + \varepsilon)I \end{bmatrix}.$$

By the hypotheses, the entries of A belong to K. Further, Theorem 3 in [JR] shows that A is subordinate to a chordal graph. Theorem 1 of [JR] (or some previous result, e.g., Theorem 1.2 in [DKW]) imply that A satisfies the hypotheses of Theorem 1.1. So there is a positive definite completion

$$\hat{B} = \begin{bmatrix} (M + \varepsilon)I & B \\ B^* & (M + \varepsilon)I \end{bmatrix}$$

of $\hat{A}$ whose entries belong to K. Then B (the right upper corner of $\hat{B}$) satisfies the requirements of Theorem 2.1.

We do not know whether one can take $\varepsilon = 0$ in Theorem 2.1. Probably this should require additional assumptions on the ring K. Some results in this direction can be deduced from Theorem 5.1 (Section 5).

It is instructive to compare Theorem 2.1 with formula (1.3) in [DKW] describing all norm-preserving completions of the matrix in the block form

$$\begin{bmatrix} A_{11} & A_{12} \\ A_{21} & ? \end{bmatrix}.$$

In this formula the square root of a positive definite matrix is involved (in the case of completion that increase the norm by ε; if norm-preserving completions are required then the formula is more complicated) Theorem 2.1 implies however, that one can in principle avoid taking the square roots. Recent report [W] contains formulas (involving square roots) and description of all strictly contractive completions of block banded matrices.

EXAMPLE 2.1. Let K be the ring of all scalar real rational functions with poles off the imaginary axis and off infinity. This ring satisfies the hypotheses of Theorem 2.1 (with $X = \{z \in \mathbf{C} | \operatorname{Re} z = 0\} \cup \{\infty\}$); note that $\overline{f(t)} = f(-t)$ for $f \in K$. So in this particular case Theorem 2.1 asserts existence for every $\varepsilon > 0$ of a completion $B(t)$ with entries from K and satisfying (2.1), of any partial matrix with a norm reserving pattern and with the specified entries in K. Completion problems of this type appear in synthesis problems in electrical engineering (see, e.g., [SJVL, N, D]).

3. Inheritance Principles.

For a given graph G, the *adjacent set* of a vertex v is defined as the set of all vertices u such that $(u,v) \in E(G)$. A *clique* of G is, by definition, a set of vertices $V_0 \subset V(G)$ such that there is an edge (u,v) in G for any pair of different vertices $u,v \in V_0$.

PROPOSITION 3.1 *Let G be a graph with* $V(G) = \{1,\ldots,n\}$, *and let* $v \in V(G)$ *be such that its adjacent set is a clique. Assume that A is a partial Hermitian matrix subordinate to G with the m.d. positive definite completion B. Then the matrix* $\hat{B}$ *obtained by crossing out column and row numbered by v is the m.d. positive definite completion of the partial Hermitian matrix A obtained from A by crossing out its v-th column and row.*

We call the result of Proposition 3.1 the first chordal inheritance principle.

PROOF. By theorem 2 of [GJSW], the matrix B is the unique positive definite completion of A such that $B^{-1} = [b_{ij}]_{i,j=1}^n$ has the property that $b_{ij} = 0$ whenever $i \neq j$ and $(i,j) \notin E(G)$. An application of a well-known result (see [GL] or Corollary 3.2 in [BJOV]) shows that the entries of $\hat{B}^{-1} = [\hat{b}_{ij}]_{i,j=1}^n$ have the same property: $\hat{b}_{ij} = 0$ whenever $i \neq j$, i and j are different from v, and $(i,j) \notin E(G)$. Now appeal to Theorem 2 of [GJSW] again to finish the proof. □

We need now the following properties of chordal graphs.

PROPOSITION 3.2. *The following statements are equivalent for a (undirected, without multiple edges, finite number of vertices, no edge from a vertex to itself) graph G with* n *vertices:*

(a) G *is chordal;*

(b) *There is a sequence of graphs* $G_0 = G$, G_1, $G_2, \ldots,$ G_s *such that* G_s *is the one-vertex graph, and each* G_j *is obtained from* G_{j-1} *be deleting (together with all adjacent edges) a vertex* v_j *whose adjacent set is a clique;*

(c) *There is a sequence of chordal graphs* $F_0 = G$, $F_1, \ldots, F_t$ *such that* F_t *is the complete graph on n vertices (i.e., there is an edge between any two different vertices), and each* F_j *is obtained from* F_{j-1} *by adding precisely one new edge in such a way that* F_j *has exactly one maximal clique which is not a clique of* F_{j-1}.

For the equivalence of (a) and (b) see [R1, R2], and for the equivalence of (a) and (c) see [GJSW].

A sequence of graphs $\{F_0 = G, F_1, \ldots, F_t\}$ with the properties described in Proposition 3.2 (c) will be called an *increasing chordal sequence* for G.

We are now ready to state and prove our second *chordal inheritance principle*. In this statement and elsewhere we denote by A(V) the principal submatrix of a partial Hermitian nxn matrix A formed by the entries with indices from $V \subset \{1, \ldots, n\}$.

THEOREM 3.3. *Let* G *be a chordal graph different from the complete graph. Then there exists a chordal graph* F *with the following properties:*

(a) F *is obtained from* G *by adding exactly one edge (between different vertices), call it* (u,v), *to the edges of G;*

(b) *There is precisely one maximal clique* V_0 *in* F *which is not a clique of G;*

(c) *For any partial hermitian matrix* A

subordinate to G with the m.d. positive definite completion B the following holds: Let A_1 be the partial hermitian matrix subordinate to F obtained from A by replacing the question mark in the (u,v) entry by a number (and replacing the (v,u) entry by the conjugate number) in such a way that $A_1(V_0)$ is the m.d. positive definite completion of $A(V_0)$. Further, let B_1 be the m.d. positive definite complete of A_1. Then B_1 = B.

Observe that the existence of the m.d. positive definite completion B ensures the existence of both m.d. positive definite completions $A_1(V_0)$ and B_1. Indeed, this follows from the criterion for existence of the m.d. positive definite completion for a partial Hermitian matrix X subordinate to a chordal graph H (see [GJSW]): Namely, all fully specified submatrices in X should be positive definite.

PROOF. For a sequence of graphs $S = \{G = G_0, G_1, \ldots, G_s\}$ as in Proposition 3.2 (b), let j(S) be the maximal index such that G_j is not the complete graph. Among all such sequences S choose one, call it S_0, for which the index $j(S_0)$ is maximal possible. In the sequal we write $j = j(S_0)$ and $S_0 = \{G_0, G_1, \ldots, G_s\}$.

The choice of G_j easily implies that by adding precisely one edge (v_0, u_0) to G_j, for some vertex u_0 in G_{j+1}, one obtains a full graph on the vertices of G_j. Now we define F to be the graph obtained from G by adding the edge (v_0, u_0).

First, let us verify that F is chordal. Indeed, letting F_k to be the graph obtained from G_k by adding the edge (v_0, u_0) (provided both vertices v_0 and u_0 belong to G_k), the sequence $F = F_0, F_1, \ldots, F_s$ satisfies the conditions of Proposition 3.2 (b), hence F is chordal.

Secondly, it is clear that $V(G_j)$is a maximal clique in F which is not a clique in G. We show that $V_0 := V(G_j)$ is the only clique in F with these properties. Suppose not; then there must be a vertex v in G but not in G_j such that both (v, u_0) and (v, v_0) are edges in G. So for some G_k $(k < j)$ the vertex v is in G_k but is not in G_{k+1}. However, as the adjacent set of v in G_k is not a clique, this contradicts the property of $\{G_0, G_1, \ldots, G_s\}$ as described in Proposition 3.2 (b).

Now let A be a partial Hermitian matrix subordinate to G with the m.d. positive definite completion B, and let A_1 be defined as in (c). By Proposition 3.1 $B(V_0)$ is the m.d. positive definite completion of $A(V_0)$. Thus, B is a positive definite completion of the matrix A_1, and hence det $B_1 \geq$ det B, where B_1 is the m.d. positive definite completion of A_1. On the other hand, B_1 is obviously a positive definite completion of A, so det $B_1 \leq$ det B. As the m.d. positive definite completion is unique (see [GJSW]), the proof is complete. □

It is worth noting that the assumption of chordality on G is, in general, important in Theorem 3.3, as indicated by the following example from [JB].

EXAMPLE 3.1. Consider the partial Hermitian matrix

$$A = \begin{bmatrix} 2 & -1 & a & -1 \\ -1 & 2 & -1 & b \\ \bar{a} & -1 & 2 & -1 \\ -1 & \bar{b} & -1 & 2 \end{bmatrix}$$

in which a and b are unspecified entries. A calculation reveals that the maximum determinant positive definite completion of A occurs for $a = b = \sqrt{3} - 1$. However, the maximum determinant positive definite completion of the upper left 3-by-3 principal submatrix of A,

$$\begin{bmatrix} 2 & -1 & a \\ -1 & 2 & -1 \\ \bar{a} & -1 & 2 \end{bmatrix},$$

occurs for $a = 1/2$.

Applying Theorem 3.3 several times, we obtain the following version of the second inheritance principle.

THEOREM 3.4. *Let G be a chordal graph. Then there exists an increasing chordal sequence* $\{F_0 = G, F_1, \ldots, F_t\}$

of G with the following property (we denote by (u_j, v_j) *the edge added to* F_{j-1} *in order to obtain* F_j*, and* V_j *is the only maximal clique in* F_j *which is not a clique in* F_{j-1}*). For every partial Hermitian matrix A subordinate to G and for which there is a positive definite completion, construct a (unique) sequence of partial Hermitian matrices as follows: Put* $A_0 =$ A*; if* A_{j-1} *is already constructed, then* A_j *is obtained from* A_{j-1} *by replacing the questions mark in the* (u_j, v_j) *entry by a number (and correspondingly replacing the* (v_j, u_j) *entry by the conjugate number) in such a way that* $A_j(V_j)$ *is the m.d. positive definite completion of* $A_{j-1}(V_j)$*. Then the last matrix in the sequence* A_t *is the m.d. positive definite completion of* A.

In connection with this theorem we conjecture (together with W. W. Barrett) that given a chordal graph G, *every* increasing chordal sequence of G satisfies the property described in theorem 3.4.

Theorem 3.4 may be viewed as a generalization of a more precise version of the permanence principle proved for banded matrices in [EGL1] (see Theorem 3.5 below). It is instructive to consider this special case of Theorem 3.4. We consider a slightly more general class than banded matrices. We say that a graph G with vertices {1,..., n} is a *generalized banded graph* if there is a number q with the property that for all pairs of indices $i = j$ with $|i - j| \le q$ there is an edge $(i,j) \in E(G)$, and if $(i,j) \in E(G)$ then $|i - j| \le q + 1$ (it may happen however that for some indices i,j with $|i - j| = q + 1$ there is *no* edge (i,j) in G). It is easy to see that generalized banded graphs are chordal and that the *banded* graphs G(n,k) (characterized by the property $(i,j) \in E(G)$ if and only if $i = j$ and $|i - j| \le k$) form a subclass of the generalized banded graphs. Also, for a generalized banded graph G there is an increasing chordal sequence all members of which are generalized banded graphs as well.

THEOREM 3.5. *Every increasing chordal sequence of a generalized banded graph G that consists of generalized banded graphs only, satisfies the property described in Theorem 3.4.*

PROOF. Applying induction on the number of edges in G, it remains to prove that any generalized banded graph F that satisfies the properties (a) and (b) of Theorem 3.3 satisfies also the property (c) of Theorem 3.3.

Let (u_0, v_0) be the edge in F but not in G $(u_0 < v_0)$. Let $\{G = G_0, G_1, \ldots, G_s\}$ be a sequence of graphs as in Proposition 3.2 (b) such that the vertices of some G_{j_0} are precisely $\{u_0, u_0 + 1, \ldots, v_0\}$ (the structure of the generalized banded graph G easily implies that such sequence exists). It is also easily verified that j_0 is the biggest index with the property that H_{j_0} is not the full graph, where H_{j_0} is taken from any sequence of graphs $\{G = H_0, H_1, \ldots, H_s\}$ satisfying the properties in Proposition 3.2 (b). Now proceed as in the proof of Theorem 3.3. □

Consider now the special case of the banded graph G(n, k).

Among the increasing chordal sequences $\{F_0 = G(n,k), F_1, \ldots, F_t\}$ where every F_j is generalized banded we distinguish two (call them C_1 and C_2) which have the additional property that

(β1) if $|i - j| = q + 1$ and $(i,j) \in E(F_p)$ then $(i - s, j - s) \in E(F_p)$ for $s = 1, \ldots, \min(i - 1, j - 1)$ (for the sequence S_1)

(β2) if $|i - j| = q + 1$ and $(i,j) \in E(F_p)$ then $(i + s, j + s) \in E(F_p)$ for $s = 1, \ldots, \max(n - 1, n - j)$ (for the sequence S_2).

(Here q is the number which appears in the definition of a generalized banded graph when applied to F_p.) Theorem 4 of [EGL1] is a particular case of the statement (implied by Theorem 3.5) that both sequences C_1 and C_2 satisfy the property described in Theorem 3.4.

4. <u>Proof of Theorem 1.1</u>.

In view of Theorem 3.4 we only have to consider the case in which G is such that by adding just one edge a full graph is obtained. Without loss of generality we can assume that this edge is (1,n). (It is implicitly assumed in Theorem 1.1 that V(G) = {1,..., n}.) Using the fact (proved in [GJSW]) that a positive definite completion $B(t) = [b_{ij}(t)]_{i,j=1}^{n}$ of A(t) is m.d. if and only if the (1,n) - entry in $B(t)^{-1}$ is zero, we see that the entry $b_{1n}(t)$ in B(t) is determined by the condition

(4.1)

$$\det \begin{bmatrix} a_{12}(t) & a_{13}(t) & \cdots & a_{1,n-1}(t) & b_{1n}(t) \\ a_{22}(t) & a_{23}(t) & \cdots & a_{2,n-1}(t) & a_{2n}(t) \\ & \vdots & & & \vdots \\ a_{n-1,2}(t) & a_{n-1,3}(t) & \cdots & & a_{n-1,n}(t) \end{bmatrix} = 0$$

By assumption, for every $t \in X$ there is a positive definite completion of A(t), so in particular

$$\det \begin{bmatrix} a_{22}(t) & a_{23}(t) & \cdots & a_{2,n-1}(t) \\ a_{32}(t) & a_{33}(t) & \cdots & a_{3,n-1}(t) \\ \vdots & & & \\ a_{n-1,2}(t) & & \cdots & a_{n-1,n-1}(t) \end{bmatrix} > 0$$

for all $t \in X$. Now clearly (4.1) defines $b_{in}(t)$ uniquely, and expansion of (4.1) along the first row together with the hypotheses on K imply that $b_{1n}(t) \in K$. This completes the proof of Theorem 1.1.

5. <u>Positive Semidefinite Completions</u>.

In this section we state one result on positive semidefinite completions that will be obtained by an application of Theorem 1.1.

Let K be a ring of functions on a set X as in Theorem 1.1, i.e, with the following property:

(α) f(t) ε K, f(t) > 0 for all t ε X $(f(t))^{-1}$ ε K.

We shall assume also that (β) all constant positive functions belong to K. Together with such a ring K, consider the ring K(e) of functions of t ε X and e > 0 of the type p(e, t)/q(e, t), in which p(e, t) and q(e, t) are polynomials in e with coefficients in K such that q(e, t) > 0 for all e > 0 and all t ε X. It is easily seen that K(e) (as a ring of functions on X x $(0, \infty)$) again satisfies the properties (α) and (β). Also, K $\subset$ K(e). We need also the following property of K:

(γ) Let g(e, t) ε K(e) be such that $|g(t, e)| \leq e + M$ for all t ε X, e > 0, where the constant M is independent of (t, e). Then there is a sequence of positive numbers $\{e_m\}_{m=1}$ tending to zero such that for every t ε X the limit $h(t) = \lim_{m\to\infty} g(t, e_m)$ exists and h(t) ε K.

THEOREM 5.1. *Let* K *be a ring of (complex-valued) functions on* X *satisfying the properties* (α) - (γ), *let* $A(t) = [a_{ij}(t)]_{i,j=1}^{n}$ *be a partial Hermitian matrix subordinate to a chordal graph* G, *with the entries* $a_{ij}(t)$ *in* K *and such that* $a_{11}(t),\ldots,a_{nn}(t)$ *are bounded functions. Assume that for every* t ε X *any fully specified principal submatrix of* A(t) *is positive semidefinite. Then there exists a completion* B(t) *of* A(t) *which is positive semidefinite for all* t ε X *and whose entries belong to* K *as functions of* t ε X.

The existence of a positive semidefinite completion for each t ε X under the hypotheses of Theorem 5.1 was proved in [GJSW]. The new fact in Theorem 5.1 is that a positive semidefinite completion can be chosen with entries in K.

PROOF. Put $A_e(t) = A(t) + eI$, where e > 0 is a parameter. Theorem 1.1 is applicable for $A_e(t)$, with K replaced by K(e), so each entry of the m.d. positive definite completion $B_e(t)$ of $A_e(t)$ belongs to K(e). Also, if $\|a_{jj}(t)\| \leq M$ for all t ε X and j = 1,...,n, then every nondiagonal entry $g(t, e)$ of $B_e(t)$ satisfies $\|g(t, e)\| \leq e + M$. It remains to pass to the limit when $e \to 0$ and use the property (γ) of K.□

Theorem 5.1 can be applied to the norm preserving completion problems in the same way as Theorem 1.1. We omit the statement of the corresponding result on norm preserving completions.

6. Lipschitz Property of Positive Definite Completions.

In this section we show yet another way in which m.d. positive definite completions are well-behaved.

THEOREM 6.1. *Let G be a chordal graph, and let* $A = [a_{ij}]_{i,j=1}^{n}$ *be a partial Hermitian matrix subordinate to G which admits a positive definite completion. Then there exist positive constants e and K such that any partial Hermitian matrix* $A' = [a'_{ij}]_{i,j=1}^{n}$ *subordinate to G with*

$$\max_{(i,j) \in E(G)} |a'_{ij} - a_{ij}| < e$$

has the m.d. positive definite completion B′, and the inequality

$$\|B' - B\| \leq K \max_{(i,j) \in E(G)} |a'_{ij} - a_{ij}|$$

holds, where B is the m.d. positive definite completion of A.

The proof is done using the same arguments as in the proof of Theorem 1.1.

We remark that the properties of m.d. positive definite completions described in Theorem 6.1 appear in the study of slowly time-varying linear systems(see, e.g., [WZ]).

Again, theorem 6.1 implies an analogous result for the norm preserving completions. We omit the statement of this result.

Appendix
The Generality of Chordal Patterns

Our results here have dealt with completion of partial Hermitian matrix functions, the graph of whose "specified" entries is chordal. Considerable work on completion problems has been and is being done for banded or "block banded" patterns of the specified entries. This has natural motivation from certain function theoretic applications, but it is known that block banded patterns are chordal. Often, results from the block banded case hold also for chordal patterns, and chordality seems to us to be the appropriate level of generality in which to consider many problems. As the generality of chordal patterns, relative to block banded patterns, is not well understood (especially in the more analytic literature), it is our purpose here to outline the precise difference as briefly and simply as possible.

The precise definition of block-banded pattern is given in Section 1. Here we consider a more general class of pattern, which may termed *generalized block banded*, and they are defined as follows.

If the i,j entry is specified, $i \leq j$, then the k,l entry is specified whenever $i \leq k \leq l \leq j$, i.e. the i,j entry guarantees an equilateral triangle of entries, with the diagonal as base. Generally, completion problems are invariant under permutation similarity, while the strict definition of block banded is not. So, to put the notion on the same footing as chordality (which is permutation invariant), we shall hereafter refer to an undirected graph (i.e. symmetric pattern) as *generalized block banded* if there exists a numbering of the vertices so that whenever i,j is an edge, then k,l is also for $i \leq k \leq l \leq j$. Clearly, the class of generalized block banded symmetric patterns as defined above contains all generalized banded graphs (defined in Section 3), as well as all block banded patterns (up to numbering of the vertices) that are defined in Section 1.

However, there are generalized block banded patters that are not block banded for any numbering of the vertices; for example,

$$\begin{bmatrix} x & x & ? & ? & ? \\ x & x & x & x & ? \\ ? & x & x & x & ? \\ ? & x & x & x & x \\ ? & ? & ? & x & x \end{bmatrix}$$

is generalized block-banded but not block banded (even after any renumbering of the vertices).

The generalized block banded graphs are properly contained among the chordal graphs, and, as all trees are chordal, the graph

G_1 = 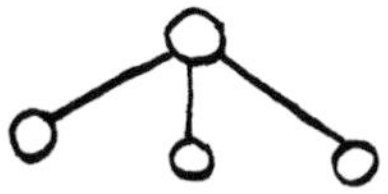

is the simplest example of a chordal graph that is not generalized block banded. The graph G_1 is often referred to as a "claw".

A key to the precise difference between chordal and generalized block banded is the strictly intermediate class of "interval graphs". An undirected graph G is called an *interval graph* if the vertices of G may be identified with a set of intervals on the real line so that an edge i,j occurs in G if and only if interval i and interval j intersect. Examples of chordal graphs that are not interval are

G_2 = 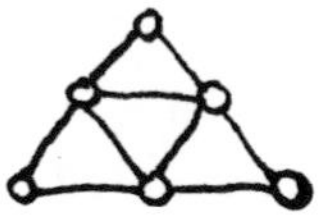

G_3 = 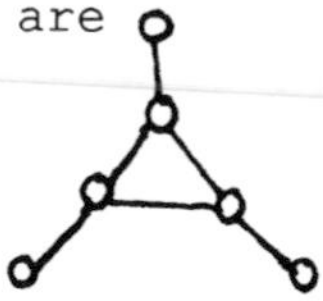

The generalized block banded graphs are interval graphs (this may be seen by using the generalized block banded ordering to construct the endpoints of the necessary intervals); in fact, the generalized block banded graphs correspond precisely to a proper subclass of the interval graphs. An interval graph is called a *proper interval graph* if it may be represented as an interval graph in such a way that no interval is contained in another. These are sometimes also called *unit interval* graphs, as, in the interval representation, each interval may be taken to have unit length. The claw G_1 is an interval graph (use three nonintersecting intervals, each of which is contained in a fourth), but it is not proper interval. It may be shown that the *generalized block banded graphs are exactly the proper interval graphs*.

Note that each of the classes of graphs we have mentioned is closed under the extraction of vertex induced subgraphs. In the matrix setting, this means that the property of having the given sort of pattern is inherited by principal submatrices. Often, such inherited graphical properties have convenient "forbidden subgraph characterizations"; i.e. a graph known to be in one class is actually in a smaller class if and only if it does not contain a vertex induced subgraph from a certain list. We have noted that the interval graphs are properly contained among the chordal graphs and that the proper interval graphs are the same as the generalized block banded graphs. In order to characterize the difference, we note forbidden subgraph characterizations of generalized block banded/proper interval relative to either chordal or interval graphs. (1) *An interval graph is proper interval if and only if it is "claw-free", i.e. contains no copy of* G_1 *as a vertex induced subgraph. (2) A chordal graph is proper interval if and only if it contains no copy of* G_1, G_2 *or* G_3 *as a vertex induced subgraph*. Unfortunately, there is no such simple way of differentiating interval from chordal, although there are several ways that require a more complicated discussion than may be given here. In any event, as G_1, G_2 and G_3 are very simple, the differences between these classes are rather large because it is easy for a chordal graph to contain a claw, for example. An interesting question which seems to be open is characterization of the class of block banded patterns (up to numbering of vertices) in terms of forbidden graphs.

Each of the classes (chordal $\subset$ interval $\subset$ generalized block banded) may be algorithmically recognized very efficiently, so that characterizations involving them are actually effective. For further reading and a variety of other facts about these classes, see either [F], [G], or [R].

Acknowledgment. We gratefully thank D. R. Shier for several helpful discussions regarding distinctions among the classes of graphs described in the appendix.

REFERENCES

[AHMR] Agler, J., Helton, J. W., McCullough S., Rodman, L.: Positive semidefinite matrices with given sparsity pattern. Submitted to Linear Algebra and Appl.

[BJOV] Barrett, W. W., Johnson, C. R., Olesky, D. D., van den Driessche, P.: Inherited matrix entries: principal submatrices of the inverse. SIAM Journal on Alg. Disc. Methods, 8(1987), 313-322.

[D] Doyle, J. C.: Synthesis of robust controllers and filters with structured plant uncertainty. Proc. IEEE Conference on Decision and Control, San Antonio, Texas, 1984.

[DG] Dym, H., Gohberg, I.: Extensions of band matrices with band inverses. Linear Algebra Appl. 36(1981), 1-24.

[DKW] Davis, C., Kahan, W. M., Weinberger, H. F.: Norm-preserving dilations and their applications to optimal error bounds. SIAM J. Numerical Anal. 19(1982), 445-469.

[EGL1] Ellis, R. L., Gohberg, I., Lay, D.: Band extensions, maximum entropy and the permanence principle. In: Maximum Entropy and Bayesian Methods in Applied Statistics, ed. J. Justice, Cambridge University Press, Cambridge, 1986.

[EGL2] Ellis, R. L., Gohberg, I., Lay, D. C.: Invertible selfadjoint extensions of band matrices and their entropy. SIAM Journal of Alg. Disc. Methods, 8(1987), 483-500.

[F] Fishburn, P. *Interval Graphs and Interval Orders*, Wiley, NY, 1985.

[G] Golumbic, M.: Algorithmic Graph Theory and Perfect Graphs. Academic Press, New York, 1980.

[GJSW] Grone, R., Johnson, C. R., de Sa', M., Wolkowicz, H.: Positive definite completions of partial Hermitian matrices. Linear Algebra Appl. 58(1984), 109-124.

[GL] George, J. A., Liu, J. W. H.: Computer solution of large sparse positive definite systems. Prentice-Hall, Englewood Cliffs, NJ, 1981.

[JB] Johnson, C. R. and Barrett, W.: Spanning Tree Extensions of the Hadamard-Fischer Inequalities, Lin. Alg. and its Applications, 66(1985), 177-193.

[JR] Johnson, C. R., Rodman, L.: Completion of Partial Matrices to Contractions. J. of Functional Analysis, 69(1986), 260-267.

[KL] Kraus, J., Larson, D. R.: Reflexivity and distance formulae. Proc. of London Math. Soc. 53(1986), 340-356.

[N] Newcombe, R. W.: Linear Multiport Synthesis, McGraw-Hill, New York, 1966.

[PP] Paulsen, V. I., Power, S. C.: Schur products and matrix completions, preprint.

[R] Roberts, F., *Applied Combinatorics*, Prentice-Hall, Englewood Cliffs, NJ, 1984.

[R1] Rose, D.: Triangulated graphs and the elimination process. J. of Math. Anal. and Appl. 32(1970), 597-609.

[R2] Rose, D.: A graph-theoretic study of the numerical solution of sparse positive definite systems of linear equations. Graph Theory and Computing, ed. R. Read, Academic Press, New York, (1973), pp. 183-217.

[SJVL] Safonov, M. G., Jonckheere, E. A., Verma, M., Limebeer, D. J. N.: Synthesis of positive real multivariable feedback systems. International J. of Control, 45(1987), 817-842.

[W] Woerdeman, H. J.: Strictly contractive and positive completions for block matrices. Rapport WS-337, Vrije Universiteit, Amsterdam, November, 1987.

[WZ] Wang, L. Y., Zames, G.: H optimization and slowly time-varying systems. Proceeding of the 26-th Conference on Decision and Control, Los Angeles, 1987, pp. 81-83.

C. R. Johnson
The College of William and Mary
Department of Mathematics
Williamsburg, Virginia 23185

L. Rodman
Arizona State University
Department of Mathematics
Tempe, Arizona 85287
Tel-Aviv University
School of Mathematical Sciences
Tel-Aviv, 69978 ISRAEL

Operator Theory:
Advances and Applications, Vol. 35

DUALITY AND UNIFORM APPROXIMATION BY SOLUTIONS OF ELLIPTIC EQUATIONS

Dmitry Khavinson*

In this paper we study the uniform approximation of continuous functions on compact subsets of $\mathbb{R}^n$ by solutions of second order elliptic equations. Also we discuss the problem of existence of a continuous best approximation and the connection of the approximation problem to some isoperimetric inequalities.

§1. Introduction.

Let $\Omega \subset \mathbb{R}^n$ be a bounded domain and $L = \sum_{i,j=1}^{n} a_{ij}(x)\frac{\partial^2}{\partial x_i \partial x_j} + \sum_{i=1}^{n} b_i(x)\frac{\partial}{\partial x_i} + h(x)$, $a_{ij}=a_{ji}$ be a second order differential operator in Ω. We assume that the operator $\mathcal{L} = \sum_{i,j=1}^{n} a_{ij}(x)\frac{\partial^2}{\partial x_i \partial x_j}$ is uniformly elliptic in Ω, i.e., there is $\mu > 0$ such that $\sum_{i,j=1}^{n} a_{ij}(x)\xi_i\xi_j \geq \mu\left[\sum_{i=1}^{n}\xi_i^2\right]$ for all $x \in \Omega$. Also, we assume that $h \leq 0$ in Ω and the coefficients a_{ij}, b_i, h are uniformly bounded in Ω and sufficiently smooth, so that L has a fundamental solution $E(x,y) \in L^1_{loc}(\Omega)$ in Ω, $L_yE(x,y)=\delta_x$ for all $x \in \Omega$ (δ denotes the Dirac mass at x). In particular, as it follows from the classical result of Malgrange and Holmgren's uniqueness theorem it sufficies to assume that all the coefficients are real-analytic in Ω (see [8], Ch. VI, VII, XI, [16], Ch. II. Also, see the discussion in [14]).

---

*This work has been supported in part by the National Science Foundation under the grant #DMS 8618755.

It is also well known, that under these assumptions, the Green function $G_{\Omega o}(x,y)$ exists for every smoothly bounded subdomain $\Omega_o \subset \Omega$ and satisfies there the standard properties (i) $G_{\Omega o}(x,y)|x-y|^{n-2}$ is bounded (in y) for each x and has a positive lower bound near x, (ii) $L_y G_{\Omega o}(x,y)=0$, $y \neq x$ (iii) $G(x,y)=0$, $x \in \Omega_o$, $y \in \partial\Omega_o$. Moveover, for any $u \in C^2(\Omega)$ the Green formula

$$u(x) = - \int_{\Omega o} G_{\Omega o}(x,y)(Lu)(y)dy + \int_{\partial\Omega o} u(y) \frac{\partial G_{\Omega o}(x,y)}{\partial n_y} dS_y \qquad (1)$$

holds for all $x \in \Omega_o$. Here, we assume $\partial\Omega_o$ to be smooth, dS_y is the Lebesgue measure on $\partial\Omega_o$ and $\frac{\partial}{\partial n_y}$ denotes the derivative in the direction of the inner normal n_y towards $\partial\Omega_o$ at y (see e.g. [16], Ch. II, §7).

Recall that if $\partial\Omega_o$ is sufficiently smooth Hopf's maximal principal holds in Ω_o.

Namely, if L is as above and $u \in C^2(\Omega)$: $Lu \geq 0$ in Ω_o, then if u attains its maximum $M \geq 0$ at an interior point of Ω_o, it follows that $u \equiv M$ in Ω_o. Furthermore, if $u(x) = M$, $x \in \partial\Omega_o$, then $\frac{\partial u}{\partial n}|_x < 0$ unless $u \equiv M$ (see [16], Ch. II).

As one of the immediate corollaries of the maximum principle, we obtain that $G_{\Omega o}(x,y) > 0$, for all $x,y \in \Omega$. Let $\mathbf{X} \subset \Omega$ be compact. In this note we study the problem of uniform approximation of continuous functions on $\mathbf{X}$ by the functions in the space $L(\mathbf{X}) \overset{def}{=}$ {uniform closure on $\mathbf{X}$ of u: $Lu=0$ in a neighborhood of $\mathbf{X}$}. More precisely, define the L-content $\lambda(\mathbf{X})$ of $\mathbf{X}$ by

$$\lambda(\mathbf{X}) = \inf_{\substack{\varphi \in C^2(\Omega) \\ L\varphi > 0 \text{ on } \mathbf{X}}} \left\{ \frac{\operatorname{dist}(\varphi, L(\mathbf{X}))_{C(\mathbf{X})}}{\min\limits_{x \in \mathbf{X}} (L\varphi)(x)} \right\}.$$

In §2 (Theorem 1), we show that $\lambda(X) = 0 \iff L(X) = C(X)$ and as a corollary we obtain that $L(X) = C(X)$ if and only if the function $f(x) \overset{def}{=} \int_X E(x,y)\,dy$ belongs to $L(X)$.

Remark, that a similar result for

$L = \frac{\partial}{\partial \bar{z}} = \frac{1}{2}\left(\frac{\partial}{\partial x} + i\frac{\partial}{\partial y}\right)$ $(n=2)$ is equivalent to the Stone-Weierstrass theorem in $\mathbb{C}$ and was first noted by S.N. Mergelyan [13]. Also, see [4], [10-12] and the discussion there. The analog of Theorem 1 for $L = \Delta \overset{def}{=} \sum_{i=1}^{n} \frac{\partial^2}{\partial x_i^2}$ was studied in [11].

In §3 we show the existence of the continuous best L-approximation to "L-sub (or super-) harmonic functions f", i.e., $Lf \geq 0$ (or $Lf \leq 0$) in smoothly bounded $X \subset \Omega$. As an illustration, using the isoperimetric inequalities related to the Schwarz symmetrization (see [1], Ch. II, [15]), we obtain in §4 the geometric estimates for the harmonic content (cf. to [11]). We note that F. Browder was probably the first to study the problem of uniform approximation by solutions of elliptic equations (of arbitrary order) systematically and obtained in [2,3], a series of fundamental results generalizing classical theorems of Runge, Walsh, Hartogs and Rosenthal, etc. The corresponding problems for the approximation in L^p-norms have been studied in [6,7,14]. The problem of existence and uniqueness of the best harmonic approximation was considered in [5]. Also see [11].

§2. Criteria for $L(X)=C(X)$.

Let $X \subset \Omega$ be a compact set.

THEOREM 1. $L(X)=C(X)$ *if and only if* $\lambda(X)=0$.

PROOF. We divide the proof into 4 lemmas. The idea of the first lemma for $L=\Delta$ goes back to A. Huber [9].

LEMMA 1. Let $\{\mathfrak{X}_\nu\}_{\nu=1}^{\infty}$ *be a decreasing sequence of smoothly bounded finitely connected compact sets, such that* $\bigcap_{\nu=1}^{\infty} \mathfrak{X}_\nu = \mathfrak{X}$. *Let* $G_\nu^i(x,y) = G_{\mathfrak{X}_\nu}^i(x,y)$ *denote the Green function of the* i^{th} *connected component* $\mathfrak{X}_\nu^i$ *of* $\mathfrak{X}_\nu$, $i=1,\dots k_\nu$, $\nu=1\dots$. *Define*

$$C_\nu = \max_{1 \le i \le k_\nu} \max_{x \in \mathfrak{X}_\nu^i} \int_{\mathfrak{X}_\nu^i} G_\nu^i(x,y)dy.$$

Then, $\lim_{\nu\to\infty} C_\nu = 0$ *implies that* $L(\mathfrak{X}) = C(\mathfrak{X})$.

Proof of Lemma 1. Let $\mu \perp L(\mathfrak{X})$. Then, the potential

$$U^\mu(x) \stackrel{def}{=} -\int_{\mathfrak{X}} E(x,y)d\mu(y)$$

is defined a.e, as $E \in L^1_{loc}$ and vanishes outside of $\mathfrak{X}$.

ASSERTION. $\int_{\mathfrak{X}} |U^\mu(x)|dx \le C_\nu \|\mu\|$.

Assume without loss of generality that $\mathfrak{X}_\nu$ is connected. Let $\mathfrak{X}_o \stackrel{def}{=} \{x \in \mathfrak{X},\ U^\mu$ is not defined$\}$. Vol $(\mathfrak{X}_o)=0$. It is easily seen, e.g. from (1), that for all $x \in \mathfrak{X}_\nu$ $G_\nu(x,y) = -E(x,y)+h^x(y)$, $L_y h^x = 0$ in $\mathfrak{X}_\nu$. Take $x \in \mathfrak{X}_\nu \setminus \mathfrak{X}_o$. Then, since $\mu \perp L(\mathfrak{X})$

$$\int_{\mathfrak{X}_\nu} G_\nu(x,y)d\mu(y) = -\int_{\mathfrak{X}_\nu} E(x,y)d\mu(y) + \int_{\mathfrak{X}_\nu} h^x(y)d\mu(y) = U^\mu(x).$$

Hence, applying Fubini's theorem we obtain ($G_\nu > 0$ in $\mathfrak{X}$)

$$\int_{\mathfrak{X}_\nu} |U^\mu(x)|dx = \int_{\mathfrak{X}_\nu} \left| \int_{\mathfrak{X}_\nu} G_\nu(x,y)d\mu(y) \right| dx \le \int_{\mathfrak{X}_\nu} \left\{ \int_{\mathfrak{X}_\nu} G_\nu(x,y)dx \right\} |d\mu(y)|$$

$$\le C_\nu \|\mu\|.$$

This proves the assertion. If $C_\nu \downarrow 0$, $U^\mu \equiv 0$. So, $\mu = L(U^\mu) \equiv 0$ in the distribution sence, and hence, $\mu \equiv 0$.

LEMMA 2. Let $\Omega_o \subset \Omega$ *be smoothly bounded, so that the Dirichlet problem for* L *is solvable in* Ω_o *and (1) holds. Fix* $x_o \in \Omega_o$. *Extend* $G_{\Omega o}(x_o,y) = G(x_o,y)$ *to* $\mathbb{R}^n$ *by setting it equal to* 0 *in* $\mathbb{R}^n\backslash\bar{\Omega}_o$. *Then,*

$$L_y\ G(x_o,y) = -\delta_{x_o} + \frac{\partial G(x_o,y)}{\partial n_y}\ dS_y|_{\partial\Omega_o}$$

in the distribution sense.

PROOF OF LEMMA 2. It is obvious that $L_yG(x_o,y) = -\delta_{xo}$ in Ω_o and vanishes in $\mathbb{R}^n\backslash\bar{\Omega}o$. So, $L_yG(x_o,y) = -\delta_{xo} + T$, where T is a distribution supported on Ω_o. Then from (1) it follows that for any $\varphi \in C^2(\Omega)$: $L\varphi=0$ in Ω_o,

$$\langle T,\varphi\rangle = \int_{\partial\Omega_o} \varphi(y)\ \frac{\partial G(x_o,y)}{\partial n_y}\ dS_y$$

Since, the Dirichlet problem is solvable on $\partial\Omega_o$, this implies the lemma.

LEMMA 3. Let $\varphi \in C^2(\Omega)$ *and let* $m=\min\limits_{x\in\mathbf{X}}(L\varphi)(x) > 0$. *Then,* $\lim\limits_{\nu\to\infty} C_\nu \le \frac{2}{m}\ \mathrm{dist}(\varphi,L(\mathbf{X}))_{C(\mathbf{X})}$, *where* C_ν *are the same as in Lemma 1.*

PROOF OF LEMMA 3. Let $f \in C^2(\Omega)$: $Lf=0$ in a neighborhood of $\mathbf{X}$. Because of continuity of φ,f we can find $\nu_o : \nu > \nu_o$, $Lf = 0$ in $\mathbf{X}_\nu$, $\min\limits_{x\in\mathbf{X}_\nu}(L\varphi)(x) > m-\varepsilon$, $\|\varphi-f\|_{\mathbf{X}_\nu} \le \|\varphi-f\|_{\mathbf{X}} + \varepsilon$. Let φ_ν denote the solution of the Dirichlet problem in $\mathbf{X}_\nu$ equal to φ on $\partial\mathbf{X}_\nu$. According to Hopf's maximal principal

$$\|\varphi_\nu-f\|_{\mathbf{X}_\nu} \le \|\varphi_\nu-f\|_{\partial\mathbf{X}_\nu} \le \|\varphi-f\|_{\mathbf{X}} + \varepsilon,\ \nu > \nu_o. \tag{2}$$

Fix $x \in \mathbf{X}_\nu$. From (1), Lemma 2, (2) we have, for $\nu > \nu_o$:

$$\int_{\mathbf{X}_\nu} G_\nu(x,y)dy \leq \frac{1}{m-\varepsilon} < L_y\varphi, \ G_\nu(x,y) > \ = \frac{1}{m-\varepsilon} <\varphi, \ L_yG_\nu(x,y)>$$

$$= \frac{1}{m-\varepsilon} \ \{-\varphi(x) \ + \ \int_{\partial \mathbf{X}_\nu} \varphi(y) \ \frac{\partial G_\nu(x,y)}{\partial n_y} \ dS_y\} \ =$$

$$= \frac{1}{m-\varepsilon} \ \{-\varphi(x) \ + \ \varphi_\nu(x)\} \leq \frac{1}{m-\varepsilon} \ \{|f(x)-\varphi(x)| \ + \ |\varphi_\nu(x)-f(x)|\}$$

$$\leq \frac{2}{m-\varepsilon} \ (\|\varphi-f\|_{C(\mathbf{X})} \ + \ \varepsilon). \tag{3}$$

Hence, for all $\nu > \nu_0$ $C_\nu \leq 2/m-\varepsilon$ $(\|\varphi-f\| + \varepsilon)$. Letting ε tend to zero and taking the infimum over $f \in L(\mathbf{X})$, we complete the proof.

Now in view of Lemma 1, the Theorem follows from the following assertion.

Lemma 4. $\lambda(\mathbf{X}) = 0 \Rightarrow \lim_{\nu \to \infty} C_\nu = 0$ *for any sequence* $\{\mathbf{X}_\nu\}$ *converging to* $\mathbf{X}$.

This last assertion follows immediately from Lemma 3.

Corollary 1. The following are equivalent,
(i) $L(\mathbf{X}) = C(\mathbf{X})$; (ii) $C_\nu \downarrow 0$ *for any sequence* $\{\mathbf{X}_\nu\}$, $\mathbf{X}_\nu \downarrow \mathbf{X}$; (iii) *the function* $f \in C(\mathbf{X})$ *defined by* $f(x) = \int_{\mathbf{X}} E(x,y) \ dy$ *belongs to* $L(\mathbf{X})$.

Proof. (i) $\Rightarrow$ (iii) is obvious. (ii) $\Rightarrow$ (i) follows from Lemma 1. (iii) $\Rightarrow$ (ii). Let $\Omega_0 \subset \Omega : \Omega_0 \supset \mathbf{X}$. It is easy to see, as $E \in L^1_{loc}$, that $g(x) = \int_{\Omega_0 \setminus \mathbf{X}} E(x,y)dy \in L(\mathbf{X})$. Hence, $(g+f) \in L(\mathbf{X})$. But $L(g+f) \equiv 1$ in Ω_0, so $\lambda(\mathbf{X})=0$ and (ii) follows from Lemma 4.

Corollary 2. (The "Hartogs-Rosenthal Theorem" - cf. to [2], [3], [4], [11]). If $Vol(\mathbf{X}) = 0$, *then* $L(\mathbf{X})=C(\mathbf{X})$.

The following example illustrates the geometric meaning of condition (ii) in Corollary 1. Let $n=1$, $L=\frac{d^2}{dx^2}$. Then $E(x)=\begin{cases} 0; & x \leq 0 \\ x; & x > 0 \end{cases}$. Let $\mathbf{X} \subset \mathbb{R}$ be compact and let

$X_\nu = \overset{n}{\underset{i=1}{\bigcup}} (a_i^\nu, b_i^\nu)$ be a disjoint union of open intervals covering

X. For each i, the Green function $G_\nu^i(x,y)$ for (a_i^ν, b_i^ν)
is readily computable and

$$G_\nu^i(x,y) = \begin{cases} \dfrac{b_\nu^i - x}{b_\nu^i - a_\nu^i} (y - a_\nu^i), & a_\nu^i \le y \le x \\[2ex] \dfrac{b_\nu^i - x}{b_\nu^i - a_\nu^i} (y - a_\nu^i) - (y - x), & x < y \le b_\nu^i. \end{cases}$$

Then, $\displaystyle\int_{a_\nu^i}^{b_\nu^i} G_\nu^i(x,y)dy = \tfrac{1}{2}(b_\nu^i - x)(x - a_\nu^i)$ attains its maximum as

$x = (a_\nu^i + b_\nu^i)/2$, and, therefore $C_\nu = 1/8 \displaystyle\max_{1 \le i \le n} (b_\nu^i - a_\nu^i)^2$.

Thus, in accordance with Corollary 1 we obtain that functions
linear over X are dense in $C(X)$ if any only if
$\displaystyle\max_{1 \le i \le n}$ length $\{(a_\nu^i, b_\nu^i)\} \to 0$ as $\nu \to \infty$, i.e., X is nowhere

dense. Of course, it is not hard to prove this directly.

§3. Existence of the Best Approximation.

Even for $L = \Delta$ and X being a nicely bounded Jordan
domain the best harmonic approximation to a continuous function
f need not to be continuous ([5], Ex. 4.3). However, if f is
L-sub (super-) harmonic, i.e., $Lf \ge 0$ (or $Lf \le 0$), as the
following theorem shows, the best L-approximation to f is
continuous and, in fact, is easily computable.

We keep the same notation as in §2. Let $X \subset \Omega$ be
a smoothly bounded finitely connected set, so that the
Dirichlet problem for L is soluable on X. Denote by $\tilde{u}$
the solution of the following Dirichlet problem $L\tilde{u} = 0$ in $\overset{o}{X}$,
$\tilde{u} \equiv 1$ on ∂X, i.e. (see (1))

$$\tilde{u}(x) = \int_{\partial X} \frac{\partial G_X(x,y)}{\partial n_y} dS_y.$$

As follows immediately from the maximum principle $0 < \tilde{u} \leq 1$ in Σ and $\tilde{u}(x) < 1$, $x \in \mathring{\Sigma}$ unless $h \equiv 0$. For $f \in C^2(\Omega)$, $\Lambda_f = \Lambda_f(\Sigma) \overset{\text{def}}{=} \text{dist}(f, L(\Sigma))_{C(\Sigma)}$, and u_f denotes the solution of the Dirichlet problem with the boundary data equal to f, i.e. $Lu_f = 0$ in Σ and $u_f = f$ on $\partial\Sigma$.

Theorem 2. Let $Lf \geq 0$ (or $Lf \leq 0$) in Σ. *Then,* $\Lambda_f = \|\frac{u_f - f}{1+\tilde{u}}\| \overset{\text{def}}{=} \sup_{x\in\Sigma} \frac{|u_f(x) - f(x)|}{1+\tilde{u}(x)}$. *Moveover, the function* $u^* = u_f - \Lambda_f\tilde{u}$ *is the best L-approximation to* f, *i.e.* $\|f - u^*\| = \Lambda_f$.

Proof. We shall conduct the argument for $Lf \geq 0$. Observe, that according to the Hahn-Banach distance formula

$$\Lambda_f(\Sigma) = \sup_{\substack{\mu \perp L(\Sigma)\\ \|\mu\|=1}} \left|\int_\Sigma f d\mu\right|.$$

Fix $x_o \in \mathring{X}$. Define the measure

$\mu^* = \frac{1}{1+\tilde{u}(x_o)} \left(\delta_{xo} - \frac{\partial G_\Sigma(x,y)}{\partial n_y} dS_y|_{\partial\Sigma}\right)$. Then, according to Lemma 2, $\mu^* \perp L(\Sigma)$ and $\|\mu^*\| = 1$. Thus,

$$\Lambda_f(\Sigma) \geq \left|\int_\Sigma f\, d\mu^*\right| = \left|\int_\Sigma (u_f - f) d\mu^*\right| = \frac{u_f(x_o) - f(x_o)}{1 + \tilde{u}(x_o)}. \tag{4}$$

Since (4) holds for all $x_o \in \mathring{\Sigma}$, it follows that $\Lambda_f(\Sigma) \geq \|\frac{u_f - f}{1+\tilde{u}}\|$. Set $a = \|\frac{u_f - f}{1+\tilde{u}}\|$. Let $u^* = u_f - a\tilde{u}$. Then, for each $x \in \Sigma$ in view of the definition of $\tilde{u}$ and since the maximum principle implies $u_f - f \geq 0$ in Σ, we have

$$|u^*(x) - f(x)| = \begin{cases} u_f(x) - f(x) - a\tilde{u}(x), & \text{if } u^*(x) \geq f(x) \\ a\tilde{u}(x) - (u_f(x) - f(x)), & \text{if } u^*(x) < f(x) \end{cases} \leq$$

$$\leq \begin{cases} a \\ a\tilde{u}(x) \end{cases} \leq a.$$

The Theorem is proved.

    Remark. One can adopt the argument in [5] by making use of the Runge type theorem due to F. Browder [2,3] and show that under the assumption of Theorem 2, u^* is the unique best L-approximation to f. We shall omit the proof.

    If $h = 0$, then $\tilde{u} = 1$ and $a = \frac{1}{2}\|u_f - f\|_{C(\mathfrak{X})}$. Therefore, we obtain the following corollary (cf. to [5], [11]).

    Corollary 3. If $L = \sum\limits_{i,j=1}^{n} a_{ij}(x)\frac{\partial^2}{\partial x_i \partial x_j} + \sum\limits_{i=1}^{n} b_i(x)\frac{\partial}{\partial x_i}$ and f is L-sub (or super-) harmonic, i.e., $Lf \geq 0$ (or $Lf \leq 0$) in $\overset{\circ}{\mathfrak{X}}$, then $\Lambda_f = \frac{1}{2}\|u_f - f\|_{\mathfrak{X}}$ and $u^* = u_f - \frac{1}{2}\|u_f - f\|$.

    §4.   Harmonic content and the isoperimetric inequality.

    Let $L = \Delta = \sum\limits_{i=1}^{n} \frac{\partial^2}{\partial x_i^2}$. For a compact set $\mathfrak{X} \subset \mathbb{R}^n$ we call the quantity $\Lambda(\mathfrak{X}) \overset{def}{=} \text{dist}\ (|x|^2, H(\mathfrak{X}))_{C(\mathfrak{X})}$ a harmonic content of $\mathfrak{X}$ (see [11]).

    (Here, $H(\mathfrak{X})(=L(\mathfrak{X}))$ is the uniform closure of functions harmonic in a neighborhood of $\mathfrak{X}$. $|x|^2 = \sum\limits_{1}^{n} x_i^2$.) Theorem 1 implies that $\Lambda(\mathfrak{X}) = 0 \iff H(\mathfrak{X}) = C(\mathfrak{X})$. Let $R_{\mathfrak{X}}$ be the volume radius of $\mathfrak{X}$, i.e. the radius of the ball B: $\text{Vol}(B) = \text{Vol}(\mathfrak{X})$. For smoothly bounded $\mathfrak{X}$, the Green Function $G(x,y)$ can be written as

$$G(x,y) = \begin{cases} \frac{1}{2\pi}\log\frac{R_y}{|x-y|} + h(x,y), & n=2 \\ \frac{1}{n(n-2)\omega_n}[|x-y|^{2-n} - R_y^{2-n}] + h(x,y), & n > 2 \end{cases}$$

where $h(y,y)=0$ and is harmonic in $\overset{\circ}{\mathfrak{X}}$, (here ω_n is the surface area of the unit sphere S^{n-1} in $\mathbb{R}^n$). The constant R_y is called the harmonic radius of $\mathfrak{X}$ at y as $n > 2$ and the conformal radius of $\mathfrak{X}$ at y as $n = 2$ (see [1], [15]).

Set $\tilde{R}_{\Sigma} = \sup_{y\in\Sigma} R_y$. For arbitrary Σ, we define $R_{\Sigma} = \lim_{\nu\to\infty} \tilde{R}_{\Sigma_\nu}$ $\{\Sigma_\nu\} \downarrow \Sigma$, Σ_ν are smoothly bounded.

Theorem 3. $\frac{1}{2}\tilde{R}_{\Sigma}^2 \le \Lambda(\Sigma) \le \frac{1}{2}R_{\Sigma}^2$ (5)

If we assume that Σ *is irreducible for* $H(\Sigma)$, *i.e.* Σ = *closure* $\{\bigcup \mathrm{supp}\,\mu : \mu \perp H(\Sigma)\}$ *then equality in either side in (5) occurs if and only if* Σ *is a ball.*

Proof. Since the proof of both inequalities is essentially the same we shall sketch the argument for the first inequality. (A proof of the second inequality based on a result of L. Payne can be found in [11]). Without loss of generality we can assume that Σ has a smooth boundary. According to Corollary 3, $\Lambda(\Sigma) = \frac{1}{2}\|u_o - |x|^2\|_{\Sigma}$, where u_o is the best harmonic majorant of $|x|^2$ in Σ. We have (see (3) and Lemma 2):

$$\Lambda(\Sigma) = \tfrac{1}{2}\|u_o - |x|^2\| = \tfrac{1}{2}\sup_{x\in\Sigma}(u_o(x) - |x|^2) =$$

$$\tfrac{1}{2}\sup_{x\in\Sigma}(-\langle |y|^2, \delta_x\rangle + \langle |y|^2, \frac{\partial G(x,y)}{\partial n_y}\Big|_{\partial\Sigma}\rangle) =$$

$$= \tfrac{1}{2}\sup_{x\in\Sigma}\langle |y|^2, \Delta_y G(x,y)\rangle = \tfrac{1}{2}\sup_{x\in\Sigma}\langle \Delta(|y|^2), G(x,y)\rangle =$$

$$= \tfrac{1}{2}\sup_{x\in\Sigma} 2n\,\{\int_{\Sigma} G(x,y)dy\} = nC_{\Sigma}. \tag{6}$$

Let $B_y = \{x: |x| < R_y(\Sigma)\}$. Then, (see [1], pp. 60-70)

$$\int_{B_y} G_{B_y}(x,o)dx \le \int_{\Sigma} G_{\Sigma}(x,y)dx. \tag{7}$$

Since

$$G_{B_y}(x,0) = \begin{cases} \frac{1}{2\pi}\log\frac{R_y}{|x|}, & n=2 \\ \frac{1}{n(n-2)\omega_n}\{|x|^{2-n} - R_y^{2-n}\}, & n > 2, \end{cases}$$

a direct calculation reveals, e.g. for n > 2, (cf. [1], p. 61):

$$C_{\Sigma} \overset{\text{def}}{=} \sup_{y\in\Sigma} \int_{\Sigma} G(x,y)dx \geq \sup_{y\in\Sigma} \int_{B_y} G_{B_y}(x,0)dx =$$

$$= \sup_{y\in\Sigma} \frac{R_y{}^2}{(n-2)^2} B\left(2, \frac{2}{n-2}\right) = \frac{\tilde{R}_{\Sigma}^2}{(n-2)^2} \frac{(n-2)^2}{2n} = \frac{\tilde{R}_{\Sigma}^2}{2n}.$$

(Here, $B(m,n) \overset{\text{def}}{=} \int_0^1 t^{m-1}(1-t)^{n-1}dt$ is the Euler beta function). Thus, (6) implies that $\Lambda(\Sigma) \geq \frac{\tilde{R}_{\Sigma}{}^2}{2}$. The case $n=2$ is even easier and left to the reader. The last statement concerning the equalities in (5) follows from the corresponding result concerning the equality in (7) (see [1], p. 61). The Theorem is proved.

Remark. The isoperimetric inequality $\tilde{R}_{\Sigma} \leq R_{\Sigma}$ which follows from (5) is known, It is sharp, since it becomes equality for the balls. We refer the reader to [1], [15] and the literature cited there, for more detail.

REFERENCES

[1] C. Bandle, Isoperimetric Inequalities and Applications, London, Pitman, 1980.

[2] F. Browder, Functional analysis and partial differential equations II, Math. Ann., Vol. 145(1961), 81-226.

[3] __________, Approximation by solutions of partial differential equations, Amer. J. Math., Vol. 84(1962), 134-160.

[4] T. Gamelin and D. Khavinson, The isoperimetric inequality and rational approximation, Amer. Math. Monthly, to appear.

[5] W. Hayman, D. Kershaw and T. Lyons, The best harmonic approximant to a continuous function, "Anniversary Volume on Approximation Theory and Functional Analysis", ed. by P.L. Butzer, R.L. Stens and B. Sz.-Nagy, ISNM, Vol. 65, Birkhäuser, 1984, 317-327.

[6] L.I. Hedberg, Approximation in the mean by the analytic functions, Trans. Amer. Math. Soc., Vol. 163(1972), 157-171.

[7] ____________, Approximation in the mean by solutions of elliptic equations, Duke. Math. J., 40(1973), 9-16.

[8] L. Hörmander, The Analysis of Linear Partial Differential Operators, Volumes I, II, III and IV, Springer-Verlag, A Series of Comprehensive Studies in Mathematics, Berlin-Heidelberg-New York-Tokyo, 1983.

[9] A Huber, Über Potentiale welche auf vorgegebenen Mengen verschwinden, Comment. Math. Helv. 43(1968), 41-50.

[10] D. Khavinson, Symmetry and uniform approximation by analytic functions, Proc. Amer. Math. Soc., to appear.

[11] ____________, On uniform approximation by harmonic functions, Mich. Math. J., to appear.

[12] ____________ and D. Luecking, On an extremal problem in the theory of rational approximation, J. Approx. Theory, Vol. 50, No. 2(1987), 127-132.

[13] S.N. Mergelyan, Uniform approximation of functions of a complex variable, Uspehi Mat. Nauk VII(2) (48), 1952, 31-122, (in Russian).

[14] J. Polking, Approximation in L^p by solutions of elliptic partial differential equations, Amer. J. Math., 94(1972) 1231-1244.

[15] G. Polya and G. Szegö, Isoperimetric Inequalities in Mathematical Physics, Ann. Math. Studies No. 27, Princeton University Press, Princeton, N.J. 1951.

[16] M. Protter and H. Weinberger, Maximum Principle in Differential Equations, Springer-Verlag, New York-Berlin Heidelberg-Tokyo, 2nd printing, 1984.

Department of Mathematics
University of Arkansas
Fayetteville, Arkansas 72701

Operator Theory:
Advances and Applications, Vol. 35

2 - CHORDAL GRAPHS

Scott McCullough

Let P be an undirected graph with vertices V and edges E. Fix an enumeration, $\{v_1, v_2, \ldots, v_n\}$, of V and let $M(P) = \{A \in M_n(\mathbb{C}) \mid \langle Ae_i, e_j\rangle = 0 \text{ if } (v_i, v_j) \notin E\}$, where e_i is the standard orthonormal basis of $\mathbb{C}^n$. $M_n(\mathbb{C})^+$ is the set of positive semi-definite $n \times n$ matrices with complex entries. For $X \subseteq M_n(\mathbb{C})^+$ a cone, define the order of X, denoted $\operatorname{ord}(X)$, to be the smallest integer k such that the elements of X of rank at most k generate X as a cone. For any set X, let $M_m(X)$ denote $m \times m$ matrices with entries from X. It is known that a graph P is chordal if and only if $\operatorname{ord}(M_m(M(P))^+) = 1$ for every positive integer m, where $M_m(M(P))^+ = \{A \in M_m(M(P)) \mid A \text{ is positive semi-definite}\}$. We characterize, in a graph theoretic way, graphs P for which $\operatorname{ord}(M_m(M(P))^+) = \operatorname{ord}(M(P)^+) \leq 2$ for every positive integer m.

INTRODUCTION

A graph P consists of a finite set $V(P)$ and a subset $E(P)$ of $V(P) \times V(P)$. $V(P)$ is the set of vertices of P. Elements of $E(P)$ are known as edges of P. Since, in the sequel, only undirected graphs will be considered, we assume that $E(P)$ is symmetric and contains the diagonal. That is, for $v, w \in V(P)$, $(v,w) \in E(P)$ if and only if $(w,v) \in E(P)$. Also, $(v,v) \in E(P)$ for each $v \in V(P)$. Given an (undirected) graph

P fix an enumeration of the vertices of P, $V(P) = \{v_1, v_2, \ldots, v_n\}$, and define $M(P)$, a subspace of the $n \times n$ matrices with complex entries by

$$M(P) = \{A \in M_n(\mathbb{C}) \mid \langle Ae_i, e_j\rangle = 0 \text{ if } (v_i, v_j) \notin E(P)\},$$

where e_i is the standard orthonormal basis for $\mathbb{C}^n$. In [AHMR], the cone $M^+(P) = \{A \in M(P) \mid A$ is a positive semi-definite matrix$\}$ is studied. In particular, the order of P, denoted $\mathrm{ord}(P)$, which is the smallest k such that $M^+(P)$ is the convex hull of its elements of rank at most k is introduced and computed for many different classes of graphs.

A central example is the class of chordal graphs. Given a graph P and $W \subseteq V(P)$, define P_W to be the graph with vertices W and edges $(w, w') \in E(P_W)$ if and only if $w, w' \in W$ and $(w, w') \in E(P)$. Q, a graph, is said to be a subgraph of P if $Q = P_W$ for some $W \subseteq V(P)$. The n-loop, denoted nLP, is the graph on n vertices $\{v_1, v_2, \ldots, v_n\}$ with $(v_i, v_j) \in E(P)$ if and only if $|i - j| \le 1$ modulo n. P is chordal if no n-loop, for $n > 3$, is a subgraph of P. For v a vertex of P, define the adjacency set of v in P, denoted $\mathrm{adj}(v;P)$, by $\mathrm{adj}(v;P) = \{w \in V(P) \mid (v,w) \in E(P)\}$. A subset W of $V(P)$ is a clique if $w, w' \in W$ implies $(w, w') \in E(P)$. An ordering, $v_1, v_2, \ldots, v_n$ of the vertices of P is a perfect elimination ordering if $\mathrm{adj}\left(v_i; P_{V(P)\setminus \bigcup_{j=1}^{i-1} v_j}\right)$ is a clique for each i.

THEOREM A. *For a graph* P, *the following are equivalent.*

i) P *has a perfect elimination ordering.*

ii) P *is chordal*

iii) $\mathrm{ord}(P) = 1$.

Theorem A is rooted in the work of Rose, [R], Grone-Johnson-Sá-Wolkowitz, [GJSW], and others. In this form, it is simultaneously due to Paulsen-Powers-Smith [PPS] and [AHMR]. The equivalence of *i*) and *ii*) is a standard fact in graph theory (see [G] p. 180). The equivalence of *i*) and *iii*) is due to [PPS] and the equivalence of *ii*) and *iii*) is due to [AHMR].

The purpose of this paper is to generalize Theorem A to graphs P for which $\mathrm{ord}(P) = 2$. Given a graph P and a positive integer m define $P^{(m)}$ to be the graph on vertices $\{v_1^1, v_1^2, \ldots, v_1^m, v_2^1, \ldots, v_n^m\}$ with edges $(v_i^k, v_j^\ell) \in E(P^{(m)})$ if and only if $(v_i, v_j) \in E(P)$. If P is chordal, then $P^{(m)}$ is chordal for every m. Hence, $\mathrm{ord}(P^{(m)}) = \mathrm{ord}(P) = 1$ for each m. Thus, a natural generalization of the class of chordal graphs is the class of graphs P for which $\mathrm{ord}(P) = \mathrm{ord}(P^{(m)}) = 2$ for each m. In section two, a (finite, given the number of vertices of P) list of graphs L is given. P is said to be 2-chordal if ℓ is not a subgraph of P for each $\ell \in L$. Also in section two, a graph is said to be 2-decomposable if there exists an ordering of the vertices of P which satisfies a condition analogous to a perfect elimination order. In section three, we prove:

THEOREM B (THEOREM 3.1). *For a graph* P, *the following are equivalent.*

i) P *is 2-decomposable.*

ii) $\mathrm{ord}(P) = \mathrm{ord}(P^{(m)}) \leq 2$ *for every* $m > 0$.

iii) P *is 2-chordal.*

Theorem B may be though of as a first step in reconciling the work of Paulsen, Powers, and Smith, [PPS], with that of Agler, Helton, McCullough, and Rodman [AHMR]. In particular, the proof of Theorem B expands upon ideas and results from [PPS] and [AHMR]. A key technique is the use of the

Cholesky decomposition to divide the graph into simpler subgraphs for which Theorem B can be verified using results from [AHRM]. This use of the Cholesky decomposition in a graph theoretic context was initiated in [PPS] to give a simple proof of the equivalence of *i*) and *iii*) in Theorem A. In a similar direction, Helton, Pierce, and Rodman [HPR] have systematically applied the Cholesky decomposition to the order problem and divised a general "divide and conquer" technique which they then use to obtain results on the orders of certain classes of graphs.

In section four, the connection between [PPS] and [AHMR] is made explicit. Let P be a graph with vertices $V(P) = \{v_1, v_2, \ldots, v_n\}$. Given $T_{ij} \in M_m(\mathbb{C})$ for each $(v_i, v_j) \in E(P)$, define $\phi_T : M(P) \longrightarrow M(P^{(m)})$ by $\phi_T(a_{ij}) = (a_{ij}T_{ij})$. ϕ_T is called an inflated Schur product map. Graphs P for which every inflated Schur product map $\phi_T : M(P) \longrightarrow M(P^{(m)})$ that is positive is automatically completely positive are characterized in [PPS] (see Theorem 4.6) by a certain condition on the positive cone of $M(P^{(m)})$. In section four, these graphs which also have order two are characterized in a graph theoretic way.

§1 PRELIMINARIES

Denote, by $M_n(\mathbb{C})$, the vector space of $n \times n$ matrices with complex entries. For M, a subspace of $M_n(\mathbb{C})$, define M^+ to be the cone of positive elements in M. That is, $M^+ = \{A \in M \mid A \text{ is a positive semi-definite matrix}\}$. Given P a graph with $V(P) = \{v_1, v_2, \ldots, v_n\}$, a function $Y : \{1,2,\ldots,n\} \longrightarrow \mathbb{C}^k$ is said to be a k dimensional representation of P if $\langle Y_i, Y_j \rangle = 0$ for $(v_i, v_j) \notin E(P)$. If Y_i is a k dimensional representation of P, then the matrix $(\langle Y_i, Y_j \rangle)_{i,j=1}^n$ is in $M^+(P)$. Conversely, if $A \in M^+(P)$ is of rank k, then there exists a k-dimensional representation

$Y_i \in \mathbb{C}^k$ of P such that $A = (\langle Y_i, Y_j\rangle)_{i,j=1}^n$. For vectors $x, y \in \mathbb{C}^k$, note that $xy^* \in M_k(\mathbb{C})$ is a rank-one matrix. Given $Y_i \in \mathbb{C}^k$, a represenation of P, define $\mathcal{F}_P(Y)$ to be the linear span of $\{Y_i Y_j^* \mid (v_i, v_j) \notin E(P)\}$. $\mathcal{F}_P(Y)$ is known as the frame space of Y. Given a cone X in a vector space V, an element $x \in X$ is said to be irreducible in X if whenever $x = x_1 + x_2$, where $x_1, x_2 \in X$, it follows that x_i are non-negative scalar multiples of x. The following theorem, which is known as the Frame Theorem, is from [AHMR].

THEOREM 1.1 (THEOREM 3.1 [AHMR]). *Let* P *be a graph on* n *vertices. Suppose* $Y_i \in \mathbb{C}^k$ *is a k-dimensioned representation of* P. *Then* $A = (\langle Y_i, Y_j\rangle)_{i,j=1}^n$ *is irreducible in* $M^+(P)$ *if and only if the dimension of* $\mathcal{F}_P(Y)$ *is* $k^2 - 1$.

For $\mathcal{A}$, a C*-algebra, and $X \subseteq \mathcal{A}$, $M_n(X)$ denotes the $n \times n$ matrices with entries from X. If $A \in M_n(X)$, A_{ij} denotes the (i,j) entry of A. Given P, a graph (see the introduction for a definition), with vertices $\{v_1, v_2, \ldots, v_n\}$ and edges $E(P)$, define $M(P) = \{A \in M_n(\mathbb{C}) \mid A_{ij} = 0$ if $(v_i, v_j) \notin E(P)\}$. $M_m(M(P))$ may be cononically identified with $M(P^{(m)})$. Given $\mathcal{A}, \mathcal{B}$ C*-algebras and $X \subseteq \mathcal{A}$, $Y \subseteq \mathcal{B}$, define $X \otimes Y = \left\{ \sum_{i=1}^k x_i \otimes y_i \,\middle|\, x_i \in X,\ y_i \in Y \right\}$. $M_m(M(P))$ may also be canonically identified with $M_m(\mathbb{C}) \otimes M(P)$ in the usual way. That is, for $X = (\bar{x}_i y_j) \in M_m(\mathbb{C})$ and $Z \in M(P)$ define $\Psi(X \otimes Z) = (\bar{x}_i Z y_j)_{i,j=1}^m$ and extend Ψ to all of $M_m(\mathbb{C}) \otimes M(P)$ by linearity. In the sequel, the above identifications will be used frequently with no further mention.

The graph L_4 , with $V(L_4) = \{v_1, v_2, v_3, v_4\}$ and $(v_i, v_j) \in E(L_4)$ if and only if $|i - j| \leq 1$ modulo four, is called the four loop.

Using the Frame Theorem, we establish,

PROPOSITION 1.2. Ord $(L_4^{(m)}) = 2$ *for every* $m \geq 1$.

Proof. Fix $m \geq 1$. Label the vertices of $L_4^{(m)}$ by $V(L_4^{(m)}) = \{v_1^1, v_1^2, \ldots, v_1^m, v_2^1, \ldots, v_4^m\}$. Suppose $Y_{i,k} \in \mathbb{C}^p$ for $i = 1, \ldots, 4$; $k = 1, 2, \ldots, m$, is a representation of $L_4^{(m)}$. Further, suppose

$$A =: ((\langle Y_{i,k}, Y_{j,l}\rangle)_{k,l=1}^m)_{i,j=1}^4 \in M^+(L_4^{(m)}) ,$$

is irreducible in $M^+(L_4^{(m)})$. For each i , let p_i be the dimension of the linear span of $\{Y_{ik} | k = 1, 2, \ldots, m\} \subseteq \mathbb{C}^p$. $\mathcal{F}_p(Y)$ is spanned by the set of matrices $\{Y_{ik}Y_{jl}^* | (i,j) \in \{(1,2), (2,1), (3,4), (4,3)\}\}$. Hence, the dimension of $\mathcal{F}_p(Y)$ is at most $2(p_1p_2 + p_3p_4)$. From here it is easy to see that if either $p_1 + p_2$, or $p_3 + p_4$ is strictly less than p , then the dimension of $\mathcal{F}_p(Y)$ is less than $p^2 - 1$, in which case by Theorem 1.1, A is not irreducible. Thus, we may assume that $p_1 + p_2 = p_3 + p_4 = p$. Arrange the vertices of $L_4^{(m)}$ such that for each i , the vectors $Y_{i1}, \ldots, Y_{ip_i}$ are a linearly independent set. Define Q to be the subgraph of $L_4^{(m)}$ on the vertices $\{v_{il} | i = 1, \ldots, 4, l = 1, \ldots, p_i\} = V(Q)$ and $(v_{il}, v_{jk}) \in E(Q)$ if and only if $(V_{il}, V_{jk}) \in E(L_4^{(m)})$. View A as an element of $M^+(Q)$. In this way,

$$A = \left[\begin{array}{cc|c} B_1 & 0 & \\ 0 & B_2 & C \\ \hline & & B_3 \quad 0 \\ C^* & & 0 \quad B_4 \end{array}\right]$$

where $B_i \in M_{p_i}(\mathbb{C})$, $C \in M_p(\mathbb{C})$. A is irreducible as an element of $M^+(Q)$ if an only if A is irreducible as an element of $M^+(L_4)$. Further, since each B_i is positive and invertible, A is irreducible in $M^+(Q)$ if and only if

$$A' = \left[\begin{array}{cc|cc} B_1^{-1/2} & 0 & & \\ 0 & B_2^{-1/2} & \multicolumn{2}{c}{\mathcal{O}} \\ \hline & & B_3^{-1/2} & 0 \\ \multicolumn{2}{c|}{\mathcal{O}} & 0 & B_4^{-1/2} \end{array}\right] \left[\begin{array}{cc|cc} B_1 & & & \\ & B_2 & \multicolumn{2}{c}{C} \\ \hline & & B_3 & \\ \multicolumn{2}{c|}{C^*} & & B_4 \end{array}\right] \times$$

$$\left[\begin{array}{cc|cc} B_1^{-1/2} & 0 & & \\ 0 & B_2^{-1/2} & \multicolumn{2}{c}{\mathcal{O}} \\ \hline & & B_3^{-1/2} & 0 \\ \multicolumn{2}{c|}{\mathcal{O}} & 0 & B_4^{-1/2} \end{array}\right] = \left[\begin{array}{cc|cc} I_{p_1} & 0 & & \\ 0 & I_{p_2} & \multicolumn{2}{c}{W} \\ \hline & & I_{p_3} & 0 \\ \multicolumn{2}{c|}{W^*} & 0 & I_{p_4} \end{array}\right]$$

is irreducible, where $W \in M_p(\mathbb{C})$. The fact that the rank of A is p implies that W is an isometry. Since $W : \mathbb{C}^p \longrightarrow \mathbb{C}^p$, W is unitary.

The reminder of the proof is devoted to showing that there exists a $D \in M(L_4^{(m)})^+$ with rank $(D) = 2$, so that the range of A' contains the range of D . This implies that there exists a $c > 0$ so that $A' - cD \geq 0$. Then, either $p = 2$, or

A' , and hence A , is not irreducible, which is the assertion of Proposition 1.2.

Write W as a block matrix with respect to the indices p_i

$$W = \begin{bmatrix} u_{11} & u_{12} \\ u_{21} & u_{22} \end{bmatrix} ,$$

where

$$u_{ij} : \mathbb{C}^{2+i} \longrightarrow \mathbb{C}^j .$$

Pick h , an eigenvector of $u_4^* u_4$ corresponding to a non-zero eigenvalue k , $0 < k \leq 1$. Let $e = u_2 h$, $f = \left[\frac{1}{k} - 1\right]^{1/2} u_4 h$. Then, since $W^*W = I$, we have

(1) $$u_1^* e = u_1^* u_2 h = -u_3^* u_4 h = \frac{1}{\left[\frac{1}{k} - 1\right]^{1/2}} u_3^* f$$

(2) $$u_2^* e = u_2^* u_2 h = h - u_4^* u_4 h = \left[\frac{1}{k} - 1\right] u_4^* u_4 h$$

and where in (2) we have used that $\frac{1}{k} u_4^* u_4 h = h$. From (1) and (2), it follows that

(3) $$(u_1^* e)(u_2^* e)^* + (u_3^* f)(u_4^* f)^* = 0 .$$

Let $x_i \in \mathbb{C}^p$ be given by $x_1 = \begin{bmatrix} e \\ f \end{bmatrix}$, $x_2 = \begin{bmatrix} e \\ -f \end{bmatrix}$. Then, computing $D = : \sum_{i=1}^{2} \begin{bmatrix} x_i \\ w^* x_i \end{bmatrix} \begin{bmatrix} x_i \\ w^* x_i \end{bmatrix}^*$ we have

$$D = \sum_{i=1}^{2} \begin{bmatrix} x_i x_i^* & x_i x^*_i w \\ w^* x_i x_i^* & w^*(x_i x_i^*) w \end{bmatrix}$$

Since $\sum_{i=1}^{2} x_i x_i^* = 2\begin{bmatrix} e^*e^* & 0 \\ 0 & ff^* \end{bmatrix}$, and since by (3)

$$w^*\left[\sum x_i x_i^*\right] w = \begin{bmatrix} u_1^* ee^* u_1 + u_3^* ee_3^* u & 0 \\ 0 & u_2^* ff^* u_2 + u_4^* ff^* u_4 \end{bmatrix},$$

it follows that $D \in M^+(L_4^{(m)})$. Further, since the range of $A = \left\{\begin{bmatrix} x \\ w^*x \end{bmatrix} \middle| x \in \mathbb{C}^k\right\}$, it follows that the range of D, which is the linear span of $\left\{\begin{bmatrix} x_i \\ w^*x_i \end{bmatrix} \middle| i = 1,2\right\}$, is a subspace of the range of A. □

§2 2-DECOMPOSABLE AND 2-CHORDAL GRAPHS

In this section, we describe a collection of graphs P which have a certain type of decomposition series, the existence of which guarantees that $\operatorname{ord}(P^{(m)}) = \operatorname{ord}(P) \le 2$ for all $m > 0$.

Given P a graph with vertices $V(P)$ and edges $E(P)$, for $W \subseteq V(P)$, define P_W to be the graph on vertices W, such that $(w_i, w_j) \in E(P_W)$ if and only if $w_i, w_j \in W$ and $(w_i, w_j) \in E(P)$. We can view $M(P_W)$ as a subspace of $M(P)$ by defining, for $A \in M(P_W)$, $(A)_{v,w} = 0$ if v or $w \in V\backslash W$. A simple consequence of this construction is:

PROPOSITION 2.1. *Let* P *be a graph. If* W *is a subset of the vertices of* P, *then* $\operatorname{ord}(P_W) \le \operatorname{ord}(P)$.

Proof. See [AHMR].

A graph Q is said to be a subgraph of graph P, denoted $Q \leq P$, if $Q = P_W$ for some $W \subseteq V(P)$. A simple corollary to Proposition 2.1 is: if $Q \leq P$, then $\mathrm{ord}(Q) \leq \mathrm{ord}(P)$.

For a graph P, we say that $v,w \in V(P)$ are equivalent, denoted $v \sim w$, if $\mathrm{adj}(v;P) = \mathrm{adj}(w;P)$. Given $v \in V(P)$, we will let $[v]$ denote the equivalence class of v in $V(P)$. For any number of vertices, $w_1, \ldots, w_k \in V(P)$, $\mathrm{adj}(w_1,\ldots,w_k;P) = \{v \mid (v,w_i) \in E(P) \text{ for some } i\}$, is the adjacency set of $w_1,\ldots,w_k$ in P. The set $\mathrm{radj}(w_1, \ldots, w_k;P) = \mathrm{adj}(w_1, \ldots, w_k;P) \setminus \{w, \ldots, w_k\}$, is known as the reduced adjacency set of $w_1, \ldots, w_k$ in P.

A pair of vertices $v,w \in V(P)$, is said to be a simplicial pair in P if $\mathrm{radj}([v],[w];P)$ is a clique and if $(v,w) \in E(P)$. Note that we allow the possibility that $[v] = [w]$, or even $v = w$.

Let $\hat{Q}$ be the graph on five vertices $\{v_1,v_2,v_3,v_4,v_5\}$ such that $\hat{Q}_{\{v_1,v_2,v_3,v_4\}} = L_4$ and $(v_5,v_i) \in E(\hat{Q})$ for each $i = 1,2,3,4$. ($\hat{Q}$ is a special case of a 2-cell, a notion which is attributable to J. Agler. In fact, $\hat{Q}$ is the protypical 2-cell with the property that $\mathrm{ord}(\hat{Q}^{(m)}) = 2$ for all m, (see Proposition 2.6).)

LEMMA 2.2. *If* v,w *is a simplicial pair in a graph* P, *then there exists an* $m > 0$ *such that* $P_{\mathrm{adj}(v,w;P)} \leq \hat{Q}^{(m)}$.

Proof. Let

$$V_1 = [v] , \quad V_2 = [w] ,$$

$$V_3 = \{x \mid (v,x) \notin E(P) , \quad (w,x) \in E(P)\}$$

$$V_4 = \{x \mid (v,x) \in E(P) , \quad (w,x) \notin E(P)\}$$

$$V_5 = \{x \mid (v,x) \in E(P) , \quad (w,x) \in E(P)\} .$$

Then, since $(v,w) \in E(P)$, the V_i are pairwise disjoint. Since $\text{radj}([v],[w];P) = V_3 \cup V_4 \cup V_5$, it is a clique. This implies that $(v_i,v_j) \notin E(P)$ for $v_i \in V_i$ if an only if $(i,j) \in \{(1,3), (3,1), (2,4), (4,2)\}$. Hence, if we let m be the maximum of the cardinalities of the V_i, then $P_{\text{adj}(v,w;P)} \leq \hat{Q}^{(m)}$. □

Given a graph P, a graph Q with $V(Q) \subseteq V(P)$, is said to be a weak subgraph of P, denoted $Q \leq_W P$, if $v_i,v_j \in V(P)$ and $(v_i,v_j) \in E(Q)$ implies $(v_i,v_j) \in E(P)$. If $Q \leq_W P$, then $M(Q) \subseteq M(P)$.

LEMMA 2.3. *Let* P *be a graph. Suppose* $Q \leq_W P$, *and* $\text{ord}(Q) = k$. *If* $A \in M^+(Q)$, *then there exist* $A_i \in M^+(P)$, *with rank* $A_i \leq k$, *such that* $A = \sum_i A_i$.

Proof. Since $A \in M^+(Q)$ and $\text{ord}(Q) = k$, there exist $A_i \in M^+(Q)$, rank $A_i \leq k$, with $A = \sum_i A_i$. Since each $A_i \in M^+(Q)$, $A_i \in M^+(P)$. □

A graph P is said to be 2-decomposable if there exists a sequence $v_1,w_1,v_2,w_2, \ldots , v_\ell,w_\ell$ where $v_i,w_i \in V(P)$, such that v_i,w_i is a simplicial pair in

$$P_{\left[V(P)\setminus\bigcup_{j=1}^{i-1}([v_j]\cup[w_j])\right]} \quad \text{and} \quad \bigcup_{i=1}^{\ell}([v_i]\cup[w_i]) = V(P) .$$

2-decomposable graphs are precisely those for which we can effectively use the Cholesky decomposition as in [PPS].

THEOREM 2.4. *Let* P *be a graph. If* P *is 2-decomposable, then* $\operatorname{ord}(P^{(m)}) = \operatorname{ord}(P) \leq 2$ *for every* $m > 0$.

The proof relies on the following lemma.

LEMMA 2.5. *Given* n_i *positive integers, suppose* $W_{ij} : \mathbb{C}^{n_j} \longrightarrow \mathbb{C}^{n_i}$ *are matrices. If the block matrix* $W = (W_{ij})$ *is positive semi-definite and* $W_{13} = W_{31} = 0$ *, then there exist matrices* $A_{ij}, B_{ij} : \mathbb{C}^{n_j} \longrightarrow \mathbb{C}^{n_i}$ *, where* $A_{3i} = A_{i3} = 0$ *and* $B_{1i} = B_{i1} = 0$ *for each* i *, such that the block matrices* $A =: (A_{ij})$ *,* $B =: (B_{ij})$ *are positive semi-definite and such that* $W = A + B$.

Proof. Suppose matrices $W_{ij} : \mathbb{C}^{n_j} \longrightarrow \mathbb{C}^{n_i}$, where $W_{13} = W_{31} = 0$ and for which $W =: (W_{ij}) \geq 0$, are given. By doing a Cholesky (or upper-lower) factorization of W , there exists matrices $X_{ij} : \mathbb{C}^{n_j} \longrightarrow \mathbb{C}^{n_i}$ with $X_{ij} = 0$ if $j > i$ such that

$$W = \begin{bmatrix} X^*_{11} & 0 & 0 \\ X^*_{12} & X^*_{22} & 0 \\ X^*_{13} & X^*_{23} & X^*_{33} \end{bmatrix} \begin{bmatrix} X_{11} & X_{12} & X_{13} \\ 0 & X_{22} & X_{23} \\ 0 & 0 & X_{33} \end{bmatrix} .$$

As an application of the polar decomposition for X_{11}, we can, by multiplying $X =: (X_{ij})_{i,j=1}^{3}$ on the left by an appropriate unitary, assume that $X_{11} = X_{11}^*$. Then, $X_{11} X_{13} = W_{13} = 0$. Let P be the orthogonal projection onto the kernel of X_{11} and let $Q = I - P \in M_{n_1}(\mathbb{C})$. Then, since $X_{11}P = 0$ and $QX_{13} = 0$, we compute

$$X^*X = X^* \begin{bmatrix} P+Q & 0 & 0 \\ 0 & I_{n_2} & 0 \\ 0 & 0 & I_{n_3} \end{bmatrix} X$$

$$= \begin{bmatrix} X_{11}^2 & X_{11}QX_{12} & 0 \\ X_{12}^*QX_{11} & X_{22}^*X_{22}+X_{12}^*(P+Q)X_{12} & X_{12}^*PX_{13}+X_{22}^*X_{23} \\ 0 & X_{23}^*X_{22}+X_{13}^*PX_{12} & X_{13}^*PX_{13}+X_{23}^*X_{23}+X_{33}^*X_{33} \end{bmatrix}$$

$$= \begin{bmatrix} X_{11}^2 & X_{11}QX_{12} & 0 \\ X_{12}^*QX_{11} & X_{12}^*QX_{12} & 0 \\ 0 & 0 & 0 \end{bmatrix}$$

$$+ \begin{bmatrix} 0 & 0 & 0 \\ 0 & X_{12}^*PX_{12}+X_{22}^*X_{22} & X_{12}^*PX_{13}+X_{22}^*X_{23} \\ 0 & X_{23}^*X_{22}+X_{13}^*PX_{12} & X_{13}^*PX_{13}+X_{23}^*X_{23}+X^*{}_{33}X_{33} \end{bmatrix} .$$

Letting A be the first summand and B the second, in the last equality above, the lemma follows. □

PROPOSITION 2.6. *Let* $\hat{Q}$ *be the graph from Lemma 2.2. Then* $\mathrm{ord}(\hat{Q}^{(m)}) = 2$ *for every* $m > 0$.

Proof. Let L_4 be the loop of length four (see Theorem 1.2). If $Y_i \in \mathbb{C}^k$ is a representation of $\hat{Q}^{(m)}$, then by eliminating those i such that $v_i \in V(\hat{Q}^{(m)})\backslash V(L_4^{(m)})$, we induce a representation, also denoted Y_i, of $L_4^{(m)}$. By Proposition 1.2, if $k > 2$, then the dimenion of $\mathcal{F}_{L_4^{(m)}}(Y) < k^2 - 1$. But, since for each $v \in V(\hat{Q}^{(m)})\backslash V(L_4^{(m)})$ and each $w \in V(\hat{Q}^{(m)})$ $(v,w) \in E(\hat{Q}^{(m)})$, the dimension of $\mathcal{F}_{\hat{Q}^{(m)}}(Y)$ equals the dimension of $\mathcal{F}_{L_4^{(m)}}(Y)$. Hence, by the Frame Theorem (Theorem 1.1), $A = : (\langle Y_i, Y_i\rangle)_{i,j=1}^{5n}$ is not irreducible. Thus $\mathrm{ord}(\hat{Q}^{(m)}) \leq 2$. □

Proof of Theorem 2.4. Suppose that P is a graph and that $x_1, y_1, x_2, y_2, \ldots, x_\ell, y_\ell$ is a 2-decomposition order for P. Let $v_1 = x_1$, $v_2 = x_2$. Order the remaining vertices of P in such a way that there exists exist k_1, k_2, k_3 positive integers such that $v_i \in [v_1] \cup [w_2]$ if and only if $1 \leq i \leq k_1$, either $(v_i, v_1) \notin E(P)$ or $(v_i, v_2) \notin E(P)$ if and only if $k_1 < i \leq k_2$, and both $(v_i, v_1) \in E(P)$ and $(v_i, v_2) \in E(P)$ if and only if $k_2 < i \leq k_3$. Fix $A \in M^+(P)$, we are to show that A may be written as a sum of elements of $M^+(P)$ each of whose rank is at most two. To this end, write $A = (A^{st})_{s,t=1}^3$ with respect to the integers $n_1 = k_1$, $n_2 = k_2 - k_1$, $n_3 = k_3 - k_2$. That is $A^{ij} : \mathbb{C}^{n_j} \longrightarrow \mathbb{C}^{n_i}$. By Lemma 2.5 we can find block matrices $B = (B^{st}) \geq 0$, $C = (C^{st}) \geq 0$ such that

$$A = B + C = \begin{bmatrix} B^{11} & B^{12} & 0 \\ B^{21} & B^{22} & 0 \\ 0 & 0 & 0 \end{bmatrix} + \begin{bmatrix} 0 & 0 & 0 \\ 0 & C^{22} & C^{23} \\ 0 & C^{32} & C^{33} \end{bmatrix} .$$

Suppose $(v_i,v_j) \notin E(P)$. If $i > k_2$ or $j > k_2$, then $B_{ij} = 0$. If $i,j \leq n_1$, then $B_{ij} = A_{ij} = 0$. If $n_1 < i,j \leq n_2$, then $v_i,v_j \in radj([v_1], [w_2]; P)$ hence $(v_i,v_j) \in E(P)$. Finally, if $i \leq n_1$, $n_2 \geq j > n_1$, then $B_{ij} = A_{ij} = 0$. Hence $B \in M^+(P)$. Since $B_{ij} = 0$ if i or $j \geq n_2$, we may view B as an element of $M^+(P_{adj([v_1],[v_2]];P)})$. Thus, by Lemma 2.2 and Lemma 2.3, B may be written as a sum of elements $B_i \in M^+(P)$, of rank at most two. Hence $A = \sum_i B_i + C$. Further, since $A,B \in M(P)$, $C \in M(P)$. Since $C^{i1} = C^{1i} = 0$ for each i , $C \in M(P_{V(P)\setminus([v_1]\cup[v_2])})$. An induction argument finishes the proof. □

Given n vertices $V_n = \{v_1,v_2,\ldots,v_n\}$, define nLN , the n-line to be the graph with vertices V_n and edges $(v_i,v_j) \in E(nLN)$ if and only if $|i - j| \leq 1$. Define nLP , the n-loop, to be the graph with vertices V_n and $(v_i,v_j) \in E(nLP)$ if and only if $|i - j| \leq 1$ modulo n . Given graphs P and Q , define (P,Q) to be the graph on vertices $V(P) \cup V(Q)$ with $(v,w) \in E((P,Q))$ if and only if either $v,w \in V(P)$ and $(v,w) \in E(P)$ or $v,w \in V(Q)$ and $(v,w) \in E(Q)$.

Given a graph P , define P^c , the complement of P , to be the graph with $V(P^c) = V(P)$ and, $(v,w) \in E(P^c)$ if and only if $(v,w) \notin E(P)$, or $v = w$. If Q is also a graph, P is said to contain Q if $Q \leq P$.

LEMMA 2.7. *Let* P *be the graph whose complement,* P^c *, equals* (2LN,2LN,2LN) . *Then* ord(P) = 2 , *but* $\mathrm{ord}(P^{(2)}) = 3$.

Proof. If P^c = (2LN,2LN,2LN) , then $(P^{(2)})^c$ contains a graph R with R^c = (3LN,3LN,2LN) . R is the graph with vertices V(R) = {1,2,...,8} and with edges E(R) determined by specifying that

$$E(R)^c = \{(1,2),(2,1),(2,3),(3,2),(4,5),(5,4),$$

$$(6,5),(5,6),(7,8),(8,7)\} .$$

Let e_k be the standard orthonormal basis for $\mathbb{C}^3$. Define $Y(i) \in \mathbb{C}^3$ $1 \leq i \leq 8$ by $Y(1) = e_1$, $Y(2) = e_2$, $Y(3) = e_3$, $Y(4) = e_1$, $Y(5) = e_2 + e_3$, $Y(6) = e_2 - e_3$, $Y(7) = e_1 + e_2$, $Y(8) = e_1 - e_2$. It is a simple matter to check that Y is a representation of R and that the dimension of $\mathcal{F}_p(Y)$ is eight. Hence $A = (\langle Y(i),Y(j)\rangle)_{i,j=1}^{8}$ is irreducible by Theorem 1.1. Since the rank of A is three, the order of R , and hence of $P^{(2)}$, is at least three. Finally, since the cardinality of the set E(P) is six, the dimension of $\bar{\mathcal{F}}_p(Y)$ is at most 6 for any representation Y . Therefore, the order of P is at most two. Reasoning as above, it is easy to verify that the order of P is at least two □

LEMMA 2.8. *Let* P *be a graph. If* P *contains a loop of length five or more, or if* P^c *contains one of the following graphs*

6LP, 6LN, (3LP,2LN), (4LN,2LN) ,

then the order of P *is at least three.*

Proof. It suffices to show by Proposition 2.1 that if P is a loop of length five or more or if P^c is one of the graphs

$$6LP,\ 6LN,\ (3LP,2LN),\ (4LN,2LN)\ ,$$

then $\mathrm{ord}(P) \geq 3$.

Claim A: If $P = nLP$ for $n \geq 5$, then $\mathrm{ord}(P) \geq n - 2 \geq 3$.

Proof. The nLP has vertices $V = \{1,2,\ldots,n\}$ and edges $(i,j) \in E$ if and only if $|i - j| \leq 1$ modulo n . Let e_i be the standard orthonormal basis for $\mathbb{C}^{n-2}$ and define a representation $Y \in \mathbb{C}^{n-2}$ of nLP by setting $Y(1) = e_1$, $Y(k) = e_k + e_{k-1}$ for $n - 2 \geq k \geq 2$ $Y(n - 1) = e_{n-2}$, and $Y(n) = \sum_{m=1}^{n-2} (-1)^m e_m$. (This representation appears in Theorem 6.5 of [AHMR]). We have

$$Y(1) \otimes Y(i) = e_1 \otimes (e_i + e_{i-1}) \in \mathcal{F}_p(Y) \quad \text{for} \quad 2 \leq i \leq n - 2$$

and

$$Y(1) \otimes Y(n - 1) = e_1 \otimes e_{n-2} \in \mathcal{F}_p(Y) \ .$$

Hence, $e_1 \otimes e_j \in \mathcal{F}_p(Y)$ for $2 \leq j \leq n - 2$. Similarly,

$$Y(2) \otimes Y(i) = (e_1 + e_2) \otimes (e_i + e_{i-1}) \in \mathcal{F}_p(Y) \quad 3 \leq i \leq n\ .$$

and

$$Y(2) \otimes Y(n-1) = e_2 \otimes e_{n-2} \in \mathcal{S}_p(Y) .$$

Hence, $e_2 \otimes e_j \in \mathcal{S}_p(Y)$ $3 \leq j \leq n-2$. Inductively, we see that $e_i \otimes e_j \in \mathcal{S}_p(Y)$ for $i < j$. Thus, since $\mathcal{S}_p(Y)$ is self adjoint $e_i \otimes e_j \in \mathcal{S}_p(Y)$ for $i \neq j$. For each $2 \leq i \leq n-2$

$$Y(i) \otimes Y(n) = (e_i \oplus e_{i-1}) \otimes \left[\sum_{m=1}^{n-2} (-1)^m e_m\right] \in \mathcal{S}_p(Y) .$$

Hence, for each $1 \leq i \leq n-3$

$$e_i \otimes e_i - e_{i+1} \otimes e_{i+1} \in \mathcal{S}_p(Y) .$$

Consequently, the dimension of $\mathcal{S}_p(Y)$ is $(n-2)^2 - 1$. By the Frame Theorem, $A = (\langle Y(i),Y(j)\rangle)_{i,j=1}^n$ is irreducible and $\text{ord}(nLP) \geq n-2$.

Claim B: If $P^c = 6LP$, then $\text{ord}(P) \geq 3$.

Proof. Let $V(P) = \{1,2,\ldots,6\}$. $(i,j) \in E(P)$ if and only if $|i-j| = 1$ modulo 6 . Therefore, if $Y(1) = e_1$, $Y(2) = e_2$, $Y(3) = e_3$, $Y(4) = e_1 + e_2$, $Y(5) = e_1 - e_2 + e_3$, $Y(6) = e_2 + e_3$ where e_i is the standard orthonornal basis for $\mathbb{C}^3$, then Y is a representation of P . To see that $B = (\langle Y(i),Y(j)\rangle)_{i,j=1}^6$ is a rank three irreducible and hence $\text{ord}(P) \geq 3$, it is enough to show that the dimension of $\mathcal{S}_p(Y)$ is eight.

Claim C: Suppose $P^c = (3LP, 2LN)$, then $\mathrm{ord}(P) \geq 3$.

Proof. Define a representation of P by letting $Y(i) \in \mathbb{C}^3$ be given by $Y(1) = e_1$, $Y(2) = e_2$, $Y(3) = e_3$, $Y(4) = \begin{bmatrix} 1 - i \\ 1 - i \\ 1 \end{bmatrix}$, and $Y(5) = \begin{bmatrix} 1 - i \\ -1 - i \\ -2 + 2i \end{bmatrix}$. Since $\langle Y_1, Y_2\rangle = \langle Y_2, Y_3\rangle = \langle Y_1, Y_3\rangle = \langle Y_4, Y_5\rangle = 0$, $Y_i \in \mathbb{C}^3$ is a representation of P . Further, it is easy to compute that the dimension of $\mathcal{F}_Q(Y) = 8$. Hence $C = (\langle Y_i, Y_j\rangle)_{i,j=1}^{5}$ is irreducible. Since the rank of C is three, the order of P is at least three.

Claim D: If $P^c = (4LN, 2LN)$, then $\mathrm{ord}(P) = 3$.

Proof. The claim follows by considering the representation of P given by $Y_1 = e_1$, $Y_2 - e_2$, $Y_3 = e_3$, $Y_4 = e_1$, $Y_5 = \begin{bmatrix} 1 - i \\ 1 - i \\ 1 \end{bmatrix}$, $Y_6 = \begin{bmatrix} 1 - i \\ -1 - i \\ -2 - 2i \end{bmatrix}$ and arguing as in Claim C. This finishes the proof of Lemma 2.8. □

A graph P is said to be 2-chordal if P contains no loops of length five or more, and if P^c contains none of the graphs

6LP, 6LN, (3LP,2LN), (4LN,2LN), (2LN,2LN,2LN) .

From Proposition 2.7 and Lemma 2.8, it follows that

THEOREM 2.9. *Let* P *be a graph. If* $\mathrm{ord}(P^{(m)}) = \mathrm{ord}(P) \leq 2$ *for all* $m > 0$, *then* P *is 2-chordal.*

§3 2-DECOMPOSABLE IS 2-CHORDAL

THEOREM 3.1 *Let* P *be a graph. The following are equivalent.*

i) P *is 2-chordal*

ii) P *is 2-decomposable*

iii) $\mathrm{ord}(P^{(m)}) = \mathrm{ord}(P) \leq 2$ *for every* $m > 0$.

From section two, Theorems 2.4 and 2.9, it follows that *ii)* implies *iii)* implies *i)*. The proof that *i)* implies *ii)* follows the same outline as a proof that every chordal graph has a perfect elimination ordering (see, for example, [G] p.83). However, because of the added complexity, the proof of Theorem 3.1, although conceptually no more difficult that the proof that chordal implies there exists a perfect elimination order, is much more tedious.

Given a graph P , define $\tilde{P}$ to be the graph P modulo the equivalence relation $\sim$; that is, $V(\tilde{P}) = \{[v] \mid v \in V(P)\}$ and $([v],[w]) \in E(\tilde{P})$ if and only if $(v,w) \in E(P)$. It is clear that P is 2-decomposable if and only if $\tilde{P}$ is 2-decomposable.

LEMMA 3.2. *Let* P *be a graph.* P *is 2-chordal if and only if* $\tilde{P}$ *is 2-chordal.*

Proof. Let P be a given graph.

If P is 2-chordal, then, since $\tilde{P}$ may be viewed as a subgraph of P , $\tilde{P}$ is also 2-chordal.

Conversely, suppose P is not 2-chordal. There exists an $m > 0$ such that $\tilde{P}^{(m)} \geq P$. Since P is not 2-chordal, either P contains nLP for $n \geq 5$ or P^c contains one of the graphs 6LP , 6LN , (3LP,2LN) , (4LN,2LN) , (2LN,2LN,2LN) . But then either $\tilde{P}^{(m)}$ contains nLP for $n \geq 5$ or $(\tilde{P}^{(m)})^c$ contains one of the graphs Q = 6LP , 6LN , (3LP,2LN) , (4LN,2LN) , or (2LN,2LN,2LN) . However, since $(\widetilde{nLP}) = nLP$ for each n , and for each graph Q above $\tilde{Q} = Q$, it follows that $(\widetilde{\tilde{P}^{(m)}}) = \tilde{P}$ contains nLP for $n \geq 5$ or one of the graphs Q above. Hence, $\tilde{P}$ is not 2-chordal. □

For the remainder of this section, we will assume that $P = \tilde{P}$.

Two pairs v_1, v_2 and w_1, w_2 of vertices of a graph P are said to be non-adjacent if $(v_i, w_j) \notin E(P)$ for each i, j . To prove Theorem 3.1, we induct on the number of vertices of P . That is, we assume that every 2-chordal graph Q on fewer vertices then P satisfies

(IH) Either Q contains two non-adjacent pairs of simplicial vertices or Q is a subgraph of $\hat{Q}^{(m)}$ for some $m > 0$.

It is to be shown that if P is 2-chordal, then P satisfies (IH). Then, either P is a subgraph of $\hat{Q}^{(m)}$, in which case P is trivially 2-decomposable, or P contains a simplicial pair and an induction argument establishes that P has a 2-decomposition series.

Fix a graph P . A sequence $(v_0, v_1, \ldots, v_n)$ is said to be a path from v_0 to v_n if $(v_i, v_{i+1}) \in E(P)$ for $i = 0, 1, 2, \ldots, n-1$. For $v \in V(P)$, the path component of v in P , denoted $C(v;P)$, is the set of vertices $w \in V(P)$ such that there exists a path from v to w in P . The sets $C(v;P)$, for $v \in V(P)$, partition $V(P)$. A path $(v_0, v_1, \ldots, v_n)$ is a minimal path if $(v_i, v_j) \notin E(P)$ if $|i - j| > 1$. $W \subseteq V(P)$ is a stable set if for each pair $w, w' \in W$, $(w, w') \notin E(P)$. For $W \subseteq V(P)$ a stable set, S a subset of $V(P) \backslash W$ is said to be a separator of W if , for each $v \neq w \in W$, there is no path from v to w in $P_{V(P) \backslash W}$. S is a minimal separator of the stable set W if S is a separator of W , but no proper subset of S separates W . The following lemma is standard (see, for example, [G] p. 83).

LEMMA 3.3. *Let* P *be a graph,* $W \subsetneq V(P)$ *a stable set. If* S *is minimal vertex separator of* W, *then for every* $w \in W$ *and every* $s \in S$ *there exists* $w(s) \in C(w;P_{V(P)-S})$ *such that* $(w(s),s) \in E(P)$.

For the rest of this section, fix P, a 2-chordal graph. Denote $V = V(P)$ and $E = E(P)$. $W \subsetneq V$ is said to be a clique if $(w,w') \in E$ for every $w,w' \in W$.

LEMMA 3.4. *If* $\{a,b,c\}$ *is a stable set in* V *and if* a,b,c *are distinct, then any minimal* $\{a,b,c\}$ *separator is a clique.*

Proof. Let S be any minimal separator of $\{a,b,c\}$. If S is not clique, then there exists $s,t, \in S$ with $(s,t) \notin E$. Let $a(s),a(t)$ be the elements of $C(a;P_{V-S})$ guaranteed by Lemma 3.3. There exists a path from $a(s)$ to $a(t)$ in $P_{C(a;P_{V-S})}$. Hence, there exists a path from s to t in $P_{S \cup C(a;P_{V-S})}$. Let $(a_0 = s,a_1,a_2,\ldots,a_{n-1},a_n = t)$ be a minimal path in $P_{S \cup C(a;P_{V-S})}$. Similarly, choose minimal paths $(b_0 = t,b_1,b_2,\ldots,b_{m-1},b_m = s)$ and $(s = c_0,c_1,\ldots,c_\ell = t)$ in $P_{S \cup C(b;P_{V-S})}$ and $P_{S \cup C(c;P_{V-S})}$ respectively. $(s,a_1,\ldots,a_{n-1},t,b_1,\ldots,b_{m-1},s)$ is a loop of length $n + m$; hence, if, for example $n > 3$, then P contains a loop of length more than four. Thus, $n = m = \ell = 2$. However, in this case, $\left[P_{\{s,t,a_1,b_1,c_1\}}\right]^c = (3LP,2LN)$, a contradiction. Therefore, $(s,t) \in E$. □

LEMMA 3.5. *If* V *contains a stable set* $\{a,b,c\}$, *where* a,b,c *are distinct, then there exists two non-adjacent simplicial pairs in* P.

Proof. Let S be a minimal separator of $\{a,b,c\}$. Since the graph $P_{S \cup C(a;P_{V-S})}$ has fewer vertices than P , either $P_{S \cup C(a;P_{V-S})}$ is a subgraph of $\hat{Q}^{(m)}$, for some m , or it has two non-adjacent pairs of simplicial vertices. In either case, since S is a clique, it follows that there exists $a_1,a_2 \in C(a;P_{v-s})$ which is simplicial in $P_{C(a;P_{v-s}) \cup S}$. Hence, a_1,a_2 is a simplicial pair in P . Similarly, there exists a simplicial pair b_1,b_2 in $C(b;P_{v-s})$. Since, for each $a' \in C(a;P_{v-s})$ and $b' \in C(b;P_{v-s})$, $(b',a') \notin E$, a_1,a_2 and b_1,b_2 are two non-adjacent simplicial pairs. □

By Lemma 3.5, if V contains a stable set consisting of three or more distinct vertices, then P satisfies (IH) . Thus, for the remainder of this section, in addition to assuming that P is 2-chordal, it will be assumed that for every triple of distinct vertices, v_1,v_2,v_3 there is an edge; i.e., there exists $i \neq j$ such that $(v_i,v_j) \in E$. Futher, if P is a clique, then trivially P is a subraph of $\hat{Q}^{(m)}$, where, for example, m is the cardinality of V . Hence, we fix for the remainder of this section vertices $a,b \in V$ with $(a,b) \notin E$. Also, fix S a minimal $\{a,b\}$ separator. For notational ease, let $A = C(a;P_{v-s})$ and $B = C(b;P_{v-s})$.

LEMMA 3.6. A *and* B *are cliques.*

Proof. Given $a_1,a_2 \in A$, if $(a_1,a_2) \notin E$, then the triple a_1,a_2,b has no edge, a contradiction. Hence $(a_1,a_2) \in E$. □

LEMMA 3.7. $A \cup B \cup S = V$.

Proof. If not, choose $c \in V\backslash(A \cup B \cup S)$. If $(a,c) \in E$, then $c \in C(a;P_{V-S})$. Hence, $(a,c) \notin E$. Similarly, $(b,c) \notin E$. Thus $\{a,b,c\}$ is a stable set. □

LEMMA 3.8. *For every* $s \in S$ *there exists* $a' \in A$, $b' \in B$ *such that* $(a',s) \in E$ *and* $(b',s) \in E$.

Proof. Fix $s_0 \in S$. Let $(a,x_1,x_2,\ldots,x_{n-1},b)$ be a minimal path from a to b in $P_{(V\backslash S)\cup\{s_0\}}$, which is guaranteed by the minimality of S. Since S separates $\{a,b\}$, there exists j such that $x_j = s_0$. As $x_i \notin S\backslash\{s_0\}$ for each i and as the path is minimal, $x_{j-1} \in A$, $x_{j+1} \in B$. □

Recall, to finish the proof of Theorem 3.1, it is enough to show that either $P \leq \hat{Q}^{(m)}$ for some $m > 0$ or P contains two non-adjacent simplicial pairs. Hence, if we show that either P contains two non-adjacent simplicial pairs or A contains a simplicial pair in P, then, by applying the same argument to B, P contains two non-adjacent simplicial pairs. In what follows the following notation will be employed. The line on n-vertices $\{v_1,v_2,\ldots,v_n\}$ will be denoted $(v_1 - v_2 - v_3 - \ldots - v_n)$. The loop on the same n vertices will be denoted $[v_1 - v_2 - v_3 - \ldots - v_n]$. The disjoint union of a line on vertices $\{v_1,v_2,\ldots,v_n\}$ and a loop on the vertices $\{w_1,w_2,\ldots,w_m\}$ will be written as $(v_1 - v_2 - \ldots - v_n) \sqcup [w_1 - w_2 - \ldots - w_m]$.

We now break the proof down into cases. In each case, we will either reach a contradiction (thus that particular case could not have occured) or we will verify the induction hypothesis (IH).

CASE A. There exists $s_1 \neq s_2 \in S$ which is a simplicial pair in $P_{A \cup S}$.

In this case, let

$$S_3 = \{s \in S | (s,s_1) \notin E , \quad (s,s_2) \in E\}$$

$$S_4 = \{s \in S | (s,s_1) \in E , \quad (s,s_2) \notin E\}$$

$$S_5 = \{s \in S | (s,s_i) \notin E \quad \text{for} \quad i = 1,2\}$$

$$S_6 = \{s \in S | (s,s_i) \in E \quad \text{for} \quad i = 1,2\}$$

$$A_1 = \{a' \in A | (a',s_i) \notin E , \quad (a',s_2) \in E\}$$

$$A_2 = \{a' \cup A | (a',s_i) \in E , \quad (a',s_2) \notin E\}$$

$$A_3 = \{a \in A | (a,s_i) \notin E \quad \text{for} \quad i = 1,2\}$$

$$A_4 = \{a \in A | (a,s_i) \in E \quad \text{for} \quad i = 1,2\} .$$

Note, as $S_3 \cup S_4 \cup S_6 \cup A_1 \cup A_2 \cup A_4$ is a subset of $\mathrm{radj}(s_1,s_2;P_{A \cup S})$ it is a clique. Also, for each $i = 1,2$ if $x \in A_i$, then $(x,s_i) \notin E$. Thus, since $(s_i,s_5) \notin E$ for each $i = 1,2$, and since for each triple of vertices there exists at least one edge, $(x,s_5) \in E$.

CASE A1. $S_5 \neq \phi$.

S_5 is a clique, since for each $t \in S_5$ and each $i = 1,2$ $(t,s_i) \notin E$.

CASE A1.1. A_1(or A_2) $\neq \phi$.

If $b' \in B$, $s_5 \in S_5$ and $(b',s_5) \notin E$, then $(b',s_2) \in E$. Otherwise, P^c contains $[s_1 - a_1 - b' - s_2 - s_5 - s_1]$, which is 5LP . Then, since $(5LP)^c = 5LP$, P contains 5LP , contradicting the assumption that P is 2-chordal.

In this case, $A_2 = \phi$. Otherwise, pick $s_5 \in S_5$, $a_1 \in A$, $a_2 \in A_2$. Choose, by Lemma 3.8, $b' \in B$ such that $(b',s_5) \in E$. Since for every triple of vertices of P there exists an edge and since $(b',a_i) \notin E$ for $i = 1,2$, it follows that $(b',s_i) \in E$ for $i = 1,2$. But then, P^c contains the graph $[s_1 - a_1 - b' - a_2 - s_2 - s_5]$, which is 6LP , contradicting the assumption that P is 2-chordal. Hence, $A_2 = \phi$. Next, we will see that $A_4 = \phi$. The alternative is that there is an $a_4 \in A_4$. Pick $s_5 \in S_5$. There are two cases; either $(a_4,s_5) \notin E$ or $(a_4,s_5) \in E$. In the first case, by choosing $b' \in B$ such that $(b',s_5) \in E$, by Lemma 3.8, it follows that P^c contains the graph $[s_1 - a_1 - b' - a_4 - s_5]$, which is 5LP . In the other case, P^c contains 6LN , $(s_2 - s_5 - s_1 - a_1 - b' - a_4)$. Hence, $A_4 = \phi$. However, since there exists an $a' \in A$ such that $(a',s_1) \in E$, $A_4 \neq \phi$. This contradiction implies Case A1.1. can not occur.

CASE A1.2. $A_1 = A_2 = \phi$.

Notice that $A_4 \neq \phi$, since, for each $a_3 \in A_3$, $(a_3,s_1) \notin E$.

CASE A1.2.1. $A_3 \neq \phi$.

Fix $a_3 \in A_3$. If $b' \in B$ then $(b',s_i) \in E$ for $i = 1,2$, as $(b',a_3) \notin E$. Thus, since $s_1 \nsim s_2$ in P , S_3 (or S_4) $\neq \phi$. Now, by choosing $b' \in B$ such that $(b',s_5) \in E$, it follows that P^c contains either $(s_2 - s_5 - s_1 - s_3) \bigsqcup (a_4 - b')$ or $(s_2 - s_5 - s_1 - s_3 - b' - a_4)$. Since P is 2-chordal, this is a contradiction. Hence, Case A1.2.1 can not occur.

CASE A1.2.2. $A_3 = \phi$.

Choose $s_5 \in S_5$. Pick $a_4 \in A_4$ such that $(a_4,s_5) \in E$ by Lemma 3.8.

If $b' \in B$ and if $(b',s_1) \notin E$, then $(b',s_2) \notin E$. Otherwise, by choosing $b'' \in B$ such that $(b'',s_1) \in E$, it follows that P^c contains one of the following three graphs $(s_2 - s_5 - s_1 - b' - a_4 - b'')$, $[s_1 - b' - a_4 - b'' - s_2 - s_5]$, $[s_1 - b' - a_4 - b'' - s_5]$. Hence, for each $b' \in B$ either $(b',s_i) \in E$ or $(b',s_i) \notin E$ for $i = 1,2$. Thus, since $s_1 \nsim s_2$ in P , S_3 (or S_4) $\neq \phi$. Pick $s_3 \in S_3$. For each $b' \in B$, $(b',s_i) \notin E$ for $i = 1$ and 2 or $i = 3$ and 5 ; otherwise, P^c contains one of the following graphs: $(s_2 - s_5 - s_1 - s_3) \bigsqcup (a_4 - b')$, $(s_2 - s_5 - s_1 - s_3 - b' - a_4)$, $(s_3 - s_1 - s_5 - b' - a_4 - b'')$, $[s_3 - b'' - a_4 - b' - s_5 - s_1]$. Now choose $b',b'' \in B$ such that (b',s_3) , $(b',s_5) \notin E$ and (b'',s_1) , $(b'',s_2) \notin E$. However, in this case P^c contains $[s_5 - b' - a_4 - b'' - s_2]$ a contradiction. Consequently, Case A1.2.2 can not occur.

CASE A2. $S_5 = \phi$.

CASE A2.1. $A_3 \neq \phi$.

Since $A_3 \neq \phi$ and $s_1 \not\sim s_2$, $P_{A \cup S} \leq \hat{Q}^{(m)}$ for any m . Thus, as $P_{A \cup S}$ satisfies (IH) , there exists v,w a simplicial pair in $P_{A \cup S}$ which is not adjacent to s_1, s_2 . Thus, $v,w \in A_3 \subseteq A$, as desired.

CASE A2.2. $A_3 = \phi$.

CASE A2.2.1. $A_1 \neq \phi$, $A_2 \neq \phi$.

Both A_1 and A_2 consist of just a single element. For example, if $a_1 \in A_1$, then $adj(a_1;P) = A_1 \cup A_2 \cup A_4 \cup S_6 \cup S_2 \cup S_4$. Hence, each $a_1 \in A_1$ has the same adjacency set and it follows that, as $P = \tilde{P}$, A_1 consists of a single element. Consequently, if $S_3 = S_4 = \phi$, then a_1, a_2 is a simplicial pair in P . If S_3 (or S_4) $\neq \phi$, then choose $b' \in B$ such that $(b', s_3) \in E$, by Lemma 3.8. But then, P^c contains $(s_3 - s_1 - a_1 - b' - a_2 - s_1)$ the 6LN , contradiction.

CASE A2.2.2. $A_2 = \phi$, $A_1 \neq \phi$.

In this case, since $(a_1, s_1) \notin E$, $A_4 \neq \phi$. Recall $A_1 = \{a_1\}$. Consequently, if $S_4 = \phi$, then $adj(a_1;P) \subseteq S_2 \cup S_3 \cup A_4$. Hence, $adj(a_1;P)$ is a clique and a_1 is a simplicial vertex in P . If $S_4 \neq \phi$, then P^c contains either $(s_1 - a_1 - b' - a_4) \sqcup (s_2 - s_4)$ or $[b' - a_1 - b'' - s_4 - s_2]$, for appropriately chosen $b', b'' \in B$. Thus $S_4 = \phi$, and Case A2.2.2 is finished.

CASE A2.2.3. $A_1 = A_2 = \phi$.

If $S_3, S_4 \neq \phi$, then P^c contains one of the graphs $(s_1 - s_2) \coprod (s_3 - s_4) \coprod (b' - a_4)$, $(s_1 - s_2 - b' - a_4) \coprod (s_3 - s_4)$ or $[b'' - s_1 - s_2 - b' - s_4 - s_3]$. Hence, S_4 (or S_3) $= \phi$.

For $b' \in B$ and $s_2 \in S_2$, $(b', s_2) \in E$, otherwise $s_2 \sim a_2$ for any $a_2 \in A_2$. There are two cases. In the first case $(s_1, b') \in E$, $(s_3, b') \in E$ for every $b' \in B$. Whence, $P = \hat{Q}$. In the second case, B breaks into two sets

$$B_1 = \{b' \in B | (b', s_1) \notin E$$

$$B_2 = \{b' \in B | (b', s_1) \in E .$$

Then $B_1 = \{b_1\}$, $B_2 = \{b_2\}$; i.e., B_1 and B_2 consist of single elements. Finally, $\text{radj}(a_4, s_1; P) = \text{adj}(b_1; P) = \{b_1, s_2\}$ which is a clique. Thus a_4, s_1 and b_1 are non-adjacent simplicial pairs in P .

CAES B. P_{AUS} contains the simplicial pairs a_1, s_1 , where $a_1 \in A$, $s_1 \in S$.

Let $$A_1 = [a_1] = \{a_1\}$$

$$A_2 = \{a' \in A | (a', s_1) \notin E\}$$

$$A_3 = \{a' \in A | (a', s_1) \in E\}$$

$$S_1 = [s_1] = \{s_1\}$$

$$S_2 = \{s \in S \mid (s_1,s) \notin E \text{ and } (a_1,s) \in E\}$$

$$S_3 = \{s \in S \mid (s_1,s) \in E \text{ and } (a_1,s) \notin E\}$$

$$S_4 = \{s \in S \mid (s_1,s),(a_1,s) \in E\}$$

$$S_5 = \{s \in S \mid (s_1,s),(a_1,s) \notin E\} \ .$$

Observe that for each $x \in A_2 \cup S_2 \cup S_3$ and $s_5 \in S_5$ we have $(x,s_5) \in E$, since every triple of vertices must have an edge. Further, since a_1,s_1 is a simplicial pair in $P_{A \cup S}$, $radj(s_1,a_1;P_{A \cup S}) = S_2 \cup S_3 \cup S_4 \cup A_2 \cup A_3$ is a clique. We now break Case B down into subcases.

CASE B1. $S_5 \neq \phi$.

In this case it follows that $A_2 = \phi$. Otherwise, by choosing $b' \in B$ such that $(b',s_1) \in E$, we find that P^c contains 5LP $(s_1 - a_2 - b' - a_1 - s_5)$.

CASE B1.1. $S_2 = \phi$.

In this case, $adj(a_1;P) \subseteq A_3 \cup S_4 \cup S_1$. Thus, since $A_3 \cup S_4$ is a clique and since $(x,s_1) \in E$ for every $x \in A_3 \cup S_4$, $adj(a_1;P)$ is a clique. Consequently, a is a simplicial vertex in P .

CASE B1.2. $S_2 \neq \phi$.

Actually, this case can not occur. To see this, choose $b' \in B$ such that $(b',s_1) \in E$, by Lemma 3.8. Also, pick $a_3 \in A_3$ such that $(a_3,s_5) \in E$. Then P^c contains one of the following two unacceptable graphs:
$(s_2 - s_1 - s_5 - a_1 - b' - a_3)$, $[s_2 - b' - a_1 - s_5 - s_1]$.

CASE B2. $S_5 = \phi$.

CASE B2.1. $S_2 \neq \phi$.

There exists $b' \in B$ such that $(b',s_1),(b',s_2) \in E$. The alternative is that P^c contains $(s_1 - s_2 - b' - a_1 - b'']$. Futher, $S_3 = \phi$, otherwise P^c contains $(s_3 - a_1 - b' - a_2 - s_1 - s_2)$ or $(s_1 - s_2) \sqcup (a_3 - b' - a_1 - s_3)$, which is (4LN,2LN). However, since $S_3 = \phi$, $a_1 \sim a_3$ for each $a_1 \in A_1$ and $a_3 \in A_3$. Since $P = \tilde{P}$, we conclude that $A_3 = \phi$.

CASE B2.1.1. $A_2 = \phi$.

There are two cases. In the first case, for each $b' \in B$, $(b',s_i) \in E$ for $i = 1,2$. It follows that $B = \{b\}$. Further, since $P = \tilde{P}$, for each $s_4 \in S_4$, $(b,s_4) \in E$. Hence $S_4 = \{s_4\}$ or $S_4 = \phi$. Consequently, $P \leq \hat{Q}$. In the second case, we may, without loss of generality, divide B into the following two sets

$$B_1 = \{b' \in B | (b',s_i) \in E \text{ for } i = 1,2\}$$

$$B_2 = \{b' \in B | (b',s_1) \notin E , (b',s_2) \in E\} .$$

If $b_1 \in B_1$ and $s_4 \in S_4$, then $(b_1,s_4) \in E$. Otherwise, there exists $b_2 \in B_2$ such that $(b_2,s_4) \in E$, in which case P^c contains $(s_2 - s_1 - b_2 - a_1 - b_1 - s_4)$ or there exists $b_1' \in B_1$ such that $(b_1',s_4) \in E$, in which case P^c contains $(s_1 - s_2) \bigsqcup (b_1' - a_1 - b_1 - s_4)$. Thus, $B_1 = \{b_1\}$. Hence, $\mathrm{radj}(s_1,a_1;P) = \{b_1\} \cup S_4 \cup S_2$ is a clique. The graph $P_{V-\{b_1\}}$ contains two pairs of non-adjacent simplicial vertices. Thus, since both pairs can not be found in $\{s_1,a_1\} \cup S_2$, a pair v,w must be in $S_4 \cup B_2$. If $v \in S_4$, then $\mathrm{radj}(v,w;P_{V-\{b_1\}}) \supseteq S_1 \cup S_2$. Since $S_1 \cup S_2$ is not a clique, this is a contradiction. Hence, $v,w \in B_2$. We have $\mathrm{radj}(v,w;P_{V-\{b_1\}}) \subseteq B \cup S_4 \cup S_2$ and since $\mathrm{adj}(b_1,P) \subseteq B \cup S_4 \cup S_2 \cup S_1$, $\mathrm{radj}(v,w;P)$ is a clique. Hence, s_1,a_1 and v,w are two non-adjacent pairs of simplicial vertices.

CASE B2.1.2. $A_2 \neq \phi$.

For each $a_2 \in A_2$, $\mathrm{adj}(a_2;P) = A_2 \cup A_1 \cup S_2 \cup S_4$. Hence, $A_2 = \{a_2\}$ and a_2 is a simplical vertex in P.

CASE B2.2. $S_2 = \phi$.

In this case, $\mathrm{adj}(a_2;P) = A_2 \cup S_3 \cup A_1 \cup A_3$ for each $a_2 \in A_2$. Hence $A_2 = \{a_2\}$. Then, $\mathrm{radj}(a_2,a_1;P) = S_3 \cup A_3 \cup S_1$ which is a clique. Consequently, a_1,a_2 is a simplicial pair in P.

CASE C. There exists $a_1 \neq a_2 \in A$ a simplicial pair in P .

CASE D. There exists $s_1, s_2 \in S$ such that $s_1 \neq s_2$ and $adj(s_i;P_{A \cup S})$ is a clique.

LEMMA 3.9. *For each* $s \in S$, *either* $s \in adj(s_1;P)$ *or* $s \in adj(s_2;P)$.

Proof. Suppose this is not the case, then the triple s, s_1, s_2 has no edge. □

According to Lemma 3.9, we may divide S into the following five sets:

$$S_1 = \{s_1\}$$

$$S_2 = \{s_2\}$$

$$S_3 = (adj(s_1;P) \backslash adj(s_2;P)) \cap S$$

$$S_4 = (adj(s_2;P) - adj(s_1;P)) \cap S$$

$$S_5 = adj(s_1;P) \cap adj(s_2;P) \cap S .$$

Observe that, if $a' \in A$ and $(a', s_1) \in E$, $(a', s_2) \in E$, then $(a', s) \in E$ for every $s \in S$, as $adj(s_i;P_{A \cup S})$ is a clique for $i = 1,2$. The analysis breaks into subcases.

CASE D1. For every $a' \in A$ and $s \in S$ we have $(a', s) \in E$.

Observe that as $P = \tilde{P}$, $A = \{a\}$. Further, since $(s_1,s_2) \notin E$, for each $b' \in B$ either (b',s_1) or (b',s_2) is an edge in P .

CASE D1.1. There exists $s_3 \in S_3$ and $s_4 \in S_4$ such that $(s_3,s_4) \in E$.

First, for each $b' \in B$, either $(b',s_3) \in E$ or $(b',s_4) \in E$. Otherwise, since for every three vertices in P there exists at least one edge, P^c contains $[s_1 - s_4 - b' - s_3 - s_2]$. Second, there does not exist $b' \in B$ such that $(b',s_i) \in E$ for $i = 1,2,3,4$. Otherwise, P^c contains $(a - b) \bigsqcup (s_3 - s_2 - s_1 - s_4)$, which is the (2LN,4LN) . Next, if $(b',s_4) \notin E$, then $(b',s_2) \notin E$ since the alternative is that P^c contains $(s_3 - s_2 - s_1 - s_4 - b' - a)$, which is the 6LN . By Lemma 3.8, choose $b' \in B$ such that $(b',s_1) \in E$. Thus, $(b',s_2) \notin E$. Next, choose $b'' \in B$ such that $(b'',s_2) \in E$. Then $(b'',s_1) \notin E$. Hence, P^c contains $[s_1 - b'' - a - b' - s_2]$ a contradiction. Thus, Case D1.1 can not occur.

CASE D1.2. For every $s_3 \in S_3$, $s_4 \in S_4$ $(s_3,s_4) \notin E$.

To begin with, S_3 (or S_4) is empty. Otherwise, fix $s_3 \in S_3$ and $s_4 \in S_4$. Then, since $s_1 \not\sim s_3$ in P and $s_2 \not\sim s_4$ in P , there exists $b_1,b_2 \in B$ such that

$$(b_1,s_i) \in E \text{ if and only if } i \neq i_0 \text{ where } i_0 = 1 \text{ or } 3$$
$$(b_2,s_j) \in E \text{ if and only if } j = j_0 \text{ where } j_0 = 2 \text{ or } 4 .$$

But then, P^c contains 5LP or 6LP ; $[s_\alpha - s_\beta - b_2 - a - b_1]$ or $[s_\beta - s_\alpha - b_2 - a - b_1 - s_\gamma]$, which contradicts the 2-chordality of P . Thus, S_3 (or S_4) = ϕ .

CASE D1.2.1. $S_3 = \phi = S_4$.

If for each $b' \in B$ and $s \in S$ we have (b',s) is an edge, then $B = \{b\}$ and P is the graph $\hat{Q}$, Otherwise, without loss of generality, we can assume there exists $b' \in B$ such that $(b',s_1) \notin E$. Then, for every $b'' \in B$, $(b'',s_2) \in E$. At this point, B breaks into two sets.

$$B_1 = \{b' \in B \mid (b',s_1) \notin E\}$$

$$B_2 = \{b'' \in B \mid (b'',s_1) \in E\} .$$

For every $b_2 \in B_2$ and every $s_5 \in S_5$, $(b_2,s_5) \in E$. Otherwise, there exists $b' \in B$ such that $(b',s_5) \in E$. If $b' \in B_2$, then P^c contains (4LN,2LN) ; $(s_1 - s_2) \sqcup (s_5 - b_2 - a_4 - b')$. If $b' \in B_1$, then P^c contains 6LN , $(s_2 - s_1 - b' - a_4 - b_2 - s_5)$. It follows that $B_2 \cup S_5 \cup S_2$ is a clique. Thus, since $radj(a,s_1;P) = B_2 \cup S_2 \cup S_5$, a,s_1 is a simplicial pair in P . The graph P_{V-B_2} contains two non-adjacent pairs of simplicial vertices, as it has fewer vertices than P . Thus, since $\{a,s_1,s_2\}$ does not contain two pairs of simplicial vertices and since $(s_1,s_2) \notin E$, it follows that there exists $v,w \in B_1$ a simplicial pair in P_{V-B_2} . Hence, $radj(v,w;P_{V-B_2}) \subsetneq S_2 \cup S_5$ is a clique. Thus, since for each $b_2 \in B_2$ and $x \in S_2 \cup S_5$,

$(b_2,x) \in E$, $radj(v,w;P) = radj(v,w;P_{V-B_2}) \dot{\cup} B_2$ is a clique and v,w is a simplicial pair in P . Since $v,w \in B_2$, v,w is not adjacent to s_1,a . Case D1.2.1 is complete.

CSAE D1.2.2. $S_3 = \phi$, $S_4 \neq \phi$.

Fix $s_4 \in S_4$. Since $s_4 \not\sim s_2$ in P , there exists $b' \in B$ such that $(b',s_2) \in E$ and $(b',s_4) \notin E$ (or vice-versa). However, since by Lemma 3.8, we may find $b'' \in B$ such that $(b'',s_4) \in E$, it follows that P^c contains one of the following three graphs: $(s_2 - s_1 - s_4 - b' - a - b'')$, $[s_2 - s_1 - s_4 - b' - a - b'']$ or $[s_1 - s_4 - b' - a - b'']$. Thus, since P is 2-chordal, it follows that case D1.2.2 can not occur.

CASE D2. There exists $a_1 \in A$ such that $(a_1,s_1) \notin E$.

In this case, since P^c does not contain 5LP , we may split A into two subsets,

$$A_1 = \{a' \in A \mid (a',s_1) \notin E\}$$

$$A_2 = \{a' \in A \mid (a',s_2) \in E\} .$$

Note that $A_2 \neq \phi$, by Lemma 3.8. If $a' \in A_2$, then $(a',s_2) \in E$, and since $adj(s_i;P_{A \cup S})$ is a clique for $i = 1,2$. Thus, $(a',s) \in E$ for every $s \in S$. Similarly, if $a' \in A_1$, then $(a',s) \in E$ for every $s \in S_2 \cup S_4 \cup S_5$. If $b' \in B$, then $(b',s_1) \in E$ since $(a_1,s_1) \notin E$ and $(b',a_1) \notin E$.

CASE D2.1. There exists $s_3 \in S_3$ and $s_4 \in S_4$ such that $(s_3,s_4) \in E$.

Choose $b' \in B$ such that $(b',s_2) \in E$, by Lemma 3.8. If $(b',s_i) \in E$ for i = 3,4 , then P^c contains the graph $(s_4 - s_1 - s_2 - s_3) \biguplus (b_1 - a_2)$, where $a_2 \in A_2$. Hence, $(b',s_i) \in E$ for i = 3 or i = 4 . If $(b',s_3) \in E$ and $(b',s_4) \notin E$, then P^c contains the graph $(s_3 - s_2 - s_1 - s_4 - b' - a_2)$. Hence, $(b',s_3) \notin E$ and $(b',s_4) \notin E$. But then, P^c contains 6LN , $(s_4 - s_1 - s_2 - s_3 - b' - a_2)$. Consequently, case D2.1 can not occur.

CASE D2.2. For every $s_3 \in S_3$ and every $s_4 \in S_4$, $(s_3,s_4) \in E$.

CASE D2.2.1. $S_3 \neq \phi$.

Suppose there exists an $a_1 \in A_1$ such that $(a_1,s_3) \notin E$ for every $s_3 \in S_3$. Then $adj(a_1;P) = S_5 \cup S_4 \cup S_2 \cup A$. For each $a \in A$, $(a,s_4) \in E$ for every $s_4 \in S_4$. Also, as $adj(s_i;P_{A \cup S})$ is a clique for i = 1,2 , if $a \in A$ and $s_5 \in S_5$, then $(a,s_6) \in E$. Hence, $S_5 \cup S_4 \cup S_2 \cup A$ is a clique. Thus a_1 is a simplicial vertex in P . On the other hand, suppose there exists $s_3 \in S_3$ such that $(a_1,s_3) \in E$ for some $a_1 \in A_1$. Choose $b' \in B$ such that $(b',s_2) \in E$, by Lemma 3.8. Then, P^c contains one of the following two graphs: $(s_3 - s_2 - s_1 - a_1 - b' - a_2)$ or $[a_1 - s_1 - s_2 - s_3 - b']$.

CASE D2.2.2. $S_3 = \phi$.

If $S_4 = \phi$, then $adj(a_1;P) \subseteq S_5 \cup S_2 \cup A$ which is a clique. Whence, a_1 is a simplicial vertex. If $S_4 \neq \phi$, then, since $s_2 \not\sim s_4$ for $s_4 \in S_4$, there exists a $b' \in B$ such that $(b',s_4) \notin E$ and $(b',s_2) \in E$ (or vice-versa). Pick $b'' \in B$ such that $(b'',s_4) \in E$, by Lemma 3.8. Then P^c contains $(s_2 - s_1 - s_4 - b' - a_2 - b'')$. Thus, $S_4 = \phi$.

We have come to the end of Case D.

The only remaining alternative is that A contains a vertex which is simplicial in P . The proof of Theorem 3.1 is thus complete. □

§4 2-SCHUR GRAPHS

For X , a subset of a vector space V we denote, by co(X) the set $\left\{ \sum_{i=1}^{n} t_i x_i \,\middle|\, t_i \geq 0 \ , \ x_i \in X \right\}$. The following proposition, though elementary, is key to linking [AHMR] to [PPS].

PROPOSITION 4.1. *Let* $X \subseteq M^+ \subseteq M_n(\mathbb{C})$, *where* M *is a subspace. If* X *is closed, and if* $x \in X$ *and* $t \geq 0$ *implies* $tx \in X$, *then* co(X) *is closed. In particular if* co(X) *is dense in* M^+ , *then* co(X) *equals* M^+ .

PROOF. We merely sketch the proof, leaving out most of the details.

Suppose y is the closure of co(X) , it is to be shown that $y \in co(X)$. To this end, assume that y has operator norm at most one, $\|y\| \leq 1$. Choose a sequence $\{y_n\} \subseteq co(X)$ converging to y . We may assume that $\|y_n\| \leq 2$. Since $X \subseteq M_n(\mathbb{C})$ and since the vector space $M_n(\mathbb{C})$ is isomorphic to $\mathbb{C}^{n^2}$, each $y \in co(X)$ is a convex linear combination of at most

$n^2 + 1$ elements of X . Write $y_k = \sum_{i=0}^{n^2} x_{ki}$. Since each x_{ki} is a positive semi-definite matrix, it follows that $\|x_{ik}\| \leq 2$. Let $X_1 = \{x \in X \mid \|x\| \leq 1\}$. X_1 is compact since it is the intersection of the unit ball of $M_n(\mathbb{C})$ with the closed set X . Define $J: [0,2]^{n^2+1} \times \prod_0^{n^2} X_1 \to co(X)$ by

$$J(t_0, t_1, \ldots, t_{n^2}, x_0, x_1, \ldots, x_{n^2}) = \sum_{i=0}^{n^2} t_i x_i .$$

Then, since $y_n \in \text{range}(J)$ for each n and since range(J) is compact, $y \in \text{range}(J)$ also. This completes the proof. □

Let $\mathscr{D}_m$ denote the diagonal matrices in $M_m(\mathbb{C})$. For P , a graph, define $\Gamma_m(P) = co\{(D_i^* x D_j)_{i,j=1}^m \mid D_i \in \mathscr{D}_m , x \in M^+(P)\} \subseteq M_m(M(P))^+$. In [PPS] , the graphs P , for which $\Gamma_m(P)$ is dense in $M_m(M(P))^+$, are characterized in terms of certain Schur product maps being positive (see Theorem 4.6 in [PPS]). We characterize graphs P with ord $(P) = 2$ for which $\Gamma_m(P) = M_m(M(P))^+$ in a graph theoretic way (see Theorem 4.8). The following is a preliminary lemma.

LEMMA 4.2. *For every graph* P *and every* $m \geq 1$, $\Gamma_m(P)$ *is closed.*

PROOF. Fix $m \geq 1$ and P a graph on n vertices. Let $S = \{(D_i^* x D_j)_{i,j=1}^m \mid D_i \in \mathscr{D}_m , x \in M^+(P)\}$. By Proposition 4.1, it is enough to show that S is closed. To this end, fix Y in the closure of S , $Y = (Y_{k\ell})$ with $Y_{k\ell} \in M(P)$. Let

$\mathfrak{a} = \{\alpha \mid (Y_{k,k})_{\alpha,\alpha} = 0$ for every $k = 1, 2, \ldots, m\}$. Since $Y \geq 0$, it follows that for each k, l, i, j and each $\alpha \in \mathfrak{a}$,

$$(Y_{kl})_{\alpha j} = (Y_{kl})_{i\alpha} = 0 .$$

Let $S_t = (D_{ti}^* X_t D_{tj})_{i,j=1}^{n} \in S$ for $t = 1, 2, \ldots$ be a sequence in S. Then, $S_k \longrightarrow Y$ if and only if, for each k, l, i, j,

$$(D_{tk}^* X_t D_{tl})_{ij} \longrightarrow (Y_{kl})_{ij} \quad \text{as} \quad t \longrightarrow \infty .$$

Thus, if $\alpha \in \mathfrak{a}$, then for each k, l, i, j both

$$(D_{tk}^* X_t D_{tl})_{\alpha j} \quad \text{and} \quad (D_{tk}^* X_t D_{tl})_{i\alpha}$$

converge to zero. Therefore, letting

$$E = \begin{bmatrix} \delta_1 & & & \mathbf{0} \\ & \delta_2 & & \\ & & \ddots & \\ \mathbf{0} & & & \delta_n \end{bmatrix} ,$$

where

$$\delta_1 = \begin{cases} 1 & \text{if} \quad i \notin \mathfrak{a} \\ 0 & \text{if} \quad i \in \mathfrak{a} \end{cases} ,$$

$$(D_{tk}^* E^* X_t ED_{tl})_{ij} \longrightarrow (Y_{kl})_{ij} \quad \text{for each} \quad k, l, i, j .$$

Consequently, by replacing D_{tl} by ED_{tl}, we can assume that $(D_{tk})_{\alpha} = 0$ for each $\alpha \in \mathfrak{a}$, where

$$D_{tk} = \begin{bmatrix} (D_{tk})_1 & & 0 \\ & \ddots & \\ 0 & & (D_{tk})_n \end{bmatrix} .$$

Further, since $E^2 = E$, X_t may be replaced by $E^* X_t E$, in which case

$$(X_t)_{i\alpha} = (X_t)_{\alpha j} = 0$$

for all i,j and all $\alpha \in a$. Hence, we may assume that $a = \phi$.

For each k , let $I_k = \{i | (Y_{kk})_{ii} = 0\}$. Since $Y \geq 0$, for every $i \in I_k$ and every j,ℓ

$$(Y_{k\ell})_{ij} = (Y_{\ell k})_{ij} = (Y_{k\ell})_{ji} = (Y_{\ell k})_{ji} = 0 .$$

Let $E_t^1 = \begin{bmatrix} E_{t1}^1 & & 0 \\ & \ddots & \\ 0 & & E_{tn}^1 \end{bmatrix}$, where $E_{t\mu}^1 = \begin{cases} 1 & \text{if } \mu \in I_1 \\ (D_{t1})_\mu & \text{if } \mu \notin I_1 \end{cases}$. By replacing X_t by $(E_t^1)^* X_t E_t^1$, we may assume $(D_1)_\mu = (D_{t1})_\mu = \begin{cases} 1 & \text{if } \mu \in I_1 \\ 0 & \text{if } \mu \notin I_t \end{cases}$. Consequently, $(X_t)_{ii} \longrightarrow (Y_{11})_{ii}$ for each $i \notin I_1$ and, by adjusting D_{tk} appropriately, $(D_{tk}^* X_t D_{tk}) \longrightarrow (Y_{k\ell})$. Let $E_2^t = \begin{bmatrix} E_{t1}^1 & & 0 \\ & \ddots & \\ 0 & & E_{tn}^1 \end{bmatrix}$, where $E_{t\mu}^2 = \begin{cases} 1 & \text{if } \mu \in I_1 \cup I_2 \\ (D_{t2})_\mu & \text{if } \mu \notin I_1 \cup I_2 \end{cases}$. Since for every $i,j \notin I_1$ $((E_t^2)^* X_t E_t^2)_{ij} = (\overline{E_t^2})_i (X_t)_{ij} (E_t^2)_j = (X_t)_{ij}$, we may replace X_t with $(E_t^2)^* X_t E_t^2$, in which case it can be assumed that

$$(D_{2t})_\mu = \begin{cases} 1 & \text{if } \mu \notin I_1 \cup I_2 \\ 0 & \text{if } \mu \in I_2 \\ (D_{2t})_\mu & \text{if } \mu \in I_1 \backslash I_2 \end{cases} .$$

Since, for each $i \notin I$, $(X_t)_{ii} \longrightarrow (Y_{11})_{ii} \neq 0$, it follows that $(D_{2t})_i \longrightarrow (D_2)_i \in \mathbb{C}$. Hence, $D_{2t} \longrightarrow D_2$ where
$(D_2)_\mu = \begin{cases} 1 & \text{if } \mu \notin I_1 \cup I_2 \\ 0 & \text{if } \mu \in I_2 \\ (D_{2t})_\mu & \text{if } \mu \in I_1 \backslash I_2 \end{cases}$. Moreover, for each $i \notin I_1 \cup I_2$, $(X_t)_{ii} \longrightarrow X_{ii} \in \mathbb{C}$. Continuing this process inductively produces $X_t \in M^+(P)$ and $D_k \in \mathcal{D}_n$ such that

$$(D_k^* X_t D_\ell) \longrightarrow (Y_{k\ell}) .$$

As $\bigcup_{k=1}^{m} I_k^c = \{1,2,\ldots,n\}$, given i and j, we can find k and ℓ such that $(D_k)_i \neq 0$ and $(D_\ell)_j \neq 0$. Thus, since $(Y_{k\ell})_{ij} = \lim_{t\to\infty} (D_k)_i (X_t)_{ij}(D_\ell)_j$, $(X_t)_{ij} \longrightarrow X_{ij} \in \mathbb{C}$. Therefore, $X_t \longrightarrow X \in M^+(P)$ and $(Y_{k\ell}) \longrightarrow (D_k^* X D_\ell)$ as desired. □

THEOREM 4.3. *If* P *is a graph for which* $\Gamma_m(P)$ *is dense in* $M_m(M(P))^+$, *then* ord $(P^{(m)})$ = ord (P) *for all* $m \geq 1$.

PROOF. Fix $m \geq 1$. Let k = ord (P). By Lemma 4.2, if $\Gamma_m(P)$ is dense in $M_m(M(P))^+$, then $\Gamma_m(P)$ equals $M_m(M(P))^+$. We suppose $\Gamma_m(P) = M_m(M(P))^+$. For $X \in M^+(P)$ and $D_i \in D_n$

$$(D_i^* X D_j)_{i,j=1}^n = (D_1^* \; D_2^* \; \dots \; D_n^*) \begin{bmatrix} X & X \dots X \\ X & X \\ \vdots & \\ X & \dots \; X \end{bmatrix} \begin{bmatrix} D_1 \\ \vdots \\ D_n \end{bmatrix} .$$

It follows that the rank of $(D_i^* X D_j)_{i,j=1}^m$ is at most the rank of X. Thus, since $M^+(P)$ is spanned by elements of rank at most k, $\Gamma_m(P)$, and hence $M_m(M(P))^+$, is spanned by elements of rank at most k. Since $M_m(M(P))^+$ can be identified with $M^+(P^{(m)})$, we conclude that $\text{ord}\,(P^{(m)}) = k = \text{ord}\,(P)$. □

EXAMPLE. If P is the compliment of the graph $(2LN, 2LN, 2LN)$, then $\text{ord}(P) = 2$, but $\text{ord}(P^{(2)}) = 3$. This is just Lemma 2.7.

The following example shows that even if $\text{ord}\,(P^{(m)}) = 2$ for all $m \geq 1$ it is still possible that $\Gamma_2(P)$ is not dense in $M_2(M(P))^+$. This example plays an important role.

PROPOSITION 4.4. $\Gamma_2(\hat{Q}) \neq M_2(M(\hat{Q}))^+$.

PROOF. Let $\hat{S}_2 = \{(D_i^* X D_j)_{i,j=1}^2 | D_i \in \mathbb{D}_5$, $X \in M^+(\hat{Q})\}$. By identifying $M_2(M(\hat{Q}))^+$ with $M(\hat{Q}^{(2)})$, we identify $(D_i^* X D_j)_{i,j=1}^2$ with

$$([(\overline{D_i})_k \, X_{kl} \, (D_j)_l]_{i,j=1}^2)_{k,l=1}^5 ,$$

where

$$D_i = \begin{bmatrix} (D_i)_1 & & 0 \\ & \ddots & \\ 0 & & (D_i)_5 \end{bmatrix} .$$

Hence,

$$[(\overline{D_i})_5 \; X_{55} \; (D_j)_5]_{i,j=1}^{2}$$

is a rank-one matrix. Suppose $M^+(\hat{Q}^{(2)}) = \Gamma_2(\hat{Q})$. Then, given an $A \in M^+(\hat{Q}^{(2)})$, $A = (A_{k,l})_{k,l=1}^{5}$, where $A_{kl} \in M_2(\mathbb{C})$, if A is irreducible in $M^+(\hat{Q}^{(2)})$, then $A \in \hat{S}_2$. Hence, $A_{55} \in M_2(\mathbb{C})$ is of rank one. Thus, to finish the proof, it suffices to exhibit an $A \in M^+(\hat{Q}^{(2)})$ which is irreducible and for which A_{55} is not rank one. To this end, define $Y_{v_i^j} \in \mathbb{C}^2$ by

$$T_{v_1^j} = \begin{bmatrix}1\\0\end{bmatrix}, \quad Y_{v_2^j} = \begin{bmatrix}1\\1\end{bmatrix}, \quad Y_{v_3^j} = \begin{bmatrix}0\\1\end{bmatrix}, \quad Y_{v_4^j} = \begin{bmatrix}1\\-1\end{bmatrix} \quad \text{for } j = 1,2$$

and

$$Y_{v_5^1} = \begin{bmatrix}1\\0\end{bmatrix}, \quad Y_{v_6^2} = \begin{bmatrix}1\\-1\end{bmatrix}.$$

Then, since $\langle Y_{v_1^j}, Y_{v_3^i}\rangle = 0 = \langle Y_{v_1^j}, Y_{v_4^i}\rangle$ for $i,j = 1,2$, it follows that

$$A =: \left[\left[\langle Y_{v_k^i}, Y_{v_l^j}\rangle\right]_{i,j=1}^{2}\right]_{k,l=1}^{5} \in M(\hat{Q}^{(2)})^+ .$$

Further, using Theorem 3.1 from [AHMR] (or see Theorem 1.1), it is a simple matter to show that A is irreducible in $M(\hat{Q}^{(2)})^+$. Finally,

$$A_{55} = \left[\langle Y_{V_5^i}, Y_{V_5^j} \rangle \right]_{i,j=1}^{2}$$

$$= \begin{bmatrix} 1 & 1 \\ 1 & 2 \end{bmatrix}$$

is not of rank one. □

THEOREM 4.5. $\Gamma_m(4LP) = M_m(M(4LP))^+$ *for each* $m \geq 1$.

PROOF. Fix $m \geq 1$. Since $\text{ord}\,(4LP^{(m)}) = 2$, by Proposition 1.2, to establish Theorem 4.5, it is enough to show, for every $A \in M^+(4LP^{(m)})$ of rank two, that $A = (D_i^* X D_j)_{i,j=1}^m$ for some $X \in M^+(4LP)$ and $D_i \in D_4$. Writing $D_i = \begin{bmatrix} (D_i)_1 & & 0 \\ & \ddots & \\ 0 & & (D_i)_4 \end{bmatrix}$ we will identify $(D_j^* X D_i)_{i,j=1}^m$ with $(((\overline{D_j})_k X_{kl} (D_i)_l)_{i,j=1}^m)_{k,l=1}^4$. Fix $A \in M(4LP^{(m)})^+$, with A of rank two. Find $Y_{ik} \in \mathbb{C}^2$ a representation of A . Hence,

$$((\langle Y_{ik}, Y_{j\ell} \rangle)_{i,j=1}^m = A .$$

There are two cases.

CASE 1: There exists k_1, k_2 so that Y_{1k_1} and Y_{2k_2} are linearly independent. And there exists k_3, k_4 so that Y_{3k_3} and Y_{4k_4} are also linearly independent.

In this case, it is easy to show that $\{Y_{ik} | i = 1, \ldots, m\}$ spans a one-dimensional space. Pick vectors X_{ik}, for $k = 1, 2, 3, 4$ and scalars c_{ik} so that $Y_{ik} = c_{ik} x_k$. Then

$$A = ((c_{ik}\bar{c}_{jl} \langle x_k, x_l \rangle)_{i,j=1}^{m})_{k,l=1}^{4} .$$

Hence, if we let $(D_j)_k = c_{ik}$ and $X = (\langle x_k, x_l \rangle)_{k,l=1}^{4}$, then $A = (D_i^* X D_j)$, as desired.

CASE 2: The vectors Y_{1k} and Y_{21} are scalar multiples of each other. In this case, we let R be the graph on vertices $\{v_1, v_2, v_3, v_4\}$ with $E(R) = V(R) \times V(R) \setminus \{(3,4), (4,3)\}$. R is a chordal graph; therefore $\operatorname{ord}(R^{(m)}) = 1$ for each m. Also,

$$A = ((\langle Y_{ik}, Y_{jl} \rangle)_{k,l=1}^{m})_{i,j=1}^{4} \in M^+(R^{(m)}) .$$

Thus, by Theorems 4.3 and 4.6 in [PPS] and Theorem 4.1 and Lemma 4.2, A is contained in the convex hull of $\{(D_i^* z D_j)_{i,j=1}^{m} | D_i \in \mathscr{D}_4, z \in M^+(R)\}$. But, $M^+(R) \subseteq M(Q)$, hence $M^+(R) \subseteq M^+(Q)$. Noting that $\{(D_i^* z D_j)_{i,j=1}^{m} | D_i \in \mathscr{D}_4, z \in M^+(R)\} \subseteq \{(D_i^* x D_j) | D_i \in D_4, x \in M^+(Q)\} \subseteq \{(D_i^* x D_j)_{i,j=1}^{m} | D_i \in \mathscr{D}_4, x \in M^+(L_4)\}$, we conclude $A \in \Gamma_m(L_4)$, as desired. □

Given a graph P, a pair of vertices $v,w \in V(P)$ is a Schur pair in P, if $P_{adj(v,w;P)} \leq (4LP)^{(m)}$ for some $m > 0$.

A sequence of vertices $v_1,w_1;v_2,w_2;\ldots;v_\ell,w_\ell$ where $v_i,w_i \in V(\tilde{P})$, is a 2-Schur decomposition of P if v_i,w_i is a Schur pair in $\tilde{P}_{V(\tilde{P})\setminus \bigcup_{j=1}^{i-1}\{v_i,w_i\}}$. P is 2-Schur decomposable if it has a 2-Schur decomposition.

PROPOSITION 4.6. *If* P *is 2-Schur decomposable, then* $\operatorname{ord}(P) = 2$ *and* $\Gamma_m(P) = M_m(M(P))^+$ *for every* $m > 0$.

PROOF. The proof is nearly identical to the proof of Theorem 2.4, thus we merely sketch it. Suppose x,y is a 2-Schur pair for a graph P. Let $v_1 = x$, $v_2 = y$ and order the remaining vertices so that there are integers $k_1 \leq k_2 \leq k_3$ as in the proof of Theorem 2.4. Fix $A \in M_m(M(P))^+$, we are to show $A \in \Gamma_m(P)$. We may write $A = (A_{st})_{s,t=1}^{3}$ with respect to the decomposition $n_1 = k_1$, $n_2 = k - k_1$, $n_3 = k_3 - k_2$, and apply Lemma 2.5 to obtain

$$A = \begin{bmatrix} B^{11} & B^{12} & 0 \\ B^{21} & B^{22} & 0 \\ 0 & 0 & 0 \end{bmatrix} + \begin{bmatrix} 0 & 0 & 0 \\ 0 & C^{22} & C^{23} \\ 0 & C^{32} & C^{33} \end{bmatrix} = B + C .$$

We may view B as an element of $M_m(M(P_{adj(v,v_2)}))^+$ and since $P_{adj(v,v_2)} = (4LP)^m$ for some m Theorem 4.5 implies $B \in \Gamma_m(P_{adj(v_1,v_2)}) \subseteq \Gamma_m(P)$. An induction argument finishes the proof. □

A graph P is said to be 2-Schur if P contains no loops of length five or more, P does not contain the graph $\hat{Q}$, and if P^c does not contain any of the graphs 6LP , 6LN , (4LN,2LN) , (3LP,2LN) , (2LN,2LN,2LN) . Thus, P is 2-Schur if and only if P does not contain $\hat{Q}$ and P is 2-chordal.

PROPOSITION 4.7. *Let* P *be a graph. If* $\Gamma_m(P) = M_m(M(P))^+$ *for every* $m > 0$ *and if* $\mathrm{ord}(P) = 2$, *then* P *is 2-Schur.*

PROOF. Since $\mathrm{ord}(P) = 2$ and $\Gamma_m(P) = M_m(P)^+$, it follows from Theorem 4.3 that $\mathrm{ord}(P^{(m)}) = \mathrm{ord}(P) = 2$ for every $m > 0$. Thus, by Theorem 3.1, P is 2-chordal. By Proposition 4.4, P does not contain $\hat{Q}$. □

THEOREM 4.8. *Given a graph* P , *the following are equivalent.*

i) P is 2-Schur decomposable.

ii) $\mathrm{ord}(P) = 2$ and $\Gamma_m(P) = M_m(M(P))^+$.

iii) P is 2-Schur.

PROOF. *ii)* implies *iii)* by Proposition 4.7. *i)* ⇏ *ii)* by Proposition 4.6. To see *iii)* implies *i)*, fix P a 2-Schur graph. P is then 2-chordal and hence, by Theorem 3.1, has a 2-decomposition series. Let (v,w) be a simplicial pair in P , then $P_{\mathrm{adj}(v,w;P)} \leq \hat{Q}$. If $P_{\mathrm{adj}(v,w;P)} \nleq 4LP$, then P is not

2-Schur. Hence (v,w) is a Schur pair in P. An induction argument finishes the proof. □

REMARK. Given P a graph and matrices $T_{ij} \in M_m(\mathbb{C})$ for each $(v_i,v_j) \in E(P)$ define the inflated Schur product map (see [PPS]) by

$$\phi_T(a_{ij}) = (a_{ij}T_{ij}) \in M(P^{(m)})$$

for $(a_{ij}) \in M(P)$. Combining Theorem 4.8 above and Theorem 4.6 in [PPS] shows that a graph P of order 2 is 2-Schur if and only if every inflated Schur product map which is positive is completely positive.

ACKNOWLEDGMENTS. The author would like to thank his ealier collaborators Jim Agler, Bill Helton, and Leiba Rodman for their continuing input and encouagement as well as Vern Paulsen for many stimulating conversations.

REFERENCES

[AHMR] Agler, J., Helton, J.W., McCullough, S., and Rodman, L., Positive Semi-definite Matrices with a Given Sparsity Pattern, to appear in Linear Algebra and its Applications.

[GJSW] Grone, R., Johnson, C., Sá, E.M., and Wolkowitz, H., Positive Completions of Partial Hermytian Matrices, Linear Algebra and its Applications 58 (1984), 109-124.

[PPS] Paulsen, V.I., Power, S.C., and Smith, R.R, Schur Products and Matrix Completions, preprint.

[PPW] Paulsen, V.I., Power, S.C., and Ward, J.P., Semi-Discreteness and Dilation Theory for Nest Algebras, preprint.

[R] Rose, D.J., A Graph Theoretic Study of the Numerical Solution of Linear Equations, Graph Theory and Computing, R. Reed Editor, Academic Press, New York, 1973, 183-217.

[D] Dirac, G.A., On Rigid Circuit Graphs, Abh. Math. Sem. Univ. Hamburg, 25 (1961), 71-76.

[FG] Fulkerson, D.R., and Gross, O.A., Incidence Matrices and Interval Graphs, Pacific J. Math., 15 (1965), 835-855.

[G] Golumbic, M.C., Algorithmic graph theory and perfect graphs, Academic Press, New York, 1980.

[HPR] Helton, J.W., Pierce, S., and Rodman, L., The ranks of extremal positive semi-definite matrices with a given sparsity pattern, preprint.

Department of Mathematics
Indiana University
Bloomington, Indiana 47405

Operator Theory:
Advances and Applications, Vol. 35

HAMILTONIAN REPRESENTATION OF STATIONARY PROCESSES

Giorgio Picci [1]

We show that any stationary m.s. continuous Gaussian process can be generated as the output of a Linear Hamiltonian System with a suitable invariant probability measure on the phase space.

1. INTRODUCTION

A good deal of the theory of "Classical" Dynamical Systems (i.e. measure preserving flows on manifolds [2]) can be viewed as an effort to understand the structure of systems which behave in a "random" or "stochastic" way in some sense. In this paper we shall pose the reverse question i.e. when can we view the trajectories of a smooth, say, sample continuous stochastic process as being generated by a Dynamical System? We shall consider (and, in fact, completely solve) this problem only for a rather restricted, but important, class of random processes, the class of $\mathbb{R}^m$-valued mean square continuous stationary Gaussian processes. In spite of the particular class of processes considered, some of the main ideas in the development which follows will be of a quite general nature. In order to illustrate these ideas, in this section we have kept an higher level of generality than what would be strictly necessary.

[1]Part of this work was done while the author was on leave at the Dept. of Electrical and Computer Engineering, Arizona State University, Tempe, AZ 85287.

KEY WORDS: Gaussian Processes, Hamiltonian Systems, Statistical Mechanics, Chaotic Dynamics.

As a first point we shall complement the classical idea of Dynamical System by introducing observation functions i.e. observables.

DEFINITION 1.1 *An autonomous, smooth, Dynamical System is a quadruple* $(M, \{\Phi(t)\}, \mu, h)$ *where* M *is a smooth manifold,* μ *is a finite measure on* M, *the maps* $\Phi(t): M \to M$ *form, for* $t \in \mathbb{R}$, *a one parameter group of measure preserving diffeomorphisms and* h *is a smooth function from* M *into a finite dimensional real space* $h: M \to \mathbb{R}^m$.

This is the notion of Dynamical System that we shall adopt in this paper. Very much as in System Theory [10], one is suggested to think of the state trajectories $t \to z(t) := \Phi(t)z$ ($z \in M$ is the initial state at time zero) as "internal" evolution of the system which is in general not directly accessible to external measurements. The state evolution is "seen" from the external world through the m read-out functions (observables) $h_1 \ldots h_m$ generating the output trajectories,

$$t \to y_k(t) = h_k(\Phi(t)z) \qquad k = 1 \ldots m$$

An important ingredient in the definition is the measure μ and the measure preserving character of the flow $\Phi(t)$. In the following we shall normalize μ to a probability measure and think of the triple $\{M, \mathcal{A}, \mu\}$ ($\mathcal{A}$ is the σ-algebra of subsets of M where μ is defined) as a bona fide probability space. The elementary event $z \in M$ chosen by "nature" is the initial state (or, equivalently, the state at any fixed reference time) of the system.

It follows that we can think of a Dynamical System in the sense of Definition 1.1, simply as a pair of *stationary processes* $\mathbf{z} = \{z(t)\}$, $\mathbf{y} = \{y(t)\}$ defined on $\{M, \mathcal{A}, \mu\}$. Namely,

$$\mathbf{z} : (t, z) \to \Phi(t)z$$
$$\mathbf{y} : (t, z) \to h(\Phi(t)z)$$

Note that $\mathbf{z}$ is a very degenerate type of *Markov process :* its present $z(0)$ determines the future (and the past) evolution exactly . The observables $y(t)$ are then functions of the Markov process $\mathbf{z}(t)$ at the corresponding time instant; $y(t)=h(\mathbf{z}(t))$.

The *finite dimensional distribution of order* n of the process y is a Borel measure $P(t_1,...,t_n,\cdot)$ on the n-fold product σ-algebra $\otimes_1^n \mathcal{B}^m$ where $\mathcal{B}^m$=Borel σ-algebra of $\mathbb{R}^m$.P is defined as

$$P(t_1,...,t_n;\ E_1,...,E_n) = \mu\{z \mid y(t_1,z) \in E_1,...,y(t_n,z) \in E_n\}$$

where $E_k \in \mathcal{B}^m$, $k=1,...,n$ and $t_1,...,t_n$ are arbitrary time instants.

Recall (e.g. [8] p. 145) that two stochastic processes are said to be *equivalent* if their finite dimensional distributions coincide (for all n).

In general terms the representation problem we are considering can be formulated in the following way: *Given a stationary* $\mathbb{R}^m$*-valued stochastic process* $\{y(t)\}$ *find (and classify) the dynamical systems whose output is equivalent to* $\{y(t)\}$.

We remark that the problem, if solvable, admits infinitely many solutions (as there certainly are infinitely many "equivalent" systems producing the same output trajectories) and the classification which is referred to above really means introducing a natural notion of "minimality" of a representation, discussing relations among minimal representations etc.

We must warn the reader that if M has finite dimension and μ is smooth (i.e. absolutely continuous), the class of random processes that one can generate is quite restricted and not very interesting. In order to generate "truly random" $\mathbb{R}^m$-valued processes we shall have to go to infinite dimensional manifolds.

2.LINEAR HAMILTONIAN SYSTEMS

We shall start with a brief digression on finite dimensional linear Hamiltonian systems as considered in classical mechanics (see e.g. [1]). Let $M:=\mathbb{R}^{2N}$ endowed with the usual (real) Euclidean metric structure and a nondegenerate antisymmetric bilinear (in one word: *simplectic*) form $\sigma(x,y) = -\sigma(y,x)$. This form, sometimes also called "antiscalar product", can be uniquely, written as $x'Jy$ (prime denote transpose) with J a nonsingular real skew symmetric ($J'=-J$) matrix. There is given on $\mathbb{R}^{2N}$ a quadratic function $H(z) = \frac{1}{2} z'Qz$, called the *Hamiltonian* which we shall assume strictly positive so that $Q=Q'>0$ (strictly positive definite). The *canonical differential equations* associated to σ and H ,

$$\dot{z}(t) = J\,Q\,z(t) \tag{2.1}$$

generate a flow $\Phi(t) : \mathbb{R}^{2N} \rightarrow \mathbb{R}^{2N}$ which is easily seen to preserve both the sympletic structure i.e. to leave invariant σ,

$$\sigma(\Phi(t)x,\Phi(t)y) = \sigma(x,y) \qquad \forall\ x,y \in \mathbb{R}^{2N} \tag{2.2}$$

and also the Hamiltonian function: $H(\Phi(t)z) = H(z)$, for all $t \in \mathbb{R}$. There is a natural family of probability measures on $\mathbb{R}^{2N}$ invariant for the flow defined by the canonical equations (2.1). These measures correspond to the so -called *Maxwell-Boltzmann* densities

$$\rho(z) = C_N \exp\left[-\frac{1}{\beta} H(z) \right] \tag{2.3}$$

(see e.g. [19]), where $\beta>0$ is a real parameter (the "temperature" of the system) and C_N is a normalization constant. In the following we shall fix β equal to one.

Together with the flow $\Phi(t)$ defined by (2.1) and the invariant measure (2.3) we consider also m linear functionals (observables) corresponding to observations of the phase vector $z(t)$ of the system along some m fixed directions $h_1,\ldots,h_m \in \mathbb{R}^{2N}$. The observations produce output trajectories $t \rightarrow y_k(t)$, $k=1,\ldots,m$ given by

$$y_k(t) = \langle h_k\ , z(t)\rangle \qquad k=1,\ldots,m \tag{2.4}$$

$\langle\cdot\ ,\ \cdot\rangle$ denoting Euclidean scalar product in $\mathbb{R}^{2N}$.

Taken together, (2.1), (2.3), (2.4) certainly define a (smooth autonomous) Dynamical System on the "simplectic" phase space $M = (\mathbb{R}^{2N}, \sigma)$, in the sense of Definition 1.1.

It is an obvious but important fact that by a coordinate change we can make the flow $\Phi(t)$ into a group of orthogonal (or unitary, which, within the present real structure amounts to the same) linear operators on $\mathbb{R}^{2N}$. In fact this is simply done by letting $\bar{z} = Q^{1/2}z$ thereby transforming the Hamiltonian function $H(z)$ into $\bar{H}(z) = 1/2 \, \| \bar{z} \|^2$. It follows that the transformed flow $\bar{\Phi}(t) = Q^{1/2}\Phi(t)\, Q^{-1/2}$ preserves Euclidean length (=twice the Hamiltonian). Note that the canonical equations (2.1) are transformed into

$$\dot{\bar{z}}(t) = Q^{1/2}J\, Q\, Q^{-1/2}\, \bar{z}(t) = Q^{1/2}J\, Q^{1/2}\, \bar{z}(t), \qquad (2.5)$$

in other words the infinitesimal generator of $\bar{\Phi}(t)$ is the skew-symmetric matrix

$$\bar{A} = Q^{1/2}J\, Q^{1/2} \qquad (2.6)$$

Note incidentally that (2.5) is not in canonical form i.e. $\bar{A}$ is not equal to $\bar{J}\,\bar{Q} = \bar{J}$, the transformed J matrix $\bar{J}$, being in fact equal to $Q^{-1/2}J\, Q^{-1/2}$, since the canonical structure is preserved only under symplectic transformations and $Q^{1/2}$ in general is not symplectic.

REMARK:

Observe that the nonsingularity of Q implies nonsingularity of the generator $\bar{A}$ (or A) which is in turn equivalent to $\bar{\Phi}(t)$ having no nontrivial fixed vectors i.e. $\bar{\Phi}(t)h=h$ for all $t \Rightarrow h=0$. This assumption, although not essential, simplifies matters considerably. In the following we shall only consider nonsingular systems of this type.

Example : Let

$$J = \begin{bmatrix} 0 & -I \\ I & 0 \end{bmatrix}, \qquad H(p,q) = 1/2(\, \|p\|^2 + q'V^2q\,) \qquad (2.7)$$

where $z \in \mathbb{R}^{2N}$ is written as $z'=[p',q']$, $p, q \in \mathbb{R}^N$ and V^2 is an NxN symmetric positive definite matrix (the potential matrix). Then the canonical equations

$$\begin{bmatrix} \dot{p}(t) \\ \dot{q}(t) \end{bmatrix} = \begin{bmatrix} 0 & -V \\ I & 0 \end{bmatrix} \begin{bmatrix} p(t) \\ q(t) \end{bmatrix} \tag{2.8.a}$$

$$y_k(t) = [\, u_k' \quad v_k'] \begin{bmatrix} p(t) \\ q(t) \end{bmatrix} \tag{2.8.b}$$

where $h_k' = [\, u_k' \,,\, v_k' \,]$, can be transformed into

$$\begin{bmatrix} \dot{\bar{p}}(t) \\ \dot{\bar{q}}(t) \end{bmatrix} = \begin{bmatrix} 0 & -V \\ V & 0 \end{bmatrix} \begin{bmatrix} \bar{p}(t) \\ \bar{q}(t) \end{bmatrix} \tag{2.9.a}$$

$$y_k(t) = [\, \bar{u}_k, \bar{v}_k] \begin{bmatrix} \bar{p}(t) \\ \bar{q}(t) \end{bmatrix} \tag{2.9.b}$$

with $\bar{p}=p$, $\bar{q}=Vq$, $\bar{u}_k= u_k$, $\bar{v}_k=v_kV^{-1}$. In this coordinate system the invariant density (2.3) becomes ($\beta=1$)

$$\rho(z) = C_N \exp(- 1/2 \, \| \bar{z} \|^2 \,) \tag{2.10}$$

i.e. it is a normalized Gaussian distribution (with zero mean and covariance matrix equal to the identity).

These preliminary observations will serve as a starting point for the generalization of the idea of Linear Hamiltonian system to infinite dimensional Hilbert spaces. This generalization will turn out to be crucial later on. For examples and more information on infinite dimensional Hamiltonian systems one may consult [13], [23] ,[22].

Let H be a real Hilbert space and $\bar{H}$ the complexification of H. A linear operator A (not necessarily everywhere defined) on $\bar{H}$ will be call *real* if it maps real vectors into real vectors.

We shall give below a general (coordinate free) definition of

Linear Hamiltonian system on a Hilbert space which will be shown to encompass the finite dimensional notion that has been discussed above.

DEFINITION 2.1

A (nonsingular) linear Hamiltonian system is a quadruple $(H, \{U(t)\}, h, \mu_0)$ *where*

i) H *is a real separable Hilbert space ;*

ii) $\{U(t);\ t \in \mathbb{R}\}$ *is a strongly continuous group of (real) unitary operators on* H *with no fixed vectors other than zero (i.e. the point 1 is not a common eigenvalue of the* $U(t)$*'s);*

iii) $h = [\langle h_1, \cdot\rangle, \ldots, \langle h_m, \cdot\rangle]'$ $h_k \in H$, $k=1,\ldots,m$ *is a collection of* m *linear functionals on* H *(the observables);*

iv) μ_0 *is the normalized Gaussian measure on* H [2].

Each initial state (or "phase") $z \in H$ originates, a state trajectory $t \to z(t) = U(t)z$ and a corresponding output trajectory $t \to y(t)$ where y is $\mathbb{R}^m$ valued with components

$$y_k : t \to \langle h_k, U(t)z\rangle \tag{2.11}$$

When y is considered as a function of (t,z) on $\mathbb{R}\times H$, H being thought of as a probability space (with Gaussian measure μ_0) i.e. when y is considered as a *stochastic process* we shall use the boldface notation **y** or $\{\mathbf{y}(t)\}$ to explicitely show that **y** is thought of as a collection of $\mathbb{R}^m$-valued random variables on H indexed by time $t \in \mathbb{R}$. Before going any further into this we need however to show (i) that Definition 2.1 naturally fits the idea of Dynamical system given in the previous section (at least in the linear case), (ii), that this definition reduces, when H is finite dimensional, to the notion of Hamiltonian system discussed at the beginning of this section.

Regarding the first point, we only need to check that μ_0 is an invariant measure for $U(t)$. To show this we shall recall

[2] See [12] p.54 or [19],[18].The definition will actually be recalled below.

that little bit of measure theory on Hilbert spaces ([7], [18], [9]) which is needed in the present linear setting.

As is well known, the natural generalization of the idea of Borel measure to infinite dimensional Hilbert spaces is a *cylinder measure*. It is a fact that, if we exclude very special cases, the Hilbert space structure in infinite dimensions is incompatible with countable additivity. Specifically, in the extension process (from algebras to σ-algebras) one has to give up the Hilbert space structure. Although countably additive on all finite dimensional subspaces of the Hilbert space H on which they are defined, cylinder measures are *not countably additive* in general. By a famous theorem of Gross [9] they can however be extended in a canonical way to a Banach space containing H as a dense subset. Hence an alternative to our present choice here could have been to work on Banach spaces. In this framework however, most of the spectral theory that we shall use rather heavily in the following would not be available and the results of this paper would conceivably be extremely hard to get.

Recall that a *cylinder set* in a (real) Hilbert space H is a subset of the form

$$C := \{ z \mid (\langle c_1 ,z\rangle,\dots,\langle c_n ,z\rangle) \in E_n\} \qquad (2.12)$$

where $c_1,\dots,c_n$ are vectors in H and E_n is a Borel subset of $\mathbb{R}^n$. Clearly $c_1,\dots,c_n$ can always be assumed linearly independent. Their span is some finite dimensional subspace H_c of H; the cylinder set (2.12) is said to have "base" in H_c. Let $\mathcal{F}$ be the family of orthogonal projections on H with finite dimensional range space. Note that any cylinder set can be written in a coordinate-free way as

$$C = \{ z ; Pz \in E_n \} \qquad (2.13)$$

for some projector $P \in \mathcal{F}$. Here (with a slight abuse of notation) E_n is a Borel subset of the (n-dimensional) range space H_n of P. The cylinder sets form an algebra $\mathcal{C}$ whose unit is the whole space H. If H is infinite dimensional this algebra however is not a σ-algebra. By a *cylinder probability measure on the Hilbert space* H we shall mean a finitely additive nonnegative set function μ on $\mathscr{C}$ such that (i) $\mu(H)=1$ and (ii) μ is contably additive whenever it is restricted to the σ-algebra of all cylinder sets having base in the same finite dimensional subspace H_n of H.

Example ([12] p. 54). The *normalized Gaussian measure,* μ_0, is defined as follows: if $P\in \mathscr{F}$ has n-dimensional range space H_n then

$$\mu_0(z|\ Pz \in E_n) := \left(\frac{1}{\sqrt{2\pi}}\right)^n \int_{E_n} \exp\ (-1/2\ \| z \|^2)\ d|z|_n \qquad (2.14)$$

where E_n is a Borel subset of H_n and $|z|_n$ is Lebesgue measure on H_n. Introducing coordinates, say, letting $(c_1,\ldots,c_n)$ be a basis for H_n, we have an invertible linear map $f_c: z \to (\langle c_1,z\rangle,\ldots,\langle c_n,z\rangle)$ from H_n onto $\mathbb{R}^n$. By composition with this map we can lift μ_0 from any finite dimensional subspace H_n to $\mathbb{R}^n$. There μ_0 (actually $\mu_0 f_c$) becomes an ordinary n-dimensional real Gaussian measure. Equivalently said, the joint distribution of the n linear functionals (components of f_c) : $\langle c_1,y\rangle,\ldots,\langle c_n,y\rangle$, considered as random variables on the cylinder probability space $(H, \mathscr{C}, \mu_0)$ *is an ordinary n-dimensional Gaussian distribution.* It is easy to check that these n Gaussian random variables are zero mean and that their covariance matrix is simply the Gramian of the c_i's,

$$\Gamma_{ij} = \langle c_i , c_j \rangle \qquad i,j=1,\ldots,n \qquad (2.15)$$

Recall that the *covariance operator* Λ of a cylinder measure μ on a Hilbert space H is defined by

$$\langle x,\Lambda y\rangle = \int_H \langle x,z\rangle\langle y,z\rangle\ \mu(dz)\ , \qquad x,y \in H \qquad (2.16)$$

If the integral on the r.h.s. exists as a bounded bilinear form in x,y then it defines Λ uniquely as a bounded self-adjoint operator on H. For the normalized Gaussian measure μ_0 the right hand side in (2.16) is equal to $\langle x,y\rangle$ (compare (2.15)). Therefore *the covariance operator of* μ_0 *is equal to the identity.*

LEMMA 2.1

Let $\{U(t)\}$ *be a continuous unitary group on a real Hilbert space* H *. Then*

$$\mu_0(U(t)^{-1}A) = \mu_0(A)$$

for all $t \in \mathbb{R}$ *and all cylinder sets A. In other words, the Gaussian measure* μ_0 *is invariant for* $\{U(t)\}$.

Proof: Let $A \in \mathcal{C}$ be represented w.r. to a basis $(c_1,\dots,c_n)$ as $A=\{ z | (\langle c_1,z\rangle,\dots,\langle c_n,z\rangle \in B\}$ with B some n-dimensional Borel set. Then

$$U(t)^{-1}A = \{ z| (\langle c_1,U(t)z\rangle,\dots,\langle c_n,U(t)z\rangle) \in B\}$$
$$= \{z \mid (\langle U(t)^*c_1,z\rangle,\dots,\langle U(t)^*c_n,z\rangle) \in B\}$$

Therefore $U(t)^{-1}A$ is also a cylinder set. Moreover the μ_0-probability of $U(t)^{-1}A$ can be computed (as indicated above) by integrating the joint Gaussian distribution of the n random variables $z \to \langle U^*(t)c_1,z\rangle,\dots,z \to \langle U^*(t)c_n,z\rangle$ over the set B. This distribution is completely determined by the mean (which is zero) and by the covariance matrix of the variables, which we denote by $\Gamma(t)$. Since $U(t)$ is unitary we have (compare (2.15))

$$\Gamma_{ij}(t) = \langle U^*(t)c_i,\ U(t)^*c_j\rangle = \Gamma_{ij} \qquad ij=1,\dots,n$$

and therefore $\mu(U(t)^{-1}A)= \mu(A)$.

As for the second point we shall show below that there is a natural simplectic structure on the real Hilbert space H which is canonically associated with the unitary group $U(t)$. With this additional structure the differential equation for the infinitesimal generator of $U(t)$ can be written as a pair of "canonical equations" which reduce to the form (2.5) or, more specifically, exactly to (2.9.a) in the finite dimensional case.

In the following "*" will denote adjoint and I will be the identity operator.

THEOREM 2.2

Let $U(t)$ *be a strongly continuous group of unitary operators on a real separable Hilbert space H. Assume there are no nontrivial fixed vectors for* $\{U(t)\}$. *Then there is,*

- *a decomposition of* H *into the sum of two orthogonal real subspaces,*

$$H = H_e + H_o , \tag{2.17}$$

- *A bounded (real) linear operator* J *on* H *with the property that* $J^* = -J$ *and* $J^2 = I$, *admitting the matrix representation (with respect to the direct sum (2.17))*

$$J = \begin{bmatrix} 0 & -E^* \\ E & 0 \end{bmatrix} \tag{2.18}$$

where $E : H_e \to H_o$ *is a unitary map,*

- *a densely defined (real) self adjoint positive operator* $V : H \to H$ *for which the direct sum decomposition* (2.17) *is reducing (i.e. both* H_e and H_o *are real invariant subspaces for* V) *which satisfies the commutation relation*

$$EV = VE . \tag{2.19}$$

With respect to the decomposition (2.17) the infinitesimal generator A of U(t) *can be written as*

$$A = \begin{bmatrix} 0 & -E^*V \\ EV & 0 \end{bmatrix} \tag{2.20}$$

and is a real skew-adjoint operator. The corresponding matrix representation of U(t) *is*

$$U(t) = \begin{bmatrix} \cos Vt & -E^* \sin Vt \\ E \sin Vt & \cos Vt \end{bmatrix} \tag{2.21}$$

so that U(t) *satisfies the identity*

$$U^*(t) J\, U(t) = J$$

i.e. it is a "simplectic map" with respect to the antiscalar product $[\, x, y \,] := \langle x, Jy \rangle$.

Although we haven't been able to find any precise reference, this result is probably well known and buried somewhere in the literature. The finite dimensional version boils down to the spectral representation of real skew-symmetric matrices and can be reconstructed e.g. from Gantmacher [6] p. 283-285 (see also [22] p.172). The infinite dimensional result seems much harder. We have been able to produce a proof starting from Stone's Theorem on the complexified space H, [16] . Note that the infinitesimal generator A in (2.20) can be written as

$$A = \begin{bmatrix} I & 0 \\ 0 & V \end{bmatrix} \begin{bmatrix} 0 & -E^* \\ E & 0 \end{bmatrix} \begin{bmatrix} I & 0 \\ 0 & V \end{bmatrix} \qquad (2.22)$$

which is of the form (2.6) for an Hamiltonian function of the form

$$H(z) = 1/2 \; [\| p \|^2 + \langle q \, , V^2 q \rangle] \qquad (2.23)$$

where $z = [p',q']'$ is the vector representation of any $z \in H_q$ relative to the direct sum decomposition (2.17).

As a last issue of this section we shall discuss the notion of *irreducibility* for linear Hamiltonian systems.

DEFINITION 2.2.

A linear Hamiltonian system $(H, U(t), h, \mu_o)$ *with output process* y *is "reducible" if there is a proper invariant subspace* $H_o \subset H$ *such that the subsystem* $(H_o, U_o(t), h_o, \nu_o)$, *where*[3]

$$U_o(t) = U(t)|_{H_0} \, , \qquad h_o = h|_{H_0} \, , \qquad \nu_o = \mu_o|_{H_0}$$

produces an output process y_o *which is equivalent to* y. *Otherwise the system is called "irreducible".*

Irreducibility is related (in fact equivalent) to the System theoretic property of *Observability.* Let $h_1, \ldots, h_m$ be the representatives in H of the m linear functionals composing the

[3]The symbol | means "restricted to".

read-out map of the system. We say that the system is *Oservable* if the $\mathbb{R}$-vector space generated by $U(t)h_1,\dots,U(t)h_m$ i.e. the set of all finite sums with real coefficients

$$\textit{span}\ \{\ U(t)h\ \}\ :=\ \{\ \Sigma\ \alpha_{kj}\ U(t)h_j\}$$

is dense in H. Alternatively said, we have observability iff $\{h_1,\dots,h_m\}$ is a *generating set* for the space H ([3] p. 63, [5] p. 105). Note that for an observable system the unitary group $U(t)$ has necessarily *finite multiplicity* (in fact multiplicity $\le m$). On the other hand everything in the phase space which can be observed from the "outside" (i.e. by looking at the output functions of the system) takes place in the *Observable subspace*

$$H_o\ :=\ \overline{\text{span}}\ \ \{\ U(t)h\ \}$$

for, any vector z orthogonal to H_0 *gives zero output for all* t as $U^*(t)h_k = U(-t)h_k \in H_o$ for all t and k 's and so,

$$y_k(t,z)\ =\ <\ U^*(t)h_k,\ z\ >\ =\ 0\quad .$$

THEOREM 2.3

A linear Hamiltonian system is irreducible if and only if it is observable.

Proof: For ease of notations we shall restrict to scalar output systems (m=1). Let the system be reducible and $H_o \oplus H_1$ the $U(t)$-reducing orthogonal direct sum decomposition of H implied by the definition. We denote by P_o the orthogonal projection onto H_o and write $(h_1 \equiv h)$ $h(t)$ for $U(t)h$. Note that by invariance

$$h_o(t)\ :=\ P_o h(t)\ =\ U_o(t)P_o h$$

Note also that the readout map $h|_{H_o}$ can be written as

$$h_o\ =\ <\ P_o\ h\ ,\ \cdot\ >$$

The equivalence of the processes y and y_o is the same thing as equality of the covariances i.e.

$$<\ h(t),\ h(s)\ >\ =\ <\ h_0(t),\ h_0(s)\ >\ =\ <P_0U(t)h,\ h(s)>$$

for all t,s. This in turn is equivalent to

$$\overline{\text{span}}\ \{ h(t) \} = \overline{\text{span}}\ \{ P_o h(t) \} \subset H_o$$

i.e. to non observability.

3. REPRESENTATION OF STATIONARY GAUSSIAN PROCESSES

Let $(\Omega, \mathscr{C}, \mu)$ be a *cylinder probability space* i.e. Ω a Hilbert space, $\mathscr{C}$ the algebra of cylinder subsets of Ω, and μ a cylinder probability measure on $\mathscr{C}$. In the following we shall always understand Ω to be a *real* Hilbert space (in which case the cylinder probability spaces is also called *real*). The inner product in Ω will still be denoted by $\langle\cdot,\cdot\rangle$. Subscripts will be appended whenever danger of confusion arises.

Let $h(\cdot): t \to [h_1(t),\dots,h_m(t)]'$ be an m-tuple of functions from $\mathbb{R}$ into Ω, usually written as a column vector. As time runs over $\mathbb{R}$, each component $t \to h_k(t)$ describes a certain "curve" in the Hilbert space Ω.

The family $y = \{ y(t) \}_{t\in\mathbb{R}}$ of linear bounded functionals

$$\omega \to y(t,\omega) = \begin{bmatrix} \langle h_1(t),\omega \rangle \\ \dots \\ \langle h_m(t),\omega \rangle \end{bmatrix} \in \mathbb{R}^m \tag{3.1}$$

will be called a *linear*, $\mathbb{R}^m$*-valued stochastic process*. (In short: a *linear process) defined on the basic space* $(\Omega,\mathscr{C}\ \mu)$. The scalar components $y_k(t) = \langle h_k(t),\cdot\rangle$ are, for each fixed t, linear real random variables on $(\Omega,\mathscr{C}\ \mu)$.

If $t \to h(t)$ is continuous (i.e. if each component $h_k(t)$ is continuous) the process is called *continuous*. If $h_k(t)=\Phi(t)h_k(o)$ for $k=1,\dots,m$ where $\Phi(t)$ is a measure preserving group of linear transformations on Ω then y is called *stationary*. The *finite dimensional distribution of order* n of the process is defined (exactly as in (1.2)) by

$$P(t_1,\dots,t_n;E_1,\dots,E_n) = \mu\{\omega;\langle h(t_1),\omega\rangle\in E_1,\dots,\langle h(t_n),\omega\rangle\in E_n\} \tag{3.2}$$

where $E_1,\dots,E_n$ are Borel sets in $\mathbb{R}^m$ and $t_1,\dots,t_n$ arbitrary time instants. By definition of cylinder measure, each $P(t_1,\dots,t_n;\dots)$ is a countably additive probability measure on the Borel σ-algebra of $(\mathbb{R}^m)^n$. By setting, say, $E_n=\mathbb{R}^m$, the base space of the cylinder set on the right in (3.2) is reduced to a subspace spanned by the first n-1 $h(t_k)$'s. It follows that $P(t_1,\dots,t_n;\dots,\mathbb{R}^m)$ coincides with the finite dimensional distribution $P(_1,\dots,t_{n-1};\cdot)$, of order n-1. This means that the finite dimensional distributions of a linear process, exactly as the finite dimensional distributions of any bonafide random process, are *consistent* in the sense of Kolmogorov. By a well known extension theorem ([8],p. 108),given any linear process y there is then a true probability space and an ordinary stochastic process defined on it which has the same finite dimensional distributions as y, i.e., *is equivalent to* y.Put it another way, *we cannot distinguish a linear process from an ordinary process by looking at probabilities of events involving any finite number of random variables of the two processes.* Later on we shall show a partial converse of this statement: every process in the family of mean square continuous vector Gaussian processes is equivalent (same finite dimensional distributions) to some linear process. Before showing this we record for future reference the following self evident fact.

PROPOSITION 3.1

The output of a Linear Hamiltonian System is a stationary continuous Gaussian linear process on the cylinder space $(H,\mathcal{C},\mu_o)$.

For, we simply have to write each $y_k(t)$ (compare (2.11)) explicitely as

$$y_k(t,z) = \langle U(t)^* h_k \, , \, z\rangle \qquad k=1,\dots,m \tag{3.3}$$

and notice that $h_k(t) := U(t)^* h_k$ evolves in time according to the unitary group $U^*(t)$.

In fact we can make this statement a bit more precise. Introduce the operation of *time average* on an m-dimensional linear stationary process y as (all quantities below are column vectors)

$$A(y) := \lim_{|t-s|\to 0} \frac{1}{t-s} \int_s^t y(r)dr = \lim_{|t-s|\to 0} < \frac{1}{|t-s|} \int_s^t \Phi^*(r)h\, dr, \cdot >$$

If y is of the form (3.3) and, more generally, if $\Phi(t)$ is *unitary*, then the time average can be shown to exist (the argument is virtually the same as in [17] pp. 24-25) and to be equal to the linear random variable $<\hat{E}(\{0\})h, \cdot>$ where $\hat{E}$ is the spectral measure of the unitary group U(t) (see e.g. [3] pp. 29-31). Consider then the following decomposition

$$y(t) = y_1(t) + y_o \qquad t \in \mathbb{R}$$

where y_o is a *constant* linear random vector and the stationary linear process $\{y_1(t)\}$ has zero average and is uncorrelated with y_o. It is easy to see that such a decomposition is unique and it must necessarily hold that $y_o = A(y)$, $y_1(t) = y(t) - A(y)$. For, any decomposition

$$<U^*(t)h,z> = <U^*(t)h_1,\ z> + <h_o,z>, \quad z \in H$$

with h orthogonal to $\overline{\{U^*(t)h\ \}}$ implies that the orthogonal direct sum decomposition $\overline{\text{span}}\ \{U(t)h_1\} \oplus \text{span}\ \{h_o\}$ is reducing for $\{U(t)\}$ and such that on span $\{h_o\}$, U(t) becomes the identity for all t. Clearly then h_o must be in the range space of $\hat{E}(\{0\})$ and in fact equal to $\hat{E}(\{0\})h$ since U(t) restricted to the first invariant subspace has a trivial spectral projector $\hat{E}_1(\{0\})=0$.

For a (non singular) linear Hamiltonian system the spectral measure $\hat{E}(\{0\})$ is always the *zero projector* since there is no common eigenvalue of the U(t)'s at 1. Therefore, we have obtained the following sharpened version of Proposition 3.1.

THEOREM 3.1

The output process of a (nonsingular) linear Hamiltonian System is a linear stationary continuous Gaussian process y *with zero average (i.e.* $A(y)=0$).

Below we shall see that this result can be inverted.

LEMMA 3.2

Every mean square continuous Gaussian process $\{\xi(t)\}$ *admits an equivalent linear process.*

Proof: For simplicity of notations we shall give the proof for scalar-valued processes (m=1). The general case will be considered briefly in the Remarks which follow. To start with we assume that $\{\xi(t)\}$ *has mean zero.*

Let $(\hat{\Omega}, \hat{\mathcal{A}}, \hat{\mu})$ be the original probability space on which the process is defined and let $H(\xi)$ be the closure in $L^2(\hat{\Omega},\hat{\mu})$ of the $\mathbb{R}$-vector space generated by the random variables $\{\xi(t)\};t\in\mathbb{R}\}$. $H(\xi)$ is called the *Gaussian space* generated by the process [14]; it is a Hilbert space of real Gaussian random variables, with inner product $<\zeta,\eta> = \hat{E}(\zeta\ \eta)$ ($\hat{E}$ means integral over $\hat{\Omega}$ w.r. to $\hat{\mu}$). By mean square continuity of the generating process, $H(\xi)$ is separable and therefore admits an orthonormal basis $\{\xi_k\}$. For each $t\in\mathbb{R}$, the representation of $\xi(t)$ with respect to the orthonormal basis

$$\xi(t) = \sum_{-\infty}^{+\infty} \alpha_j(t)\xi_j \tag{3.4}$$

converges in mean square and since $\hat{E}\ \xi(t)^2 < \infty$ we have

$$\sum_{-\infty}^{+\infty} \alpha_j(t)^2 < \infty \qquad \forall t \in \mathbb{R} \tag{3.5}$$

Thus the sequence $\alpha(t) := \{\alpha_j(t)\}_{j\in\mathbb{Z}}$ belongs to the real Hilbert space $l^2 := l^2(\mathbb{Z};\mathbb{R})$ for all t. Notice that the *covariance function* $\Lambda(t,s)$ of the process can be expressed from (3.4) as

$$\Lambda(t,s) = \hat{E}\ \xi(t)\xi(s) = \sum_{-\infty}^{+\infty} \alpha_j(t)\ \alpha_j(s) = <\alpha(t),\alpha(s)>_{l^2}. \tag{3.6}$$

We now introduce a cylinder probability space with $\Omega = l^2$, $\mathcal{C}$ the algebra of cylinder sets of l^2, $\mu=\mu_o$, the normalized Gaussian measure on Ω, and a linear process $\{y(t)\}$ defined as

$$y(t,\omega) = <\alpha(t),\omega>_\Omega \qquad t \in \mathbb{R} \tag{3.7}$$

It is clear that ξ and y have the same covariance function, in fact this follows immediately from formula (2.15) which in the present situation reads

$$E[y(t)y(s)] = <\alpha(t),\alpha(s)>_\Omega \tag{3.8}$$

E denoting integral w.r. to μ_o. Thus, ξ and y being both Gaussian, zero mean, with the same covariance function, have the same finite dimensional distributions.

If now $\{\xi(t)\}$ has nonzero mean, say $\hat{E}\,\xi(t)=m(t)$, then it is enough to repeat the first part of the argument above for $\xi(t)=\xi(t)-m(t)$ and then add $m(t)$ on the right hand side of (3.6).

REMARKS

i) In certain degenerate situations $H(\xi)$ is *finite dimensional*. In these cases $\{\xi_j\}$ is a finite set and thus $\alpha(t)$ is simply a vector in a finite dimensional euclidean space. We use the symbol Ω (instead of l^2) to accomodate for this possibility as well.

ii) In case $\{\xi(t)\}$ is $\mathbb{R}^m$-valued there are m different representations of the form (3.4) one for each component $\xi_k(t)$, $k=1,\dots,m$. We shall then write

$$y_k(t,\omega) = \langle\alpha_k(t),\omega\rangle_\Omega \qquad k=1,\dots,m \tag{3.9}$$

with the understanding that $\alpha_k(t)$ is now a vector in Ω (for each t). Single components of $\alpha_k(t)$ will be denoted by $\alpha_{kj}(t)$.

iii) By means of the representation (3.4) we can define a map $V:H(\xi)\to\Omega$ as

$$V\,\xi_k(t) := \alpha_k(t) \tag{3.10}$$

It is evident that V is *linear* on the $\mathbb{R}$-vector space $\text{span}\{\xi_k(t);\ k=1,\dots,m,\ t\in\mathbb{R}\}$ and *isometric*, since by formula (3.6) (in the expression below c_{kj} are real numbers),

$$\|\sum_{kj} c_{kj}\,\xi_k(t_j)\|_{H(\xi)} = \|\sum_{kj} c_{kj}\alpha_k(t_j)\|_\Omega$$

hence it extends to a unitary map from $H(\xi)$ onto its range space which we denote by $\mathbf{H}\subset\Omega$. Each element $h\in\mathbf{H}$ defines in turn a linear functional $\langle h,\cdot\rangle_\Omega$ on the cylinder space $(\Omega,\mathcal{C},\mu_\sigma)$. The Hilbert space of these functionals will be denoted by $\mathbf{H}^*$. *There* *is then a unitary map* $V : H(\xi) \to H^*$ *mapping each real random variable* $x \in H(\xi)$ (recall that x is defined on the original probability space $(\hat{\Omega},\hat{\mathcal{A}},\hat{\mu})$ and is real - Gaussian) *into a linear random variable* $\mathbf{x}:\omega \to \langle h, \omega\rangle_\Omega$ defined on the cylinder space $(\Omega,\mathcal{C},\mu_o)$, where $h^*=Vx$. Note that H^* is the analog of $H(\xi)$ in terms of linear random variables on the cylinder space $(\Omega,\mathcal{C},\mu_o)$. In fact it is immediate to check that it is the closure of the $\mathbb{R}$-vector space generated by the variables of the *linear process* $\mathbf{y}$ i.e. the closure of the space of linear functionals

$$\{ \sum_{kj} c_{kj}\langle\alpha_k(t_j), \cdot\rangle_\Omega \}$$

with respect to the metric

$$\| \langle h, \cdot\rangle_\Omega \|^2 := \int_\Omega |\langle h,\omega\rangle|^2 \mu_o(d\omega)$$

the latter integral being actually equal to $\| h \|^2_\Omega$.

THEOREM 3.2

Every zero average stationary m.s. continuous $\mathbb{R}^m$*-valued Gaussian process* $\{\xi(t)\}$ *can be generated*[4] *as the output of a linear Hamiltonian system.*

Proof: Let $U(t) : H(\xi) \to H(\xi)$ be the strongly continuous unitary group (the "shift group") acting on the random variables of the process as

$$U(t)\xi_k(s) = \xi_k(t+s), \qquad k=1,..m, \qquad t,s \in \mathbb{R}$$

(see e.g. [17] p. 14). We define a family of operators $T^*(t):H \to H$ by setting

$$T^*(t)\alpha_k(s) := \alpha_k(t+s), \quad k=1,...m, \quad t,s \in \mathbb{R} \qquad (3.11)$$

Since

$$T^*(t) = V\,U(t)V^{-1} \qquad (3.12)$$

$\{ T^*(t) \}$ is a strongly continuous unitary group on H. Its adjoint

[4] In the sense that we can reproduce all its finite dimensional probability distributions.

also acts on H, considered as a subspace of Ω. In fact, since $U(t)\xi_1(0),\ldots,U(t)\xi_m(0)$ generate $H(\xi)$ it follows that, likewise,

$$\overline{\text{span}}\ \{\ T(t)\alpha_k(0);\ k=1\ldots m,\ t\in\mathbb{R}\ \}\ =\mathbf{H}\ . \qquad (3.13)$$

Now since $\{U(t)\}$ has no nonzero fixed vectors (as ξ is zero average) the same is true for $T(t)$. Pick any strongly continuous group $T_1(t)$ on the orthogonal complement of H in Ω, also without nonzero fixed vectors. Then any linear Hamiltonian system of the type

$$\{\Omega,\ T(t)\oplus T_1(t)\ ,\ (\langle\alpha_1(0),.\rangle,\ldots,\langle\alpha_m(0),.\rangle),\ \mu_o\} \qquad (3.14)$$

will produce an output process which is a *linear* $\mathbb{R}^m$-valued, stationary Gaussian process y with exactly the same covariance matrix function of ξ. In fact by unitarity of V, (3.11) and (3.12), we get

$$E[y_j(t)y_k(s)]\ =\ \langle\alpha_j(t),\alpha_k(s)\rangle_\Omega\ =\ \langle\xi_j(t),\ \xi_k(s)\rangle_{H(\xi)}$$

$$=\ \hat{E}[\xi_j(t),\ \xi_k(s)]\qquad .$$

An *irreducible* linear Hamiltonian system generating a process equivalent to ξ is obtained by taking Ω = H and $T(t)$ in place of $T(t)\oplus T_1(t)$. Compare (3.13).

Taken together with Theorem 3.1, this result may be viewed as a characterization of a certain class of Gaussian processes.

COROLLARY 3.3

The set of all zero average stationary m.s. continuous Gaussian processes constitutes exactly the class of random processes that can be generated as output of linear non singular Hamiltonian dynamical systems.

The above is probably the simplest instance of an equivalence between stochastic processes and (deterministic) dynamical systems. Eqivalences of this kind are important to provide rigorous foundations to the "stochastic aggregation" procedures of statistical mechanics. Typically,in this setting one is interested in describing the external variables of a deterministic Hamiltonian system in "thermal equilibrium" (i.e. with an invariant measure of the Maxwell-Boltzmann type), having a "very large" number of degrees of freedom. The goal is to prove that the external variables, defining the macroscopic physics of the system, behave in some sense in a "random" way so that the Thermodynamic (i.e. average macroscopic) behaviour can be deduced rigorously from the microscopic dynamics. See e.g. [11], [13], [15].

We refer the reader to [21] or [17] for the definition of a *purely non deterministic* (or regular) process. This is what is meant to be a truly (or completely) "random" process. We want to end this note by a characterization of the situations where an interesting (i.e. purely non deterministic) random behaviour of the observables is obtained. In general this occurs *only if the dimension* (i.e. the number of degrees of freedom) *of the system is infinite* .

THEOREM 3.4

An irreducible linear Hamiltonian system $(H_o\{U(t)\},h,\mu_o)$, *generates a purely non deterministic output process if and only if*

i) H *is infinite dimensional* .

ii) *The real self adjoint operator* V, *i.e. the (square root of the) potential operator of the system (compare* (2.20), (2.23)) *has Lebesgue spectrum, necessarily of finite multiplicity* $\le m$.

iii) *The spectral density matrix* $M=[M_{jk}]$

$$M_{jk}(\lambda) = \langle h_j, dE(\lambda)h_k\rangle/d\lambda \qquad j,k=1,\ldots,m$$

admits analytic factors

$$M(\lambda) = W^*(\lambda)W(\lambda)$$

i.e. matrix factors W *with rows in the* m-*dimensional Hardy space* H^2_m *of the half plane.*

For the proof of this Theorem we shall have to refer the reader to the paper [15] where the general technical background for this sort of arguments is discussed in detail. Note that Theorem 3.4 can also be read in a slightly different key, more in the spirit of the theory of Classical Dynamical Systems. It gives an answer to a question like "when is a linear Hamiltonian system chaotic (i.e. a K-system)"?

REFERENCES

[1] ARNOLD V.I.(1979) *Mathematical methods of classical Mechanics*, Springer.

[2] ARNOLD V.I., AVEZ A. (1968) *Ergodic Problems of Classical Mechanics*, Benjamin.

[3] AKHIEZER N.I., GLAZMAN I.M. (1963) *Theory of Linear Operators in Hilbert Space*, Vol. II, Ungar.

[4] BLOCH A. (1985) Completely integrable Hamiltonian Systems and Total Least Squares. Doctoral Dissertation, Harvard University.

[5] FUHRMANN P.A (1981) *Linear Systems and Operators in Hilbert Space*, Mc Graw Hill.

[6] GANTMACHER F.R. (1959) *Matrix Theory* Vol. I, Chelsea.

[7] GELFAND I.M., VILENKIN N.Y. (1964) *Generalized Functions*, Vol. 4, Ac. Press.

[8] GIKHMAN I.I., SHOROKHOD A.N. (1965) *Introduction to the Theory of Random Processes*, Saunders.

[9] GROSS L. (1965) "Abstract Wiener Spaces", *Proc. 5th Berkeley Symp. Math. Stat. Prob.*, 2, pp. 31-42.

[10] KALMAN R.E., FALB P.L., ARBIB M.A. (1979) *Topics in Mathematical System Theory*, Mc Graw Hill.

[11] KINTCHINE A. (1949) *Mathematical Foundations of Statistical Mechanics*, Dover.

[12] KUO H.H. (1975) *Gaussian Measures in Banach Spaces*, Springer Lect. Notes Math., 463.

[13] LEWIS J.T., MAASSEN H. (1984) "Hamiltonian Models of Classical and Quantum Stochastic Processes", *Proc. Workshop Quantum Probability and Applications to the Quantum Theory of Irreversible Processes*, L. Accardi, A. Frigerio, V. Gorini eds. Springer Lect. Notes Math. 1055.

[14] NEVEU J.(1968) *Processus Alatoires Gaussiens*, Presses de l'Universit de Montral.

[15] PICCI G. (1986) "Application of Stochastic Realization Theory to a Fundamental Problem of Statistical Physics" in *Modelling Identification and Robust Control* C.J. Byrnes and A. Lindquist eds. North Holland.

[16] PICCI G. (1987) "The Spectral Theory of Unitary groups on a real Hilbert space and Hamiltonian systems". Preprint.

[17] ROZANOV Y.A. (1967) *Stationary Random Processes*. Holden Days.

[18] SEGAL I.E. (1965) "Algebraic Integration Theory" *Bull A.M.S.*, 71, pp. 419-489.

[19] THOMPSON C.J. (1972) *Mathematical Statistical Mechanics*, Princeton Univ. Press.

[20] VON NEUMANN J. (1932) "Zur Operatorenmethoden in der klassischen Mechanik" *Ann. Math.*, 33, pp. 587-648.

[21] WIENER N., MASANI P. (1957) "The Prediction Theory of Multivariate Stochastic Processes" I, *Acta Math.*, 98, pp. 111-150, II *Acta Math.*, 99, pp. 93-137.

[22] ABRAHAM R.,MARSDEN J.E. (1978) *Foundations of Mechanics* Benjamin/Cummings.

[23] CHERNOFF P.R., MARSDEN J.E. (1974) *Properties of infinite dimensional Hamiltonian Systems.* Springer Lect. Notes in Mathematics 425.

Dipartimento di Elettronica e Informatica
Universita' di Padova
35131 PADOVA, ITALY
and
LADSEB-C.N.R.
PADOVA,ITALY

Operator Theory:
Advances and Applications, Vol. 35

END POINT RESULTS FOR ESTIMATES OF SINGULAR VALUES OF SINGULAR INTEGRAL OPERATORS

Richard Rochberg[1] and Stephen Semmes[2]

We study the singular values of the commutator between multiplication by a function b(x) and singular integral operators acting on $L^2(\mathbb{R})$. The relation between the smoothness of b(x) (measured using the Besov scale) and the decay of the singular values of the commutator (measured using the Schatten ideals) is well understood when the index, p, is greater than one. Here we offer results for the case $p = 1$. The simplest example, when the integral operator is the Hilbert transform, is atypical because of the algebraic simplicity of the kernel. Our methods are designed for more general kernels.

We also give results for the case $p = n$ for analogously defined operators on $L^2(\mathbb{R}^n)$.

INTRODUCTION AND SUMMARY

Suppose b(x) is a function defined on the real line and let $T = T_b$ be the operator on $L^2(\mathbb{R})$ obtained by commuting multiplication by b and the Hilbert transform. T has the integral kernel

$$k(x,y) = \frac{b(x) - b(y)}{x - y} . \tag{1.1}$$

We quantify the smoothness of b using the Besov scale. Let Pb denote the Poisson extension for b from $\mathbb{R}$ to $\mathbb{R}^2_+$. For $0 < p < \infty$ and $0 \leq q \leq \infty$ we will say that b is in the (Lebesgue-Lorentz) Besov space $B^{p,q}$ if b is in the space BMO and the gradients $\nabla^k Pb$ satisfy

$$y^k \nabla^k Pb(x,y) \in L^{p,q}(\mathbb{R}^2_+, y^{-2}\, dxdy) \tag{1.2}$$

---

[1] Partially supported by NSF grant DMS 8701271.

[2] Partially supported by an NSF postdoctoral fellowship.

for $k > 1/p$. Here $L^{p,q}$ denotes the Lebesque-Lorentz space. The requirement that b be in BMO is for control at infinity. It is well known that these are complete (quasi-)normed spaces with the natural (quasi-)norm and that different allowable choices of k produce equivalent quasinorms.

We measure the size of operators using the (Lebesgue-Lorentz) Schatten ideals. For a compact linear operator A acting on a Hilbert space we set $|A| = (A^*A)^{1/2}$ and denote the eigenvalues of $|A|$, repeated according to multiplicity and in decreasing order, by $s_n = s_n(A)$; $n = 0,1,\ldots$ We say that A is in the (Lebesgue-Lorentz) Schatten ideal $\mathcal{S}^{p,q}$ if the sequence $\{s_n\}$ is in the Lebesgue-Lorentz space of the nonnegative integers, $\ell^{p,q}(\mathbb{Z}^+)$. Again we use the natural (quasi-)norm.

For the model case of T_b we have complete results.

THEOREM 1.3. (Peller [Pe1,2], Semmes [S]): For $0 < p < \infty$, $0 \le q \le \infty$, T_b is in $\mathcal{S}^{p,q}$ if and only if b is in $B^{p,q}$.

(The proofs in the references are given only for the diagonal case, $p = q$; but they extend without difficulty.)

The original proofs of Theorem 1.3 made substantial use of harmonic analysis, fucntion theory, and the particular algebraic structure of the kernel (1.1). As an example of how the particular structure of $k(x,y)$ can be decisive, note that if $b(x) = (x - a)^{-1}$ for some a in $\mathbb{C}\backslash\mathbb{R}$ then we compute

$$k(x,y) = -(x - a)^{-1}(y - a)^{-1}.$$

Because the kernel is a product of a function of x and a function of y, T_b is a one dimensional operator and certainly in all the spaces $\mathcal{S}^{p,q}$. We will see that a slight change in the form of the kernel leads to a class of operators which contain no non-trivial operators in the trace class $\mathcal{S}^{1,1}$.

In [RS] we presented techniques for studying the relation between the integral kernel of integral operators and the singular values of the operator. Those techniques didn't use function theory, Fourier transform, or the particular algebraic structure of the kernel. The results apply, for instance, to the operator R_b acting on $L^2(\mathbb{R})$ with integral kernel given by

$$k(x,y) = \frac{b(x) - b(y)}{|x - y|}. \tag{1.4}$$

A particular case of the results of [RS] is

THEOREM 1.5. For $1 < p < \infty$, $1 \leq q \leq \infty$, R_b is in $\mathcal{S}^{p,q}$ if and only if b is in $B^{p,q}$.

Here we describe what happens for $p \leq 1$. We will establish

THEOREM A. For $p < 1$ or $p = 1$ and $q < \infty$, R_b is in $\mathcal{S}^{p,q}$ if and only if b is constant (and hence R_b is trivial).

This type of degenerate behavior below a critical index was found by Janson and Wolff [JW] in their study of commutators acting on $L^2(\mathbb{R}^n)$. In that case $p = n$ is the critical index.

By Theorem A the map from functions, b, to operators, R_b, which is of strong type (p,p) for $1 < p < \infty$ is not of strong type (1,1). We will, however, show it is of weak type (1,1). Let $Op^{1,\infty}$ be the space of b for which R_b is in $\mathcal{S}^{1,\infty}$. We will obtain

THEOREM B.

$$B^{1,1} \subset Op^{1,\infty}. \tag{1.6}$$

The proof of Theorem B uses the machinery of [RS] but not the particular form of R_b. Hence a similar result holds for any operator to which the methods of [RS] apply. For instance, the result holds if the denominator in (1.4) is replaced by

$$|x - y|^{1+i\gamma}$$

for some real γ.

These results are similar in spirit to the results of Arazy, Fisher, and Peetre [AFP] on Hankel operators on Bergman spaces. They obtain an analog of Theorem 1.5, an analog of Theorem A, and a result similar to Theorem B involving the Maceev ideal (which is slightly larger than $\mathcal{S}^{1,\infty}$).

We actually prove a result about function spaces. Let $\mathcal{Q}$ be the collection of the triples of the dyadic intervals in $\mathbb{R}$. For Q in $\mathcal{Q}$ and any locally integrable b defined on $\mathbb{R}$, let $m_Q(b)$ be the mean of b on Q;

$$m_Q(b) = |Q|^{-1}\int_Q b.$$

Here $|Q|$ denotes the length of Q. Define the mean oscillation of b on Q, osc(b,Q) by

$$\operatorname{osc}(b,Q) = m_Q(|b - m_Q(b)|).$$

Let $\operatorname{Osc}^{p,q}$ be the set of functions b in BMO for which the sequence on numbers $\{\operatorname{osc}(b,Q)\}_{Q\in\mathcal{Q}}$ is in $\ell^{p,q}(\mathcal{Q})$. We will prove

THEOREM C.

(1.7) $$B^{1,1} \subset \operatorname{Osc}^{1,\infty} \subset B^{1,\infty}$$

and both inclusions are proper.

Corollary 2.8 of [RS] has as an instance

(1.8) $$\operatorname{Osc}^{1,\infty} \subset \operatorname{Op}^{1,\infty}.$$

The combination of this and (1.7) gives Theorem B.

Theorems A and C are proved in the next section. In the third section we consider the analogs of these results for operators acting on $L^2(\mathbb{R}^n)$, $n \geq 2$. The final section contains a few remarks and questions.

PROOFS

We will be a bit sketchy with those details that are very similar to those in [RS].

<u>Proof of Theorem A:</u> If b is constant then R_b is the zero operator.

If $p < 1$, $1 \leq q \leq \infty$, then $\mathcal{S}^{p,q} \subset \mathcal{S}^{1,1}$. Thus we must show that if we are given b with R_b in $\mathcal{S}^{1,q}$ for some q, $1 \leq q < \infty$ then b is constant. Let $s_n = s_n(R_b)$, $n = 0,1,\ldots$ By definition of $\mathcal{S}^{1,q}$ we must have

(2.1) $$\sum s_n{}^q\, n^{q-1} < \infty.$$

Given N, by Holder's inequality,

$$\sum_{n=1}^{2^N} s_n \le \left[\sum_{n=1}^{2^N} s_n{}^q\, n^{q-1}\right]^{1/q} \left[\sum_{n=1}^{2^N} n^{-1}\right]^{(q-1)/q}.$$

Hence, using (2.1) we find

(2.2) $$\sum_{n=1}^{2^N} s_n \le c\, N^{(q-1)/q}.$$

If T is a compact operator and $\{h_j\}$, $\{k_j\}$ are orthonormal sequences then

$$\sum_{n=1}^{2^N} |(Th_j, k_j)| \le \sum_{n=1}^{2^N} s_n$$

(pg. 47 of [GK]).

Suppose that b is non-constant and suppose, for the moment, that b is smooth. We can find a dyadic interval J and constants c_1, c_2 with $c_1 \neq 0$ so that , for x in J

(2.3) $$|b'(x) - c_1| \ge |c_1|/2$$

and

(2.4) $$|b''(x)| \le c_2.$$

Let $\{S_j\}_{j\in\mathbb{Z}}$ be the dyadic subintervals of J indexed so that $|S_j|$ is nonincreasing. For each j, let L_j be the left half of S_j, let h_j be the Haar function associated with S_j, let k_j be the Haar function associated with L_j, and let x_j be the common left end point of S_j and L_j.

We wish to compute

$$(2.5) \qquad (R_b h_j, k_j) = \iint \frac{b(x) - b(y)}{|x - y|} h_j(y) k_j(x)\, dy\, dx.$$

The integrand is zero unless (y,x) is in $S_j \times L_j$. On that region we can use Taylor's theorem twice and (2.4) to write

$$b(y) = b(x) + (y - x)b'(x) + O(|x - y|^2)$$

and

$$b'(x) = b'(x_j) + O(|S_j|).$$

Thus

$$b(x) - b(y) = b'(x_j)(x - y) + O(|x - y|\ |S_j|).$$

Using this in (2.5) we find

$$(2.6) \quad (R_b h_j, k_j) = \int\int_{L_j X S_j} b'(x_j) \operatorname{sgn}(x - y)\ h_j(y) k_j(x)\, dy\, dx$$

$$+ \int\int_{L_j X S_j} O(|S_j|)\ |S_j|^{-1/2}\ |L_j|^{-1/2}\, dy\, dx.$$

The second integral is $O(|S_j|^2)$. The first can be evaluated explicitly as $2^{-3/2}\, b'(x_j)\ |S_j|$. We now use (2.3) and find that for large j (for which $|S_j|^2 << c_1|S_j|$) and some positive c,

$$|(R_b h_j, k_j)| \geq c\ |S_j|.$$

The number of $|S_j|$ of size 2^{-k} is $2^k|J|$. Thus, for large k,

$$\sum_{|S_j| = 2^{-k}} |(R_b h_j, k_j)| \geq c.$$

Summing this for $n \leq k$ gives a contradiction to (2.2) and thus to (2.3). Hence $b' \equiv 0$ and b is constant.

To remove the assumption that b is smooth, first consider the case $q = 1$. If T_b is in $\mathcal{S}^{1,1}$ and φ is any test function then, changing the order of integration and noting that

$\mathcal{S}^{1,1}$ is a Banach space, we find $T_{b*\varphi}$ is in $\mathcal{S}^{1,1}$. The previous discussion applies to the smooth function $b*\varphi$ and we conclude that $b*\varphi$ is constant. Since φ is any test function we conclude b is constant. If $q > 1$ then $\mathcal{S}^{1,q}$ is not a Banach space. However $T_{b*\varphi}$ will still be in the Banach space of operators whose singular numbers satisfy (2.2). Thus, as before, we conclude that b is constant.

<u>Proof of Theorem C:</u> The two halves are independent. First suppose f is in $B^{1,1}$. Let $F(u,v)$ be the Poisson extension of f to $\mathbb{R}^2_+$. Define F^* on $\mathbb{R}^2_+$ by

$$F^*(x,t) = t \sup\left\{|\nabla F(u,v)| : (u,v)\in\mathbb{R}^2_+,\ |x-u|<t,\ t/2<v<t\right\}.$$

By Proposition 4.1 of [RS], in order to show that f is in $Osc^{1,\infty}$ it is sufficient to show that F^* is in $L^{1,\infty}(\mathbb{R}^2_+, y^{-2}\,dxdy)$. $\nabla F = (F_x, F_y)$. Both F_x and F_y are Poisson integrals of functions in the real Hardy space Re H^1. F_x is in Re H^1 because of the classical inclusions between the Besov spaces and the potential spaces. F_y is the conjugate harmonic function to F_x and hence is also in Re H^1. (For all this see [T].) The nontangential Poisson maximal function takes Re H^1 to $L^1(\mathbb{R})$ and thus $g(x)$, the nontangential maximal function of ∇F, is in L^1. By definition $F^*(x,y) \le y\, g(x)$. Hence

$$S_1 = \{(x,y): F^*(x,y) \ge \lambda\} \subset \{(x,y): y\,g(x) \ge \lambda\} = S_2.$$

Thus

$$\begin{aligned} |S_1| \le |S_2| &= \iint_{S_2} y^{-2}\,dy\,dx \\ &= \int_{\mathbb{R}} \int_{yg(x)>\lambda} y^{-2}\,dy\,dx \\ &= \int_{\mathbb{R}} \lambda^{-1} g(x)\,dx \le c\,\lambda^{-1} \end{aligned}$$

as required. The fact that the inclusion is strict follows from the fact that the space $B^{1,1}$ is strictly contained in the potential space of the Hardy space (again, [T]) and the Hardy space estimate is all that we used.

(Note: The proof of the inclusion doesn't need the theory of Hardy spaces. The required estimate on the nontangential maximal function can be obtained for $B^{1,1}$ using the atomic decomposition of $B^{1,1}$ and doing the (elementary) verification one atom at a time. Alternatively, the weak type estimate can be obtained by direct computation on sequence spaces (this is done in [RT]). However, the use of Hardy spaces does give a quick way to see that the inclusion is proper.)

We now go to the second part. First suppose f is in $\mathrm{Osc}^{1,\infty}$. Let F^* be defined by (2.4). By differentiating the Poisson integral representation on small disks in $\mathbb{R}^2_+$ we get the pointwise estimate

$$y^2\ |\nabla^2 F(x,y)| \le c\ y\ F^*(x,y).$$

By Proposition 4.1 of [RS], F^* is in $L^{1,\infty}$. The pointwise estimate now insures that $y^2\ |\nabla^2 F(x,y)|$ will also be in $L^{1,\infty}$.

Pick and fix a smooth function b with support on I = [0,1] and of which we will say more later. For dyadic subintervals Q of I denote the left end point by x_Q and set

$$b_Q(x) = b((x-x_Q)/|Q|).$$

Given $\{\lambda_Q\}$ in $\ell^{1,\infty}$ then

$$\left\|\sum \lambda_Q\ b_Q\right\|_{B^{1,\infty}} \le c\ \|\{\lambda_Q\}\|_{\ell^{1,\infty}}. \tag{2.7}$$

(A proof that this map from sequences to functions takes ℓ^p to $B^{p,p}$ for $0 < p < \infty$ is given in [FJ]. The Lebesgue-Lorentz case follows by interpolation.)

We will be done if we can rule out the possibility that there is an estimate of the form

$$\left\|\left\{\mathrm{osc}_R\left(\sum \lambda_Q\ b_Q\right)\right\}\right\|_{B^{1,\infty}} \le c\|\{\lambda_Q\}\|_{\ell^{1,\infty}}. \tag{2.8}$$

Suppose (2.8) holds. Let E be an arbitrary finite collection of the Q's. Let $r_Q(t)$ be the Radamacher functions defined on X = (0,1). Pick p, 0 < p < 1. Using (2.7), (2.8), and Holder's inequality we get,

$$\|\{\lambda_R\}\|_{\ell^{1,\infty}} = \Big[\int_X \|\{r_R(t)\lambda_R\}\|^p_{\ell^{1,\infty}}\, dt\Big]^{1/p}$$

$$\geq c^{-1}\Big[\int_X \Big\|\Big\{\mathrm{osc}_Q(\sum r_R(t)\ \lambda_R\ b_R)\Big\}\Big\|^p_{B^{1,\infty}} dt\ \Big]^{1/p}$$

$$\geq c^{-1}\Big[\int_X \sum_{Q\in E} \Big|\mathrm{osc}_Q(\sum r_R(t)\ \lambda_R\ b_R)\Big|^p\ |E|^{p-1} dt\ \Big]^{1/p}.$$

Writing $(b_R)_Q$ for the mean of b_R on Q we continue with

$$\geq c\Big[\sum_{Q\in E}\int_X \Big[\frac{1}{|Q|}\int_Q \Big|\sum r_R(t)\lambda_R(b_R - (b_R)_Q)\Big|\ dx\Big]^p dt\Big]^{1/p}\ |E|^{1-1/p}$$

$$\geq c\Big[\sum_{Q\in E}\int_X \frac{1}{|Q|}\int_Q \Big|\sum r_R(t)\lambda_R(b_R - (b_R)_Q)\Big|^p\ dx\ dt\Big]^{1/p}\ |E|^{1-1/p}$$

By Khinchin's inequality (see [G]) we continue with

$$\geq c\Big[\sum_{Q\in E}\frac{1}{|Q|}\int_Q \Big[\sum_R |\lambda_R|^2\ |b_R - (b_R)_Q|^2\Big]^{p/2} dx\ \Big]^{1/p}\ |E|^{1-1/p}.$$

We now describe a choice of $\{\lambda_Q\}$ and a function b for which this cannot hold. Suppose b(x), which is smooth and supported in I = [0,1], satisfies b(x) = x for x in (.2,.8). Let λ_Q be zero unless Q is a dyadic subinterval of I and for those intervals let $\lambda_Q = |Q|$. Given such a Q, let U(Q) be the collection of dyadic subintervals of I which contain Q in their center half. If R is in U(Q) then, on Q, and denoting the center of Q by c_Q,

$$|\lambda_R|^2 \; |b_R - (b_R)_Q|^2 = (x - c_Q)^2.$$

We can continue the previous estimate with

$$\geq c \left[\sum_{Q \in E} \frac{1}{|Q|} \int_Q \left[\sum_{R \in U(Q)} (x - c_Q)^2 \right]^{p/2} dx \right]^{1/p} |E|^{1-1/p}$$

$$\geq c \left[\sum_{Q \in E} \frac{1}{|Q|} \int_Q |U(Q)|^{p/2} |x - c_Q|^p \, dx \right]^{1/p} |E|^{1-1/p}$$

Doing the integration gives

$$\geq c \left[\sum_{Q \in E} |U(Q)|^{p/2} \; |Q|^p \right]^{1/p} |E|^{1-1/p}.$$

We pick N large and let E be the set of intervals Q with $|Q| = 2^{-N}$. Thus $|E|^{1-1/p} = 2^{N-N/p}$. The function $|U(Q)|$ varies between 0 and N. Pick a small positive α. The number of Q in E for which $|U(E)| \geq \alpha N$ is approximately

$$\sum_{k > \alpha N}^{k \leq N} \begin{bmatrix} N \\ k \end{bmatrix} 2^{N-k}.$$

Using the Central Limit Theorem to approximate the binoimial distribution by a normal we find that, for large N, $|U(Q)| \geq \alpha N$ on at least $\alpha 2^N$ of the intervals in E. Thus we can continue the previous inequality with

$$\geq c \left[\alpha \; 2^N \; (\alpha \; N)^{p/2} \; 2^{-pN}\right]^{1/p} 2^{N-N/p} = c \; N^{1/2}.$$

Since the sequence $\{\lambda_R\}$ is in $\ell^{1,\infty}$ and N is arbitrary this is a contradiction.

THE HIGHER DIMENSIONAL CASE

We now consider operators acting on $L^2(\mathbb{R}^n)$ for $n \geq 2$. In this case the information from [RS] is more complete. We consider the operator, again denoted R_b, given by the integral kernel

$$k(x,y) = \frac{b(x) - b(y)}{|x - y|^n} .$$

(Similar comments apply to a much more general class of operators.)

Again we quantify the smoothness of b using the Besov scale. Now we let Pb denote the Poisson extension of b from $\mathbb{R}^n$ to $\mathbb{R}^{n+1}_+$. For $0 < p < \infty$ and $0 \leq q \leq \infty$ we will say that b is in the (Lebesgue-Lorentz) Besov space $B^{p,q} = B^{p,q}(\mathbb{R}^n)$ if b is in the space BMO and the gradients $\nabla^k Pb$ satisfy

$$y^k \nabla^k Pb(x,y) \in L^{p,q}(\mathbb{R}^{n+1}_+, y^{-n+1} dxdy)$$

for $k > n/p$. As before, these are complete (quasi-)normed spaces and the topology is independent of k for allowable k.

By [RS] the analogs of Theorem 1.5, Theorem A, and a stronger version of (1.8) hold in this case. The cut point for change in behavior is now at $p = n$.

Before stating the result, we need to define the function spaces $Osc^{p,q}(\mathbb{R}^n)$. Define the numbers osc(b,Q) as in Section 1, but using dyadic cubes to replace dyadic intervals. Then define the spaces $Osc^{p,q}(\mathbb{R}^n)$ exactly as in Section 1.

THEOREM 2.1.

A. For $n < p < \infty$, $1 \leq q \leq \infty$, R_b is in $\mathcal{S}^{p,q}$ if and only if b is in $B^{p,q}$.

B. For $p < n$ or $p = n$ and $q < \infty$, R_b is in $\mathcal{S}^{p,q}$ if and only if b is constant (and hence R_b is trivial).

C. R_b is in $Osc^{n,\infty}(\mathbb{R}^n)$ if and only if R_b is in $\mathcal{S}^{n,\infty}$.

The proof in [RS] of part B of this theorem uses a duality argument which fails when $p = 1$. That is why a separate proof was needed for Theorem A. Similarly, half of the proof of part C fails in one dimension. That is why we don't know if equality holds in (1.8).

Because the space $Osc^{n,\infty}$ gives the sharp end point result we want to know how it compares to other, more classical, spaces. Let L_1^n be the space of potentials of order one of functions in $L^n(\mathbb{R}^n)$. That is $L_1^n = \{f\colon \nabla f \in L^n(\mathbb{R}^n)\}$.

THEOREM 2.2.

$$B^{n,1} \subset L_1^n \subset \mathrm{Osc}^{n,\infty} \subset B^{n,\infty}.$$

This is the analog of Theorem C. L_1^n replaces the space of potentials of functions in the Hardy space, H^1, which, although it wasn't mentioned in the statement of Theorem C, was used in the proof.

Proof: As we noted following (2.7) we may make use of the decomposition theorems for the Besov spaces. Thus we write f in $B^{n,1}$ as $f(x) = \sum \lambda_Q b_Q(x)$. Here the index Q runs over distinct dyadic cubes, each b_Q is supported on the cube 10Q, $\|b_Q\|_\infty \leq 1$, $\|\nabla b_Q\|_\infty \leq |Q|^{-1/n}$, and the $\ell^{n,1}$ norm of the sequence $\{\lambda_Q\}$ is comparable to the norm of f. Furthermore, any f of norm one is essentially a convex combination terms

$$g(x) = K^{-1/n} \sum_{j=1}^{j=K} b_{Q_j}$$

where the b_Q satisfy the estimates just described and $Q_1, \ldots, Q_K$ are distinct. (This is easily seen by working with the coeffieient sequence $\{\lambda_Q\}$.) Pick and fix such a g. We must show $\|g\|_{L_1^n} \leq A$ for some constant A.

Suppose the cubes are numbered so that $|Q_j|$ is a nondecreasing function of j. For each x in the union $\cup(10Q_j)$ let j(x) be the smallest j for which $x \in 10Q_j$. Let $E_j = \{x\colon j(x) = j\}$. The construction insures the E_j are disjoint. Using the fact that for fixed k the set $\{10Q\colon Q$ a dyadic cube and $|Q| = 2^k\}$

is a locally finite cover, and summing a geometric series, we see that

$$(4.1) \qquad |\nabla g(x)| \lesssim c\, K^{-1/n} \sum |Q_j|^{-1/n} \chi_{10Q_j}(x)$$
$$\lesssim c\, K^{-1/n} \sum |Q_j|^{-1/n} \chi_{E_j}(x).$$

Raising both sides to the nth power and integrating gives the required estimate.

The proof of the inclusion of L_1^n in $\mathrm{Osc}^{n,\infty}$ is similar to the one dimensional proof. However, instead of using the boundedness of the nontangential Poission maximal function on H^1 we need only the boundedness on $L^n(\mathbb{R}^n)$, $n \geq 2$. Using that fact, the previous proof adapts easily.

For the final inclusion, the one dimensional proof extends directly.

REMARKS

1. One of our goals was to understand why the distinction in behavior between $p > 1$ and $p \leq 1$ occurs for some operators (e.g. R_b) and not for others (e.g. T_b). (A similar split occurs for the two types of Hankel operators considered in [AFP]. That fact led us to look at this simpler model case.) The crucial issue here is the first term on the right hand side of (2.6). The analogous integral for T_b would not have "sgn(x-y)" and the integral would be zero. The operator would then see through the first order oscillation and respond to the second order behavior of b.

2. Is $\mathrm{Osc}^{1,\infty} = \mathrm{Op}^{1,\infty}$ for functions on $\mathbb{R}$? We know that $\mathrm{Osc}^{n,\infty} = \mathrm{Op}^{n,\infty}$ for functions on $\mathbb{R}^n$?

3. How far can Theorem C be refined? That is, where does $\mathrm{Osc}^{1,\infty}(\mathbb{R})$ fit inside the classical scales of spaces; the (Lebesgue-Lorentz) Besov scale, and/or the (Lebesgue-Lorentz) Tribel-Lizorkin scale (see [T])? There is a similar question for

the $Osc^{n,\infty}(\mathbb{R}^n)$. We already have enough information to know that $Osc^{n,\infty}(\mathbb{R}^n)$ can be used as an interpolation endpoint. Here is a precise formulation; stated for convenience with n = 1.

Corollary 4.1: Suppose $p > 1$, $1 \leq r \leq \infty$, $\theta > 1$, and $1 \leq q \leq \infty$. Let $(\cdot,\cdot)_{\theta,q}$ denote the intermediate spaces obtained by real interpolation. Define s by $s^{-1} = (1 - \theta) + \theta/p$. We have

$$(Osc^{1,\infty}, B^{p,r})_{\theta,q} = (B^{1,1}, B^{p,r})_{\theta,q} = B^{s,q}.$$

Proof: By Theorem C we must have

$$(B^{1,1}, B^{p,r})_{\theta,q} \subset (Osc^{1,\infty}, B^{p,r})_{\theta,q} \subset (B^{1,\infty}, B^{p,r})_{\theta,q}$$

However, the standard facts about interpolation in the Lebesgue-Lorentz scale insures that the first and third of these spaces are the same and also give the identification of the spaces as $B^{s,q}$.

REFERENCES

[AFP] J. Arazy, S. Fisher and J. Peetre, Hankel operators on weighted Bergman spaces, preprint 1986.

[FJ] M. Frazier and B. Jawerth, Decomposition of Besov Spaces, Indiana. U. Math. J. (1985) 777-799.

[G] J. Garnett, Bounded Analytic Functions, Academic Press, New York, 1981.

[GK] I. C. Gohberg and M. G. Krein, Introduction to the Theory of Nonselfadjoint Operators, Amer. Math. Soc, Providence RI, 1969.

[JW] S. Janson and T. Wolff, Schatten classes and commutators of singular integral operators, Ark. Mat 20 (1982) 301-310.

[Pe1] V. Peller, Hankel operators of class S_p and their applications (rational approximation, Gaussian processes, and the problem of majorizing operators), Math. USSR Sbornik, 41 (1982) 443-479.

[Pe2] ___________, A description of Hankel operators of class S_p

for p > 0, an investigation of the rate of rational approximation, and other applications, Math. USSR Sbornik, 50, (1985), 465-494.

[RS] R. Rochberg and S. Semmes, Nearly weakly orthonormal sequences, singular value estimates, and Calderon-Zygmund operators, Manuscript, 1987.

[RT] R. Rochberg and M. Taibleson, An Averaging Operator on a Tree, preprint, 1987.

[Se] S. Semmes, Trace ideal criteria for Hankel operators and applications to Besov spaces, Int. Equations and Op. Theory. 7, (1984) 241-281.

[T] H. Triebel, Theory of Function Spaces, Birkhauser, Bassel, 1983.

Current Addresses:

RR: Mathematics Department
Washington University
St. Louis MO 63130

SS: Mathematics Department
Rice University
Houston TX 77251

Operator Theory:
Advances and Applications, Vol. 35

ON LIFTING TO THE COMMUTANT

Waclaw Szymanski

It is shown that the lifting to the commutant problem in dilation theory is a particular case of the general dilation theorem for semigroups without involution. Applications are given to subnormal and contraction homomorphisms.

1. INTRODUCTION

The lifting to the commutant problem for a single operator arises naturally in two classical cases: contractions and subnormals. A general formulation of this problem is:

(L) Suppose that an operator $A \in B(H)$ = the algebra of all linear bounded operators on a complex Hilbert space H can be extended to a, usually "better", operator $B \in B(K)$, where H is a subspace of the Hilbert space K, B leaves H invariant, and $A = B|H$. Under what condition can an operator $C \in B(H)$ be extended to $C' \in B(K)$ so that C' leaves H invariant, $C = C'|H$, and C' commutes with B ?

The obvious necessary condition is that C commutes with A.

(C) If A is a contraction and B is its (minimal) coisometric extension, then the answer to (L) is that the obvious necessary condition is also sufficient, which was proved by Ando, cf. [9, Ch.1, Theorem 6.1], as well as by Sz.-Nagy and Foias in a different, but equivalent form [9, Ch.2, Theorem 2.3].

(S) If A is subnormal and B is its (minimal) normal extension, then it is well-known that the obvious necessary condition is not sufficient - see e.g. [5] and [4, p. 195].

It is worth noticing that, although the question (L)

looks the same in both cases, it, in fact, is not the same. Requiring C' to commute with the normal B in case (S) forces C' to commute also with B*, by Fuglede's theorem, whereas if C' commutes with the coisometry B in case (C), it is far from commuting with B*. The only known necessary and sufficient condition for an operator to lift to the commutant in case (S) given by Bram [3, Theorem 7], see also [4, Ch.3. Theorem 11.2], resembles a boundedness condition known from the general dilation theory.

In this paper a general approach to the lifting to the commutant is discussed. It occurs that one has to use in an essential way the most general form of the bounded dilation theory - for semigroups without involution. This theory originated and found applications mostly in the theory of stochastic processes (see e.g. [8]). It seems that, apart from the application to the characterization of subnormal homomorphisms as the ones that have quasinormal extensions in [13, Theorem (3.4)], the solution of the lifting problem presented here is the only other application of that theory to operators. The lifting to the commutant for *-semigroups is discussed in Ch. 8 of [7], for C*- algebras in [2, Ch. 1.3.] - both rely heavily on the von Neumann algebra theory. The approach in this paper is different, straightforward, and results concern functions on arbitrary, not necessarily * - , semigroups. The main result states essentially that the lifting to the commutant question does not exist as a separate problem - it is a particular case of the general dilation problem on semigroups without involution. This result will then be applied to both (S) and (C) /in general semigroup setting, following [13] and [11]/. It will become clear that not only Bram's condition in (S) is natural, but also, why. The application to (C) gives results different from the results of Ando and Sz.-Nagy - Foias, for the reasons stated after (S).

2. NOTATIONS AND PRELIMINARY RESULTS

Let S be a set. Let H, H_1 be Hilbert spaces (always assumed to be complex). $B(H_1,H)$ is the linear space of all linear bounded mappings from H_1 to H. $B(H) = B(H,H)$. $F(S,H)$ denotes the linear space of all functions from S to H that vanish off a finite subset of S. A function $A:S\times S \to B(H)$ is called *positive definite* PD if $\Sigma(A(s,t)f(s),f(t)) \geq 0$ for each $f \in F(S,H)$. If A is PD, then $A(s,t)^* = A(t,s)$, $s,t \in S$ (cf. [7, p. 18]). Hence $A(S\times S)$ contains the adjoint of each of its members and its commutant $A(S\times S)'$ is a von Neumann algebra. Suppose Ω, S are sets, H_1, H are Hilbert spaces, $A:S\times S \to B(H)$, $C:\Omega \to B(H_1,H)$ are functions. Define $A^C:(S\times\Omega)\times(S\times\Omega) \to B(H_1)$ by

(2.1) $A^C(s,\alpha,t,\beta) = C(\beta)^*A(s,t)C(\alpha)$, $s,t \in S$, $\alpha,\beta \in \Omega$.

(2.2) PROPOSITION. (a) *If* A *is PD, then so is* A^C.

(b) *If* $H = H_1$, $Q \in B(H)$ *is a positive operator commuting with* $A(S\times S)$, *and* A *is PD, then the function* $QA:S\times S \to B(H)$ *defined by* $(QA)(s,t) = QA(s,t)$, $s,t \in S$, *is PD.*

(c) *If* $H = H_1$, $T \in B(H)$ *commutes with* $A(S\times S)$, *and* A *is PD, then* $\Sigma(T^*A(s,t)Tf(s),f(t)) \leq \|T\|^2\, \Sigma(A(s,t)f(s),f(t))$, for $f \in F(S,H)$.

PROOF. (a) Let $f \in F(S\times\Omega,H)$. Define $h:S \to H$ by $h(s) = \Sigma_\alpha C(\alpha)f(s,\alpha)$, $s \in S$. Then $h \in F(S,H)$, and

$\Sigma(A^C(s,\alpha,t,\beta)f(s,\alpha),f(t,\beta)) =$

$\Sigma(A(s,t)C(\alpha)f(s,\alpha),C(\beta)f(t,\beta)) =$

$\Sigma(A(s,t)h(s),h(t)) \geq 0.$

(b) Apply (a) with $\Omega = \{\alpha\}$, $C(\alpha) = Q^{\frac{1}{2}}$.

(c) Since $A(S\times S)'$ is a symmetric algebra, $Q = \|T\|^2 I - T^*T$ belongs to $A(S\times S)'$. Since $Q \geq 0$, it follows from (b) that QA is PD, which is exactly the inequality in (c), because $T \in A(S\times S)'$. Q.E.D.

Let now S be a semigroup. It will always be assumed that semigroups have unit and that semigroup homomorphisms preserve units. (K,τ,R) is called a *dilation* of $A:S\times S \to B(H)$ if K is a Hilbert space, $\tau:S \to B(K)$ is a semigroup homomorphism, $R \in B(H,K)$, and $A(s,t) = R^*\tau(t)^*\tau(s)R$, $s,t \in S$.

If $A(1,1) = I$, then R is an isometric embedding of H into K. In such case H will be treated as a subspace of K and $R^* = P_H$ as the projection of K onto H. Also, the notation (K,τ,R) will be shortened to (K,τ). A dilation (K,τ,R) of A is called *minimal* if K equals the closed linear span $[\tau(S)RH]$ of $\tau(S)RH$. If there is a dilation of A, then there is a minimal one and it is unique up to a unitary isomorphism, because S has unit (if S has no unit, the last statement fails [10]).

DILATION THEOREM. ([8,1]) *Let* S *be a semigroup.* $A:S\times S \to B(H)$ *has a dilation if and only if* A *is PD and for each* $u \in S$ *there is a non-negative real number* $c(u)$ *such that*

BC: $\Sigma(A(us,ut)f(s),f(t)) \le c(u)\ \Sigma(A(s,t)f(s),f(t))$.

It follows from the construction of the dilation (cf. e.g. [1]) that if (K,τ,R) is a dilation of A, then

(2.3) $\|\tau(u)\|^2 \le c(u),\ u \in S$.

In general, the dilation theorem fails without BC (called the boundedness condition), although in several particular circumstances BC can be dropped - cf. [1,12] for a detailed discussion. It will be shown in the next section that BC is crucial for the "lifting to the commutant" problem.

(2.4) LEMMA. *Let* S *be a semigroup, let* $A:S\times S \to B(H)$ *be a function. If* A *satisfies BC for* $u,v \in S$ *with* $c(u)$, $c(v)$, *respectively, then* A *satisfies BC for* uv *with* $c(u)c(v)$.

PROOF. Take $f \in F(S,H)$, $v \in S$, and define

$$f(t) = \Sigma_{s:vs=t} f(s).$$

Clearly, $f_v \in F(S,H)$. Suppose A satisfies BC for $u,v \in S$ with $c(u)$, $c(v)$, respectively. Then

$$\Sigma(A(uvs,uvt)f(s),f(t)) = \Sigma(A(us,ut)f_v(s),f_v(t)) \le$$
$$c(u)\ \Sigma(A(s,t)f_v(s),f_v(t)) = c(u)\ \Sigma(A(vs,vt)f(s),f(t)) \le$$
$$c(u)c(v)\ \Sigma(A(s,t)f(s),f(t)). \qquad \text{Q.E.D.}$$

3. LIFTING TO THE COMMUTANT.

Let S be a semigroup. Suppose $A:S\times S \to B(H)$ satisfies $A(1,1) = I$ and has a dilation (K,τ). Let Ω be a set and let $C:\Omega \to B(H)$ be a function. It will be said that C *lifts to the commutant of* τ if there is a function $\sigma:\Omega \to B(K)$, called the *lifting* of C, such that $\sigma(\alpha)$ leaves H invariant, $\sigma(\alpha)|H = C(\alpha)$, and $\sigma(\alpha)$

commutes with $\tau(s)$, for each $\alpha \in \Omega$, $s \in S$. The last condition will be abbreviated to: σ commutes with τ. A single operator $C \in B(H)$ lifts to the commutant of τ if the above conditions are satisfied for the constant function $C:\Omega \to B(H)$, $C(\alpha) = C$, on any set Ω. It is clear that if $C,D \in B(H)$ lift to the commutant of τ, then so does their product CD. Since the identity operator lifts to the commutant of τ, with no loss of generality and without any additional restrictions in the above definition it can and will always be assumed that Ω is a semigroup, $C:\Omega \to B(H)$ is a semigroup homomorphism, and required that the lifting $\sigma:\Omega \to B(K)$ of C is also a semigroup homomorphism.

The following simple lemma on semigroup homomorphisms is of essential importance.

(3.1) LEMMA. *Let* S_1, S_2, S_3 *be semigroups. Suppose* $\pi:S_1 \to S_3$, $\sigma:S_2 \to S_3$ *are semigroup homomorphisms. Then* $\pi(s_1)$ *commutes with* $\sigma(s_2)$ *for each* $s_1 \in S_1$, $s_2 \in S_2$ *if and only if the mapping* $\pi\sigma:S_1 x S_2 \to S_3$ *defined by* $\pi\sigma(s_1,s_2) = \pi(s_1)\sigma(s_2)$, $s_1 \in S_1$, $s_2 \in S_2$, *is a semigroup homomorphism of the product semigroup* $S_1 x S_2$ *to* S_3.

PROOF. If all values of π commute with all values of σ, then for all $s_1,t_1 \in S_1$, $s_2,t_2 \in S_2$:

$$\pi\sigma((s_1,s_2)(t_1,t_2)) = \pi\sigma(s_1t_1,s_2t_2) =$$
$$\pi(s_1t_1)\sigma(s_2t_2) = \pi(s_1)\pi(t_1)\sigma(s_2)\sigma(t_2) =$$
$$\pi(s_1)\sigma(s_2)\pi(t_1)\sigma(t_2) = \pi\sigma(s_1,s_2)\pi\sigma(t_1,t_2).$$

To prove the converse take $s_1 \in S_1$, $s_2 \in S_2$ and compute:

$$\sigma(s_2)\pi(s_1) = \pi(1)\sigma(s_2)\pi(s_1)\sigma(1) = \pi\sigma(1,s_2)\pi\sigma(s_1,1) =$$
$$\pi\sigma((1,s_2)(s_1,1)) = \pi\sigma(s_1,s_2) = \pi(s_1)\sigma(s_2). \qquad \text{Q.E.D.}$$

Now everything is ready to state and prove the following :

(3.2) THEOREM. *Let* S, Ω *be semigroups.* $Sx\Omega$ *is the product semigroup. Let* $A:SxS \to B(H)$, $C:\Omega \to B(H)$ *be functions such that* $A(1,1) = C(1) = I$. *The following conditions are equivalent:*

(a) the function $A^C:(Sx\Omega)x(Sx\Omega) \to B(H)$ *defined by (2.1) has a dilation,*

(b) A *has a dilation* (K,τ) *and* C *lifts to the commutant of* τ,

(c) A *has a dilation,* C *is a semigroup homomorphism, and for each* $\delta \in \Omega$ *there is* $d(\delta) \geq 0$ *such that*

$$(3.3)\quad \Sigma(A(s,t)C(\delta)h(s),C(\delta)h(t)) \leq d(\delta)\ \Sigma(A(s,t)h(s),h(t)),$$
$$\text{for each } h \in F(S,H).$$

Moreover, (a) and (b) are related as follows: If (K^C,τ^C) *is a dilation of* A^C, *then* (K,τ) *is a dilation of* A *with* $K = K^C$, $\tau:S \dashrightarrow B(K)$, $\tau(s) = \tau^C(s,1)$, *for* $s \in S$, *and the semigroup homomorphism* $\sigma:\Omega \dashrightarrow B(K)$ *lifting* C *is* $\sigma(\alpha) = \tau^C(1,\alpha)$, $\alpha \in \Omega$. *Conversely, if* (K,τ) *is a dilation of* A *and* $\sigma:\Omega \dashrightarrow B(K)$ *is the semigroup homomorphism lifting* C, *then* (K^C,τ^C) *is a dilation of* A^C *with* $K^C = K$ *and* $\tau^C:S\times\Omega \dashrightarrow B(K)$, $\tau^C(s,\alpha) = \tau(s)\sigma(\alpha)$, $s \in S$, $\alpha \in \Omega$. *If* σ *is the lifting of* C, *then*

$$(3.4)\quad \|C(\delta)\|^2 \leq \|\sigma(\delta)\|^2 \leq d(\delta) \quad \text{for each } \delta \in \Omega.$$

Finally, the dilation of A^C *is minimal if and only if the dilation of* A *is minimal. If* (K^C,τ^C) *is the minimal dilation of* A^C, *then the lifting of* C *to the commutant of* τ *is unique.*

PROOF. (a) ==> (b). Suppose (K,τ^C) is a dilation of A^C. Then

$$(3.5)\quad C(\beta)^*A(s,t)C(\alpha) = P_H\ \tau^C(t,\beta)^*\tau^C(s,\alpha)|H\ ,$$
$$s,t \in S,\ \alpha,\beta \in \Omega.$$

Define $\tau:S \dashrightarrow B(K)$ by $\tau(s) = \tau^C(s,1)$, $s \in S$, and $\sigma:\Omega \dashrightarrow B(K)$ by $\sigma(\alpha) = \tau^C(1,\alpha)$, $\alpha \in \Omega$. Both τ, σ are semigroup homomorphisms. Let $\alpha = \beta = 1$ in (3.5). Then (3.5) proves that (K,τ) is a dilation of A. Now let $s = t = 1$, $\alpha = \beta$ in (3.5). Then $C(\alpha)^*C(\alpha) = P_H\sigma(\alpha)^*\sigma(\alpha)|H$, which proves (see e.g. [11]) that $\sigma(\alpha)$ leaves H invariant and $\sigma(\alpha)|H = C(\alpha)$, $\alpha \in \Omega$. Since $\tau^C = \tau\sigma$ is a semigroup homomorphism, it follows from Lemma (3.1) that σ commutes with τ.

(b) ==> (c). Since $C(\alpha) = \sigma(\alpha)|H$, $\alpha \in \Omega$, and σ is a semigroup homomorphism, so is C. Fix $\delta \in \Omega$, $h \in F(S,H)$. Then

$$\Sigma_{s,t}(A(s,t)C(\delta)h(s),C(\delta)h(t)) =$$
$$\Sigma(\tau(s)\sigma(\delta)h(s),\tau(t)\sigma(\delta)h(t)) =$$
$$\|\Sigma\tau(s)\sigma(\delta)h(s)\|^2 \leq \|\sigma(\delta)\|^2\ \Sigma(A(s,t)h(s),h(t)).$$

(c) ==> (a). Here the Dilation Theorem will be used. Since A has a dilation, A is PD. By Proposition (2.2)(a), A^C is PD. It remains to be shown that for each $(u,\delta) \in S\times\Omega$ there is $c(u,\delta) \geq 0$ such that

$$(3.6)\quad \Sigma(A^C((u,\delta)(s,\alpha),(u,\delta)(t,\beta))f(s,\alpha),f(t,\beta)) \leq c(u,\delta)\ \Sigma(A^C(s,\alpha,t,\beta)f(s,\alpha),f(t,\beta)),$$
$$\text{for each } f \in F(S\times\Omega,H),$$

which is BC written for A^C. Take $\delta \in \Omega$, $f \in F(S\times\Omega,H)$. Define $h(s) = \Sigma_\alpha C(\alpha)f(s,\alpha)$. Then $h \in F(S,H)$, and

$$\Sigma(A^C((1,\delta)(s,\alpha),(1,\delta)(t,\beta))f(s,\alpha),f(t,\beta)) =$$
$$\Sigma(A(s,t)C(\delta\alpha)f(s,\alpha),C(\delta\beta)f(t,\beta)) =$$
$$\Sigma(A(s,t)C(\delta)h(s),C(\delta)h(t)) \leq d(\delta)\ \Sigma(A(s,t)h(s),h(t)) =$$
$$d(\delta)\ \Sigma(A^C(s,\alpha,t,\beta)f(s,\alpha),f(t,\beta)).$$

This proves that A^C satisfies BC for each $(1,\delta)$, $\delta \in \Omega$ - cf. (3.6). Since A has a dilation, A satisfies BC. Hence, computing similarly as above, one proves that A^C satisfies BC for each $(u,1)$, $u \in S$. By Lemma (2.4), A^C satisfies BC for each $(u,\delta) = (u,1)(1,\delta) \in S\times\Omega$. Now the conditions (a), (b), and (c) are proved to be equivalent.

Since $C(\delta) = \sigma(\delta)|H$, it follows that $\|C(\delta)\| \leq \|\sigma(\delta)\|$, $\delta \in \Omega$. The second inequality in (3.4) is a consequence of (2.3). If (K,τ) is a minimal dilation of A and $\sigma:\Omega \dashrightarrow B(K)$ is a lifting of C to the commutant of τ, then $[\tau(S)H] = K$, and for each $x \in H$, $\alpha \in \Omega$, $s \in S$:

$$\sigma(\alpha)\tau(s)x = \tau(s)\sigma(\alpha)x = \tau(s)C(\alpha)x,$$

which proves that the lifting σ of C is unique.

The remaining assertion follows from Lemma (3.1). Q.E.D.

Notice that if A has a dilation then the condition (3.3) is equivalent to BC for A^C (3.6). Moreover, there is no "a priori" relationship between the functions A and C in this theorem, like, e.g. $C(\alpha)$ commutes with $A(S\times S)$, $\alpha \in \Omega$. This particular one is very restrictive - see Theorem (3.8). Also notice that if the condition (3.3) is satisfied for δ, $\delta' \in \Omega$, then it is satisfied for $\delta\delta'$, which can be proved similarly as Lemma (2.4).

(3.7) COROLLARY. *Suppose* $A:S\times S \dashrightarrow B(H)$ *has a dilation* (K,τ). *An operator* $C \in B(H)$ *lifts to the commutant of* τ *if and only if there is* $d \geq 0$ *such that*

$\Sigma(A(s,t)Ch(s),Ch(t)) \leq d\, \Sigma(A(s,t)h(s),h(t))$, $h \in F(S,H)$.

PROOF. C lifts to the commutant of τ if and only if the semigroup homomorphism $C(\ ):N \to B(H)$, $C(n) = C^n$, $n \in N$ of the additive semigroup N of non-negative integers into B(H) lifts to the commutant of τ. If the second condition in the statement of this corollary (which is (3.3) for δ = one = the generator of the semigroup N) is satisfied, then the remark immediately preceding this corollary proves (3.3) for each $\delta \in N$. Apply Theorem (3.2). Q.E.D.

Now a refinement of Theorem (3.2) will be proved under additional assumptions about the relationship between A and C.

(3.8) THEOREM. *Let* S *be a semigroup. Let* $A:S\times S \to B(H)$ *be a function satisfying* $A(1,1) = I$. *Suppose* A *has a dilation. Let* (K,τ) *be the minimal dilation of* A. *Let* P_H *be the projection of* K *onto* H.

(a) Each operator $T \in B(H)$ *that commutes with* $A(S\times S)$ *lifts uniquely to the commutant of* τ.

Let L(T) *be the lifting of* T.

(b) The mapping $L:A(S\times S)' \to W^*(\tau(S))' \cap \{P_H\}'$ *defined by* $T \to L(T)$ *is an isometric *-isomorphism from the von Neumann algebra* $A(S\times S)'$ *onto the von Neumann algebra* $W^*(\tau(S))' \cap \{P_H\}'$.

PROOF. (a) The existence of the lifting follows from Proposition (2.2)(c) and Corollary (3.7). The uniqueness follows from the minimality of the dilation of A and Theorem (3.2).

(b) It is plain that the mapping L is an algebra homomorphism. L is an isometry, which is a consequence of Proposition (2.2)(c) and (3.4). Now it will be shown that L preserves involutions. Take $T \in A(S\times S)'$, $s,t \in S$, $x,y \in H$. Then $T^* \in A(S\times S)'$, and

$$(L(T)^*\tau(s)x,\tau(t)y) = (\tau(s)x,\tau(t)L(T)y) = (\tau(s)x,\tau(t)Ty) =$$
$$(A(s,t)x,Ty) = (A(s,t)T^*x,y) = (\tau(s)L(T^*)x,\tau(t)y) =$$
$$(L(T^*)\tau(s)x,\tau(t)y).$$

Since (K,τ) is minimal, the vectors $\tau(s)x$, $s \in S$, $x \in H$, are linearly dense in K. Thus $L(T)^* = L(T^*)$. Now if T commutes with A(SxS), then H is invariant for both L(T) and $L(T)^* = L(T^*)$, hence H reduces L(T).

Finally it will be proved that L is onto.

Let $X \in W^*(\tau(s))' \cap \{P_H\}'$. Put $T = X|H$. By the uniqueness of the lifting it suffices to prove that T commutes with A(SxS). Take $x,y \in H$, $s,t \in S$. Then

$$(TA(s,t)x,y) = (A(s,t)x,T^*y) = (\tau(s)x,\tau(t)X^*y) = (\tau(s)Xx,\tau(t)y) = (A(s,t)Tx,y). \qquad \text{Q.E.D.}$$

A comment on *-semigroups and C*-algebras is now in order. Assume S is a *-semigroup, i.e. a semigroup with an involution *:S --> S satisfying $(s^*)^* = s$, $(st)^* = t^*s^*$, $s,t \in S$, and $1^* = 1$. Let $\Phi:S \to B(H)$ be a function. Define $A_\Phi:SxS \to B(H)$ by $A_\Phi(s,t) = \Phi(t^*s)$, $s,t \in S$. Assume that $A = A_\Phi$ has a *-dilation (K,τ), i.e. (K,τ) is a dilation of A and τ preserves involutions. In this particular case (b)<==>(c) of Theorem (3.2) implies Lemma 1 in Ch.8 of [7], and Theorem (3.8) becomes Theorem 1 in Ch.8 of [7]. If S is a C*-algebra and Φ is a completely positive map on S, then Theorem (3.8) with $A = A_\Phi$ implies the results of [2, Ch. 1.3].

4. APPLICATION I: SUBNORMAL HOMOMORPHISMS.

Here the results of the preceding sections will be applied to a special function that arises when dealing with subnormal homomorphisms. In particular, Bram's results on lifting of the commutant of a subnormal operator [3, Theorems 7,8], will be explained. The notations and terminology follow [13]. Let Y be a semigroup. A semigroup homomorphism $\tau:Y \to B(K)$ is called *normal* if $\tau(s)\tau(t)^* = \tau(t)^*\tau(s)$, $s,t \in Y$, i.e. the values of τ are commuting normal operators. A semigroup homomorphism $\pi:Y \to B(H)$ is called *subnormal* if there is a Hilbert space K containing H and a normal homomorphism $\tau:Y \to B(K)$, called a normal extension of π, such that $\tau(s)$ leaves H invariant and $\tau(s)|H = \pi(s)$, $s \in Y$. Let Y be a semigroup. Let $\pi:Y \to B(H)$ be a semigroup homomorphism. Let S = YxY be the product semigroup. The involution $(s,s')^* = (s',s)$ for $(s,s') \in S$ completes the structure of a *-semigroup on S. Define $\Phi:S \to B(H)$ by $\Phi(s,s')$

$= \pi(s')^*\pi(s)$, for $(s,s') \in S$, and $A{:}S\times S \dashrightarrow B(H)$ by $A(s_0,t_0) = \Phi(t_0{}^*s_0)$, $s_0,t_0 \in S$, as at the end of Section 3. A part of Theorem (3.4) of [13] says that π is a subnormal homomorphism with a (the minimal) normal extension (K,τ_0) if and only if A_Φ has a (the minimal) $*$-dilation (K,τ). The relationship between τ_0 and τ is: $\tau(s,s') = \tau_0(s')^*\tau_0(s)$, $s,s' \in Y$.

(4.1) THEOREM. *Let* Y, Ω *be semigroups. Suppose* $\pi{:}Y \dashrightarrow B(H)$ *is a subnormal homomorphism and* $C{:}\Omega \dashrightarrow B(H)$ *is a semigroup homomorphism. Let* $\tau_0{:}Y \dashrightarrow B(K)$ *be a normal extension of* π. *The following are equivalent:*

(a) $A_\Phi{}^C{:}(S\times\Omega)\times(S\times\Omega) \dashrightarrow B(H)$ *defined by (2.1) has a dilation,*

(b) C *lifts to the commutant of* τ_0 *,*

(c) all values of C *commute with all values of* π, *and for each* $\delta \in \Omega$ *there is* $d(\delta) \geq 0$ *such that for each* $h \in F(Y,H)$:

(4.2) $\Sigma(\pi(t)C(\delta)h(s),\pi(s)C(\delta)h(t)) \leq$
$d(\delta)\ \Sigma(\pi(t)h(s),\pi(s)h(t))$.

If τ_0 *is the minimal normal extension of* π *and* C *lifts to the commutant of* τ_0, *then the lifting of* C *is unique.*

PROOF. Since $\tau_0(Y)$ consists of commuting normal operators, it follows from the relationship between τ_0 and τ stated before this theorem and from Fuglede's theorem that $\tau_0(Y)' = \tau(S)'$. Hence the lifting to the commutant of τ is the same as the lifting to the commutant of τ_0. It has to be pointed out that this very particular situation is caused by the normality of τ_0. Hence (a) <==> (b), by Theorem (3.2) (a) <==> (b), and [13] Theorem (3.4) (a) <==> (b). Now it will be shown that (c) above is the condition (c) in Theorem (3.2) for $A = A_\Phi$, which, by Theorem (3.2), will finish the proof. Suppose that (c) above holds. Take $\delta \in \Omega$, $f \in F(S,H)$, and define $h \in F(Y,H)$ by $h(s') = \Sigma_s\pi(s)f(s,s')$, $s' \in Y$. Let $s_0 = (s,s')$, $t_0 = (t,t') \in S$.

(4.3) $\Sigma(A_\Phi(s_0,t_0)C(\delta)f(s_0),C(\delta)f(t_0)) =$
$\Sigma(\pi(t')\pi(s)C(\delta)f(s,s'),\pi(t)\pi(s')C(\delta)f(t,t')) =$
$\Sigma(\pi(t')C(\delta)h(s'),\pi(s')C(\delta)h(t')) \leq$
$d(\delta)\ \Sigma(\pi(t')h(s'),\pi(s')h(t')) =$
$d(\delta)\ \Sigma(A(s_0,t_0)f(s_0),f(t_0))$.

For the converse assume that $h \in F(Y,H)$. Define $f \in F(S,H)$ by $f(1,s') = h(s')$, $s' \in Y$, $f(s,s') = 0$ if $s \neq 1$. Then the condition (3.3) translates into (4.2) by a computation similar to (4.3). Q.E.D.

The equivalence of (a) and (b) of this theorem applied to $Y = \Omega = N$, i.e. for a single subnormal operator A ($\pi(n) = A^n$, $n \in N$) and a single operator C to be lifted ($C(n) = C^n$, $n \in N$), is Bram's Theorem 7 of [3]. To be completely precise, Corollary (3.7) shows that Bram's boundedness condition $\Sigma(A^m Ch(n), A^n Ch(m)) \leq d\, \Sigma(A^m h(n), A^n h(m))$ for some $d \geq 0$, and each $h \in F(N,H)$, is equivalent to the boundedness condition BC for $A_\Phi{}^C$.

(4.4) THEOREM. *Let* Y *be a semigroup. Let* $\pi: Y \dashrightarrow B(H)$ *be a subnormal homomorphism. Let* τ_0 *be its minimal normal extension.*

(a) Each operator $T \in B(H)$ *that commutes with* $\pi(s)$ *and* $\pi(s)^*$ *for each* $s \in Y$, *lifts uniquely to the commutant of* τ_0.

(b) The von Neumann algebras $W^*(\pi(S))'$ and $W^*(\tau_0(Y))' \cap \{P_H\}'$ *are isometrically *-isomorphic (via the mapping* $T \dashrightarrow$ *the lifting of* T*).*

This theorem is the translation of Theorem (3.8) to the subnormal situation. Notice that $W^*(\pi(Y))' = A_\Phi(SxS)'$, and $W^*(\tau(S))' = W^*(\tau_0(Y))'$. If $S = N$, i.e. for a single subnormal operator, Theorem (4.4) is Theorem 8 in [3].

5. APPLICATION II: CONTRACTIONS.

The lifting to the commutant question will be discussed here following the approach to contraction semigroups in [6], [11]. G denotes a commutative group ordered by a subsemigroup G_+ satisfying: $G_+ \cap (-G_+) = \{0\}$, $G_+ \cup (-G_+) = G$. If $m,n \in G$, then $m \leq n$ if $n - m \in G_+$. In $G_+ x G_+$ the involution is defined by $(m,n)^* = (n,m)$, $m,n \in G_+$, and the algebraic operation # is introduced by the formula: $(j,k) \# (m,n) = (m+j-n,k)$ if $j \geq n$, and $(j,k) \# (m,n) = (m,k+n-j)$ if $j < n$. The set $G_+ x G_+$ with this operation and involution is a *-semigroup denoted by $G^\#$ - cf. [11, Proposition 1]. *-semigroup homomorphisms of $G^\#$ are in a bijective correspondence with coisometric homomorphisms of G_+

(i.e. each value is a coisometry) by Proposition 2 of [11]. Let $\pi:G_+ \to B(H)$ be a semigroup homomorphism. Define $\Phi:G^\# \to B(H)$ by $\Phi(m,n) = \pi(n)^*\pi(m)$, $m,n \in G_+$, and $A_\Phi:G^\# x G^\# \to B(H)$ by $A_\Phi(\beta,\alpha) = \Phi(\alpha^*\#\beta)$, $\alpha,\beta \in G^\#$. Assume that π is contractive, i.e. $\|\pi(n)\| \le 1$, $n \in G_+$. Then π has a coisometric extension $\tau_0:G_+ \to B(K)$ This is equivalent to the existence of a $*$-dilation (K,τ) of A_Φ related to τ_0 as follows: $\tau(m,n) = \tau_0(n)^*\tau_0(m)$, $m,n \in G_+$ - [11, Theorem]. Let Ω be a semigroup. Let $C:\Omega \to B(H)$ be a semigroup homomorphism. The next theorem gives a necessary and sufficient condition for C to lift to the commutant of τ. The lifting σ of C will commute not only with each coisometry $\tau_0(n)$, $n \in G_+$, but also with its adjoint. Notice that, unlike in the subnormal case, the commutants of $\tau(G^\#)$ and $\tau_0(G_+)$ have, in general, no reason to be equal. The above notations will be preserved.

(5.1) THEOREM. *Let* $\pi:G_+ \to B(H)$ *be a contractive semigroup homomorphism. Put* $D(n) = (I - \pi(n)^*\pi(n))^{\frac{1}{2}}$, $n \in G_+$. *Let* Ω *be a semigroup. Let* $C:\Omega \to B(H)$ *be a semigroup homomorphism. The following conditions are equivalent:*

(a) $A_\Phi{}^C:(G^\# x\Omega)x(G^\# x\Omega) \to B(H)$ *defined in (2.1) has a dilation,*

(b) C *lifts to the commutant of* τ.

(c) The values of C *commute with the values of* π *and for each* $\delta \in \Omega$ *there is* $d(\delta) \ge 0$ *such that*

$$(5.2)\quad \|D(n)C(\delta)x\|^2 \le d(\delta)\ \|D(n)x\|^2, \quad x \in H,\ n \in G_+.$$

If τ_0 *is the minimal coisometric extension of* π *and* C *lifts to the commutant of* τ, *then the lifting of* C *is unique.*

PROOF. By Theorem (3.2) and Theorem of [11], it has to be proved only that (c) is equivalent to (c) in Theorem (3.2). This is done by a rather lengthy and sometimes involved computation, only the final results of which will be shown here. More details can be found in [14] where a computation based on a similar idea proves a part of Theorem (4.1). Take $f \in F(G^\#,H)$, $\alpha = (k,j)$, $\beta = (m,n) \in G^\#$. Define $h \in F(G_+,H)$ by $h(n) = \Sigma_p\pi(p)f(p,n)$, $n \in G_+$. Let $j_0 < \ldots < j_\mu$ be the elements of G_+ for which the value of h is not zero. Define $g:G_+ \to H$ by $g(j) = \Sigma_{n<j}\pi(j-n)h(n)$ if $j > j_0$, and

$g(j) = 0$ if $j \le j_0$. Then, assuming that the values of C commute with the values of π, one gets for a fixed $\delta \in \Omega$:

$$(5.3)\ \Sigma_{\alpha,\beta}\ (A_\Phi(\beta,\alpha)C(\delta)f(\beta),C(\delta)f(\alpha)) = \Sigma_{j\ge n}\ (\pi(j-n)C(\delta)h(n),C(\delta)h(j)) + \Sigma_{j<n}\ (C(\delta)h(n),\pi(n-j)C(\delta)h(j)) = \|C(\delta)h(j_0)\|^2 - \|\pi(j_1 - j_0)C(\delta)h(j_0)\|^2 + \Sigma_{1\le i\le\mu-1}\ [\|C(\delta)(g(j_i) + h(j_i))\|^2 - \|\pi(j_{i+1} - j_i)C(\delta)(g(j_i) + h(j_i))\|^2] + \|C(\delta)(g(j_\mu) + h(j_\mu))\|^2.$$

The inequality in (5.2) reads:

$$(5.4)\ \|C(\delta)x\|^2 - \|\pi(n)C(\delta)x\|^2 \le d(\delta)\ [\|x\|^2 - \|\pi(n)x\|^2],\quad x \in H,\ n \in G_+.$$

By (3.4), $\|C(\delta)\|^2 \le d(\delta)$, $\delta \in \Omega$. Hence, by (5.3), (c) above implies (c) in Theorem (3.2). For the converse fix $x \in H$, $n \in G_+$, and choose f so that $h(0) = x$, $h(n) = -\pi(n)h(0)$, $h(j) = 0$ elsewhere. Take $\mu = 1$, $j_0 = 0$, $j_1 = n$. Since $g(j) = \pi(j - j_0)h(j_0)$ if $j_0 < j \le j_1$, in the last sum in (5.3) only the first two terms are non-zero. Exactly the same happens in the sum in (5.3) corresponding to $\delta = 1$, $C(\delta) = I$. Hence, by (5.4), the inequality (3.3) reduces to (5.2). Q.E.D.

If G = the group of integers, $G_+ = \Omega = N$, this theorem gives a necessary and sufficient condition for an operator C to lift to the commutant of a (the minimal) coisometric extension B of a single contraction in such a manner that the lifting commutes also with B^*. Unlike in the case considered by Ando and Sz.-Nagy - Foias, here the lifting is unique, if the coisometric extension is minimal.

Finally, Theorem (3.8) has the following form for contraction semigroups:

(5.5) THERORЕМ. *Suppose* $\pi:G_+ \to B(H)$ *is a contractive semigroup homomorphism. Let* $\tau_0:G_+ \to B(K)$ *be its minimal coisometric extension. and let* (K,τ) *be the minimal *-dilation of* A_Φ .

(a) Each operator $T \in B(H)$ *that commutes with* $\pi(n)$ *and* $\pi(n)^*$ *for each* $n \in G_+$ *lifts to the commutant of* τ *(the lifting commutes with* $\tau_0(n)$ and $\tau_0(n)^*$, $n \in G$).

(b) *The von Neumann algebras* $W^*(\pi(G_+))'$ *and* $W^*(\tau_0(G_+)' \cap \{P_H\}'$ *are isometrically *-isomorphic (via the mapping* $T \dashrightarrow$ *the lifting of T).*

Notice that $W^*(\pi(G_+))' = A_\Phi(G^\# x G^\#)'$, and $W^*(\tau_0(G_+))'$ $W^*(\tau(G^\#))'$. For a single contraction $A \in B(H)$ and its minimal coisometric extension $B \in B(K)$ Theorem (5.5) says that the von Neumann algebras $W^*(A)'$ and $W^*(B)' \cap \{P_H\}'$ are isometrically *-isomorphic.

Deddens gave a simple example of a subnormal operator A and an operator C commuting with A which does not lift to the commutant of the minimal normal extension of A ([5], see also [4, p. 195]). His idea will now be used to illustrate how the theorems of Ando and Sz.-Nagy - Foias differ from the equivalence (b) <==> (c) in Theorem (5.1).

(5.6) EXAMPLE. H_1 is an infinite dimensional Hilbert space, $V \in B(H_1)$ is a non-unitary isometry, $E = I - VV^*$. In $H = H_1 \oplus H_1$ consider

$$A = \begin{bmatrix} V & 0 \\ 0 & 0 \end{bmatrix} \qquad C = \begin{bmatrix} 0 & 0 \\ E & 0 \end{bmatrix}$$

Then $AC = CA = 0$. By the theorem of Ando or Sz.-Nagy - Foias, C lifts to the commutant of the minimal coisometric extension of the contraction A. If $n \in N$, then

$$D(n) = (I - A^{*n}A^n)^{\frac{1}{2}} = 0 \oplus I, \text{ and } D(n)C = C.$$

Choose $x \in H_1$, not in the kernel of E. Then

$$\|D(n)C(x \oplus 0)\| = \|C(x \oplus 0)\| = \|Ex\|, \text{ and } \|D(n)(x \oplus 0)\| = 0.$$

Hence (5.2) fails. By Theorem (5.1), the lifting of C cannot commute with the adjoint of the coisometric extension of A.

It should be noticed that, by Theorem (4.1) and Theorem (5.1), Deddens's example and Example (5.6) seen as a part of the general dilation theory are two more examples of PD functions on semigroups that fail to satisfy BC and because of that have no bounded dilations.

All the results of this paper remain true if "commuting" is replaced by "intertwining", by the well-known Berberian matrix method.

R E F E R E N C E S

[1] Ando, T., Szymanski W.: Order structure and Lebesgue decomposition of positive definite operator functions Indiana Univ. Math. J. 35 (1986), 157-173.

[2] Arveson, W.B.: Subalgebras of C*-algebras, I, Acta Math. 123 (1969), 142-224.

[3] Bram, J.: Subnormal operators, Duke Math. J. 22 (1955), 75-94.

[4] Conway, J.B.: Subnormal operators, Pitman, London, 1981.

[5] Deddens, J.A.: Intertwiwning analytic Toeplitz operators, Mich. Math. J. 18 (1971), 243-246.

[6] Mlak, W: Unitary dilations in case of ordered groups Annales Polon. Math. 17 (1966), 321-328.

[7] Mlak, W: Dilations of Hilbert space operators (General theory), Dissertationes Math. 153 (1978), 1-65.

[8] Mlak, W., Weron, A: Dilations of Banach space valued functions - Annales Polon. Math. 38 (1980), 295-303.

[9] Sz.-Nagy, B., Foias, C: Harmonic analysis of operators in Hilbert spaces, North Holland - Amsterdam, London, Akad. Kiado, Budapest, 1970.

[10] Stochel, J., Szymanski, W.: On the uniqueness of minimal R-dilations for unstarred semigroups, Indiana Univ. Math. J. 32 (1983), 793-800.

[11] Szymanski, W.: Coisometric extensions of contraction semigroups, Proc. Amer. Math. Soc. 97 (1986), 418-422.

[12] Szymanski, W.: Positive forms and dilations, Trans. Amer. Math. Soc. 301 (1986), 761-780.

[13] Szymanski, W.: Dilations and subnormality, Proc. Amer. Math. Soc. 101 (1987) 251-259.

[14] Szymanski, W.: The boundedness condition of dilation theory characterizes subnormals and contractions, to appear in Rocky Mountain Jour. of Math.

Department of Mathematical Sciences
West Chester University
West Chester, PA 19383
USA

Operator Theory:
Advances and Applications, Vol. 35

THE SMOOTH MAPPINGS WHICH PRESERVE THE HARDY SPACE $H^2(B_n)$

W. R. Wogen[1)]

Holomorphic self–maps φ of the open unit ball in $\mathbb{C}^n$ which extend to be C^3 on the closed unit ball are considered. For such φ we characterize those with the property that composition by φ preserves the Hardy space H^2.

1. INTRODUCTION.

Let B_n be the open unit ball in $\mathbb{C}^n$, let $H^2 = H^2(B_n)$ denote the Hardy space on B_n, and suppose $\varphi : B_n \to B_n$ is holomorphic on B_n. The composition operator on H^2 induced by φ is the map $C_\varphi : f \longmapsto f \circ \varphi$, $f \in H^2$. By the Closed Graph Theorem, C_φ is a bounded operator on H^2 if and only if φ preserves H^2; that is, if and only if the range of C_φ is a subset of H^2.

It is well known that for $n = 1$, C_φ is always bounded (see [7] and its references). It is also known that when $n > 1$, C_φ need not be bounded. Note the examples in [1], [2], [3], and [4]. In fact, the main result of [2] is the construction of polynomial self–map φ of the closed ball $\overline{B}_2$ which is one–to–one on $\overline{B}_2$ and such that C_φ is unbounded.

In this paper a necessary and sufficient condition is given for a smooth (i.e., C^3) map $\varphi : \overline{B}_n \longrightarrow \overline{B}_n$ to induce a bounded C_φ. In Sections 2 and 3 we give detailed proofs for the $n = 2$ case. The notation is slightly simpler for this case. Then in Section 4 we comment briefly on the $n > 2$ case.

---

1) Supported in part by a grant from the National Science Foundation

We remark that sufficient conditions for boundedness of C_φ are given in [6, Theorem 6.4] and in [5]. Our necessary and sufficient condition for boundedness (see Theorems 1 and 2) is a strict inequality relating certain directional derivatives. This inequality leads to a "local Lipschitz invertibility" condition (Lemma 4) at points ξ on the unit sphere such that $\varphi(\xi)$ is on the unit sphere.

Our notation will follow [8]. Let $B_2 = B$ and let $S = \partial B$ be the unit sphere in $\mathbb{C}^2$. $<.,.>$ denotes the complex inner product in $\mathbb{C}^2$, and $|\cdot|$ denotes the Euclidean norm. Let $e = e_1 = (1,0)$ and $e_2 = (0,1)$.

For $z, w \in \overline{B}$, let $d(z,w) = |1-<z,w>|^{1/2}$. Then the triangle inequality for d holds on $\overline{B}$ and d is a metric on S which induces the same topology as the Euclidean metric (see [8, pp. 65–67]). For $\xi \in S$, $\delta > 0$, let $S(\xi,\delta) = \{z \in \overline{B} : d(z,\xi)\} < \delta\}$ and let $Q(\xi,\delta) = S \cap S(\xi,\delta)$. This terminology agrees with [8] but differs slightly from [2] and [5]. The set $S(\xi,\delta)$ above is the set $S(\xi,\delta^2)$ of [2] and [5].

Let σ denote surface measure on S. Recall that a positive measure μ on $\overline{B}$ is a σ–Carleson measure if there is a positive constant C so that $\mu(S(\xi,t)) \le Ct^4$ for all $\xi \in S$ and $t > 0$. For $\varphi : B \to B$ holomorphic on B and $\xi \in S$, let $\varphi^*(\xi) = \lim_{r\to 1} \varphi(r\xi)$. φ^* exists a.e. σ. In this paper, φ will always have a continuous extension to the closed ball. We will also use the symbol φ to denote the boundary function $\varphi^* = \varphi|S$. We will use the following Carleson measure criterion for the boundedness of C_φ.

Theorem [5]. *Suppose that* $\varphi : B \to B$ *is holomorphic. Then* C_φ *is bounded on* H^2 *if and only if* $\sigma\varphi^{-1}$ *is a* σ*–Carleson measure.*

2. UNBOUNDED C_φ.

We assume throughout the rest of the paper that $\varphi = (\varphi_1,\varphi_2) : \overline{B} \to \overline{B}$ is a C^3 map on $\overline{B}$ which is holomorphic on B. We begin with a lemma.

Lemma 1. *If* $\varphi(e) = e$ *(i.e.,* $\varphi_1(e) = 1$*), then*

(i) $$D_1\varphi_1(e) \ge \frac{1 - |\varphi_1(0)|}{1 + |\varphi_1(0)|},$$

(ii) $D_2\varphi_1(e) = 0$,

(iii) $D_1\varphi_1(e) \geq |D_{22}\varphi_1(e)|$.

Proof. Note that $D_1\varphi_1(e)$ is the angular derivative of φ_1 at e. (See [8, pp. 174–181].) If $\varphi_1(0) = 0$, then it is easy to see that $D_1\varphi_1(e) \geq 1$, by Schwarz' Lemma. If $\varphi_1(0) \neq 0$, let

$$g(z_1) = \lambda \frac{\varphi_1(z_1 e) - \varphi_1(0)}{1 - \overline{\varphi_1(0)}\ \varphi_1(z_1 e)}$$

where λ is chosen so that $|\lambda| = 1$ and $g(1) = 1$. Then as above, $g'(1) \geq 1$, which easily yields (i). (ii) follows directly from [8, Theorem 8.5.6 (v)]. We will obtain another proof of (ii) as part of the proof of (iii). For each λ with $|\lambda| = 1$, let $h_\lambda(t) = \operatorname{Re} \varphi_1(\cos t, \lambda \sin t)$. h_λ has a maximum when $t = 0$, so $h_\lambda'(0) = 0$ and $h_\lambda''(0) \leq 0$. But $h_\lambda'(t) = -\operatorname{Re} D_1\varphi_1(\cos t, \lambda\sin t) \sin t + \operatorname{Re} D_2\varphi_1(\cos t, \lambda \sin t)\lambda \cos t$, so $0 = \operatorname{Re} \lambda D_2\varphi_1(e)$, for all t. Thus $D_2\varphi_1(e) = 0$. A similar computation shows that $h_\lambda''(0) = -D_1\varphi_1(e) + \operatorname{Re} \lambda^2 D_{22}\varphi_1(e) \leq 0$, for all λ . Thus $|D_{22}\varphi_1(e)| \leq D_1\varphi_1(e)$.

<u>Lemma</u> 2. *If* $\varphi(e) = e$ *and* $D_1\varphi_1(e) = D_{22}\varphi_1(e)$, *then* C_φ *is unbounded on* H^2 .

Proof. Let $G = \{u \in \mathbb{R}^3 : |u| < 1/2\}$. Parametrize a neighborhood of e in S by $\Lambda : G \to S$, where $\Lambda(u) = (\sqrt{1-|u|^2} + iu_1 , u_2 + iu_3)$. It is easy to check that

$$d\sigma = \frac{dm_3}{\sqrt{1-|u|^2}} , \tag{1}$$

where $dm_3 = du_1 du_2 du_3$ is volume measure in $\mathbb{R}^3$.

Choose δ_0 , $0 < \delta_0 < 1$, so that $Q(e,\delta_0) \subset \Lambda(G)$. For $0 < \delta \leq \delta_0$, let $E(\delta) = \{u \in \mathbb{R}^3 : |u_1| < \delta^2, |u_2| < \delta, |u_3| < \delta\}$. It is elementary to check that

(2) $$\Lambda(E(\delta/2)) \subset Q(e,\delta) \subset \Lambda(E(2\delta)) .$$

To apply the Carleson measure criterion, we must estimate $\sigma\{z \in S : \varphi(z) \in S(e,\delta)\} = \sigma\{z \in S : |1-\varphi_1(z)| < \delta^2\}$. Using (1), it will suffice to estimate $m_3\{u \in \mathbb{R}^3 : \varphi(\Lambda(u)) \in S(e,\delta)\}$. Now it follows from (2) and Lemma 4 of Section 3 (or see the proof of [2, Theorem 1]) that there is a constant $C > 0$ so that $E(C\delta) \subset \{u : \varphi(\Lambda(u)) \in S(e,\delta)\}$. Thus $m_3\{u : \varphi(\Lambda(u)) \in S(e,\delta)\} \geq C'\delta^4$ for some $C' > 0$. We will show that a stronger estimate holds.

Let $g(u) = \varphi_1(\Lambda(u))-1$, $u \in G$. Then g is a C^3 function. It follows from the Chain Rule that

(3) $$g(0) = 0 , D_{u_2}g(0) = D_{u_3}g(0) = 0 , \text{ and } D_{u_2u_2}g(0) = 0 .$$

The vanishing of the first order partials is a consequence of Lemma 1(ii), while the vanishing to second order in the u_2 direction follows from the condition $D_1\varphi_1(e) = D_{22}\varphi_1(e)$.

Apply Taylor's Theorem to g at $u = 0$. We have

(4) $$g(u) = D_{u_1}g(0)u_1 + 1/2 \sum_{j,k=1}^{3} D_{u_ju_k}g(0)u_ju_k + 0(|u|^3) ,$$

where $D_{u_2u_2}g(0) = 0$.

For $0 < \delta \leq \delta_0$, define

$$\Omega(\delta) = \{u \in \mathbb{R}^3 : |u_1| < \delta^2, |u_3| < \delta , |u_2| < \min\{\delta^{2/3}, \delta^2/|u_3|\}\} .$$

A straightforward iterated integration (as in [2, p. 481]) shows that $m_3(\Omega(\delta)) \approx \delta^4 \log 1/\delta$. From the definition of $\Omega(\delta)$ we see that each term of the righthand side of (4) is $0(\delta^2)$. Thus there is a constant $C > 0$ so that $|g(u)| \leq (C\delta)^2$ for $u \in \Omega(\delta)$. This inequality shows that $\varphi(\Lambda(\Omega(\delta))) \subset S(e,C\delta)$. Thus $\dfrac{\sigma\varphi^{-1}S(e,\delta)}{\delta^4} \approx \log 1/\delta$ so that $\sigma\varphi^{-1}$ is not a σ–Carleson measure.

Before stating the main theorem of this section, we introduce some notation. Let $K = \{\xi \in S : \varphi(\xi) \in S\}$. For each $\eta \in S$, $\varphi_\eta(z) = <\varphi(z),\eta>$, $z \in \overline{B}$. Thus φ_η is the coordinate of φ in the η direction. For $\xi \in S$, let $\xi^\perp = (\overline{\xi}_2, -\overline{\xi}_1)$, so that $<\xi,\xi^\perp> = 0$. Also denote the directional derivative in the ξ direction by D_ξ. We have the following generalization of Lemma 1.

Lemma 1'. *If* $\xi \in K$ and $\eta = \varphi(\xi)$, *then*

(i) $$D_\xi \varphi_\eta(\xi) \geq \frac{1 - |\varphi(0)|}{1 + |\varphi(0)|},$$

(ii) $$D_{\xi^\perp} \varphi_\eta(\xi) = 0,$$

(iii) $$D_\xi \varphi_\eta(\xi) \geq |D_{\xi^\perp \xi^\perp} \varphi_\eta(\xi)|.$$

Theorem 1. *Suppose* $\varphi : \overline{B} \to \overline{B}$ *is holomorphic on* B *and is* C^3 *on* $\overline{B}$. *Suppose there is a* $\xi \in K$ *so that for* $\eta = \varphi(\xi)$ *we have* $D_\xi \varphi_\eta(\xi) = |D_{\xi^\perp \xi^\perp} \varphi_\eta(\xi)|$. *Then* C_φ *is unbounded on* H^2.

Proof. For each $\tau \in S$, define a unitary map $V_\tau : \mathbb{C}^2 \to \mathbb{C}^2$ by $V_\tau e = \tau$ and $V_\tau e_2 = \tau^\perp$. Note that V_τ induces a unitary composition operator on H^2. Let $\psi = V_\eta^{-1} \circ \varphi \circ V_\xi$. Then C_φ is bounded if and only if C_ψ is bounded. But $\psi(e) = e$. Also, the hypothesis on φ in the theorem translates to the equality $D_1\psi_1(e) = |D_{22}\psi_1(e)|$. Now we choose $\lambda, |\lambda| = 1$, so that the unitary change of variable $U : (z_1,z_2) \longmapsto (z_1,\lambda z_2)$ gives $D_{22}\psi_1(U(e)) > 0$. By Lemma 2, $C_{\psi \circ U}$ is unbounded, so C_φ is unbounded.

3. BOUNDED C_φ.

In this section we prove the following converse of Theorem 1.

Theorem 2. *Suppose the* $\varphi : \overline{B} \to \overline{B}$ *is holomorphic on* B *and is* C^3 *on* $\overline{B}$. *If* $D_\xi \varphi_\eta(\xi) > |D_{\xi^\perp \xi^\perp} \varphi_\eta(\xi)|$ *for all* $\xi \in K$ *and* $\eta = \varphi(\xi)$, *then* C_φ *is bounded on* H^2.

We will need several lemmas. We begin by defining $A_0 = \inf\{D_\xi\varphi_\eta(\xi) - |D_{\xi^\perp\xi^\perp}\varphi_\eta(\xi)| : \xi \in K, \eta = \varphi(\xi)\}$. Since K is compact, A_0 is positive.

For ξ and η in S, let $P_\eta(z,\xi)$ be the second order Taylor polynomial at ξ of $\varphi_\eta(z)$, $z \in \overline{B}$. Let $E_\eta(z,\xi) = \varphi_\eta(z) - P_\eta(z,\xi)$.

Lemma 3. *There is a constant* $M > 0$, *independent of* ξ *and* η, *so that* $|E_\eta(z,\xi)| = |\varphi_\eta(z) - P_\eta(z,\xi)| \le M\, d(z,\xi)^3$, *for* $z \in S$.

Proof. This follows directly from Taylor's Theorem, since the metric d satisfies

$$|z-\xi|^2 \le 2d(z,\xi)^2 \text{ for } z,\xi \in S .$$

M can be taken to be the sum of the sup norms of the third order partials of φ_1 and φ_2.

Lemma 4. *There is a* $\delta_0 > 0$ *and there are constants* $A,B > 0$ *so that if* $\xi \in K$ *and* $d(z,\xi) < \delta_0$, *then* $B\, d(z,\xi)^2 \ge d(\Phi(\delta),\Phi(\xi))^2 \ge A\, d(z,\xi)^2$.

Proof. Let $M_1 = \sup\{|D\varphi_\eta(z)| : z, \eta \in S, D$ a directional derivative of order $\le 2\}$. We will consider Taylor's Theorem (Lemma 3) applied to φ_η at ξ, where $\eta = \varphi(\xi)$. To simplify the notation, we write $D_1 = D_\xi$, $D_2 = D_{\xi^\perp}$. Also let $w_1 = \langle z,\xi\rangle$ and $w_2 = \langle z,\xi^\perp\rangle$. w_1 and w_2 are the coordinates of z relative to the basis $\{\xi,\xi^\perp\}$. Note that $|w_2|^2 = 1 - |w_1|^2 \le 2|1-w_1|$ and that $D_2\varphi_\eta(\xi) = 0$ by Lemma 1'. Thus

$$(5)\qquad P_\eta(z,\xi) = 1 + D_1\varphi_\eta(\xi)(w_1-1) + \tfrac{1}{2}\{D_{11}\varphi_\eta(\xi)(w_1-1)^2$$

$$+ 2D_{12}\varphi_\eta(\xi)(w_1-1)w_2 + D_{22}\varphi_\eta(\xi)w_2^{\,2}\} .$$

Hence

$$d(\varphi(z),\eta)^2 = |1-\varphi_\eta(z)|$$

$$\geq (D_1\varphi_\eta(\xi) - |D_{22}\varphi_\eta(\xi)|)|1-w_1|$$

$$-\tfrac{1}{2}|D_{11}\varphi_\eta(\xi)||1-w_1|^2 - |D_{12}\varphi_\eta(\xi)||1-w_1||w_2| - M|1-w_1|^{\frac{3}{2}}$$

$$\geq A_0|1-w_1| - (\tfrac{1}{2}M_1|1-w_1| + 2M_1|1-w_1|^{\frac{1}{2}} + M|1-w_1|^{\frac{1}{2}})|1-w_1| .$$

Choose δ_0 small enough that

$$(6)\qquad \tfrac{1}{2}M_1|1-w_1| + 2M_1|1-w_1|^{\frac{1}{2}} + M|1-w_1|^{\frac{1}{2}} < A_0/16$$

if $d(z,\xi)^2 = |1-w_1| < \delta_0^{\,2}$. Then for $d(z,\xi) < \delta_0$ we have $d(\varphi(z),\eta)^2 = |1-\varphi_\eta(z)| \geq (A_0/2)\, d(z,\xi)^2$, and we can choose $A = A_0/2$. The choice of the constant B is more straightforward. In fact only first order Taylor approximation is needed. (See also [2, Lemma 1].) We omit the details.

We may (and do) assume that the δ_0 of Lemma 4 has these additional properties.

(7) If $\xi,\eta \in S$ and $\xi^0 \in K$ and if $d(\xi,\xi^0) < \delta_0$, $d(\eta,\varphi(\xi^0)) < \delta_0$,
then $\mathrm{Re}\, D_\xi\, \varphi_\eta(\xi) - |D_{\xi^\perp\xi^\perp}\varphi_\eta(\xi)| \geq A_0/2 = A$,
and $\mathrm{Im}\, D_\xi\, \varphi_\eta(\xi) < A/8$.

(8) If $\xi,\eta \in S$, $\xi^0 \in K$ and if $d(\xi,\xi^0) < \delta_0$, $d(\eta,\varphi(\xi^0)) < \delta_0$,
then $|\text{Arg}\, D_\xi\, \varphi_\eta(\xi)| < \pi/6$.

For (7), note that if D is a directional derivative of order ≤ 2, then $D\varphi_\eta(\xi)$ is continuous in ξ and η. This fact, together with Lemma 1'(i) and the definition of A_0, shows that (7) holds. (8) follows from (7). In fact from (7) we get

$$\frac{|\text{Im}\; D_\xi\; \varphi_\eta(\xi)|}{\text{Re}\; D_\xi\; \varphi_\eta(\xi)} < \frac{1}{8},$$

which surely implies

$$|\text{Arg}\, D_\xi\, \varphi_\eta(\xi)| < \pi/6 .$$

For the estimates of Lemma 4, it is crucial that $D_2\varphi_\eta(\xi) = 0$. This is because the best estimate on $|w_2|$ is $|w_2| \leq (2|1-w_1|)^{\frac{1}{2}}$. We need a version of Lemma 4 which holds at certain points $\xi \in S\backslash K$.

We continue to use the notation in the proof of Lemma 4.

For $\xi,\eta \in S$, let $R_\eta(z,\xi) = \varphi_\eta(z) - \varphi_\eta(\xi) - D_2\varphi_\eta(\xi)w_2$.

Lemma 5. *If* $\xi,\eta \in S$, $\xi^0 \in K$ *and if* $d(\xi,\xi^0) < \delta_0$, $d(\eta,\varphi(\xi^0)) < \delta_0$, *then*

(i) $B\, d(z,\xi)^2 \geq |R_\eta(z,\xi)| \geq \frac{A}{2}\, d(z,\xi)^2$ *if* $d(z,\xi) < \delta_0$.

(ii) $|\text{Arg}\, R_\eta(z,\xi)| \geq \pi/3$ *if* $R_\eta(z,\xi) \neq 0$ *and* $d(z,\xi) < \delta_0$.

Proof. Let $\eta^0 = \varphi(\xi^0)$. Note that by Lemma 4, if $d(z,\xi^0) < \delta_0$, then $|R_{\eta^0}(z,\xi^0)| = d(\varphi(\xi),\varphi(\xi^0))^2 \geq A\, d(z,\xi^0)^2$. Now $R_\eta(z,\xi) = P_\eta(z,\xi) + E_\eta(z,\xi) - \varphi_\eta(\xi) - D_2\varphi_\eta(\xi)w_2$. We imitate the proof of Lemma 4.

$$|R_\eta(z,\xi)| \geq |D_1\, \varphi_\eta(\xi)(w_1-1) + \tfrac{1}{2}D_{22}\, \varphi_\eta(\xi)w_2{}^2|$$

$$- |\text{the remaining second order terms} + \text{the error term}|$$

$$\geq (|D_1\varphi_\eta(\xi)| - |D_{22}\varphi_\eta(\xi)|)|1-w_1| - \frac{A}{8}\,d(z,\xi)^2$$

$$\geq \frac{A}{2}\,d(z,\xi)^2\,,\ \text{using (7) and (6).}$$

The other inequality in (i) follows exactly as in Lemma 4.

To establish (ii) we need the inequality $|w_2|^2 \leq 2(1-\mathrm{Re}\,w_1)$ for $|w| = 1$. Since also

$$\mathrm{Re}\,D_1\,\varphi_\eta(\xi) - |D_{22}\,\varphi_\eta(\xi)| > 0 \ \text{ by (7),}$$

we have $|\frac{1}{2}D_{22}\,\varphi_\eta(\xi)w_2{}^2| \leq (\mathrm{Re}\,D_1\,\varphi_\eta(\xi))(1-\mathrm{Re}\,w_1)$. Thus $\mathrm{Re}\{\mathrm{Re}\,D_1\,\varphi_\eta(\xi)(w_1-1) + \frac{1}{2}D_{22}\,\varphi_\eta(\xi)w_2{}^2\} \leq 0$. It follows that

$$\mathrm{Re}\,R_\eta(z,\xi) \leq \mathrm{Re}\{(\mathrm{Im}\,D_1\varphi_\eta(\xi))(w_1-1) + \text{remaining second order terms}$$
$$+\ \text{error term}\} \leq \frac{A}{8}|1-w_1| + \frac{A}{8}|1-w_1| = \frac{A}{4}d(z,\xi)^2\,,\ \text{using (6) and (7).}$$

If $R_\eta(z,\xi) \neq 0$, then the above shows that $\dfrac{\mathrm{Re}\ R_\eta(z,\xi)}{|R_\eta(z,\xi)|} < \frac{1}{2}$. Thus $|\mathrm{Arg}\,R_\eta(z,\xi)| > \frac{\pi}{3}$.

<u>Lemma 6</u>. *Suppose that* $\eta \in S$ *and that* $d(\varphi(z),\eta)^2 = |1-\varphi_\eta(z)|$, $z \in S$, *has a local minimum at* $z = \xi$. *Then*

(i) $D_2\varphi_\eta(\xi) = 0$,

(ii) $1-\varphi_\eta(\xi) = \mu D_1\varphi_\eta(\xi)$ for some $\mu \geq 0$,

and (iii) $d(\varphi(\xi),\eta)^2 + B\,d(z,\xi)^2 \geq d(\varphi(z),\eta)^2 \geq \frac{A}{4}\,d(z,\xi)^2$ for $d(z,\xi) < \delta_0$.

Proof. If $\varphi_\eta(\xi) = 1$, then Lemmas 1' and 4 apply. Hence let $g(z) = 1-\varphi_\eta(z)$ and suppose $g(\xi) \neq 0$. We know that for some δ_1 , $0 < \delta_1 < \delta_0$, we have $|g(\xi)| \le |g(z)|$ if $z \in Q(\xi,\delta_1)$.

Suppose that $\gamma(t) = \gamma_1(t)\xi + \gamma_2(t)\xi^\perp$ is a C^1 curve in $Q(\xi,\delta_1)$ with $\gamma(0) = \xi$. Then $\tilde{\gamma} = g \circ \varphi$ is a C^1 curve in $\{w \in \mathbb{C} : |g(\xi)| \le |w| \le 1\}$, and $g(\gamma(0)) = g(\xi)$. Thus the tangent vector to $\tilde{\gamma}$ at $t = 0$ is perpendicular to $g(\xi)$. (Here "perpendicular" is in the sense of the real inner product in $\mathbb{R}^2$.) So we have

$$D_1\varphi_\eta(\xi)\gamma_1'(0) + D_2\varphi_\eta(\xi)\gamma_2'(0) = a\, i\, g(\xi) \text{ for some } a \in \mathbb{R} . \tag{9}$$

Taking $\gamma(t) = (\cos t)\xi + (\sin t)\ \xi^\perp$, (9) gives $D_2\varphi_\eta(\xi) = a_1\ i\ g(\xi)$, while for $\gamma(t) = (\cos t)\ \xi + (i \sin t)\xi^\perp$, (9) gives $i\, D_2\ \varphi_\eta(\xi) = a_2\ i\ g(\xi)$ for some $a_1, a_2 \in \mathbb{R}$. Since $g(\xi) \neq 0$, we must conclude $D_2\varphi_\eta(\xi) = 0$. Now consider $\gamma(t) = e^{it}\xi$. Then (9) gives $i\, D_1 \varphi_\eta(\xi) = ai(1-\varphi_\eta(\xi))$ for some $a \in \mathbb{R}$, $a \neq 0$. Clearly $|\text{Arg}\,(1-\varphi_\eta(\xi))| < \frac{\pi}{2}$. Also $|\text{Arg}\, D_1\varphi_\eta(\xi)| < \frac{\pi}{6}$ by (8). Thus $a > 0$ and (ii) holds with $\mu = a$. Now write

$$|1-\varphi_\eta(z)| = |(1-\varphi_\eta(\xi)) - R_\eta(z,\xi)| . \tag{10}$$

From above, $|\text{Arg}\,(1-\varphi_\eta(\xi))| = |\text{Arg}\, D_1\varphi_\eta(\xi)| < \frac{\pi}{6}$. Also $|\text{Arg}\, R_\eta(z,\xi)| > \frac{\pi}{3}$ by Lemma 5. It follows (e.g., by the Law of Sines) that

$$d(\varphi(z),\eta)^2 = |1-\varphi_\eta(z)| \ge \tfrac{1}{2}|R_\eta(z,\xi)| \quad \text{for } z \in Q(z,\delta_0) .$$

By Lemma 5, $d(\varphi(z),\eta)^2 \ge \frac{A}{4}d(z,\xi)^2$ for $z \in Q(z,\delta_0)$. From (10) and Lemma 5, $d(\varphi(z),\eta)^2 \le d(\varphi(\xi),\eta)^2 + |R_\eta(z,\xi)| \le d(\varphi(\xi),\eta)^2 + B\, d(z,\xi)^2$.

Let $A_1 = \min\{1,\frac{A}{4}\}$.

<u>Lemma 7</u>. *Suppose that* t_0 *satisfies* $0 < t_0 < \sqrt{A_1}\,\delta_0$ *and that* $\eta \in S$. *Suppose that* $\mathcal{O}$ *is a component in* S *of* $S \cap \varphi^{-1}(S(\eta,t_0))$. *Then there is a* $\xi^0 \in \mathcal{O}$ *so that* $\mathcal{O} \subset Q(\xi^0,t_0/\sqrt{A_1})$. *Also, if* $0 < t \leq t_0$, *then* $\mathcal{O} \cap \varphi^{-1}(S(\eta,t)) \subset Q(\xi^0,t/\sqrt{A_1})$.

<u>Proof</u>. If ξ is on the boundary of $\mathcal{O}$, then $|1-\varphi_\eta(\xi)| = t_0^2$, by continuity of φ. Thus $d(\varphi(z),\eta)^2 = |1-\varphi_\eta(z)|$ attains a minimum at some point $\xi^0 \in \mathcal{O}$. We apply Lemma 6 to conclude that

$$\text{if } d(z,\xi^0) < \delta_0 \text{, then } d(\varphi(z),\eta)^2 \geq A_1 d(z,\xi^0)^2 . \tag{11}$$

Hence if $d(z,\xi^0) < \delta_0$, and $d(\varphi(z),\eta) < t_0$, then $A_1 d(z,\xi^0)^2 < t_0^2$, and $d(z,\xi^0) < t_0/\sqrt{A_1}$. This says $\mathcal{O} \cap Q(\xi^0,\delta_0) \subset Q(\xi^0,t_0/\sqrt{A_1})$. Since $\mathcal{O}$ is connected and $t_0/\sqrt{A_1} < \delta_0$, we have that $\mathcal{O} \subset Q(\xi^0,t_0/\sqrt{A_1})$. (11) also shows that for $0 < t \leq t_0$, we have $\varphi^{-1}(S(\eta,t)) \cap \mathcal{O} \subset Q(\xi^0,t/\sqrt{A_1})$.

We are now in a position to prove Theorem 2.

<u>Proof of Theorem 2</u>. Let $B_1 = \max\{1,B\}$. Let $\Omega = \bigcup_{\xi \in K} Q(\xi,\delta_0/\sqrt{4B_1})$. Let $M = \max\{|\varphi(\xi)| : \xi \in S\backslash\Omega\}$, so that $M < 1$. Choose t_0 so that $0 < t_0 < \min\{\sqrt{1-M},\delta_0/2,\delta_0/\sqrt{A_1}\}$. It will suffice to check the Carleson condition for $0 < t \leq t_0/2$.

First suppose $\eta \in S$ and $d(\eta,\varphi(K)) \geq \delta_0$. If $z \in S \cap \varphi^{-1}(S(\eta,t_0))$, then $|1-<\varphi(z),\eta>| < t_0^2$, so $|\varphi(z)| \geq |<\varphi(z),\eta>| \geq 1-t_0^2 > M$. Thus $z \in \Omega$. But if $\xi \in K$ and $d(z,\xi)^2 < \delta_0^2/4B_1$, then $d(\varphi(z),\varphi(\xi))^2 < \delta_0^2/4$, by Lemma 4. But $d(\varphi(z),\eta)^2 < t_0^2 < \delta_0^2/4$, so $d(\varphi(\xi),\eta) < \delta_0$, a contradiction. Thus $S \cap \varphi^{-1}(S(\eta,t_0))$ is empty. This means that we need only check the Carleson condition at those $\eta \in S$ with $d(\eta,\varphi(K)) < \delta_0$. Let J_0 be a positive integer with the property that if $\{\xi^j\}_{j=1}^J \subset S$ and if $\{Q(\xi^j,t_0/\sqrt{4B_1})\}_{j=1}^J$ are pairwise disjoint, then $J \leq J_0$.

Fix $\eta \in S$ with $d(\eta,\varphi(K)) < \delta_0$. Let $\{\mathcal{O}_\alpha\}_{\alpha\in\Lambda}$ be the components of

$S \cap \varphi^{-1}(S(\eta,t_0))$. We only consider the components which meet $\varphi^{-1}(S(\eta,t_0/2))$. Denote these by $\{\mathcal{O}_j\}_{j=1}^{J}$. Choose $\xi^j \in \mathcal{O}_j$ as in the conclusion of Lemma 7. We first apply Lemma 6. If $d(z,\xi^j) < t_0/\sqrt{4B_1}$, then

$$d(\varphi(z),\eta)^2 \le d(\varphi(\xi^j),\eta)^2 + B\, d(z,\xi^j)^2$$

$$\le (\frac{t_0}{2})^2 + \frac{B t_0^{\,2}}{4B_1} \le \frac{t_0^{\,2}}{2} .$$

Thus $Q(\xi^j,t_0/\sqrt{4B_1}) \subset \mathcal{O}_j$, and $J \le J_0$.

By Lemma 7, for $0 < t \le t_0/2$ we have

$$\mathcal{O}_j \cap \varphi^{-1}(S(\eta,t)) \subset Q(\xi^j,t/\sqrt{A_1}) .$$

Thus

$$\sigma\varphi^{-1}(S(\eta,t)) \le \sum_{j=1}^{J} \sigma(Q(\xi^j,t/\sqrt{A_1}) \approx \frac{J}{A_1^{\,2}} t^4 .$$

Thus $\sigma\varphi^{-1}$ is a σ–Carleson measure.

4. REMARKS AND COMMENTS.

We now consider briefly the question of generalizing Theorems 1 and 2 to the $n > 2$ setting. First note in particular that Lemma 1'(iii) generalizes:

Suppose that $\xi,\eta,\tau \in S$ and that $\varphi(\xi) = \eta$, $\varphi_\eta(z) = \langle\varphi(z),\eta\rangle$, and $\langle\xi,\tau\rangle = 0$. Then $D_\xi\varphi_\eta(\xi) \ge |D_{\tau\tau}\varphi_\eta(\xi)|$.

The results of section 3 extend easily to prove

<u>Theorem 2'</u>. *If $\varphi : \overline{B}_n \to \overline{B}_n$ is holomorphic on B_n and C^3 on $\overline{B}_n$ and if $D_\xi\varphi_\eta(\xi) > |D_{\tau\tau}\varphi_\eta(\xi)|$ for all $\xi \in S$ so that $\varphi(\xi) = \eta \in S$ and for all $\tau \perp \xi$, then C_φ is bounded on $H^2(B_n)$.*

Theorem 1 also generalizes.

Theorem 1'. *If* $\varphi : \overline{B}_n \to \overline{B}_n$ *is holomorphic on* B_n *and* C^3 *on* $\overline{B}_n$ *and if* $D_{\xi}\varphi_{\eta}(\xi) = |D_{\tau\tau}\varphi_{\eta}(\xi)|$ *for some* $\xi, \tau \in S$ *with* $\varphi(\xi) = \eta \in S$ *and* $\tau \perp \xi$, *then* C_{φ} *is unbounded on* $H^2(B_n)$.

The key step is to generalize Lemma 2, where we assume $\xi = \eta = e_1$ and $\tau = e_2$. Modify the proof of Lemma 2 as follows.

Let $G = \{u \in \mathbb{R}^{2n-1} : |u| < \frac{1}{2}\}$ and define $\Lambda : G \to S$ by $\Lambda(u) : (\sqrt{1-|u|^2} + iu_1, u_2 + iu_3, \ldots, u_{2n-2} + iu_{2n-1})$. Then $d\sigma = \dfrac{dm_{2n-1}}{\sqrt{1-|u|^2}}$. Let $g(u) = \varphi_1(\Lambda(u)) - 1$. By Taylor's Theorem,

$$g(u) = D_{u_1} g(0) u_1 + \frac{1}{2} \sum_{j,k=1}^{2n-1} D_{u_j u_k} g(0) u_j u_k + 0(|u|^3), \tag{12}$$

and $D_{u_2 u_2} g(0) = 0$.

We consider two cases.

If $D_{u_2 u_k} g(0) = 0$ for all $k \geq 3$, we let

$$\Omega(\delta) = \{ u \in \mathbb{R}^{2n-1} : |u_1| < \delta^2, |(u_3, \ldots, u_{2n-1})| < \delta, |u_2| < \delta^{\frac{2}{3}} \}.$$

Then $m_{2n-1}(\Omega(\delta)) \approx \delta^{2n-1/3}$. Also each term on the righthand side of (12) is $0(\delta^2)$, so there is a $C > 0$ such that $|g(u)| \leq C\delta^2$ for $u \in \Omega(\delta)$. Thus $\sigma\varphi^{-1}$ is not σ–Carleson.

If $D_{u_2 u_k} g(0) \neq 0$ for some $k \geq 3$, we let

$$\Omega(\delta) = \{ u \in \mathbb{R}^{2n-1} : |u_1| < \delta^2, |(u_3, \ldots, u_{2n-1})| < \delta, |u_2| < \min\{\delta^{2/3}, \delta^2 / |\sum_{k=3}^{2n-1} D_{u_2 u_k} g(0) u_k|\}\}.$$

The definition of $\Omega(\delta)$ yields that for some $C > 0$ we have $|g(u)| \le C\delta^2$ for $u \in \Omega(\delta)$. It remains to estimate $m_{2n-1}(\Omega(\delta))$. Consider an orthogonal change of coordinates

$$u = (u_1,u_2,u_3,\dots,u_{2n-1}) \longmapsto (u_1,u_2,u_3',\dots,u_{2n-1}') = u',$$

which is chosen so that

$$u_3' = A \sum_{k=3}^{2n-1} D_{u_2 u_k} g(0) u_k \quad \text{for some } A > 0 .$$

Then $\Omega(\delta) \supset \{u' \in \mathbb{R}^{2n-1} : |u_1| < \delta^2 , |u_k'| < \delta/\sqrt{2n-3}$ for $3 \le k \le 2n-1$, and $|u_2| < \min\{\delta^{2/3}, A\,\delta^2/|u_3'|\}\}$. A straightforward iterated integration shows that $m_{2n-1}(\Omega(\delta)) \approx \delta^{2n} \log 1/\delta$. Thus $\sigma\varphi^{-1}$ is not σ–Carleson.

We remark that the Carleson measure criterion [5] characterizes the bounded composition operators on $H^P(B_n)$, $1 \le p < \infty$. Thus the above theorems extend from H^2 to H^p, $1 \le p < \infty$.

We also note that the differentiability hypothesis on φ can be relaxed slightly. It is enough to require that all second order partials be Lipschitz. In particular the Taylor estimates of Lemma 2 will persist under this weaker assumption.

The results in this paper yield trivial proofs of the boundedness assertions for the examples of [2]. Theorem 1 does not, however, generate new examples of unbounded C_φ in any easy way. It is a fairly delicate matter, for instance, to construct a map $\varphi : \mathbb{C}^2 \to \mathbb{C}^2$ with $\varphi(e) = e$ so that one has both $\varphi(B_2) \subset B_2$ and $D_1\varphi_1(e) = |D_{22}\varphi_1(e)|$.

These results say nothing about nonsmooth φ. There exist highly nonsmooth φ (constructed from inner functions on B_2) which induce unbounded composition operators (see[1]).

In conclusion, the author would like to express his gratitude to his friend and colleague, J. A. Cima, for many fruitful discussions on the material presented here.

REFERENCES

1. J. A. Cima, C. S. Stanton, and W. R. Wogen, On boundedness of composition operators on $H^2(B_2)$, Proc. Amer. Math. Soc. **91** (1984), 217–222.

2. J. A. Cima and W. R. Wogen, Unbounded composition operators on $H^2(B_2)$, Proc. Amer. Math. Soc. **99** (1987), 477–483.

3. B. D. Figura, Composition operators on Hardy space in several complex variables, J. Math Anal. Appl. **109** (1985), 340–354.

4. B. D. MacCluer, Spectra of compact composition operators on $H^p(B_N)$, Analysis **4** (1984), 87–103.

5. ________________, Compact composition operators on $H^P(B_N)$, Michigan Math. J. **32** (1985), 237–248.

6. B. D. MacCluer and J. H. Shapiro, Angular derivatives and compact composition operators on the Hardy and Bergman spaces, Canad. J. Math. **38** (1986), 878–906.

7. E. Nordgren, Composition operators on Hilbert spaces, Hilbert Space Operators, Lecture Notes in Math., vol. **693**, Springer–Verlag, Berlin, 1978, 37–63.

8. W. Rudin, Function Theory on the Unit Ball of $\mathbb{C}^N$, Grundlehren Math. Wiss., vol. 241, Springer–Verlag, Berlin and New York, 1980.

Department of Mathematics
University of North Carolina
Chapel Hill, North Carolina 27514

Operator Theory:
Advances and Applications, Vol. 35

SHIFT INVARIANT SUBSPACES, PASSIVITY, REPRODUCING KERNELS AND H^∞-OPTIMIZATION

Joseph A. Ball* and J. William Helton *

Various notions of passivity are introduced for a lossless circuit, or equivalently, for a rational matrix function θ which is J-unitary on the unit circle. These notions, as well as how they are related to each other, are analyzed from several points of view: energy bookkeeping in the circuit, analytic conditions on θ and on the associated scattering matrix U, geometry of shift invariant subspaces, positive definiteness conditions on associated reproducing kernel functions, connections with classical interpolation problems, and state space representations. This gives a circuit theoretic interpretation for several modern approaches to interpolation such as the geometric one of Ball-Helton.

Introduction. A rational matrix function θ which is J-unitary on the imaginary axis (or equivalently via a conformal change of variable, on the unit circle) can be viewed in a number of ways: (1) as the chain matrix for a lossless circuit, (2) as generating a shift invariant subspace θH^2, (3) as inducing a kernel function $\frac{J - \theta(z)J\theta(w)^*}{1 - z\overline{w}}$ which generates a reproducing kernel Hilbert (or more generally, Pontrjagin) space, (4) as inducing a linear fractional map which parametrizes all solutions of a matrix Nevanlinna-Pick- or Nehari-type interpolation problem, or (5) in terms of a state space realization $\theta(z) = D + C(z - A)^{-1}B$. The fourth view in turn subdivides in several ways, depending on which language one chooses to express the interpolation conditions. In this paper we introduce several notions of passivity and interpret the meaning of each of these notions in terms of the five different ways of viewing θ listed above. We also discuss how these various notions of passivity are related among themselves. In illustrating the viability of

* Supported in part by the National Science Foundation, the Air Force Office of Scientific Research and the Office of Naval Research.

each of these points of view, sometimes a proof is done entirely in the framework of one of the points of view even though it may be easier when done in the framework of another. On some occasions two proofs of the same result are given using different points of view. The interested reader is also referred to [FF] which gives circuit interpretations of their approach to interpolation.

Physically the notion of *passivity* is that power put out by the circuit up to time T is no more than the power put into the circuit up to the same time T; this is to be distinguished from *losslessness*, which means that the power in over all time balances with the power out over all time. New weaker notions of passivity arise by demanding that only some smaller subcircuit of θ be passive. In particular, the well known positive-definiteness test for a Nevanlinna-Pick interpolation problem to be solvable can be interpreted as the passivity of a circuit associated with the interpolation conditions. For the Nehari problem, the associated circuit is never passive in the usual sense; the (suboptimal) Nehari problem is solvable if and only if the associated circuit satisfies our weakest notion of passivity. It is this weakest notion which provides a unification of Nevanlinna-Pick and Nehari type results.

In section 1 we define precisely our four notions of passivity, and state characterizations of each of them in terms of analytic properties of the chain matrix θ and the scattering matrix U. We then obtain characterizations in terms of the geometry of the associated shift invariant subspace θH^2, and finally in terms of analytic properties of a block upper triangular matrix function L (which arises naturally in the context of interpolation problems) for which $LH^2 = \theta H^2$. In section 1 we also state results which indicate how these notions of passivity are related to each other. In section 2 we give proofs of the results stated in section 1. In section 3 we characterize the various forms of passivity introduced in section 1 in terms of positive definiteness of certain kernel functions associated with θ. Section 4 gives the connections with interpolation theory and section 5 with state space representations.

1. Passivity of Circuits and Shift Invariant Subspaces

Consider the following circuit:

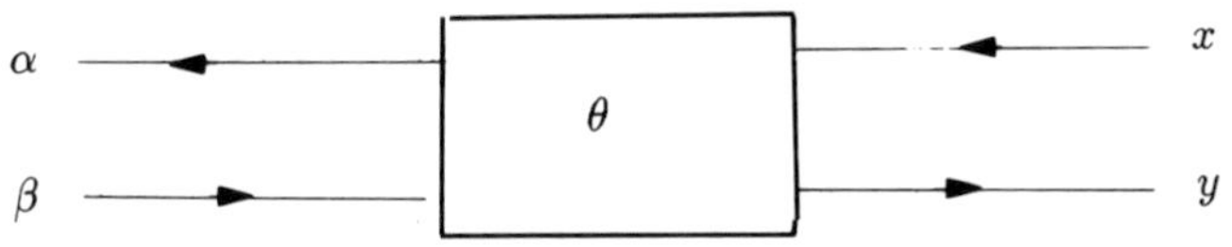

Figure 1.

Arrows in denote inputs, arrows out denote outputs. Algebraically, the circuit is described in the *chain formalism* by a 2×2 block matrix function $\theta(z) = \begin{bmatrix} \alpha_1(z) & \alpha_2(z) \\ \beta_1(z) & \beta_2(z) \end{bmatrix}$ via the system of equations

$$\begin{bmatrix} \alpha(z) \\ \beta(z) \end{bmatrix} = \begin{bmatrix} \alpha_1(z) & \alpha_2(z) \\ \beta_1(z) & \beta_2(z) \end{bmatrix} \begin{bmatrix} x(z) \\ y(z) \end{bmatrix}.$$

Thus the chain formalsim relates not inputs to outputs but rather right side signals to left side signals. The *scattering formalism* on the other hand uses a 2×2 block matrix function $U(z) = \begin{bmatrix} a(z) & b(z) \\ c(z) & d(z) \end{bmatrix}$ to relate inputs to outputs:

$$\begin{bmatrix} \alpha(z) \\ y(z) \end{bmatrix} = \begin{bmatrix} a(z) & b(z) \\ c(z) & d(z) \end{bmatrix} \begin{bmatrix} \beta(z) \\ x(z) \end{bmatrix}.$$

While the scattering formalsim is easier to interpret physically, the chain formalism has better algebraic properties with respect to cascade connections. The chain matrix $\theta = \begin{bmatrix} \alpha_1 & \alpha_2 \\ \beta_1 & \beta_2 \end{bmatrix}$ and the scattering matrix $U = \begin{bmatrix} a & b \\ c & d \end{bmatrix}$ for the same circuit are related to each other by the algebraic formulas

$$\begin{aligned} a &= \alpha_2 \beta_2^{-1} \\ b &= \alpha_1 - \alpha_2 \beta_2^{-1} \beta_1 \qquad (1.1) \\ c &= \beta_2^{-1} \\ d &= -\beta_2^{-1} \beta_1. \end{aligned}$$

For mathematical convenience we consider our circuits as acting in discrete time (positive as well as negative). After Fourier transform, a signal x supported in positive time and having finite power (or energy) corresponds to a function in the Hardy space H^2 of the unit disk. Signals in negative time having finite energy will be in $H^{2\perp}$; thus all such signals are in L^2 of the circle. For our general setting we take θ to be an $M+N$ port; thus α and x will be $\mathbb{C}^M$-valued functions with components in L^2 (i.e., $\alpha,\ x \in L^2_M$), while β and y are in L^2_N.

The concepts of "lossless" and "stable" arise when one imposes energy considerations on the circuit. *Lossless* means simply

$$\text{Power in over all time} = \text{Power out over all time}$$

while *stable* means

$$\text{Power out up to time } n \leq \gamma \text{ [Power in up to time } n]$$

If the circuit is both stable and lossless, then it is automatically *passive*, i.e., γ may be chosen ≤ 1:

$$\text{Power out up to time } n \leq \text{Power in up to time } n.$$

In this section we shall be interested in studying which properties of the circuit are captured by the geometry of various shift invariant subspaces associated with the circuit. To describe this connection we consider two experiments.

E1 Apply the circuit to all inputs in H^2_{M+N} to get a set $\mathcal{M}$ of outputs. Then the circuit is stable if and only if $\mathcal{M} \subset H^2_{M+N}$.

The usual Beurling-Lax theorem can be interpreted as saying that given any full range shift invariant subspace $\mathcal{M}$ of H^2_{M+N}, there exists a lossless circuit consistent with the result $\mathcal{M}$ of this experiment, and the circuit is stable if $\mathcal{M} \subset H^2_{M+N}$. Here the circuit is really described using U from the scattering formalism. The next experiment is more complicated as it involves "negative time," that is, time before the experiment begins.

E2 The "experiment" is to generate the set $\mathcal{M}$ of signals f measured at the left ports of the circuit with the property that what one observes at the right side of the circuit exactly equals 0 for time ≤ 0. The set of signals thus observed is just $\theta \cdot H^2_{M+N}$, where θ comes from the chain formalism description of the circuit. Just from observing the outcome $\mathcal{M}$ of this experiment, we would like to deduce whether there exists a corresponding circuit, and if yes, whether it is lossless, stable, etc.?

We first analyze losslessness from the point of view of the experiment (E2). Observe that:

$$\begin{aligned} \|y\|^2 - \|x\|^2 &= \text{power consumed by the circuit} \\ &\qquad \text{from the right side signals;} \\ \|\beta\|^2 - \|\alpha\|^2 &= \text{power consumed by the circuit} \\ &\qquad \text{from the left side signals.} \end{aligned}$$

Lossless thus means

$$\left\langle J\theta \begin{bmatrix} x \\ y \end{bmatrix}, \; \theta \begin{bmatrix} x \\ y \end{bmatrix} \right\rangle_{L^2_{M+N}} = \left\langle J \begin{bmatrix} x \\ y \end{bmatrix}, \begin{bmatrix} x \\ y \end{bmatrix} \right\rangle_{L^2_{M+N}}$$

where $J = I_M \oplus -I_N$, i.e., $\theta(z)$ is J unitary on the unit circle $\{z: |z| = 1\}$. The issue of whether a lossless circuit exists compatible with the result $\mathcal{M}$ of the experiment reduces to the question of which subspaces $\mathcal{M}$ of L^2_{M+N} can be represented as $\mathcal{M} = \theta H^2_{M+N}$ for a J-unitary matrix function θ. The answer, roughly that $\mathcal{M}$ be a full range, simply invariant subspace of L^2_{M+N} which is *regular* (i.e., $\mathcal{M} + \mathcal{M}^{\perp J} = L^2_{M+N}$) with respect to the J-inner product, corresponds to the generalized Buerling-Lax theorem obtained by the authors in [BH1]. Note that losslessness can also be expressed as

$$\begin{aligned} \text{Total power of output signals} &= \text{Total power of input signals} \\ \|\alpha\|^2 + \|y\|^2 &= \|\beta\|^2 + \|x\|^2, \end{aligned}$$

i.e.,

$$\left\| U \begin{bmatrix} \beta \\ x \end{bmatrix} \right\|^2 = \left\| \begin{bmatrix} \beta \\ x \end{bmatrix} \right\|^2.$$

Thus losslessness in terms of the scattering matrix U is that $U(z)$ be unitary for $|z| = 1$.

An irony of circuits is that power conservation over all time can hold without the circuit being passive. If P_n denotes the orthogonal projection of L^2 onto $z^{n+1}H^{2\perp}$ (i.e., the Fourier transform of the projection of ℓ^2 onto $\ell^2[-\infty, n]$—the space of signals which are 0 after time n), then when signals x, y, α, β are measured

$$\begin{aligned} \|P_n x\|^2 + \|P_n \beta\|^2 &= \text{power put into the circuit up to time } n \\ \|P_n \alpha\|^2 + \|P_n y\|^2 &= \text{power put out by the circuit up to time } n. \end{aligned}$$

A passive circuit has the property that for each time n,

(PAS1) $\quad c_n :=$ power in up to time $n -$ power out up to time $n \geq 0$,

and power conservation over all time in no way guarantees this. Thus θ corresponds to a passive circuit if and only if

$$\left\langle JP_n\theta\begin{bmatrix}x\\y\end{bmatrix}, P_n\theta\begin{bmatrix}x\\y\end{bmatrix}\right\rangle = \|P_n\alpha\|^2 - \|P_n\beta\|^2 \leq \|P_nx\|^2 - \|P_ny\|^2$$
$$= \left\langle JP_n\begin{bmatrix}x\\y\end{bmatrix}, P_n\begin{bmatrix}x\\y\end{bmatrix}\right\rangle,$$

i.e.,

$$\theta^* P_n J\theta \leq P_n J$$

as an operator on L^2_{M+N} for all n. In terms of the scattering matrix, the passivity condition

$$\|P_n\alpha\|^2 + \|P_ny\|^2 \leq \|P_n\beta\|^2 + \|P_nx\|^2$$

can be expressed as

$$U^* P_n U \leq P_n$$

for $n = \cdots, -1, 0, 1, \cdots$. Thus $P_nx = 0 \Rightarrow P_nUx = 0$, so in particular $P_0x = 0 \Rightarrow P_0Ux = 0$, i.e., multiplication by U leaves H^2_{M+N} invariant, so $U \in H^\infty$. Conversely, if $U \in H^\infty$ and is unitary for $|z| = 1$ (i.e., if U is *inner*), then by shift invariance $P_nU = P_nUP_n$ follows for all n from its validity for $n = 0$, so the passivity condition $U^*P_nU \leq P_n$ follows. We have thus established: *a circuit is passive* (PAS1) *if and only if its scattering matrix U is inner.*

To get the equivalent condition for the chain matrix, note that given that U is unitary for $|z| = 1$, then $U \in H^\infty$ is equivalent to $\|U(z)\| \leq 1$ for $|z| \leq 1$, i.e.,

$$\|\alpha(z)\|^2 + \|y(z)\|^2 \leq \|\beta(z)\|^2 + \|x(z)\|^2$$

for $|z| \leq 1$. Rewrite this inequality in the form

$$\left\langle J\begin{bmatrix}\alpha(z)\\\beta(z)\end{bmatrix}, \begin{bmatrix}\alpha(z)\\\beta(z)\end{bmatrix}\right\rangle = \|\alpha(z)\|^2 - \|\beta(z)\|^2$$
$$\leq \|x(z)\|^2 - \|y(z)\|^2 = \left\langle J\begin{bmatrix}x(z)\\y(z)\end{bmatrix}, \begin{bmatrix}x(z)\\y(z)\end{bmatrix}\right\rangle$$

for $|z| < 1$ to deduce that (PAS1) is equivalent to the chain matrix θ (besides being J-unitary for $|z| - 1$) satisfying

$$\theta(z)^* J\theta(z) \leq J$$

for $|z| \leq 1$ (at all points z of analyticity in the unit disk). An equivalent formulation is had by using (2.1): a circuit satisfies (PAS1) if and only if its chain matrix $\theta = \begin{bmatrix} \alpha_1 & \alpha_2 \\ \beta_1 & \beta_2 \end{bmatrix}$ satisfies

$$\alpha_2\beta_2^{-1}, \quad \alpha_1 - \alpha_2\beta_2^{-1}\beta_1, \quad \beta_2^{-1} \quad \text{and} \quad \beta_2^{-1}\beta_1$$

$$\text{all are} \quad H^\infty \quad \text{matrix functions.}$$

Weaker notions of passivity which arise in the context of generalized Nevanlinna-Pick interpolation are:

(PAS2) The subcircuit $\beta \to \alpha, y$ is passive, i.e.,

$$\|P_n\beta\|^2 \geq \|P_n y\|^2 + \|P_n\alpha\|^2$$

when $x = 0$.

An alternative weakening of passivity is

(PAS3) The subcircuit $x \to \alpha, y$, is passive, i.e.,

$$\|\beta\|^2 + r\|P_n x\|^2 \geq \|P_n\alpha\|^2 + \|P_n y\|^2$$

for $n = \cdots, -1, 0, 1, \cdots$.

It turns out that taking $r < 1$ rules out only circuits having certain degeneracies which we do not wish to consider, so we shall refer to (PAS3) as the above condition holding for some $r < 1$. Similar conventions will also pertain to (PAS3) to follow . A notion weaker than both (PAS2) and (PAS3) is:

(PAS4) The subcircuit $x \to y$ is stable, i.e.,

$$\|\beta\|^2 + r\|P_n x\|^2 \geq \|P_n y\|^2$$

for $n = \cdots, -1, 0, 1, \cdots$.

Each of these physical notions corresponds to an analytic condition on the scattering matrix U or the chain matrix θ. The derivation is exactly as was done above for (PAS1), so we omit the details of the proof.

PROPOSITION 1.1. *Suppose* $\theta = \begin{bmatrix} \alpha_1 & \alpha_2 \\ \beta_1 & \beta_2 \end{bmatrix}$ *is the chain matrix and* $U = \begin{bmatrix} a & b \\ c & d \end{bmatrix}$ *is the scattering matrix for the same lossless circuit. Then*

the circuit satisfies:	*if and only if the scattering matrix satisfies:*	*if and only if the chain matrix satisfies:*
(PAS1): $\|P_n\alpha\|^2 + \|P_n y\|^2 \leq \|P_n\beta\|_+^2 \|P_n x\|^2$.	$U(z)$*is contractive on* $\mathcal{D}$.	$\theta(z)$ *is* J*-contractive on* $\mathcal{D}$.
(PAS2): $\|P_n\beta\|^2 \geq \|P_n y\|^2 + \|P_n\alpha\|^2$ when $x = 0$.	$\begin{bmatrix} a(z) \\ c(z) \end{bmatrix}$ *is contractive on* $\mathcal{D}$.	$\begin{bmatrix} \alpha_2 \\ \beta_2 \end{bmatrix}$ J*-contractive on* $\mathcal{D}$.
(PAS3): $\|\beta\|^2 + r\|P_n x\|^2 \geq \|P_n\alpha\|^2 + \|P_n y\|^2$.	$\begin{bmatrix} b(z) \\ d(z) \end{bmatrix}$ *contractive on* $\mathcal{D}$.	$\beta_2^{-1}\beta_1$ and $\alpha_1 - \alpha_2\beta_2^{-1}\beta_1 \in H^\infty$, with $\beta_2(z)^*\beta_2(z) > (1+\delta)I_N$ on $\mathcal{D}$.
(PAS4): $\|\beta\|^2 + r\|P_n x\|^2 \geq \|P_n y\|^2$	$d(z)$ *contractive on* $\mathcal{D}$.	$\beta_2^{-1}\beta_1 \in H^\infty$.

One of the main new results of this paper is a characterization of the physical conditions (PAS1)—(PAS4) in terms of the Krein space geometry of the associated shift invariant subspace $\mathcal{M} = \theta H^2_{M+N}$ with respect to the decomposition $L^2_{M+N} = H^{2\perp} + H^2_{M+N}$ of L^2_{M+N}. We set $\mathcal{M}^x$ to be the J-orthogonal complement of $\mathcal{M}$, $\mathcal{M}^{\perp J}$. Besides $\mathcal{M}$ itself being *regular*, i.e.,

$$\mathcal{M} \boxplus \mathcal{M}^x = L^2_{M+N},$$

we also assume that

$$\mathcal{M} \cap H^2_{M+N} \quad \text{is regular}$$

and

$$\mathcal{M}^x \cap H^{2\perp}_{M+N} \quad \text{is regular.}$$

As this situation is generic, these extra assumptions will not affect the validity of the results to follow. With this assumption in force, if we define subspaces $\mathcal{M}_{\mathcal{R}}$ and $\mathcal{M}^x_{\mathcal{R}}$ by

$$\mathcal{M}_{\mathcal{R}} = \mathcal{M} \boxminus (\mathcal{M} \cap H^2_{M+N}) \tag{1.2}$$

(i.e., the J-orthogonal complement of $\mathcal{M} \cap H^2_{M+N}$ inside $\mathcal{M}$), and analogously

$$\mathcal{M}^x_{\mathcal{R}} = \mathcal{M}^x \boxminus (\mathcal{M}^x \cap H^{2\perp}_{M+N}) \tag{1.3}$$

then we have the J-orthogonal direct sum decompositions

$$\mathcal{M} = \mathcal{M}_{\mathcal{R}} \boxplus (\mathcal{M} \cap H^2_{M+N})$$

and

$$\mathcal{M}^x = \mathcal{M}^x_{\mathcal{R}} \boxplus (\mathcal{M}^x \cap H^{2\perp}_{M+N}).$$

We also introduce subspaces χ^+ and χ^- by

$$\chi^+ = P_{H^2_{M+N}} \mathcal{M}^x \tag{1.4}$$

and

$$\chi^- = P_{H^{2\perp}_{M+N}} \mathcal{M}. \tag{1.5}$$

Then it is not difficult to verify that χ^+ is the J-orthogonal complement of $\mathcal{M} \cap H^2_{M+N}$ inside H^2_{M+N}, i.e.,

$$H^2_{M+N} = \chi^+ \boxplus (\mathcal{M} \cap H^2_{M+N}).$$

Similarly,

$$H^{2\perp}_{M+N} = \chi^- \boxplus (\mathcal{M} \cap H^{2\perp}_{M+N}).$$

From the definitions we see that for each $f \in \chi^-$ there must exist a unique $g_f \in \chi^+$ such that $f + g_f \in \mathcal{M}_{\mathcal{R}}$. The mapping $f \to g_f$ defines a bounded linear operator $T: \chi^- \to \chi^+$ by

$$T(f) = g_f \quad \text{for} \quad f \in \chi^-.$$

Then $\mathcal{M}_{\mathcal{R}}$ may be expressed as the *graph of* T, i.e.,

$$\mathcal{M}_{\mathcal{R}} = (I+T)\chi^{-}. \tag{1.6}$$

Similarly, the subspace $\mathcal{M}^{x}_{\mathcal{R}}$ may be expressed as the graph of a unique operator $T^{x}: \chi^{+} \to \chi^{-}$; since $\mathcal{M}_{\mathcal{R}}$ is J-orthogonal to $\mathcal{M}^{x}_{\mathcal{R}}$ and χ^{-} is J-orthogonal to χ^{+}, one can easily check that

$$T^{x} = -T^{+}$$

where $T^{+}: \chi^{+} \to \chi^{-}$ is the J-adjoint of T as an operator from χ^{-} to χ^{+}. We thus have

$$\mathcal{M}^{x}_{\mathcal{R}} = (I-T^{+})\chi^{+}. \tag{1.7}$$

Finally we introduce subspaces α^{+} and α^{-} by

$$\alpha^{+} = (\mathcal{M} \cap H^2_{M+N}) \boxminus \{[\mathcal{M} \cap (H^2_M \oplus 0)] + [\mathcal{M} \cap (0 \oplus H^2_N)]\} \tag{1.8}$$

and

$$\alpha^{-} = (\mathcal{M}^{x} \cap H^{2\perp}_{M+N}) \boxminus \{[\mathcal{M}^{x} \cap (H^{2\perp}_{M} \boxplus 0)] + [\mathcal{M}^{x} \cap (0 \boxplus H^{2\perp}_{N})]\}. \tag{1.9}$$

For the case where $\mathcal{M} = \theta H^2_{M+N}$ and θ is rational, all the subspaces $\mathcal{M}_{\mathcal{R}}$, $\mathcal{M}^{x}_{\mathcal{R}}$, χ^{+}, χ^{-}, α^{+}, α^{-} are finite dimensional. The next result gives characterizations of the various notions of passivity (PAS1)–(PAS4) in terms of the geometry of these various subspaces. The proof will be given in the next section.

THEOREM 1.2. *Let $\mathcal{M} \subset L^2_{M+N}$ be the outcome $\mathcal{M} = \theta H^2_{M+N}$ of the experiment (E2) performed on a lossless circuit with chain matrix θ. In addition to $\mathcal{M}$ being regular, assume also that $\mathcal{M} \cap H^2_{M+N}$ is regular. Associate with $\mathcal{M}$ the subspaces $\mathcal{M}_{\mathcal{R}}, \chi^{+}, \chi^{-}, \mathcal{M}^{x}_{\mathcal{R}}, \alpha^{+}$, α^{-} and the operator $T: \chi^{-} \to \chi^{+}$ as in (1.2)–(1.9). Then*

the circuit satisfies	*if and only if it satisfies the operator condition*	*if and only if it satisfies the subspace condition*
(PAS1)	$JP_{\chi^+} - P_M J \geq 0$, *or equivalently,* $\begin{bmatrix} -I & T^+ \\ T & I \end{bmatrix}$ *is* J*-postive on* $\chi^- \oplus \chi^+$.	χ^+ *positive and* $\mathcal{M}_{\mathcal{R}}$ *negative.*
(PAS2)	$P_{\chi^+} J \geq 0$	χ^+ *positive.*
(PAS3)	$P_{P_+\chi^+} - P_{\mathcal{M}_{\mathcal{R}}} J - P_{\alpha^+} J \geq 0$	α^+ *and* $\mathcal{M}_{\mathcal{R}}$ *negative.*
(PAS4)	$P_- P_{\mathcal{M}} P_- \geq 0$, *or equivalently* $P_- P_{\mathcal{M}_{\mathcal{R}}} P_- + P_- P_{\alpha^+} P_- \geq 0$	$\rho^+ \boxminus \{[\rho^+ \cap (L^2 \oplus 0)] + [\rho^+ \cap (0 \oplus L^2)]\}$ *negative where* $\rho^+ := \mathcal{M}_{\mathcal{R}} \boxplus \alpha^+$.

The next result makes apparent the close interrelationships among the various passivity conditions.

THEOREM 1.3. *The following implications hold:*

(i) (PAS4) *together with*

$$\mathcal{M} \cap (L^2_M \oplus 0) = \mathcal{M} \cap (H^2_M \oplus 0)$$

is equivalent to (PAS3).

(ii) (PAS2) *is equivalent to* α^+ *being negative together with*

$$\chi^+ \cap (0 \oplus H^2_N) = (0).$$

(iii) (PAS2) *and* (PAS3) *holding simultaneously is equivalent to* (PAS1).

(iv) (PAS4) *together with*

$$\mathcal{M} \cap (L^2_M \oplus 0) = \mathcal{M} \cap (H^2_M \oplus 0)$$

and

$$\chi^+ \cap (0 \oplus H^2_N) = 0$$

is equivalent to (PAS1).

We remark that statement (iii) is trivial if one uses the characterizations of passivity in terms of the scattering matrix $U(z) = \begin{bmatrix} a(z) & b(z) \\ c(z) & d(z) \end{bmatrix}$ in Proposition 1.1. We think it instructive however to give a proof using exclusively the subspace characterizations of Theorem 1.2; this will be done in section 2.

For some of the assertions of Theorem 1.3 it is possible to give physical arguments. We now sketch one such argument. Specifically, we argue from physical grounds that χ^+ is necessarily positive if θ is (PAS1)-lossless—for the special case where θ is an H^∞-matrix function (so $\mathcal{M} \subset H^2_{M+N}$). The key point is that in this case χ^+ can be identified with the state space of the system. To see this, consider the "experiment" of feeding in ℓ^2_{M+N} signals on the right until time 0. These typically are enough to drive the system to any state it possesses at time 0. After time 0 insist upon no signal appearing on the right. Record all signals which do appear on the left after time 0; by the Nerode construction (see eg. [Ka]), these signals can be identified with states and moreover the energy of the signal can be identified with the energy of the corresponding state. On the other hand, this set of signals from the definitions can be seen to be $P_{\ell^{2+}_{M+N}}(\theta\ell^2_{M+N})$, which in turn is (after Fourier transform) χ^+. Passivity implies that the energy stored by a state is positive; thus necessarily $\langle Jx, x\rangle \geq 0$ for all $x \in \chi^+$ as asserted.

There exists yet another way to represent the set $\mathcal{M}$ arising as the result of the experiment (E2) for a circuit θ. Namely, $\mathcal{M} = LH^2_{M+N}$ where

$$L = \begin{bmatrix} \psi & K\varphi^{-1} \\ 0 & \varphi^{-1} \end{bmatrix} H^2_{M+N}$$

where $K, \psi, \varphi \in L^\infty_{M\times N}, L^\infty_{M\times M}, L^\infty_{N\times N}$ respectively with $\psi^{-1} \in L^\infty_{M\times M}$, $\varphi^{-1} \in L^\infty_{N\times N}$. How one obtains L from $\mathcal{M}$ is described in [BH1]. Here we record the result; the proof will be given in the next section.

THEOREM 1.4. *The following characterizations of* (PAS1)—(PAS4) *hold for the circuit* θ if $\mathcal{M} = LH^2_{M+N}$ *where L has the triangular form* $L = \begin{bmatrix} \psi & K\varphi^{-1} \\ 0 & \varphi^{-1} \end{bmatrix}$:

$$\text{PAS1} \iff K, \psi, \varphi \in H^\infty \text{ and } \|\Gamma_K\| < 1$$

$$\text{PAS2} \iff \varphi \in H^\infty, \Gamma_K : H^2_N \to H^2_M \text{ and } \|\Gamma_K|_{H^2_N}\| < 1$$

$$\text{PAS3} \iff \|\Gamma_K\| < 1 \text{ and } \psi \in H^\infty$$

$$\text{PAS4} \iff \|\Gamma_K\| < 1$$

Here $\Gamma_K : \varphi^{-1} H_N^2 \to L_M^2 \Theta \psi H_M^2$ *is the operator of Hankel type*

$$\Gamma_K : \varphi^{-1} f \to P_{L_M^2 \Theta \psi H_M^2}(K \varphi^{-1} f).$$

(Note that Γ_K *depends on* φ *and* ψ *as well as on* K.*)*

Remark. All results hold equally well in continuous time. To go from the time domain to the frequency domain, instead of the Fourier transform $\mathcal{F}: \ell^2 \to L^2$ of the circle ($\mathcal{F}: \{a_n\}_{-\infty}^{\infty} \to \sum_{n=-\infty}^{\infty} a_n z^n$), we use the bilateral Laplace transform $\mathcal{L}: L^2(-\infty, \infty) \to L^2(-i\infty, i\infty)$ ($\mathcal{L}: f(t) \to \hat{f}(s) = \frac{1}{\sqrt{2\pi}} \int_{-\infty}^{\infty} e^{-st} f(t)\, dt$). A linear time invariant operator in the time domain is given by convolution with a distribution, or in the frequency domain by multiplication by an L^∞ (of the imaginary axis) function. The chain matrix $\theta(s)$ and the scattering matrix $U(s)$ for a lossless circuit is a matrix function which is J-unitary (resp. unitary) for $\operatorname{Re} s = 0$. (PAS1)—(PAS4) may be defined in exactly the same way, but with $n = \cdots, -1, 0, 1, \cdots$ replaced by $-\infty < t < \infty$. Then the characterizations of Proposition 1.1 hold, but with the unit disk replaced by the right half plane (so e.g. H^∞ now refers to bounded analytic functions on the right half plane. Theorems 1.2–1.4 retain exactly the same form (with the right half plane replacing the unit disk) for continuous time as discrete time; the proofs we give in section 2 are also valid in continuous time with the obvious modifications, so we do not give the continuous time versions explicitly. □

We close this section with a circuit interpretation of interpolation conditions; interpolation problems will be discussed in more detail in sections 4 and 5.

So far we have been considering lossless circuits as in Fig. 1 in isolation. Next we consider the effect of loading a passive circuit S onto the lossless circuit on the right side ports as in Fig. 2.

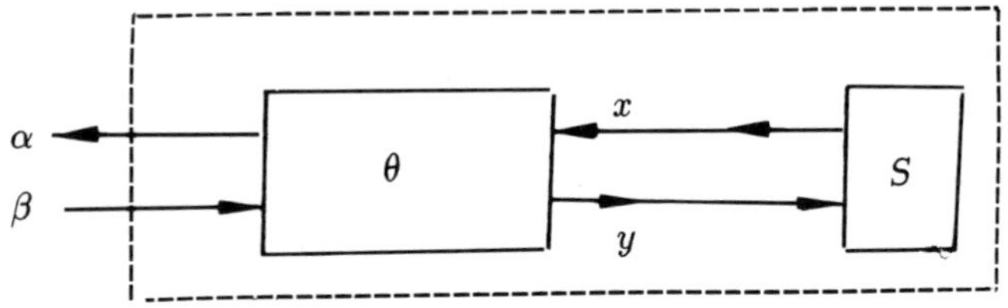

Figure 2.

The composition circuit has input signal β and output signal α. Inside the workings of the composite circuit, the output y of θ is fed into S producing an output $S(y)$ which is fed back into θ at the right input port as the input signal $x = S(y)$. In the chain formalism we have the system of equations

$$\alpha = \alpha_1 x + \alpha_2 y$$

$$\beta = \beta_1 x + \beta_2 y$$

$$x = Sy.$$

Solving for α in terms of β and eliminating x and y we get

$$\alpha = (\alpha_1 S + \alpha_2)(\beta_1 S + \beta_2)^{-1}\beta.$$

On the other hand, in the scattering formalism we have the system of equations

$$\alpha = a\beta + bx$$

$$y = c\beta + dx$$

$$x = Sy$$

which reduces to

$$\alpha = [a + bS(I - dS)^{-1}c]\beta.$$

The set of all circuits $\mathcal{G}_\theta(S)\colon \beta \to \alpha$ arising in this way from loading some passive circuit S onto a given lossless circuit θ can be characterized as all solutions of an interpolation problem. When we represent $\mathcal{M} = \theta H^2_{M+N}$ as LH^2_{M+N} with $L = \begin{bmatrix} \psi & K\varphi^{-1} \\ 0 & \varphi^{-1} \end{bmatrix}$, the range $\{\mathcal{G}_\theta(S)\colon S \text{ passive}\}$ is characterized as

$$[K + \psi H^\infty_{M\times N}(\ell)\varphi] \cap \mathcal{B}L^\infty_{M\times N}$$

where $\ell =$ the number of negative eigenvalues of $I - \Gamma_K^* \Gamma_K$, $H^\infty_{M\times N}(\ell)$ denotes the class of functions $H^\infty_{M\times N} + \mathcal{R}_{M\times N}(\ell)$ where $\mathcal{R}_{M\times N}(\ell)$ is the class of rational $M \times N$ matrix functions with McMillan degree ℓ, and $\mathcal{B}L^\infty_{M\times N}$ is the unit ball in $L^\infty_{M\times N}$. When $\ell = 0$, (i.e., the *stable* case where (PAS1) holds), one possible choice of K, ψ, φ is $K = a$, $\psi = b$ and $\varphi = c$ where $\begin{bmatrix} a & b \\ c & d \end{bmatrix}$ is as in the scattering formalism for the circuit θ. Then the zeros of b are called the *backward transmission zeros* and the zeros of c are called the forward transmission zeros for physical reasons. Intuitively, every circuit $\tilde{S}$ of the form $\tilde{S} = \tilde{\theta} * S$ has value $\tilde{S}(z_j)$ at the backward transmission zero z_j of the degenerate form $a(z_j) + b(z_j)X$ for some $N \times N$ matrix X, since the back reflection $\beta \to \alpha$ at this frequency is degenerate. Similarly the value $\tilde{S}(w_j)$ of $\tilde{S}$ at a forward transmission zero w_j is necessarily of the degenerate form $a(w_j) + Yc(w_j)$ for some $M \times M$ matrix Y, since the forward transmission $\beta \to y$ at this frequency is degenerate. In terms of the chain formalism (still only for the (PAS1) case), the backward transmission zeros are the zeros of $\theta = \begin{bmatrix} \alpha_1 & \alpha_2 \\ \beta_1 & \beta_2 \end{bmatrix}$ and the forward transmission zeros are the poles of θ. As we shall see in sections 4 and 5, the usual Pick matrix condition for the solution of a Nevanlinna-Pick interpolation problem to be solvable is just the condition which guarantees that the associated circuit is passive (PAS1).

2. Passivity and Shift Invariant Subspaces: Proofs

In this section we give complete proofs of Theorems 1.2–1.4. We shall need the following general lemma, valid for any subspace $\mathcal{M}$ in a Krein space $\mathcal{K}$ with a fundamental decomposition $\mathcal{K}_+ \oplus \mathcal{K}_-$.

LEMMA 2.1. *$\mathcal{M} \boxminus \{[\mathcal{M} \cap (\mathcal{K}_+ \oplus 0)] + [\mathcal{M} \cap (0 \oplus \mathcal{K}_-)]\}$ is negative if and only if $\mathcal{M} \boxminus (\mathcal{M} \cap [\mathcal{K}_+ \oplus 0])$ is negative.*

Proof. Note that we have the orthogonal decomposition

$$\begin{aligned} &\mathcal{M} \boxminus [\mathcal{M} \cap (\mathcal{K}_+ \oplus 0)] = \\ &\mathcal{M} \boxminus \{[\mathcal{M} \cap (\mathcal{K}_+ \oplus 0)] + [\mathcal{M} \cap (0 \oplus \mathcal{K}_-)]\} \\ &\qquad \boxplus [\mathcal{M} \cap (0 \oplus \mathcal{K}_-)] \end{aligned}$$

where $\mathcal{M} \cap (0 \oplus \mathcal{K}_-)$ is automatically negative. Thus the direct sum space is negative if and only if the first direct summand is negative.

Proof of Theorem 1.2. From the definition of (PAS1) we get that (PAS1) is equivalent to

$$JP_n - \theta^* JP_n \theta \geq 0$$

for $n = \ldots, -1, 0, 1, \ldots$ Conjugate by θJ and use that $\theta J \theta^* = J$ to see the equivalence of this with

$$\theta P_n J \theta^* - JP_n \geq 0$$

for $n = \ldots, -1, 0, 1, \ldots$ Write $P_n = S^{n+1} P_{-1} S^{*n+1}$ where S is the bilateral shift on L^2 and use that θ and J commute with S to get the equivalence of this with

$$S^{n+1}[\theta P_{-1} J \theta^* - JP_{-1}] S^{*n+1} \geq 0,$$

i.e.,

$$\theta P_{-1} J \theta^* - JP_{-1} \geq 0.$$

Write next $P_{-1} = I - P_{H^2_{M+N}}$ and use $\theta J \theta^* = J$ to get

$$JP_{H^2_{M+N}} - \theta P_{H^2_{M+N}} J \theta^* \geq 0.$$

Now the operator $\theta P_{H^2_{M+N}} J \theta^* J$ can be identified with the J-orthogonal projection $P_{\mathcal{M}}$ of L^2_{M+N} onto $\mathcal{M} = \theta H^2_{M+N}$. Thus we arrive at

$$JP_{H^2_{N+N}} - P_{\mathcal{M}} J \geq 0.$$

Now $H^2_{M+N} = \chi^+ \boxplus (\mathcal{M} \cap H^2_{M+N})$ and $\mathcal{M} = \mathcal{M}_{\mathcal{R}} \boxplus (\mathcal{M} \cap H^2_{M+N})$, and thus $JP_{H^2_{M+N}} - P_{\mathcal{M}} J = JP_{\chi^+} - P_{\mathcal{M}_{\mathcal{R}}} J$. This gives us the operator form of (PAS1).

To get the subspace version of (PAS1) requires an argument involving a Schur complement. We write $\mathcal{M}_{\mathcal{R}}$ in terms of the angle operator $T \colon \chi^- = P_- \mathcal{M} \to \chi^+$ as $\mathcal{M} = (I+T)\chi^-$. If we write elements of $\chi^- \oplus \chi^+$ as block column vectors $\left(\chi^- \oplus \chi^+ \approx \begin{bmatrix} \chi^- \\ \chi^+ \end{bmatrix}\right)$, then $\mathcal{M}_{\mathcal{R}} = \begin{bmatrix} I \\ T \end{bmatrix} \chi^-$. In terms of this coordinate system it is easy to compute $P_{\mathcal{M}_{\mathcal{R}}}$ as a block 2×2 matrix:

$$P_{\mathcal{M}_{\mathcal{R}}} = \begin{bmatrix} I \\ T \end{bmatrix} (I + T^+ T)^{-1} [I \; T^+]$$

where T^+ is the adjoint of T with respect to the J-inner products on χ^- and χ^+. [The assumption that $\mathcal{M}_{\mathcal{R}}$ is regular guarantees that $(I+T^+T)$ is invertible.] Since the decomposition $\chi^- \oplus \chi^+$ is J-orthogonal, P_{χ^+} has the simple block matrix form $\begin{bmatrix} 0 & 0 \\ 0 & I \end{bmatrix}$. We conclude that

$$P_{\chi^+} - P_{\mathcal{M}_{\mathcal{R}}} = \begin{bmatrix} -Z & -ZT^+ \\ -TZ & I - TZT^+ \end{bmatrix}$$

is J-positive on $\chi^- \oplus \chi^+$ where we have set $Z = (I + T^+T)^{-1}$. As the upper left corner $-Z$ is invertible, we can use the Schur complement test for positive definiteness. Namely, the block matrix $\begin{bmatrix} -Z & -ZT^+ \\ -TZ & I - TZT^+ \end{bmatrix}$ is J-positive if and only if

$$-Z \text{ is } J\text{-positive on } \chi^-$$

and

the Schur complement of $-Z$,

$$(I - TZT^+) - (TZ)(-Z^{-1})(ZT^+) = I,$$

is J-positive on χ^+.

Note that this criterion is easily verified from the factorization

$$\begin{bmatrix} -Z & -ZT^+ \\ -TZ & I - TZT^+ \end{bmatrix} = \begin{bmatrix} I & 0 \\ T & I \end{bmatrix} \begin{bmatrix} -Z & 0 \\ 0 & I \end{bmatrix} \begin{bmatrix} I & T^+ \\ 0 & I \end{bmatrix}.$$

The second statement simply says that χ^+ is a J-positive subspace. The first statement says that $I + T^+T$ is J-negative, i.e., for all $x \in \chi^-$,

$$\begin{aligned} 0 &\geq \langle J(I+T^+T)x, x\rangle \\ &= \langle Jx, x\rangle + \langle JTx, Tx\rangle \\ &= \langle J(I+T)x, (I+T)x\rangle, \end{aligned}$$

i.e., $\mathcal{M}_{\mathcal{R}} = (I+T)\chi^-$ is a negative subspace. As all the steps are reversible, we have established that (PAS1) is equivalent (at least for the generic situation where χ^+ and $\mathcal{M}_{\mathcal{R}}$ are regular) to χ^+ being positive combined with $\mathcal{M}_{\mathcal{R}}$ being negative.

Another Schur complement argument gives that χ^+ is positive (i.e., $I \mid \chi^+$ is J-positive) and $\mathcal{M}_{\mathcal{R}}$ is negative (i.e., $I + T^+T$ is J-negative) if and only if $\begin{bmatrix} -I & T^+ \\ T & I \end{bmatrix}$ is J-positive on $\chi^- \oplus \chi^+$; the argument involves taking Schur complement with respect to the $(2,2)$ block entry. Note that if we take the Schur complement with respect to the $(1,1)$ block entry, we see that $\begin{bmatrix} -I & T^+ \\ T & I \end{bmatrix}$ being J-positive is equivalent to $-I \mid \chi^-$ being J-positive (i.e., χ^- is negative) together with $I + TT^+$ being J-positive (i.e., $\mathcal{M}_{\mathcal{R}}^x = \mathcal{M}^x \boxminus \mathcal{M}^x \cap H_{M+N}^{2\perp}$ is positive, where $\mathcal{M}^x = \mathcal{M}^{\perp J}$).

We next consider (PAS2). From the definition of (PAS2) we get the equivalent formulation $[\alpha_2^*\beta_2^*]P_n J \begin{bmatrix} \alpha_2 \\ \beta_2 \end{bmatrix} + P_n \leq 0$ on L_N^2, i.e.,

$$\alpha_2^* P_n \alpha_2 + P_n \leq \beta_2^* P_n \beta_2.$$

Conjugating with β_2^{-1} gives

$$\beta_2^{-*}\alpha_2^* P_n \alpha_2 \beta_2^{-1} + \beta_2^{-*} P_n \beta_2^{-1} \leq P_n$$

for $n = \dots, -1, 0, 1, \dots$ Using shift invariance we see that this is equivalent to $\alpha_2\beta_2^{-1}$ and β_2^{-1} being H^∞ matrix functions. As θ is J-unitary and $\mathcal{M} = \theta H_{M+N}^2$, certainly the subspace

$$\begin{bmatrix} \alpha_2 \\ \beta_2 \end{bmatrix} H_N^2 = \theta\{0 \oplus H_N^2\}$$

is $\mathcal{M}$-maximal negative. As $\beta_2^{-1} \in H_{N\times N}^\infty$ we see that $\beta_2^{-1}H_N^2 \subset H_N^2$. Moreover, as $\alpha_2\beta_2^{-1} \in H_{M\times N}^\infty$, $\alpha_2\beta_2^{-1}H_N^2 \subset H_M^2$. Thus we deduce precisely

$$\begin{aligned} \begin{bmatrix} \alpha_2 \\ \beta_2 \end{bmatrix} H_N^2 \cap H_{M+N}^2 &= \begin{bmatrix} \alpha_2 \\ \beta_2 \end{bmatrix} \beta_2^{-1} H_N^2 \\ &= \begin{bmatrix} \alpha_2\beta_2^{-1} \\ I \end{bmatrix} H_N^2. \end{aligned}$$

As $\begin{bmatrix} \alpha_2 \\ \beta_2 \end{bmatrix} H_N^2$ is $\mathcal{M}$-maximal negative, it is easy to deduce that $\mathcal{N} := \begin{bmatrix} \alpha_2 \\ \beta_2 \end{bmatrix} H_N^2 \cap H_{M+N}^2$ is $(\mathcal{M} \cap H_{M+N}^2)$-maximal negative. As $P_-\mathcal{N}$ is equal to all of H_N^2, then also $\mathcal{N}$ is H_{M+N}^2-maximal negative as well. Then by Lemma 1.1 from [BH1], necessarily $\chi^+ := H_{M+N}^2 \boxminus (\mathcal{M} \cap H_{M+N}^2)$ is positive.

Conversely, if χ^+ is positive then any $(\mathcal{M}\cap H^2_{M+N})$-maximal negative subspace (e.g. $\begin{bmatrix}\alpha_2\\ \beta_2\end{bmatrix} H^2_N \cap H^2_{M+N}$) is also H^2_{M+N}-maximal negative (by the reverse direction of Lemma 1.1 from [BH1]). This in turn is equivalent to $\beta_2^{-1} \in H^\infty_{N\times N}$ and $\alpha_2\beta_2^{-1} \in H^\infty_{M\times N}$. But this we have seen is equivalent to (PAS2). We have thus proved the subspace characterization (χ^+ positive) of (PAS2). In general, it is easy to see that a regular subspace $\mathcal{G}$ is positive if and only if $JP_{\mathcal{G}}$ ($P_{\mathcal{G}}$ = the J-orthogonal projection onto $\mathcal{G}$) is positive; this gives the operator form $JP_{\chi^+} \geq 0$ for (PAS2).

An immediate equivalent formulation of (PAS3) is

$$\theta^* J(P_n \oplus I_N)\theta \leq JP_n$$

for $n = \ldots, -1, 0-, 1, \ldots$ Conjugate by θJ to rewrite this as

$$\theta J\{\theta^* J(P_n \oplus I_N)\theta\} J\theta^* \leq \theta JP_n\theta^*,$$

i.e.,

$$P_n \oplus -I_N \leq \theta JP_n\theta^*$$

for $n = \ldots, -1, 0, 1, \ldots$ Then write $P_n = S^{n+1}P_{-1}S^{*n+1}$ and conjugate by S^{*n+1} to get the single condition

$$P_{-1} \oplus -I_N \leq \theta JP_{-1}\theta^*.$$

Replace P_{-1} with $I - P_{H^2_{M+N}}$ and use again $\theta J\theta^* = J$ to get

$$(P_{H^2_M} \oplus 0) - P_{\mathcal{M}}J \geq 0.$$

As $H^2_M \oplus 0 = P_+\chi^+ \boxplus (\mathcal{M} \cap (H^2_M \oplus 0))$ and

$$\mathcal{M} = \mathcal{M}_{\mathcal{R}} \boxplus \alpha^+ \boxplus [\mathcal{M} \cap (H^2_M \oplus 0)] \boxplus [\mathcal{M} \cap (0 \oplus H^2_N)]$$

we get

$$(P_{H^2_M} \oplus 0) - P_{\mathcal{M}}J = P_{P_+\chi^+} - P_{\mathcal{M}_{\mathcal{R}}}J - P_{\alpha^+}J - P_{\mathcal{M}\cap(0\oplus H^2_N)}J.$$

This in turn is positive if and only if

$$P_{P_+\chi^+} - P_{\mathcal{M}_{\mathcal{R}}}J - P_{\alpha^+}J \geq 0.$$

This gives the operator characterization of (PAS3).

The subspace characterization follows by a Schur complement argument as was done for (PAS1). Using the coordinate system

$$L^2_{M+N} = H^{2\perp}_{M+N} \oplus H^2_{M+N},$$

we write $\mathcal{M}_{\mathcal{R}} = \begin{bmatrix} I \\ T \end{bmatrix} \chi^-$ where $\chi^- \subset H^{2\perp}_{M+N}$ and $T: \chi^- \to \chi^+ \subset H^2_{M+N}$. Then we compute

$$P_{\mathcal{M}_{\mathcal{R}}} = \begin{bmatrix} I \\ T \end{bmatrix} Z[I\, T^+]$$

where $Z = (I + T^+T)^{-1}$. Thus $P_{P_+\chi^+} - P_{\mathcal{M}_{\mathcal{R}}} - P_{\alpha^+}$ has the form

$$\begin{bmatrix} -Z & -ZT^+ \\ -TZ & P_{P_+\chi^+} - P_{\alpha^+} - TZT^+ \end{bmatrix}.$$

This is J-positive if and only if $-Z$ is J-positive and its Schur complement

$$P_{P_+\chi^+} - P_{\alpha^+} - TZT^+ + TZT^+ = P_{P_+\chi^+} - P_{\alpha^+}$$

is J-positive. We saw in the discussion for (PAS1) that $-Z$ is J-positive if and only if $\mathcal{M}_{\mathcal{R}}$ is negative. Next note that by definition of α^+, $\alpha^+ \cap P_+\chi^+ = (0)$. Thus α^+ has the form $(I + \tilde{T})\mathcal{G}$ when $\mathcal{G} \subset P_-\chi^-$ and $\tilde{T}: \mathcal{G} \to P_+\chi^+$. Now by another Schur complement argument, we deduce that $P_{P_+\chi^+} - P_{\alpha^+}$ is positive if and only if $P_+\chi^+$ is positive (which is always true, as it is contained in $H^2_M \oplus 0$) and α^+ is negative. This gives the subspace characterization of (PAS3).

For (PAS4), we use the equivalent formulation

$$\theta^*(0 \oplus -P_{L^2_N})\theta \le JP_n$$

for $n = \ldots, -1, 0, 1, \ldots$ Conjugate by θJ to write instead

$$J(0 \oplus -P_{L^2_N})J \le \theta J P_n \theta^*$$

for $n = \ldots, -1, 0, 1, \ldots$ As $P_n = S^{n+1}P_{-1}S^{*n+1}$ and θ commutes with S, this reduces to the single condition

$$\begin{aligned} 0 \oplus -P_{L^2_N} &\le \theta J(I - P_{H^2_{M+N}})\theta^* \\ &= J - P_{\mathcal{M}} J \end{aligned}$$

or equivalently

$$(1)\qquad (P_{L^2_M} \oplus 0) - P_{\mathcal{M}} J \geq 0$$

on L^2_{M+N}. Next, with respect to the coordinate system $L^2_{M+N} = L^2_M \oplus L^2_N$, we write

$$\mathcal{M} = \begin{bmatrix} \hat{T} \\ I \end{bmatrix} \mathcal{L} + \begin{bmatrix} \mathcal{M} \cap (L^2_M \oplus 0) \\ 0 \end{bmatrix}$$

so $P_{\mathcal{M}}$ has the form

$$P_{\mathcal{M}} = \begin{bmatrix} \hat{T} \\ I \end{bmatrix} \hat{Z}[\hat{T}^* - I] + \begin{bmatrix} P_{\mathcal{M}_0} & 0 \\ 0 & 0 \end{bmatrix}$$

where $\hat{Z} = (\hat{T}^*\hat{T} - I)^{-1}$ and $\mathcal{M}_0 = \mathcal{M} \cap (L^2_M \oplus 0)$. Thus

$$(P_{L^2_M} \oplus 0) - P_{\mathcal{M}} J = \begin{bmatrix} I + P_{\mathcal{M}_0} - T\hat{Z}T^* & -T\hat{Z} \\ -\hat{Z}T^* & -\hat{Z} \end{bmatrix}.$$

By a Schur complement argument again, (1) holds if and only if

$$-\hat{Z} \text{ is positive and } I + P_{\mathcal{M}_0} \text{ is positive.}$$

As $I + P_{\mathcal{M}_0}$ is automatically positive, this is equivalent to the single condition $-\hat{Z}$ being positive, i.e., $\hat{T}$ being a contraction. This in turn is the same as

$$\mathcal{M} \boxminus \mathcal{M} \cap (L^2_M \oplus 0) \text{ is negative.}$$

By Lemma 2.1 this is the same as

$$\mathcal{M} \boxminus \{[\mathcal{M} \cap (L^2_M \oplus 0)] + [\mathcal{M} \cap (0 \oplus L^2_N)]\} \text{ is negative.}$$

As $\mathcal{M} = \rho^+ \boxplus \{[\mathcal{M} \cap (H^2_M \oplus 0)] + [\mathcal{M} \cap (0 \oplus H^2_N)]\}$, this is the same as

$$\rho^+ \boxminus \{[\rho^+ \cap (L^2_M \oplus 0)] + [\rho^+ \cap (0 \oplus L^2_N)]\} \text{ is negative.}$$

This gives the subspace characterization of (PAS4).

The operator characterization ($P_- P_{\mathcal{M}} P_- \geq 0$) of (PAS4) follows immediately from the subspace characterization obtained above ($\mathcal{M} \boxminus \{[\mathcal{M} \cap (L^2_M \oplus 0)] + [\mathcal{M} \cap (0 \oplus L^2_N)]\}$ negative) once we have the following general lemma. □

LEMMA 2.2. *Suppose $\mathcal{K}$ is a Krein space with fundamental decomposition $\mathcal{K} = \mathcal{K}_+ \oplus \mathcal{K}_-$ and $\mathcal{M}$ is a regular subspace of $\mathcal{K}$. Let P_- be the projection onto $\mathcal{K}_-$ along $\mathcal{K}_+$. Then $P_- P_{\mathcal{M}} P_- \geq 0$ on $\mathcal{K}_-$ if and only if $\mathcal{M} \boxminus \{\mathcal{M} \cap (\mathcal{K}_+ \oplus 0) + \mathcal{M} \cap (0 \oplus \mathcal{K}_-)\}$ is negative.*

Proof. Write $\mathcal{M}$ as

$$\mathcal{M} = \begin{bmatrix} T \\ I \end{bmatrix} \mathcal{N} + \begin{bmatrix} \mathcal{M}_0 \\ 0 \end{bmatrix}$$

where $\mathcal{N} \subset \mathcal{K}_-$, $T\colon \mathcal{N} \to \mathcal{K}_+ \Theta \mathcal{M}_0$ and $\mathcal{M}_0 = [I_{\mathcal{K}_+} \;\; 0]\{\mathcal{M} \cap \left[\begin{smallmatrix} \mathcal{K}_+ \\ 0 \end{smallmatrix}\right]\}$. Then

$$\mathcal{M} \boxminus \{\mathcal{M} \cap (\mathcal{K}_+ \oplus 0)\} = \begin{bmatrix} T \\ I \end{bmatrix} \mathcal{N}$$

and hence is negative if and only if $\|T\| < 1$. By Lemma 2.1, $\|T\| < 1$ is also equivalent to $\mathcal{M} \boxminus \{\mathcal{M} \cap (\mathcal{K}_+ \oplus 0) + \mathcal{M} \cap (0 \oplus \mathcal{K}_-)\}$ being negative. We next compute

$$P_{\mathcal{M}} = \begin{bmatrix} T \\ I \end{bmatrix} Z [T \quad -I] + \begin{bmatrix} P_{\mathcal{M}_0} & 0 \\ 0 & 0 \end{bmatrix}$$

where $Z = (T^*T - I)^{-1}$. Thus $P_- P_{\mathcal{M}} P_- = -Z$. Clearly this is positive if and only if $\|T\| < 1$. □

We are now ready for the proof of Theorem 1.3.

Proof of Theorem 1.3. The subspace characterization of (PAS4) is equivalent to

$$\mathcal{M} \boxminus \{\mathcal{M} \cap (L^2_M \oplus 0)\} \text{ is negative.}$$

by Lemma 2.1. With the extra assumption that $\mathcal{M} \cap (L^2_M \oplus 0) = \mathcal{M} \cap (H^2_M \oplus 0)$, we therefore get

$$\mathcal{M} \boxminus \{\mathcal{M} \cap (H^2_M \oplus 0)\} \text{ is negative.}$$

As in Lemma 2.1, this holds if and only if

$$\mathcal{M} \boxminus \{\mathcal{M} \cap (H^2_M \oplus 0) + \mathcal{M} \cap (0 \oplus H^2_M)\}.$$

This last space by definition is $\mathcal{M}_{\mathcal{R}} \boxplus \alpha^+$. We thus have obtained the subspace characterization of (PAS3). Conversely if (PAS3) holds, then $\mathcal{M} \boxminus \{\mathcal{M} \cap (H^2_M \oplus 0)\}$ is negative.

As $\{\mathcal{M}\cap(L^2_M\oplus 0)\}\boxminus\{\mathcal{M}\cap(H^2_M\oplus 0)\}$ is a positive subspace of $\mathcal{M}\boxminus\{\mathcal{M}\cap(H^2_M\oplus 0)\}$, this forces $\mathcal{M}\cap(L^2_M\oplus 0)=\mathcal{M}\cap(H^2_M\oplus 0)$. This proves (i) in Theorem 1.3.

To prove (ii) in Theorem 1.3, note first that

$$P_+\chi^+\oplus P_-\chi^+=\chi^+\boxplus\alpha^+. \tag{1}$$

Indeed, check that

$$\begin{aligned}P_+\chi^+\oplus H^2_N&=\{\chi^{+\perp J}\cap(H^2_M\oplus 0)\}^{\perp J}\\&=\{\mathcal{M}\cap(H^2_M\oplus 0)\}^{\perp J}\end{aligned}$$

where the orthogonal complements are with respect to H^2_{M+N}. Similarly,

$$H^2_M\oplus P_-\chi^+=\{\mathcal{M}\cap(0\oplus H^2_N)\}^{\perp J}$$

so, taking intersections gives

$$P_+\chi^+\oplus P_-\chi^+=\{\mathcal{M}\cap(H^2_M\oplus 0)+\mathcal{M}\cap(0\oplus H^2_N)\}^{\perp J}.$$

But also

$$\alpha^+=\mathcal{M}\cap H^2_{M+N}\boxminus\{\mathcal{M}\cap(H^2_M\oplus 0)+\mathcal{M}\cap(0\oplus H^2_N)\}$$

while $\chi^+=H^2_{M+N}\boxminus\mathcal{M}\cap H^2_{M+N}$. Putting all this together gives (1). In particular the space $P_+\chi^+\oplus P_-\chi^+=\chi^+\boxplus\alpha^+$ has dim $P_+\chi^+$ positive squares and dim $P_-\chi^+$ negative squares in the J-inner product.

If χ^+ is positive (i.e., (PAS2) holds), then certainly $\chi^+\cap(0\oplus H^2_N)=(0)$, but then also χ^+ is necessarily maximal positive in $P_+\chi^+\oplus P_-\chi^+$. Therefore its J-orthogonal complement α^+ in $P_+\chi^+\oplus P_-\chi^+$ must be negative. Conversely, if $\chi^+\cap(0\oplus H^2_N)=(0)$ then dim $\chi^+=$ dim $P_+\chi^+$. By dimension count, its complement α_+ in $P_+\chi^+\oplus P_-\chi^+$ must have dim $\alpha_+=$ dim $P_-\chi^+$, and therefore is maximal negative in $P_+\chi^+\oplus P_-\chi^+$ if it is negative. Therefore its J-orthogonal complement χ^+ must therefore be positive. This establishes (ii) in Theorem 1.3.

If (PAS1) holds, then by Theorem 1.2 χ^+ is positive (so (PAS2) holds) and $\mathcal{M}_{\mathcal{R}}$ is negative. By part (ii) of Theorem 1.3 just proven, (PAS2) implies α^+ is negative. By the characterization in Theorem 1.2, this gives (PAS3). Conversely, if (PAS2) and

(PAS3), then by Theorem 1.3 χ^+ is positive and $\mathcal{M}_{\mathcal{R}}$ is negative, so (PAS1) holds. In this way (iii) in Theorem 1.3 is established.

Consider next (iv). We saw in the discussion immediately preceding Lemma 2.2 that (PAS4) is equivalent to the subspace $\mathcal{M} \boxminus \{\mathcal{M} \cap (L_M^2 \oplus 0)\}$ being negative. If also $\mathcal{M} \cap (L_M^2 \oplus 0) = \mathcal{M} \cap (H_M^2 \oplus 0)$, then certainly $\mathcal{M} \boxminus \{\mathcal{M} \cap (H_M^2 \oplus 0)\}$ is negative, and hence by Lemma 2.1,

$$\mathcal{M}_{\mathcal{R}} \boxplus \alpha^+ = \mathcal{M} \boxminus \{[\mathcal{M} \cap (H_M^2 \oplus 0)] + [\mathcal{M} \cap (0 \oplus H_N^2)]\}$$

is negative. But if we also have $\chi^+ \cap (0 \oplus H_M^2) = 0$, then, as we saw in the proof of part (ii), α^+ is negative if and only if χ^+ is positive. Moreover, since we established above that $\mathcal{M}_{\mathcal{R}} \boxplus \alpha^+$ is negative, certainly $\mathcal{M}_{\mathcal{R}}$ is negative. We thus have arrived at the subspace characterization of (PAS1) in Theorem 1.2.

Conversely, supposse (PAS1) holds. Then by Theorem 1.2 χ^+ is positive; trivially this forces $\chi^+ \cap (0 \oplus H_M^2) = 0$. By the argument in the proof of part (ii), then α^+ is negative. Again by Theorem 1.2, (PAS1) implies that $\mathcal{M}_{\mathcal{R}}$ is negative. We have thus arrived at the subspace characterization of (PAS3) in Theorem 1.2. Then $\rho^+ = \mathcal{M}_{\mathcal{R}} \boxplus \alpha^+$ is negative, so trivially any subspace is also negative; this establishes the subspace characterization of (PAS4). Finally by Theorem 1.2 (PAS1) implies that $\mathcal{M}_{\mathcal{R}}$ is negative. But

$$\{\mathcal{M} \cap (L_M^2 \oplus 0)\} \boxminus \{\mathcal{M} \cap (H_M^2 \oplus 0)\}$$

is a positive subspace of $\mathcal{M}_{\mathcal{R}}$, and so must be 0 since $\mathcal{M}_{\mathcal{R}}$ is negative. [Here we use regularity of the various subspaces.] Thus $\mathcal{M} \cap (L_M^2 \oplus 0) = \mathcal{M} \cap (H_M^2 \oplus 0)$. This establishes sufficiency in part (iv) and completes the proof of Theorem 1.3. □

We now consider Theorem 1.4.

Proof of Theorem 1.4. We suppose now that $\mathcal{M}$ has the form

$$\mathcal{M} = \begin{bmatrix} \psi & K\varphi^{-1} \\ 0 & \varphi^{-1} \end{bmatrix} H_{M+N}^2$$

where $K \in L_{M\times N}^\infty$, $\psi^{\pm 1} \in L_M^\infty$, $\varphi^{\pm 1} \in L_N^\infty$. We wish to characterize in terms of K, ψ, φ when (PAS1)–(PAS4) hold.

We compute

$$\mathcal{M} \boxminus \{\mathcal{M} \cap (L^2_M \oplus 0)\} = \begin{bmatrix} \Gamma_K \\ I \end{bmatrix} \varphi^{-1} H^2_N.$$

As was observed in the proof of (iv) in Theorem 1.2, (PAS4) is equivalent to this space being negative, i.e., to $\|\Gamma_K\| < 1$. Next note $\mathcal{M} \cap (L^2_M \oplus 0) = \psi H^2_M \oplus 0$. Thus $\mathcal{M} \cap (L^2_M \oplus 0) = \mathcal{M} \cap (H^2_M \oplus 0)$ if and only if $\psi \in H^\infty_{M \times M}$. Now the characterization of (PAS3) in Theorem 1.4 follows from Theorem 1.4(i).

Finally, by Lemma 1.1 of [BH1], (PAS2) (i.e., χ^+ positive) is equivalent to a subspace being H^2_{M+N}-maximal negative whenever it is $(\mathcal{M} \cap H^2_{M+N})$-maximal negative. In particular then $P_-(\mathcal{M} \cap H^2_{M+N}) = H^2_N$ so $\varphi^{-1} H^2_N \supset H^2_N$, i.e., $\varphi \in H^\infty_{N \times N}$. An $\mathcal{M}$-maximal negative subspace is $\begin{bmatrix} \Gamma_K \\ I \end{bmatrix} \mathcal{D}$ where $\mathcal{D}$ is the image of $E([0,1])$ with E the spectral measure for $\Gamma_K^* \Gamma_K$, thus an $(\mathcal{M} \cap H^2_{M+N})$-maximal negative subspace is $\begin{bmatrix} \Gamma_K I \\ I \end{bmatrix} \mathcal{D} \cap H^2_{M+N}$. For this to be H^2_{M+N}-maximal negative we must have

$$\begin{bmatrix} \Gamma_K \\ I \end{bmatrix} \mathcal{D} \cap H^2_{M+N} = \begin{bmatrix} \Gamma_K \\ I \end{bmatrix} H^2_N.$$

This has two consequences, namely, $\mathcal{D} \supset H^2_N$ so $\Gamma_K \mid H^2_N$ is a contraction, and moreover, Γ_K must map H^2_N into H^2_M. As the argument is reversible, this establishes the characterization of (PAS2) in Theorem 1.2.

To obtian the characterization of (PAS1), simply use the equivalence of (PAS1) with (PAS2) and (PAS3) holding simultaneously (Theorem 1.3(iii)). Note that $K \in H^\infty_{M \times N}$ and $\psi \in H^2_{M \times M}$ is equivalent to $\psi \in H^\infty_{M \times M}$ combined with $\Gamma_K : H^2_N \to H^2_M$. □

3. Reproducing Kernel Functions

In this section we express our passivity conditions and analyze the relations among them in terms of positive definiteness properties of various kernel functions. This will also yield an operator theoretic interpretation for some classical positive definiteness conditions on various kernel functions which gives another point of view to the recent work of [AD1, AD2].

If $K(z, w)$ is an $N \times N$ matrix function of two complex variables, meromorphic in z and conjugate meromorphic in w on some domain $\mathcal{D}$ in the complex plane, we say that K is a *positive definite* kernel on $\mathcal{D}$ if the matrix

$$[x_i^* K(z_i, z_j) x_j]_{1 \leq i,j \leq n}$$

is positive semidefinite for all choices of vectors $x_1, \ldots, x_n$ in $\mathbb{C}^n$ and of points $z_1, \ldots, z_n$ in $\mathcal{D}$ at which K is analytic. In particular necessarily $K(z_i, z_j)^* = K(z_j, z_i)$. In the case we write $K(z, w) \geq 0$. We now state the passivity conditions (PAS1), (PAS3) and (PAS4) in terms of positive definiiteness of certain kernel functions; we did not find a similar simple condition for (PAS2).

THEOREM 3.1. *Suppose* $\theta(z) = \begin{bmatrix} \alpha_1(z) & \alpha_2(z) \\ \beta_1(z) & \beta_2(z) \end{bmatrix}$ *is the chain matrix for a lossless circuit. Then the following equivalences hold.*

(i) (PAS1) $\Longleftrightarrow \frac{J - \theta(z) J \theta(w)^*}{1 - z\overline{w}} \geq 0$ *on* $\mathcal{D}$.

(ii) (PAS3) $\Longleftrightarrow \frac{(I_M \oplus 0) - \theta(z) J \theta(w)^*}{1 - z\overline{w}} \geq 0$,

(iii) (PAS4) $\Longleftrightarrow P_- \frac{J - \theta(z) J \theta(w)^*}{1 - z\overline{w}} P_-^* \geq 0$.

Proof. By Proposition 1.1, (PAS1) is equivalent to $\theta(z)$ being J-contractive at all points of analyticity in the unit disk $\mathcal{D}$. This means that θ satisfies a J-Pick matrix condition (see [BH3]) on arbitrary finite subsets of $\mathcal{D}$; this in turn is equivalent to the positive definiteness of the kernel $\frac{J - \theta(z) J \theta(w)^*}{1 - z\overline{w}}$. Conversely, if the kernel is positive definite, then the J-contractiveness of $\theta(z)$ for $z \in \mathcal{D}$ follows from the diagonal entries of a positive semidefinite matrix being nonnegative. Similarly, by Proposition 1.1 (PAS4) is equivalent to $\beta_2^{-1}\beta_1 \in H^\infty$. Since $\theta(z)$ is J-unitary for $|z| \leq 1$, $\|\beta_2^{-1}(z)\beta_1(z)\| \leq 1$ for $|z| = 1$, so by the maximum modulus theorem $\|\beta_2(z)^{-1}\beta_1(z)\| \leq 1$ for $z \in \mathcal{D}$. By the necessity of the usual Pick condition, we conclude that the kernel $\frac{I - \beta_2(z)^{-1}\beta_1(z)\beta_1(w)^*\beta_2(w)^{-*}}{1 - z\overline{w}}$ is positive definite. From this we get that

$$\beta_2(z)\left\{\frac{I - \beta_2(z)^{-1}\beta_1(z)\beta_1(w)^*\beta_2(w)^{-*}}{1 - z\overline{w}}\right\}\beta_2(w)^* = \frac{\beta_2(z)\beta_2(w)^* - \beta_1(z)\beta_1(w)^*}{1 - z\overline{w}} \geq 0.$$

Here β^{-*} stands for β^{-1*}. □

We now give a direct kernel function proof of the last part of Theorem 1.4.

THEOREM 3.2. *(= kernel function form of Theorem 1.4(iii)). (PAS1) is equivalent to (PAS2) and (PAS3) holding simultaneously.*

Proof. Assume (PAS1), i.e.,

$$\frac{J-\theta(z)J\theta(w)^*}{1-z\overline{w}} \geq 0.$$

Then also

$$P_-\left\{\frac{J-\theta(z)J\theta(w)^*}{1-z\overline{w}}\right\}P_- \geq 0,$$

i.e.,

$$\frac{-I-\beta_1(z)\beta_1(w)^*+\beta_2(z)\beta_2(w)^*}{1-z\overline{w}} \geq 0. \tag{1}$$

From this we have

$$\frac{\beta_2(z)\beta_2(w)^*-\beta_1(z)\beta_2(w)^*}{1-z\overline{w}} \geq \frac{I}{1-z\overline{w}} \geq 0$$

from which (PAS4) follows. To get (PAS2), rearrange (1) in another way to get

$$\frac{\beta_2(z)\beta_2(w)^*-I}{1-z\overline{w}} \geq \frac{\beta_1(z)\beta_1(w)^*}{1-z\overline{w}} \geq 0.$$

For (PAS3), note that (PAS1) implies that

$$[I,-\alpha_2(z)\beta_2(z)^{-1}]\left\{\frac{J-\theta(z)J\theta(w)^*}{1-z\overline{w}}\right\}\begin{bmatrix} I \\ -\beta_2(w)^{-*}\alpha_2(w)^* \end{bmatrix} \geq 0,$$

i.e.,

$$\frac{I-\alpha_2(z)\beta_2(z)^{-1}\beta_2(w)^{-*}\alpha_2(w)^*}{1-z\overline{w}} \geq \frac{b(z)b(w)^*}{1-z\overline{w}}$$

where $b(z)=\alpha_1(z)-\alpha_2(z)\beta_2(z)^{-1}\beta_1(z)$. Thus

$$\frac{I-b(z)b(w)^*}{1-z\overline{w}} \geq \frac{\alpha_2(z)\beta_2(z)^{-1}\beta_2(w))^{-*}\alpha_2(w)^*}{1-z\overline{w}} \geq 0$$

and (PAS3) follows.

In [AD] (see also [AG]) the reproducing kernel Hilbert space $\mathcal{K}(\theta)$ based on the kernel $\frac{J-\theta(z)J\theta(w)^*}{1-z\overline{w}}$ associated with (PAS1) plays a prominent role. We now obtain an operator interpretation for the kernel $\frac{J-\theta(z)J\theta(w)^*}{1-z\overline{w}}$ and the reproducing kernel Hilbert space $\mathcal{K}(\theta)$.

THEOREM 3.3. *Suppose $\theta(z)$ is the chain matrix for a lossless circuit. Choose a scalar inner function ψ such that $\psi\theta$ is analytic in $\mathcal{D}$. Denote by Q the operator on L^2_{M+N} given by*

$$Q = JP_{H^2_{M+N}} - \theta P_{H^2_{M+N}} J\theta^*$$
$$= JP_{H^2_{M+N}} - P_{\mathcal{M}}J = JP_{\chi^+} - P_{\mathcal{M}_{\mathcal{R}}}J.$$

For $z \in \mathcal{D}$ and $x \in \mathbb{C}^{M+N}$, $k_z x$ denotes the element $[k_z x](e^{i\theta}) = \frac{1}{1-e^{i\theta}\overline{z}}x \in H^2_{M+N} \subset L^2_{M+N}$.

(1i) *Then, for z, w points of analyticity for θ inside $\mathcal{D}$ and $x, y \in \mathbb{C}^{M+N}$, we have*

$$y^* \frac{J - \theta(z)J\theta(w)^*}{1 - z\overline{w}} x = \langle Q\psi^* k_w \psi(w)^{-*}x, \psi^* k_z \psi(z)^{-*}y\rangle.$$

If $h \in \psi^* H^{2\perp}_{M+N}$, then $Qh = 0$.

(1ii) *The reproducing kernel Hilbert space $\mathcal{K}(\theta)$ can be identified explicitly as $\operatorname{Im} Q = \chi^- \oplus \chi^+ \subset L^2_{M+N}$ with reproducing kernel inner product given by*

$$\langle Qh, Qk\rangle_{\mathcal{K}(\theta)} = \langle Qh, k\rangle_{L^2_{M+N}}.$$

(Here $\chi^- = P_{H^{2\perp}_{M+N}}\mathcal{M}$, $\chi^+ = H^2_{M+N} \boxminus (\mathcal{M} \cap H^2_{M+N})$.)

(1iii) (PAS1) *is equivalent to $Q \geq 0$, i.e. to $\mathcal{K}(\theta)$ being a Hilbert space in its reproducing kernel inner product.*

(2i) *If $\theta(z) = \begin{bmatrix} \alpha_1(z) & \alpha_2(z) \\ \beta_1(z) & \beta_2(z) \end{bmatrix}$ then, for $x, y \in \mathbb{C}^n$ and z, w points of analyticity for θ,*

$$y^* \left[\frac{\beta_2(z)\beta_2(w)^* - \beta_1(z)\beta_1(w)^*}{1 - z\overline{w}}\right] x = \langle P_- P_{\mathcal{M}} P_-^* \psi^* k_w \psi(w)^{-*}x, \psi^* k_z \psi(z)^{-*}y\rangle.$$

(2ii) *The reproducing kernel space $\mathcal{K}(-P_-\theta P_-)$ with reproducing kernel*

$$\mathcal{K}(z, w) = \frac{\beta_2(z)\beta_2(w)^* - \beta_1(z)\beta_1(w)^*}{1 - z\overline{w}}$$

can be identified concretely as $\operatorname{Im} P_- P_{\mathcal{M}} P_-^* \subset L^2_N$ with reproducing kernel inner product

$$\langle P_- P_{\mathcal{M}} P_-^* h, P_- P_{\mathcal{M}} P_-^* k\rangle_{\mathcal{K}} = \langle P_- P_{\mathcal{M}} P_-^* h, k\rangle_{L^2_N}.$$

(2iii) (PAS4) *is equivalent to* $P_- P_{\mathcal{M}} P_-^* \geq 0$ *on* L^2_N, *i.e., to* $\mathcal{K}(-P_-\theta P_-)$ *being a Hilbert space in its reproducing kernel inner product.*

Remark. Note that assertion (2iii) overlaps Theorem 1.4 which was obtained by purely Krein space geometry methods. We shall now obtain an alternative derivation based on classical kernel function arguments.

Proof. We use the well known general identity

$$P_{H^2_N} A^* k_w x = k_w A(w)^* x$$

if $A \in H^\infty_{N\times N}, x \in \mathbb{C}^N$. For completeness we give the short proof: For $h \in H^2_N$,

$$\begin{aligned}\langle h, P_{H^2_N} A^* k_w x\rangle &= \langle Ah, k_w x\rangle \\ &= \langle A(w)h(w), c\rangle \\ &= \langle h(w), A(w)^* x\rangle \\ &= \langle h, k_w A(w)^* x\rangle.\end{aligned}$$

Thus if $B \in H^\infty_{N\times N}$ we also have

$$\begin{aligned}\langle BP_{H^2_N} A^* k_w x, k_z y\rangle &= \langle [BP_{H^2_N} A^* k_w x](z), y\rangle \\ &= y^* \frac{B(z)A(w)^*}{1 - z\overline{w}} x.\end{aligned}$$

If the scalar inner function such that $\psi\theta$ is analytic, then the above applies in particular to $A = \psi I_{M+N}$, $B = \psi J$ and to $A = \psi\theta$, $B = \psi\theta J$. We conclude

$$\begin{aligned}\langle \psi Q\psi^* k_w x, k_z y\rangle &= \langle [\psi J P_{H^2_{M+N}} \psi^* - \psi\theta J P_{H^2_{M+N}} \theta^* \psi^*] k_w x, k_z y\rangle \\ &= y^* \left[\frac{\psi(z) J \psi(w)^* - \psi(z)\theta(z) J \theta(w)^* \psi(w)^*}{1 - z\overline{w}}\right] x \\ &= y^* \psi(z) \left[\frac{J - \theta(z) J \theta(w)^*}{1 - z\overline{w}}\right] \psi(w)^* x.\end{aligned}$$

If we replace x with $\psi(w)^{-*}x$ and y with $\psi(z)^{-*}y$, we get the desired identity (1i) in Theorem 3.3. Also, as θ is J-unitary and $\theta H^2_{M+N} \subset \psi^* H^2_{M+N}$ it follows that

$$\begin{aligned}\psi^* H^{2\perp}_{M+N} &= (\psi^* H^2_{M+N})^{\perp J} \subset (\theta H^2_{M+N})^{\perp J} \\ &= \theta H^{2\perp J}_{M+N} = \theta H^{2\perp}_{M+N}.\end{aligned}$$

Thus

$$\psi^* H^{2\perp}_{M+N} = J\psi^* H^{2\perp}_{M+N} \subset J\theta H^{2\perp}_{M+N}$$

so

$$\begin{aligned}\theta^*[\psi^* H^{2\perp}_{M+N}] \subset \theta^* J\theta H^{2\perp}_{M+N} &= JH^{2\perp}_{M+N} \\ &= H^{2\perp}_{M+N}\end{aligned}$$

so $P_{H^2_{M+N}}\theta^*$ is zero on $\psi^* H^{2\perp}_{M+N}$. As $\psi^* H^{2\perp}_{M+N} \subset H^{2\perp}_{M+N}$, we also have $JP_{H^2_{M+N}}$ is zero on $\psi^* H^{2\perp}_{M+N}$, so $Q = 0$ on $\psi^* H^{2\perp}_{M+N}$. This completes the proof of (1i).

The inner product identity in (1ii) is an immediate consequence of the identity in (1i). To identify $\mathcal{K}(\theta)$, we note that the kernel function $\mathcal{K}(z,w)x = \frac{J-\theta(z)J\theta(w)^*}{1-z\overline{w}}x$ by the computation above in the proof of (1i) can be identified as $\mathcal{K}(\cdot,w)x = Q\psi^* k_w \psi(w)^{-*}x$. Thus the span of the kernel functions, namely $\mathcal{K}(\theta)$, is contained in $\operatorname{Im} Q$. Conversely, since $\{\psi^* k_w \psi(w)^{-*}x,\ w \in \mathcal{D} \text{ with } \psi(w) \neq 0,\ x \in \mathbb{C}^{M+N}\}$ is dense in $\psi^* H^2_{M+N}$, it is clear the $\operatorname{Im} Q$ is contained in the closure in L^2_{M+N} of the span of $\{\mathcal{K}(\cdot,w)x : w \in \mathcal{D},\ \psi(w) \neq 0,\ x \in \mathbb{C}^{M+N}\}$. For the rational case, this span is finite dimensional, so is equal to its closure. [For the general case, if $Q \geq 0$ then more precisely $\mathcal{K}(\theta) = \operatorname{Im} Q^{1/2}$.] Thus $\mathcal{K}(\theta) = \operatorname{Im} Q$ and (1ii) follows.

In the proof of Theorem 1.3 in section 2 it was shown that (PAS1) is equivalent to $Q = JP_{H^2_{M+N}} - \theta JP_{H^2_{M+N}}\theta^* \geq 0$. From this and the form of the reproducing kernel inner product on $\mathcal{K}(\theta)$ established in (1ii), (1iii) follows easily.

Since $\mathcal{M} = \theta H^2_{M+N}$ and θ is J-unitary, it is easy to deduce that $P_{\mathcal{M}} = \theta P_{H^2_{M+N}} J\theta^* J$ ($P_{\mathcal{M}}$ = the J-orthogonal project). Thus

$$\begin{aligned}P_- P_{\mathcal{M}} P_-^* &= [\beta_1 P_{H^2_{M+N}}\beta_1^* - \beta_2 P_{H^2_{M+N}}\beta_2^*][P_- J P_-] \\ &= \beta_2 P_{H^2_{M+N}}\beta_2^* - \beta_1 P_{H^2_{M+N}}\beta_1^*.\end{aligned}$$

As in the proof of (1i) it follows from this that

$$y^*\left[\frac{\beta_2(z)\beta_2(w)^* - \beta_1(z)\beta_1(w)^*}{1-z\overline{w}}\right]x = \langle P_- P_{\mathcal{M}} P_-^* \psi^* k_w \psi(w)^{-*}x,\ \psi^* k_z \psi(z)^{-*}y\rangle$$

and (2i) follows. (2ii) then follows in exactly the same way as (1ii). In Theorem 3.1 it was noted that (PAS4) is equivalent to the positive definiteness of the kernel $\left[\frac{\beta_2(z)\beta_2(w)^* - \beta_1(z)\beta_1(w)^*}{1-z\overline{w}}\right]$. By an argument as done above for (1ii), it follows that the positive definiteness of this kernel is equivalent to $P_-P_{\mathcal{M}}P_-^* \geq 0$ on L^2_N. From this (2iii), and hence all of Theorem 3.3, follows.

4. Passivity and Interpolation

In this section we explore the meaning of (PAS1)–(PAS4) in the contexts of special examples.

a. The Nehari problem. The Nehari problem is: Given $K \in L^\infty_{M\times N}$, find $F \in K + H^\infty_{M\times N}$ so that $\|F\|_\infty \leq 1$. In the approach of the authors [BH1] to the problem, the subspace associated with this problem is

$$\mathcal{M} = LH^2_{M+N}$$

where $L = \begin{bmatrix} I & K \\ 0 & I \end{bmatrix}$. Solutions to the Nehari problem exist if and only if $\|\mathcal{H}_K\| \leq 1$, where $\mathcal{H}_K: H^2_N \to H^{2\perp}_M$ is the Hankel operator

$$\mathcal{H}_K: f \to P_{H^{2\perp}_M}(Kf).$$

When $\|\mathcal{H}_K\| < 1$ then the subspace $\mathcal{M}$ is regular, and so can be represented as

$$\mathcal{M} = \theta H^2_{M+N}$$

where $\theta(z)$ is J-unitary for $|z| = 1$ (with $J = I_M \oplus -I_N$). If K is rational then θ is also rational; more generally, if K is smooth (eg. if the Fourier coefficients of K are absolutely summable), then θ and θ^{-1} are in $L^\infty_{(M+N)\times(M+N)}$. In any case, given that $\|\mathcal{H}_K\| < 1$, then the set of all solutions F of the Nehari problem is given by

$$F = [\alpha_1 G + \alpha_2][\beta_1 G + \beta_2]^{-1}$$

where G is an arbitrary element of $H^\infty_{M\times N}$ with $\|G\|_\infty \leq 1$ and where $\theta = \begin{bmatrix} \alpha_1 & \alpha_2 \\ \beta_1 & \beta_2 \end{bmatrix}$. Physically this has the interpretation that solutions of the Nehari problem arise as the scattering matrices F of the circuits resulting from loading the lossless (but as we shall see unstable) circuit θ with an arbitrary passive circuit G. All this information (with the exception of the physical interpretation) is given in more detail in [BH1].

What we wish to analyze here is the various passivity conditions (PAS1)–(PAS4) for a lossless circuit θ of the special form

$$\theta H^2_{M+N} = \mathcal{M} = LH^2_{M+N}$$

with $L = \begin{bmatrix} I & K \\ 0 & I \end{bmatrix}$. Note that $\mathcal{M}$ has the J-orthogonal decomposition

$$\mathcal{M} = \begin{bmatrix} \mathcal{H}_K \\ I \end{bmatrix} H^2_N \boxplus \begin{bmatrix} H^2_M \\ 0 \end{bmatrix}$$

and

$$\mathcal{M} \cap (H^2_M \oplus 0) = H^2_M \oplus 0$$

$$\mathcal{M} \cap (0 \oplus H^2_N) = 0 \oplus (\ker \mathcal{H}_K)^{\perp}.$$

We assume that $\mathcal{M}$ is regular, so $I - \mathcal{H}^*_K \mathcal{H}_K$ is invertible. Thus we have

$$\mathcal{M} \boxminus \{[\mathcal{M} \cap (H^2_M \oplus 0)] + [\mathcal{M} \cap (0 \oplus H^2_N)]\} = \begin{bmatrix} \mathcal{H}_K \\ I \end{bmatrix} (\ker \mathcal{H}_K)^{\perp}.$$

Thus this space is negative (i.e., (PAS4) holds) if and only if $\|\mathcal{H}_K\| < 1$. We thus have a physical interpretation of Nehari's Theorem: The Nehari problem is solvable if and only if the corresponding circuit θ satisfies (PAS4).

We next analyze (PAS3). By Theorem 1.4 (PAS3) holds if and only if (PAS4) holds and $\mathcal{M} \cap (L^2_M \oplus 0) \subset H^2_M \oplus 0$. For our case here, $\mathcal{M} \cap (L^2_M \oplus 0) = H^2_M \oplus 0$. Thus for the situation of the Nehari problem, (PAS4) and (PAS3) are equivalent.

By Theorem 1.4, (PAS2) is equivalent to α^+ being negative together with $\chi^+ \cap (0 \oplus H^2_N) = 0$. For our case here we compute

$$\mathcal{M} \cap H^2_{M+N} = H^2_M \oplus \ker \mathcal{H}_K$$

so

$$\chi^+ = 0 \oplus (\ker \mathcal{H}_K)^{\perp} \subset 0 \oplus H^2_M.$$

For χ^+ of this simple form, $\alpha^+ = (0)$. Thus the condition "α^+ negative" is satisfied vacuously, but the other condition $\chi^+ \cap (0 \oplus H^2_N) = (0)$ is violated in a fundamental way. Therefore (PAS2) (and hence also (PAS1)) always fails for the setting of the Nehari problem.

b. Bitangential Nevanlinna-Pick interpolation. The simplest case of the bitangential Nevanlinna-Pick interpolation problem is the following: We are given $m+n$ distinct points $w_1, \dots, w_m, w_{m+1}, \dots, w_{m+n}$ in the unit disk, $m+n$ nonzero vectors $x_1, \dots, x_m, x_{m+1}, \dots, x_{m+n}$ in $\mathbb{C}^M$ and $m+n$ nonzero vectors $y_1, \dots, y_m, y_{m+1}, \dots, y_{m+n}$ in $\mathbb{C}^N$. The problem is to find all $M \times N$ matrix functions $F(z)$ analytic on the disk with H^∞-norm $\|F\|_\infty \le 1$ such that

$$F(w_k)y_k = x_k \quad \text{for} \quad 1 \le k \le m, \tag{4.1}$$

$$x_k^* F(w_k) = y_k^* \quad \text{for} \quad m+1 \le k \le m+n. \tag{4.2}$$

(if any exist at all). The problem has been well-studied (see [BH1,2,4;BR1;F1,2;Ki,LA]). We review the approach of [BH1,BH4,BR1]. Introduce a subspace $\mathcal{M} \subset L^2_{M+N}$ by

$$\mathcal{M} = \left\{ \sum_{k=1}^m c_k \frac{1}{z-w_k} \begin{bmatrix} x_k \\ y_k \end{bmatrix} + h(z) : c_k \in \mathbb{C},\ h \in H^2_{M+N} \right. \\ \text{such that} \quad [x_j^*, -y_j^*] h(w_j) = \sum_{k=1}^m c_k \frac{x_j^* x_k - y_j^* y_k}{w_k - w_j} \\ \left. \text{for} \qquad m+1 \le j \le m+n \right\}. \tag{4.3}$$

If we introduce matrix functions $\mathcal{K}$, ψ, φ according to the rule

(4.4i) $K \in H^\infty_{M\times N}$ and satisfies the interpolation conditions (4.1) and (4.2).

(4.4ii) ψ is an $M \times M$ matrix Blaschke product such that $\det \psi$ has only simple zeros at $w_{m+1}, \dots, w_{m+n}$ and such that $x_k^* \psi(w_k) = 0$ for $m+1 \le k \le m+n$.

(4.4iii) φ is an $N \times N$ matrix Blaschke product such that $\det \varphi$ has only simple zeros at $w_1, \dots, w_m$ and such that $\varphi(w_k) y_k = 0$ for $1 \le k \le m$,

then the same space $\mathcal{M}$ as in (4.3) can also be expressed in the same form as was used in Theorem 1.4

$$\mathcal{M} = L H^2_{M+N} \quad \text{where} \quad L = \begin{bmatrix} \psi & K\varphi^{-1} \\ 0 & \varphi^{-1} \end{bmatrix} \tag{4.4}$$

and $\mathcal{K}, \psi, \varphi$ are as in (4.4i)–(4.4iii).

We mention that the form (4.4) was the main tool of analysis in [BH1, BH3] while (4.3) was presented in [BR]. The main result on the interpolation problem is

THEOREM 4.1. *If $\mathcal{M}$ is a subspace of the form (4.3) or equivalently (4.4), then (PAS1) holds if and only if (PAS4) holds. In this case, if $\mathcal{M}$ is regular and $\mathcal{M}$ is represented as $\mathcal{M} = \theta H^2_{M+N}$ where $\theta(z) = \begin{bmatrix} \alpha_1(z) & \alpha_2(z) \\ \beta_1(z) & \beta^2(z) \end{bmatrix}$ is J-unitary for $|z| = 1$, then solutions $F \in H^\infty_{M\times N}$ with $\|F\|_\infty \leq 1$ satisfying (4.1) and (4.2) are given by*

$$F = (\alpha_1 G + \alpha_2)(\beta_1 G + \beta_2)^{-1}$$

where G is an arbitrary function in the unit ball of $H^\infty_{M\times N}$.

Proof. The first assertion is an immediate consequence of Theorem 1.4 if we use the representation (4.4) for $\mathcal{M}$. The second assertion is the main result of [BH1] if one uses the characterization $\|\Gamma_{\mathcal{K}}\| < 1$ for (PAS4) given in Theorem 1.4. □

By the results of this paper we now have a physical interpretation for the Nevanlinna-Pick interpolation problem to have a solution. Namely, there exists an F in the unit ball $\mathcal{B}H^\infty_{M\times N}$ of $H^\infty_{M\times N}$ satisfying (4.1) and (4.2) if and only if the circuit θ which has the set of signals $\mathcal{M}$ built from the data according to (4.3) or (4.4) as the result of the experiment (E2) is a passive circuit.

In [BH3] a Pick matrix test for solutions to exist was obtained by analyzing the condition $\|\Gamma_{\mathcal{K}}\| < 1$ (i.e., (PAS4)). We now know that for subspaces $\mathcal{M}$ associated with Nevanlinna-Pick interpolation problems, (PAS4) and (PAS1) are equivalent. Theorem 1.3 gives other forms of (PAS1) which are more convenient for computation. In this way we can derive a form of the Pick matrix for the bitangential problem which is cleaner than that obtained in [BH3]; this form of the Pick matrix for the bitangential problem was first obtained by D. Limebeer and B. D. O. Anderson [LA] who used a matrix generalization of the Schur algorithm.

THEOREM 4.2. (see [LA]) *There exists a solution F in $\mathcal{B}H^\infty_{M\times N}$ of the interpolation conditions (4.1) and (4.2) (i.e., $\mathcal{M}$ given by (4.3) satisfies (PAS1)) if and only if the $(m+n)\times(m+n)$ matrix*

$$\Lambda = [\Lambda_{kj}]_{1\leq k,j\leq m+n}$$

where

$$\Lambda_{k,j} = \frac{y_j^* y_k - x_j^* x_k}{1 - w_k \overline{w}_j} \quad \textit{if } 1 \le k, j \le m$$

$$\Lambda_{k,j} = \frac{x_j^* x_k - y_j^* y_k}{w_k - w_j} \quad \textit{if } 1 \le k \le m, m+1 \le j \le m+n$$

$$\Lambda_{k,j} = \overline{\Lambda}_{j,k} \quad \textit{if } m+1 \le k \le m+n, 1 \le j \le m,$$

and

$$\Lambda_{k,j} = \frac{x_j^* x_k - y_j^* y_k}{1 - w_j \overline{w}_k} \quad \textit{if } m+1 \le k, j \le m_n,$$

is positive semidefinite.

Proof. If $\mathcal{M}$ is given by (4.3) then a basis for $\chi^- = P_{H^{2\perp}_{M+N}} \mathcal{M}$ is

$$e_k(z) = \frac{1}{z - w_k} \begin{bmatrix} x_k \\ y_k \end{bmatrix}, \quad 1 \le k \le m$$

while a basis for $\chi^+ = H^2_{M+N} \boxminus (\mathcal{M} \cap H^2_{M+N})$ is given by the kernel functions

$$e_k(z) = \frac{1}{1 - z\overline{w}_k} \begin{bmatrix} x_k \\ y_k \end{bmatrix}, \quad m+1 \le k \le m+n.$$

By the previous theorem, solutions of the interpolation problem (4.1) and (4.2) in $\mathcal{B}H^\infty_{M \times N}$ exist if and only if $\mathcal{M}$ satisfies (PAS1). We use the criterion for (PAS1)

$$\begin{bmatrix} -I & T^+ \\ T & I \end{bmatrix} \quad \text{is} \quad J\text{-positive on} \quad \chi^- \oplus \chi^+$$

from Theorem 1.3. Here $T: \chi^- \to \chi^+$ is such that $\mathcal{M} \boxminus (\mathcal{M} \cap H^2_{M+N}) = (I+T)\chi^-$. Theorem 4.2 then follows immediately once we verify

$$\langle -Je_k, e_j \rangle = \frac{y_j^* y_k - x_j^* x_k}{1 - w_k \overline{w}_j} \quad \text{for } 1 \le k, j \le m, \tag{4.5}$$

$$\langle JTe_k, e_j \rangle = \frac{x_j^* x_k - y_j^* y_k}{w_k - w_j} \quad \text{for } 1 \le k \le m,\ m+1 \le j \le m+n, \tag{4.6}$$

and

$$\langle Je_k, e_j \rangle = \frac{x_j^* x_k - y_j^* y_k}{1 - w_j \overline{w}_k} \quad \text{for } m+1 \le k, j \le m+n. \tag{4.7}$$

Identities (4.5) and (4.7) are direct computations using the residue theorem. To verify (4.6), write $(I+T)e_k$ (where $1 \leq k \leq m$ and k is fixed) in the form (4.3)

$$\frac{1}{z-w_k}\begin{bmatrix} x_k \\ y_k \end{bmatrix} + h(z)$$

for $h = Te_k \in \chi^+$. Then from the representation (4.3) we see that necessarily

$$[x_j^*, -y_j^*](Te_k)(w_j) = \frac{x_j^* x_k - y_j^* y_k}{w_k - w_j}$$

for each j, $m+1 \leq j \leq n$. But on the other hand, since $Te_k \in H^2_{M+N}$ and $\frac{1}{1-z\overline{w}}$ is the kernel function for H^2 we have

$$\begin{aligned}[x_j^*, -y_j^*](Te_k)(w_j) &= \left\langle Te_k, \frac{1}{1-z\overline{w}}\begin{bmatrix} x_j \\ -y_j \end{bmatrix}\right\rangle \\ &= \langle Te_k, Je_j\rangle = \langle JTe_k, e_j\rangle.\end{aligned}$$

This verifies (4.6) as needed. □

The analysis is completely similar for the continuous time setting where the right half plane replaces the unit disk. In this case we assume that the $m+n$ points $w_1, \ldots, w_m, \ldots, w_{m+n}$ are in the open right half plane and we seek a matrix function F in $\mathcal{B}H^\infty_{M\times N}$ of the right half plane satisfying the interpolation conditions (4.1) and (4.2). Then we take the subspace $\mathcal{M}$ of precisely the same form (4.3) and compute the gramian of a basis for $\chi^- \oplus \chi^+$ with respect to the inner product induced by $\begin{bmatrix} J & 0 \\ 0 & J \end{bmatrix}\begin{bmatrix} -I & T^+ \\ T & I \end{bmatrix}$. In this case a basis for χ^- is still given by

$$e_k(z) = \frac{1}{z-w_k}\begin{bmatrix} x_k \\ y_k \end{bmatrix} \quad \text{for } 1 \leq k \leq m$$

while a basis for χ^+ is given by

$$e_k(z) = \frac{1}{z+\overline{w}_k}\begin{bmatrix} x_k \\ y_k \end{bmatrix} \quad \text{for } m+1 \leq k \leq m+n.$$

The details involved in converting an L^2-inner product to a contour integral to which one can apply the theory of residues is different since the contour is now the imaginary axis rather than the unit circle. The result is

THEOREM 4.3. *There exists a solution F in $\mathcal{B}H^{\infty}_{M\times N}$ (right half plane) of the interpolation conditions (4.1) and (4.2) (where $w_1, \ldots, w_{m+n}$ are distinct points in the open right half plane) if and only if the matrix*

$$\Lambda = [\Lambda_{kj}]_{1\le k,j\le m+n}$$

given by

$$\Lambda_{kj} = \frac{y_j^* y_k - x_j^* x_k}{\overline{w}_j + w_k} \quad \text{if } 1 \le j,k \le m$$

$$\Lambda_{kj} = \frac{x_j^* x_k - y_j^* y_k}{w_k - w_j} \quad \text{if } 1 \le k \le m,\ m+1 \le j \le m+n$$

$$\Lambda_{kj} = \overline{\Lambda}_{jk} \quad \text{if } m+1 \le k \le m+n,\ 1 \le j \le m$$

and

$$\Lambda_{kj} = \frac{x_j^* x_k - y_j^* y_k}{w_j + \overline{w}_k} \quad \text{if } m+1 \le k,j \le m+n$$

is positve semidefinite.

Higher multiplicities as well as allowing left-side and right-side interpolation conditions to occur at the same point can be handled in the same way. The analogue of the representation (4.3) for $\mathcal{M}$ is given for the most complicated case in [BR] (see Theorems 5.2 and 2.2 there). However more compact formulas, including an explicit formula for the J-unitary chain matrix θ with $\mathcal{M} = \theta H^2_{M+N}$, are obtained by using state space representations for the interpolation conditions themselves. This is explained in the next section.

5. State Space Representation

In this section we suppose that the shift invariant subspace $\mathcal{M}$ has a representation as $\mathcal{M} = LH^2_{M+N}$ where L is a regular rational matrix function (not necessarily block upper triangular) for which a realization is known. For technical convenience we assume that L is regular at ∞, so without loss of generality we may assume that the realization has the form

$$L(z) = I + \underline{C}(z - \underline{A})^{-1}\underline{B}.$$

In this section we wish to characterize the passivity conditions (PAS1) and (PAS4) explicitly in term of $\underline{A}$, $\underline{B}$, $\underline{C}$. The work in [BR2] and [BCR] gives explicit realization formulas (in terms of $\underline{A}$, $\underline{B}$, $\underline{C}$) for the J-unitary matrix θ such that $LH^2_{M+N} = \theta H^2_{M+N}$ (i.e., for the J-phase factor θ in a J-phase-outer factorization $L = \theta Q$ for L) but does not identify explicitly when the J-phase factor is J-inner (i.e., J-contractive inside $\mathcal{D}$) for example.

To describe $\mathcal{M} = LH^2_{M+N}$ in state space terms one does not need all the information in a realization $[\underline{A}, \underline{B}, \underline{C}]$ for L but only a *canonical set of spectral data* (c.s.s.d) for L over the unit disk $\mathcal{D}$. We say that the quintuple of matrices (C, A_p, A_z, B, S) is a c.s.s.d. for L over $\mathcal{D}$ if

(5.1) $$(C, A_p) \text{ is an observable pair } (\ker \operatorname*{col}_{j\geq 0} (CA^j) = (0))$$
$$\text{and } \sigma(A_p) \subset \mathcal{D}.$$

(5.2) $$(A_z, B) \text{ is a controllable pair } (\operatorname{Im}[B, A_zB, A_z^2B, \ldots] = \mathbb{C}^{n_z})$$
$$\text{and } \sigma(A_z) \subset \mathcal{D},$$

and

(5.3) $$\mathcal{M} = LH^2_{M+N} \text{ is characterized as}$$
$$\mathcal{M} = \left\{ C(z - A_p)^{-1}x + h(z) \colon x \in \mathbb{C}^{n_p},\ h \in H^2_{M+N} \text{ such that} \right.$$
$$\left. \frac{1}{2\pi i} \int_{|z|=1} (z - A_z)^{-1} Bh(z)\, dz = Sx \right\}.$$

Here the matrices C, A_p, A_z, B, S have sizes (say) $(M+N) \times n_p$, $n_p \times n_p$, $n_z \times n_z$, $n_z \times (M+N)$, and $n_z \times n_p$. If $L(z) = I + \underline{C}(z - \underline{A})^{-1}\underline{B}$ is a minimal realization for L, one choice for c.s.s.d. for L over $\mathcal{D}$ is

$$C = \underline{C} \mid \operatorname{Im} P, \qquad A_p = \underline{A} \mid \operatorname{Im} P$$
$$A_z = \underline{A}^x \mid \operatorname{Im} P^x, \qquad B = P^x \underline{B}$$
$$S = P^x \mid \operatorname{Im} P.$$

Here P (resp. P^x) is the Riesz spectral projection for $\underline{A}$ (resp. $\underline{A}^x$) for eigenvalues in $\mathcal{D}$

$$P^{(x)} = \frac{1}{2\pi i} \int_{|z|=1} (z - \underline{A}^{(x)})^{-1}\, dz$$

and $\underline{A}^x = \underline{A} - \underline{BC}$. Any other c.s.s.d. for L over $\mathcal{D}$ is *similar* to this one. For details, see [BR2] or [GK] for two different approaches.

We thus assume that we have a c.s.s.d. (C, A_p, A_z, B, S) for L over $\mathcal{D}$, so $\mathcal{M}$ is represented as in (iii).

THEOREM 5.1. *Suppose $\mathcal{M} = LH^2_{M+N}$ and (C, A_p, A_z, B, S) is a c.s.s.d. for L over $\mathcal{D}$. Then $\mathcal{M}$ is regular if and only if*

$$\Lambda = \begin{bmatrix} -\sum_{j\geq 0} A_p^{*j} C^* J C A_p^j & S^* \\ S & \sum_{j\geq 0} A_z^j B J B^* A_z^{*j} \end{bmatrix} \tag{5.4}$$

is invertible. In this case, $\mathcal{M}$ satisfies (PAS1) *if and only if Λ is positive definite.*

Proof. Use the Fourier transforms $\mathcal{F}_+ : H^2_{M+N} \to \ell^{2+}_{M+N}$ and $\mathcal{F}_- : H^{2\perp}_{M+N} \to \ell^{2+}_{M+N}$

$$\mathcal{F}_+ : \sum_{j=0}^{\infty} c_j z^j \to \{c_j\}_{j\geq 0}$$

$$\mathcal{F}_- : \sum_{j=0}^{\infty} d_j z^{-j-1} \to \{d_j\}_{j\geq 0}$$

to identify H^2_{M+N} with ℓ^{2+}_{M+N} and $H^{2\perp}_{M+N}$ with ℓ^{2+}_{M+N}. With these identifications

$$\chi^- = \operatorname{Im} \operatorname*{col}_{j\geq 0} (C A_p^j)$$

$$\chi^+ = \operatorname{Im} \operatorname*{col}_{j\geq 0} (J B^* A_z^{*j})$$

and the connection between S and T (where $T: \chi^- \to \chi^+$ characterizes $\mathcal{M}_{\mathcal{R}} = \mathcal{M} \boxminus (\mathcal{M} \cap (0 \oplus \ell^{2+}_{M+N}))$ as $\mathcal{M}_{\mathcal{R}} = (I + T)\chi^-$) is given by

$$S = [\operatorname*{row}_{j\geq 0} (A_z^j B)] \cdot T \cdot [\operatorname*{col}_{j\geq 0} (C A_p^j)].$$

(see [BR2] for details.) By Theorem 1.3, we know that [PAS1] is equivalent to $\begin{bmatrix} -I & T^+ \\ T & I \end{bmatrix}$ being J-positive on $\chi^- \oplus \chi^+$. As (C, A_p) is observable and (A_z, B) is controllable, this is equivalent to the matrix Λ equal to

$$\begin{bmatrix} \operatorname*{row}_{j\geq 0} (A_p^{*j}(C^*) & 0 \\ 0 & \operatorname*{row}_{j\geq 0} (A_z B J) \end{bmatrix} \begin{bmatrix} -J & JT^+ \\ JT & J \end{bmatrix} \begin{bmatrix} \operatorname*{col}_{j\geq 0} (C A_p^j) & 0 \\ 0 & \operatorname*{col}_{j\geq 0} J B^* A_z^{*j} \end{bmatrix}$$

being positive definite on $\mathbb{C}^{n_p} \oplus \mathbb{C}^{n_z}$. □

Remark 1. We remark that the Hermitian matrix appearing in Theorem 5.1 satisfies a Lyapunov equation and, with appropriate choice of zero and pole pair for θ inside the disk, is the same as the key matrix $\hat{T}$ appearing in the realization formula for θ in [BR2] (see also [GKLR]). There the point of view was to build a matrix function J-unitary on the circle with given left zero and right pole data inside the disk. In [AG] the problem of constructing a rational matrix function θ with given zero data for the whole complex plane is given; the matrix H, arising as the solution of a certain Lyapunov equation, is identical to the matrix Λ in Theorem 5.1, and occurs in a realization formula for θ. There also the condition $H = \Lambda \geq 0$ is obtained as the test for [PAS1].

Remark 2. If $\mathcal{M}$ has the form (4.3) associated with bitangential Nevanlinna-Pick interpolation problem, then $\mathcal{M}$ can also be expressed as in (5.3) with

(5.5a) $$C = \begin{bmatrix} x_1 & x_2 & \cdots & x_m \\ y_1 & y_2 & \cdots & y_m \end{bmatrix}$$

(5.5b) $$A_p = \operatorname{diag}(w_1, \ldots, w_m)$$

(5.5c) $$A_z = \operatorname{diag}(w_{m+1}, \ldots, w_{m+n})$$

(5.5d) $$B = \begin{bmatrix} x^*_{m+1} & -y^*_{m+1} \\ \vdots & \vdots \\ x^*_{m+n} & -y^*_{m+n} \end{bmatrix}$$

(5.5e) $$S = [S_{kj}]_{m+1 \leq k \leq m+n,\, 1 \leq j \leq m}$$

where

(5.5f) $$S_{kj} = \frac{x^*_k x_j - y^*_k y_j}{w_k - w_j},$$

(see [BR1]). Then it is a direct check to verify that the matrix Λ as in Theorem 5.1 with the c.s.s.d. of this special form specializes exactly to the matrix Λ in Theorem 4.2. This of course is no accident.

More complicated interpolation problems involving higher multiplicities can be handled quite compactly using the same formalism. Specifically, suppose one is given rational matrix functions K, ψ, φ in $H^\infty_{M\times N}$, $H^\infty_{M\times M}$ and $H^\infty_{N\times N}$ such that $\psi^{-1}\in L^\infty_{M\times M}$, $\varphi^{-1}\in L^\infty_{N\times N}$, and the interpolation problem one wants to consider is to describe all F in $H^\infty_{M\times N}$ with $\|F\|_\infty \le 1$ such that

$$F\in K+\psi H^\infty_{M\times N}\varphi. \tag{5.6}$$

Set $L=\begin{bmatrix}\psi & K\varphi^{-1}\\ 0 & \varphi^{-1}\end{bmatrix}$ and let $\mathcal{M}=LH^2_{M+N}$. Then if $\mathcal{M}$ is expressed in terms of matrices (C,A_p,A_z,B,S) as in (5.3), then the interpolation condition (5.4) is equivalently expressed as the set of conditions

$$\frac{1}{2\pi i}\int_{|z|=1}(z-A_z)^{-1}B_+F(z)\,dz=-B_-, \tag{5.7a}$$

$$\frac{1}{2\pi i}\int_{|z|=1}F(z)C_-(zI-A_\pi)^{-1}\,dz=C_+, \tag{5.7b}$$

and

$$\frac{1}{2\pi i}\int_{|z|=1}(zI-A_z)^{-1}B_+F(z)C_-(zI-A_\pi)^{-1}\,dz=S. \tag{5.7c}$$

These formulas are a sort of state space representation for the interpolation conditions themselves. When (C,A_p,A_z,B,S) have the form (5.5), it is easy to check that the conditions (5.7) collapse to the (multiplicity one) bitangential interpolation conditions (4.1), (4.2). When A_p and A_z are allowed to have more general Jordan forms, (5.7) gives a compact way to write more complicated interpolation conditions (involving higher order derivatives of F in various directions). Matrix Nevanlinna-Pick interpolation problem with the interpolation condition expressed in the general form (5.7a) was first introduced and studied by Nudelman [N]. Finally we note that the analogue of Theorem 4.1 applies for these more general interpolation conditions; in particular, there is an F in $H^\infty_{M\times N}$ with $\|F\|_\infty\le 1$ which satisfies the set of interpolation conditions (5.7) if and only if the matrix Λ given by (5.4) is positive semidefinite; this again has the interpretation that an associated circuit be (PAS1). The state space form (5.4) for the Pick matrix associated with an interpolation problem has also been obtained by Kimura [Ki]. A fuller exposition on these and other related matters will appear in the forthcoming monograph [BGR].□

The following characterization of (PAS4) is less satisfactory since the test involves an operator on an infinite dimensional space (although it is an operator of finite rank).

THEOREM 5.2. *Suppose* $\mathcal{M} = LH^2_{M+N}$ and (C, A_p, A_z, B, S) *is a c.s.s.d. for* L *over* $\mathcal{D}$. *Block decompose* C *and* B *as* $C = \begin{bmatrix} C_+ \\ C_- \end{bmatrix}$, $B = [B_+, B_-]$ *conformal with* $\mathbb{C}^{M+N} = \mathbb{C}^M \oplus \mathbb{C}^N$. *Define observability and controllability operators by*

$$\mathcal{O} = \operatorname*{col}_{j\geq 0} (CA_p^j): \mathbb{C}^{n_p} \to \ell^{2+}_{M+N}$$

$$\mathcal{C} = \operatorname*{row}_{j\geq 0} (A_z^j B): \ell^{2+}_{M+N} \to \mathbb{C}^{n_z}$$

$$\mathcal{C}_+ = \operatorname*{row}_{j\geq 0} (A_z^j B_+): \ell^{2+}_M \to \mathbb{C}^{n_z}$$

$$\mathcal{C}_- = \operatorname*{row}_{j\geq 0} (A_z^j B_-): \ell^{2+}_N \to \mathbb{C}^{n_z}$$

$$J = I_M \oplus -I_N$$

$$\mathcal{O}_+ = \operatorname*{col}_{j\geq 0} (C_+ A_p^j): \mathbb{C}^{n_p} \to \ell^{2+}_M$$

$$\mathcal{O}_- = \operatorname*{col}_{j\geq 0} (C_- A_p^j): \mathbb{C}^{n_p} \to \ell^{2+}_N$$

Assume $\mathcal{M}$, χ^+ and $\mathcal{M}_\mathcal{R}$ are regular. Then $\mathcal{M} = LH^2_{M+N}$ satisfies (PAS4) if and only if the operator Z on $\ell^{2+}_N \oplus \ell^{2+}_N$ given by

$$Z = \begin{bmatrix} \mathcal{O}_- \\ -\mathcal{C}_-^*(\mathcal{C}J\mathcal{C}^*)^{-1}S \end{bmatrix} (-\mathcal{O}^* J \mathcal{O} - S^*(\mathcal{C}J\mathcal{C}^*)^{-1}S)^{-1} [\mathcal{O}_-^*, -S^*(\mathcal{C}J\mathcal{C}^*)^{-1}\mathcal{C}_-] + \begin{bmatrix} 0 & 0 \\ 0 & \mathcal{C}_-^*(\mathcal{C}_-\mathcal{C}_-^*)^{-1}\mathcal{C}_+\mathcal{C}_+^*(\mathcal{C}J\mathcal{C}^*)^{-1}\mathcal{C}_- \end{bmatrix}$$

is positive semidefinite.

Proof. We identify L^2_{M+N} with $\ell^{2+}_{M+N} \oplus \ell^{2+}_{M+N}$ as in the previous theorem. By Theorem 1.3, (PAS4) is equivalent to $P_-(P_{\mathcal{M}_\mathcal{R}} + P_{\alpha+})P_- \geq 0$. To compute $P_{\mathcal{M}_\mathcal{R}} + P_{\alpha+}$, we use

$$\mathcal{M}_\mathcal{R} = \operatorname{Im} \begin{bmatrix} \mathcal{O} \\ J\mathcal{C}^*(\mathcal{C}J\mathcal{C}^*)^{-1}S \end{bmatrix}$$

and $\alpha_+ = (P_+\chi^+ \oplus P_-\chi^+) \boxminus \chi^+$ where

$$P_+\chi^+ \oplus P_-\chi^+ = \operatorname{Im} \mathcal{C}_+^* \oplus \mathcal{C}_-^*$$

and

$$\mathcal{X}^+ = \operatorname{Im} J\mathcal{C}^*.$$

In general, if a subspace $\mathcal{G}$ of a Krein space $\mathcal{K}$ is the image ImX of an injective operator $X: \mathcal{H} \to \mathcal{K}$, then $\mathcal{G}$ is regular if and only if X^*JX is invertible on $\mathcal{H}$, and then the J-orthogonal projection $P_{\mathcal{G}}$ is given by $P_{\mathcal{G}} = X(X^*JX)^{-1}X^*J$. Using this principle, we compute

$$P_{\mathcal{M}_{\mathcal{R}}} = \begin{bmatrix} \mathcal{O} \\ J\mathcal{C}^*(\mathcal{C}J\mathcal{C}^*)^{-1}\mathcal{S} \end{bmatrix} [\mathcal{O}^*J\mathcal{O} + \mathcal{S}^*(\mathcal{C}J\mathcal{C}^*)^{-1}\mathcal{S}]^{-1}[\mathcal{O}^*J, \mathcal{S}^*(\mathcal{C}J\mathcal{C}^*)^{-1}\mathcal{C}]$$

on $\ell^{2+}_{M+N} \oplus \ell^{2+}_{M+N}$

$$P_{P_+\mathcal{X}^+ \oplus P_-\mathcal{X}^+} = \begin{bmatrix} \mathcal{C}_+^*(\mathcal{C}_+\mathcal{C}_+^*)^{-1}\mathcal{C}_+ & 0 \\ 0 & \mathcal{C}_-^*(\mathcal{C}_-\mathcal{C}_-^*)^{-1}\mathcal{C}_- \end{bmatrix}$$

as an operator on $0 \oplus \ell^{2+}_{M+N} \approx \ell^{2+}_M \oplus \ell^{2+}_N$ and

$$P_{\mathcal{X}^+} = J\mathcal{C}^*(\mathcal{C}J\mathcal{C}^*)^{-1}\mathcal{C}$$

as an operator on $0 \oplus \ell^{2+}_{M+N} \approx \ell^{2+}_{M+N}$. We then compute $P_-(P_{\mathcal{M}_{\mathcal{R}}} + P_{\alpha^+})P_- = P_-(P_{\mathcal{M}_{\mathcal{R}}} + P_{P_+\mathcal{X}^+ \oplus P_-\mathcal{X}^+} - P_{\mathcal{X}^+})P_-$ to reach the desired conclusion. □

It is amusing to check that the criterion $Z \geq 0$ in Theorem 5.2 gives the correct answer for the situation of the Nehari problem. In this situation (see [G] or [BR2]) we are given an $M \times N$ matrix function $K(z) = C(z - A)^{-1}B$ with all poles in $\mathcal{D}$, and form

$$L(z) = \begin{bmatrix} I & K(z) \\ 0 & I \end{bmatrix} = \begin{bmatrix} I & 0 \\ 0 & I \end{bmatrix} + \begin{bmatrix} C \\ 0 \end{bmatrix} (z - A)^{-1}[0 \ \ B].$$

We know that (PAS4) in this situation is equivalent to $\|\mathcal{H}_K\| < 1$, where $\mathcal{H}_K: H^2_N \to H^{2\perp}_M$ is the Hankel operator $\mathcal{H}_K f \to P_{H^{2\perp}_M}(Kf)$. In terms of the realization $K(z) = C(z - A)^{-1}B$ and the identifications of $H^{2\perp}_M$ and H^2_N with ℓ^{2+}_M and ℓ^{2+}_N as used above, $\mathcal{H}_K$ is given as the product

$$\mathcal{H}_K = \underline{\mathcal{O}}\,\underline{\mathcal{C}}$$

where

$$\underline{\mathcal{O}} = \operatorname*{col}_{j \geq 0} CA^j : \mathbb{C}^n \to \ell^{2+}_M$$

and

$$\underline{\mathcal{C}} = \operatorname*{row}_{j \geq 0} A^j B : \ell_N^{2+} \to \mathbb{C}^n.$$

Therefore $\|\mathcal{H}_\mathcal{K}\| < 1$ is equivalent to $\mathcal{H}_\mathcal{K}^* \mathcal{H}_\mathcal{K} = \underline{\mathcal{C}}^* \underline{\mathcal{O}}^* \mathcal{O} \underline{\mathcal{C}}$ having all eigenvalues < 1, or equivalently (using $\sigma(AB) \backslash \{0\} = \sigma(BA) \backslash \{0\}$) to $\hat{P}\hat{Q}$ having all eigenvalues < 1 where

$$\hat{P} = \underline{\mathcal{C}}\, \underline{\mathcal{C}}^* = \text{ controllability gramian}$$

and

$$\hat{Q} = \underline{\mathcal{O}}^* \underline{\mathcal{O}} = \text{ observability gramian.}$$

On the other hand we can plug data of this special form into the operator Z in Theorem 5.2. The result collapses to

$$Z = \begin{bmatrix} 0 \\ \underline{\mathcal{C}}^* (\underline{\mathcal{C}}\, \underline{\mathcal{C}}^*)^{-1} \end{bmatrix} (-\hat{Q} + \hat{P}^{-1})^{-1} [0, (\underline{\mathcal{C}}\, \underline{\mathcal{C}}^*)^{-1} \underline{\mathcal{C}}].$$

By the controllability of (A, B), $Z \geq 0$ if and only if $(-\hat{Q} + \hat{P}^{-1})^{-1} \geq 0$, i.e., $\hat{P}^{-1} - \hat{Q} \geq 0$. Conjugating by $\hat{P}^{1/2}$ gives the equivalence of this with

$$I - \hat{P}^{1/2} \hat{Q} \hat{P}^{1/2} \geq 0,$$

i.e., the eigenvalues of $\hat{P}^{1/2} \hat{Q} \hat{P}^{1/2}$ must be < 1. Again since in general $\sigma(AB) \backslash \{0\} = \sigma(BA) \backslash \{0\}$, we get that this is equivalent to all eigenvalues of $\hat{P}\hat{Q}$ being < 1, as it should be. We thus see that Theorem 5.2 does give a somewhat (complicated) generalization of known results on the Nehari problem to a more general situation.

References

[AD1] D. Alpay and H. Dym, Hilbert spaces of analytic functions inverse scattering, and operator models I, Integral Equations and Operator theory, **7** (1984), 589–641.

[AD2] D. Alpay and H. Dym, On applications of reproducing kernel spaces to the Schur algorithm J-unitary factorization, in: Methods in Operator Theory and Signal Processing (ed. I. Gohberg), Operator Theory: Advances and Applications, **18** Birkhäuser (Basel), 1986.

[AG] D. Alpay and I. Gohberg, Unitary rational matrix functions and orthogonal matrix polynomials, Integral Equations and Operator Theory, to appear in Operator Theory: Advances and Applications volume, Birkhäuser (Basel).

[BCR] J. A. Ball, N. Cohen and A. C. M. Ran, Inverse spectral problems for regular improper rational matrix functions, to appear in Operator Theory: Advances and Applications volume, Birkhäuser (Basel).

[BGR] J. A. Ball, I. Gohberg and L. Rodman, Interpolation problems for matrix valued functions, Part I: rational functions, monograph in preparation.

[BH1] J. A. Ball and J. W. Helton. A Beurling-Lax Theorem for the Lie group $U(m, n)$ which contains most classical interpolation theory, J. Operator Theory, **9** (1983), 107–142.

[BH2] J. A. Ball and J. W. Helton. Interpolation problems of Pick-Nevanlinna and Loewner types for meromorphic matrix functions: parametrization of the set of all solutions, Integral Equations and Operator Theory, **9** (1986), 155–203.

[BH3] J. A. Ball and J. W. Helton, Lie groups over the field of rational functions, signed spectral factorization, signed interpolation, and amplifier design, J. Operator Theory, **8** (1982), 19–64.

[BH4] J. A. Ball and J. W. Helton. Beurling-Lax representations using classical Lie groups with many applications III: groups preserving forms, Amer. J. Math., **108** (1986), 95–174.

[BR1] J. A. Ball and A. C. M. Ran. Local inverse spectral problems for rational matrix functions, Integral Equations and Operator Theory, **10** (1987), 349–415.

[BR2] J. A. Ball and A. C. M. Ran. Global inverse spectral problems for rational matrix functions, Lin. Alg. and Appl., **86** (1987), 237–282.

[F1] I. I. Fedchin, Description of solutions of the tangential Nevanlinna-Pick problem, Akad. Nauk. Armjan. SSR. Dokl., **60:1** (1975), 37–42 (in Russian).

[F2] I. I. Fedchin, Tangential Nevanlinna-Pick problem with multiple points, Akad. Nauk. Armjan. SSR. Dokl., **60:1** (1975), 37–42 (in Russian).

[FF] C. Foias and A. Frazho, On the Schur representation in the commutant lifting theorem, I, Operator Theory, Advances and Applications, Birkhäuser **18** (1986).

[G] K. Glover, All optimal Hankel-norm approximations of linear multivariable systems and their L^{∞}-error bounds, Inter. J. Control, **39** (1984), 1115–1193.

[GK] I. Gohberg and M. A. Kaashoek, An inverse spectral problem for rational matrix functions and minimal divisibility, Integral Equations and Operator Theory, **10** (1987), 437–465.

[GKLR] I. Gohberg, M. A. Kaashoek, L. Lerer and L. Rodman, Minimal divisors of rational matrix functions with prescribed zero and pole struture, in Topics in Operator Theory Systems and Networks, (ed. H. Dym and I. Gohberg), **OT 12** Birkhäuser (Basel) (1983), 241–275.

[Ka] T. Kailath, *Linear Systems*, Prentice Hall, Engelwood Cliffs, New Jersey, 1980.

[Ki] H. Kimura, Directional interpolation in the state space, Lecture presented at SIAM Workshop on Linear Systems and Signal Processing, Stanford University, September 1987.

[LA] D. J. N. Limebeer and B.D. O. Anderson, An interpolation theory approach to H^∞ controller degree bounds, Lin. Alg. and Appl., to appear.

[N] A. A. Nudelman, On a new problem of moment problem type, Soviet Math. Doklady, **18** (1977), 507–510 [Doklady Akademii Nauk SSSR (1977)].

Joseph A. Ball
Department of Mathematics
Virginia Tech
Blacksburg, Virginia 24061

J. William Helton
Department of Mathematics
University of California, San Diego
La Jolla, California 92093

Operator Theory:
Advances and Applications, Vol. 35

TOEPLITZ OPERATORS ON MULTIPLY CONNECTED DOMAINS AND THETA FUNCTIONS

Kevin F. Clancey

The Fredholm spectral picture of Toeplitz operators acting on the least harmonic majorant Hardy space of a multiply connected planar domain as described by M.B. Abrahamse is refined. This is accomplished by viewing the planar domain as a domain on its double and applying the methods of Hilbert barrier problems associated with divisors as developed by R.N. Abdulaev, N. Koppelman, Yu.L. Rodin and E.I. Zverovich. In essence the results on barrier problems are obtained by reducing to the classical Riemann-Roch Theorem and the Riemann Singularity Theorem for theta functions. The barrier problems encountered are associated with the critical Green's divisor and the results are considerably enhanced by the work on theta functions by J.D. Fay.

0. INTRODUCTION

Let D be a bounded multiply connected planar domain having g holes. It is assumed the positively oriented boundary ∂D is the union $\partial D = b_0 \cup b_1 \cup \dots \cup b_g$ of finitely many simple closed disjoint analytic curves $b_0, b_1, \dots, b_g$, with b_0 the boundary of the unbounded component and $b_1, \dots, b_g$ the (negatively oriented) boundaries of the g holes. Fix a point q_0 in D and let m_0 denote harmonic measure on ∂D based at q_0. The least harmonic majorant Hardy space of D based at q_0 is the space $H^2(m_0)$ consisting of the closure in $L^2(m_0)$ of functions analytic on a neighborhood of $\overline{D} = D \cup \partial D$. For a continuous function on ∂D one defines the Toeplitz operator T_a on $H^2(m_0)$ by $T_a f = Paf$.

---

[1]The author was supported by a grant from the National Science Foundation.

There have been extensive investigations of Toeplitz operators on $H^2(m_0)$ for the case when D is the unit disc $\mathbb{D} = \{z: |z| < 1\}$. See, e.g., the bibliographies of Douglas [8,9]. The basics of spectral theory for Toeplitz operators on multiply connected domains have been developed by Abrahamse [3,4].

In this report we will focus on the following phenomena noted by Abrahamse [4]. Unlike the case of genus zero (D - simply connected), a Fredholm Toeplitz operator of index zero on a multiply connected domain can have kernel.

We expand on this last statement. If a is continuous on ∂D, then the Toeplitz operator T_a on $H^2(m_0)$ is a Fredholm operator if and only if a doesn't vanish on ∂D and, moreover, in this case the Fredholm index $\text{ind}\, T_a$ of the operator T_a is minus the winding number $j(a) = \frac{1}{2\pi} \sum_{j=0}^{g} \text{Var}_{b_j}(\arg a)$ of the symbol a. This result is due to Abrahamse [4].

In the classical case where D is the unit disc there is a well known alternative of Coburn [7] that states for a non-zero a in $L^\infty(m_0)$ either the kernel of T_a or the kernel of T_a^* is trivial. (This result was noted earlier when a is a non-vanishing continuous function. See, the remarks in Gohberg and Krupnik [13, Chap VII].) In contrast, to this on multiply connected domains Abrahamse [4] provides examples of Fredholm Toeplitz operators of index zero which have non-trivial kernels.

The point of this paper is to outline a method for studying this Fredholm kernel phenomena. Roughly the method goes as follows: Consider the domain D as a domain on its Schottky double X. (The double X (defined below) of a planar domain with g holes is a compact Riemann surface of genus g on which one has a anti-conformal reflection $J: X \to X$.) The orthogonal decomposition $L^2(m_0) = H^2(m_0) \oplus [H^2(m_0)]^\perp$ has a natural function theoretic explanation on the double involving non-tangential limits of analytic functions on D for $H^2(m_0)$ and non-tangential limits of meromorphic functions on the "reflection" $JD = X - (D \cup \partial D)$ for $[H^2(m_0)]^\perp$. See, Heins [14,15]. The meromorphic functions on JD occuring in this orthogonal decomposition must vanish at Jq_0 and can only have poles at the the reflection of the critical points of the Green's function $G(\cdot,q_0)$ for D based at q_0. Thus the Toeplitz equation $T_a f = 0$ is easily reduced to a Hilbert barrier problem on X having the form

$$(0.1) \qquad a\phi_+ = \phi_- \ , \quad (\phi) + J\mathcal{D}_{c.v.} \geq 0 \ .$$

The solution space of this barrier problem consists of all sectionally meromorphic functions on $X - \partial D$ whose non-tangential limits ϕ_+ (from inside D) and ϕ_- (from inside JD) satisfy (0.1) on ∂D and whose (pole-zero) divisor (ϕ) on $X - \partial D$ satisfies $(\phi) + J\mathcal{D}_{c.v.} \geq 0$, where $\mathcal{D}_{c.v.} = p_1 + \ldots + p_g - q_0$ is the critical Green's divisor.

Barrier problems of the form (0.1) on compact Riemann surfaces have been studied in considerable detail. An expository account of these barrier problems is given in Zverovich [33]. The Fredholm and index theory for such barrier problems was given by Koppelman [16,17] and Rodin [24]. Criteria for non-trivial solutions of (0.1) are due to Abdulaev [1,2] and Zverovich [33]. Indeed, the multiplicative Cauchy kernel on a compact Riemann surface allows one to easily reduce (0.1) to a global meromorphic function problem whose index is given by the classical Riemann-Roch formula and dimension of the solution space is fully explained by the remarkable Riemann Singularity Theorem. We have included a streamlined version of the results on the Hilbert barrier problem (0.1) that have been obtained by the above cited authors.

We close the introduction with the statements of two typical results which will be proved using the above methods.

THEOREM 0.1 *Let* X *be the Schottky double of the planar domain* D *with canonical homology basis* $a_1,\ldots,a_g$: $b_1,\ldots,b_g$. *Let* $\vec{dw} = (dw_1,\ldots,dw_g)^t$, *where* $dw_1,\ldots,dw_g$ *is a dual basis of holomorphic one forms. Let* ξ_0: $\mathrm{Div}(X) \to \mathrm{Jac}(X)$ *be the Abel-Jacobi map (based at* $p_0 \in b_0$) *from the divisor group of* X *to the Jacobian variety* $\mathrm{Jac}(X) = \mathbb{C}^g/\mathbb{Z}^g + \tau\mathbb{Z}^g$, *here* $\tau = [\int_{b_j} dw_i]$ *is the Riemann period matrix. If* a *is a non-vanishing Hölder continuous function on* ∂D *with zero winding number on each component of* ∂D *, then the (Fredholm) Toeplitz operator* T_a *has a non trivial kernel if and only if*

$$\xi_0(\mathcal{D}_{c.v.}) - \left[\frac{1}{2\pi i}\int_{\partial D} \log a \, d\vec{w}\right] + [\Delta_0] \tag{0.2}$$

is a zero of Riemann's θ*-function* $\theta(z,\tau)$ *, where* $\mathcal{D}_{c.v.}$ *is the critical divisor of the Green's function for* D *having pole at* q_0 *, and* Δ_0 *is the vector of Riemann constants.*

It should be noted that in (0.2), $[\underline{z}]$ denotes the equivalence class of $\underline{z} = (z_1,\ldots,z_g)^t$ in $\mathbb{C}^g$ modulo the period lattice $\mathbb{Z}^g + \tau\mathbb{Z}^g$, i.e., $[\underline{z}]$ is a point in Jac(X) . Further, the location of $\xi_0(\mathcal{D}_{c.v.})$ in the Jacobian variety is given implicitly by Fay [11] (see, below) and the value $[\Delta_0]$ depends only on the base point p_0 and the fixed homology basis for X . Also it is interesting to observe that, unlike the case of genus zero, the question of when T_a has a non-trivial kernel depends on the base point q_0 .

The alternative of Coburn mentioned earlier can be generalized to multiply connected domains as follows:

PROPOSITION 0.1. *Let* a *be a non-vanishing Hölder continuous function on the boundary of the g-holed planar domain* D *and* T_a *the corresponding Toeplitz operator on* $H^2(m_0)$. *One of the following three alternatives holds. Either,*

(i) dim Ker $T_a = 0$ *and* dim Ker $T_a^* = j(a)$ *, or*

(ii) dim Ker $T_a^* = 0$ *and* dim Ker $T_a = -j(a)$ *, or*

(iii) $0 <$ dim Ker $T_a \le g$, $0 <$ dim Ker $T_a^* \le g$ *and* $0 \le |j(a)| \le g - 1$ *, with* $j(a) =$ dim Ker $T_a -$ dim Ker T_a^* .

Note that in case $|j(a)| \ge g$, the usual Coburn alternative holds.

The remainder of this paper is structured as follows. Section 1 contains capsulated preliminaries from the theory of compact Riemann surfaces. Section 2 gives the details of the theory of Hilbert barrier problems for a regular domain on a compact Riemann surface. Proofs are given in Section 2 to indicate how the multiplicative Cauchy kernel can be used to easily reduce the analysis of such barrier problems to the classic work of Riemann. Section 3 contains a discussion of the symmetric function theory of Schottky double of a planar domain. Section 4 applies the results in Sections 2 and 3 to Toeplitz operators on multiply connected domains. The results formulated above as Theorem 0.1, Proposition 0.1 as well as related results are proved in this final section.

1. NOTATIONS AND CONVENTIONS.

It is necessary to set up and review some standard notations and conventions from the theory of Riemann surfaces. Further explanation of this theory can be found in Farkas and Kra [10], Schiffer and Spencer [27] and Springer [24].

In Section 3 much of this material is specialized to the case where X is the double of a planar domain.

1.1. Let X be a compact Riemann surface of genus g. The notation $\eta_1 = a_1, \dots, \eta_g = a_g$; $\eta_{g+1} = b_1, \dots, \eta_{2g} = b_g$ will be used for a fixed system of closed curves that form a canonical homology basis for X. Thus the $2g \times 2g$ intersection matrix $[\eta_i \cdot \eta_j]$ has the block form $\begin{bmatrix} 0 & I \\ -I & 0 \end{bmatrix}$.

Let $\Omega(X)$ denote the vector space of holomorphic one forms on X. There is a unique basis $dw_1, \dots, dw_g$ for $\Omega(X)$ which is dual to the fixed homology basis subject to the normalization

$$(1.1) \qquad [\int_{a_1} d\vec{w}, \dots, \int_{a_g} d\vec{w} \; ; \int_{b_1} d\vec{w}, \dots, \int_{b_g} d\vec{w}] = [I;\tau]$$

of the $g \times 2g$ Riemann period matrix, here $d\vec{w} = (dw_1, \dots, dw_g)^t$. It is a consequence of Riemann's bilinear relations that the matrix τ in (1.1) belongs to $\mathcal{H}_g$, the Siegel upper half-space of genus g. Recall $\mathcal{H}_g$ denotes the set of complex $g \times g$ symmetric matrices with positive definite imaginary parts.

1.2 The notation Div(X) will be used for the divisor group on X . The typical element $\mathcal{D}$ in Div(X) is a finite sum $\mathcal{D} = \sum_{p \in X} n_p p$, where n_p is in $\mathbb{Z}$. Addition and comparison of divisors is done pointwise and the degree of $\mathcal{D}$ is the integer $\deg \mathcal{D} = \Sigma n_p$. The notation 0 is used for the divisor of a (non-zero) constant function. Given an element f in the space $\mathcal{M}(X)$ of meromorphic functions on X , then f has a well defined order $\mathrm{ord}_p(f)$ at each p in X . The divisor of f is $(f) = \Sigma \mathrm{ord}_p(f)p$ and is called a principal divisor. The quotient group $\mathrm{Div}(X)/\mathrm{Div}_*(X)$ of divisors modulo the subgroup $\mathrm{Div}_*(X)$ of principal divisors is called the divisor class group. Two divisors $\mathcal{D}_1$ and $\mathcal{D}_2$ (necessarily of the same degree) are called equivalent in case $D_1 = D_2 + (f)$ for some meromorphic function f .

An element dw in the space $\mathcal{M}^{(1)}(X)$ of meromorphic differentials has a well defined order $\mathrm{ord}_p(dw)$ at each point p in X . In fact, $\mathrm{ord}_p(dw) = \mathrm{ord}_p(f)$, where $dw = f(z)dz$ in local coordinates (z,U) at p in U . The divisor of a non-zero differential dw is $(dw) = \sum_{p \in X} \mathrm{ord}_p(dw)p$ and called a canonical divisor. Since for any two non-zero elements dw_1, dw_2 in $\mathcal{M}^{(1)}(X)$, $f = \frac{dw_1}{dw_2}$ is in $\mathcal{M}(X)$, then all canonical divisors are equivalent. The notation K_X will be used for the divisor class of the meromorphic differentials. The class K_X is called the canonical class. The degree of a canonical divisor is $2g - 2$.

1.3 For $\mathcal{D}$ a divisor we will use the standard notations

$$L(\mathcal{D}) = \{f \in \mathcal{M}(X) : (f) + \mathcal{D} \geq 0\}$$

and

$$(dw) = \{dw \in \mathcal{M}^{(1)}(X) : (dw) - \mathcal{D} \geq 0\} .$$

The spaces $L(\mathcal{D})$ and $\Omega(\mathcal{D})$ are finite dimensional vector spaces over $\mathbb{C}$ and we write $l(\mathcal{D}) = \dim_{\mathbb{C}} L(\mathcal{D})$, $i(\mathcal{D}) = \dim_{\mathbb{C}} \Omega(\mathcal{D})$. Of course, $l(\mathcal{D})$ and $i(\mathcal{D})$ depend only on the divisor class of $\mathcal{D}$ and $\Omega(\mathcal{D})$ is naturally isomorphic to $L(Z - \mathcal{D})$, where Z is any canonical divisor. It is clear that $l(\mathcal{D}) = 0$ if $\deg \mathcal{D} < 0$ and $i(\mathcal{D}) = 0$ if $\deg \mathcal{D} > 2g - 2$.

The Riemann-Roch theorem says that on a compact Riemann surface of genus g one has the index formula

(1.2) $$l(\mathcal{D}) - i(\mathcal{D}) = \deg \mathcal{D} - g + 1 .$$

1.4 Let $\pi: |\mathcal{M}| \to X$ be the sheaf of meromorphic germs on the compact Riemann surface. A multiple valued meromorphic function on X is a component $\mathfrak{F}$ of the space of germs $|\mathcal{M}|$ such that $\pi: \mathfrak{F} \to X$ is surjective and such that given a curve $c: [0,1] \to X$ and a germ f_0 in $\mathfrak{F}$ over $c(0)$ there is a (necessarily unique) lift $\hat{c}: I \to \mathfrak{F}$ such that $\hat{c}(0) = f_0$. A multiple valued meromorphic function determines through the natural evaluation $ev: |\mathcal{M}| \to \hat{\mathbb{C}}$ a single valued meromorphic function on the Riemann surface $\mathfrak{F}$.

A homomorphism χ from the fundamental group $\pi_1(X)$ to the multiplicative group $\mathbb{C}^* = \mathbb{C} - \{0\}$ is called a character. A multiple valued meromorphic function $\mathfrak{F}$ on X is said to be a multiplicative meromorphic function belonging to a character χ in case given a closed curve $c: I \to X$ the lift $\hat{c}: I \to \mathfrak{F}$ satisfies $\hat{c}(1) = \chi(c)\,\hat{c}(0)$. In other terms the continuation of the germ f_0 in $\pi^{-1}(p) \cap \mathfrak{F}$ along a closed path c beginning and ending at p is the germ $\chi(c)\,f_0$.

We mention the following facts concerning multiplicative meromorphic functions. The order $\mathrm{ord}_p(f)$ of a multiplicative meromorphic function f at each point in the fibre $\pi^{-1}(p) \cap \mathfrak{F}$ over a point p in X is the same. Thus a multiplicative meromorphic has a well defined divisor $(f) = \sum_{p \in X} \mathrm{ord}_p(f)p$. This divisor is of degree zero and every divisor of degree zero is the divisor of some multiplicative meromorphic function belonging to a character $\chi: \pi_1(X) \to \mathbb{C}^*$. In fact, given a divisor $\mathcal{D}$ of degree zero there is a unique (up to a constant factor) multiplicative meromorphic function f belonging to a unique unimodular character with $(f) = \mathcal{D}$. Further given a character $\chi: \pi_1(X) \to \mathbb{C}^*$ there is a multiplicative meromorphic function belonging to χ.

1.5 The period lattice associated with the canonical homology basis in 1.1 is the subset $L(X) = \mathbb{Z}^g + \tau\mathbb{Z}^g$ of $\mathbb{C}^g$. The complex torus $\mathrm{Jac}(X) = \mathbb{C}^g/L(X)$ is called the Jacobian variety of X (associated with the fixed homology basis). The projection of e in $\mathbb{C}^g$ into $\mathrm{Jac}(X)$ will be denoted by $[e]$.

Fix a point p_0 in X. The Abel-Jacobi map (with base point p_0) is the map $\xi_0: X \to \mathrm{Jac}(X)$ defined by $\xi_0(p) = [\int_{p_0}^{p} d\vec{w}]$. The map ξ_0 is extended to elements $\mathcal{D} = \sum_{p\in X} n_p p$ in the divisor group $\mathrm{Div}(X)$ by setting $\xi_0(\mathcal{D}) = \sum_{p\in X} n_p \xi_0(p)$.

The famous theorem of Abel asserts that for divisors $\mathcal{D}_1, \mathcal{D}_2$ of the same degree $\xi_0(\mathcal{D}_1) = \xi_0(\mathcal{D}_2)$ if and only if $\mathcal{D}_1 - \mathcal{D}_2 = (f)$ for some meromorphic function on X. The equally famous theorem of Jacobi asserts that ξ_0 is surjective when restricted to the collection of positive divisors of degree n provided $n \geq g$.

The following multiplicative version of Abel's theorem will be used in the sequel. The theorem appears in Farkas and Kra [10, p. 127]. It is easy to give a proof of this theorem using the Riemann theta function introduced below.

THEOREM 1.1. *Let X be a compact Riemann surface, $a_1,\ldots,a_g$; $b_1,\ldots,b_g$ a fixed canonical homology basis on X, $\mathrm{Jac}(X) = \mathbb{C}^g/\mathbb{Z}^g + \tau\mathbb{Z}^g$ the associated Jacobian variety and $\xi_0: \mathrm{Div}(X) \to \mathrm{Jac}(X)$ the Abel-Jacobi map with base point p_0 in X. Let $\chi_0: \pi_1(X) \to \mathbb{C}^*$ be a character and $\mathcal{D}$ in $\mathrm{Div}(X)$. A necessary and sufficient condition that $\mathcal{D}$ be the divisor of a multiplicative meromorphic function belonging to the character χ_0 is that*

$$\xi_0(\mathcal{D}) = \frac{1}{2\pi i}\left[\sum_{j=1}^{g} (\log \chi_0(b_j)e_j - \log \chi_0(a_j)\tau_j)\right],$$

where $e_1,\ldots,e_g$ *is the standard basis in* $\mathbb{C}^g$ *and* $\tau_1,\ldots,\tau_g$ *are the columns of* τ .

1.6 This paragraph concerns theta functions. Fuller explanation of this material can be found in some of the references cited at the beginning of this section. Further references for this material are Fay [11], Lewittes [18], Mumford [19] and Rauch and Farkas [22].

Given an element τ in the Siegel upper half-space $\mathcal{H}_g$ the Riemann theta function is the entire function defined for z in $\mathbb{C}^g$ by

$$\theta(z,\tau) = \sum_{n\in\mathbb{Z}^g} \exp\{2\pi i(\tfrac{1}{2}\, n^t\tau n + n^t z)\} .$$

Usually in the discussion below τ is fixed (as the "B-period" matrix of a compact Riemann surface), so that, we simply write $\theta(z)$ for $\theta(z,\tau)$.

The theta function has the fundamental quasi-periodicity

$$\theta(z + \mu' + \tau\mu) = \exp\{2\pi i(-\tfrac{1}{2}\,\mu^t\tau\mu - \mu z)\}\,\theta(z)$$

for μ, μ' in $\mathbb{Z}^g$. Note also θ is an even function on $\mathbb{C}^g$.

A consequence of the quasi-periodicity of the function θ is that if $\theta(e) = 0$, then θ vanishes on the coset $[e]$ of e in $\mathbb{C}^g/L$ where L is the lattice $\mathbb{Z}^g + \tau\mathbb{Z}^g$. In particular, if Θ_0 denotes the zero set of θ on $\mathbb{C}^g$, then

$$[\Theta_0] = \{[e] \in \mathbb{C}^g/L\colon\ \theta \equiv 0 \ \text{ on } \ [e]\}$$

is an analytic subset of $\mathbb{C}^g/L$. Similarly, if for $r \geq 0$, Θ_r denotes the subset of $\mathbb{C}^g$ where all partial derivatives of order at most r vanish, then $[\Theta_r]$ equals the set of all $[e]$ in in $\mathbb{C}^g/L$ such that θ vanishes to order r on each representative of $[e]$. Thus $[\Theta_r]$ is an analytic set in $\mathbb{C}^g/L$.

Remarkable theorems of Riemann [23] describe the analytic subsets $[\Theta_r]$ when L is the period lattice of a compact Riemann surface. Let X be a compact Riemann surface with

$d\vec{w} = (dw_1, \ldots, dw_g)^t$ a basis for $\Omega(X)$ normalized so that (1.1) holds relative to the fixed homology basis. Let $\mathrm{Jac}(X)$ be the corresponding Jacobian variety. From this point on we will consider the Riemann theta function $\theta(z) = \theta(z,\tau)$ associated with the period lattice of X. For p_0 fixed in X and e fixed in $\mathbb{C}^g$ consider the multiple valued holomorphic function f defined on X by

$$f(p) = \theta\left(\int_{p_0}^{p} d\vec{w} - e\right) .$$

The function f is not multiplicative, nevertheless, the quasi-periodicity of θ implies that the zero set of f is a well defined subset of X. This zero set has been characterized by Riemann in the following:

THEOREM 1.2. *(Riemann) There is an absolute constant* Δ_0 *in* $\mathbb{C}^g$ *depending only on the base point* p_0 *(and the homology basis) such that for* e *fixed in* $\mathbb{C}^g$ *either* $\theta(\int_{p_0}^{p} d\vec{w} - e)$ *vanishes identically on* X *or has precisely* g *zeros* $P_1, \ldots, P_g$ *such that*

$$\xi_0(P_1 + \ldots + P_g) + [\Delta_0] = [e] .$$

The following celebrated singularity theorem of Riemann gives a remarkable description of the index of divisors of degree $g - 1$.

THEOREM 1.3. *(Riemann). Fix* p_0 *in* X *and for* $r \geq 0$ *let* W_{g-1}^{r} *be the image in* $\mathrm{Jac}(X)$ *under the map* ξ_0 *of the non-negative divisors* $\mathcal{D}$ *of degree* $g - 1$ *with* $l(\mathcal{D}) \geq r + 1$ *. Then*

$$[\Theta_r] = W_{g-1}^{r} + [\Delta_0] ,$$

where Δ_0 *is the Riemann constant with base point* p_0 *.*

COROLLARY 1.1. *Let* $\mathcal{D}$ *be a divisor on* X *of degree* $g - 1$ *and* e *in* $\mathbb{C}^g$ *any representative of* $\xi_0(\mathcal{D}) + [\Delta_0]$ *. The index* $i(\mathcal{D})$ *is the order of the zero of* θ *at* e *. In particular,*

$i(\mathcal{D}) > 1$ *if and only if* e *is in* Θ_1 *, the singular set of* Θ .

REMARK. For latter purposes we mention that the vector Δ_0 of Riemann constants has the explicit form

$$[\Delta_0] = -\left\{\sum_{k=1}^{g} \int_{a_k} \vec{w}_0 dw_k - \frac{1}{2}\tau_{kk}e_k\right\},$$

where $\vec{w}_0(p) = \int_{p_0}^{p} d\vec{w}$ and $e_1,\ldots,e_g$ is the standard basis in $\mathbb{C}^g$.

2. HILBERT BARRIER PROBLEMS

This section contains proofs of the basic results of Koppelman [17], Rodin [24], Abdulaev [1] and Zverovich [33] concerning Hilbert barrier problems on compact Riemann surfaces. The specific factorization theorem (Theorem 2.2) formulated below should be of interest to readers familar with the case of genus zero.

2.1 The barrier problems will be formulated on the boundary of regular regions. A regular region on the compact Riemann surface X is a domain D whose positively oriented boundary Γ is a finite disjoint union $\Gamma = \Gamma_1 \cup \ldots \cup \Gamma_N$ of simple closed analytic curves $\Gamma_1,\ldots,\Gamma_N$ such that D lies on one side of Γ . To say that D lies on one side of Γ means the following: The orientability of X implies that each of the curves Γ_j has a neighborhood U_j such that Γ_j separates $U_j \backslash \Gamma_j$ into two components. The domain D lies on one side of Γ in case D intersects only one of the components of $U_j \backslash \Gamma_j$ for $j = 1,\ldots, N$. The positive orientation of Γ is then the one such that D lies to the left as one proceeds along Γ .

A natural example of a regular region is given by a component of $f^{-1}(\mathbb{D})$, where $f\colon X \to \hat{\mathbb{C}}$ is a meromorphic function that is unbranched over the boundary ∂D of the unit disc $\mathbb{D}$.

It should be noted that the barrier problems discussed below can be formulated in the case of an arbitrary finite disjoint union of oriented simple closed analytic curves. See, e.g., Koppelman [17].

Given a point p in an analytic curve Γ on X , there is a coordinate chart (z,U) defined in a neighborhood U

of p such that z maps $U \cap \Gamma$ to the real axis with $z(p) = 0$. When we speak of a function f on Γ being Hölder continuous at p, we mean that considered as a function on the real axis near zero, the function $f \circ z^{-1}$ is Hölder continuous.

The barrier problems treated here will be assumed to have Hölder continuous coefficients. This is a technical advantage over the general case of continuous coefficients. Much of what is said probably remains true for arbitrary continuous coefficients; however, one would have to consider generalized measurable factorizations to solve barrier problems with continuous coefficients. See, e.g., Gohberg-Krupnik [13] and Clancey-Gohberg [6].

We are now ready to formulate the barrier problems. Assume D is a fixed regular region with boundary Γ. Let $\mathcal{D}$ be a divisor with support, supp $\mathcal{D}$, satisfying $\Gamma \cap \operatorname{supp} \mathcal{D} = \phi$ and let G denote a function which is non-singular and Hölder continuous on Γ.

Homogeneous Hilbert barrier problem: Find the space $L(\mathcal{D}:G)$ of all sectionally meromorphic ϕ in $\mathcal{M}(X-\Gamma)$ which have Hölder continuous extensions ϕ_+ (respectively, ϕ_-) to Γ from inside (respectively, outside) D and solve the barrier problem

$$(2.1) \qquad \phi_+ = G\phi_- \quad \text{on} \quad \Gamma, \quad (\phi) + \mathcal{D} \geq 0 .$$

The classical case of this barrier problem is the case where X is the Riemann sphere with D a bounded domain on $\hat{\mathbb{C}}$ and $\mathcal{D} = -\infty$. This classical barrier problem is studied in detail in Muskhelishvili [20].

We remark that the inhomogeneous problem is formulated as follows. Given a Hölder continuous function h on Γ, find all solutions ϕ in $\mathcal{M}(X-\Gamma)$ possessing Hölder continuous extensions ϕ_+ (respectively, ϕ_-) to Γ from inside (respectively, outside) D and satisfy

$$(2.2) \qquad \phi_+ = G\phi_- + h \quad \text{on} \quad \Gamma, \quad (\phi) + \mathcal{D} \geq 0 .$$

The adjoint of problem (2.1) is for differentials. This problem is formulated as follows:

Homogeneous adjoint Hilbert barrier problem. Find the space $\Omega(\mathcal{D}:G)$ of all sectionally meromorphic differentials $d\psi$ in $\mathcal{M}^{(1)}(X-\Gamma)$ which have Hölder continuous extensions $d\psi_+$ (respectively, $d\psi_-$) to Γ from inside (respectively, outside) D and satisfy

$$d\psi_+ = G^{-1}d\psi_- \quad \text{on} \quad \Gamma\ , \quad (d\psi) - \mathcal{D} \geq 0\ . \tag{2.3}$$

The adjoint problem is a true adjoint of (2.1) in the sense that (2.2) has a solution if and only if $\int_\Gamma h\, d\psi_+ = 0$ for all $d\psi$ in $\Omega(\mathcal{D}:G)$.

Note as in the Riemann-Roch theory there is a natural isomorphism between $L(Z - \mathcal{D}:G^{-1})$ and $\Omega(\mathcal{D}:G)$ which sends f in $L(Z - \mathcal{D}:G^{-1})$ to fdw , where $Z = (dw)$ is a fixed canonical divisor with support disjoint from Γ .

The notations $l(\mathcal{D}:G)$, $i(\mathcal{D}:G)$ will be used for the dimensions of $L(\mathcal{D}:G)$, $\Omega(\mathcal{D}:G)$, respectively. The following theorem describing the index of the Hilbert barrier problem was established independently by Koppelman [17] and Rodin [24].

THEOREM 2.1. *(Koppelman-Rodin). Let* G *be a non-singular Hölder continuous function on the boundary* Γ *of a regular region* D *and* $\mathcal{D}$ *a divisor with* $\Gamma \cap \operatorname{supp} \mathcal{D} = \phi$. *The dimensions* $l(\mathcal{D}:G)$ *and* $i(\mathcal{D}:G)$ *of the solution spaces of the homogeneous Hilbert problem (2.1) and its adjoint (2.3) are related by*

$$l(\mathcal{D}:G) - i(\mathcal{D}:G) = \deg \mathcal{D} + \kappa - g + 1\ , \tag{2.4}$$

where $\kappa = \sum_{j=1}^{N} \operatorname{ind}_{\Gamma_j} G$ *with* $\operatorname{ind}_{\Gamma_j} G$ *denoting the winding number about the origin of the curve* $G \circ \Gamma_j$, $j = 1,\ldots,N$.

Obviously, the choice $G = 1$ on Γ in the Koppelman-Rodin theorem yields the Riemann-Roch theorem. Indeed, Koppelman [17] establishes (2.4) as a consequence of the index theory of one-dimensional singular integral operators on the Riemann sphere and thus gives an independent proof of the classical Riemann-Roch theorem. However, the usual method is to derive (2.4) from the Riemann-Roch theorem. This reduction is sketched below.

2.2 The multiplicative Cauchy kernel. The familiar Cauchy kernel

$$A(z,w)\,dz = \frac{dz}{z - w} \tag{2.5}$$

on the sphere is exploited via the Plemelj-Sokhotskii jump formulae to solve many barrier problems of the form (2.1) and (2.2) on planar domains by factorizing the function G. In this paragraph we note the basic properties of the multiplicative analogue of the Cauchy kernel on a compact Riemann surface of genus $g > 0$. The principal result described below is multiplicative factorization of the symbol G appearing in the problems (2.1) - (2.3).

The basic characteristics of the kernel (2.5) on the Riemann sphere are the following: (i) For w fixed, $w \neq \infty$, $A(z,w)dz$ is a meromorphic differential with divisor $(A(z,w)dz) = -w - \infty$ and $\operatorname{Res}_{z=w} A(z,w)dz = +1$. (ii) For z fixed, $A(z,w)$ is a meromorphic function on the sphere with divisor $(A(z,w)) = \infty - z$.

It is not difficult to generalize the kernel $A(z,w)dz$ to arbitrary compact Riemann surfaces such that (i) holds. For condition (ii) on an arbitrary compact Riemann surface one has two options. The first of these is to allow $A(z,w)$ be multiple valued as a function of w and this leads to the multiplicative Cauchy kernel of Behnke and Stein [5] developed below. The second option is to maintain $A(z,w)$ a meromorphic function and allow the polar divisor of $A(z,w)$ to be increased. This leads to a class of Cauchy kernels $A_{\mathcal{D}}(a,w)dz$ associated with certain minimal divisors $\mathcal{D}$. These Cauchy kernels have been introduced and studied by Behnke-Stein [5], Fay [11], Koppelman [17], Röhrl [25], Tietze [30], Vaccaro [32], Zverovich [33] and others. The kernels $A_{\mathcal{D}}(z,w)dz$ associated with divisors are the key to both explicit solutions of the inhomogeneous barrier problem (2.2) and the theory reproducing kernels on compact Riemann surfaces. Unfortunately, we do not have enough room to discuss the theory of Cauchy kernels associated with divisors. The reader is referred to Žverovich [33] for a relatively complete discussion of Cauchy kernels.

The construction of the multiplicative Cauchy kernel is accomplished (as one would expect) by means of normalized differentials of the third kind. Recall that we have fixed on X a canonical homology bases $a_1,\ldots,a_g$; $b_1,\ldots,b_g$. Now fix w_0 in X . (The role of w_0 is played by ∞ in (2.5).) For $w \neq w_0$ we will use the notation $d\lambda_{w-w_0}$ for the unique meromorphic differential having zero periods along $a_1,\ldots,a_g$ and simple poles at w, w_0 with $\operatorname{Res}_{z=w} d\lambda_{w-w_0}(z) = +1$.

Two basic results concerning the normalized differentials of the third kind are the formulae of Riemann

$$(2.6) \qquad \int_{b_j} d\lambda_{w-w_0} = -2\pi i \int_{w_0}^{w} dw_j \ , \ j = 1,\ldots,g$$

for the "B-periods" and the law of "interchange of argument and parameter"

$$(2.7) \qquad \lambda_{w-w_0}(z) - \lambda_{w-w_0}(z_0) = \lambda_{z-z_0}(w) - \lambda_{z-z_0}(w_0)$$

for appropriate branches of λ_{w-w_0} , λ_{z-z_0} .

It is apparent from (2.6) and (2.7) that

$$(2.8) \qquad A(z,w)dz = d\lambda_{w-w_0}(z)$$

has the following properties:

1. For fixed, $w \neq w_0$, $A(z,w)dz$ is in $\mathcal{M}^{(1)}(X)$ with divisor $(A(z,w)dz) \geq -w - w_0$ and expansion in local coordinates near w of the form

$$(2.9)\qquad A(z,w)\,dz = \frac{dz}{z-w} + dh(z,w) ,$$

where $h = h(z,w)$ is holomorphic at $z = w$.

2. For z fixed $A(z,w)dz$ is an abelian integral in its dependence on w which satisfies

$$(2.10)\qquad \int_{a_j} d_w\, A(z,w)dz = 0 , \quad \int_{b_j} d_w\, A(z,w)dz = 2\pi i dw_j(z) ,$$

$j = 1,\ldots,g$.

The derivation of (2.10) is easily achieved with the aid of (2.6) and (2.7).

The remainder of this subsection will show how the Cauchy kernel (2.8) can be used to produce factorizations relative to the contour Γ of the function G appearing in the barrier problem (2.1). Unlike the classical cases of genus zero, the factorizations relative to a contour developed below are also relative to a (multiplicative) divisor class associated to G.

Before describing precisely the factorization relative to a contour some preliminary material is needed.

Let Γ be the boundary of a regular region D on X and $G = G(t)$ a non-vanishing Hölder continuous function on Γ. Select p_j in the component Γ_j of Γ such that p_j does not belong to the union $a_1 \cup \ldots \cup a_g$, $j = 1,\ldots,N$. (This may require a homotopic deformation of the homology basis.) For $j = 1,\ldots,N$, let $\log_j G$ be a (Hölder) continuous branch of $\log G$ on $\Gamma_j - \{p_j\}$ so that

$$\begin{aligned}\kappa_j &= \frac{1}{2\pi i}\{\log_j G(p_j+) - \log_j G(p_j-)\}\\ &= \operatorname{ind}_{\Gamma_j} G .\end{aligned}$$

We refer to $\mathcal{D}_I = \kappa_1 p_1 + \ldots + \kappa_N p_N$ as the index divisor of G. The notation $\log G$ will be used for the function which agrees on Γ_j with $\log_j G$, $j = 1,\ldots,g$.

Consider the character

$$(2.11)\qquad \chi(a_j) = 1 , \quad \chi(b_j) = e^{\int_\Gamma \log G\, dw_j} , \; j = 1,\ldots,g$$

and let f be a multiplicative meromorphic function belonging to the character χ appearing in (2.11). This function f is not unique but the divisor class of (f) modulo principal divisors is uniquely determined by the character χ. We let $\mathcal{D}_G = \mathcal{D}_I - (f)$. A priori $\mathcal{D}_G$ depends also on $p_1,\ldots,p_g$ and the various branches of $\log G$. We will see below that the divisor class of $\mathcal{D}_G$ depends only on G.

Fix w_0 in $X - (D \cup \Gamma)$ and let $A(z,w)dz$ be the Cauchy kernel defined in (2.8). Set

$$E(w) = \frac{H(w)}{f(w)}, \quad w \notin \Gamma, \tag{2.12}$$

where $H(w)$ is the multiple valued meromorphic function

$$H(w) = \exp\left\{\frac{1}{2\pi i}\int_\Gamma \log G(z)\, A(z,w)dz\right\}.$$

The function $E(w)$ has the following properties:

1°. E is a single valued element in $\mathcal{M}(X - \Gamma)$.

2°. At every z_0 in $\Gamma\text{-supp}(\mathcal{D}_G)$, E has (Hölder) continuous limits $E_+(z_0)$ (respectively, $E_-(z_0)$) from inside (respectively, outside) D which satisfy

$$E_+(z_0) = G(z_0)\, E_-(z_0).$$

3°. Let $\mathcal{D}_G = \sum_{p\in X} n_p p$. For $p \in \Gamma$, $\operatorname{ord}_p E = n_p$ and for $p \in \Gamma$, there is a neighborhood U of p, so that in local coordinates $z: U \to \mathbb{C}$ with $z(p) = 0$

$$|E(z)| = O(|z|^{n_p}) \quad z \in U - \Gamma$$
$$|E_\pm(z)| = O(|z|^{n_p}) \quad z \in \Gamma \cap - \{p\}.$$

The proof of properties 1° - 3° follow from (2.9), (2.10) and the familiar Plemelj-Sokhotskii formulae.

It is natural to make the following definition. Let G be a non-singular Hölder continuous function defined on the boundary

Γ of a regular region D and $\mathcal{D}_0$ an element in $\mathrm{Div}(X)$. The function G is said to admit a factorization relative to the contour Γ and divisor $\mathcal{D}_0 = \sum_{p \in X} n_p p$ in case: (i) On $\Gamma - \operatorname{supp} \mathcal{D}$, $G = E_+ E_-^{-1}$ where E_+ (respectively, E_-) are the Hölder continuous restrictions to $\Gamma - \operatorname{supp}(\mathcal{D}_0)$ of the limiting values of E in $\mathcal{M}(X - \Gamma)$ from inside (respectively, outside) D. (ii) In local coordinates $z\colon U \to \mathbb{C}$ at p in X with $z(p) = 0$, $|E(z)| = O(|z|^{n_p})$, $z \in U - (\Gamma \cup \{p\})$ and $|E_{\pm}(z)| = O(|z|^{n_p})$, $z \in \Gamma \cap U - \{p\}$.

It is clear that if a non-singular function G admits a factorization relative to the contour Γ and divisor class $\mathcal{D}_0$, then it admits a factorization relative to the contour Γ and any divisor $\mathcal{D}_1$ equivalent to $\mathcal{D}_0$. Thus we will say G admits a factorization relative to the contour Γ and divisor class $[\mathcal{D}_0]$ in case G admits a factorization relative to Γ and any divisor equivalent to $\mathcal{D}_0$.

The existence of the function (2.12) satisfying 1° - 3° can be summarized as follows.

THEOREM 2.2. *Let* $G = G(t)$ *be a non-vanishing Hölder continuous function on the boundary* Γ *of a regular region* D. *The function* G *admits factorization relative to the contour* Γ *and divisor class* $[\mathcal{D}_G]$ *of degree* $\mathrm{ind}_\Gamma(G)$, *where the image of* $\mathcal{D}_G$ *under the Abel-Jacobi map is*

$$\xi_0(\mathcal{D}_G) = \xi_0(\mathcal{D}_I) - \frac{1}{2\pi i} \int_\Gamma \log G \, d\vec{w} \, , \tag{2.13}$$

here $\mathcal{D}_I = \kappa_1 p_1 + \ldots + \kappa_N p_N$, $p_i \in \Gamma_i$, *and* $\kappa_i = \mathrm{ind}_{\Gamma_i} G$ *is the index divisor.*

We remark that the divisor class $[\mathcal{D}_G]$ is independent of the base points $p_1, \ldots, p_N$ and the branches of $\log G$ appearing in (2.13). This follows since any second factorization $E'_+ = GE'_-$, where E' is given by (2.12) with a different choice $p'_1, \ldots, p'_N$ of "cut points" on Γ and branches of $\log G$ will satisfy $(E/E')_+ = (E/E')_-$ on Γ and, consequently, the values on the right in (2.13) will be the same when the second set of "cut points" and branches of $\log G$ are used. The equality (2.13) follows directly from Theorem 1.1 in Section 1.

In order that $G = G(t)$ admit the factorization as described in Theorem 2.2 it is necessary that G be Hölder continuous. If G is merely assumed to be continuous on , then to obtain an analogous result the notion of factorization must be "generalized". (See, e.g. Gohberg and Krupnik [13].) Similarly, the hypothesis of Hölder continuity is essential in the following useful lemma from Koppelman [17, p. 259].

LEMMA 2.1. *Suppose* G *is a non-vanishing Holder continuous function on* Γ *and let* ϕ *be a solution of the homogeneous barrier problem (2.1). Given* q *fixed on* Γ *there is a neighborhood* U *of* q *such that in* $U - \Gamma$

$$\phi = Xh ,$$

where h *is holomorphic on* U *and* X *is a non-vanishing holomorphic function on* $U - \Gamma$ *possessing non-vanishing Hölder continuous limits* X_+ *(respectively,* X_-*) on* $U \cap \Gamma$ *from inside (respectively, outside)* D *. In particular, there are only finitely many zeros of* $\phi_\pm$ *on* Γ *and these zeros have a well defined order given by*

$$\mathrm{ord}_q \phi_+ = \mathrm{ord}_q \phi_- = \mathrm{ord}_q h$$

PROOF. Choose a coordinate chart (z,U) at q with the additional property that $\log G$ is single valued on $U \cap \Gamma$ and such that $\mathrm{supp}\, \mathcal{D} \cap U$ is empty. The function G admits the factorization

$$G = X_+ X_-^{-1}$$

on $U \cap \Gamma$, where $X(z) = \exp\left[\frac{1}{2\pi i} \int_{\Gamma\cap U} \log G(t) \frac{dt}{t - z}\right]$. The function X has the required properties. It is clear that given any solution ϕ of (2.1), the function $h = \phi/X$ extends to be holomorphic on $\Gamma \cap U$. The proof is complete.

Let ϕ solve (2.1). For q in ∂D we will let $\mathrm{ord}_q\phi$ denote the common value of $\mathrm{ord}_q\phi_\pm$ as described in Lemma 2.1. It follows easily from Lemma 2.1 and the argument principal that for any solution of (2.1)

$$(2.14) \qquad \sum_{p \in X} \mathrm{ord}_p \phi = \kappa$$

The result in (2.14) can be derived using the factorization result in Theorem 2.2, however, the result is best viewed as a consequence of the argument principle.

2.3 Proof of the Koppelman-Rodin theorem and complementary results. The Koppelman-Rodin theorem can be proved easily using the factorization theorem of the preceding section and the Riemann-Roch theorem. Indeed, let $E_+ = GE_-$ be a factorization of G relative to Γ and the divisor class $[\mathcal{D}_G]$. The map $\phi \to \phi E^{-1}$ is an isomorphism of $L(\mathcal{D}:G)$ onto $L(\mathcal{D} + \mathcal{D}_G)$. Similarly, $\Omega(\mathcal{D}:G)$, which has been noted to be isomorphic to $L(Z - \mathcal{D}:G^{-1})$, is isomorphic to $L(Z - (\mathcal{D} + \mathcal{D}_G))$, for some fixed canonical divisor Z.

The Riemann Roch theorem implies.

$$\begin{aligned} l(\mathcal{D}:G) = l(\mathcal{D} + \mathcal{D}_G) &= \deg \mathcal{D} + \deg \mathcal{D}_G - g + 1 + i(\mathcal{D} + \mathcal{D}_G) \\ &= \deg \mathcal{D} + \kappa - g + 1 + l(Z - (\mathcal{D} + \mathcal{D}_G)) \\ &= \deg \mathcal{D} - \kappa - g + 1 + i(\mathcal{D}:G) . \end{aligned}$$

This is (2.4) and completes the proof of the Koppelman-Rodin theorem.

In the above proof there appears the equality $l(\mathcal{D}:G) = l(\mathcal{D} + \mathcal{D}_G)$ which leads to the following version of results of Abdulaev [1] and Zverovich [33,34].

PROPOSITION 2.1. *The dimension of the solution space of the homogeneous Hilbert barrier problem (2.1) satisfies*

$$l(\mathscr{D}:G) = l(\mathscr{D} + \mathscr{D}_G) .$$

In case $\deg(\mathscr{D}_G + \mathscr{D}) = \kappa + \deg \mathscr{D} = g - 1$ *, then* $l(\mathscr{D}:G)$ *is the order of the zero of the Riemann theta function at any point in*

$$\xi_0(\mathscr{D}_G + \mathscr{D}) + [\Delta_0] = \xi_0(\mathscr{D}) + \xi_0(\mathscr{D}_I) - \left[\frac{1}{2\pi i} \int_\Gamma \log G \, d\vec{w}\right] + [\Delta_0] .$$

In particular, in the interesting case where the component winding numbers $\kappa_j (j = 1,\ldots,g)$ *are all zero and* $\deg \mathscr{D} = g - 1$ *, then* $l(\mathscr{D}:G) = i(\mathscr{D}:G)$ *is the order of the zero of the Riemann theta function at*

$$\xi_0(\mathscr{D}) - \left[\frac{1}{2\pi i} \int_\Gamma \log G \, d\vec{w}\right] + [\Delta_0] .$$

We remark that the isomorphism $L(\mathscr{D}:G) \cong L(\mathscr{D} + \mathscr{D}_G)$ is not given explicitly in Abdulaev [1] or Zverovich [33,34]. The result in Theorem 1 of Zverovich [34] is an immediate consequence of this isomorphism and Abel's theorem.

EXAMPLE: Consider the case where X is the torus $X = \mathbb{C}/(\mathbb{Z} + \tau\mathbb{Z})$, where $\operatorname{Im}\tau > 0$, with fixed homology basis $a_1 = [-1/2, 1/2)$ and b_1 the directed line segment from $-\tau/2$ to $\tau/2$. The normalized basis of $\Omega(X)$ dual to this homology basis is given in local coordinates z by $dw_1 = dz$ and the Abel-Jacobi map with base poin the origin is the identity. Let D be a regular region with boundary Γ (see, e.g., Figure 1) and G a non-vanishing Hölder continuous function on Γ having zero winding number with respect to the origin along any component of Γ .

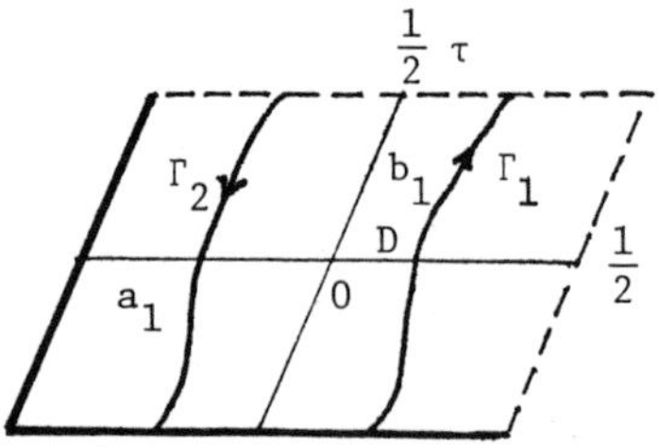

Figure 1

Let $\mathcal{D} = \sum_{j=1}^{k} r_j - \sum_{j=1}^{k} s_j$ be a divisor on X of degree zero. The homogeneous Hilbert barrier problem

$$\phi_+ = G\phi_- \text{ on } \Gamma \text{ , } (\phi) + \mathcal{D} \geq 0$$

has a non-trivial solution if and only if

$$\sum_{j=1}^{k} r_j - \sum_{j=1}^{k} s_j \equiv \frac{1}{2\pi i} \int_\Gamma \log G(z)dz \bmod (\mathbb{Z} + \tau\mathbb{Z}) \text{ .}$$

This follows directly from the identity $l(\mathcal{D}:G) = l(\mathcal{D} + \mathcal{D}_G)$ and the fact that on the torus $l(\mathcal{D} + \mathcal{D}_G) > 0$ if and only if the divisor $\mathcal{D} + \mathcal{D}_G$ is principal. The result in this paragraph is due to Zverovich [34].

As a final remark in this section, we observe that in formulating the barrier problems (2.1) - (2.3) it was assumed that the support of the divisor $\mathcal{D} = \sum_{p \in X} n_p p$ was disjoint from Γ . The results in this section remain valid in case $\operatorname{supp} \mathcal{D} \cap \Gamma$ is non-empty provided solutions ϕ of these barrier problems are assumed to have Holder continuous extensions ϕ_+ (respectively, ϕ_-) from inside (respectively, outside) D such that in a neighborhood U of p in Γ, $|\phi(z)| = O(|z|^{n_p})$ on $U \cap (X - \Gamma)$ and $|\phi_\pm(z)| = O(|z|^{n_p})$ on $\Gamma \cap (U - \{p\})$.

3. THE DOUBLE OF A MULTIPLY CONNECTED DOMAIN.

In this section we will describe the basic properties of the double of a multiply connected planar domain. The double was first introduced by Schottky [28]. References for this material are Fay [11], Heins [14] and Schiffer and Spencer [27].

3.1 Let D be a domain in the complex plane $\mathbb{C}$ whose positively oriented boundary $\Gamma = \partial D$ is a finite disjoint union $\partial D = b_0 \cup b_1 \cup \ldots \cup b_g$ of simple closed oriented analytic curves $b_0, b_1, \ldots, b_g$. The orientation along each of the curves $b_0, b_1, \ldots, b_g$ is the orientation inherited from D. It is assumed that the component b_0 is the boundary of the unbounded component of the complement of D and that $b_1, \ldots, b_g$ bound the g holes of D.

One constructs a compact Riemann surface X called the double of D as follows. Let D' be a second copy of D. As a topological space $X = D \cup \partial D \cup D'$ with D glued to D' along ∂D. On D one takes the usual complex structure and local coordinates of a domain in $\mathbb{C}$. On D' local coordinates are of the form $(\overline{z}, U')$ where (z,U) is a local coordinate for D and U' is the subset of D' corresponding to the subset U of D. Given a point $p_0 \in \partial D$ there is a conformal mapping f of a neighborhood V of p_0 such that $f(p_0) = 0$, $f(V \cap D)$ is contained in the upper half-plane and $f(V \cap \partial D)$ is contained in the real axis. Set $U = V \cap (D \cup \partial D) \cup (V \cap D)'$ and define

$$z(q) = \begin{cases} f(p) & q = p \in V \cap (D \cup \partial D) \\ \overline{f(p)} & q = p' \in (V \cap D)' . \end{cases}$$

The chart (z,U) defines local coordinates at p_0 in ∂D compatible with those complex charts already introduced on $D \cup D'$. In this manner X is given the complex structure of a compact Riemann surface of genus g.

There is a natural anti-conformal involution $J: X \to X$ defined by

$$J(q) = \begin{cases} p' & q = p \in D \\ p & q = p \in \ D \\ p & q = p' \in D' . \end{cases}$$

Clearly J fixes ∂D and interchanges D with D'. The mapping J induces an involution $J: \mathrm{Div}(X) \to \mathrm{Div}(X)$, where for $\mathcal{D} = \sum_{p \in X} n_p p$ in $\mathrm{Div}(X)$, $J\mathcal{D} = \sum_{p \in X} n_p \, Jp$.

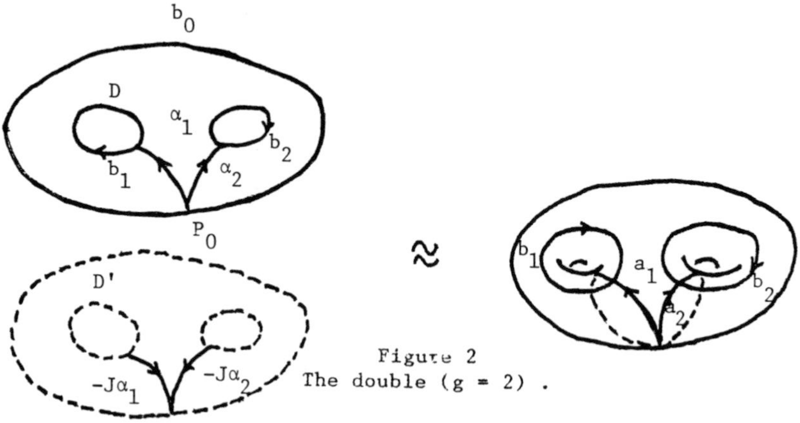

Figure 2
The double ($g = 2$) .

3.2 The curves $b_1,\ldots,b_g$ are completed to a canonical homology basis $a_1,\ldots,a_g;\ b_1,\ldots,b_g$ by choosing crosscuts $\alpha_1,\ldots,\alpha_g$ joining p_0 in b_0 to $b_1,\ldots,b_g$ and setting $a_j = \alpha_j \cup -J\alpha_j$ $j = 1,\ldots,g$, see Fig 2. Note that b_j intersects a_j once from left to right so that the $2g \times 2g$ intersection matrix of the basis $\eta_1 = a_1,\ldots,\eta_g = a_g;\ \eta_{g+1} = b_1,\ldots,\eta_{2g} = b_g$ has the requisite form $\begin{bmatrix} 0 & I_g \\ -I_g & 0 \end{bmatrix}$.

The reader is cautioned that some authors use the components of ∂D as the "A-cycles" in the homology basis (see, e.g. Fay [11], p. 108]). The basis for the space of holomorphic differentials $\Omega(X)$ dual to the above canonical homology basis has a nice description in terms of harmonic measure on D .

For $j = 1,\ldots,g$, let $\omega_j(z)$ be the harmonic measure of b_j based at z in D . Thus ω_j is the solution of the Dirichlet problem $\Delta u = 0$ on D , $u|_{\partial D} = \chi_{b_j}$ where χ_{b_j} denotes the characteristic function of b_j . The function $\tilde{\omega}_j$ extends to be smooth in a neighborhood of ∂D with $d\omega_j = 0$ on ∂D . Recall that $*d\omega_j = d\tilde{\omega}_j$ on D , where $\tilde{\omega}_j$ denotes the multiple-valued harmonic conjugate of ω_j . We remark that also for any ω smooth on a neighborhood of ∂D , $*d\omega = \frac{\partial\omega}{\partial\eta}\,ds$ on ∂D , where $\frac{\partial}{\partial\eta}$ denotes the differentiation in the outward normal direction and ds denotes the element of arclength on ∂D .

Introduce the holomorphic differentials

$$dw_j(q) = \begin{cases} \frac{1}{2}\,[d\omega_j + i{*}d\omega_j](p) & q = p \in D \cup \partial D \\ -\frac{1}{2}\,[d\omega_j - i{*}d\omega_j](p) & q = p' \in D' \end{cases}$$

$j = 1,\dots,g$. The remarks above make it clear that $dw_1,\dots,dw_g$ are elements in $\Omega(X)$. Further

$$\int_{a_j} dw_i = \delta_{ij}\ , \int_{b_j} dw_i = \frac{i}{2}\int_{b_j} {*}d\omega_i = ip_{ij}\ ,$$

where p_{ij} is real $(i,j = 1,\dots,g)$. In particular, the differentials $dw_1,\dots,dw_g$ form a basis of $\Omega(X)$ dual to the homology basis $\eta_1,\dots,\eta_{2g}$.

It is immediate from the above remarks that the $g \times 2g$ Riemann period matrix has the form

$$\left[\int_{\eta_j} dw_i\right] = [I,\ iP] = [I,\tau]\ ,$$

where we have introduced the notation $\tau = iP$. The $g \times g$ symmetric matrix $P = [p_{ij}]$ is real and positive definite. The last fact can be obtained from the general theory of Riemann's period relations (See, e.g. Farkas and Kra [10, p.62]) or by direct verification (See, Nehari [21, p.37 ff]).

The above basis of $\Omega(X)$ has the symmetry

$$J^{*}dw_j = -\overline{dw_j}\ ,\quad j = 1,\dots,g\ .$$

3.3 For the case of the double, with homology basis as described above, the period lattice $L(X) = \mathbb{Z}^g + \tau\mathbb{Z}^g$ is invariant under the anticonformal involution $J\colon \mathbb{C}^g \to \mathbb{C}^g$ defined by $Je = -\bar{e}$. Consequently, $J[e] = [Je]$ is well defined on $\mathrm{Jac}(X)$.

When dealing with the double of a planar domain the base point p_0 for the Abel-Jacobi map $\xi_0\colon X \to \mathrm{Jac}(X)$ will always be chosen in b_0 . This leads to the symmetry

$$\xi_0 J = J\xi_0 \ .$$

The explicit form of the vector of Riemann constants implies the identity

$$J[\Delta_0] = [\Delta_0] \ .$$

The theta function associated with the period lattice of the double of the planar domain has the symmetry $\overline{J^*\theta} = \theta$. In particular, $J[\Theta_0] = [\Theta_0]$.

3.4 Fix a point q_0 in D and denote by $d\Omega_{Jq_0 - q_0}$ the unique meromorphic differential of the third kind having only simple poles at Jq_0, q_0 with residue -1 at q_0 and normalized to have the real parts of all periods zero. Note that

$$J^* d\Omega_{Jq_0 - q_0} = \overline{-d\Omega_{Jq_0 - q_0}} \ .$$

As usual fix p_0 in b_0 . The single valued function defined for p in X by

$$\begin{aligned} G(p,q_0) &= \operatorname{Re} \int_{p_0}^{p} d\Omega_{Jq_0 - q_0} \\ &= \frac{1}{2} \int_{p_0}^{p} (d\Omega_{Jq_0 - q_0} - J^* d\Omega_{Jq_0 - q_0}) \end{aligned}$$

is the Green's function with pole at q_0 . To see that G has the usual properties of the Green's function observe that

$$G(p,q_0) + \log|p - q_0|$$

is harmonic on D . Further, $G(p,q_0)$ is non-negative on D and vanishes on ∂D . This last fact is clear from the definition on b_0 .

From the identity

$$\operatorname{Re} \int_{\alpha_k} d\Omega_{Jq_0-q_0} = \frac{1}{2} \int_{\alpha_k} \left(d\Omega_{Jq_0-q_0} - J^* d\Omega_{Jq_0-q_0} \right)$$
$$= \frac{1}{2} \int_{a_k} d\Omega_{Jq_0-q_0} \; .$$

and the hypothesis $\operatorname{Re} \int_{a_k} d\Omega_{Jq_0-q_0} = 0$ we conclude that $G(p,q_0)$ vanishes on b_k , $k = 1,\ldots,g$.

Note that the last argument shows not only is $\operatorname{Re} \int_{a_k} d\Omega_{Jq_0-q_0} = 0$ but $\int_{a_k} d\Omega_{Jq_0-q_0} = 0$, $k = 1,\ldots,g$. Thus $d\Omega_{Jq_0-q_0}$ is also the unique normalized differential of the third kind with the simple poles at Jq_0 , q_0 , residue -1 at q_0 and having zero "A-periods". In terms of our earlier notation this means $d\Omega_{Jq_0-q_0} = d\lambda_{Jq_0-q_0}$; however, we'll continue to use the notation $d\Omega_{Jq_0-q_0}$ since the requirement here is more appropriately that the real parts of all periods are zero. The completion of the description of the periods of $d\Omega_{Jq_0-q_0}$ follows from the identities

$$\int_{b_k} d\Omega_{Jq_0-q_0} = i \int_{b_k} {}^*dG(p,q_0)$$
$$= i \int_{b_k} \frac{\partial G}{\partial \eta}(p,q_0)\, ds$$
$$= -2\pi i \; \omega_k(q_0) \; ,$$

where ω_k denotes the harmonic measure of b_k , $k = 1,\ldots,g$.

It is important to note that $\frac{\partial G}{\partial \eta} < 0$ on ∂D . This result is seen as follows. If $\frac{\partial G}{\partial \eta}$ were to vanish at some p in ∂D , then since $dG = 0$ on ∂D , the gradient $\vec{\nabla} G$ would vanish at p . Transplanting G via local coordinates at p one obtains a harmonic function u on some disc $|z| < r$ with the following properties (i) $u < 0$ on $\operatorname{Im} z > 0$, (ii) $u = 0$ on $\operatorname{Im} z = 0$ (iii) $u(x,y) = -u(x,-y)$ (iv) $\vec{\nabla} u = 0$ at $z = 0$. The Fourier series of such a u has the form $u(re^{i\theta}) = \sum_{j=k}^{g} u_j r^j \sin(j\theta)$, where $k \geq 2$ and $u_k \neq 0$. Such a series cannot be always negative when $0 < \theta < \pi$. This contradiction shows $\frac{\partial G}{\partial \eta} < 0$ on ∂D . This last argument is from Tsuji [31, p.15].

One consequence of the result in the last paragraph is that the divisor of $d\Omega_{Jq_0 - q_0}$ has the form

$$\left(d\Omega_{Jq_0 - q_0}\right) = \mathcal{D}_{c.v.} + J\mathcal{D}_{c.v.} \,,$$

where $\mathcal{D}_{c.v.} = p_1 + \ldots + p_g - q_0$ is supported in D . The divisor $\mathcal{D}_{c.v.}$ will be called the critical Green's divisor. This is a natural terminology since $p_1, \ldots, p_g$ are the point in D where $\vec{\nabla}G = 0$.

The location of the critical Green's divisor is an important consideration for the spectral picture of Toeplitz operators. Fortunately, Fay [11] has implicitly characterized the value $\xi_0(\mathcal{D}_{c.v.})$. This characterization involves the concept of symmetric definite differentials.

The canonical cocylce $\{g_{\alpha\beta}\} = \{\frac{dz_\alpha}{dz_\beta}\}$ associated with the atlas $\mathcal{A} = \{(z_\alpha, U_\alpha) : \alpha \in A\}$ that has been introduced on the double X has the property that $g_{\alpha\beta}$ is positive on ∂D . Thus a meromorphic differential dw which is real on ∂D has a well defined sign away from the zeros and poles of dw . A differential dw which is real on ∂D will be called definite in case it has constant sign on each component of ∂D .

A meromorphic differential dw on X is called symmetric in case $J^*dw = \overline{dw}$. Clearly a symmetric definite differential is real valued on ∂D away from its poles.

The following characterization of symmetric definite differentials is due to Fay [11, p.118].

PROPOSITION 3.1. *(Fay) The subvariety* $T = \{t \in \mathrm{Jac}(X) : JT = -t\}$ *is a disjoint union*

$$T = \bigcup_{\nu \in \mathbb{Z}^g / 2\mathbb{Z}^g} T_\nu$$

of the 2^g *real g-dimensional torii*

$$T_\nu = \{[z]: \ z = \mu + \frac{1}{2}\tau\nu,\ \mu \in \mathbb{R}^g\} .$$

Each torus T_ν , $\nu = (\nu_1,\ldots,\nu_g) \in \mathbb{Z}^g/2\mathbb{Z}^g$ *consists of all points* $t = \xi_0(\mathscr{D}) + [\Delta_0]$ *with* $\mathscr{D} + J\mathscr{D}$ *the divisor of a symmetric definite meromorphic differential on* X *which is non-negative on* b_0 *and has sign* $(-1)^{\nu_k}$ *on* b_k, $k = 1,\ldots,g$. *The symmetric definite meromorphic differential associated with* t *in* T *is holomorphic if and only if* t *is in* $[\Theta_0] \cap T$.

From the observation that on ∂D , $id\Omega_{Jq_0-q_0} = -{*dG} > 0$ we conclude that $id\Omega_{Jq_0-q_0}$ is a definite symmetric differential. Consequently, by Proposition 3.1, the point $t_{c.v}$ in Jac(X) defined by

$$t_{c.v.} = \xi_0(\mathscr{D}_{c.v.}) + [\Delta_0]$$

is in $T_{0,\ldots,0}$. Moreover, since $T_{0,\ldots,0} \cap [\Theta_0] = \phi$, we have that

$$i(\mathscr{D}_{c.v.}) = 1(\mathscr{D}_{c.v.}) = 0$$

The following result due to Fay [11] characterizes implicitly the critical Green's divisor.

THEOREM 3.1 *(Fay). The critical Green's divisor has the property that* $t_{c.v.} = \xi_0(\mathscr{D}_{c.v.}) + [\Delta_0]$ *is a point in* $T_{0,\ldots,0}$, *where*

$$(3.1) \qquad \frac{d}{dz_j} \log \frac{\theta(z + \vec{\omega}(q_0))}{\theta(z)} = 0 \ , \ j = 1,\ldots,g \ ,$$

here $\vec{\omega}(q_0) = (\omega_1(q_0),\ldots,\omega_g(q_0))^t$ *is the vector of harmonic measures of* $b_1,\ldots,b_g$ *based at* q_0 .

Unfortunately, we cannot include a proof of the result in the last theorem. The general idea of the proof involves two representations of $d\Omega_{Jq_0-q_0} = d\lambda_{Jq_0-q_0}$ in terms of theta functions. The reader will also notice a difference in the formula (3.1) and formula (134) of Fay [11, p.126]. This difference is accounted for by the different choice of the "A-cycles" and normalization of the Riemann period matrix in Fay [11] versus the normalization here.

3.6 For q_0 fixed in D let $H^2 = H^2(D:q_0)$ denote the space of anlytic functions on D for which $|f|^2$ has at least harmonic majorant $u_{|f|^2}$. Endowed with the norm $\|f\| = [u_{|f|^2}(q_0)]^{1/2}$ the space H^2 becomes a Hilbert space which is often called the least harmonic majorant Hardy space. Let m_0 denote harmonic measure on ∂D based at q_0. Each element f in H^2 has non-tangential limits a.e. with respect to m_0 on ∂D. Let f^* denote this non-tangential limit function. The map $f \to f^*$ is an isometric isomorphism between H^2 and the subspace $H^2(m_0)$ of $L^2(m_0)$. (Recall that as noted in the introduction $H^2(m_0)$ is defined the closure in $L^2(m_0)$ of the functions analytic in a neighborhood of $\bar{D} = D \cup \partial D$.)

Note further that the measure dm_0 on ∂D has the alternate descriptions

$$dm_0 = -\frac{1}{2\pi i}\, d\Omega_{Jq_0-q_0} = -\frac{1}{2\pi}\, {*dG} = -\frac{1}{2\pi}\frac{\partial G}{\partial \eta}\, ds ,$$

where as usual $\partial/\partial\eta$ denotes differentiation in the direction of the exterior normal and $G = G(p,q_0)$ is the Green's function with pole at q_0. The space H^2 can also be characterized as the space of analytic functions f on D for which

$$\|f\|^2 = \lim_{\varepsilon \downarrow 0} -\frac{1}{2\pi}\int_{G=\varepsilon} |f|^2\, {*dG} \tag{3.2}$$

is finite. The reproducing kernel for H^2 is given in terms of theta functions on the double in Fay [11, p.126].

Let $\mathcal{D}$ be a divisor in D. The notation $H^2_{\mathcal{D}} = H^2_{\mathcal{D}}(D:q_0)$ will be used for the meromorphic functions f on D with $(f) + \mathcal{D} \geq 0$ such that the norm (3.2) is finite. It is clear that $H^2_{\mathcal{D}} = k\, H^2$, where k is any function meromorphic on a neighborhood of D with divisor $-\mathcal{D}$ on this neighborhood. We denote by $H^2_{\mathcal{D}}(m_0)$ the subspace of $L^2(m_0)$ consisting of the space of non-tangential limit functions from elements in $H^2_{\mathcal{D}}$.

Of course one can contruct spaces analogous to H^2 and $H^2_{\mathcal{D}}$ for the domain $D' = JD$ on X. The easiest way to handle this is to consider the conjugate linear operator R which sends an analytic function f defined on D to the function

$$Rf = \overline{f \circ J}$$

defined on D'. The image of $H^2_{\mathcal{D}}$ under the operator R will be denoted by $K^2_{\mathcal{D}}$. We note that $K^2_{\mathcal{D}}$ is the space of meromorphic g analytic on D'-$\mathrm{supp}(J\mathcal{D})$ with $(g) + J\mathcal{D} \geq 0$ and such that

$$\|g\|^2 = \lim_{\varepsilon \uparrow 0} -\frac{1}{2\pi} \int_{G=\varepsilon} |g|^2 \, {*dG}$$

is finite, where as usual $G(p,q_0) = \mathrm{Re}\,\Omega_{Jq_0 - q_0}(p)$ is the Green's function on X.

The space of non-tangential limits of elements in $K^2_{\mathcal{D}}$ on Γ from outside of D (or inside D') is denoted by $K^2_{\mathcal{D}}(m_0)$ and satisfies $K^2_{\mathcal{D}}(m_0) = \overline{H^2_{\mathcal{D}}(m_0)}$.

The most important divisor for the development here is the critical Green's divisor $\mathcal{D}_{c.v.}$. Note that $\mathcal{D}_{c.v.}$ is the divisor of the function

$$\text{(3.3)} \qquad v = \frac{d}{dz}\, \Omega_{Jq_0 - q_0}$$

on $D \cup \partial D$. Clearly, $H^2_{\mathcal{D}_{c.v.}} = v^{-1} H^2$.

The following decomposition of $L^2(m_0)$ appears in Heins [14,15]. See also Abrahamse [4, Theorem 1.7] and Fisher [12].

PROPOSITION 3.2. *The space* $L^2(m_0)$ *admits the orthogonal decomposition*

$$\begin{aligned} L^2(m_0) &= H^2(m_0) \oplus \overline{v^{-1} H^2(m_0)} \\ &= H^2(m_0) \oplus K^2_{\mathcal{D}_{c.v.}}(m_0) , \end{aligned} \tag{3.4}$$

where v *is the function in (3.3). The above orthogonal decomposition can also be written in the form*

$$L^2(m_0) = H^2(m_0) \oplus \overline{H^2(m_0)} \oplus N \tag{3.5}$$

where N *is the* g *dimensional subspace spanned by the functions* $h_j = \overline{\frac{\partial\omega_j}{\partial\eta}\left\{\frac{\partial G}{\partial\eta}\right\}^{-1}}$, $j = 1,\ldots,g$.

We do not include a proof of this proposition; however, we observe that the decompositions (3.4) - (3.5) are intimately related to barrier problems and the Riemann Roch theorem discussed in the preceding section. It is a consequence of the fact that $i(\mathcal{D}_{c.v.}) = 0$ that the homogeneous barrier problem

$$\phi_+ = \phi_- , \quad (\phi) + J\mathcal{D}_{c.v.} \geq 0$$

and its adjoint

$$d\psi_+ = d\psi_- , \quad (d\psi) - \mathcal{D}_{c.v.} \geq 0$$

have only the trivial solution. Consequently, for every (Hölder) continuous h on $\Gamma = \partial D$ the inhomogeneous barrier problem

$$\phi_+ = \phi_- + h , \quad (\phi) + J\mathcal{D}_{c.v.} \geq 0$$

has a unique solution ϕ in $\mathcal{M}(X - \Gamma)$. The decomposition $f_1 + f_2 = h$, where $f_1 = \phi_+$ is in $H^2(m_0)$ and $f_2 = -\phi_-$ is in $K^2_{\mathcal{D}_{c.v.}}(m_0)$ is the orthogonal decomposition of h which is given in (3.4)

Similarly, the solution space of the homogeneous adjoint barrier problem

$$d\psi_+ = d\psi_- \ , \ (d\ ) \geq 0$$

is clearly $\Omega(X)$ and is spanned by $dw_1,\ldots,dw_g$. Thus $\int_\Gamma h dw_{j+} = -i\int_\Gamma h\bar{h}_j \, dm_0 = 0, j = 1,\ldots,g$ for any Hölder continuous h such that the barrier problem

$$\phi_+ = \phi_- + h \ , \quad (\phi) \geq 0$$

is solvable. This should explain the nature of the orthogonal complement N of $H^2(m_0) \oplus H^2(m_0)$ appearing in (3.5).

We close this section with some remarks related to regularity of solutions of generalized barrier problems.

Using local coordinates one can establish the following continuation results.

(i) Suppose f_1 is in $H^2(m_0)$, f_2 is in $K^2_{\mathcal{D}_{c.v.}}(m_0)$ and $f_1 = f_2$ on some arc γ of ∂D , then f_1 and f_2 are analytic continuations of each other across γ .

(ii) Suppose G is non-singular and holomorphic on an arc γ of D with $f_1 = Gf_2$ for some f_1 in $H^2(m_0)$ and f_2 in $K^2_{\mathcal{D}_{c.v.}}(m_0)$. Then f_1 and f_2 admit analytic continuations across γ .

(iii) Suppose G is non-singular and Holder continuous on D . Then any solution ϕ in $\mathcal{M}(X - \Gamma)$ of the homogeneous barrier problem

$$\phi_+ = G\phi_- \ , \ (\phi) + \mathcal{D}_{c.v.} \geq 0 \ ,$$

where ϕ restricted to D is in $H^2(m_0)$ and ϕ restricted to D' is in $K^2_{\mathcal{D}_{c.v.}}(m_0)$, has Hölder continuous limiting values on ∂D . It follows that ϕ actually belongs to $L(\mathcal{D}_{c.v.} : G)$.

The proof of (iii) in addition to the methods of Clancey and Gohberg [6, Section 2] uses the form of the factorization of

G established in Theorem 2.2 of Section 2.

4. TOEPLITZ OPERATORS ON MULTIPLY CONNECTED DOMAINS

4.1 The earlier established notations and conventions relating to a multiply connected domain D and its double X will be maintained in this section.

For a in $L^\infty(m_0)$ one defines the Toeplitz operator T_a on $H^2(m_0)$ by

$$(4.1) \qquad T_a f = Paf \ , \quad f \in H^2(m_0) \ ,$$

where P denotes the orthogonal projection of $L^2(m_0)$ onto $H^2(m_0)$. Obviously, $T_{\alpha a+\beta b} = \alpha T_a + \beta T_b$, a, b in $L^\infty(m_0)$ and α, β in $\mathbb{C}$. Further, $T_a^* = T_{\bar{a}}$, where the star denotes the Hilbert space adjoint.

The inversion of the operator T_a in (4.1) is a special case of the solution of Hilbert barrier problems on the double of D. In fact, it follows from the orthogonal decomposition (3.4) of Proposition 3.2 that for g in $H^2(m_0)$ equation

$$(4.2) \qquad T_a x = g$$

is solvable if and only if there is a solution ϕ in $\mathfrak{M}(X - \Gamma)$ of the (generalized) barrier equation

$$(4.3) \qquad a\phi_+ = \phi_- + g \ , \ (\phi) + J\mathcal{D}_{c.v.} \geq 0 \ ,$$

where ϕ restricted D is in $H^2(m_0)$, ϕ restricted to D' is in $K^2_{\mathcal{D}_{c.v.}}(m_0)$ and the equality (4.3) holds a.e. with respect to m_0 on $\Gamma = \partial D$. Moreover, given such a solution ϕ of (4.3), then $x = \phi_+$ solves (4.2).

The point is that the Toeplitz operator T_a is related to the barrier problem on the double associated with the specific divisor $J\mathcal{D}_{c.v.}$. The reader should contrast this barrier problem on the double and the familiar analytic barrier problem on the sphere of finding ϕ in $\mathfrak{M}(\hat{\mathbb{C}} - \Gamma)$ solving

$$\alpha\phi_+ = \phi_- + g \, , \ (\phi) - \infty \geq 0 \, . \tag{4.4}$$

The problems (4.4) and (4.3) agree (after a conformal mapping) only when D is simply connected. The barrier problem (4.4) is studied in detail in Muskhelishvili [20].

The connection between least harmonic majorant Toeplitz operators and the barrier problem (4.3) belonging to the critical Green's divisor has not been exploited in earlier works. The principal references on this class of Toeplitz operators are Abrahamse [3,4]. It is interesting to note that the H^p function theory in Abrahamse [4] is the (modulus) automorphic function theory on the universal cover (see, [26].) and the double lurks only in the background. The double has appeared explicitly in other planar barrier problems. See, for example, Zverovich [39; §9-10].

The Fredholm theory of the Toeplitz operators T_a when a is continuous on Γ is completely developed by Abrahamse [4]. It is apparent from the connection between the problems (4.2) and (4.3) that this Fredholm theory also falls out of the general Fredholm theory of barrier operators which was established by Koppelman [17] and Rodin [24] on spaces of Hölder continuous functions and generalized to H^p spaces by Rodin [24] and Abdulaev [2] However, the approach in Abrahamse [4] is a novel C*-approach. For example, among the results established in Abrahamse [4, Theorem 3.1] is an isomorphism of the C*-algebra generated by the operators T_a , a in $L^\infty(m_0)$, modulo compact operators, and the direct sum of the corresponding $g + 1$ C*-algebras on the components $b_0, b_1, \ldots, b_g$ of ∂D .

For a continuous function a on the boundary of D the Toeplitz operator T_a is Fredholm if and only if $a(t) \neq 0$ for t in $\Gamma = \partial D$ and in this case the Fredholm index $i(T_a)$ satisfies

(4.5) $i(T_a) = -j(a)$

See, Abrahamse [4, Theorem 2.15].

In the sequel we will only treat the case where $a(t) \neq 0$ and is Hölder continuous on the boundary of D. In this case (4.5) can be derived as follows:

The equivalence of (4.2) and (4.3) and the final remark in the preceding section imply that the kernel $\text{Ker } T_a$ satisfies

(4.6) $$\dim \text{Ker } T_a = l(J\mathcal{D}_{c.v.} : a^{-1}) .$$

It is convenient to recall the conjugate linear operator $R: \mathcal{M}(X - \Gamma) \to \mathcal{M}(X - \Gamma)$ defined

$$R\phi = \overline{\phi o J} .$$

Note that for G a (Hölder) continuous non-singular function on Γ and $\mathcal{D}$ in $\text{Div}(X)$

(4.7) $$RL(\mathcal{D}:G) = L(J\mathcal{D}:\overline{G}^{-1})$$

Combining (4.6) and (4.7), we obtain

$$\dim \text{Ker } T_a^* = l(\mathcal{D}_{c.v.}:a)$$

and, therefore,

(4.8) $$\dim \text{Ker } T_a = i(J\mathcal{D}_{c.v.} : a^{-1}) .$$

The Koppelman-Rodin result (2.4) yields

$$\begin{aligned} i(T_a) &= \dim \text{Ker } T_a - \dim \text{Ker } T_a^* \\ &= l(J\mathcal{D}_{c.v.} : a^{-1}) - i(J\mathcal{D}_{c.v.} : a^{-1}) \\ &= j(a^{-1}) + \deg(J\mathcal{D}_{c.v.}) - g + 1 \\ &= -j(a) . \end{aligned}$$

The last statement shows how (at least for Hölder continuous symbols) the Koppelman-Rodin theorem implies the index result in (4.5).

4.2 PROOF OF PROPOSITION 0.1. Let a be a non-vanishing Hölder continuous function on ∂D. Using the isomorphism

$$\operatorname{Ker} T_a \cong L(J\mathcal{D}_{c.v.} : a^{-1})$$

and the (conjugate linear) isomorphism

$$\operatorname{Ker} T_a^* \cong L(J\mathcal{D}_{c.v.} : \overline{a}^{-1}) \cong L(\mathcal{D}_{c.v.} : a)$$

one obtains (by multiplication) a bilinear map

$$B : \operatorname{Ker} T_a \times \operatorname{Ker} T_a^* \to L(\mathcal{D}_{c.v.} + J\mathcal{D}_{c.v.}) \cong \Omega(X) .$$

Since, $\dim \Omega(X) = g$ the result in Proposition 0.1 follows easily.

4.3 The following result is a direct consequence of Proposition 2.1 in Section 2.

THEOREM 4.1. *Let a be a non-singular Hölder continuous function on the boundary $\Gamma = \partial D = b_0 \cup b_1 \cup \ldots \cup b_g$ of the multiply connected planar domain D viewed as a domain on its double X, where the canonical homology basis $a_1, \ldots, a_g; b_1, \ldots, b_g$ has been chosen. Fix t_j in b_j and let $\log a$ denote a branch of the logarithm of a which is continuous on each $b_j \backslash \{t_j\}$ with*

$$\kappa_j = \operatorname{ind}_{b_j} a = (2\pi i)^{-1} [\log a(t_j^+) - \log a(t_j^-)] ,$$

$j = 0,1,\ldots,g$. Let $\mathcal{D}_I$ be the divisor $\mathcal{D}_I = \sum_{j=0}^{g} \kappa_j t_j$ and $\zeta_0 : X \to \operatorname{Jac}(X)$ the Abel-Jacobi map based at t_0 into the Jacobian variety $\mathbb{C}^g/\mathbb{Z}^g + \tau\mathbb{Z}^g$ associated with the fixed homology basis. Let $[\mathcal{D}_a]$ be the divisor class given by

$$\xi_0(\mathcal{D}_a) = \xi_0(\mathcal{D}_I) - \left[\frac{1}{2\pi i} \int_\Gamma \log a \, d\vec{w}\right] .$$

The kernel of T_a *satisfies*

$$\dim \operatorname{Ker} T_a = l(J\mathcal{D}_{c.v.} - \mathcal{D}_a) .$$

In case, $\operatorname{ind}_\Gamma a = \deg \mathcal{D}_I = 0$ *, then* $\dim \operatorname{Ker} T_a$ *is the order of the zero of the Riemann theta function* $\theta(z,\tau)$ *at*

$$(4.9) \qquad t_{c.v.} + \xi_0(\mathcal{D}_a) ,$$

where $t_{c.v.} = \xi_0(\mathcal{D}_{c.v.}) + [\Delta_0]$ *is a point in the torus* $T_{0,\dots,0}$ *satisfying (3.1).*

We remark that Theorem 0.1 which was formulated in the introduction is an immediate consequence of Theorem 4.1.

4.4 EXAMPLE. We spell out the above result for the case when D is the annulus

$$D_r = \{z: r < |z| < 1\} ,$$

where $0 < r < 1$. The canonical homology basis on the double X_r will be fixed by choosing a_1 the path consisting of the line segments from 1 to r in D_r and r to 1 in D_r' . The curve b_1 will be the circle $|z| = r$ with the clockwise orientation. The basis of $\Omega(X_r)$ dual to the fixed homology basis $a_1; b_1$ is given in local coordinates by

$$dw_1 = \begin{cases} \dfrac{1}{2\log r} \dfrac{dz}{z} & \text{on } D_r \\ -\dfrac{1}{2\log r} \dfrac{d\bar{z}}{\bar{z}} & \text{on } D_r' . \end{cases}$$

The periods of dw_1 are

$$\int_{a_1} dw_1 = 1 ; \int_{b_1} dw_1 = \frac{\pi i}{-\log r} .$$

Set $\tau = \pi i/(-\log r)$. The Abel-Jacobi map ξ_0 is a conformal iromorphism of X_r onto the torus $\mathbb{C}/(\mathbb{Z} + \tau\mathbb{Z})$ and with base point $p_0 = 1$ is given explicitly by

$$\xi_0(p) = \begin{cases} \left[\dfrac{\log z}{2 \log r}\right] & p = z \quad \text{in} \quad D_r \cup \partial D_r \\ \left[\dfrac{-\log z}{2 \log r}\right] & p = z' \quad \text{in} \quad D_r' . \end{cases}$$

Without loss of generality it can be assumed that the pole q_0 of the Green's function is in the interval $(r,1)$ on the real axis. (Otherwise q_0 can be rotated to this interval by a conformal automorphism of D_r .)

The critical divisor of the Green's function $G(p; q_0)$ has the form $\mathcal{D}_{c.v.} = p_1 - q_0$ and $t_{c.v.} = \xi_0(\mathcal{D}_{c.v.}) + [\Delta_0]$ is in the torus $T_0 = \{[\mu]: \mu \in \mathbb{R}\}$. The Riemann constant Δ_0 has the explicit form $[\Delta_0] = [-\frac{1}{2} + \frac{1}{2}\tau]$. (This value $-\frac{1}{2} + \frac{1}{2}\tau$ of Δ_0 , can be computed from the form of Δ_0 given in Section 1.) It follows that $\operatorname{Im} \xi_0(\mathcal{D}_{c.v.}) = [\frac{1}{2 \log r} (\arg p_1 - \arg q_0)] = [\frac{1}{2} \tau]$. Thus $\arg p_1 - \arg q_0 \equiv \pi \bmod(2\pi\mathbb{Z})$. This says that the point p_1 lies in the interval $(-1, -r)$.

Let $e = \frac{1}{2} + \frac{1}{2}\tau$. The value e is the only zero of $\theta(z,\tau)$ in the fundamental parallelogram and has multiplicity one. The Green's function is given in terms of the function $\theta(z) = \theta(z,\tau)$ by the formula

$$\text{(4.10)} \qquad d\Omega_{Jq_0-q_0}(p) = d \log \left[\frac{\theta(\int_1^p dw_1 + \lambda + e)}{\theta(\int_1^p dw_1 - \lambda + e)}\right],$$

where $\lambda = \log |q_0|/2 \log r$ and the integral $\int_1^p dw_1$ is taken along the same path in both occurences.

It follows from (4.10) that

$$t_{c.v.} = \left[\frac{1}{2 \log r} \log \left(\frac{|p_1|}{|q_0|}\right)\right]$$

is a solution of

$$\text{(4.11)} \qquad \frac{d}{dt} \log \frac{\theta(t + w(q_0))}{\theta(t)} = 0$$

in T_0 , here $w(q_0) = 2\lambda = \log q_0 / \log r$ is the harmonic measure of b_1 based at q_0 . Of course, the last fact is also a special case of Fay's result in Theorem 3.1.

Let a be a nonvanishing (Hölder) continuous function on the boundary of D_r . For simplicity, it will be assumed that the component indices $\kappa_j = \mathrm{ind}_{b_j}(a)$ $(j = 0, 1)$ are zero. It was established in Theorem 4.1 that $\dim \mathrm{Ker}\, T_a = 1(J\mathcal{D}_{c.v.} - \mathcal{D}_a)$, where $\mathcal{D}_a$ is the divisor class given by $\xi_0(\mathcal{D}_a) =$ $[-\frac{1}{2\pi i}\int_\Gamma \log a \, dw_1]$.

It follows that $\dim \mathrm{Ker}\, T_a$ is non-zero if and only if $\xi_0(J\mathcal{D}_{c.v.} - \mathcal{D}_a) = 0$. Since $J(\xi_0(\mathcal{D}_{c.v.}) + [\Delta_0]) =$ $-(\xi_0(\mathcal{D}_{c.v.}) + [\Delta_0])$ and $[-2\,\Delta_0] = 0$, then $\xi_0(J\mathcal{D}_{c.v.} - \mathcal{D}_a) = 0$ if and only if $\xi_0(\mathcal{D}_{c.v.}) + \xi_0(\mathcal{D}_a) = 0$.

It is now easy to establish the following:

COROLLARY 4.1. *Let* a *be a nonvanishing (Hölder) continuous function on the boundary of the annulus* $D_r =$ $\{z: r < |z| < 1\}$ *which has zero index on the circles* $|z| = 1$ *and* $|z| = r$. *The Toeplitz operator* T_a *on the least harmonic majorant Hardy space* $H^2(m_0)$ *has a non-trivial kernel if and only if*

$$(4.12)\qquad \frac{1}{2\pi}\int_0^{2\pi} \log a(e^{i\theta})\,d\theta - \frac{1}{2\pi}\int_0^{2\pi} \log a(re^{i\theta})\,d\theta = \left(\log \frac{|p_1|}{|q_0|} - \pi i\right) \mathrm{mod}(2 \log r\,\mathbb{Z} + 2\pi i\mathbb{Z}) ,$$

where p_1 *is the critical value of the Green's function* $G(p; q_0)$ *The value* p_1 *is given implicitly by the fact that*

$\frac{1}{2 \log r} \log \frac{|p_1|}{|q_0|}$ *is a solution of (4.11).*

Let us consider the case where the symbol a of the Toeplitz operator T_a is a constant α on $|z| = 1$ and the constant $\beta(\beta \neq \alpha)$ on $|z| = r$. It follows from (4.12) that the eigenvalues of T_a consist of the sequence

$$\lambda_k = \frac{q_0\alpha - p_1\beta r^{2k}}{q_0 - p_1 r^{2k}}, \ k \in \mathbb{Z} ,$$

where p_1 is the critical value of the Green's function. Each of these eigenvalues is simple and the only other points in the spectrum are the limit points α, β of the sequence $\{\lambda_k\}_{k=-\infty}^{\infty}$. It is interesting to note that (unlike the case of the unit disc) the spectrum of T_a depends on the pole of the Green's function. This phenomena is related to the fact that the conformal automorphism group of the annulus is not transitive.

4.5 The Toeplitz operator T_a is self-adjoint if and only if the symbol a is real valued. The extra symmetry of the self-adjoint case pairs up nicely with the result of Fay in Proposition 3.1 describing the symmetric definite meromorphic differentials on the double.

In fact, let a be a non-vanishing Hölder continuous real valued function on the boundary of D. As observed above there is an isomorphism between $\text{Ker } T_a$ and $L(JD_{c.v.} : a^{-1})$. Suppose $\text{Ker } T_a$ is non-empty. Then there is a non-zero element ϕ in $L(J\mathcal{D}_{c.v.} : a^{-1})$. It follows from (2.14) that

$$\sum_{p\in X} \text{ord}_p(\phi)p + J\mathcal{D}_{c.v.} = R_1 + \ldots + R_{g-1}$$

for some $R_1,\ldots,R_{g-1}$ in X.

The function $R\phi = \overline{\phi o J}$ is in $L(\mathcal{D}_{c.v.} : a)$ and, consequently,

$$dw = i\phi R\phi \, d\Omega_{Jq_0 - q_0}$$

is an element in $\mathcal{M}^{(1)}(X)$. The differential dw on the boundary of D has the form

$$\begin{aligned} dw &= \phi_+(R\phi)_+ \ (-{*}dG) \\ &= a^{-1} \ |\phi_+|^2 \ (-{*}dG) . \end{aligned}$$

Thus dw is a symmetric definite differential with sign equal to $\operatorname{sgn} a$ on the boundary of D. Of course, the function $\operatorname{sgn} a$ is a constant $(-1)^{\nu_j}$, $\nu_j = 0$ or 1 on each component b_j $(j=0,1,\ldots,g)$ of the boundary of D. If necessary, we can multiply a by -1 to arrange that a be positive on b_0. With this convention it follows from Proposition 3.1 that

$$(dw) = \mathcal{D} + J\mathcal{D} ,$$

where $\mathcal{D} = R_1+\ldots+R_{g-1} = \sum_{p\in X} \operatorname{ord}_p(\phi)p + J\mathcal{D}_{c.v.}$, satisfies $\xi_0(\mathcal{D}) + [\Delta_0]$ is in $T_\nu \cap [\Theta_0]$, $\nu = (\nu_1,\ldots,\nu_g)^t$. We have the equality $\xi_0(\mathcal{D}) = -\xi_0((f))$, where f is a multiplicative meromorphic function belonging to the character

$$\chi(a_j) = 1 \; ; \quad \chi(b_j) = \exp(- \int_\Gamma \log a \; dw_j)$$

$j = 1,\ldots,g$. Combining these facts with Theorem 4.1 we obtain the following.

PROPOSITION 4.2. *Let* a *be a non-vanishing real valued Hölder continuous function on the boundary of* D *which is positive on* b_0. *The kernel of the self-adjoint operator* T_a *is non-trivial if and only if*

$$\left[\frac{1}{2\pi i} \int_\Gamma \log a \; d\vec{w}\right] + t_{c.v.} \tag{4.13}$$

is in $T_\nu \cap [\Theta_0]$, *where* $\operatorname{sgn} a = (-1)^{\nu_k}$ *on* $b_k (k = 1,\ldots,g)$ *and* T_ν *is the torus* $T_\nu = \{[z]: \; z = \mu + \frac{1}{2}\tau\nu, \; \mu \in \mathbb{R}^g\}$ *characterized in Proposition 3.1.*

We remark that the fact that $t_{c.v.}$ is in $T_{0,\ldots,0}$ and a direct computation of $\operatorname{Im}[\frac{1}{2\pi i} \int_\Gamma \log a \; d\vec{w}]$ can also be used to show that the expression in (4.13) is in T_ν. However, the argument preceding the statement of Proposition 4.2, shows the direct connection between $\operatorname{Ker} T_a$ and the symmetric definite meromorphic differentials.

REFERENCES

[1] Abdulaev, R.N., On the solvability conditions of the Riemann homogeneous problem on closed Riemann surfaces, Dokl. Adad. Nauk SSSR 152 (1963), 1279-1281.

[2] Abdulaev, R.N., The discontinuous Riemann-Hilbert problem for analytic functions on a Riemann surface, Dokl. Adad. Nauk. SSSR 172 (1967), 751-754 Soviet Math. Dokl. 8 (1967), 144-148.

[3] Abrahamse, M.B., Toeplitz operators in multiply connected regions, Bull. Amer. Math. Soc., 77 (1971), 449-454.

[4] Abrahamse, M.B., Toeplitz operators in multiply connected regions, Amer. Jour. Math., 96 (1974), 261-297.

[5] Behnke, H. and Stein, K., Entwicklung analytischer Functionen auf Riemanschen Flachen , Mat. Ann., 120 (1949), 430-461.

[6] Clancey, K. and Gohberg, I., Local and global factorizations of matrix valued functions, Trans. Amer. Math. Soc., 232 (1977), 155-167.

[7] Coburn, L.A., Weyl's theorem for non-normal operators, Michigan Math. J. 13 (1966), 285-286.

[8] Douglas, R.G., Banach Algebra Techniques in Operator Theory, Academic Press, New York, 1972.

[9] Douglas, R.G., Banach Algebra Techniques in the theory of Toeplitz Operators, C.B.M.S. Regional Conference Series in Mathematics, No. 15, 1972.

[10] Farkas, H.M. and Kra, I., Riemann Surfaces, Springer-Verlag, New York, 1980.

[11] Fay, J.D., Theta Functions on Riemann Surfaces, Lecture Notes in Mathematics No. 352, Springer-Verlag, New York, 1973.

[12] Fisher, S.D., Function Theory on Planar Domains: A Second Course in Complex Analysis, Wiley, New York, 1983.

[13] Gohberg, I. and Krupnik, N.Ya., Introduction to the Theory of One-Dimensional Singular Integral Operators, German transl., Birkhauser Verlag, Basel, 1979.

[14] Heins, M., Hardy Classes on Riemann Surfaces, Lecture Notes in Mathematics, No. 98, Springer-Verlag, New York, 1969.

[15] Heins, M., Symmetric Riemann surfaces and boundary problems, Proc. L.M.S. 3rd ser. 14a (1965), 129-143.

[16] Koppelman, W., The Riemann-Hilbert problem for finite Riemann surfaces, Comm. Pure App. Math. XII (1959), 13-35.

[17] Koppelman, W., Singular integral equations, boundary value problems and the Riemann-Roch theorem, Jour. of Math. and Mechanics, 10 (1961), 247-277.

[18] Lewittes, T., Riemann surfaces and the theta functions, Acta Math., 111 (1964), 37-61.

[19] Mumford, D., Tata Lectures on Theta I, II, Birkhauser Verlag, Basel, 1983.

[20] Muskhelishvili, N.I., Singular Integral Equations, Boundary Problems of Function Theory and their Applications to Mathematical Physics, 2nd ed., Fizmatgiz, Moscow, 1962; English transl. of 1st ed., Noordhoff, Groningen, 1953.

[21] Nehari, Z., Conformal Mapping, McGraw-Hill, New York, 1952.

[22] Rauch, H.E. and Farkas, H.M., Theta Functions with Applications to Riemann Surfaces, Williams and Wilkins; Baltimore, Maryland, 1973.

[23] Riemann, B., Collected Works, Dover, 1953.

[24] Rodin, Yu.L., On the solubility conditions for Riemann's and Hilbert's boundary value problem in Riemann surfaces, Dokl. Adad. Nauk SSSR 129 (1959), 1234-1237.

[25] Röhrl, H., Ω-degenerate singular integral equations and holomorphic affine bundles over compact Riemann surfaces, I., Comment. Math. Helv. 38 (1963), 84-120.

[26] Sarason, D., The H^p spaces of an annulus, Memoirs Amer. Math. Soc. 56 (1965).

[27] Schiffer, M. and Spencer, D.C., Functionals of Finite Riemann Surfaces, Princeton Univ. Press, Princeton, N.J., 1954.

[28] Schottky, F., Uber die comforme abbildung mehrfach zusammehänzenduebener Flachen, Crelles Journal 83 (1977), 300-351.

[29] Springer, G., Introduction to Riemann Surfaces, Chelsea, New York, 1981.

[30] Tretze, H., Fabersche Entiwicklungen auf geschlossenen Riemanschen Flächen, J. Reine Angew. Math. 190 (1952), 22-33.

[31] Tsuji, M., Potential Theory in Modern Function Theory, Maruzen, Tokyo, 1959.

[32] Vaccaro, M., Sui funzionali analitici lineari definiti per le funzioni analitici uniformi sopra una curva algebrica, Ann. Scuola Norm. Sup. Pisa V., series 3a (1951), 39-59.

[33] Zverovich, E.I., Boundary value problems in the theory of analytic functions in Hölder classes on Riemann surfaces, Russian Mathematical Surveys, 26 (1971), 117-192.

[34] Zverovich, E.I., The Behnke-Stein kernel and a solution in closed form of Riemann's boundary value problem on the torus, Dokl. Adad. Nauk SSSR 188 (1969), 27-30 ≡ Soviet Math. Doklady 10 (1969), 1064-1068.

Department of Mathematics
University of Georgia
Athens, Georgia 30602
USA

Operator Theory:
Advances and Applications, Vol. 35

INTEGRAL REPRESENTATIONS OF BOUNDED HANKEL FORMS DEFINED IN SCATTERING SYSTEMS WITH A MULTIPARAMETRIC EVOLUTION GROUP

MISCHA COTLAR and CORA SADOSKY[1]

The notion of Hankel and Toeplitz forms acting in algebraic scattering systems is introduced. Particular examples of such systems are the classical scattering structures on Hilbert spaces as well as the trigonometric polynomials under the shift operator. In this last example, the Hankel and Toeplitz forms acting in it coincide with the usual ones. Given two positive Toeplitz forms in a scattering system, the Hankel forms bounded with respect to the hilbertian seminorms they define, have Toeplitz extensions similarly bounded, as well as Fourier representations. These results still hold when the discrete 1-parametric evolution group of the system is replaced by a continuous or a d-parametric one. Several applications to harmonic analysis are obtained.

INTRODUCTION

The notion of Hankel or Toeplitz forms acting in so-called algebraic scattering systems with a d-parametric evolution group is formulated, and integral representations and lifting properties are obtained for bounded Hankel forms in this setting.

The study of such lifting properties was initiated in [7], in the special case where $d = 1$ and the forms arise from hermitian kernels. The consideration of forms in the general setting of scattering systems allows us now to treat cases where the evolution is given by a continuous or by a multiparametric group, to deal by the same method with scalar or operator-valued kernels, and to give for them explicit Fourier representations of classical type. In particular, the treatment through forms enables us, in the case $d = 1$, to get a generalized Bochner theorem [6] for distribution-valued kernels in $\mathbf{R}$, which contains as special cases an extension of the Bochner-Schwartz theorem for generalized Toeplitz kernels, even in the case of a prescribed number of vanishing moments, englobing the

[1] Author partially supported by grants from the National Science Foundation (USA).

theorems of Nehari, Helson-Szegő and Helson-Sarason in $\mathbf{R}$. Some of these results where announced in [10] and [9]. On the other hand, when the Hankel form is given by an inner product, the integral representation of Theorem 2, together with Remark 3, lead to a definition of scattering functions, even for systems where condition (3a) below is not satisfied.

The theorems for multiparametric groups open the possibility of applications to several dimensional problems. Here we consider the liftings of Hankel forms defined on half-planes of Helson-Lowdenslager [12], and through them, related extensions of the Nehari theorem and the Paley lacunary inequality in a d-dimensional context.

Section 1 deals with the definition of algebraic scattering systems, of which both the classical scattering structures and the trigonometric model arising in one-dimensional Fourier analysis are special instances. Section 2 discusses the notion of Hankel and Toeplitz forms acting in such algebraic systems, as well as the notion of boundedness which leads to an interpolation or lifting problem. The Fourier representations and lifting properties of forms acting in classical scattering systems with a discrete evolution are given in Section 3, and those for forms acting in general algebraic systems, in Section 4. In Section 5, the liftings of forms invariant with respect to a discrete multiparametric evolution group are given, through the introduction of a concept of conditional Toeplitz forms. In Section 6, the results of the preceding sections are extended to continuous groups. Finally, Section 7 contains the applications mentioned above.

Basic notations used throughout the text follow. For $1 \le p \le \infty$, $L^p(\mathbf{T};N) = \left\{f : \mathbf{T} \to N \,;\, \int |f|^p\, dt < \infty\right\}$, $H_1^p(\mathbf{T};N) = \{f \in L^p(\mathbf{T};N)\,;\, \hat{f}(n) = 0\,, n < 0\}$, $H_2^p(\mathbf{T};N) = \{f \in L^p(\mathbf{T};N)\,;\, \hat{f}(n) = 0\,, n \ge 0\}$, where $\hat{f}$ is the usual Fourier transform of f. For N_1, N_2 two Hilbert spaces, $L(N_1,N_2)$ stands for the space of all bounded linear operators from N_1 to N_2, $L^\infty(\mathbf{T};L(N_1,N_2))$ for the space of $L(N_1,N_2)$-valued bounded functions defined in $\mathbf{T}$, and $N_1 \vee N_2$ is the minimal closed space spanned by N_1 and N_2.

1. ALGEBRAIC SCATTERING SYSTEMS

Let V be a Hilbert space, W_1, W_2 two closed subspaces of V, τ a unitary operator in V, and let $V^\alpha = \bigvee_{n=-\infty}^{\infty} \tau^n W_\alpha$ for $\alpha = 1$ or 2. $[V;W_1,W_2;\tau]$ is called an *Adamjan-Arov* $(A-A)$ *scattering system* if (i) $\tau W_1 \subset W_1$, $\tau^{-1}W_2 \subset W_2$; (ii) $\bigcap_{n=1}^{\infty} \tau^n W_1 = \bigcap_{n=1}^{\infty} \tau^{-n} W_2 = \{0\}$; (iii) $V = V^1 \vee V^2$. If, in addition, $W_1 \perp W_2$ and $V^1 = V^2 = V$, then the classical Lax-Phillips systems are obtained. By (i), we may set

$$N_1 = W_1 \ominus \tau W_1 \quad , \quad N_2 = W_2 \ominus \tau^{-1} W_2 \,. \tag{1}$$

Each $A - A$ scattering system is known to have the following functional realization [1], [2]: a function $S \in L^\infty(\mathbf{T}; L(N_1, N_2))$, $\|S(t)\| \leq 1$ for $t \in \mathbf{T}$, and an isometric mapping $\mathcal{F}$ of V onto $L^2(N_2) \oplus L^2_\Sigma(N_1)$, where $\Sigma(t) = \left(I_{N_1} - S^*(t)\, S(t)\right)^{1/2}$ and $L^2_\Sigma(N_1)$ is the closure of the set

$$\{\phi \in L^2(N_1)\,;\, \phi(t) = \Sigma(t)\, h(t)\,,\, h \in L^2(\mathbf{T}; N_1)\}\,, \tag{2}$$

such that

$$\mathcal{F}(\tau f)\,(t) = e^{it}\, \mathcal{F}(f)\,(t) \quad , \quad \forall\ f \in V\,, \tag{2a}$$

$$\mathcal{F}(W_2) = H^2_2(N_2) \oplus \{0\} \tag{2b}$$

and

$$\mathcal{F}(W_1) = \{\phi; \phi(\varsigma) = S(\varsigma)\,\phi_1(\varsigma) \oplus \Sigma(\varsigma)\,\phi_1(\varsigma) \ ,\ \phi_1 \in H^2_1(N_1)\}\,. \tag{2c}$$

Here S is called the Heisenberg scattering function of the given $A - A$ scattering system.

From (2)-(2c) it follows in particular that there are two isometries $j_\alpha : W_\alpha \to H^2_\alpha(\mathbf{T}; N_\alpha)$, $\alpha = 1, 2$, such that for $(f_1, f_2) \in W_1 \times W_2$,

$$\mathcal{F}(f_2) = j_2 f_2 \oplus \{0\} \tag{2d}$$

$$\mathcal{F}(f_1) = S(\varsigma)(j_1 f_1)(\varsigma) \oplus \Sigma(\varsigma)(j_1 f_1)(\varsigma) \tag{2e}$$

$$j_1(\tau f_1) = e^{it}(j_1 f_1)(t) \ ,\ j_2(\tau^{-1} f_2) = e^{-it}(j_2 f_2)(t) \tag{2f}$$

For our purposes it is necessary to consider the following more general setting, where there are two underlying spaces V_1, V_2, that need not be Hilbert spaces. $[V_1, V_2; W_1, W_2; \tau_1, \tau_2]$ is called a (discrete) *algebraic scattering system* if V_1, V_2 are vector spaces, and $\tau_1 : V_1 \to V_1$, $\tau_2 : V_2 \to V_2$, are two algebraic isomorphisms such that

$$\tau_1 W_1 \subset W_1 \quad , \quad \tau_2^{-1} W_2 \subset W_2\,. \tag{3}$$

If, in addition,

$$\bigcap_{n=1}^{\infty} \tau_1^n W_1 = \bigcap_{n=1}^{\infty} \tau_2^{-n} W_2 = \{0\}\,, \tag{3a}$$

then $[V_1, V_2; W_1, W_2; \tau_1, \tau_2]$ is called an $A - A$ *algebraic scattering system*. If $V_1 = V_2 = V$ is a Hilbert space, W_1 and W_2 are closed subspaces and $\tau_1 = \tau_2 = \tau$ is a unitary operator, then we obtain again the notion of an $A - A$ scattering structure. The simplest example of an $A - A$ algebraic scattering system, that in what follows will be referred to as the *trigonometric example*, is where $V_1 = V_2 = \mathcal{P}$ = the set of trigonometrical polynomials in $\mathbf{T}$, $W_1 = \mathcal{P}_+$ = the set of analytic polynomials, $W_2 = \mathcal{P}_-$ = the set of conjugate analytic polynomials, and $\tau_1 = \tau_2 = \tau$ is the shift, $\tau f(t) = e^{it} f(t)$. Note that in the trigonometric example $V = W_1 \oplus W_2$, while in the case of Lax-Phillips scattering structures the opposite condition, $V \neq W_1 \oplus W_2$, is of interest. In this setting condition (3a) means that, if $\alpha = 1$ or 2, for every $f_\alpha \in W_\alpha$, the *trajectory* $\{\tau_\alpha^m f_\alpha : n \in Z\}$ contains some element of the complement of W_α. Thus, if $\alpha = 1$ (resp. $\alpha = 2$) there is an integer $m \leq 0$ (resp. $m \geq 0$) such that $\tau_1^m f_1 \in W_1$, while $\tau_1^{m-1} f_1 \notin W_1$ (resp. $\tau_2^m f_2 \in W_2$, while $\tau_2^{m+1} f_2 \notin W_2$). Of special interest are the $A - A$ algebraic scattering systems satifying

$$\bigvee_{m=-\infty}^{\infty} \tau_1^m W_1 = V_1 \quad , \quad \bigvee_{m=-\infty}^{\infty} \tau_2^m W_2 = V_2 \,, \tag{3b}$$

which means that each element of V_α is in some trajectory $\{\tau_\alpha^m f_\alpha\}$ for $f_\alpha \in W_\alpha$, $\alpha = 1, 2$. If both conditions (3a) and (3b) are satisfied, then if $\alpha = 1$ or 2, for each $f_\alpha \in V_\alpha$ there is an element $e_\alpha \in W_\alpha$, such that $f_\alpha = \tau_\alpha^n e_\alpha$ for some n, and $\tau_1^m e_1 \in W_1$ iff $m \geq 0$, $\tau_2^m e_2 \in W_2$ iff $m \leq 0$. Therefore, we can fix two sets $\mathcal{E}_1 \subset W_1$, $\mathcal{E}_2 \subset W_2$ such that, for $\alpha = 1$ of 2, each $f \in V_\alpha$ has a unique representation

$$f = \tau_\alpha^{n(f)} e_\alpha \,, \quad \text{with } e_\alpha \in \mathcal{E}_\alpha$$

and

$$f \in W_1 \text{ iff } n(f) \geq 0 \text{ or } f \in W_2 \text{ iff } n(f) \leq 0 \,. \tag{3c}$$

The notion of algebraic scattering system extends to continuous one-parametric groups: let V_1, V_2, $W_1 \subset V_1$, $W_2 \subset V_2$ be as before, but consider, instead of two isomorphisms, $\{\tau_\alpha^t : V_\alpha \to V_\alpha \,,\ t \in \mathbf{R}\}$, $\alpha = 1, 2$, such that

$$\tau_1^t W_1 \subset W_1 \,,\ \tau_2^{-t} W_2 \subset W_2 \,,\ \forall\ t \geq 0 \,. \tag{4}$$

If V_1, V_2 have a topology then $(t, f) \to \tau_\alpha^t f$, $\alpha = 1, 2$, are assumed to be continuous. If in addition the condition corresponding to (3a) holds, we speak of an $A - A$ algebraic evolution in $\mathbf{R}$. When $V_1 = V_2 = V$ is a Hilbert space, W_1 and W_2 are closed subspaces, and $\{\tau_1^t\}$, $\{\tau_2^t\}$ two unitary groups, we obtain the notion of $A - A$ scattering system in $\mathbf{R}$. In such case there is a functional realization of the scattering system, similar to the one given by (2)–(2f), but where $L^2(\mathbf{T}; N_\alpha)$ is replaced by $L^2(\mathbf{R}; N_\alpha)$, $\alpha = 1, 2$, and τ^t is transformed into the operator $f \to e^{itx} f(x)$ (see [2]).

2. TOEPLITZ AND HANKEL FORMS DEFINED ON ALGEBRAIC SCATTERING SYSTEMS

Let $[V_1, V_2; W_1, W_2; \tau_1, \tau_2]$ be a (discrete) algebraic scattering system. The trigonometric example suggest the following definitions.

For $\alpha, \beta = 1$ or 2, a sesquilinear form $B : V_\alpha \times V_\beta \to \mathbf{C}$ is called $(\tau_\alpha, \tau_\beta)$-*Toeplitz* if

$$B(\tau_\alpha f, \tau_\beta g) = B(f, g) \quad , \quad \forall\ (f, g) \in V_\alpha \times V_\beta \,. \tag{5}$$

For $\alpha = 1$ or 2, the restrictions of a $(\tau_\alpha, \tau_\alpha)$-Toeplitz form to $W_\alpha \times W_\alpha$ is again Toeplitz, but since W_2 is not τ_2-invariant, the restriction of a (τ_1, τ_2)-Toeplitz form to $W_1 \times W_2$ is not Toeplitz, but Hankel in the following sense: a sesquilinear form $B^\circ : W_1 \times W_2 \to \mathbf{C}$ is (τ_1, τ_2)-*Hankel* if

$$B^\circ(\tau_1 f_1, f_2) = B^\circ(f_1, \tau_2^{-1} f_2) \quad , \quad \forall\ (f_1, f_2) \in W_1 \times W_2 . \tag{5a}$$

In the trigonometric example these definitions coincide with the usual ones for Toeplitz and Hankel forms.

Consider now B_1 and B_2, two positive sesquilinear forms, $B_\alpha : V_\alpha \times V_\alpha \to \mathbf{C}$, $B_\alpha(f, f) \geq 0$, $\forall\ f \in V_\alpha$, $\alpha = 1, 2$, so that each defines in V_1 and V_2 two (possibly degenerate) scalar products. Given the sesquilinear forms $B : V_1 \times V_2 \to \mathbf{C}$ or $B^\circ : W_1 \times W_2 \to \mathbf{C}$, we write $B \leq (B_1, B_2)$ or $B^\circ \prec (B_1, B_2)$ if B or B° are bounded by the corresponding seminorms, more precisely,

$$B \leq (B_1, B_2) \text{ if } |B(f_1, f_2)| \leq B_1(f_1, f_1)^{1/2} B_2(f_2, f_2)^{1/2} \ , \ \forall\ (f_1, f_2) \in V_1 \times V_2 \tag{6a}$$

or

$$B^\circ \prec (B_1, B_2) \text{ if } |B^\circ(f_1, f_2)| \leq B_1(f_1, f_1)^{1/2} B_2(f_2, f_2)^{1/2} \ , \ \forall\ (f_1, f_2) \in W_1 \times W_2 \tag{6b}$$

respectively. We also write $B \prec (B_1, B_2)$ if $B|_{W_1 \times W_2} \prec (B_1, B_2)$.

Setting $B_{11} = B_1$, $B_{22} = B_2$, $B_{12} = B$, $B_{21}(f_2, f_1) = B_{12}(f_1, f_2)$, triple B_1, B_2, B can be identified with the 2×2 matrix $(B_{\alpha\beta})$, $\alpha, \beta = 1, 2$, which in turn identifies with the sesquilinear form $\mathcal{B} : (V_1 \times V_2) \times (V_1 \times V_2) \to \mathbf{C}$ given by

$$\mathcal{B}((f_1, f_2), (g_1, g_2)) = \sum_{\alpha, \beta = 1, 2} B_{\alpha\beta}(f_\alpha, g_\beta) . \tag{7}$$

Thus the subordination condition $B \leq (B_1, B_2)$ is equivalent to the positiveness of the associated $\mathcal{B}$.

Similarly, the triple B_1, B_2, B° is identified with the 2×2 matrix $(B^\circ_{\alpha\beta})$, where $B^\circ_{\alpha\alpha} = B_{\alpha|W_\alpha \times W_\alpha}$, $\alpha = 1, 2$, $B^\circ_{12} = B^\circ$, and with the form $\mathcal{B}^\circ : (W_1 \times W_2) \times (W_1 \times W_2) \to \mathcal{C}$, so that $B^\circ \prec (B_1, B_2)$ is equivalent to $\mathcal{B}^\circ \geq 0$.

Defining the operator $\tau : V_1 \times V_2 \to V_1 \times V_2$ by $\tau(f_1, f_2) = (\tau_1 f_1, \tau_2 f_2)$ for $(f_1, f_2) \in V_1 \times V_2$, we say that $\mathcal{B}$ is τ-*Toeplitz* if for $\alpha, \beta = 1, 2$, the four forms $B_{\alpha\beta}$ are $(\tau_\alpha, \tau_\beta)$-Toeplitz. Since the subspace $W_1 \times W_2$ of $V_1 \times V_2$ is not τ-invariant, the restriction $\mathcal{B}^\circ$ of a τ-Toeplitz form $\mathcal{B}$ to $(W_1 \times W_2) \times (W_1 \times W_2)$ is not τ-Toeplitz but *generalized* τ-*Toeplitz*, in the sense that the restrictions B°_{12} of B_{12} is (τ_1, τ_2)-Hankel, while for $\alpha = 1, 2$, the restriction $B^\circ_{\alpha\alpha}$ of $B_{\alpha\alpha}$ are $(\tau_\alpha, \tau_\alpha)$-Toeplitz.

Given B_1 and B_2 two positive sesquilinear forms such that, for $\alpha = 1,2$, $B_\alpha : V_\alpha \times V_\alpha \to \mathbf{C}$, $B_\alpha(\tau_\alpha,\tau_\alpha)$-Toeplitz, define the families of forms

$$\Lambda = \Lambda(B_1,B_2) = \{B : V_1 \times V_2 \to \mathbf{C} \ , \ B \ (\tau_1,\tau_2) - \text{Toeplitz} \ , \ B \le (B_1,B_2)\} \qquad (8)$$

and

$$\Lambda^\circ = \Lambda^\circ(B_1,B_2) = \{B^\circ : W_1 \times W_2 \to \mathbf{C} \ , \ B^\circ \ (\tau_1,\tau_2) - \text{Hankel} \ , \ B^\circ \prec (B_1,B_2)\} \qquad (8a)$$

Then $B \in \Lambda$ *if and only if the associated* $\mathcal{B}$ *is a positive* τ*-Toeplitz form, and* $B^\circ \in \Lambda^\circ$ *if and only if the associated* $\mathcal{B}^\circ$ *is a positive generalized* τ*-Toeplitz form.*

For an arbitrary family Λ of sesquilinear forms (in $V_1 \times V_2$), and $\Lambda^\circ \supset \Lambda_{|W_1 \times W_2}$, the following *lifting* (or *interpolation*)*problem* can be posed: Given $B^\circ \in \Lambda^\circ$, does there exist a lifting $B \in \Lambda$, such that $B = B^\circ$ on $W_1 \times W_2$? The family Λ has the lifting property with respect to $W_1 \times W_2$ if every element in Λ° has a lifting Λ. We shall see that the lifting problem has positive solution in the case of $\Lambda = \Lambda(B_1,B_2)$, as defined in (8), and that the solution is closely related to integral representations, of Fourier type, of the associated matrices $(B^\circ_{\alpha\beta})$.

REMARK 1. In proving that an element $B^\circ \in \Lambda^\circ(B_1,B_2)$ has a lifting in $\Lambda(B_1,B_2)$ it is enough to show that there is a lifting defined only on $V_1^1 \times V_2^2$, where, as in (iii), $V_\alpha^\alpha = \bigvee_{n\in Z} \tau_\alpha^n W_\alpha$, $\alpha = 1,2$. In fact, assume that $B : V_1^1 \times V_2^2 \to \mathbf{C}$ satisfies $B(\tau_1 f_1, \tau_2 f_2) = B(f_1,f_2)$ and $|B(f_1,f_2)| \le B_1(f_1,f_1)^{1/2} B_2(f_2,f_2)^{1/2}$ for $(f_1,f_2) \in V_1^1 \times V_2^2$, and that $B = B^\circ$ on $W_1 \times W_2 \subset V_1^1 \times V_2^2$. Then B is bounded in $V_1^1 \times V_2^2$ with respect to the seminorms defined in V_1 and V_2 by B_1 and B_2. It is enough to observe then that for $\alpha = 1,2$, the projection P_α of V_α on $\overline{V_\alpha^\alpha}$ commute with τ_α (since $\overline{V_\alpha^\alpha}$ is invariant under τ_α and τ_α^{-1}), so that, setting $B'(f_1,f_2) = B(P_1 f_1, P_2 f_2)$, one obtains the required lifting to $V_1 \times V_2$.

3. FOURIER REPRESENTATIONS AND LIFTING THEOREMS ON DISCRETE SCATTERING SYSTEMS

Given four finite complex measures in $\mathbf{T}$, $\mu_{11},\mu_{12},\mu_{21},\mu_{22}$, we write $(\mu_{\alpha\beta})_{\alpha,\beta=1,2} \ge 0$ if, for every Borel set $\Delta \subset \mathbf{T}$, $(\mu_{\alpha\beta}(\Delta))$ is a positive definite 2×2 matrix. If N_1 and N_2 are two Hilbert spaces and if for $\alpha,\beta = 1,2$, $\mu_{\alpha\beta}$ is a $L(N_\alpha,N_\beta)$-valued measure, then we write $(\mu_{\alpha\beta}) \ge 0$ if $\sum_{\alpha,\beta=1,2} < \mu_{\alpha\beta}(\Delta)\,\xi_\alpha, \xi_\beta > \ge 0$ for all $\xi_1 \in N_1$, $\xi_2 \in N_2$, $\Delta \in \mathbf{T}$.

Consider an $A-A$ scattering system $[V;W_1,W_2;\tau]$. By (2d), (2e), for every $f_\alpha \in W_\alpha$ we have $\varphi_\alpha = j_\alpha(f_\alpha) = \sum \xi_n e^{int} \in H^2_\alpha(N_\alpha)$, $\xi_n \in N_\alpha$, $\alpha = 1,2$. Thus, if for $\alpha,\beta = 1,2$, $B^\circ_{\alpha\beta} : W_\alpha \times W_\beta \to \mathbf{C}$ is a continuous form, then $B^\circ_{\alpha\beta}$ will be determined in $W_\alpha \times W_\beta$ if we give the values $B^\circ_{\alpha\beta}(j_\alpha(\xi_\alpha e^{int}), j_\beta(\xi_\beta e^{imt})$ for all $\xi_1 \in N_1$, $\xi_2 \in N_2$, $n \in \mathbf{Z}_+$, $m \in \mathbf{Z}_-$.

If $B^\circ \prec (B_1, B_2)$ and $(B^\circ_{\alpha\beta})$ is its associated matrix as in (7), we say that $(B^\circ_{\alpha\beta})$ has a *Fourier representation* by a positive matrix measure if there exists a matrix measure $(\mu_{\alpha\beta}) \geq 0$, where, for $\alpha, \beta = 1, 2$, each $\mu_{\alpha\beta}$ is a $L(N_\alpha, N_\beta)$-valued measure in $\mathbf{T}$, such that

$$B^\circ_{\alpha\beta}(j_\alpha(\xi_\alpha e^{int}), j_\beta(\xi_\beta e^{imt})) =< \widehat{\mu}_{\alpha\beta}(m-n)\, \xi_\alpha, \xi_\beta >_{N_2} \tag{9}$$

if $\xi_1 \in N_1$, $\xi_2 \in N_2$, $n \in \mathbf{Z}_+$ and $m \in \mathbf{Z}_-$.

If for each $\alpha, \beta = 1, 2$, $B^\circ_{\alpha\beta}$ is continuous, then (9) is equivalent to

$$B^\circ_{\alpha\beta}(f_\alpha, f_\beta) = \int < \mu_{\alpha\beta}\varphi_\alpha, \varphi_\beta > dt \tag{9a}$$

for all $(f_\alpha, f_\beta) \in W_\alpha \times W_\beta$ with $f_\alpha = j_\alpha^{-1}(\varphi_\alpha)$.

If H is a Hilbert space and $U \in L(H)$ is a unitary operator, U is a *unitary dilation* of the matrix $(B^\circ_{\alpha\beta})$ if there exist two maps $\varrho_1 : N_1 \to H$, $\varrho_2 : N_2 \to H$ such that, for $\alpha, \beta = 1, 2$,

$$B^\circ_{\alpha\beta}(j_\alpha(\xi_\alpha e^{int})), j_\beta(\xi_\beta e^{imt})) =< U^{m-n}\varrho_\alpha\xi_\alpha, \varrho_\beta\xi_\beta > . \tag{9b}$$

As was already observed, then $(\mu_{\alpha\beta})$ determines the forms B_1, B_2 and B° in $W_1 \times W_1$, $W_2 \times W_2$ and $W_1 \times W_2$ respectively, and, if condition (3b) holds, then it determines also B_1 and B_2 in the whole of $V_1 \times V_1$ and $V_2 \times V_2$.

THEOREM 1. *Let $[V; W_1, W_2; \tau]$ be an $A - A$ scattering system, B_1 and B_2, two positive τ-Toeplitz forms in $V \times V$, and $B^\circ : W_1 \times W_2 \to \mathbf{C}$, a (τ, τ)-Hankel form such that $B^\circ \prec (B_1, B_2)$. If B_1 and B_2 are continuous forms then, for $(B^\circ_{\alpha\beta})$ the matrix associated to B_1, B_2, B°, there exist, for each $\alpha, \beta = 1, 2$, a $L(N_\alpha, N_\beta)$-valued measure $\mu_{\alpha\beta}$ defined in $\mathbf{T}$, such that $(\mu_{\alpha\beta}) \geq 0$ gives the Fourier representation* (9).

PROOF. Since B_1 and B_2 are continuous, from $B^\circ \prec (B_1, B_2)$ it follows that B° is also continuous and thus the elements of $(B^\circ_{\alpha\beta})$ are determined by their value on the elements $(j_\alpha(\xi_\alpha e^{int}), (j_\beta(\xi_\beta e^{imt}))$, $\alpha, \beta = 1, 2$, for all $\xi_1 \in N_1$, $\xi_2 \in N_2$, $n \in \mathbf{Z}_+$, $m \in \mathbf{Z}_-$. For $\alpha, \beta = 1, 2$ and $(n, m) \in \mathbf{Z}_\alpha \times \mathbf{Z}_\beta$, where $\mathbf{Z}_1 = \mathbf{Z}_+$, $\mathbf{Z}_2 = \mathbf{Z}_-$, let us define a kernel $K : \mathbf{Z} \times \mathbf{Z} \to L(N_\alpha, N_\beta)$, where N_1 and N_2 are given by (1) and, for all $(\xi_\alpha, \xi_\beta) \in N_\alpha \times N_\beta$,

$$< K(n, m)\, \xi_\alpha, \xi_\beta >= B^\circ_{\alpha\beta}(j_\alpha(\xi_\alpha e^{int}), j_\beta(\xi_\beta e^{imt})) . \tag{9c}$$

Since the forms $B^\circ_{\alpha\beta}$ are either τ-Toeplitz or τ-Hankel, the kernel K satisfies the property $K(n+1, m+1) = K(n, m)$ whenever $n \neq -1$, $m \neq -1$, i.e., K is a so-called generalized Toeplitz kernel in $\mathbf{Z} \times \mathbf{Z}$. Since $\sum\limits_{\alpha,\beta=1,2} B^\circ_{\alpha\beta}(f_\alpha, f_\beta) \geq 0$ if $f_1 \in W_1$, $f_2 \in W_2$, setting $f_1 = j_1^{-1}\left(\sum\limits_{n=0}^{N} \xi_n e^{int}\right)$ with $\xi_n \in N_1$, $f_2 = j_2^{-1}\left(\sum\limits_{m=-N}^{-1} \xi_m e^{imt}\right)$ with $\xi_m \in N_2$, we get by

(9c), that $\sum_{n,m} < K(n,m)\, \xi_n, \xi_m > \geq 0$ for every sequence (ξ_n) of finite support such that $\xi_n \in N_\alpha$ if $n \in \mathbf{Z}_\alpha$, $\alpha = 1,2$. This means that K is a positive definite operator-valued generalized Toeplitz kernel, and by the basic property of such kernels (established in [6] for scalar-valued K and generalized in [3] for operator-valued K), there is a matrix measure $(\mu_{\alpha\beta}) \geq 0$ such that

$$< K(n,m)\, \xi_\alpha, \xi_\beta > = < \widehat{\mu}_{\alpha\beta}(m-n)\, \xi_\alpha, \xi_\beta >$$

for $(n,m) \in \mathbf{Z}_\alpha \times \mathbf{Z}_\beta$, $(\xi_\alpha, \xi_\beta) \in N_\alpha \times N_\beta$, $\alpha, \beta = 1,2$, which is equivalent to (9). ■

REMARK 2. Observe that in the proof above B_1 and B_2 are required to be defined and to satisfy the positivity and τ-invariance conditions only on $W_1 \times W_1$ and $W_2 \times W_2$, respectively.

THEOREM 1A. *Under the same assumptions of* Theorem 1, *the following lifting and dilation properties hold:*

(i) *there exists a τ-Toeplitz form $B : V \times V \to \mathbf{C}$ such that $B \leq (B_1, B_2)$ and $B = B^\circ$ in $W_1 \times W_2$, which is given explicitely by*

$$B(\tau^n f_1, \tau^m f_2) = \int < d\mu_{12}\, e^{int}\varphi_1, e^{imt}\varphi_2 > \tag{9d}$$

whenever $\varphi_\alpha = j_\alpha(f_\alpha)$, $\alpha = 1,2$ (see (2f)).

(ii) *There exists a unitary dilation $U \in L(H)$ of $(B^\circ_{\alpha\beta})$* (see (9b)).

PROOF. (i) Let $(\mu_{\alpha\beta}) \geq 0$ be as in Theorem 1, so that (9c) holds and define $B(\tau^n f_1, \tau^m f_2) = \int < d\mu_{12} e^{int}\varphi_1, e^{imt}\varphi_2 >$. This is well-defined, since if $\tau^n f_1 = \tau^k g_1$ and $\varphi_1 = j_1 f_1$, $\psi_1 = j_1 g_1$, then $e^{int}\varphi_1 = e^{ikt}\psi_1$, and B is clearly τ-invariant, since $e^{i(n+1)t}\varphi_1 = j_1(\tau(\tau^n f_1))$, and similarly for f_2, φ_2. Finally, $B = B^\circ$ on $W_1 \times W_2$. Moreover, by the positivity of $(\mu_{\alpha\beta})$,

$$\begin{aligned} 2\,| < \mu_{12}(\Delta_j)\, e^{int_j}\varphi_1(t_j), e^{imt_j}\varphi_2(t_j) > | \leq \\ \leq < \mu_{11}(\Delta_j)\, e^{int_j}\varphi_1, e^{int_j}\varphi_1 > + < \mu_{22}(\Delta_j)\, e^{imt_j}\varphi_2, e^{imt_j}\varphi_2 > = \\ = < \mu_{11}(\Delta_j)\varphi_1(t_j), \varphi_1(t_j) > + < \mu_{22}(\Delta_j)\varphi_2(t_j), \varphi_2(t_j) >, \end{aligned}$$

and approximating the integral in (9d) by Riemann sums, we have

$$\begin{aligned} 2\,|B(\tau^n f_1, \tau^m f_2)| &\leq B_1(f_1, f_1) + B_2(f_2, f_2) = \\ &= B_1(\tau^n f_1, \tau^n f_1) + B_2(\tau^m f_2, \tau^m f_2) \end{aligned}$$

and, hence,

$$|B(\tau^n f_1, \tau^m f_2)| \leq B_1(\tau^n f_1, \tau^n f_1)^{1/2} B_2(\tau^m f_2, \tau^m f_2)^{1/2}.$$

(ii) Let $(\mu_{\alpha\beta}) \geq 0$ be as in (i) and let $\mathcal{H} = \{\varphi = (\varphi_1, \varphi_2);\ \varphi_\alpha \in L^2(\mathbf{T}; N_\alpha),\ \alpha = 1,2,$ with $<\varphi, \varphi> = \sum_{\alpha,\beta} <\mu_{\alpha\beta}\varphi_\alpha, \varphi_\beta> < \infty\}$. Then $\mathcal{H}$ gives rise to a Hilbert space, informally also denoted by $\mathcal{H}$, and $U(\varphi_1, \varphi_2) = <e^{it}\varphi_1, e^{it}\varphi_2>$ is a unitary operator in $\mathcal{H}$. Define $\varrho_1\xi_1 = (\xi e_0, 0)$, $\varrho_2\xi_2 = (0, \xi_2 e_0)$. Then, for $\xi_1 \in N_1$, $\xi_2 \in N_2$, $m \in \mathbf{Z}_+$, $n \in \mathbf{Z}_-$,

$$\begin{aligned} <U^{m-n}\varrho_1\xi_1, \varrho_2\xi_2> &= <U^n\varrho_1\xi_1, U^m\varrho_2\xi_2> = \\ &= <(e^{int}\xi e_0, 0), (0, e^{imt}\xi_2 e_0)> = \\ &= \int <d\mu_{12} e^{int}\xi_1, e^{imt}\xi_2> = \\ &= B^\circ(j_1\xi_1 e^{int}, j_2\xi_2 e^{imt}), \end{aligned}$$

and similarly for the remaining cases. ■

4. FOURIER REPRESENTATIONS AND LIFTING THEOREMS ON DISCRETE ALGEBRAIC SCATTERING SYSTEMS

The Fourier representation theorem on classical scattering systems can be extended to algebraic ones by imposing on the forms B_1, B_2 a regularity condition defined below, suggested by the notion of regular stochastic process, that allows to convert the algebraic situation into a classical one.

Given an algebraic scattering system $[V_1, V_2; W_1, W_2; \tau_1, \tau_2]$, a pair of positive forms B_1, B_2, such that for $\alpha = 1,2$, $B_\alpha : V_\alpha \times V_\alpha \to \mathbf{C}$, $(\tau_\alpha, \tau_\alpha)$-Toeplitz, is called *regular* if there exists no sequence $(f_n)_{n=1}^{\infty}$ such that $f_n \in \tau_1^n W_1$ for all $n \geq 0$ and $B_1(f_n - f_m, f_n - f_m) \to 0$ or $f_n \in \tau_2^{-n} W_2$ for all $n \geq 0$ and $B_2(f_n - f_m, f_n - f_m) \to 0$, $n, m \to \infty$.

Since for $\alpha = 1,2$, each B_α defines a hilbertian pseudometric in W_α, if B_1, B_2 is a regular pair then $\bigcap_{n=1}^{\infty} \tau_1^n \overline{W_1} = \bigcap_{n=1}^{\infty} \tau_2^{-n} \overline{W_2} = \{0\}$, where the closure $\overline{W_\alpha}$ are taken in the corresponding pseudometrics.

THEOREM 2. *Let $[V_1, V_2; W_1, W_2; \tau_1, \tau_2]$ be an algebraic scattering system, B_1, B_2, a regular pair of positive forms, $B_\alpha : V_\alpha \times V_\alpha \to \mathbf{C}$, $(\tau_\alpha, \tau_\alpha)$-Toeplitz, for $\alpha = 1,2$, and $B^\circ : W_1 \times W_2 \to \mathbf{C}$, a (τ_1, τ_2)-Hankel form such that $B^\circ \prec (B_1, B_2)$. Then there exists an $A - A$ scattering system $[H; \overline{W}_1, \overline{W}_2; U]$ such that, if N_1, N_2, S, j_1, j_2, correspond to its functional realization* (2)–(2f), *then the matrix $(B^\circ_{\alpha\beta})$ associated to B_1, B_2, B° has the Fourier representation*

$$B^\circ_{\alpha\beta}(f_\alpha, f_\beta) = \int <d\mu_{\alpha\beta}\varphi_\alpha, \varphi_\beta>$$

where

$$d\mu_{11} = I_{N_1}\, dt\,,\ d\mu_{22} = I_{N_2}\, dt\,,\ d\mu_{12} = S(t)\, dt\,. \tag{10}$$

Moreover, there is a lifting B of B° given by the explicit formula (9d).

PROOF. The positive form $\mathcal{B}$, associated with B_1, B_2, B° as in Section 2, determines a pre-hilbertian pseudometric in $W_1 \times W_2$, such that, for all $(f_1, f_2), (g_1, g_2) \in W_1 \times W_2$,

$$\begin{aligned} &< (f_1,0),(g_1,0) >_{\mathcal{B}} = B_1(f_1,g_1) \\ &< (0,f_2),(0,g_2) >_{\mathcal{B}} = B_2(f_2,g_2) \\ &< (f_1,0),(0,g_2) >_{\mathcal{B}} = B^\circ(f_1,g_2) \end{aligned} \tag{11}$$

Let $\tau : W_1 \times W_2 \to V_1 \times V_2$ be defined by $\tau(f_1, f_2) = (\tau_1 f_1, \tau_2 f_2)$. Indentifying $(f_1, 0)$ with $f_1 \in W_1$ and $(0, f_2)$ with $f_2 \in W_2$, we may consider W_1 and W_2 as subspaces of $W_1 \times W_2$, and the regularity condition on the pair B_1, B_2 insures that $\bigcap_{n=1}^{\infty} \overline{\tau^n W_1} = \bigcap_{n=1}^{\infty} \overline{\tau^{-n} W_2} = \{0\}$, where the closures are taken in the $\mathcal{B}$ pseudometric in $W_1 \times W_2$. The restriction of τ to $\overline{W_1 \times (\tau_2^{-1} W_2)}$ is an isometry with range $\overline{(\tau_1 W_1) \times W_2}$, and thus can be extended by the usual procedure to a unitary operator U acting in a larger Hilbert space H (that contains $\overline{W_1 \times W_2}$ as a subspace), and such that $U = \tau$ in $\overline{W}_1$ and $U^{-1} = \tau^{-1}$ in $\overline{W}_2$. Therefore $[H; \overline{W}_1, \overline{W}_2; U]$ is an $A - A$ scattering structure that has a functional realization as (2)–(2f). Then, by (11), since $\mathcal{F}$ respects scalar products and $\Sigma^*\Sigma = I - S^*S$, setting $\varphi_1 = j_1(f_1) = j_1(f_1, 0)$, $\varphi_2 = j_2 f_2$, $\psi_1 = j_1 g_1$, $\psi_2 = j_2 g_2$, we get

$$\begin{aligned} B_1(f_1,g_1) &= < (f_1,0), g_1, 0) > = < \mathcal{F}(f_1,0), \mathcal{F}(g_1,0) > = \\ &= \int < S(t)\,\varphi_1(t), S(t)\,\psi_1(t) > \,dt + \\ &\qquad + \int < \Sigma(t)\,\varphi_1(t), \Sigma(t)\,\psi_1(t) > \,dt \\ &= \int < \varphi_1(t), \psi_1(t) > \,dt\,. \end{aligned}$$

Similarly, $B_2(f_2, g_2) = \int < \varphi_2(t), \psi_2(t) > \,dt$ and $B^\circ(f_1, g_2) = \int < S(t)\,\varphi_1(t), \psi_2(t) > \,dt$.

The existence of the lifting B of B° given by (9d) follows from the considerations above, as in the proof of Theorem 1a. ■

REMARK 3. The representations $(\mu_{\alpha\beta})$ of subordinated Hankel forms $B^\circ \prec (B_1, B_2)$ can be seen as a generalization of the Heinsenberg scattering function, since in the particular case of Theorem 2 the density of the measure μ_{12} coincides with the scattering function $S(t)$, while μ_{11} and μ_{22} are given by the corresponding identities in N_1 and N_2. Moreover, in the special case of the trigonometric example, in which, for $\alpha = 1, 2$,

$B_\alpha(f_\alpha, g_\alpha) = \int f_\alpha \overline{g}_\alpha \, dt$, μ_{12} turns out to be an absolutely continuous measure with density in BMO (cf. [4]). Thus the Fourier representation unifies the notion of Heinsenberg scattering functions and of BMO.

As shown in [10], the lifting property holds on any algebraic scattering system, even if regularity is not required to the pair of forms B_1, B_2, but in such case the lifting is not given in the precise form (9d), and the proof of its existence is not based on the functional representation (2)–(2f). More precisely,

THEOREM 2A. *Let $[V_1, V_2; W_1, W_2; \tau_1, \tau_2]$ be an algebraic scattering system, B_1, B_2 a pair of positive forms, (τ_1, τ_1) and (τ_2, τ_2)-Toeplitz, respectively, and $B^\circ : W_1 \times W_2 \to \mathbf{C}$, a (τ_1, τ_2)-Hankel form such that $B^\circ \prec (B_1, B_2)$. Then there exists a (τ_1, τ_2)-Toeplitz form $B : V_1 \times V_2 \to \mathbf{C}$, such that $B \leq (B_1, B_2)$ and $B = B^\circ$ in $W_1 \times W_2$.*

Two different proofs of this theorem were given in [7] and [10] for the case $V_1 = V_2$, $\tau_1 = \tau_2$, and their extension to general systems is immediate.

REMARK 4. As observed in [7] and [10], for every Hankel form $B^\circ \in \Lambda^\circ(B_1, B_2)$, its liftings in $\Lambda(B_1, B_2)$ are in $1-1$ correspondance with the Nagy-Foias liftings of a certain intertwining contraction (cf. also [9]).

In [9] it was also shown that triples of forms B_1, B_2, B°, defined on $A-A$ algebraic systems have a dilation property as well as a Fourier representation, although of a different nature from that of Theorem 1.

THEOREM 2B. *Let $[V_1, V_2; W_1, W_2; \tau_1, \tau_2]$ be an $A-A$ algebraic scattering system such that $V_1 = V_1^1$, $V_2 = V_2^2$ (as defined by (3b)). Let the triple B_1, B_2, B° be as in Theorem 2. Then for every pair $(e_1, e_2) \in \mathcal{E}_1 \times \mathcal{E}_2$ (as defined in (3c))*

(i) *there is a scalar-valued matric measure $(\nu_{\alpha\beta}) \geq 0$, defined in $\mathbf{T}$, $\nu_{\alpha\beta} = \nu_{\alpha\beta}(e_1, e_2)$ such that, for $\alpha = 1, 2$,*

$$B_\alpha(\tau_\alpha^n e_\alpha, \tau_\alpha^n e_\alpha) = \widehat{\nu}_{\alpha\beta}(m-n) \quad , \quad \forall\ (m,n) \in \mathbf{Z} \times \mathbf{Z}$$

and

$$B^\circ(\tau_1^n e_1, \tau_2^m e_2) = \widehat{\nu}_{12}(m-n) \quad , \quad \forall\ (m,n) \in \mathbf{Z}_+ \times \mathbf{Z}_- \tag{12}$$

(ii) *there is an unitary operator $U \in L(H)$, where H is a Hilbert space, and two mappings, $\varrho_1 : W_1 \to H$, $\varrho_2 : W_2 \to H$, giving the dilation, for $\alpha = 1, 2$,*

$$B_\alpha(\tau_\alpha^n, \tau_\alpha^m e_\alpha) = < U^{n-m} \varrho_\alpha e_\alpha, \varrho_\alpha e_\alpha > \quad , \quad (n,m) \in \mathbf{Z}_\alpha \times \mathbf{Z}_\alpha$$

and

$$B^\circ(\tau_1^n e_1, \tau_2^m e_2) = < U^{n-m} \varrho_1 e_1, \varrho_2 e_2 > \quad , \quad (n,m) \in \mathbf{Z}_1 \times \mathbf{Z}_2 \tag{13}$$

where $\mathbf{Z}_1 = \mathbf{Z}_+$, $\mathbf{Z}_2 = \mathbf{Z}_-$.

The relations between the two kinds of Fourier representations given by Theorem 1 and 2a for particular scattering systems will be discussed elsewhere.

5. LIFTINGS OF FORMS INVARIANT WITH RESPECT TO SEVERAL PAIRS OF ISOMORPHISMS

For simplicity, let us consider here the case of two pairs of isomorphisms. Let $[V_1, V_2; W_1, W_2; \tau_1, \tau_2]$ be a (discrete) algebraic scattering system, and let σ_1, σ_2, be another pair of linear isomorphisms, $\sigma_\alpha : V_\alpha \to V_\alpha$, such that $\tau_\alpha \sigma_\alpha = \sigma_\alpha \tau_\alpha$ for $\alpha = 1, 2$.

A sesquilinear form $B : V_\alpha \times V_\beta \to \mathbf{C}$, where $\alpha, \beta = 1, 2$, is called (τ, σ)-*Toeplitz* if B is invariant with respect to $(\tau_\alpha, \tau_\beta)$ as well as to $(\sigma_\alpha, \sigma_\beta)$, i.e.: if for all $m, n \in \mathbf{Z}$,

$$B(\tau_\alpha^m \sigma_\alpha^n f_\alpha, \tau_\beta^m \sigma_\beta^n f_\beta) = B(f_\alpha, f_\beta) \ , \ \forall \ (f_\alpha, f_\beta) \in V_\alpha \times V_\beta \tag{14}$$

Since for σ_1, σ_2 there are no conditions similar to $\tau_1 W_1 \subset W_1$, $\tau_2^{-1} W_2 \subset W_2$, we adopt the following definition: a form $B^\circ : W_1 \times W_2 \to \mathbf{C}$ is called (τ, σ)-*Hankel* if it is the restriction to $W_1 \times W_2$ of a (τ, σ)-Toeplitz form.

Now, let for $\alpha = 1, 2$,

$$W_\alpha^\sigma = \{f \in W_\alpha : \sigma_\alpha^p f \in W_\alpha \ , \ \forall \ p \in \mathbf{Z}\} \tag{15}$$

A form $B : V_1 \times V_2 \to \mathbf{C}$ is called *conditionally* (τ, σ)-*Toeplitz with respect to* W_1, W_2 if it is (τ_1, τ_2)-Toeplitz and if, for all $m \in \mathbf{Z}$,

$$B(\sigma_1^m f_1, \sigma_2^m f_2) = B(f_1, f_2) \ \text{ whenever } \ (f_1, f_2) \in W_1^\sigma \times W_2^\sigma . \tag{16}$$

Observe that this definition is equivalent to have, for all $m \in \mathbf{Z}$,

$$B(\sigma_1^m f_1, \sigma_2^m f_2) = B(f_1, f_2) \ \text{ whenever } \ (f_1, f_2) \in (\tau_1^r W_1^\sigma) \times (\tau_2^r W_2^\sigma) \tag{16a}$$

for some $r \in \mathbf{Z}$.

The definition of conditionally (τ, σ)-Toeplitz forms is motivated by the following property, of easy verification.

LEMMA 1. *Let* $[V_1, V_2; W_1, W_2; \tau_1, \tau_2]$ *be an algebraic scattering system. If* B *and* B' *are two forms defined in* $V_1 \times V_2$, *such that* B *is* (τ_1, τ_2)-*Toeplitz and* B' *is* (τ, σ)-*Toeplitz, and* B *coincides with* B' *on* $W_1^\sigma \times W_2^\sigma$, *then* B *is conditionally* (τ, σ)-*Toeplitz.*

The lifting property stated in Section 4, together with Lemma 1, immediately imply

COROLLARY 1. *Let* $[V_1, V_2; W_1, W_2; \tau_1, \tau_2]$ *be an algebraic scattering system, and let* B_1, B_2 *be two positive forms,* $B_\alpha : V_\alpha \times V_\alpha \to \mathbf{C}$, $(\tau_\alpha, \tau_\alpha)$-*Toeplitz for* $\alpha = 1, 2$,

$B^\circ : W_1 \times W_2 \to \mathbf{C}$, be a (τ,σ)-Hankel form such that $B^\circ \prec (B_1, B_2)$. Then there exists a conditionally (τ,σ)-Toeplitz form, $B : V_1 \times V_2 \to \mathbf{C}$, such that $B \leq (B_1, B_2)$, and B coincides with B° on $\mathcal{E}_1^\sigma \times \mathcal{E}_2^\sigma$.

PROPOSITION 1. *Let $[V_1, V_2; W_1, W_2; \tau_1, \tau_2]$ be an algebraic scattering system, and σ_1, σ_2 two isomorphisms, $\sigma_\alpha : V_\alpha \to V_\alpha$, such that $\sigma_\alpha \tau_\alpha = \tau_\alpha \sigma_\alpha$ for $\alpha = 1,2$. Given two positive forms B_1, B_2, $B_\alpha : V_\alpha \times V_\alpha \to \mathbf{C}$, $(\sigma_\alpha,\sigma_\alpha)$-Toeplitz, for $\alpha = 1,2$, and a conditionally (τ,σ)-Toeplitz form, $B : V_1 \times V_2 \to \mathbf{C}$, such that $B \leq (B_1, B_2)$, there exists a (τ,σ)-Toeplitz form, $B' : V_1 \times V_2 \to \mathbf{C}$, such that $B' \leq (B_1, B_2)$, and B' coincides with B on $W_1^\sigma \times W_2^\sigma$, where W_α^σ is given by (15).*

PROOF. Since for each $k = 1, 2, \cdots$,

$$|B(\sigma_1^k f_1, \sigma_2^k f_2)| \leq B_1(\sigma_1^k f_1, \sigma_1^k f_1)^{1/2} B_2(\sigma_2^k f_2, \sigma_2^k f_2)^{1/2} = \\ = B_1(f_1, f_1)^{1/2} B_2(f_2, f_2)^{1/2}, \tag{17}$$

fixing the pair f_1, f_2, we have that $\left(B(\sigma_1^k f_1, \sigma_2^k f_2)\right)_{k=1}^\infty$ is a bounded numerical sequence, so that the generalized Banach-Mazur limit (cf. [11], p. 73) of this sequence exists, and we may set

$$B'(f_1, f_2) = \operatorname*{LIM}_{k\to\infty} B(\sigma_1^k f_1, \sigma_2^k f_2) \tag{17a}$$

B' is easily seen to be a sesquilinear form. Since B is (σ_1,σ_2)-invariant on $W_1^\sigma \times W_2^\sigma$, we have that $B(\sigma_1^k f_1, \sigma_2^k f_2) = B(f_1, f_2)$ for $(f_1, f_2) \in W_1^\sigma \times W_2^\sigma$, and B' coincides with B on $W_1^\sigma \times W_2^\sigma$. From inequality (17) and the properties of LIM for complex-valued sequences, it follows that

$$|\text{Re } B'(f_1, f_2) \leq B_1(f_1, f_1)^{1/2}\, B_2(f_2, f_2)^{1/2} \quad , \quad \forall\ f_1, f_2$$

This, combined with the sesquilinearity of B', gives $B' \leq (B_1, B_2)$. Finally, since

$$B'(\sigma_1 f_1, \sigma_2 f_2) = \operatorname*{LIM}_{k\to\infty} B(\sigma_1^{k+1} f_1, \sigma_2^{k+1} f_2) = \\ = \operatorname*{LIM}_{k\to\infty} B(\sigma_1^k f_1, \sigma_2^k f_2) = B'(f_1, f_2),$$

B' is (σ_1,σ_2)-invariant, and since

$$B'(\tau_1 f_1, \tau_2 f_2) = \operatorname*{LIM}_{k\to\infty} B(\sigma_1^k \tau_1 f_1, \sigma_2^k \tau_2 f_2) = \\ = \operatorname*{LIM}_{k\to\infty} B(\sigma_1^k f_1, \sigma_2^k f_2) = B'(f_1, f_2),$$

B' is also (τ_1,τ_2)-invariant. Thus, B' is (τ,σ)-Toeplitz. ■

Combining Proposition 1 with Corollary 1, the following lifting theorem for (τ,σ)-Hankel forms is obtained as an immediate corollary.

THEOREM 3. *Let* $[V_1, V_2; W_1, W_2; \tau_1, \tau_2]$ *be an algebraic scattering system, and* σ_1, σ_2 *two isomorphisms,* $\sigma_\alpha : V_\alpha \to V_\alpha$*, such that* $\sigma_\alpha \tau_\alpha = \tau_\alpha \sigma_\alpha$*,* $\alpha = 1, 2$*. Given two positive* (τ, σ)*-Toeplitz forms,* B_1 *and* B_2*,* $B_\alpha : V_\alpha \times V_\alpha \to \mathbf{C}$*,* $\alpha = 1, 2$*, and a* (τ, σ)*-Hankel form,* $B^\circ : W_1 \times W_2 \to \mathbf{C}$*, such that* $B^\circ \prec (B_1, B_2)$*, there exists a* (τ, σ)*-Toeplitz form* $B' : V_1 \times V_2 \to \mathbf{C}$*, such that* $B' \leq (B_1, B_2)$*, and* B' *coincides with* B *in* $W_1^\sigma \times W_2^\sigma$*, where* W_1^σ, W_2^σ *are defined by* (15).

REMARK 5. Observe that (17a) is an explicit expression for B' in terms of B, and that in the cases discussed in Theorems 1 and 2, B is also given by explicit formulae. Therefore in these cases there are explicit representations of the liftings in all preceding results.

In the same framework we can consider the case of d different pairs of isomorphisms $(\sigma_1^{(1)}, \sigma_2^{(1)}), \ldots, (\sigma_1^{(d)}, \sigma_2^{(d)})$, $\sigma_\alpha^{(j)} : V_\alpha \to V_\alpha$, such that $\tau_\alpha \sigma_\alpha^{(j)} = \sigma_\alpha^{(j)} \tau_\alpha$, $j = 1, \ldots, d$, $\alpha = 1, 2$, and all the definitions and results of this Section extend to such situation.

6. EXTENSIONS TO CONTINUOUS SCATTERING SYSTEMS

Let us describe briefly what extensions to $\mathbf{R}$ are valid for the results of the preceding Sections.

The proof of Theorem 2 is based only on the functional realization (2)–(2f) of the discrete $A - A$ scattering system which extends to consider an evolution group $(\tau^t, t \in \mathbf{R})$ [2], and therefore the theorem holds, with only obvious modifications, also in the continuous case. In the proof of Theorem 1, the functional realization was used only to reduce the problem to the known Fourier representation of certain generalized Toeplitz kernels. A similar reduction still holds in the case of $\mathbf{R}$, but now it has to be followed by a Fourier representation theorem for a different kind of generalized Toeplitz kernels considered in [7].

Thus, Theorems 1 and 2a extend to the case of a continuous $A - A$ scattering system $[V; W_1, W_2; \tau^t, t \in \mathbf{R}]$, and Theorem 2 extends to continuous algebraic scattering systems $[V_1, V_2; W_1, W_2; \tau_1^t, \tau_2^t, t \in \mathbf{R}]$ for regular pairs of positive forms B_1, B_2.

Finally, the lifting property for general classes $\Lambda(B_1, B_2)$, in the case of continuous algebraic systems $[V_1, V_2; W_1, W_2; \tau_1^t, \tau_2^t, t \in \mathbf{R}]$, is given by Theorem 2 of [10].

Similarly, Proposition 1 and Theorem 4 extend, with obvious modifications, to the case of continuous algebraic systems $[V_1, V_2; W_1, W_2; \tau_1^t, \tau_2^t, t \in \mathbf{R}]$, where two continuous groups of isomorphisms $(\sigma_1^t : V_1 \to V_1, t \in \mathbf{R})$, $(\sigma_2^t : V_2 \to V_2, t \in \mathbf{R})$, operate, such that, for $\alpha = 1, 2$, $s, t \in \mathbf{R}$, $\sigma_\alpha^t \tau_\alpha^s = \tau_\alpha^s \sigma_\alpha^t$. Similar extensions hold for d different pairs of continuous evolutions, as in the discrete case.

7. APPLICATIONS

The study of forms developed above has a counterpart for hermitian kernels, that initiated in [7].

Consider a system $[X_1, X_2; E_1, E_2; \tau_1, \tau_2]$, where X_1, X_2 are given sets, $E_1 \subset X_1$, $E_2 \subset X_2$ are subsets, and, for $\alpha = 1,2$, $\tau_\alpha : X_\alpha \to X_\alpha$ are bijections in X_α such that

$$\tau_1 E_1 \subset E_1 \quad , \quad \tau_2^{-1} E_2 \subset E_2 \,. \tag{18}$$

To such a system is associated a discrete algebraic scattering structure $[V_1, V_2; W_1, W_2; \tau_1, \tau_2]$, where, for $\alpha = 1,2$,

$$V_\alpha = \{f : X_\alpha \to \mathbf{C}\,;\, \operatorname{supp} f \text{ finite}\}\,, W_\alpha = \{f \in V_\alpha \,;\, \operatorname{supp} f \subset E_\alpha\} \tag{19}$$

and

$$(\tau_\alpha f)(x) = f(\tau_\alpha x) \quad , \quad \forall\, f \in V_\alpha \,,\; x \in X_\alpha \tag{19a}$$

To each hermitian kernel $K : X_\alpha \times X_\beta \to \mathbf{C}$, $\alpha, \beta = 1,2$, is associated the sesquilinear form $B = B_K : V_\alpha \times V_\beta \to \mathbf{C}$, given by

$$B_K(f_\alpha, f_\beta) = \sum_{(x,y) \in X_\alpha \times X_\beta} K(x,y)\, f_\alpha(x)\, \overline{f_\beta(y)}\,. \tag{20}$$

If $\alpha = \beta$, K is said to be positive definite, p.d., if $B_K(f,f) \geq 0$, and we write $K \leq (K_1, K_2)$ if $B_K \leq (B_{K_1}, B_{K_2})$. Similarly, if $K^\circ : E_1 \times E_2 \to \mathbf{C}$ and $B^\circ = B_{K^\circ} : W_1 \times W_2 \to \mathbf{C}$, we write $K^\circ \prec (K_1, K_2)$ if $B^\circ \prec (B_{K_1}, B_{K_2})$. Also K, K_1, K_2 and K° are called respectively $(\tau_1, \tau_2)-$, $(\tau_1, \tau_1)-$, (τ_2, τ_2)-Toeplitz, and (τ_1, τ_2)-Hankel if the associated sasquilinear forms are of such types.

If $X_1 = X_2 = \mathbf{Z}$, $E_1 = \mathbf{Z}_+$, $E_2 = \mathbf{Z}_-$, $\tau_1 = \tau_2 =$ the translation in $\mathbf{Z}$, then we are (within a Fourier isomorphism) in the case of the trigonometric example. In this special case, every sesquilinear form in $V_\alpha \times V_\beta$ arises from a kernel K defined on $E_\alpha \times E_\beta$, and both studies, of forms and kernels, are equivalent. The proof of Theorem 1 shows that also the study of forms defined in an $A - A$ scattering system can be reduced to that of operator-valued kernels. However, this is not so for general algebraic structures. The result for kernels in [7] can therefore be obtained as a special case of Theorem 2a and given a different direct proof. Moreover, the generalization of Section 6 extends these results to $\mathbf{R}$. Even in the trigonometric example the results of Section 6 allow to extend the basic properties of the generalized Toeplitz kernels to distribution-valued ones, and give, in particular, the Nehari theorem in $\mathbf{R}$ (for details see [9]; that extension was obtained independently by R. Bruzual [5] through different methods). Finally the extension of forms in Section 6 gives also the refinements of the theorems of Helson-Szegő and Helson-Sarason in $\mathbf{R}$, stated in [4] without complete proofs.

The notions and results of Section 5 give corresponding results for kernels when in the scattering system $[V_1, V_2; W_1, W_2; \tau_1, \tau_2]$ operate other pairs of isomorphisms $(\sigma_1^{(j)}, \sigma_2^{(j)})$, $j = 1, \ldots, d$, which commute with the given (τ_1, τ_2). Let us remark that the analogue for kernels of Proposition 1 and Theorem 3 can be obtained directly with a different approach.

The results of Section 5 allow the treatment of different moment problems in several dimensions, in particular the extension of the Nehari theorem to Helson-Lowdenslager halplanes in $\mathbf{Z}^2$ (cf. [12]).

The subset $S \subset \mathbf{Z}^2$ is a $H-L$ halfplane if (i) $(0,0) \notin S$; (ii) $(m,n) \in S$ iff $(-m,-n) \notin S$ unless $m = n = 0$, and (iii) if $(m,n) \in S$ and $(m',n') \in S$ then $(m+m', n+n') \in S$. Here we shall limit ourselves to $H-L$ halfplanes S such that there exists a $(m_0, n_0) \in \mathbf{Z}^2$ satisfying $(m_0, n_0) + S \subset S$, thus also $(m_0, n_0) + (-S) \subset -S$, and for simplicity we concentrate on the case where

$$S = S_k = \{(m,n); n > k \text{ if } m < 0, n > 0 \text{ if } m = 0, n \geq -k \text{ if } m > 0\}$$

for k a non-negative integer, and $(m_0, n_0) = (0, 1)$. For such S_k, we set $X_1 = X_2 = \mathbf{Z}^2 = S_k \cup (-S_k) \cup \{(0,0)\}$, $E_1 = S_k$, $E_2 = -S_k$, $\tau_1 = \tau_2 = \tau$ defined by $\tau(m,n) = (m, n+1)$, $[V; W_1, W_2; \tau]$ the associated algebraic scattering structure, and $\sigma_1 = \sigma_2 = \sigma$ defined on $\mathbf{Z}^2$ by $\sigma(m,n) = (m+1, n)$. Observe that V can be identified through the Fourier isomorphism with the set of trigonometric polynomials in two variables.

Now we have that the subspaces defined in (15) in this case are, for $\alpha = 1, 2$, $W_\alpha(k) = \{f \in V; \operatorname{supp} \hat{f} \subset E_\alpha^k\}$, where

$$E_1^k = \{(m,n)\,;\, n > k\} \quad , \quad E_2^k = \{(m,n)\,;\, n < -k\} \tag{21}$$

are regular halfplanes.

In this setting a kernel $K : \mathbf{Z}^2 \times \mathbf{Z}^2 \to \mathbf{C}$, or a form $B : V \times V \to \mathbf{C}$, is (τ, σ)-Toeplitz iff it is Toeplitz in the usual sense with respect to both the horizontal and the vertical translations. Similarly, B° is *(τ, σ)-Hankel with respect to S_k* if it is the restriction of a (τ, σ)-Toeplitz form to

$$W_1 \times W_2 = \{(f_1, f_2) \in V \times V\,;\, \operatorname{supp} \hat{f}_1 \subset S_k\,,\, \operatorname{supp} \hat{f}_2 \subset -S_k\} \tag{22}$$

Theorem 3 reads in this context as

COROLLARY 2. *Given the $H-L$ halfplane S_k and B_1, B_2 two positive (τ, σ)-Toeplitz forms in $V \simeq$ the set of trigonometric polynomials in two variables, if B° is a (τ, σ)-Hankel form with respect to S_k* (as in (22)), *such that $|B^\circ(f_1, f_2)|^2 \leq B_1(f_1, f_1)\, B_2(f_2, f_2)$ whenever $(f_1, f_2) \in W_1 \times W_2$, then there exists a (τ, σ)-Toeplitz form B' such that $|B'(f_1, f_2)|^2 \leq B_1(f_1, f_1)\, B_2(f_2, f_2)$ for all $(f_1, f_2) \in V \times V$, and $B'(f_1, f_2) = B^\circ(f_1, f_2)$ whenever $(f_1, f_2) \in W_1(k) \times W_2(k)$.*

Writing, for $\alpha = 1,2$, $B_{\alpha\alpha} = B_\alpha$, $B_{12} = B'$, $B_{21} = (B')^*$, the forms of Corollary 2 satisfy $\sum_{\alpha,\beta=1,2} B_{\alpha\beta}(f_\alpha, f_\beta) \geq 0$ for all $(f_\alpha, f_\beta) \in V \times V$, so that $(B_{\alpha\beta})$ is a matrix-valued positive Toeplitz form and, by the Herglotz-Bochner theorem, there exists a positive definite 2×2 matrix $(\mu_{\alpha\beta})$, where each $\mu_{\alpha\beta}$ is a finite complex measure in $\mathbf{T}^2$, such that $B_{\alpha\beta}(f_\alpha, f_\beta) = \int\int f_\alpha \overline{f}_\beta \, d\mu_{\alpha\beta}$.

This gives

COROLLARY 3. *If B_1, B_2, B° are as in Corollary 2, then there exists a positive definite 2×2 matrix measure $(\mu_{\alpha\beta})$, defined in $\mathbf{T}^2$, such that, for $\alpha = 1,2$,*

$$B_\alpha(f,g) = \int\int f\overline{g}\, d\mu_{\alpha\alpha} \quad , \quad \forall\ f,g \in V$$

and

$$B^\circ(f_1,f_2) = \int\int f_1\overline{f}_2\, d\mu_{12} \text{ whenever } f_1 \in W_1(k)\,,\ f_2 \in W_2(k)\,.$$

In particular, if $B_1(f,g) = B_2(f,g) = M\int\int f\overline{g}\,dt$, then $d\mu_{11} = d\mu_{22} = M\,dt$, and from the positive definiteness of $(\mu_{\alpha\beta})$ one gets easily that $d\mu_{12} = p(t)\,dt$ with $|p(t)| \leq M$ for $t \in \mathbf{T}^2$. Thus, the following extension of the theorem of Nehari holds.

COROLLARY 4. *Given the $H - L$ halfplane S_k and a form B°, Hankel with respect to S_k, such that $|B^\circ(f_1,f_2)| \leq M\,\|f_1\|_2\,\|f_2\|_2$ for all $(f_1,f_2) \in W_1 \times W_2$, there is a bounded function p, $|p(t)| \leq M$ for $t \in \mathbf{T}^2$, such that $B^\circ(f_1,f_2) = \int\int f_1\overline{f}_2\,p\,dt$, whenever $(f_1,f_2) \in W_1(k) \times W_2(k)$.*

Observe that Corollary 3 allows also the extension of the Helson-Szegő theorem to $H - L$ halfplanes, which will be developed in a forthcoming paper.

Finally, let us indicate an application to bidimensional lacunary series, with a viewpoint similar to that developed in [8] for the onedimensional case. Again, let $X_1 = X_2 = \mathbf{Z}^2$, $E_1 = S_k$, $E_2 = -S_k$, $\tau_1 = \tau_2 = \tau$, the vertical translation in $\mathbf{Z}^2$, and $\sigma_1 = \sigma_2 = \sigma$, the horizontal translation in $\mathbf{Z}^2$. Given B_1, B_2, two positive Toeplitz forms in the associated $V \times V$, a countable set $Y \subset S_k + S_k$ is called a *(B_1,B_2)-Paley set with respect to S_k* if there is a $C(Y)$, such that for every function $\Phi(t)$, $\operatorname{supp}\widehat{\Phi} \subset S_k + S_k$,

$$\Big(\sum_{(m,n)\in Y} |\widehat{\Phi}(m,n)|^2\Big)^{1/2} \leq C(Y)\,B_1(\Phi,\Phi)\,B_2(\Phi,\Phi)$$

holds.

An argument similar to those in [8] allows to deduce from Corollary 4 the following

LEMMA 2. *A necessary and sufficient condition for a countable set* $Y \subset S_k + S_k$ *to be* (B_1, B_2)*-Paley with respect to* S_k *is that, for every* $\nu \in l^2(Y)$, $B^\circ \prec (cB_1, cB_2)$, *where* $B^\circ(f_1, f_2) \equiv \int\int \Phi f_1 \overline{f}_2 \, dt$, $\widehat{\Phi}(m,n) = \nu(m,n)$ *if* $(m,n) \in Y$ *and zero if* $(m,n) \in (S_k + S_k) \setminus Y$, *and* $c = C(Y) \, \|\nu\|_2$.

A countable set $Y \subset S_k + S_k$ is called *lacunary* if there exists a lacunary sequence of positive integers (n_k), $n_{k+1}/n_k > \gamma > 1$ for all k, and a family (Y_k) of finite subsets of $\mathbf{Z}$, $\operatorname{card} Y_k \leq c$ for all k, such that for each $(m,n) \in Y$ there is a k such that $m \in Y_k$ and $n = n_k$.

From Lemma 2 follows

COROLLARY 5. *Every lacunary set* $Y \subset S_k + S_k$ *is a* (B_1, B_2)*-Paley set with respect to* S_k, *for* $B_1(f,g) = B_2(f,g) = \int\int f\overline{g} \, dt$.

REMARK 6. The Bochner integral representation of positive definite functions in $\mathbf{R}$ was extended by M.G. Krein for the "reduced" case of positive definite functions defined in a finite interval $(-a, a)$. As shown in a forthcoming paper of R. Bruzual and the authors, a similar reduced version can be given for Theorem 2a, whenever the forms B_1, B_2, B° are associated to hermitian kernels. Reduced versions of Theorem 4 and Corollary 3 also hold, which lead to applications to reduced bidimensional moment problems, and, in particular, to the extension for generalized Toeplitz kernels of a theorem of Livshitz and Devinatz, however lack of space does not allow us to go into this matter here.

REFERENCES

[1] V.M. Adamjan, *Non-degenerate unitary coupling of semiunitary operators*, Funk. An. Priloz, **7**: 4 (1973), 1–16 (in Russian).

[2] V.M. Adamjan and D.Z. Arov, *On unitary couplings of semiunitary operators*, Matem. Issledovanya, **1**: 2 (1966), 3–64 (in Russian).

[3] R. Arocena and M. Cotlar, *Dilations of generalized Toeplitz kernels and L^2-weighted problems*, Lecture Notes in Math., **908**, Springer-Verlag, New York, 1982, 169–188.

[4] R. Arocena, M.Cotlar and C. Sadosky, *Weighted inequalities in L^2 and lifting properties*, Math. Anal. & Appl., Adv. in Math. Suppl. Stud., **7A** (1981), 95–128.

[5] R. Bruzual, Acta Cient. Venez., to appear.

[6] M. Cotlar and C. Sadosky, *On the Helson-Szegő theorem and a related class of modified Toeplitz kernels*, Proc. Symp. Pure Math. AMS, **25**: I (1979), 383–407.

[7] M. Cotlar and C. Sadosky, *A lifting theorem for subordinated invariant kernels*, J. Funct. Anal., **67** (1986), 345–359.

[8] M. Cotlar and C. Sadosky, *Lifting properties, Nehari theorem and Paley lacunary inequality*, Rev. Mat. Iberoamericana, **2**, 55–71.

[9] M. Cotlar and C. Sadosky, *Toeplitz liftings of Hankel forms*, in "Function Space & Applications, Lund 1981", (Eds.: J. Peetre, Y. Sagher & H. Wallin), Lecture notes in Math., Springer-Verlag, New York, 1987.

[10] M. Cotlar and C. Sadosky, *Prolongements des formes de Hankel généralisées en formes de Toeplitz*, C.R. Acad. Sci. Paris **A**, # (1987).

[11] N. Dunford and J.T. Schwartz, *Linear Operators*, Part I: General Theory, Interscience Publ., New York, 1958.

[12] H. Helson & D. Lowdenslager, *Prediction theory and Fourier series in several variables*, Acta Math., **99** (1958), 165–202.

M. Cotlar
Fac. de Ciencias
Univ. Central de Venezuela
Caracas 1050, Venezuela

C. Sadosky
Dept. of Mathematics
Howard University
Washington, D.C. 20059, USA

Operator Theory:
Advances and Applications, Vol. 35

RANDOM TOEPLITZ AND HANKEL OPERATORS*

Raúl Curto, Paul Muhly, and Jingbo Xia

An analogue of Hartman's theorem on completely continuous Hankel operators is proved for Hankel operators with random symbols.

§1 INTRODUCTION

In recent work [CMX], we have been studying operators that arise from flows in the following fashion. Let X be a compact Hausdorff space on which $\mathbb{R}$ acts and for $(x,t) \in X \times \mathbb{R}$, write $x + t$ for the translate of x by t. Also, let m be a fixed ergodic, invariant, probability measure on X. Given $\varphi \in L^\infty(m)$ and $x \in X$, we write $\varphi_x(t)$ for $\varphi(x + t)$ and we write T_{φ_x} for the Toeplitz operator on $H^2(\mathbb{R})$ determined by φ_x. The Hankel operator determined by φ_x, H_{φ_x}, is the operator from $H^2(\mathbb{R})$ to $H^2(\mathbb{R})^\perp$ defined by the formula $H_{\varphi_x}\xi = P^\perp\varphi_x\xi$, where $\xi \in H^2(\mathbb{R})$, P is the projection from $L^2(\mathbb{R})$ onto $H^2(\mathbb{R})$ and $P^\perp = I - P$. Thus, for each $\varphi \in L^\infty(m)$, we obtain operator–valued random variables on X, $x \longrightarrow T_{\varphi_x}$ and $x \longrightarrow H_{\varphi_x}$, and our ultimate interest is in how the dynamical properties of $(X, \mathbb{R}, m)$ are reflected in these random variables and vice versa.

Given $\varphi \in L^\infty(m)$, let $T_\varphi = \int_X^\oplus T_{\varphi_x}\, dm(x)$ and let $H_\varphi = \int_X^\oplus H_{\varphi_x}\, dm(x)$. The operator T_φ is unitarily equivalent to an operator in a II_∞ factor and, as is shown in [CMX], this fact leads to interesting spectral information about (almost) every T_{φ_x}. The operator H_φ also is unitarily equivalent to an operator in a II_∞ factor, a factor closely related to the one for T_φ. In this note we describe the factor for H_φ and address the problem of deciding when H_φ is relatively compact with respect to the factor. We prove

*Research supported by the National Science Foundation.

an analogue of Hartman's theorem [H], but in a sense that we shall make precise, it falls a bit short of what one might expect. Our analysis leads to interesting questions about relatively compact operators and function theory on flows.

§2 THE FACTOR

In this section, we describe the factor in which we do our analysis. It is really the well known group measure algebra of Murray and von Neumann built from $(X, \mathbb{R}, m)$. We call attention to certain features of it which arise in our calculations. Details which are omitted here may be found in [CMX].

The linear space $C_c(X \times \mathbb{R})$ of compactly supported continuous function on $X \times \mathbb{R}$ is a $*$–algebra under the product and involution given by the formulae

$$f * g(x,t) = \int g(x,s)f(x + s, t - s)ds,$$

and

$$f^*(x,t) = \overline{f(x + t, - t)},$$

$f, g \in C_c(X \times \mathbb{R})$. Also, the functional τ on $C_c(X \times \mathbb{R})$ defined by the formula $\tau(f) = \int f(x,0)\, dm(x)$ is a faithful trace on $C_c(X \times \mathbb{R})$ and $(C_c(X \times \mathbb{R}), \tau)$ is a Hilbert algebra. The inner product on $C_c(X \times \mathbb{R})$ determined by τ is really that on $L^2(X \times \mathbb{R})$ because $(f,g)_\tau = \tau(g^* * f) = \int_{\mathbb{R}} \int_X \overline{g(x,t)}\, f(x,t)\, dm(x)\, dt$, and so the left von Neumann algebra, $\mathfrak{M}$, of the Hilbert algebra $(C_c(X \times \mathbb{R}), \tau)$ is the von Neumann algebra on $L^2(X \times \mathbb{R})$ generated by the operators $\pi(f)$, $f \in C_c(X \times \mathbb{R})$, where $\pi(f)$ is given by the formula

$$\pi(f)\, \xi(x,t) = \int_{\mathbb{R}} f(x,s)\, \xi(x + s, t - s)\, ds, \quad \xi \in L^2(X \times \mathbb{R}).$$

Assuming, as we shall, that m is not supported on a periodic orbit, the von Neumann algebra $\mathfrak{M}$ is a II_∞ factor. One may think of the elements of $\mathfrak{M}$ as integral operators with kernels k supported on $X \times \mathbb{R}$ and one may think of the trace of such an operator as $\int k(x,0)\, dm(x)$. Of course these assertions are <u>not</u> strictly correct, but they do aid the intuition.

The algebra $\mathfrak{M}$ is generated by the operators $\sigma(\varphi)$, $\varphi \in L^\infty(m)$, and $\{U_t\}_{t \in \mathbb{R}}$ where $\sigma(\varphi)\, \xi *(x,s) = \varphi(x)\, \xi(x,s)$ and $(U_t\xi)(x,s) = \xi(x + t, s - t)$, $\xi \in L^2(X \times \mathbb{R})$. These operators satisfy the key covariance relation:

(2.1) $$U_t\sigma(\varphi)U_t^* = \sigma(\varphi_t)$$

where $\varphi_t(x) = \varphi(x + t)$.

Write $U_s = \int e^{i\lambda s} dE(\lambda)$ and let M be a Borel subset of $\mathbb{R}$ with finite Lebesque measure $|M|$. Then an easy calculation shows that E(M) is given by the formula $(E(M)\xi)(x,t) = \int_{\mathbb{R}} \hat{1}_M(s)\ \xi(x + s, t - s)ds$ where 1_M is the characteristic function of M and $\hat{1}_M$ is the Fourier transform of 1_M. Thus we see that E(M) <u>is</u> an "integral operator" with kernel $k(x,t) = \hat{1}_M(t)$. Moreover, even though $\hat{1}_M$ does not have compact support, a summability argument shows that E(M) is trace class relative to $\mathfrak{R}$ with $\tau(E(M)) = \int k(x,0)dm(x) = \hat{1}_M(0) = |M|$. (Once one knows $\mathfrak{R}$ is a factor, a fact which follows easily from the ergodicity of m, this calculation shows that the range of the trace on the projections of $\mathfrak{R}$ is $[0,\infty]$, thereby proving that $\mathfrak{R}$ is a II_∞ factor.)

We define P to be the spectral projection $E[0,\infty]$ and we define $H^2(X \times \mathbb{R})$ to be $PL^2(X \times \mathbb{R})$. For $\varphi \in L^\infty(m)$, we set

$$T_\varphi = P\sigma(\varphi) \mid H^2(X \times \mathbb{R}),$$

and we set

$$H_\varphi = P^\perp \sigma(\varphi)P.$$

We call T_φ the *generalized Toeplitz* operator determined by φ and we call H_φ the *generalized Hankel* operator determined by φ. Define V on $L^2(X \times \mathbb{R})$ by $(V\xi)(x,t) = \xi(x - t,t)$. Then V is a unitary operator on $L^2(X \times \mathbb{R})$ that carries $H^2(X \times \mathbb{R})$ onto $L^2(X) \otimes H^2(\mathbb{R})$, viewed as a subspace of $L^2(X \times \mathbb{R})$ in the usual way. If we think of $L^2(X \times \mathbb{R})$ as $\int_X^\oplus L^2(\mathbb{R})\ dm(x)$ with $L^2(X) \otimes H^2(\mathbb{R})$ viewed as $\int_X^\oplus H^2(\mathbb{R})\ dm(x)$, then for $\varphi \in L^\infty(m)$,

$$VT_\varphi V^{-1} = \int_X^\oplus T_{\varphi_x}\ dm(x)$$

(2.2) $$V(H_\varphi \mid H^2(X \times \mathbb{R}))V^{-1} = \int_X^\oplus H_{\varphi_x}\ dm(x).$$

This indicates why the II_∞ factor $\mathfrak{R}$ might be useful in the analysis of the operator–valued random variables $\{T_{\varphi_x}\}_{x \in X}$ and $\{H_{\varphi_x}\}_{x \in X}$.

Recall that a projection in a semifinite von Neumann algebra is called *finite* if it has finite trace. In particular, we have just seen that each E(M), $|M| < \infty$, is a finite projection in $\mathfrak{R}$. By definition, the *Breuer ideal*, or the ideal of *relatively compact operators*, in a semifinite von Neumann algebra is the norm closed *algebra* generated by the finite projections. The fact that this algebra is, indeed, an ideal follows from the unitary invariance of the trace. We write $K(\mathfrak{M})$ for the Breuer ideal in our factor $\mathfrak{M}$.

Problem: When does $H_\varphi \in K(\mathfrak{M})$?

In the next section we give a necessary and sufficient condition on φ that H_φ lies in a certain subalgebra of $K(\mathfrak{M})$.

§3. HARTMAN'S THEOREM REVISITED.

Set $\mathfrak{M}_1 = E[0,1]\mathfrak{M}E[0,1]$. Then $\mathfrak{M}_1$ is a II_1 factor and $\mathfrak{M}$ is isomorphic to $\mathfrak{M}_1 \otimes \mathcal{L}(\ell^2(\mathbb{Z}))$. (This is the von Neumann algebra tensor product.) Indeed, $I = \sum_{n\in\mathbb{Z}} E[n,n+1]$ and the projections $E[n,n+1]$ are all equivalent in $\mathfrak{M}$ to $E[0,1]$ because $\tau(E[n,n+1]) = 1$. Let $\mathcal{LC}(\ell^2(\mathbb{Z}))$ denote the compact operators on $\ell^2(\mathbb{Z})$ and write $\mathfrak{M}_1 \otimes \mathcal{LC}(\ell^2(\mathbb{Z}))$ for the *norm closed* subalgebra of $\mathfrak{M}_1 \otimes \mathcal{L}(\ell^2(\mathbb{Z}))$ generated by the operators of the form $A \otimes K$ where $A \in \mathfrak{M}_1$ and $K \in \mathcal{LC}(\ell^2(\mathbb{Z}))$. Then it is easy to see that under the identification of $\mathfrak{M}$ with $\mathfrak{M}_1 \otimes \mathcal{L}(\ell^2(\mathbb{Z}))$, $\mathfrak{M}_1 \otimes \mathcal{LC}(\ell^2(\mathbb{Z}))$ is identified with $\{T \in \mathfrak{M} \mid \lim_{n\to\infty} E[-n,n]T\,E[-n,n] = T \text{ in norm}\}$. Henceforth we will make these identifications without further comment.

Remark 3.1. At first glance, one might think that $\mathfrak{M}_1 \otimes \mathcal{LC}(\ell^2(\mathbb{Z})) = K(\mathfrak{M})$. Certainly every operator in $\mathfrak{M}_1 \otimes \mathcal{LC}(\ell^2(\mathbb{Z}))$ is also in $K(\mathfrak{M})$. However, the inclusion is proper! Indeed, the projection $Q = \sum_{n\in\mathbb{Z}} E[n, n+2^{-|n|}]$ lies in $K(\mathfrak{M})$ because $\tau(Q) = 3$, but since $E[-n,n]Q\,E[-n,n]$ does not converge in norm to Q, $Q \notin \mathfrak{M}_1 \otimes \mathcal{LC}(\ell^2(\mathbb{Z}))$. It is not difficult to see that $K(\mathfrak{M})$ is simple and so one concludes, in particular, that $\mathfrak{M}_1 \otimes \mathcal{LC}(\ell^2(\mathbb{Z}))$ is not an ideal in $\mathfrak{M}$. Finally, we note that since $\mathfrak{M}_1 \otimes \mathcal{LC}(\ell^2(\mathbb{Z}))$ contains a projection with trace r for each $r \in [0,\infty)$, every projection in $K(\mathfrak{M})$ is equivalent in $\mathfrak{M}$ to a projection in $\mathfrak{M}_1 \otimes \mathcal{LC}(\ell^2(\mathbb{Z}))$.

We let $L^\infty_c(m) = \{\varphi \in L^\infty(m) \mid t \longrightarrow \varphi_t \text{ is continuous in } L^\infty(m)\text{-norm}\}$. (Recall, $\varphi_t(x)$ is defined to be $\varphi(x+t)$, $x \in X$.) By a descendant of Cohen's famous factorization theorem, $L^\infty_c(m) = \{\varphi * f \mid \varphi \in L^\infty(m), f \in L^1(\mathbb{R})\}$, where

$(\varphi * f)(x) = \int_{\mathbb{R}} \varphi(x+t)f(t)dt$. See [HR, Theorem 32.23]. Also, we let $H^\infty(m) = \{\varphi \in L^\infty(m) \mid \varphi_x$ lies in $H^\infty(\mathbb{R})$ for m almost all $x\}$. Then $H^\infty(m)$ is a weak-$*$ closed subalgebra of $L^\infty(m)$ containing the constants such that $H^\infty(m) + \overline{H^\infty(m)}$ is weak-$*$ dense in $L^\infty(m)$ [M]. From equation (2.2), it follows that $H_\varphi = 0$ precisely when $\varphi \in H^\infty(m)$. Also, it can be proved using techniques of [R] that $L_c^\infty(m) + H^\infty(m)$ is a norm closed linear subspace of $L^\infty(m)$. In fact, as we shall see in Theorem 4.1, $L_c^\infty(m) + H^\infty(m)$ is a subalgebra of $L^\infty(m)$.

THEOREM 3.2. *For* $\varphi \in L^\infty(m)$, H_φ *lies in* $\mathfrak{M}_1 \otimes \mathcal{LC}(\ell^2(\mathbb{Z}))$ *if and only if* $\varphi \in L_c^\infty(m) + H^\infty(m)$.

COROLLARY 3.3. *If* $\varphi \in C(X)$, *then* H_φ *lies in* $K(\mathfrak{M})$.

Of course we are led naturally to the

CONJECTURE. $H_\varphi \in K(\mathfrak{M})$ if and only if $\varphi \in L_c^\infty(m) + H^\infty(m)$.

The conjecture is appealing, but since $K(\mathfrak{M})$ is so much bigger than $\mathfrak{M}_1 \otimes \mathcal{LC}(\ell^2(\mathbb{Z}))$ we are not at all confident that it is true.

To prove Theorem 3.2, we begin by letting $\{\alpha_t\}_{t\in\mathbb{R}}$ denote the inner automorphism group implemented by $\{U_t\}_{t\in\mathbb{R}}$, i.e., for $T \in \mathfrak{M}$, $\alpha_t(T) = U_t T U_t^*$. Then since $\alpha_t(\sigma(\varphi)) = \sigma(\varphi_t)$ by equation (2.1), we see that $\alpha_t(P) = P$. It follows that for $f \in L^1(\mathbb{R})$, $H_\varphi *_\alpha f = H_{\varphi * f}$ where $H_\varphi *_\alpha f$ is the weakly convergent integral $\int_{\mathbb{R}} \alpha_t(H_\varphi)f(t)dt$. Note, too, that for $T \in \mathfrak{M}_1 \otimes \mathcal{LC}(\ell^2(\mathbb{Z}))$, the function $t \longrightarrow \alpha_t(T)$ is *norm* continuous. Indeed, for each fixed k, $\alpha_t(E[-k,k]T\,E[-k,k])$ $= (E[-k,k]U_t\,E[-k,k])(T)(E[-k,k]U_t^*\,E[-k,k])$ and $t \longrightarrow E[-k,k]U_t\,E[-k,k]$ is norm continuous. This implies our assertion.

Suppose now that H_φ lies in $\mathfrak{M}_1 \otimes \mathcal{LC}(\ell^2(\mathbb{Z}))$. Then by what we just noted, $t \longrightarrow \alpha_t(H_\varphi)$ is norm continuous. By the descendant of Cohen's factorization theorem cited above, there is an $f \in L^1(\mathbb{R})$ such that $H_\varphi = H_\varphi *_\alpha f$. Since $H_\varphi *_\alpha f = H_{\varphi * f}$ we conclude that $\varphi - \varphi * f$ lies in $H^\infty(m)$. Since $\varphi * f \in L_c^\infty(m)$, we conclude that $\varphi \in L_c^\infty(m) + H^\infty(m)$.

To prove the converse, we require the following assertion which is an immediate consequence of equation (2.1) and [LM, Scholium 2.8], Forelli's Spectral Commutation Theorem.

ASSERTION. Let $\varphi \in L^\infty(m)$, let $f \in L^1(\mathbb{R})$, and let K be the support of $\hat{f}$. Then $\sigma(\varphi * f)\, H^2(X \times \mathbb{R}) = \sigma(\varphi * f)\, E[0,\infty)\, L^2(X \times \mathbb{R}) \subseteq E(K + [0,\infty))\, L^2(X \times \mathbb{R})$.

To show that $\varphi \in L^\infty_c(m) + H^\infty(m)$ implies that H_φ lies in $\mathfrak{R}_1 \otimes \mathcal{LC}(\ell^2(\mathbb{Z}))$, we may assume without loss of generality that $\varphi \in L^\infty_c(m)$. Choose an approximate identity $\{f_n\}_{n=1}^\infty$ for $L^1(\mathbb{R})$ such that for each n, the support of $\hat{f}_n$ is compact. Then because $\varphi \in L^\infty_c(m)$, $\varphi * f_n \longrightarrow \varphi$ in $L^\infty(m)$–norm and so $H_{\varphi * f_n} \longrightarrow H_\varphi$ in operator norm. On the other hand our Assertion implies that for each n there is an N_n such that $H_{\varphi * f_n} = E[-N_n, N_n]\, H_{\varphi * f_n}\, E[-N_n, N_n]$. Thus each $H_{\varphi * f_n}$ lies in $\mathfrak{R}_1 \otimes \mathcal{LC}(\ell^2(\mathbb{Z}))$ and so, therefore, does H_φ. This completes the proof.

§4. ON $L^\infty_c(m) + H^\infty(m)$

Our objective in this section is to prove

THEOREM 4.1. *The space* $L^\infty_c(m) + H^\infty(m)$ *is a norm closed subalgebra of* $L^\infty(m)$.

We are indebted to Don Sarason for pointing out this result and for suggesting that a proof might be given along the lines found in §5 of [S].

Recall that if $\varphi \in L^\infty(m)$, then $sp(\varphi)$ is the intersection $\cap\{\lambda \mid \hat{f}(\lambda) = 0\}$ where the intersection is taken over all functions $f \in L^1(\mathbb{R})$ such that $\varphi * f = 0$. For $\varphi \in L^\infty(m)$, $sp(\varphi)$ is a closed subset of $\mathbb{R}$ which is nonempty, if $\varphi \neq 0$. It is not difficult to show that $sp(\varphi) \subseteq [a,\infty)$ if and only if $\varphi * f = 0$ for all $f \in L^1(\mathbb{R})$ such that $\hat{f}(\lambda) = 0$ for all $\lambda \in [a,\infty)$. We note, in particular, that $H^\infty(m) = \{\varphi \in L^\infty(m) \mid sp(\varphi) \subseteq [0,\infty)\}$ [M]. The following is an analogue of Lemma 6 in [S].

LEMMA 4.2. *If* φ *is a function in* $L^\infty(m)$ *with* $sp(\varphi) \subseteq [a,\infty)$, *where* $a < 0$, *then* $\varphi \in L^\infty_c(m) + H^\infty(m)$.

PROOF. Choose a function $f \in L^1(\mathbb{R})$ such that $\hat{f}$ has compact support and such that $\hat{f}$ is identically 1 on $[a,0]$, and write $\varphi = \varphi * f + (\varphi - \varphi * f)$. Then, as noted earlier, $\varphi * f \in L^\infty_c(m)$. To show that $\varphi - \varphi * f \in H^\infty(m)$, we need to show that if $g \in L^1(\mathbb{R})$ satisfies $\hat{g}(\lambda) = 0$, $\lambda \geq 0$, then $(\varphi - \varphi * f) * g = 0$. But $(\varphi - \varphi * f) * g = \varphi * (g - f * g)$ and $(g - f * g)\hat{}\,(\lambda) = (1 - \hat{f}(\lambda))\hat{g}(\lambda) = 0$ when $\lambda \in [a,0]$ because $\hat{f}(\lambda) = 1$ there, while $(1 - \hat{f}(\lambda))\hat{g}(\lambda) = 0$ when $\lambda \in [0,\infty)$ by the hypothesis on

g. Consequently, since $\mathrm{sp}(\varphi) \subseteq [a,\infty)$, by assumption, $\varphi *(g - f*g) = 0$, proving the lemma.

Since $\mathrm{sp}(\varphi\psi) \subseteq \mathrm{sp}(\varphi) + \mathrm{sp}(\psi)$, by a corollary of the Forelli Spectral Commutation Theorem, we see that the collection of $\varphi \in L^\infty(m)$ such that $\mathrm{sp}(\varphi) \subseteq [a,\infty)$, for some a depending on φ, is an algebra A_0 contained in $L_c^\infty(m) + H^\infty(m)$. On the other hand, since $L^1(\mathbb{R})$ has an approximate identity consisting of functions with compactly supported Fourier transforms and since $\mathrm{sp}(\varphi * f) \subseteq \sup(\hat{f})$, it follows that $L_c^\infty(m) + H^\infty(m)$ is contained in the norm closure of A_0. Hence, to complete the proof of Theorem 4.1, it suffices to prove

LEMMA 4.3. *The space* $L_c^\infty(m) + H^\infty(m)$ *is norm closed.*

PROOF. It suffices to show that the conditions of Rudin's Theorem 1.2 in [R] are satisfied. We follow the notation there. The Banach space X is $L^\infty(m)$, $Y = L_c^\infty(m)$ and $Z = H^\infty(m)$. The space Φ of operators on X is $\{\Lambda_y\}_{y>0}$ where $\Lambda_y(\varphi) = \frac{1}{\pi}\int_{\mathbb{R}} \varphi(x+t)\frac{y}{y^2+t^2}\,dt$; i.e. Λ_y is convolution with respect to the Poisson kernel for the upper half–plane evaluated at $y > 0$. Then $\Lambda_y(X) \subseteq Y$ since, as we noted earlier $L^\infty(m) * L^1(\mathbb{R}) = L_c^\infty(m)$. So, Rudin's condition a) is satisfied. Since each Λ_y commutes with translation, Λ_y maps Z into Z; i.e., Rudin's condition b) is satisfied. Clearly $\sup\{\|\Lambda_y\|\} = 1$, so his condition c) is satisfied. Finally, since the Poisson kernel is an approximate identity for $L^1(\mathbb{R})$ and since translation on $L_c^\infty(m)$ is continuous in norm, we see that $\lim_{y\to 0} \|\varphi - \Lambda_y(\varphi)\| = 0$ for all $\varphi \in Y$. Thus Rudin's last condition, condition d), is satisfied. This completes the proof of the lemma, and with it, the proof of Theorem 4.1.

REFERENCES

[CMX] R. Curto, P. Muhly, and J. Xia, Toeplitz operators on flows, preprint.

[H] P. Hartman, On completely continuous Hankel matrices, Proc. Amer. Math. Soc. 9(1958), 362–366.

[HR] E. Hewitt and K. Ross, Abstract Harmonic Analysis, Springer Verlag, Berlin, Vol. 2, 1970.

[LM] R. Loebl and P. Muhly, Analyticity and flows in von Neumann algebras, J. Functional Anal. 29(1978), 214–252.

[M] P. Muhly, Function algebras and flows, Acta Sci. Math. (Szeged) 35(1973), 111–121.

[R] W. Rudin, Spaces of type $H^\infty + C$, Ann. L'Inst. Fourier (Grenoble) XXV(1975), 99–125.

[S] D. Sarason, Functions of vanishing mean oscillation, Trans. Amer. Math. Soc. 207 (1975), 391–405.

R. Curto and P. Muhly
Department of Mathematics
University of Iowa
Iowa City, Iowa 52242
U.S.A.

J. Xia
Department of Mathematics
State University of New York
Buffalo, NY 14214
U.S.A.

Operator Theory:
Advances and Applications, Vol. 35

BLOCK TOEPLITZ OPERATORS WITH RATIONAL SYMBOLS

I. Gohberg and M.A. Kaashoek

Semi-infinite block Toeplitz operators with rational matrix symbols are inverted explicitly by using the factorization method and by a method of reduction to singular systems with boundary conditions. The case of finite block Toeplitz matrices is also included. Fredholm characteristics are computed. All formulas are explicit and based on a realization of the symbol as a transfer function of a singular system.

0. INTRODUCTION

This paper concerns block Toeplitz equations of the form:

$$\sum_{\nu=0}^{\infty} \Phi_{k-\nu} x_\nu = y_k, \qquad k = 0, 1, 2, \ldots, \tag{0.1}$$

where Φ_k, $k = 0, \pm 1, \pm 2, \ldots$, are the Fourier coefficients of a rational $m \times m$ matrix function

$$\Phi(\zeta) = \sum_{\nu=-\infty}^{\infty} \zeta^\nu \Phi_\nu, \qquad |\zeta| = 1.$$

Equation (0.1) has been analyzed and solved explicitly in [1,2] for the case when the symbol Φ is, additionally, analytic at infinity and $\Phi(\infty)$ is invertible. Here we consider the general rational matrix case without any restriction on the behaviour at infinity.

Our analysis is based on a special representation of the symbol Φ, namely

$$\Phi(\zeta) = I + C(\zeta G - A)^{-1} B, \qquad |\zeta| = 1. \tag{0.2}$$

Here A and G are square matrices of which the order n may be larger than m, the pencil $\zeta G - A$ is regular on the unit circle $|\zeta| = 1$, and the matrices B and C have sizes $n \times m$ and $m \times n$, respectively. The representation (0.2) comes from mathematical systems theory and is called a *realization*. The main ideas from [1,2], where G is the $n \times n$ matrix I, are extended to the general case considered here. First we make an explicit canonical factorization of Φ in terms of A, G, B and C with factors also expressed in realized form. The construction is based on a separation of spectra argument for linear pencils which may be found in F. Stummel [9]. Next, we use this factorization to write explicitly the inverse operator.

Also the method from [2,3], which is based on an equivalence with linear systems with boundary conditions, is extended to the general rational case. The systems which appear now are singular (cf. [10]) and have the following form:

$$\tag{0.3} \begin{cases} A\rho_{k+1} &= G\rho_k + Bx_k, \qquad k=0,1,2,\dots, \\ y_k &= -C\rho_{k+1} + x_k, \quad k=0,1,2,\dots, \\ (I-Q)\rho_0 &= 0. \end{cases}$$

Here A, G, B and C are as in (0.2), and Q is the projection

$$Q = \frac{1}{2\pi i} \int\limits_{|\zeta|=1} (\zeta G - A)^{-1} G d\zeta.$$

The equivalence between (0.1) and (0.3) provides an alternative way to invert (0.1) and allows one to compute different Fredholm characteristics. This second method is also used to invert finite block Toeplitz matrices. In both cases the inversion formulas are obtained in a form which is similar to the formula for the general solution of a system of ordinary differential equation with constant coefficients. It turns out that also for the general rational case considered here the coupling method from [4] can be applied. We use this method to construct a generalized inverse.

The paper consists of 10 sections. The first section has a preliminary character. We recall the factorization method [7] and introduce some notations. In Section 2 we present in a form which is suitable for our purposes, the extension to linear operator pencils [9] of the classical Riesz theory of separation of spectra. Section 3 concerns the construction of the realized form (0.2). In Section 4 double infinite block Toeplitz operators with rational symbols are inverted explicitly. Here appears the associate pencil $\zeta G - A + BC$ which plays also an essential role in the explicit construction of the canonical factorization (Section 5) and in the explicit inversion of semi-infinite block Toeplitz operators with rational symbols (Section 6). In Section 7 the second method based on equivalence with discrete boundary value systems is developed. Section 8 contains the applications to finite block Toeplitz matrices. Fredholm characteristics and generalized inverses are computed in Section 9. The results of Section 9 can be extended to singular integral equations with rational symbols defined on arbitrary closed curves. In the last section we illustrate the results of this paper on an example.

1. PRELIMINARIES

This section has a preliminary character. We introduce some terminology and notation, and we recall (from [7]) the usual procedure to invert a block Toeplitz operator with symbol in the Wiener class using the factorization method.

We begin with some notation. The unit circle in the complex plane $\mathbb{C}$ will be denoted by $\mathbb{T}$. We write $\mathbb{D}_+$ for the open unit disc and $\mathbb{D}_-$ is the complement on the Riemann sphere $\mathbb{C}_\infty = \mathbb{C} \cup \{\infty\}$ of the set $\mathbb{D}_+ \cup \mathbb{T}$. A *Cauchy contour* Γ will mean the positively oriented boundary of a bounded Cauchy domain in $\mathbb{C}$. Such a contour consists of a finite number of nonintersecting closed rectifiable Jordan curves. The set of points inside Γ is called the *inner domain* of Γ and will be denoted by Δ_+. The *outer domain* of Γ is the set $\Delta_- = \mathbb{C}_\infty \backslash (\Delta_+ \cup \Gamma)$. We shall always assume that 0 belongs to Δ_+. By definition $\infty \in \Delta_-$. For $1 \leq p \leq \infty$ we denote by ℓ_p^m the Banach space of all sequences $(x_0, x_1, x_2, \ldots)$ of vectors in $\mathbb{C}^m$ such that the corresponding sequence of norms, $(\|x_k\|)_{k=1}^\infty$, belongs to ℓ_p. The space of all double infinite sequences of this type is denoted by $\ell_p^m(\mathbb{Z})$.

Consider the block Toeplitz operator $T = [\Phi_{k-j}]_{k,j=0}^\infty$, where the Φ_k are complex $m \times m$ matrices such that

$$(1.1)\qquad \sum_{\nu=-\infty}^{\infty} \|\Phi_k\| < \infty.$$

Here the norm is the usual operator norm on an $m \times m$ matrix. Condition (1.1) means that the *symbol*,

$$(1.2)\qquad \Phi(\zeta) = \sum_{\nu=-\infty}^{\infty} \zeta^\nu \Phi_\nu, \qquad \zeta \in \mathbb{T},$$

belongs to the Wiener class $\mathcal{W}^{m\times m}$ of all absolutely convergent sequences of complex $m \times m$ matrices. Fix $1 \leq p \leq \infty$. The block Toeplitz operator T induces a bounded linear operator (also denoted by T) on ℓ_p^m, namely

$$(1.3)\qquad (Tx)_k = \sum_{\nu=0}^{\infty} \Phi_{k-\nu} x_\nu, \qquad k = 0, 1, 2, \ldots,$$

where $x = (x_0, x_1, x_2, \ldots) \in \ell_p^m$. To invert T one looks for a so-called right canonical factorization of its symbol.

Let Γ be a Cauchy contour with Δ_+ and Δ_- as inner and outer domain, respectively. A continuous $m \times m$ matrix-valued function Φ on Γ is said to admit a *right canonical factorization* relative to Γ if Φ can be written as

$$\Phi(\zeta) = \Phi_-(\zeta)\Phi_+(\zeta), \qquad \zeta \in \Gamma, \tag{1.4}$$

where for $\alpha = +, -$ the function Φ_α is an $m \times m$ matrix function which is continuous on $\Delta_\alpha \cup \Gamma$, analytic on Δ_α and $\det \Phi_\alpha(\lambda) \neq 0$ for each $\lambda \in \Delta_\alpha \cup \Gamma$. In particular, the factor Φ_- is analytic at ∞ and $\det \Phi_-(\infty) \neq 0$. If Φ admits such a factorization, then $\det \Phi(\zeta) \neq 0$ for each $\zeta \in \Gamma$, but, in general, this condition is only necessary and not sufficient for (1.4) to exist. One speaks about a *left canonical factorization* if in (1.4) the order the the factors is interchanged.

A block Toeplitz operator T on ℓ_p^m with symbol Φ from the Wiener class $\mathcal{W}^{m\times m}$ is invertible (see [7]) if and only if Φ admits a right canonical factorization relative to the unit circle. In that case the factors Φ_- and Φ_+ in a right canonical factorization of Φ relative to $\mathbb{T}$ are also in $\mathcal{W}^{m\times m}$ and (see [6])

$$(T^{-1}y)_k = \sum_{j=0}^{\infty} \Gamma_{kj} y_j, \qquad k = 0, 1, 2, \ldots, \tag{1.5}$$

where

$$\Gamma_{kj} = \sum_{r=0}^{\min(k,j)} \gamma_{k-r}^+ \gamma_{r-j}^-, \tag{1.6}$$

with

$$\Phi_-(\zeta)^{-1} = \sum_{j=-\infty}^{0} \zeta^j \gamma_j^-, \quad \Phi_+(\zeta)^{-1} = \sum_{j=0}^{\infty} \zeta^j \gamma_j^+ \qquad (\zeta \in \mathbb{T}). \tag{1.7}$$

The inversion of a double infinite block Toeplitz operator $L = [\Phi_{k-j}]_{k,j=-\infty}^{\infty}$ on $\ell_p^m(\mathbb{Z})$ is much easier. We shall use the following result (see [7]): If the symbol Φ of L belongs to the Wiener class, then L is invertible if and only if $\det \Phi(\zeta) \neq 0$ for each $\zeta \in \mathbb{T}$ and in that case $L^{-1} = [\Phi_{k-j}^\times]_{k,j=-\infty}^{\infty}$, where the $\Phi_k^\times$ are the Fourier coefficients of the function $\Phi(\cdot)^{-1}$.

In what follows we identify a $p \times q$ matrix with the linear transformation from $\mathbb{C}^q$ into $\mathbb{C}^p$ defined by the canonical action of the matrix relative to the standard bases in $\mathbb{C}^q$ and $\mathbb{C}^p$. The symbol I denotes an identity operator or a square identity matrix. If necessary an index will indicate on which space I acts.

2. LINEAR OPERATOR PENCILS

The main result in this section is a spectral decomposition theorem which summarizes in a way suitable for our purposes the extension (see [9]) to operator pencils of the classical Riesz theory about separation of spectra.

Let X be a complex Banach space, and let G and A be bounded linear operators on X. The expression $\lambda G - A$, where λ is a complex parameter, will be called a (*linear*) *pencil* of operators on X. Given a nonempty subset Δ of the Riemann sphere $\mathbb{C}_\infty$, we say that $\lambda G - A$ is Δ-*regular* if $\lambda G - A$ (or just G if $\lambda = \infty$) is invertible for each λ in Δ. In what follows we study Γ-regular pencils, where Γ is a Cauchy contour (see Section 1). We assume that 0 is in the inner domain of Γ.

THEOREM 2.1. *Let Γ be a Cauchy contour with Δ_+ and Δ_- as inner and outer domain, respectively, and let $\lambda G - A$ be a Γ-regular pencil of operators on the Banach space X. Then there exists a projection P and an invertible operator E, both acting on X, such that relative to the decomposition $X = \operatorname{Ker} P \oplus \operatorname{Im} P$ the following partitioning holds true*:

$$(2.1) \qquad (\lambda G - A)E = \begin{bmatrix} \lambda\Omega_1 - I_1 & 0 \\ 0 & \lambda I_2 - \Omega_2 \end{bmatrix} : \operatorname{Ker} P \oplus \operatorname{Im} P \to \operatorname{Ker} P \oplus \operatorname{Im} P,$$

where I_1 (resp. I_2) denotes the identity operator on $\operatorname{Ker} P$ *(resp.* $\operatorname{Im} P$*), the pencil $\lambda\Omega_1 - I_1$ is $(\Delta_+ \cup \Gamma)$-regular and $\lambda I_2 - \Omega_2$ is $(\Delta_- \cup \Gamma)$-regular. Furthermore P and E (and hence also the operators Ω_1 and Ω_2) are uniquely determined. In fact,*

$$(2.2) \qquad P = \frac{1}{2\pi i} \int_\Gamma G(\zeta G - A)^{-1} d\zeta.$$

$$(2.3) \qquad E = \frac{1}{2\pi i} \int_\Gamma (1 - \zeta^{-1})(\zeta G - A)^{-1} d\zeta.$$

$$(2.4) \qquad \Omega = \begin{bmatrix} \Omega_1 & 0 \\ 0 & \Omega_2 \end{bmatrix} = \frac{1}{2\pi i} \int_\Gamma (\zeta - \zeta^{-1}) G(\zeta G - A)^{-1} d\zeta.$$

To see the connections with the classical Riesz theory about separation of spectra, let us assume that the operator G in Theorem 2.1 is the identity operator on X. Then the Γ-regularity of the pencil means that Γ splits the spectrum of A into two disjoint compact sets and the projection P is just the Riesz projection corresponding to the part of the spectrum of A inside Γ. Furthermore, in that case

$$E = \begin{bmatrix} (A \mid \operatorname{Ker} P)^{-1} & 0 \\ 0 & I_2 \end{bmatrix}, \qquad \Omega_1 = (A \mid \operatorname{Ker} P)^{-1}, \quad \Omega_2 = A \mid \operatorname{Im} P.$$

Note that $A \mid \operatorname{Ker} P$ has its spectrum in the outer domain Δ_-, and hence, since $0 \in \Delta_+$, the operator $A \mid \operatorname{Ker} P$ is invertible.

PROOF OF THEOREM 2.1. We have to modify the arguments which are used to derive the properties of the Riesz projections. Only the main differences will be explained. Let P be defined by (2.2). We also need the following operator

$$Q = \frac{1}{2\pi i} \int_\Gamma (\zeta G - A)^{-1} G d\zeta. \tag{2.5}$$

We shall see that P and Q are projections. For a pencil a generalized resolvent identity holds true, namely

$$(\zeta G - A)^{-1} - (\mu G - A)^{-1} = (\mu - \zeta)(\zeta G - A)^{-1} G (\mu G - A)^{-1}, \tag{2.6}$$

where ζ and μ are points where the pencil is invertible. Introduce the following auxiliary operator

$$K = \frac{1}{2\pi i} \int_\Gamma (\zeta G - A)^{-1} d\zeta.$$

Note that

$$KG = Q, \qquad GK = P. \tag{2.7}$$

Using (2.6), the usual contour integration arguments show that $KGK = K$, and hence the identities in (2.7) imply that P and Q are projections. We also have

$$GQ = PG, \qquad AQ = PA, \qquad K = KP = QK. \tag{2.8}$$

The first identity in (2.8) is obvious, the third is a corollary of (2.7) and the fact that $K = KGK$, and the second identity in (2.8) is an easy consequence of the following formula:

$$A(\zeta G - A)^{-1} G = G(\zeta G - A)^{-1} A. \tag{2.9}$$

Formula (2.8) allows us to partition the operators G, A and K in the following way:

$$G = \begin{bmatrix} G_1 & 0 \\ 0 & G_2 \end{bmatrix} : \operatorname{Ker} Q \oplus \operatorname{Im} Q \to \operatorname{Ker} P \oplus \operatorname{Im} P, \tag{2.10}$$

$$A = \begin{bmatrix} A_1 & 0 \\ 0 & A_2 \end{bmatrix} : \operatorname{Ker} Q \oplus \operatorname{Im} Q \to \operatorname{Ker} P \oplus \operatorname{Im} P, \tag{2.11}$$

$$K = \begin{bmatrix} 0 & 0 \\ 0 & L \end{bmatrix} : \operatorname{Ker} P \oplus \operatorname{Im} P \to \operatorname{Ker} Q \oplus \operatorname{Im} Q. \tag{2.12}$$

The identities in (2.7) imply that G_2 is invertible and $G_2^{-1} = L$. Next, consider

$$T(\lambda) = \frac{1}{2\pi i} \int_\Gamma (\lambda - \zeta)^{-1} (\zeta G - A)^{-1} d\zeta, \qquad \lambda \notin \Gamma.$$

One checks that

$$T(\lambda)(\lambda G - A) = \begin{cases} Q - I & \text{for} \quad \lambda \in \Delta_+, \\ Q & \text{for} \quad \lambda \in \Delta_-; \end{cases} \tag{2.13}$$

$$(\lambda G - A) T(\lambda) = \begin{cases} P - I & \text{for} \quad \lambda \in \Delta_+, \\ P & \text{for} \quad \lambda \in \Delta_-. \end{cases} \tag{2.14}$$

Here I is the identity operator on X. From the generalized resolvent identity (2.6) it follows that $T(\lambda)P = QT(\lambda)$, $\lambda \in \Gamma$, and hence $T(\lambda)$ partitions as follows:

$$T(\lambda) = \begin{bmatrix} T_1(\lambda) & 0 \\ 0 & T_2(\lambda) \end{bmatrix} : \operatorname{Ker} P \oplus \operatorname{Im} P \to \operatorname{Ker} Q \oplus \operatorname{Im} Q, \qquad \lambda \notin \Gamma.$$

From (2.13) and (2.14) we may conclude that

$$(\lambda G_1 - A_1)^{-1} = -T_1(\lambda), \qquad \lambda \in \Delta_+ \tag{2.15}$$

$$(\lambda G_2 - A_2)^{-1} = T_2(\lambda), \qquad \lambda \in \Delta_-. \tag{2.16}$$

In particular, since $0 \in \Delta_+$, the operator A_1 is invertible. Now, put

$$E = \begin{bmatrix} A_1^{-1} & 0 \\ 0 & G_2^{-1} \end{bmatrix} : \operatorname{Ker} P \oplus \operatorname{Im} P \to \operatorname{Ker} Q \oplus \operatorname{Im} Q, \tag{2.17}$$

$$\Omega_1 = G_1 A_1^{-1}, \qquad \Omega_2 = A_2 G_2^{-1}. \tag{2.18}$$

With P, E, Ω_1 and Ω_2 defined in this way (2.1) holds true and the pencils $\lambda\Omega_1 - I_1$ and $\lambda I_2 - \Omega_2$ have the desired regularity properties.

Next we prove the uniqueness of P and E. So, let us assume that for some projection P and invertible operator E the identity (2.1) holds true, with $\lambda\Omega_1 - I_1$ and $\lambda I_2 - \Omega_2$ regular in $\Delta_+ \cup \Gamma$ and $\Delta_- \cup \Gamma$, respectively. Formula (2.1) implies that

$$GE = \begin{bmatrix} \Omega_1 & 0 \\ 0 & I_2 \end{bmatrix}, \qquad AE = \begin{bmatrix} I_1 & 0 \\ 0 & \Omega_2 \end{bmatrix}. \tag{2.19}$$

Thus

$$\begin{aligned}
\frac{1}{2\pi i}\int_\Gamma G(\zeta G - A)^{-1} d\zeta &= \frac{1}{2\pi i}\int_\Gamma GE[(\zeta G - A)E]^{-1} d\zeta \\
&= \frac{1}{2\pi i}\int_\Gamma \begin{bmatrix} \Omega_1(\zeta\Omega_1 - I_1)^{-1} & 0 \\ 0 & (\zeta I_2 - \Omega_2)^{-1} \end{bmatrix} d\zeta \\
&= \begin{bmatrix} 0 & 0 \\ 0 & I_2 \end{bmatrix},
\end{aligned}$$

because of the regularity conditions on the pencils $\lambda\Omega_1 - I_1$ and $\lambda I_2 - \Omega_2$. Hence P is given by (2.2) and so P is uniquely determined. From

$$(\zeta G - A)^{-1} = E\begin{bmatrix} (\zeta\Omega_1 - I_1)^{-1} & 0 \\ 0 & (\zeta I_2 - \Omega_2)^{-1} \end{bmatrix}, \qquad \zeta \in \Gamma,$$

and the properties of the pencils $\lambda\Omega_1 - I_1$ and $\lambda I_2 - \Omega_2$ it follows that

$$\frac{1}{2\pi i}\int_\Gamma (\zeta G - A)^{-1} d\zeta = E\begin{bmatrix} 0 & 0 \\ 0 & I_2 \end{bmatrix} = EP,$$

$$\frac{1}{2\pi i}\int_\Gamma -\zeta^{-1}(\zeta G - A)^{-1} d\zeta = E\begin{bmatrix} I_1 & 0 \\ 0 & 0 \end{bmatrix} = E(I - P).$$

To prove the last formula one uses that for some $\varepsilon > 0$

$$-\zeta^{-1}(\zeta\Omega_1 - I_1)^{-1} = \sum_{\nu=0}^{\infty} \zeta^{\nu-1}\Omega_1^\nu, \qquad 0 < |\zeta| < \varepsilon,$$

$$-\zeta^{-1}(\zeta I_2 - \Omega_2)^{-1} = \sum_{\nu=0}^{\infty} -\zeta^{-\nu-2}\Omega_2^\nu, \qquad 0 < |\zeta^{-1}| < \varepsilon.$$

We conclude that E is given by (2.3), and hence E is uniquely determined.

It remains to prove (2.4). Since $G_2^{-1} = L$, formulas (2.12) and (2.17) imply that $EP = K$. So

$$\begin{aligned}\Omega = \begin{bmatrix} \Omega_1 & 0 \\ 0 & \Omega_2 \end{bmatrix} &= \begin{bmatrix} G_1A_1^{-1} & 0 \\ 0 & A_2G_2^{-1} \end{bmatrix} \\ &= GE(I-P) + AEP \\ &= GE - GK + AK \\ &= \frac{1}{2\pi i}\int_\Gamma -\zeta^{-1}G(\zeta G - A)^{-1}d\zeta + \frac{1}{2\pi i}\int_\Gamma A(\zeta G - A)^{-1}d\zeta.\end{aligned}$$

Now replace A by $A - \zeta G + \zeta G$ in the last integral. Then the term $(A - \zeta G)(\zeta G - A)^{-1}$ drops out, and we obtain the desired formula for Ω. □

We shall refer to the 2×2 operator matrix in (2.1) as the *Γ-spectral decomposition* of the pencil $\lambda G - A$, and the operator Ω in (2.4) will be called the *associated operator* corresponding to $\lambda G - A$ and Γ. For the projection P and the operator E in Theorem 2.1 we shall use the words *separating projection* and *right equivalence operator*, respectively. Note that formula (2.17) implies that the projection Q in (2.5) is also given by $Q = EPE^{-1}$. For later purposes (see Section 8) we prove the following lemma.

LEMMA 2.2. *Let Γ be a Cauchy contour, and let $\lambda G - A$ be a Γ-regular pencil of operators on the Banach space X. Let $\varphi_0, \ldots, \varphi_N$ be vectors in X. Then the general solution of the difference equation*

$$A\rho_{k+1} = G\rho_k + \varphi_k, \qquad k = 0, \ldots, N, \tag{2.20}$$

is given by

$$\begin{aligned}\rho_k = E\Omega^k x + E\Omega^{N+1-k}y + \sum_{\nu=0}^{k-1} E\Omega^{k-1-\nu}(I-P)\varphi_\nu \\ - \sum_{\nu=k}^{N} E\Omega^{\nu-k}P\varphi_\nu, \qquad k = 0, \ldots, N+1.\end{aligned} \tag{2.21}$$

Here P, E and Ω are as in (2.2)–(2.4) *and x and y are arbitrary vectors in* $\operatorname{Ker} P$ *and* $\operatorname{Im} P$, *respectively.*

PROOF. Let $\rho_0, \dots, \rho_{N+1}$ be given by (2.21). To prove that these vectors satisfy (2.20) we use the following identities:

$$AE(I-P) = I-P, \qquad AEP = \Omega P, \tag{2.22a}$$

$$GE(I-P) = \Omega(I-P), \qquad GEP = P. \tag{2.22b}$$

Indeed,

$$\begin{aligned}
A\rho_{k+1} &= AE\Omega^{k+1}x + AE\Omega^{N-k}y + \sum_{\nu=0}^{k} AE\Omega^{k-\nu}(I-P)\varphi_\nu \\
&\quad - \sum_{\nu=k+1}^{N} AE\Omega^{\nu-k-1}P\varphi_\nu \\
&= \Omega^{k+1}x + \Omega^{N+1-k}y + \sum_{\nu=0}^{k} \Omega^{k-\nu}(I-P)\varphi_\nu \\
&\quad - \sum_{\nu=k+1}^{N} \Omega^{\nu-k}P\varphi_\nu \\
&= GE\Omega^{k}x + GE\Omega^{N+1-k}y + \sum_{\nu=0}^{k-1} GE\Omega^{k-1-\nu}(I-P)\varphi_\nu + (I-P)\varphi_\nu \\
&\quad - \sum_{\nu=k}^{N} GE\Omega^{k-\nu}P\varphi_\nu + P\varphi_k \\
&= GE\rho_k + \varphi_k.
\end{aligned}$$

Thus (2.20) holds true.

To prove the converse statement one uses the Γ-spectral decomposition of $\lambda G - A$ and rewrite (2.20) as two separate difference equations, one going forwards and the other going backwards. It is then easily seen that any solution of (2.20) is of the form (2.21). □

To get the general solution of (2.20) it is not necessary to assume that $\lambda G - A$ is a Γ-regular pencil. One can work with any (not necessarily spectral) decomposition of the type (2.1) to get the general solution of (2.20) in the form (2.21).

In what follows we shall often take Γ to be the unit circle $\mathbb{T}$. In that case the regularity conditions on the pencils $\lambda\Omega_1 - I_1$ and $\lambda I_2 - \Omega_2$ in (2.1) are just equivalent to the requirement that Ω_1 and Ω_2 have their spectra in the open unit disc.

COROLLARY 2.3. *Let $\lambda G - A$ be a $\mathbb{T}$-regular pencil of operators. Then the corresponding associated operator Ω has its spectrum in the open unit disc.*

PROOF. Use that Ω is given by the first identity in (2.4) and apply the remark preceding the present corollary. □

3. REALIZATION AND POWER REPRESENTATION

This section concerns the special representation (0.2). Throughout this section Γ is a Cauchy contour with Δ_- and Δ_+ as inner and outer domain, respectively. As before we assume that $0 \in \Delta_+$.

THEOREM 3.1. *A rational $m \times m$ matrix function Φ without poles on Γ admits the following representation:*

$$\Phi(\zeta) = I + C(\zeta G - A)^{-1}B, \qquad \zeta \in \Gamma. \tag{3.1}$$

Here G and A are square matrices of the same size, $n \times n$ say, the pencil $\zeta G - A$ is Γ-regular, and B and C are matrices of sizes $n \times m$ and $m \times n$, respectively.

PROOF. Let $\lambda_1, \ldots, \lambda_p$ be the poles of Φ in Δ_+. Fix $1 \le j \le p$, and consider the Laurent series expansion of Φ in a punctured neighbourhood of λ_j:

$$\Phi(\lambda) = \sum_{\nu=-q_j}^{\infty} (\lambda - \lambda_j)^{\nu} A_{j,\nu}.$$

Introduce the following block matrices:

$$N_j = \begin{bmatrix} \lambda_j I & I & & & \\ & \lambda_j I & I & & \\ & & \ddots & \ddots & \\ & & & \lambda_j I & I \\ & & & & \lambda_j I \end{bmatrix}, \qquad Q_j = \begin{bmatrix} A_{j,-1} \\ A_{j,-2} \\ \vdots \\ A_{j,-q_j} \end{bmatrix},$$

$$R_j = [I \quad 0 \quad \cdots \quad 0].$$

Here I denotes the $m \times m$ identity matrix, the blanks in N_j stand for zero entries, and N_j has size $q_j \times q_j$. The matrix $\lambda - N_j$ is invertible for $\lambda \ne \lambda_j$, and the first row in the block matrix representation of $(\lambda - N_j)^{-1}$ is given by

$$[(\lambda - \lambda_j)^{-1} I \quad (\lambda - \lambda_j)^{-2} I \quad \cdots \quad (\lambda - \lambda_j)^{-q_j} I].$$

It follows that $\Phi(\lambda) - R_j(\lambda - N_j)^{-1}Q_j$ is analytic in λ_j. We carry out this construction for each j and define

$$\Omega_2 = \begin{bmatrix} N_1 & & & \\ & N_2 & & \\ & & \ddots & \\ & & & N_p \end{bmatrix}, \qquad B_2 = \begin{bmatrix} Q_1 \\ Q_2 \\ \vdots \\ Q_p \end{bmatrix},$$

$$C_2 = [R_1 \quad R_2 \quad \cdots \quad R_p].$$

Note that Ω_2 is a block diagonal matrix with diagonal elements $N_1, N_2, \ldots, N_p$. So the eigenvalues of Ω_2 are precisely the poles $\lambda_1, \ldots, \lambda_p$. In particular the pencil $\lambda - \Omega_2$ is $(\Delta_- \cup \Gamma)$-regular. Observe that

$$C_2(\lambda - \Omega_2)^{-1}B_2 = \sum_{j=1}^{p} R_j(\lambda - N_j)^{-1}Q_j,$$

and hence $\Phi_+(\lambda) = \Phi(\lambda) - C_2(\lambda - \Omega_2)^{-1}B_2$ has no poles on $\Delta_+ \cup \Gamma$.

Put $\Gamma' = \{\lambda^{-1} \mid \lambda \in \Gamma\}$. We define the orientation on Γ' to be the reverse of the orientation it inherits from Γ. Then Γ' is again a Cauchy contour with inner domain $\Delta'_+ = \{\lambda^{-1} \mid \lambda \in \Delta_-\}$ and outer domain $\Delta'_- = \{\lambda^{-1} \mid \lambda \in \Delta_+\}$. The function

$$\Psi(\lambda) = \frac{1}{\lambda}\left[I - \Phi_+\left(\frac{1}{\lambda}\right)\right] \tag{3.2}$$

is analytic on $\Delta'_- \cup \Gamma'$ and

$$\lim_{\lambda \mapsto \infty} \Psi(\lambda) = 0. \tag{3.3}$$

Now repeat the above construction for Ψ instead of Φ (with Γ replaced by Γ' and Δ_+ by Δ'_+). So there exist matrices Ω_1, B_1 and C_1 such that Ω_1 is a square matrix and the pencil $\lambda - \Omega_1$ is $(\Delta'_- \cup \Gamma')$-regular and

$$\Psi(\lambda) - C_1(\lambda - \Omega_1)^{-1}B_1 \tag{3.4}$$

is analytic on Δ'_+. Since both terms in (3.4) are analytic on $\Delta'_- \cup \Gamma'$, we conclude that (3.4) defines an entire function which tends to 0 if $\lambda \to \infty$, because of (3.3). Thus $\Psi(\lambda) = C_1(\lambda - \Omega_1)^{-1}B_1$. Together with (3.2) this yields

$$\Phi(\lambda) = C_1(\lambda\Omega_1 - I_1)B_1 + I + C_2(\lambda I_2 - \Omega_2)^{-1}B_2 \tag{3.5}$$

where I_ν is the identity matrix of the same order as Ω_ν ($\nu = 1,2$). Note that the pencil $\lambda\Omega_1 - I_1$ is $(\Delta_+ \cup \Gamma)$-regular. Now put

$$G = \begin{bmatrix} \Omega_1 & 0 \\ 0 & I_2 \end{bmatrix}, \qquad A = \begin{bmatrix} I_1 & 0 \\ 0 & \Omega_2 \end{bmatrix}, \tag{3.6}$$

$$C = [C_1 \quad C_2], \qquad B = \begin{bmatrix} B_1 \\ B_2 \end{bmatrix}. \tag{3.7}$$

Then

$$\zeta G - A = \begin{bmatrix} \zeta\Omega_1 - I_1 & 0 \\ 0 & \zeta I_2 - \Omega_2 \end{bmatrix}. \tag{3.8}$$

Hence the pencil $\zeta G - A$ is Γ-regular and with C and B defined by (3.7) formula (3.1) holds true. □

If Φ is as in (3.1), then we shall say that Φ is in *realized form*, and we shall call the right hand side of (3.1) a *realization* of Φ. This terminology comes from mathematical systems theory and refers to the fact that the right hand side of (3.1) is the transfer function of a (possibly singular) system (cf. [10]).

The pencil $\zeta G - A$ constructed in the proof of Theorem 3.1 is Γ-regular, and hence Theorem 2.1 applies. From the construction of the pencil it is clear that the right hand side of (3.8) is precisely the Γ-spectral decomposition of $\zeta G - A$. The separating projection corresponding to $\zeta G - A$ and Γ is given by

$$\begin{bmatrix} 0 & 0 \\ 0 & I_2 \end{bmatrix},$$

and the corresponding right equivalence operator is the identity operator.

If one specifies Theorem 3.1 for Γ equal to the unit circle $\mathbb{T}$, then the realization in (3.1) can be used to compute the Fourier coefficients of Φ. This leads to the following corollary.

COROLLARY 3.2. *Let Φ be a rational $m \times m$ matrix function without poles on the unit circle $\mathbb{T}$, and let*

$$\Phi(\zeta) = I + C(\zeta G - A)^{-1}B, \qquad \zeta \in \mathbb{T}, \tag{3.9}$$

be a realization of Φ*. Then the k-th Fourier coefficient* Φ_k *of* Φ *admits the following representation:*

$$\Phi_k = \begin{cases} -CE\Omega^k(I-P)B, & k=1,2,\ldots, \\ I-CE(I-P)B, & k=0, \\ CE\Omega^{-k-1}PB, & k=-1,-2,\ldots . \end{cases} \tag{3.10}$$

Here P*,* E *and* Ω *are, respectively, the separating projection, the right equivalence operator and the associated operator corresponding to* $\zeta G - A$ *and* $\mathbf{T}$*, that is,* P*,* E *and* Ω *are given by* (2.2)–(2.4)*. In particular,* Ω *has all its eigenvalues in the open unit disc and* Ω *commutes with* P*.*

PROOF. Let Ω be as in (2.4). According to Theorem 2.1,

$$\Phi(\zeta) = I + CE\begin{bmatrix} (\zeta\Omega_1 - I_1)^{-1} & 0 \\ 0 & (\zeta I_2 - \Omega_2)^{-1} \end{bmatrix} B, \qquad \zeta \in \mathbf{T}.$$

Since $\lambda\Omega_1 - I_1$ is regular on $\mathbf{D}_+ \cup \mathbf{T}$ and $\lambda I_2 - \Omega_2$ is regular on $\mathbf{D}_- \cup \mathbf{T}$, the matrices Ω_1 and Ω_2 have all their eigenvalues in $\mathbf{D}_+$. Hence the eigenvalues of the matrix Ω have the required location. Furthermore,

$$(\zeta\Omega_1 - I_1)^{-1} = \sum_{\nu=0}^{\infty} -\zeta^\nu \Omega_1^\nu, \qquad \zeta \in \mathbf{T},$$

$$(\zeta I_2 - \Omega_2)^{-1} = \sum_{\nu=0}^{\infty} \zeta^{-\nu-1} \Omega_2^\nu, \qquad \zeta \in \mathbf{T}.$$

It follows that

$$\Phi_k = -CE\begin{bmatrix} \Omega_1^k & 0 \\ 0 & 0 \end{bmatrix} B = -CE\Omega^k(I-P)B, \qquad k > 0,$$

$$\Phi_0 = I - CE\begin{bmatrix} I_1 & 0 \\ 0 & 0 \end{bmatrix} B = I - CE(I-P)B,$$

$$\Phi_k = CE\begin{bmatrix} 0 & 0 \\ 0 & \Omega_2^{-k-1} \end{bmatrix} B = CE\Omega^{-k-1}PB, \qquad k < 0,$$

and the corollary is proved. □

We shall refer to (3.10) as the *power representation* of the Fourier coefficients of Φ corresponding to the realization (3.9).

4. INVERSION OF A DOUBLE INFINITE BLOCK TOEPLITZ OPERATOR WITH A RATIONAL SYMBOL

In this section $L = [\Phi_{i-j}]_{i,j=-\infty}^{\infty}$ is a double infinite block Toeplitz operator on $\ell_p^m(\mathbb{Z})$. We assume that the symbol

$$\Phi(\zeta) = \sum_{\nu=-\infty}^{\infty} \zeta^\nu \Phi_\nu, \qquad \zeta \in \mathbb{T},$$

is a rational matrix function. Since Φ has no poles on $\mathbb{T}$, it admits a realization. The next theorem describes the inversion of L in terms of the data appearing in a realization of its symbol.

THEOREM 4.1. *Let L be a double infinite block Toeplitz operator on $\ell_p^m(\mathbb{Z})$ with a rational symbol*

$$\Phi(\zeta) = I + C(\zeta G - A)B, \qquad \zeta \in \mathbb{T}, \tag{4.1}$$

given in realized form. Put $A^\times = A - BC$. Then L is invertible if and only if the pencil $\zeta G - A^\times$ is $\mathbb{T}$-regular, and in that case $L^{-1} = [\Phi_{i-j}^\times]_{i,j=-\infty}^{\infty}$, with

$$\Phi_k^\times = \begin{cases} CE^\times(\Omega^\times)^k(I - P^\times)B, & k = 1, 2, \ldots, \\ I + CE^\times(I - P^\times)B, & k = 0, \\ -CE^\times(\Omega^\times)^{-k-1}P^\times B, & k = -1, -2, \ldots\ . \end{cases} \tag{4.2}$$

Here $P^\times$, $E^\times$ and $\Omega^\times$ are, respectively, the separating projection, the right equivalence operator and the associated operator corresponding to the pencil $\zeta G - A^\times$ and $\mathbb{T}$, that is

$$P^\times = \frac{1}{2\pi i} \int_{\mathbb{T}} G(\zeta G - A^\times)^{-1} d\zeta, \tag{4.3}$$

$$E^\times = \frac{1}{2\pi i} \int_{\mathbb{T}} (1 - \zeta^{-1})(\zeta G - A^\times)^{-1} d\zeta, \tag{4.4}$$

$$\Omega^\times = \frac{1}{2\pi i} \int_{\mathbb{T}} (\zeta - \zeta^{-1}) G(\zeta G - A^\times)^{-1} d\zeta. \tag{4.5}$$

For the proof of Theorem 4.1 we need the following theorem. In this theorem as well as in the lemma at the end of this section Γ is an arbitrary Cauchy contour.

THEOREM 4.2. *Let* $\Phi(\zeta) = I + C(\zeta G - A)^{-1}B$, $\zeta \in \Gamma$, *be a given realization. Put* $A^\times = A - BC$. *Then* $\det \Phi(\zeta) \neq 0$ *for each* $\zeta \in \Gamma$ *if and only if the pencil* $\zeta G - A^\times$ *is* Γ*-regular, and in that case*

$$\Phi(\zeta)^{-1} = I - C(\zeta G - A^\times)^{-1}B, \qquad \zeta \in \Gamma. \tag{4.6}$$

PROOF. We shall prove a stronger (pointwise) version of the lemma. Take a fixed $\lambda \in \Gamma$. Since $\det(I - TS) = \det(I - ST)$, we have

$$\begin{aligned} \det \Phi(\lambda) &= \det[I + C(\lambda G - A)^{-1}B] \\ &= \det[I + (\lambda G - A)^{-1}BC] \\ &= \det[(\lambda G - A)^{-1}(\lambda G - A^\times)] \\ &= \frac{\det(\lambda G - A^\times)}{\det(\lambda G - A)}. \end{aligned}$$

It follows that $\det \Phi(\lambda) \neq 0$ if and only if $\det(\lambda G - A^\times) \neq 0$. In particular, $\det \Phi(\zeta) \neq 0$ for each $\zeta \in \Gamma$ if and only if $\zeta G - A^\times$ is Γ-regular.

Next, assume $\det(\lambda G - A^\times) \neq 0$, and let us solve the equation $\Phi(\lambda)x = y$. Introduce a new unknown by setting $z = (\lambda G - A)^{-1}Bx$. Then given y we have to compute x from

$$\begin{cases} \lambda G z = Az + Bx, \\ y \quad\; = Cz + x. \end{cases} \tag{4.7}$$

This is easy. Apply B to the second equation in (4.7) and subtract the result from the first equation in (4.7). This yields the following equivalent system:

$$\begin{cases} \lambda G z = A^\times z + By, \\ x \quad\; = -Cz + x. \end{cases} \tag{4.8}$$

Hence $z = (\lambda G - A^\times)^{-1}By$ and

$$\Phi(\lambda)^{-1}y = x = y - C(\lambda G - A^\times)^{-1}By,$$

which proves (4.6). □

PROOF OF THEOREM 4.1. Note that the symbol Φ is continuous on $\mathbb{T}$. It is known (see Section 1) that L is invertible if and only if $\det \Phi(\zeta) \neq 0$ for each $\zeta \in \mathbb{T}$, and in that case $L^{-1} = [\Phi^{\times}_{i-j}]_{i,j=-\infty}^{\infty}$, where $\Phi^{\times}_k$ is the k-th Fourier coefficient of $\Phi(\cdot)^{-1}$. Now apply Theorem 4.2 with $\Gamma = \mathbb{T}$. We conclude that L is invertible if and only if $\zeta G - A^{\times}$ is $\mathbb{T}$-regular.

Next, assume that L is invertible. Theorem 4.2 implies that

$$\Phi(\zeta)^{-1} = I - C(\zeta G - A^{\times})^{-1}B, \qquad \zeta \in \mathbb{T}. \tag{4.9}$$

Apply Corollary 3.2 and compute the power representation of the Fourier coefficients of $\Phi(\cdot)^{-1}$ corresponding to the realization (4.9). This yields precisely the formula (4.2). □

The following lemma will be used in the next section.

LEMMA 4.3. *Let* $\Phi(\zeta) = I + C(\zeta G - A)^{-1}B$, $\zeta \in \Gamma$, *be a given realization, and assume* $\det \Phi(\zeta) \neq 0$ *for each* $\zeta \in \mathbb{T}$. *Put* $A^{\times} = A - BC$. *Then for* $\zeta \in \Gamma$

$$C(\zeta G - A^{\times})^{-1} = \Phi(\zeta)^{-1} C(\zeta G - A)^{-1},$$
$$(\zeta G - A^{\times})^{-1}B = (\zeta G - A)^{-1} B \Phi(\zeta)^{-1},$$
$$(\zeta G - A^{\times})^{-1} = (\zeta G - A)^{-1} - (\zeta G - A)^{-1} B \Phi(\zeta)^{-1} C(\zeta G - A)^{-1}.$$

PROOF. From Theorem 4.2 we know that $\zeta G - A^{\times}$ is invertible for $\zeta \in \mathbb{T}$. A direct computation, using (4.6) and the fact that

$$BC = A - A^{\times} = (\zeta G - A^{\times}) - (\zeta G - A), \tag{4.10}$$

gives the desired formulas. □

5. EXPLICIT CANONICAL FACTORIZATION

In this section we construct explicitly a canonical factorization of a rational matrix function given in realized form. Necessary and sufficient conditions for the existence of such a factorization and the formulas for the factors are stated explicitly in terms of the data appearing in the realization. Another factorization theorem which describes all minimal factorizations of a general rational matrix function in terms of a realization different from the one used here is obtained in [5]. It is not clear how one can identify a spectral factorization employing the factorization theorem in [5], and therefore the latter theorem cannot be used to get the inverse of a block Toeplitz operator.

Throughout this section Γ is a Cauchy contour with Δ_+ and Δ_- as inner and outer domain, respectively. As before, $0 \in \Delta_+$ and $\infty \in \Delta_-$.

THEOREM 5.1. *Let Φ be a rational $m \times m$ matrix function without poles on the contour Γ, and let Φ be given in realized form:*

$$\Phi(\zeta) = I + C(\zeta G - A)^{-1}B, \qquad \zeta \in \Gamma. \tag{5.1}$$

Put $A^\times = A - BC$. Then Φ admits a right canonical factorization relative to Γ if and only if the following two conditions hold true:

(i) *the pencil $\zeta G - A^\times$ is Γ-regular,*

(ii) $\mathbb{C}^n = \operatorname{Im} Q \oplus \operatorname{Ker} Q^\times$ *and* $\mathbb{C}^n = \operatorname{Im} P \oplus \operatorname{Ker} P^\times$.

Here n is the order of the matrices G and A, and

$$Q = \frac{1}{2\pi i}\int_\Gamma (\zeta G - A)^{-1} G\, d\zeta, \qquad P = \frac{1}{2\pi i}\int_\Gamma G(\zeta G - A)^{-1} d\zeta,$$

$$Q^\times = \frac{1}{2\pi i}\int_\Gamma (\zeta G - A^\times)^{-1} G\, d\zeta, \qquad P^\times = \frac{1}{2\pi i}\int_\Gamma G(\zeta G - A^\times)^{-1} d\zeta.$$

In that case a right canonical factorization $\Phi(\zeta) = \Phi_-(\zeta)\Phi_+(\zeta)$ of Φ relative to Γ is obtained by taking

$$\Phi_-(\zeta) = I + C(\zeta G - A)^{-1}(I - \rho)B, \qquad \zeta \in \Gamma, \tag{5.2}$$

$$\Phi_+(\zeta) = I + C\tau(\zeta G - A)^{-1}B, \qquad \zeta \in \Gamma, \tag{5.3}$$

$$\Phi_-(\zeta)^{-1} = I - C(I - \tau)(\zeta G - A^\times)^{-1}B, \qquad \zeta \in \Gamma, \tag{5.4}$$

$$\Phi_+(\zeta)^{-1} = I - C(\zeta G - A^\times)^{-1}\rho B, \qquad \zeta \in \Gamma. \tag{5.5}$$

Here τ is the projection of $\mathbb{C}^n$ along $\operatorname{Im} Q$ onto $\operatorname{Ker} Q^\times$ and ρ is the projection along $\operatorname{Im} P$ onto $\operatorname{Ker} P^\times$. Furthermore, the two equalities in (ii) *are not independent; in fact, the first equality in* (ii) *implies the second and conversely.*

PROOF. From the definition of a right canonical factorization (see Section 1) it is clear that $\det \Phi(\zeta) \neq 0$ for each $\zeta \in \mathbb{T}$ is a necessary condition in order that Φ admits such a factorization. By Lemma 4.2 this necessary condition is fulfilled if and only if (i) holds true. So in what follows we shall assume that condition (i) is satisfied.

First, let us prove the last statement of the theorem. Consider the operators

$$Q^{\times} \mid \operatorname{Im} Q\colon \operatorname{Im} Q \to \operatorname{Im} Q^{\times}, \qquad P^{\times} \mid \operatorname{Im} P\colon \operatorname{Im} P \to \operatorname{Im} P^{\times}. \tag{5.6}$$

It is straightforward to check that the first (resp. second) equality in (ii) is equivalent to the invertibility of the operator $Q^{\times} \mid \operatorname{Im} Q$ (resp. $P^{\times} \mid \operatorname{Im} P$). From the results of Section 2, applied to $\zeta G - A$ as well as to $\zeta G - A^{\times}$, we know that

$$GQ = PG, \qquad GQ^{\times} = P^{\times} G. \tag{5.7}$$

Furthermore, G maps $\operatorname{Im} Q$ (resp. $\operatorname{Im} Q^{\times}$) in a one-one manner onto $\operatorname{Im} P$ (resp. $\operatorname{Im} P^{\times}$). Thus the operators

$$F = G \mid \operatorname{Im} Q\colon \operatorname{Im} Q \to \operatorname{Im} P, \qquad F^{\times} = G \mid \operatorname{Im} Q^{\times}\colon \operatorname{Im} Q^{\times} \to \operatorname{Im} P^{\times}$$

are invertible and $F^{\times}(Q^{\times} \mid \operatorname{Im} Q) = (P^{\times} \mid \operatorname{Im} P)F$. So the operators in (5.6) are equivalent, and hence the first operator in (5.6) is invertible if and only if the same is true for the second operator in (5.6). This proves that the first equality in (ii) implies the second and conversely.

Next, we assume that (i) and the direct sum decompositions in (ii) hold true. Write A, G, B, C and $A^{\times} = A - BC$ as block matrices relative to these decompositions:

$$A = \begin{bmatrix} A_{11} & A_{12} \\ 0 & A_{22} \end{bmatrix} : \operatorname{Im} Q \oplus \operatorname{Ker} Q^{\times} \to \operatorname{Im} P \oplus \operatorname{Ker} P^{\times}, \tag{5.8}$$

$$G = \begin{bmatrix} G_{11} & 0 \\ 0 & G_{22} \end{bmatrix} : \operatorname{Im} Q \oplus \operatorname{Ker} Q^{\times} \to \operatorname{Im} P \oplus \operatorname{Ker} P^{\times}, \tag{5.9}$$

$$B = \begin{bmatrix} B_1 \\ B_2 \end{bmatrix} : \mathbb{C}^m \to \operatorname{Im} P \oplus \operatorname{Ker} P^{\times}, \tag{5.10}$$

$$C = [C_1 \quad C_2]\colon \operatorname{Im} Q \oplus \operatorname{Ker} Q^{\times} \to \mathbb{C}^m, \tag{5.11}$$

$$(5.12)\qquad A^\times = \begin{bmatrix} A_{11}^\times & 0 \\ A_{21}^\times & A_{22}^\times \end{bmatrix} : \operatorname{Im} Q \oplus \operatorname{Ker} Q^\times \to \operatorname{Im} P \oplus \operatorname{Ker} P^\times .$$

Formula (2.8) applied to $\zeta G - A$ as well as to $\zeta G - A^\times$ yields

$$(5.13)\qquad AQ = PA, \qquad A^\times Q^\times = P^\times A^\times .$$

The first identity in (5.13) implies that A maps $\operatorname{Im} Q$ into $\operatorname{Im} P$. This explains the zero entry in the left lower corner of the block matrix for A. From (5.7) we conclude that G has the desired block diagonal form. From the second identity in (5.13) it follows that $A^\times$ maps $\operatorname{Ker} Q^\times$ into $\operatorname{Ker} P^\times$, which justifies the zero in the right upper corner of the block matrix for $A^\times$. The fact that $A^\times = A - BC$ implies

$$(5.14)\qquad A_{12} = B_1 C_2, \qquad A_{21}^\times = -B_2 C_1,$$

$$(5.15)\qquad A_{11}^\times = A_{11} - B_1 C_1, \qquad A_{22}^\times = A_{22} - B_2 C_2.$$

We shall prove that the pencils $\lambda G_{22} - A_{22}$ and $\lambda G_{22} - A_{22}^\times$ are $(\Delta_+ \cup \Gamma)$-regular and the pencils $\lambda G_{11} - A_{11}$ and $\lambda G_{11} - A_{11}^\times$ are $(\Delta_- \cup \Gamma)$-regular. To do this we employ the Γ-spectral decompositions of $\lambda G - A$ and $\lambda G - A^\times$:

$$(\lambda G - A)E = \begin{bmatrix} \lambda \Omega_1 - I_1 & 0 \\ 0 & \lambda I_2 - \Omega_2 \end{bmatrix} : \operatorname{Ker} P \oplus \operatorname{Im} P \to \operatorname{Ker} P \oplus \operatorname{Im} P,$$

$$(\lambda G - A^\times)E^\times = \begin{bmatrix} \lambda \Omega_1^\times - I_1^\times & 0 \\ 0 & \lambda I_2^\times - \Omega_2^\times \end{bmatrix} : \operatorname{Ker} P^\times \oplus \operatorname{Im} P^\times \to \operatorname{Ker} P^\times \oplus \operatorname{Im} P^\times .$$

Here E is the right equivalence operator corresponding to $\lambda G - A$ and Γ, and $E^\times$ is the analogous operator for $\lambda G - A^\times$. Recall that $Q = EPE^{-1}$ and $Q^\times = E^\times P^\times (E^\times)^{-1}$. Since

$$\lambda G_{22} - A_{22}^\times = (\lambda G - A^\times) \mid \operatorname{Ker} Q^\times ,$$

the $(\Delta_+ \cup \Gamma)$-regularity of $\lambda \Omega_1^\times - I_1^\times$ implies that $\lambda G_{22} - A_{22}^\times$ is $(\Delta_+ \cup \Gamma)$-regular. To prove the analogous result for $\lambda G_{22} - A_{22}$, we first show that the operators

$$(5.16)\qquad J = (I - Q) \mid \operatorname{Ker} Q^\times : \operatorname{Ker} Q^\times \to \operatorname{Ker} Q,$$

$$(5.17)\qquad H = (I - P) \mid \operatorname{Ker} P^\times : \operatorname{Ker} P^\times \to \operatorname{Ker} P,$$

are invertible. In fact,

$$J^{-1} = \tau \mid \operatorname{Ker} Q, \qquad H^{-1} = \rho \mid \operatorname{Ker} P,$$

where τ is the projection along $\operatorname{Im} Q$ onto $\operatorname{Ker} Q^{\times}$ and ρ is the projection along $\operatorname{Im} P$ onto $\operatorname{Ker} P^{\times}$. Next, take $x \in \operatorname{Ker} Q^{\times}$. Then

$$\begin{aligned}(\lambda G_{22} - A_{22})x &= \rho(\lambda G - A)x \\ &= \rho(\lambda G - A)(I - Q)x \\ &= \rho(\lambda G - A)Jx,\end{aligned}$$

which shows that

(5.18) $$H(\lambda G_{22} - A_{22}) = [(\lambda G - A) \mid \operatorname{Ker} Q]J.$$

Since $\lambda\Omega_1 - I_1$ is $(\Delta_+ \cup \Gamma)$-regular, the identity (5.18) implies that the same is true for $\lambda G_{22} - A_{22}$. From

$$\lambda G_{11} - A_{11} = (\lambda G - A) \mid \operatorname{Im} Q$$

and the $(\Delta_- \cup \Gamma)$-regularity of $\lambda I_2 - \Omega_2$, we may conclude that $\lambda G_{11} - A_{11}$ is $(\Delta_- \cup \Gamma)$-regular. To get the desired regularity for $\lambda G_{11} - A_{11}^{\times}$, we use that

(5.19) $$H^{\times}(\lambda G_{11} - A_{11}^{\times}) = [(\lambda G - A^{\times}) \mid \operatorname{Im} Q^{\times}]J^{\times}$$

where

$$\begin{aligned}J^{\times} &= Q^{\times} \mid \operatorname{Im} Q \colon \operatorname{Im} Q \to Q^{\times}, \\ H^{\times} &= P^{\times} \mid \operatorname{Im} P \colon \operatorname{Im} P \to \operatorname{Im} P^{\times}\end{aligned}$$

are invertible linear transformations of which the inverses are given by

$$(J^{\times})^{-1} = (I - \tau) \mid \operatorname{Im} Q^{\times}, \qquad (H^{\times})^{-1} = (I - \rho) \mid \operatorname{Im} P^{\times}.$$

Since $\lambda I_2^{\times} - \Omega_2^{\times}$ is $(\Delta_- \cup \Gamma)$-regular, the identity (5.19) implies that the same is true for $\lambda G_{11} - A_{11}^{\times}$.

Now, let Φ_+ and Φ_- be the matrix functions defined by (5.2) and (5.3), respectively. By using the block matrix representations (5.8)–(5.11) we rewrite Φ_- and Φ_+ in the following form:

(5.20) $$\Phi_-(\zeta) = I + C_1(\zeta G_{11} - A_{11})^{-1}B_1, \qquad \zeta \in \Gamma,$$

(5.21) $$\Phi_+(\zeta) = I + C_2(\zeta G_{22} - A_{22})^{-1}B_2, \qquad \zeta \in \Gamma.$$

From (5.8) and the first identity in (5.14) we see that

$$\begin{aligned}\Phi_-(\zeta)\Phi_+(\zeta) &= I + [C_1 \quad C_2]\begin{bmatrix} \zeta G_{11} - A_{11} & -B_1C_2 \\ & \zeta G_{22} - A_{22}\end{bmatrix}^{-1}\begin{bmatrix} B_1 \\ B_2\end{bmatrix} \\ &= I + C(\zeta G - A)^{-1}B = \Phi(\zeta), \qquad \zeta \in \Gamma,\end{aligned}$$

which gives us the desired factorization. Since the pencils $\zeta G_{11} - A_{11}^\times$ and $\zeta G_{22} - A_{22}^\times$ are Γ-regular we can apply Theorem 4.2 to show that

(5.22) $$\Phi_-(\zeta)^{-1} = I - C_1(\zeta G_{11} - A_{11}^\times)^{-1}B_1, \qquad \zeta \in \Gamma,$$

(5.24) $$\Phi_+(\zeta)^{-1} = I - C_2(\zeta G_{22} - A_{22}^\times)^{-1}, \zeta \in \Gamma.$$

Here we used the two identities in (5.15). From the partitionings in (5.9)–(5.12) it follows that (5.22) and (5.23) yield the formulas (5.4) and (5.5), respectively. Since $\lambda G_{11} - A_{11}$ and $\lambda G_{11} - A_{11}^\times$ are $(\Delta_- \cup \Gamma)$-regular, (5.20) and (5.22) imply that $\Phi_-^{\pm 1}$ has no poles on $\Delta_- \cup \Gamma$. The $(\Delta_+ \cup \Gamma)$-regularity of $\lambda G_{22} - A_{22}$ and $\lambda G_{22} - A_{22}^\times$ implies that $\Phi_+^{\pm 1}$ has no poles on $\Delta_+ \cup \Gamma$ (cf. formulas (5.21) and (5.23)). Thus the factorization $\Phi(\zeta) = \Phi_-(\zeta)\Phi_+(\zeta)$, $\zeta \in \Gamma$, is a right canonical factorization.

Next we prove the necessity of the equalities in (ii). So in what follows we assume that Φ admits a right canonical factorization relative to Γ:

(5.24) $$\Phi(\zeta) = \Phi_-(\zeta)\Phi_+(\zeta), \qquad \zeta \in \Gamma.$$

Take $x \in \operatorname{Im} P \cap \operatorname{Ker} P^\times$, and put

$$\varphi_-(\zeta) = C(\zeta G - A)^{-1}x, \quad \varphi_+(\zeta) = C(\zeta G - A^\times)^{-1}x \qquad (\zeta \in \Gamma).$$

Since $x \in \operatorname{Im} P$, the Γ-spectral decomposition of the pencil $\lambda G - A$ allows us to rewrite φ_- as follows:

$$\varphi_-(\zeta) = CE(\zeta I_2 - \Omega_2)^{-1}x, \qquad \zeta \in \Gamma.$$

It follows that φ_- has an analytic continuation to Δ_- (which we also denote by φ_-) and $\varphi_-(\lambda) \to 0$ if $\lambda \to \infty$. Similarly, since $x \in \operatorname{Ker} P^\times$,

$$\varphi_+(\zeta) = CE^\times(\zeta\Omega_1^\times - I_1^\times)^{-1}x, \qquad \zeta \in \Gamma,$$

and we conclude that φ_+ has an analytic continuation to Δ_+, which is also denoted by φ_+. Note that $\Phi(\zeta)^{-1}\Phi_-(\zeta) = \varphi_+(\zeta)$, $\zeta \in \Gamma$, because of Lemma 4.3. It follows (use the factorization (5.24)) that

$$\Phi_-(\zeta)^{-1}\varphi_-(\zeta) = \Phi_+(\zeta)\varphi_+(\zeta), \zeta \in \Gamma. \tag{5.25}$$

Now employ the properties of the factors Φ_- and Φ_+. We conclude that $\Phi_-(\cdot)^{-1}\varphi_-(\cdot)$ has an analytic continuation to Δ_- and $\Phi_-(\lambda)^{-1}\varphi_-(\lambda) \to 0$ if $\lambda \to \infty$. On the other hand $\Phi_+(\cdot)\varphi_+(\cdot)$ has an analytic continuation to Δ_+. Liouville's theorem implies that both terms in (5.25) are identically zero. It follows that $\varphi_-(\zeta) = 0$ for each $\zeta \in \Gamma$. But then we can apply the third identity in Lemma 4.3 to show that

$$(\zeta G - A^\times)^{-1}x = (\zeta G - A)^{-1}x, \qquad \zeta \in \Gamma. \tag{5.26}$$

Apply G to both sides of (5.26) and integrate over the contour Γ. One sees that $x = Px = P^\times x = 0$. We proved that $\operatorname{Im} P \cap \operatorname{Ker} P^\times = \{0\}$. Since G maps $\operatorname{Im} Q \cap \operatorname{Ker} Q^\times$ in a one-one way into $\operatorname{Im} P \cap \operatorname{Ker} P^\times$, also $\operatorname{Im} Q \cap \operatorname{Ker} Q^\times = \{0\}$.

We proceed by showing that $\operatorname{Im} Q + \operatorname{Ker} Q^\times = \mathbb{C}^n$. Take $y \in \mathbb{C}^n$ such that $y \perp (\operatorname{Im} Q + \operatorname{Ker} Q^\times)$. Let y^* be the row vector of which the j-th entry is equal to the complex conjugate of the j-th entry of y ($j = 1, \dots n$). Put

$$\psi_-(\zeta) = y^*(\zeta G - A^\times)^{-1}B, \quad \psi_+(\zeta) = y^*(\zeta G - A)^{-1}B \qquad (\zeta \in \Gamma).$$

Since $y^*(I - Q^\times) = 0$, the function ψ_- has an analytic continuation on Δ_- and $\psi_-(\zeta) \to 0$ if $\zeta \to \infty$. From $y^*Q = 0$, it follows that ψ_+ has an analytic continuation on Δ_+. The second identity in Lemma 4.3 shows that

$$\psi_+(\zeta)\Phi_+(\zeta)^{-1} = \psi_-(\zeta)\Phi_-(\zeta), \qquad \zeta \in \Gamma, \tag{5.27}$$

and Liouville's theorem implies that both terms in (5.7) are zero. It follows that $\psi_+(\zeta) = 0$ for each $\zeta \in \Gamma$, and we can use the third identity in Lemma 4.3 to show that

$$y^*(\zeta G - A^\times)^{-1} = y^*(\zeta G - A)^{-1}, \qquad \zeta \in \Gamma. \tag{5.28}$$

Now multiply both sides of (5.28) on the right by G and integrate over Γ. This yields $y^*Q^\times = y^*Q = 0$, and hence $y \perp \operatorname{Im} Q^\times$, which implies $y = 0$. Then $\mathbb{C}^n = \operatorname{Im} Q + \operatorname{Ker} Q^\times$.

We have now proved the first equality in (ii), which is sufficient (according to the result proved in the second paragraph of the proof). □

In a similar way (or using an inversion argument) one can show that the matrix function Φ in (5.1) admits a left canonical factorization if and only if $\mathbb{C}^n = \operatorname{Im} P^{\times} \oplus \operatorname{Ker} P$. It follows that Φ admits both a left and right canonical factorization if and only if

$$\det[(I - P^{\times})(I - P) + P^{\times} P] \neq 0. \tag{5.29}$$

6. EXPLICIT INVERSION OF A BLOCK TOEPLITZ OPERATOR WITH A RATIONAL SYMBOL

In this section the factorization formulas derived in the previous section are applied to construct explicitly the inverse of a block Toeplitz operator with a rational symbol. The necessary and sufficient conditions for invertibility and the formula for the inverse are expressed explicitly in terms of the data appearing in a realization of the symbol.

THEOREM 6.1. *Let T be a block Toeplitz operator on ℓ_p^m with a rational symbol*

$$\Phi(\zeta) = I + C(\zeta G - A)^{-1} B, \qquad \zeta \in \mathbb{T},$$

given in realized form. Put $A^{\times} = A - BC$. Then T is invertible if and only if the following two conditions hold true:

(α) *the pencil $\zeta G - A^{\times}$ is $\mathbb{T}$-regular,*

(β) $\mathbb{C}^n = \operatorname{Im} P \oplus \operatorname{Ker} P^{\times}$,

where n is the order of the matrices G and A, and

$$P = \frac{1}{2\pi i} \int_{\mathbb{T}} G(\zeta G - A)^{-1} d\zeta, \qquad P^{\times} = \frac{1}{2\pi i} \int_{\mathbb{T}} G(\zeta G - A^{\times})^{-1} d\zeta.$$

In that case the inverse of T is obtained in the following. Put

$$E^{\times} = \frac{1}{2\pi i} \int_{\mathbb{T}} (1 - \zeta^{-1})(\zeta G - A^{\times})^{-1} d\zeta, \tag{6.1}$$

(6.2) $$\Omega^{\times} = \frac{1}{2\pi i}\int_{\mathbb{T}} (\zeta - \zeta^{-1})G(\zeta G - A^{\times})^{-1} d\zeta.$$

Then the entries of the inverse $T^{-1} = [\Gamma_{ij}]_{i,j=0}^{\infty}$ *are given by*

$$\Gamma_{ij} = \Phi_{i-j}^{\times} + K_{ij}, \qquad i,j = 0,1,2,\dots,$$

$$\Phi_k^{\times} = \begin{cases} CE^{\times}(\Omega^{\times})^k(I - P^{\times})B, & k = 1,2,\dots, \\ I + CE^{\times}(I - P^{\times})B, & k = 0, \\ -CE^{\times}(\Omega^{\times})^{-k-1}P^{\times}B, & k = -1,-2,\dots, \end{cases}$$

$$K_{ij} = CE^{\times}(\Omega^{\times})^i(I - P^{\times})\rho P^{\times}(\Omega^{\times})^j B,$$

where ρ *is the projection of* $\mathbb{C}^n$ *along* $\operatorname{Im} P$ *onto* $\operatorname{Ker} P^{\times}$.

PROOF. We know (see Section 1) that T is invertible if and only if Φ admits a right canonical factorization relative to $\mathbb{T}$. So we can apply Theorem 5.1 (with $\Gamma = \mathbb{T}$) to show that (α) and (β) are the necessary and sufficient conditions in order that T is invertible.

In the remaining part of the proof we assume that (α) and (β) are satisfied. Let $\Phi(\zeta) = \Phi_-(\zeta)\Phi_+(\zeta)$, $\zeta \in \mathbb{T}$, be the right canonical factorization of Φ described in Theorem 5.1 with $\Gamma = \mathbb{T}$. To find the entries Γ_{ij} of T^{-1} we have (see Section 1) to compute the Fourier coefficients of the functions Φ_-^{-1} and Φ_+^{-1}. The latter functions are given by the formulas (5.4) and (5.5). We use the right equivalence operator $E^{\times}$ and the associated operator $\Omega^{\times}$ corresponding to $\zeta G - A^{\times}$ and $\mathbb{T}$ to rewrite the functions Φ_-^{-1} and Φ_+^{-1} as follows:

(6.3) $$\Phi_-(\zeta)^{-1} = I - C(I - \tau)E^{\times}(\zeta - \Omega^{\times})^{-1}P^{\times}B, \qquad \zeta \in \mathbb{T},$$

(6.4) $$\Phi_+(\zeta)^{-1} = I - CE^{\times}(\zeta\Omega^{\times} - I)^{-1}(I - P^{\times})\rho B, \zeta \in \mathbb{T}.$$

Here we used that $(I - \tau)E^{\times}(I - P^{\times}) = 0$ and $P^{\times}\rho = 0$. Note that $E^{\times}$ and $\Omega^{\times}$ are given by (6.1) and (6.2) (cf. Theorem 2.1). Since $\Omega^{\times}$ has all its eigenvalues in the open unit disc (Corollary 2.3), the formulas (6.3) and (6.4) imply that

$$\Phi_-(\zeta)^{-1} = \sum_{j=-\infty}^{0} \zeta^j \gamma_j^-, \qquad \Phi_+(\zeta)^{-1} = \sum_{j=0}^{\infty} \zeta^j \gamma_j^+,$$

where

$$\begin{aligned}
\gamma_0^- &= I,\ \gamma_j^- = -C(I-\tau)E^\times(\Omega^\times)^{-j-1}P^\times B, \qquad j=-1,-2,\dots,\\
\gamma_0^+ &= I + CE^\times(I-P^\times)\rho B,\\
\gamma_j^+ &= CE^\times(\Omega^\times)^j(I-P^\times)\rho B, \qquad j=1,2,\dots\,.
\end{aligned}$$

Now recall (see Section 1) that the (i,j)-th entry Γ_{ij} of T^{-1} is given by

$$\Gamma_{ij} = \sum_{r=0}^{\min(i,j)} \gamma_{i-r}^+\gamma_{r-j}^-. \tag{6.5}$$

To compute the products in (6.5) we first show that

$$\Omega^\times(I-P^\times)\rho BC(I-\tau)E^\times P^\times = (I-P^\times)[\rho-\Omega^\times\rho\Omega^\times]P^\times. \tag{6.6}$$

Recall that $BC = A - A^\times$. From the definitions of τ and ρ (see Theorem 5.1) it follows that $\rho A(I-\tau)=0$ and $\rho A^\times\tau = A^\times\tau$. Thus

$$\rho BC(I-\tau) = A^\times\tau - \rho A^\times. \tag{6.7}$$

Next, observe that the following identities hold true:

$$\Omega^\times A^\times\tau = G\tau = \rho G, \tag{6.8}$$

$$A^\times E^\times P^\times = \Omega^\times P^\times, \qquad GE^\times P^\times = P^\times. \tag{6.9}$$

From these identities and the fact that $\Omega^\times P^\times = P^\times\Omega^\times$ it follows that

$$\begin{aligned}
\Omega^\times(I-P^\times)\rho BC(I-\tau)E^\times P^\times &= (I-P^\times)\Omega^\times A^\times\tau E^\times P^\times - (I-P^\times)\Omega^\times\rho A^\times E^\times P^\times\\
&= (I-P^\times)\rho GE^\times P^\times - (I-P^\times)\Omega^\times\rho\Omega^\times P^\times\\
&= (I-P^\times)\rho P^\times - (I-P^\times)\Omega^\times\rho\Omega^\times P^\times\\
&= (I-P^\times)[\rho-\Omega^\times\rho\Omega^\times]P^\times,
\end{aligned}$$

and (6.6) is proved. From (6.6) and $\Omega^\times P^\times = P^\times\Omega^\times$ one derives that for $p>0$ and $q<0$

$$\begin{aligned}
\gamma_p^+\gamma_q^- &= CE^\times(\Omega^\times)^p(I-P^\times)\rho P^\times(\Omega^\times)^{-q}B\\
&\quad - CE^\times(\Omega^\times)^{p-1}(I-P^\times)\rho P^\times(\Omega^\times)^{-q-1}B.
\end{aligned}$$

We are now ready to compute the (i,j)-th entry Γ_{ij}. First, assume that $i > j$. Then

$$\begin{aligned}
\Gamma_{ij} &= \sum_{r=0}^{j} \gamma_{i-r}^{+}\gamma_{r-j}^{-} \\
&= \gamma_{i-j}^{+} + \sum_{r=0}^{j-1} \gamma_{i-r}^{+}\gamma_{r-j}^{-} \\
&= CE^{\times}(\Omega^{\times})^{i-j}(I-P^{\times})\rho B \\
&\quad + \sum_{r=0}^{j-1} CE^{\times}(\Omega^{\times})^{i-r}(I-P^{\times})\rho P^{\times}(\Omega^{\times})^{j-r}B \\
&\quad - \sum_{r=0}^{j-1} CE^{\times}(\Omega^{\times})^{i-r-1}(I-P^{\times})\rho P^{\times}(\Omega^{\times})^{j-r-1}B \\
&= CE^{\times}(\Omega^{\times})^{i-j}(I-P^{\times})\rho B \\
&\quad + CE^{\times}(\Omega^{\times})^{i}(I-P^{\times})\rho P^{\times}(\Omega^{\times})^{j}B \\
&\quad - CE^{\times}(\Omega^{\times})^{i-j}(I-P^{\times})\rho P^{\times}B \\
&= CE^{\times}(\Omega^{\times})^{i-j}(I-P^{\times})\rho(I-P^{\times})B + K_{ij}.
\end{aligned}$$

Since $\rho(I-P^{\times}) = I-P^{\times}$, we proved that

$$\Gamma_{ij} = \Phi_{i-j}^{\times} + K_{ij} \tag{6.10}$$

for $i > j$. Next, take $i = j$. Then

$$\begin{aligned}
\Gamma_{ii} &= \gamma_{0}^{+} + \sum_{r=0}^{i-1} \gamma_{i-r}^{+}\gamma_{r-i}^{-} \\
&= I + CE^{\times}(I-P^{\times})\rho B \\
&\quad + \sum_{r=0}^{i-1} CE^{\times}(\Omega^{\times})^{i-r}(I-P^{\times})\rho P^{\times}(\Omega^{\times})^{i-r}B \\
&\quad - \sum_{r=0}^{i-1} CE^{\times}(\Omega^{\times})^{i-r-1}(I-P^{\times})\rho P^{\times}(\Omega^{\times})^{i-r-1}B \\
&= I + CE^{\times}(I-P^{\times})\rho B \\
&\quad + CE^{\times}(\Omega^{\times})^{i}(I-P^{\times})\rho P^{\times}(\Omega^{\times})^{i}B \\
&\quad - CE^{\times}(I-P^{\times})\rho P^{\times}B \\
&= I + CE^{\times}(I-P^{\times})B + K_{ii},
\end{aligned}$$

and (6.10) is proved for $i=j$. Finally, take $i<j$. Then

$$\begin{aligned}\Gamma_{ii} &= \gamma_0^+\gamma_{i-j}^- + \sum_{r=0}^{i-1}\gamma_{i-r}^+\gamma_{r-j}^- \\ &= \gamma_0^+\gamma_{i-j}^- + \sum_{r=0}^{i-1} CE^\times(\Omega^\times)^{i-r}(I-P^\times)\rho P^\times(\Omega^\times)^{j-r}B \\ &\quad - \sum_{r=0}^{i-1} CE^\times(\Omega^\times)^{i-r-1}(I-P^\times)\rho P^\times(\Omega^\times)^{j-r-1}B \\ &= -C(I-\tau)E^\times(\Omega^\times)^{j-i-1}P^\times B \\ &\quad - CE^\times(I-P^\times)\rho BC(I-\tau)E^\times(\Omega^\times)^{j-i-1}P^\times B \\ &\quad + CE^\times(\Omega^\times)^i(I-P^\times)\rho P^\times(\Omega^\times)^j B \\ &\quad - CE^\times(I-P^\times)\rho P^\times(\Omega^\times)^{j-i}B.\end{aligned}$$

To simplify this further we use (6.7), (6.9) and $E^\times A^\times\tau=\tau$ to compute that

$$\begin{aligned}E^\times(I-P^\times)\rho BC(I-\tau)E^\times P^\times &= -E^\times(I-P^\times)\rho A^\times E^\times P^\times + E^\times(I-P^\times)\rho A^\times\tau E^\times P^\times \\ &= -E^\times(I-P^\times)\rho\Omega^\times P^\times + E^\times A^\times\tau E^\times P^\times \\ &= -E^\times(I-P^\times)\rho\Omega^\times P^\times + \tau E^\times P^\times.\end{aligned}$$

Since $\Omega^\times P^\times = P^\times\Omega^\times$, we see that for $i<j$

$$\begin{aligned}\Gamma_{ij} &= -C(I-\tau)E^\times(\Omega^\times)^{j-i-1}P^\times B \\ &\quad + CE^\times(I-P^\times)\rho P^\times(\Omega^\times)^{j-i}B \\ &\quad - C\tau E^\times(\Omega^\times)^{j-i-1}P^\times B \\ &\quad + K_{ij} - CE^\times(I-P^\times)\rho P^\times(\Omega^\times)^{j-i}B \\ &= -CE^\times(\Omega^\times)^{j-i-1}P^\times B + K_{ij},\end{aligned}$$

which proves (6.10) for $i<j$. □

7. EQUIVALENCE TO BOUNDARY VALUE SYSTEMS

In this section we develop an alternative approach for inverting block Toeplitz operators with rational symbols. This second approach does not use factorization and is based on connections between Toeplitz operators and discrete singular systems with boundary conditions.

THEOREM 7.1. *Let $1 \leq p \leq \infty$, and let $T = [\Phi_{j-k}]_{j,k=0}^{\infty}$ be a block Toeplitz operator on ℓ_p^m with symbol*

$$\Phi(\zeta) = I + C(\zeta G - A)^{-1}B, \qquad \zeta \in \mathbb{T}, \tag{7.1}$$

given in realized form. Then the Toeplitz equation

$$Tx = z, \qquad z \in \ell_p^m \tag{7.2}$$

is equivalent to the following discrete boundary value system:

$$\begin{cases} A\rho_{k+1} &= G\rho_k + Bu_k, \qquad k = 0,1,2,\ldots, \\ y_k &= -C\rho_{k+1} + u_k, \quad k = 0,1,2,\ldots, \\ (I - Q)\rho_0 = 0. \end{cases} \tag{7.3}$$

Here Q is the projection given by (2.5) with $\Gamma = \mathbb{T}$ and the equivalence between (7.2) and (7.3) has to be understood in the following sense: If $x = (x_k)_{k=0}^{\infty}$ in ℓ_p^m is a solution of (7.2), then the system (7.3) with input $u_k = x_k$ $(k = 0,1,2,\ldots)$ has output $y_k = z_k$ $(k = 0,1,2,\ldots)$, and, conversely, if the system (7.3) with input $u = (u_k)_{k=0}^{\infty}$ from ℓ_p^m has output $y_k = z_k$ $(k = 0,1,2,\ldots)$, then $x = u$ is a solution of (7.2).

To make the statement of the theorem precise, we mention that the system (7.3) with input $u = (u_k)_{k=0}^{\infty}$ from ℓ_p^m is said to have output $y = (y_k)_{k=0}^{\infty}$ if and only if there exists $\rho = (\rho_k)_{k=0}^{\infty}$ in ℓ_p^n, where n is the order of the square matrices A and G, such that $(I - Q)\rho_0 = 0$ and the sequence $\rho_0, \rho_1, \ldots$ satisfies the two equations in (7.3). In the proof of Theorem 7.1 we shall see that in that case ρ is uniquely determined by the input u. Thus Theorem 7.1 tells us that the system (7.3) has a well-defined input/output map which is equal to the block Toeplitz operator T. For the proof of Theorem 7.1 we need the following lemma.

LEMMA 7.2. *Let $\zeta G - A$ be a $\mathbb{T}$-regular pencil of $n \times n$ matrices. Fix $1 \leq p \leq \infty$, and let $(\varphi_k)_{k=0}^{\infty}$ be in ℓ_p^n. Then the general solution in ℓ_p^n of the equation*

$$A\rho_{k+1} = G\rho_k + \varphi_k, \qquad k = 0,1,2,\ldots, \tag{7.4}$$

is given by

$$\rho_k = E\Omega^k\eta + \sum_{\nu=0}^{k-1} E\Omega^{k-1-\nu}(I-P)\varphi_\nu - \sum_{\nu=k}^{\infty} E\Omega^{\nu-k}P\varphi_\nu, \qquad k = 0,1,2,\ldots . \tag{7.5}$$

Here P, E *and* Ω *are given by* (2.2)–(2.4) *with* $\Gamma = \mathbb{T}$ *and* η *is an arbitrary vector in* $\operatorname{Ker} P$.

PROOF. Let η be an arbitrary vector in $\mathbb{C}^n$, and let $\rho = (\rho_k)_{k=0}^{\infty}$ be given by (7.5). We first prove that ρ is in ℓ_p^n. Since Ω has its eigenvalues in the open unit disc, the sequence

$$g = (E\Omega^k \eta)_{k=0}^{\infty} \in \ell_p^n$$

and the series in (7.5) converges for each k. Put

$$M_k = \begin{cases} E\Omega^{k-1}(I-P), & k = 1,2,\ldots, \\ -E\Omega^{-k}P, & k = 0,-1,-2,\ldots, \end{cases}$$

and consider the operator $S \colon \ell_p^n \to \ell_p^n$ defined by

$$(Su)_k = \sum_{\nu=0}^{\infty} M_{k-\nu} u_\nu, \qquad k = 0,1,2,\ldots .$$

Because of the location of the eigenvalues of Ω, the operator S is a well-defined block Toeplitz operator on ℓ_p^n. Note that $\rho = g + S\varphi$. Thus $\rho \in \ell_p^n$.

Take $N \geq 0$. Then the first $N+1$ elements in ρ may be rewritten in the form:

$$\rho_k = E\Omega^k \eta + E\Omega^{N+1-k} y_{N+1} + \sum_{\nu=0}^{k-1} E\Omega^{k-1-\nu}(I-P)\varphi_\nu - \sum_{\nu=k}^{N} E\Omega^{\nu-k} P\varphi_\nu, \qquad k = 0,\ldots,N+1,$$

where

$$y_{N+1} = \sum_{\nu=0}^{\infty} E\Omega^\nu P\varphi_{\nu+N+1} \in \operatorname{Im} P.$$

But then we can apply Lemma 2.2 to show that $\rho_0,\ldots,\rho_{N+1}$ satisfy the equation

$$A\rho_{k+1} = G\rho_k + \varphi_k, \qquad k = 0,\ldots,N+1. \tag{7.6}$$

Since N is arbitrary, this implies that ρ is a solution of (7.4).

To prove the converse, let $\rho = (\rho_k)_{k=0}^{\infty}$ in ℓ_p^n be a solution of (7.4). Take $N \geq 0$. Then $\rho_0,\ldots,\rho_{N+1}$ is a solution of (7.6). So, by Lemma 2.2, there exist $x_{N+1} \in \operatorname{Ker} P$

and $y_{N+1} \in \operatorname{Im} P$ such that

$$
\begin{aligned}
\rho_k = {} & E\Omega^k x_{N+1} + E\Omega^{N+1-k} y_{N+1} \\
& + \sum_{\nu=0}^{k-1} E\Omega^{k-1-\nu}(I-P)\varphi_\nu \\
& - \sum_{\nu=k}^{N} E\Omega^{\nu-k} P\varphi_\nu, \qquad k = 0, \dots, N+1.
\end{aligned} \tag{7.7}
$$

From (7.7) it follows that

$$
(I-Q)\rho_0 = Ex_{N+1}, \qquad Q\rho_{N+1} = Ey_{N+1}, \tag{7.8}
$$

where Q is given by (2.5) with $\Gamma = \mathbb{T}$. The first identity in (7.8) implies that x_{N+1} does not depend on N. Put $\eta = E^{-1}(I-Q)\rho_0$. Then $\eta = x_{N+1}$ for each N and $\eta \in \operatorname{Ker} P$. Since $(\rho_k)_{k=0}^{\infty}$ is in ℓ_p^n, the sequence $\rho_0, \rho_1, \dots$ is bounded in $\mathbb{C}^n$, and thus the same is true for the sequence $y_1, y_2, y_3, \dots$. It follows that $E\Omega^{N+1-k} y_{N+1} \to 0$ if $N \to \infty$, because of the location of the eigenvalues of Ω. Furthermore, since $(\varphi_k)_{k=0}^{\infty}$ is in ℓ_p^n and the eigenvalues of Ω are in the open unit disc, the series

$$
\sum_{\nu=k}^{\infty} E\Omega^{\nu-k} P\varphi_\nu
$$

converges for each k. We conclude that in (7.7) we may take the limit for $N \to \infty$. The resulting formula is precisely (7.5). □

PROOF OF THEOREM 7.1. Since the symbol Φ is given by (7.1), the entries of T admit the following power representation:

$$
\Phi_k = \begin{cases} -CE\Omega^k(I-P)B, & k = 1, 2, \dots, \\ I - CE(I-P)B, & k = 0, \\ CE\Omega^{-k-1}PB, & k = -1, -2, \dots, \end{cases} \tag{7.9}
$$

where P, E and Ω are given by (2.2)–(2.4) with $\Gamma = \mathbb{T}$. Assume $x = (x_k)_{k=0}^{\infty} \in \ell_p^m$ is a solution of (7.2). Put

$$
\rho_k = \sum_{\nu=0}^{k-1} E\Omega^{k-1-\nu}(I-P)Bx_\nu - \sum_{\nu=k}^{\infty} E\Omega^{\nu-k} PBx_\nu, \qquad k = 0, 1, 2, \dots . \tag{7.10}
$$

Note that ρ_k $(k = 0,1,2,\ldots)$ is as in (7.5) provided that in (7.5) we take $\eta = 0$ and $\varphi_k = Bx_k$, $k = 0,1,2,\ldots$. So Lemma 7.2 implies that $\rho = (\rho_k)_{k=0}^{\infty}$ is in ℓ_p^n and the sequence $\rho_0, \rho_1, \ldots$ satisfies the first equation in (7.3) with $u_k = x_k$, $k = 0,1,2,\ldots$. The power representation (7.9) implies that $(\rho_k)_{k=0}^{\infty}$ satisfies the second equation in (7.3) with $y_k = z_k$ and $u_k = x_k$, $k = 0,1,2,\ldots$. From $\Omega P = P\Omega$ and $EP = QE$ it follows that $(I-Q)\rho_0 = 0$. Thus $(\rho_k)_{k=0}^{\infty} \in \ell_p^n$ is a solution of (7.3) with $u_k = x_k$ and $y_k = z_k$, $k = 0,1,2,\ldots$.

To prove the converse, let $\rho = (\rho_k)_{k=0}^{\infty}$ be a solution in ℓ_p^n of (7.3) with $u = (u_k)_{k=0}^{\infty}$ from ℓ_p^m. Put $x_k = u_k$ and $z_k = y_k$, $k = 0,1,2,\ldots$. Then x and z are in ℓ_p^m, and we shall prove that (7.2) is satisfied. Note that Lemma 7.2 implies that

$$\rho_k = E\Omega^k\eta + \sum_{\nu=0}^{k-1} E\Omega^{k-1-\nu}(I-P)Bx_\nu - \sum_{\nu=k}^{\infty} E\Omega^{\nu-k}PBx_\nu, \qquad k = 0,1,2,\ldots,$$

where η is some vector in $\operatorname{Ker} P$. One computes that

$$(I-Q)\rho_0 = (I-Q)E\eta = E(I-P)\eta = E\eta.$$

Thus the boundary condition in (7.3) implies that $\eta = 0$. So the sequence $\rho_0, \rho_1, \ldots$ is uniquely determined and given by (7.10). But then we can use the second equation in (7.3) and the power representation (7.9) to show that x in ℓ_p^m is a solution of (7.2). □

Note that the last part of the proof of Theorem 7.1 shows that for given input and output in ℓ_p^m the solution $\rho = (\rho_k)_{k=0}^{\infty}$ of (7.3) in ℓ_p^n is unique (assuming it exists).

The equivalence in Theorem 7.1 implies that we may get solutions of equation (7.2) by inverting the system (7.3). The first step is to interchange in (7.3) the roles of the input and output. This is easy. Apply B to the second equation and subtract the result from the first equation. This yields the following system:

$$\text{(7.11)} \qquad \begin{cases} A^{\times}\rho_{k+1} = G\rho_k + By_k, & k = 0,1,2,\ldots, \\ u_k = C\rho_{k+1} + y_k, & k = 0,1,2,\ldots, \\ (I-Q)\rho_0 = 0. \end{cases}$$

Here $A^{\times} = A - BC$, and we may assume that $y = (y_k)_{k=0}^{\infty}$ is a given element in ℓ_p^m. The problem is now to find $(\rho_k)_{k=0}^{\infty}$ in ℓ_p^n satisfying the first equation in (7.11) and the boundary condition $(I-Q)\rho_0 = 0$. Note that the projection Q comes from the pencil $\zeta G - A$ and is not directly related to $\zeta G - A^\times$, and hence it is not straightforward to find a sequence $(\rho_k)_{k=0}^\infty$ with the desired properties. In fact, the problem may not be solvable or if it is solvable it may have many solutions. However if such a sequence $(\rho_k)_{k=0}^\infty$ has been found, then a solution of the equation $Tu = y$ is obtained by taking $u_k = C\rho_{k+1} + y_k$, $k = 0, 1, 2, \ldots$. In this way we come to the following theorem.

THEOREM 7.3. *Let $1 \le p \le \infty$, and let $y = (y_k)_{k=0}^\infty$ be in ℓ_p^m. Consider the block Toeplitz equation*

$$\sum_{\nu=0}^{\infty} \Phi_{k-\nu} u_\nu = y_k, \qquad k = 0, 1, 2, \ldots, \tag{7.12}$$

where the Φ_k are the Fourier coefficients of a rational matrix function

$$\Phi(\zeta) = I + C(\zeta G - A)^{-1} B, \qquad \zeta \in \mathbf{T}, \tag{7.13}$$

given in realized form. Put $A^\times = A - BC$, and assume that the pencil $\zeta G - A^\times$ is $\mathbf{T}$-regular. Then the equation (7.12) is solvable in ℓ_p^m if and only if

$$\sum_{\nu=0}^{\infty} (\Omega^\times)^\nu P^\times B y_\nu \in \operatorname{Im} P + \operatorname{Ker} P^\times, \tag{7.14}$$

and in that case the general solution in ℓ_p^m of (7.12) is given by

$$u_k = CE^\times(\Omega^\times)^k \eta + \sum_{\nu=0}^{\infty} \Phi_{k-\nu}^\times y_\nu, \qquad k = 0, 1, 2, \ldots . \tag{7.15}$$

Here P is the separating projection corresponding $\zeta G - A$ and $\mathbf{T}$, the operators $P^\times$, $E^\times$ and $\Omega^\times$ are, respectively, the separating projection, the right equivalence operator and the associate operator corresponding to $\zeta G - A^\times$ and $\mathbf{T}$,

$$\Phi_k^\times = \begin{cases} CE^\times(\Omega^\times)^k (I - P^\times) B, & k = 1, 2, \ldots, \\ I + CE^\times (I - P^\times) B, & k = 0, \\ -CE^\times (\Omega^\times)^{-k-1} B, & k = -1, -2, \ldots, \end{cases} \tag{7.16}$$

and η is an arbitrary vector in $\operatorname{Ker} P^\times$ such that

$$\eta - \sum_{\nu=0}^{\infty} (\Omega^\times)^\nu P^\times B y_\nu \in \operatorname{Im} P. \tag{7.17}$$

In particular, the general solution in ℓ_p^m *of the homogeneous equation*

$$\sum_{\nu=0}^{\infty} \Phi_{k-\nu} u_\nu = 0, \qquad k = 0,1,2,\ldots, \tag{7.18}$$

is given by

$$u_k = CE^\times(\Omega^\times)^k \eta, \qquad k = 0,1,2,\ldots, \tag{7.19}$$

where η *is an arbitrary vector in* $\operatorname{Ker} P^\times \cap \operatorname{Im} P$.

PROOF. Let Q be the projection defined by (2.5), and let $Q^\times$ be the corresponding projection for $\zeta G - A^\times$. From Theorem 7.1 and the remarks made in the paragraph preceding the present theorem it follows that (7.12) is solvable in ℓ_p^m if and only if there exists $(\rho_k)_{k=0}^\infty$ in ℓ_p^n satisfying the first equation in (7.11) and the boundary condition $(I-Q)\rho_0 = 0$. According to Lemma 7.2 the general solution in ℓ_p^n of the first equation in (7.11) is given by

$$\begin{aligned} \rho_k = {} & E^\times(\Omega^\times)^k \gamma + \sum_{\nu=0}^{k-1} E^\times(\Omega^\times)^{k-1-\nu}(I-P^\times)By_\nu \\ & - \sum_{\nu=k}^{\infty} E^\times(\Omega^\times)^{\nu-k} P^\times By_\nu, \qquad k = 0,1,2,\ldots, \end{aligned} \tag{7.20}$$

where γ is an arbitrary vector in $\operatorname{Ker} P^\times$. Note that

$$\rho_0 = E^\times \gamma - \sum_{\nu=0}^{\infty} E^\times(\Omega^\times)^\nu P^\times By_\nu.$$

Since $E^\times\gamma \in \operatorname{Ker} Q^\times$ we conclude that the first equation in (7.11) has a solution $(\rho_k)_{k=0}^\infty$ in ℓ_p^n satisfying the boundary condition $(I-Q)\rho_0 = 0$ if and only if

$$\sum_{\nu=0}^{\infty} E^\times(\Omega^\times)^\nu P^\times By_\nu \in \operatorname{Ker} Q^\times + \operatorname{Im} Q, \tag{7.21}$$

and in that case the outputs $u = (u_k)_{k=0}^\infty$ of (7.11) are given by

$$u_k = CE^\times(\Omega^\times)^{k+1}\gamma + \sum_{\nu=0}^{\infty} \Phi_{k-\nu}^\times y_\nu, \qquad k = 0,1,2,\ldots, \tag{7.22}$$

where the $\Phi_k^\times$ are defined by (7.16) and γ is an arbitrary vector in $\operatorname{Ker} P^\times$ such that

$$E^\times\gamma - \sum_{\nu=0}^{\infty} E^\times(\Omega^\times)^\nu P^\times B y_\nu \in \operatorname{Im} Q. \tag{7.23}$$

We conclude that (7.21) is the necessary and sufficient condition in order that (7.12) has a solution in ℓ_p^m, and if this condition is satisfied, then the general solution $(u_k)_{k=0}^\infty$ in ℓ_p^m of (7.12) is given by (7.22).

To finish to proof it remains to show that (7.14) is equivalent to (7.21) and (7.15) gives the same set of sequences as (7.22). Denote the left hand side of (7.14) by x_0. Note that $x_0 \in \operatorname{Im} P^\times$. So $GE^\times x_0 = x_0$ (cf. the second identity in (6.9)). Next, recall that the operators in (5.6) are equivalent. In fact

$$(G \mid \operatorname{Im} Q^\times)(Q^\times \mid \operatorname{Im} Q) = (P^\times \mid \operatorname{Im} P)(G \mid \operatorname{Im} Q). \tag{7.24}$$

It follows that

$$\begin{aligned} E^\times x_0 \in \operatorname{Ker} Q^\times + \operatorname{Im} Q &\iff E^\times x_0 \in \operatorname{Im}(Q^\times \mid \operatorname{Im} Q) \\ &\iff GE^\times x_0 \in \operatorname{Im}(P^\times \mid \operatorname{Im} P) \\ &\iff x_0 \in \operatorname{Im}(P^\times \mid \operatorname{Im} P) \\ &\iff x_0 \in \operatorname{Ker} P^\times + \operatorname{Im} P, \end{aligned}$$

which proves the equivalence of (7.14) and (7.21). Next, note that $\Omega^\times(I - P^\times) = GE^\times(I - P^\times)$ (cf. formula (2.22b)). Hence

$$\Omega^\times\gamma = GE^\times\gamma, \qquad \gamma \in \operatorname{Ker} P^\times.$$

Let L_1 be the set of all $\gamma \in \operatorname{Ker} P^\times$ satisfying (7.23), and let L_2 be the set of all $\eta \in \operatorname{Ker} P^\times$ such that (7.17) holds true. To prove that (7.15) and (7.22) define the same set of sequences, it suffices to show that $GE^\times(L_1) = L_2$. Take $\gamma \in L_1$. Thus $E^\times\gamma - E^\times x_0 \in \operatorname{Im} Q$. Since G maps $\operatorname{Im} Q$ into $\operatorname{Im} P$, this implies that $GE^\times\gamma - x_0 \in \operatorname{Im} P$. Also $GE^\times(\operatorname{Ker} P^\times) \subset \operatorname{Ker} P^\times$. So $GE^\times\gamma \in L_2$. Conversely, take $\eta \in L_2$. Then there exists $u \in \operatorname{Im} Q$ such that $\eta - x_0 = Gu$. It follows that

$$-GE^\times x_0 = -x_0 = -P^\times x_0 = P^\times Gu = GQ^\times u,$$

and hence $-E^\times x_0 = Q^\times u$ because G is one-one on $\operatorname{Im} Q^\times$. But then there exists $\gamma \in \operatorname{Ker} P^\times$ such that $E^\times\gamma - E^\times x_0 = u$. So $\gamma \in L_1$ and

$$GE^\times\gamma - x_0 = GE^\times\gamma - GE^\times x_0 = Gu = \eta - x_0.$$

Thus $\eta = GE^{\times}\gamma \in GE^{\times}(L_1)$. The theorem is proved. □

Theorem 7.3 may be used to derive the inversion formula in Theorem 6.1. Indeed, assume that $\mathbb{C}^n = \operatorname{Ker} P^{\times} \oplus \operatorname{Im} P$, where n is the order of the matrices G and A. Then Theorem 7.3 implies that for each $(y_k)_{k=0}^{\infty}$ in ℓ_p^m equation (7.12) has a unique solution in ℓ_p^m which is given by (7.15) with

$$\eta = \sum_{\nu=0}^{\infty} \rho(\Omega^{\times})^{\nu} P^{\times} B y_{\nu}. \tag{7.25}$$

Here ρ is the projection of $\mathbb{C}^n$ along $\operatorname{Im} P$ onto $\operatorname{Ker} P^{\times}$. Since $(I - P^{\times})\rho = \rho$, the expression for η in (7.25) inserted in (7.15) yields precisely the formula for the inverse in Theorem 6.1.

The condition in Theorem 7.3 that the pencil $\zeta G - A^{\times}$ is $\mathbb{T}$-regular is equivalent to the requirement that the block Toeplitz operator on ℓ_p^m defined by the symbol (7.13) is Fredholm. We shall come back to this statement in Section 9.

In Theorem 7.1 the space ℓ_p^m may be replaced by larger sequence spaces. In fact with minor modifications the equivalence in Theorem 7.1 remains true if one allows as solutions of (7.2) any sequence $(x_k)_{k=0}^{\infty}$ such that the series

$$\sum_{\nu=0}^{\infty} \Omega^{\nu} P B x_{\nu}$$

converges in $\mathbb{C}^n$. Here n is the order of the matrices G and A, and the operators P and Ω are, respectively, the separating projection and associated operator corresponding to $\zeta G - A$ and $\mathbb{T}$. The sequence space which one obtains in this way depends on the realization (7.1) and is the largest sequence space which one can use for the given realization.

8. INVERSION OF FINITE BLOCK TOEPLITZ MATRICES

In this section the inversion method based on equivalence to linear systems, which was used in the previous section, is developed further for finite block Toeplitz matrices.

THEOREM 8.1. *Consider the finite block Toeplitz equation*

$$\sum_{\nu=0}^{N} \Phi_{k-\nu} x_{\nu} = z_k, \qquad k = 0, \ldots, N, \tag{8.1}$$

where $\Phi_{-N},\dots,\Phi_N$ *are the* $-N$ *to* N *Fourier coefficients of a rational matrix function*

$$\Phi(\zeta) = I + C(\zeta G - A)^{-1}B, \qquad \zeta \in \mathbb{T} \tag{8.2}$$

given in realized form. The equation (8.1) *is equivalent to the following discrete boundary value system:*

$$\begin{cases} A\rho_{k+1} &= G\rho_k + Bu_k, \qquad k = 0,1,\dots,N, \\ y_k &= -C\rho_{k+1} + u_k, \qquad k = 0,1,\dots,N, \\ (I-Q)\rho_0 = 0, & Q\rho_{N+1} = 0, \end{cases} \tag{8.3}$$

where Q *is the projection given by* (2.5) *with* $\Gamma = \mathbb{T}$. *The equivalence between* (8.1) *and* (8.3) *has to be understood in the following sense: If* $x = (x_k)_{k=0}^N$ *is a solution of* (8.1), *then the system* (8.3) *with input* $u_k = x_k$ $(k = 0,1,\dots,N)$ *has output* $y_k = z_k$ $(k = 0,1,\dots,N)$, *and, conversely, if the system* (8.3) *with input* $u = (u_k)_{k=0}^N$ *has output* $y_k = z_k$ $(k = 0,1,\dots,N)$, *then* $x = u$ *is a solution of* (8.1).

PROOF. Since the symbol Φ is given by (8.1), the matrix coefficients $\Phi_{-N},\dots,\Phi_N$ in (8.1) are given by

$$\Phi_k = \begin{cases} -CE\Omega^k(I-P)B, & k = 1,\dots,N, \\ I - CE(I-P)B, & k = 0, \\ CE\Omega^{-k-1}PB, & k = -1,\dots,-N, \end{cases} \tag{8.4}$$

where P, E and Ω are given by (2.2)–(2.4) with $\Gamma = \mathbb{T}$. Assume $x_0,\dots,x_N$ is a solution of (8.1). Put

$$\rho_k = \sum_{\nu=0}^{k-1} E\Omega^{k-1-\nu}(I-P)Bx_\nu - \sum_{\nu=k}^{N} E\Omega^{\nu-k}PBx_\nu, \qquad k = 0,1,\dots,N+1. \tag{8.5}$$

Lemma 2.2 implies that $\rho_0,\dots,\rho_{N+1}$ is a solution of the first equation in (8.3) with $u_k = x_k$, $k = 0,1,\dots,N$. The power representation (8.4) and the fact that $x_0,\dots,x_N$ solve (8.1) implies that $\rho_0,\dots,\rho_{N+1}$ satisfy the second equation in (8.3) with $u_k = x_k$ and $y_k = z_k$, $k = 0,1,\dots,N$. From $\Omega P = P\Omega$ and $EP = QE$ it is clear that $(I-Q)\rho_0 = 0$ and $Q\rho_{N+1} = 0$. Thus with input $u_k = x_k$ $(k = 0,\dots,N)$ the system (8.3) responses with output $y_k = z_k$ $(k = 0,\dots,N)$.

To prove the converse statement, let $\rho_0,\dots,\rho_N$ be a solution of (8.3) with $y_k = z_k$, $k = 0,1,\dots,N$. We shall prove that $x_k = u_k$, $k = 0,1,\dots,N$, is a solution of

(8.1). The boundary conditions in (8.3) and Lemma 2.2 imply that again $\rho_0, \ldots, \rho_{N+1}$ are given by (8.5). So the sequence $\rho_0, \ldots, \rho_{N+1}$ is uniquely determined. Since $\rho_0, \ldots, \rho_{N+1}$ satisfy the second equation in (8.3), the power representation (8.4) implies that (8.1) is satisfied. □

Using the equivalence in Theorem 8.1 one may solve equation (8.1). The final result is the following theorem.

THEOREM 8.2. *Let $y_0, y_1, \ldots, y_N$ be given vectors in $\mathbb{C}^m$, and consider the equation*

$$\sum_{\nu=0}^{\infty} \Phi_{k-\nu} u_\nu = y_k, \qquad k = 0, \ldots, N, \tag{8.6}$$

where $\Phi_{-N}, \ldots, \Phi_N$ are the $-N$ to N Fourier coefficients of a rational matrix function

$$\Phi(\zeta) = I + C(\zeta G - A)^{-1} B, \qquad \zeta \in \mathbb{T},$$

given in realized form. Put $A^\times = A - BC$, and assume that the pencil $\zeta G - A^\times$ is $\mathbb{T}$-regular. Introduce

$$\begin{aligned} V_N = {} & (I - Q)E^\times(I - P^\times) + (I - Q)E^\times(\Omega^\times)^{N+1}P^\times \\ & + QE^\times(\Omega^\times)^{N+1}(I - P^\times) + QE^\times P^\times, \end{aligned} \tag{8.7}$$

where Q is the projection given by (2.5) with $\Gamma = \mathbb{T}$ and $P^\times$, $E^\times$ and $\Omega^\times$ are, respectively, the separating projection, the right equivalence operator and the associated operator corresponding to $\zeta G - A^\times$ and $\mathbb{T}$. Then equation (8.6) is solvable if and only if

$$\sum_{\nu=0}^{N} [(I - Q)E^\times(\Omega^\times)^\nu P^\times - QE^\times(\Omega^\times)^{N-\nu}(I - P^\times)]By_\nu \in \operatorname{Im} V_N, \tag{8.8}$$

and in that case the general solution of (8.6) is given by

$$\begin{aligned} u_k = {} & CE^\times(\Omega^\times)^{k+1}(I - P^\times)\eta + CE^\times(\Omega^\times)^{N-k}P^\times\eta \\ & + \sum_{\nu=0}^{N} \Phi^\times_{k-\nu} y_\nu, \qquad k = 0, 1, \ldots, N, \end{aligned} \tag{8.9}$$

where η is an arbitrary vector in $\mathbb{C}^n$ (with n the order of the matrices G and A) such that $V_N\eta$ is equal to the left hand side of (8.8) and

$$\Phi^\times_k = \begin{cases} CE^\times(\Omega^\times)^k(I - P^\times)B, & k = 1, \ldots, N, \\ I + CE^\times(I - P^\times)B, & k = 0, \\ -CE^\times(\Omega^\times)^{-k-1}P^\times B, & k = -1, \ldots, -N. \end{cases} \tag{8.10}$$

In particular, the general solution of the homogeneous equation

$$\sum_{\nu=0}^{N} \Phi_{k-\nu} u_\nu = 0, \qquad k = 0, 1, \ldots, N,$$

is given by

$$(8.11) \qquad u_k = CE^\times(\Omega^\times)^{k+1}(I - P^\times)\eta + CE^\times(\Omega^\times)^{N-k}P^\times\eta, \qquad k = 0, 1, \ldots, N,$$

where η *is an arbitrary vector in* $\operatorname{Ker} V_N$. *Furthermore, the block Toeplitz matrix*

$$T_N = [\Phi_{k-j}]_{k,j=0}^{N}$$

is invertible if and only if $\det V_N \neq 0$, *and in that case the entries of the inverse* $T_N^{-1} = [\Gamma_{kj}^N]_{k,j=0}^N$ *admits the following representation:*

$$(8.12) \qquad \Gamma_{kj}^N = \Phi_{k-j}^\times + K_{kj}^N, \qquad k, j = 0, \ldots, N,$$

where $\Phi_{-N}^\times, \ldots, \Phi_N^\times$ *are as in* (8.10) *and*

$$\begin{aligned} K_{kj}^N = {} & CE^\times(\Omega^\times)^{k+1}(I - P^\times)V_N^{-1}(I - Q)E^\times(\Omega^\times)^j P^\times B \\ & - CE^\times(\Omega^\times)^{N-k}P^\times V_N^{-1} Q E^\times(\Omega^\times)^{N-j}(I - P^\times)B. \end{aligned}$$

PROOF. By Theorem 8.1 the sequence $u = (u_k)_{k=0}^N$ is a solution of (8.6) if and only if there exist $\rho_0, \rho_1, \ldots, \rho_{N+1}$ satisfying (8.3). Now multiply the second equation in (8.3) by B and subtract the result from the first equation. This leads to the following equivalent system:

$$(8.13) \qquad \begin{cases} A^\times \rho_{k+1} = G\rho_k + By_k, & k = 0, 1, \ldots, N, \\ u_k = C\rho_{k+1} + y_k, & k = 0, 1, \ldots, N, \\ (I - Q)\rho_0 = 0, \quad Q\rho_{N+1} = 0. \end{cases}$$

From Lemma 2.2 we know that the general solution of the first equation in (8.13) is given by

$$(8.14) \qquad \begin{aligned} \rho_k = {} & E^\times(\Omega^\times)^k(I - P^\times)\eta + E^\times(\Omega^\times)^{N+1-k}P^\times\eta \\ & + \sum_{\nu=0}^{k-1} E^\times(\Omega^\times)^{k-1-\nu}(I - P^\times)By_\nu \\ & - \sum_{\nu=k}^{N} E^\times(\Omega^\times)^{\nu-k}P^\times By_\nu, \qquad k = 0, 1, \ldots, N+1, \end{aligned}$$

where η is an arbitrary vector in $\mathbb{C}^n$. The vectors $\rho_0, \ldots, \rho_{N+1}$ in (8.14) satisfy the boundary conditions in (8.12) if and only if

$$V_N\eta = \sum_{\nu=0}^{N}[(I-Q)E^\times(\Omega^\times)^\nu P^\times - QE^\times(\Omega^\times)^{N-\nu}(I-P^\times)]By_\nu,$$

and in that case the output of (8.13) is given by (8.9). From these remarks the proof of Theorem 8.2 is clear. □

General two point boundary value singular systems, which include systems of the type (8.3), are considered in [8]. In particular, in [8] the input/output operator of such a system is computed. The inversion result obtained in this section can also be extended to the more general class of systems considered in [8].

Note that the matrix V_N in (8.7) has size $n \times n$, where n is the order of the matrices G and A. In particular, the size of V_N is independent of N and the invertibility of the $Nm \times Nm$ matrix T_N is decided by an $n \times n$ matrix regardless how large N is. Since $\Omega^\times$ has its eigenvalues in the open unit disc (Corollary 2.3),

$$V_N \to (I-Q)(I-Q^\times)E^\times + QQ^\times E^\times \qquad (N \to \infty). \tag{8.15}$$

Let us denote the limit in (8.15) by V. The matrix V is invertible if and only if

$$\mathbb{C}^n = \operatorname{Ker} Q^\times \oplus \operatorname{Im} Q, \qquad \mathbb{C}^n = \operatorname{Ker} Q \oplus \operatorname{Im} Q^\times, \tag{8.16}$$

and thus we can apply Theorem 5.1 to show that the invertibility of V is equivalent to the requirement that the symbol Φ in (8.2) admits a left and right canonical factorization relative to the unit circle (cf. the last paragraph of Section 5).

Let T be the block Toeplitz operator on ℓ_p^m with symbol Φ as in (8.2). Note that the N-th section of T is precisely the block Toeplitz matrix considered in the last part of Theorem 8.2. Assume that the symbol Φ of T admits a left and right canonical factorization. In that case the operator T is invertible and it is known (cf. [6]) that the solutions of the equation $Tu = y$ may be obtained as the limit (for $N \to \infty$) of the solutions of the finite sections $T_N x_N = y_N$ (the projection method). In our framework this result may be derived from (8.15). Indeed, the hypothesis on Φ implies (see the preceding paragraph) that the limit V in (8.15) is invertible. So for N sufficiently large

V_N is invertible, and hence, by Theorem 8.2, the matrix T_N is invertible. Furthermore, if $T_N^{-1} = [\Gamma_{kj}^N]_{k,j=0}^N$, then (8.12) implies that for each k and j

$$\lim_{N\to\infty} \Gamma_{kj}^N = \Phi_{k-j}^\times + CE^\times(\Omega^\times)^{k+1}(I-P^\times)V^{-1}(I-Q)E^\times(\Omega^\times)^j P^\times B. \tag{8.17}$$

It remains to show that the right hand side of (8.17) is the (k,j)-th entry Γ_{kj} in the block matrix representation of T^{-1}. From the formula for Γ_{kj} given in Theorem 6.1 it is clear that it is sufficient to show that

$$\Omega^\times(I-P^\times)V^{-1}(I-Q)E^\times P^\times = (I-P^\times)\rho P^\times, \tag{8.18}$$

where ρ is the projection of $\mathbb{C}^n$ along $\operatorname{Im} P$ onto $\operatorname{Ker} P^\times$. Let τ be the projection of $\mathbb{C}^n$ along $\operatorname{Im} Q$ onto $\operatorname{Ker} Q^\times$. Take $x \in \mathbb{C}^n$. Then

$$\begin{aligned}(I-Q)x &= (I-Q)\tau x \\ &= (I-Q)(I-Q^\times)\tau x = V(E^\times)^{-1}\tau x.\end{aligned}$$

Next, use (2.22b) for the pencil $\zeta G - A^\times$ instead of $\zeta G - A$, apply the second identity in (6.8) and use the formulas $E^\times P^\times = Q^\times E^\times$ and $(I-Q^\times)\tau = \tau$. We conclude that

$$\begin{aligned}\Omega^\times(I-P^\times)V^{-1}(I-Q)E^\times P^\times &= \Omega^\times(I-P^\times)(E^\times)^{-1}\tau E^\times P^\times \\ &= GE^\times(I-P^\times)(E^\times)^{-1}\tau E^\times P^\times \\ &= G(I-Q^\times)\tau E^\times P^\times \\ &= \rho GE^\times P^\times = \rho P^\times.\end{aligned}$$

Since $(I-P^\times)\rho = \rho$, this yields (8.18).

We end this section with the remark that Theorems 8.1 and 8.2 apply to any finite block Toeplitz equation. To see this we have to prove that for any finite sequence $\Phi_{-N}, \dots, \Phi_N$ of $m \times m$ matrices there exists a rational $m \times m$ matrix function Φ without poles on $\mathbb{T}$ such that $\Phi_{-N}, \dots, \Phi_N$ are the $-N$ to N Fourier coefficients of Φ and $\det \Phi(\zeta) \neq 0$ for each $\zeta \in \mathbb{T}$. Let us construct such a Φ. Put $P(\zeta) = \sum_{\nu=-N}^N \zeta^\nu \Phi_\nu$, and set

$$r = \max\{\|P(\zeta)\| \mid \zeta \in \mathbb{T}\}.$$

Take $\Phi(\zeta) = P(\zeta) + (r+1)\zeta^{N+1}I$, where I is the $m \times m$ identity matrix. This Φ has the desired properties. Obviously, Φ has no poles on $\mathbb{T}$ and $\Phi_{-N}, \dots, \Phi_N$ are the $-N$ to N

Fourier coefficients of Φ. Assume $\det \Phi(\zeta_0) = 0$ for some $\zeta_0 \in \mathbb{T}$. Choose $x_0 \neq 0$ in $\mathbb{C}^m$ such that $\Phi(\zeta_0)x_0 = 0$, and put $\lambda_0 = -(r+1)\zeta_0^{N+1}$. Then $P(\zeta_0)x_0 = \lambda_0 x_0$, and thus λ_0 is an eigenvalue of $P(\zeta_0)$ with absolute value equal to $r+1$. Since $\|P(\zeta_0)\| \leq r$, this is impossible. Thus $\det \Phi(\zeta) \neq 0$ for each $\zeta \in \mathbb{T}$.

9. FREDHOLM CHARACTERISTICS AND GENERALIZED INVERSE

In this section the coupling method of [4] is used to derive Fredholm characteristics and a generalized inverse for a block Toeplitz operator with a rational symbol. Again the symbol is given in realized form and all results are expressed explicitly in terms of the data appearing in the realization. In what follows the term generalized inverse is used in a weak sense, i.e., an operator S is said to have a *generalized inverse* S^+ whenever $S = SS^+S$. If S is a Fredholm operator, then, by definition, its *index* is the integer

$$\operatorname{ind}(S) = n(S) - d(S),$$

where $n(S) = \dim \operatorname{Ker} S$ and $d(S) = \operatorname{codim} \operatorname{Im} S$.

THEOREM 9.1. *Let T be a block Toeplitz operator on ℓ_p^m with a rational symbol*

$$\Phi(\zeta) = I + C(\zeta G - A)^{-1}B, \qquad \zeta \in \mathbb{T}, \tag{9.1}$$

given in realized form. Put $A^\times = A - BC$. Then T is a Fredholm operator if and only if $\zeta G - A^\times$ is a $\mathbb{T}$-regular pencil. Assume that the latter condition holds true. Then

$$\operatorname{Ker} T = \{(CE^\times(\Omega^\times)^k x)_{k=0}^\infty \mid x \in \operatorname{Im} P \cap \operatorname{Ker} P^\times\}, \tag{9.2}$$

$$\operatorname{Im} T = \left\{(\varphi_k)_{k=0}^\infty \in \ell_p^m \,\middle|\, \sum_{\nu=0}^\infty P^\times(\Omega^\times)^\nu B\varphi_\nu \in \operatorname{Im} P + \operatorname{Ker} P^\times\right\}, \tag{9.3}$$

$$n(T) = \dim(\operatorname{Im} P \cap \operatorname{Ker} P^\times), \qquad d(T) = \dim \frac{\mathbb{C}^n}{\operatorname{Im} P + \operatorname{Ker} P^\times}, \tag{9.4}$$

$$\operatorname{ind}(T) = \operatorname{rank} P - \operatorname{rank} P^\times, \tag{9.5}$$

and a generalized inverse of T is given by $T^+ = [\Gamma_{ij}^+]_{i,j=0}^{\infty}$ *with*

$$\Gamma_{ij}^+ = \Phi_{i-j}^\times + K_{ij}^+, \qquad i,j = 0,1,2,\dots, \tag{9.6}$$

$$\Phi_k^\times = \begin{cases} CE^\times(\Omega^\times)^k(I-P^\times)B, & k = 1,2,\dots, \\ I + CE^\times(I-P^\times)B, & k = 0, \\ -CE^\times(\Omega^\times)^{-k-1}P^\times B, & k = -1,-2,\dots, \end{cases} \tag{9.7}$$

$$K_{ij}^+ = -CE^\times(\Omega^\times)^i(I-P^\times)(J^\times)^+P^\times(\Omega^\times)^jB, \tag{9.8}$$

where $(J^\times)^+$ *is a generalized inverse of the operator*

$$J^\times = P^\times \mid \operatorname{Im} P\colon \operatorname{Im} P \to \operatorname{Im} P^\times. \tag{9.9}$$

Here P is the separating projection corresponding to $\zeta G - A$ and $\mathbb{T}$, and the operators $P^\times$, $E^\times$ and $\Omega^\times$ are, respectively, the separating projection, the right equivalence operator and the associate operator corresponding to $\zeta G - A^\times$ and $\mathbb{T}$.

PROOF. From [6] we know that T is Fredholm if and only if $\det \Phi(\zeta) \neq 0$ for each $\zeta \in \mathbb{T}$. By Theorem 4.2 the latter condition is equivalent to the requirement that $\zeta G - A^\times$ is $\mathbb{T}$-regular.

In what follows we assume that the pencil $\zeta G - A^\times$ is $\mathbb{T}$-regular. To establish the Fredholm properties of T we use the method of matricial coupling (see [4]). Introduce the following operators:

$$\begin{bmatrix} T & U \\ R & J \end{bmatrix} : \ell_p^m \oplus \operatorname{Im} P^\times \to \ell_p^m \oplus \operatorname{Im} P,$$

$$\begin{bmatrix} T^\times & U^\times \\ R^\times & J^\times \end{bmatrix} : \ell_p^m \oplus \operatorname{Im} P \to \ell_p^m \oplus \operatorname{Im} P^\times,$$

$$(Ux)_j = -CE\Omega^j(I-P)x, \qquad x \in \operatorname{Im} P^\times,$$

$$(U^\times x)_j = -CE^\times(\Omega^\times)^j(I-P^\times)x, \qquad x \in \operatorname{Im} P,$$

$$R\eta = \sum_{j=0}^{\infty} P\Omega^j B\varphi_j, \qquad \eta = (\varphi_0, \varphi_1, \dots) \in \ell_p^m,$$

$$R^{\times}\eta = -\sum_{j=0}^{\infty} P^{\times}(\Omega^{\times})^{j}B\varphi_{j}, \qquad \eta = (\varphi_0, \varphi_1, \ldots) \in \ell_p^m,$$

$$Jx = Px \quad (x \in \operatorname{Im} P^{\times}), \qquad J^{\times}x = P^{\times}x \quad (x \in \operatorname{Im} P).$$

Here E and Ω are the right equivalence operator and associate operator corresponding to $\zeta G - A$ and $\mathbb{T}$. The operator $T^{\times}$ is the block Toeplitz operator on ℓ_p^m with symbol $\Phi(\cdot)^{-1}$. Note that $J^{\times}$ is the operator defined by (9.9). Since Ω and $\Omega^{\times}$ have their eigenvalues in the open unit disc (Corollary 2.3), the operators U, $U^{\times}$, R and $R^{\times}$ are well-defined. We shall prove that

$$\begin{bmatrix} T & U \\ R & J \end{bmatrix}^{-1} = \begin{bmatrix} T^{\times} & U^{\times} \\ R^{\times} & J^{\times} \end{bmatrix}. \tag{9.10}$$

Proving (9.10) comes down to verifying eight identities. Here we shall establish four of them, namely

$$TT^{\times} + UR^{\times} = I_{\ell_p^m}, \tag{9.11}$$

$$RT^{\times} + JR^{\times} = 0, \tag{9.12}$$

$$TU^{\times} + UJ^{\times} = 0, \tag{9.13}$$

$$RU^{\times} + JJ^{\times} = I_{\operatorname{Im} P}. \tag{9.14}$$

The other four identities can be obtained by interchanging the roles of Φ and $\Phi(\cdot)^{-1}$.

We first consider the case $p = 2$. Let $L_2^m(\mathbb{T})$ be the Hilbert space of all $\mathbb{C}^m$-valued square integrable functions on $\mathbb{T}$, and let $H_2^m(\mathbb{T})$ be the subspace consisting of all $\varphi \in L_2^m(\mathbb{T})$ with Fourier coefficients $c_n = 0$ for $n = -1, -2, \ldots$. The orthogonal projection of $L_2^m(\mathbb{T})$ onto $H_2^m(\mathbb{T})$ will be denote by $\mathbb{P}$. If $g \in L_2(\mathbb{T})$, then $\mathbb{P}g$ has a natural extension to an analytic function on $\mathbb{D}_+$ (also denoted by $\mathbb{P}g$), and we shall use the fact that

$$(\mathbb{P}g)(\zeta) = \frac{1}{2\pi i}\int_{\mathbb{T}} \frac{g(\mu)}{\mu - \zeta}\,d\mu, \qquad |\zeta| < 1. \tag{9.15}$$

It will be convenient to use the Fourier transform

$$F: H_2^m(\mathbf{T}) \to \ell_2^m, \qquad F\varphi = (c_j)_{j=0}^{\infty},$$

where c_j is the j-th Fourier coefficient of φ. Put

$$S_\Phi = F^{-1}TF, \qquad V = F^{-1}U, \qquad N = RF,$$

$$S_{\Phi^{-1}} = F^{-1}T^\times F, \qquad V^\times = F^{-1}U^\times, \qquad N^\times = R^\times F.$$

Then

$$(Vx)(\zeta) = C(\zeta G - A)^{-1}(I - P)x, \qquad x \in \operatorname{Im} P^\times, \zeta \in \mathbf{T},$$

$$(V^\times x)(\zeta) = C(\zeta G - A^\times)^{-1}(I - P^\times)x, \qquad x \in \operatorname{Im} P, \zeta \in \mathbf{T},$$

$$N\varphi = \frac{1}{2\pi i}\int_{\mathbf{T}} PG(\zeta G - A)^{-1}B\varphi(\zeta)d\zeta, \qquad \varphi \in H_2^m(\mathbf{T}),$$

$$N^\times\varphi = \frac{-1}{2\pi i}\int_{\mathbf{T}} P^\times G(\zeta G - A^\times)^{-1}B\varphi(\zeta)d\zeta, \qquad \varphi \in H_2^m(\mathbf{T}),$$

$$S_\Phi\varphi = \mathbb{P}M_\Phi\varphi, \qquad S_{\Phi^{-1}}\varphi = PM_{\Phi^{-1}}\varphi, \qquad \varphi \in H_2^m(\mathbf{T}),$$

where $\mathbb{P}$ is the orthogonal projection of $L_2^m(\mathbf{T})$ onto $H_2^m(\mathbf{T})$ and M_Φ (resp. $M_{\Phi^{-1}}$) is the operator of multiplication by Φ (resp. Φ^{-1}). We have to prove the following identities:

(9.16) $$S_\Phi S_{\Phi^{-1}} + VN^\times = I_{H_2^m(\mathbf{T})},$$

(9.17) $$NS_{\Phi^{-1}} + JN^\times = 0,$$

(9.18) $$S_\Phi V^\times + VJ^\times = 0,$$

(9.19) $$NV^\times + JJ^\times = I_{\operatorname{Im} P}.$$

First we compute $S_\Phi S_{\Phi^{-1}}$. Note that

(9.20) $$BC = (\mu G - A^\times) - (\zeta G - A) - (\mu - \zeta)G.$$

Thus

$$\begin{aligned}\Phi(\zeta)\Phi(\mu)^{-1} &= [I + C(\zeta G - A)^{-1}B][I - C(\mu G - A^{\times})^{-1}B] \\ &= I - C(\mu G - A^{\times})^{-1}B + C(\zeta G - A)^{-1}B \\ &\quad - C(\zeta G - A)^{-1}BC(\mu G - A^{\times})^{-1}B \\ &= I + (\mu - \zeta)C(\zeta G - A)^{-1}G(\mu G - A^{\times})^{-1}B.\end{aligned}$$

Take $g \in H_2^m(\mathbb{T})$, and assume g is a polynomial. Then, by formula (9.15),

$$(S_{\Phi^{-1}}g)(\zeta) = \frac{1}{2\pi i}\int_{\mathbb{T}} \frac{\Phi(\mu)^{-1}g(\mu)}{\mu - \zeta}d\mu, \qquad |\zeta| < 1.$$

It follows that for $|\zeta| < 1$

$$\begin{aligned}(M_{\Phi}S_{\Phi^{-1}}g)(\zeta) &= \frac{1}{2\pi i}\int_{\mathbb{T}} \frac{\Phi(\zeta)\Phi(\mu)^{-1}g(\mu)}{\mu - \zeta}d\mu \\ &= g(\zeta) + C(\zeta G - A)^{-1}\Big(\frac{1}{2\pi i}\int_{\mathbb{T}} G(\mu G - A^{\times})^{-1}Bg(\mu)d\mu\Big).\end{aligned}$$

Now use the $\mathbb{T}$-spectral decomposition of the pencil $\lambda G - A^{\times}$ (Theorem 2.1). It follows that $(I - P^{\times})G(\lambda G - A^{\times})^{-1}$ is analytic on $\mathbb{D}_+$. Since $g \in H_2^m(\mathbb{T})$, we conclude that

$$\frac{1}{2\pi i}\int_{\mathbb{T}} (I - P^{\times})G(\mu G - A^{\times})^{-1}Bg(\mu)d\mu = 0. \tag{9.21}$$

Thus

$$(M_{\Phi}S_{\Phi^{-1}}g)(\zeta) = g(\zeta) - C(\zeta G - A)^{-1}N^{\times}g, \qquad |\zeta| < 1.$$

The $\mathbb{T}$-spectral decomposition of $\lambda G - A$ implies that $C(\lambda G - A)^{-1}P$ is analytic on $\mathbb{D}_-$ and $C(\lambda G - A)^{-1}(I - P)$ is analytic on $\mathbb{D}_+$. Note that all functions involved are rational. Thus $S_{\Phi}S_{\Phi^{-1}}g = g - VN^{\times}g$ for each polynomial in $H_2^m(\mathbb{T})$. But the polynomials are dense in $H_2^m(\mathbb{T})$. So the identity (9.16) is proved.

Again let $g \in H_2^m(\mathbb{T})$ be a polynomial. Put $h = (I - \mathbb{P})M_{\Phi^{-1}}g$. Then h is a rational $\mathbb{C}^m$-valued function which is analytic on $\mathbb{D}_-$ and $h(\lambda) \to 0$ if $\lambda \to \infty$. The $\mathbb{T}$-spectral decomposition of $\lambda G - A$ implies that $PG(\lambda G - A)^{-1}Bh(\lambda)$ is analytic on $\mathbb{D}_-$ and has a zero of order 2 at infinity. It follows that

$$\frac{1}{2\pi i}\int_{\mathbb{T}} P(\zeta G - A)^{-1}Bh(\zeta)d\zeta = 0.$$

Note that $S_{\Phi^{-1}}g = \mathbb{P}M_{\Phi^{-1}}g = M_{\Phi^{-1}}g - h$. Hence

$$\begin{aligned} NS_{\Phi^{-1}}g &= \frac{1}{2\pi i}\int_{\mathbb{T}} PG(\zeta G - A)^{-1}B(M_{\Phi^{-1}}g - h)(\zeta)d\zeta \\ &= \frac{1}{2\pi i}\int_{\mathbb{T}} PG(\zeta G - A)^{-1}B\Phi(\zeta)^{-1}g(\zeta)d\zeta. \end{aligned}$$

Now apply Lemma 4.3 and formula (9.21). We get

$$\begin{aligned} NS_{\Phi^{-1}}g &= \frac{1}{2\pi i}\int_{\mathbb{T}} PG(\zeta G - A^{\times})^{-1}Bg(\zeta)d\zeta \\ &= P\Big(\frac{1}{2\pi i}\int_{\mathbb{T}} P^{\times}G(\zeta G - A^{\times})^{-1}Bg(\zeta)d\zeta\Big) \\ &= -JN^{\times}g. \end{aligned}$$

Since the polynomials are dense in $H_2^m(\mathbb{T})$, formula (9.17) is proved.

Next, we take $x \in \operatorname{Im} P$. Note that $(I-P)(I-P^{\times})x = -(I-P)P^{\times}x$. Thus, using lemma 4.3,

$$\begin{aligned} (M_{\Phi}V^{\times}x)(\zeta) &= \Phi(\zeta)C(\zeta G - A^{\times})^{-1}(I-P^{\times})x \\ &= C(\zeta G - A)^{-1}(I-P^{\times})x \\ &= C(\zeta G - A)^{-1}P(I-P^{\times})x - (VJ^{\times}x)(\zeta). \end{aligned}$$

Now use that $(\lambda G - A)^{-1}P$ is analytic on $\mathbb{D}_{-}$, it follows that $S_{\Phi}V^{\times} = -VJ^{\times}$, and (9.18) is proved.

Formula (9.20) (with $\mu = \zeta$) implies that

$$(\zeta G - A)^{-1}BC(\zeta G - A^{\times})^{-1} = (\zeta G - A)^{-1} - (\zeta G - A^{\times})^{-1}.$$

Thus for $x \in \operatorname{Im} P$

$$\begin{aligned} NV^{\times}x &= \frac{1}{2\pi i}\int_{\mathbb{T}} PG[(\zeta G - A)^{-1} - (\zeta G - A^{\times})^{-1}](I-P^{\times})x\,d\zeta \\ &= P(I-P^{\times})x - PP^{\times}(I-P^{\times})x \\ &= x - JJ^{\times}x, \end{aligned}$$

which proves (9.19).

We have now proved the identities (9.11)–(9.14) for $p = 2$. Next, take an arbitrary p, $1 \le p \le \infty$. Since T and $T^\times$ are block Toeplitz operators with symbols from the Wiener class, the operator $TT^\times$ on ℓ_p^m has a matrix representation, that is,

$$(TT^\times x)_k = \sum_{j=0}^{\infty} M_{kj} x_j, \qquad k = 0, 1, 2, \ldots,$$

for each $x = (x_0, x_1, x_2, \ldots)$ in ℓ_p^m. The same is true for $UR^\times$. So to check (9.11) for arbitrary p it suffices to show that $(TT^\times + UR^\times)x = x$ for all sequences $x = (x_k)_{k=0}^\infty$ with a finite number of non-zero elements. But the latter sequences are all in ℓ_2^m, and hence (9.11) holds true for any $1 \le p \le \infty$. A similar argument proves that (9.12) holds for any $1 \le p \le \infty$. This identities (9.13) and (9.14) do not depend on p.

We have now shown that the operator T on ℓ_p^m is matricially coupled to the operator $J^\times$ via the formula (9.10). But then we can apply Theorems I.1.1 and I.2.1 in [4] to show that

(9.22) $$\operatorname{Ker} T = \{U^\times x \mid x \in \operatorname{Ker} J^\times\},$$

(9.23) $$\operatorname{Im} T = \{\eta = (\varphi_j)_{j=0}^\infty \in \ell_p^m \mid R^\times \eta \in \operatorname{Im} J^\times\},$$

(9.24) $$n(T) = \dim \operatorname{Ker} J^\times, \qquad d(T) = \dim[\operatorname{Im} P^\times / \operatorname{Im} J^\times].$$

Note that

(9.25) $$\operatorname{Ker} J^\times = \operatorname{Im} P \cap \operatorname{Ker} P^\times,$$

(9.26) $$P^\times z \in \operatorname{Im} J^\times \iff z \in \operatorname{Im} P + \operatorname{Ker} P^\times.$$

From (9.22) and (9.25) we get the desired description of $\operatorname{Ker} T$. Formulas (9.23) and (9.26) yield (9.3). Note that (9.26) also implies

(9.27) $$\dim[\operatorname{Im} P^\times / \operatorname{Im} J^\times] = \dim \frac{\mathbb{C}^n}{\operatorname{Im} P + \operatorname{Ker} P^\times}.$$

From (9.24), (9.25) and (9.27) our formulas for $n(T)$ and $d(T)$ in (9.4) are clear. According to (9.24) and the definition of $J^\times$:

$$n(T) = \operatorname{rank} P - \operatorname{rank} J^\times, \qquad d(T) = \operatorname{rank} P^\times - \operatorname{rank} J^\times,$$

which proves (9.5). Finally, if $(J^\times)^+$ is a generalized inverse of $J^\times$, then

$$T^+ = T^\times - U^\times (J^\times)^+ R^\times$$

is a generalized inverse of T. The operator $T^\times$ is the block Toeplitz operator defined by $\Phi(\cdot)^{-1}$. Thus $T^\times = [\Phi^\times_{i-j}]_{i,j=0}^\infty$ with $\Phi^\times_k$ given by (9.7) (see Theorem 4.1). But then $T^+ = [\Gamma^+_{ij}]_{i,j=0}^\infty$ with Γ^+_{ij} as in (9.6). □

Note that the operator $J^\times$ in (9.9) is invertible if and only if $\mathbb{C}^n = \operatorname{Im} P \oplus \operatorname{Ker} P^\times$, and in that case $(J^\times)^{-1} = (I-\rho) \mid \operatorname{Im} P^\times$, where ρ is the projection of $\mathbb{C}^n$ along $\operatorname{Im} P$ onto $\operatorname{Ker} P^\times$. It follows that Theorem 9.1 provides an alternative proof for Theorem 6.1. In a somewhat other form formulas (9.2) and (9.3) also appear in Theorem 7.3.

Theorem 9.1 can be extended to Toeplitz operators defined with respect to arbitrary curves, and hence with some modifications the results of this section can also be applied to singular integral equations with rational symbols (cf. [4], Chapter III).

10. AN EXAMPLE

In this section we illustrate the results of this paper on an example. Let T be the block Toeplitz operator with symbol

$$\Phi(\lambda) = \begin{bmatrix} 1-\lambda^{-1} & (2\lambda)^{-1} \\ -3\lambda & 1+\lambda \end{bmatrix}. \tag{10.1}$$

As a semi-infinite block matrix T is tridiagonal and the off diagonal elements are singular 2×2 matrices. We shall compute the Fourier coefficients of $\Phi(\cdot)^{-1}$, construct a right canonical factorization of Φ and compute the inverses of T and its finite sections by applying the recipes given by Corollary 3.2 and Theorems 5.1, 6.1 and 8.2.

The first step is to write Φ as a transfer function of a system. Such a representation may be constructed by using the procedure described in the proof of Theorem 3.1. Introduce

$$A = \begin{bmatrix} -1 & 0 & 0 \\ 0 & -1 & 0 \\ 0 & 0 & 0 \end{bmatrix}, \qquad G = \begin{bmatrix} 0 & 1 & 0 \\ 0 & 0 & 0 \\ 0 & 0 & 1 \end{bmatrix},$$

$$B = \begin{bmatrix} 0 & 0 \\ 3 & -1 \\ -1 & \frac{1}{2} \end{bmatrix}, \qquad C = \begin{bmatrix} 0 & 0 & 1 \\ 1 & 0 & 0 \end{bmatrix}.$$

The pencil $\lambda G - A$ is $\mathbb{T}$-regular and one computes that

$$(\lambda G - A)^{-1} = \begin{bmatrix} 1 & -\lambda & 0 \\ 0 & 1 & 0 \\ 0 & 0 & \lambda^{-1} \end{bmatrix}, \qquad \lambda \in \mathbb{T},$$

and thus

$$\Phi(\lambda) = I + C(\lambda G - A)^{-1}B, \qquad \lambda \in \mathbb{T}, \tag{10.2}$$

which is a desired realization. Note that

$$G(\lambda G - A)^{-1} = (\lambda G - A)^{-1}G = \begin{bmatrix} 0 & 1 & 0 \\ 0 & 0 & 0 \\ 0 & 0 & \lambda^{-1} \end{bmatrix},$$

and hence the projections P and Q (cf. (2.2) and (2.5)) are given by

$$P = Q = \begin{bmatrix} 0 & 0 & 0 \\ 0 & 0 & 0 \\ 0 & 0 & 1 \end{bmatrix}. \tag{10.3}$$

The next step is to analyze the pencil $\lambda G - A^{\times}$, where

$$A^{\times} = \begin{bmatrix} -1 & 0 & 0 \\ 1 & -1 & -3 \\ -\frac{1}{2} & 0 & 1 \end{bmatrix}.$$

One computes that $\det(\lambda G - A^{\times}) = (\lambda + 2)(\lambda - \frac{1}{2})$, and thus the pencil $\lambda G - A^{\times}$ is $\mathbb{T}$-regular. According to Theorem 4.2 this implies that

$$\Phi(\lambda)^{-1} = I - C(\lambda G - A^{\times})^{-1}B, \qquad \lambda \in \mathbb{T}, \tag{10.4}$$

and we can apply Corollary 3.2 to determine the Fourier coefficients $\Phi_k^{\times}$ of $\Phi(\cdot)^{-1}$. This requires to compute the separating projection $P^{\times}$, the right equivalence operator $E^{\times}$ and the associate operator $\Omega^{\times}$ corresponding to pencil $\lambda G - A^{\times}$ and $\mathbb{T}$. The first step is the inversion of $\lambda G - A^{\times}$,

$$(\lambda G - A^{\times})^{-1} = (\lambda + 2)^{-1}(\lambda - \frac{1}{2})^{-1} \begin{bmatrix} \lambda - 1 & \lambda(1-\lambda) & 3\lambda \\ \lambda + \frac{1}{2} & \lambda - 1 & -3 \\ -\frac{1}{2} & \frac{1}{2}\lambda & \lambda + 1 \end{bmatrix},$$

and next one uses the contour integrals in (4.3), (4.4) and (4.5) to compute that

$$P^{\times} = \frac{1}{5}\begin{bmatrix} 2 & -1 & -6 \\ 0 & 0 & 0 \\ -1 & \frac{1}{2} & 3 \end{bmatrix}, \tag{10.5}$$

$$E^{\times} = \frac{1}{5}\begin{bmatrix} -4 & -\frac{1}{2} & -3 \\ \frac{1}{2} & -4 & -9 \\ -\frac{3}{2} & -\frac{1}{2} & 2 \end{bmatrix}, \tag{10.6}$$

$$\Omega^{\times} = \frac{1}{5}\begin{bmatrix} -\frac{1}{2} & -\frac{7}{2} & -6 \\ 0 & 0 & 0 \\ -1 & -\frac{3}{4} & 1 \end{bmatrix}. \tag{10.7}$$

We have now all ingredients to compute the power representation of $\Phi_k^{\times}$ corresponding to the realization in (10.4) (cf. formula 4.2)). To simplify the computations note that $\Omega^{\times}$ has three different eigenvalues, namely $\frac{1}{2}$, $-\frac{1}{2}$ and 0. This allows us to diagonalize $\Omega^{\times}$. Put

$$D = \begin{bmatrix} \frac{1}{2} & 0 & 0 \\ 0 & -\frac{1}{2} & 0 \\ 0 & 0 & 0 \end{bmatrix}, \qquad S = \begin{bmatrix} 2 & 3 & -2 \\ 0 & 0 & 2 \\ -1 & 1 & -1 \end{bmatrix}.$$

Then S is invertible,

$$S^{-1} = \frac{1}{5}\begin{bmatrix} 1 & -\frac{1}{2} & -3 \\ 1 & 2 & 2 \\ 0 & \frac{5}{2} & 0 \end{bmatrix}, \qquad \Omega^{\times} = SDS^{-1}.$$

Furthermore

$$E^{\times}S = \begin{bmatrix} -1 & -3 & 2 \\ 2 & -\frac{3}{2} & 0 \\ -1 & -\frac{1}{2} & 0 \end{bmatrix}, \qquad S^{-1}P^{\times}S = \begin{bmatrix} 1 & 0 & 0 \\ 0 & 0 & 0 \\ 0 & 0 & 0 \end{bmatrix}.$$

It follows that

$$CE^{\times}S = \begin{bmatrix} -1 & -\frac{1}{2} & 0 \\ -1 & -3 & 2 \end{bmatrix},$$

$$S^{-1}P^{\times}B = (S^{-1}P^{\times}S)S^{-1}B = \frac{1}{10}\begin{bmatrix} 3 & -2 \\ 0 & 0 \\ 0 & 0 \end{bmatrix},$$

$$S^{-1}(I-P^{\times})B = \frac{1}{10}\begin{bmatrix} 0 & 0 \\ 8 & -2 \\ 15 & -5 \end{bmatrix}.$$

Using these expressions in (4.2) yields

$$\Phi_k^{\times} = \begin{cases} \frac{1}{10}\left(-\frac{1}{2}\right)^k \begin{bmatrix} -4 & 1 \\ -24 & 6 \end{bmatrix}, & k = 1,2,\dots, \\ \frac{1}{10}\begin{bmatrix} 6 & 1 \\ 6 & 6 \end{bmatrix}, & k = 0, \\ -\frac{1}{10}\left(\frac{1}{2}\right)^{-k-1}\begin{bmatrix} -3 & 2 \\ -3 & 2 \end{bmatrix}, & k = -1,-2,\dots . \end{cases} \tag{10.8}$$

For the canonical factorization we also need the operator

$$Q^{\times} = \frac{1}{2\pi i}\int_{\mathbb{T}} (\lambda G - A^{\times})^{-1} G\, d\lambda = \frac{1}{5}\begin{bmatrix} 0 & -1 & 3 \\ 0 & 2 & -6 \\ 0 & -1 & 3 \end{bmatrix}.$$

One checks that

$$\operatorname{Im} P = \operatorname{span}\left\{\begin{bmatrix} 0 \\ 0 \\ 1 \end{bmatrix}\right\}, \qquad \operatorname{Ker} P^{\times} = \operatorname{span}\left\{\begin{bmatrix} 3 \\ 0 \\ 1 \end{bmatrix}, \begin{bmatrix} -2 \\ 2 \\ -1 \end{bmatrix}\right\},$$

$$\operatorname{Im} Q = \operatorname{span}\left\{\begin{bmatrix} 0 \\ 0 \\ 1 \end{bmatrix}\right\}, \qquad \operatorname{Ker} Q^{\times} = \operatorname{span}\left\{\begin{bmatrix} 1 \\ 0 \\ 0 \end{bmatrix}, \begin{bmatrix} 0 \\ 3 \\ 1 \end{bmatrix}\right\}.$$

Hence

$$\mathbb{C}^3 = \operatorname{Im} P \oplus \operatorname{Ker} P^{\times}, \qquad \mathbb{C}^3 = \operatorname{Im} Q \oplus \operatorname{Ker} Q^{\times}, \tag{10.9}$$

and Theorem 5.1 implies that Φ admits a right canonical factorization relative to $\mathbb{T}$. To compute the factors we have to determine the projections corresponding to the decompositions in (10.9). This is easily done. Put

$$\rho = \begin{bmatrix} 1 & 0 & 0 \\ 0 & 1 & 0 \\ \frac{1}{3} & -\frac{1}{6} & 0 \end{bmatrix}, \qquad \tau = \begin{bmatrix} 1 & 0 & 0 \\ 0 & 1 & 0 \\ 0 & \frac{1}{3} & 0 \end{bmatrix}.$$

Then ρ is the projection of $\mathbb{C}^3$ onto $\operatorname{Ker} P^\times$ along $\operatorname{Im} P$ and τ is the projection onto $\operatorname{Ker} Q^\times$ along $\operatorname{Im} Q$. Now use formulas (5.2) and (5.3), and insert the present data. One computes that

$$\Phi_-(\lambda) = \begin{bmatrix} 1-(2\lambda)^{-1} & (3\lambda)^{-1} \\ 0 & 1 \end{bmatrix},$$

$$\Phi_+(\lambda) = \begin{bmatrix} 2 & -\frac{1}{3} \\ -3\lambda & \lambda+1 \end{bmatrix},$$

are the factors in a right canonical factorization of Φ relative to $\mathbb{T}$.

We know now that the block Toeplitz operator T with symbol Φ is invertible. The next step is to compute its inverse. The recipe to find the entries of the inverse $T^{-1} = [\Gamma_{ij}]_{i,j=0}^{\infty}$ is given in Theorem 6.1. We already computed $\Phi_k^\times$. It remains to compute

$$K_{ij} = CE^\times(\Omega^\times)^i(I-P^\times)\rho P^\times(\Omega^\times)^j B.$$

First we determine $S^{-1}(I-P^\times)\rho P^\times S$. Since

$$S^{-1}(I-P^\times)\rho P^\times S = S^{-1}(I-P^\times)S(S^{-1}\rho S)S^{-1}P^\times S,$$

it suffices to compute the $(2,1)$ and $(3,1)$ entries in $S^{-1}\rho S$. This is simple to do, and one finds that

$$S^{-1}(I-P^\times)\rho P^\times S = \begin{bmatrix} 0 & 0 & 0 \\ \frac{2}{3} & 0 & 0 \\ 0 & 0 & 0 \end{bmatrix}. \tag{10.10}$$

Using (10.10) together with the formulas for $CE^\times S$ and $S^{-1}P^\times B$ which we derived earlier, one finds that

$$K_{ij} = \frac{1}{10}(-1)^i\left(\frac{1}{2}\right)^{i+j}\begin{bmatrix} -1 & \frac{2}{3} \\ -6 & 4 \end{bmatrix}, \qquad i,j = 0,1,2,\dots . \tag{10.11}$$

So $T^{-1} = [\Phi_{i-j}^\times + K_{ij}]_{i,j=0}^{\infty}$, where $\Phi_k^\times$ is given by (10.8) and K_{ij} by (10.11).

Next, we consider the N-th section T_N of our block Toeplitz operator T. Thus T_N is the $(N+1)\times(N+1)$ block Toeplitz matrix in the left upper corner of T. To see whether or not T_N is invertible we first determine the matrix $V_N S$, where V_N is the matrix defined by (8.7). Note that in our case V_N (and also $V_N S$) is just a 3×3 matrix. To compute this matrix, we use that

$$\begin{aligned}V_NS &= (I-Q)E^\times S[S^{-1}(I-P^\times)S]+(I-Q)E^\times SD^{N+1}(S^{-1}P^\times S)\\&\quad+QE^\times SD^{N+1}[S^{-1}(I-P^\times)S]+QE^\times S(S^{-1}P^\times S).\end{aligned}$$

A straighforward computation yields

$$V_NS=\begin{bmatrix}(-\frac{1}{2})^{N+1} & -3 & 2\\ (\frac{1}{2})^N & -\frac{3}{2} & 0\\ -1 & (-\frac{1}{2})^{N+2} & 0\end{bmatrix}.$$

Put $d_N=\det(V_NS)=\frac{1}{2}(\frac{1}{2})^N(-\frac{1}{2})^N-3$. Obviously, $d_N\neq 0$, and so Theorem 8.2 implies that T_N is invertible. To compute its inverse we just specify the inversion formula in Theorem 8.2 for the case considered here. First one computes that

$$S^{-1}P^\times S(V_NS)^{-1}Q=\begin{bmatrix}0&0&3\\0&0&0\\0&0&0\end{bmatrix},$$

$$S^{-1}(I-P^\times)S(V_NS)^{-1}(I-Q)=\begin{bmatrix}0&0&0\\0&2(d_N)^{-1}&0\\\frac{1}{2}&*&0\end{bmatrix},$$

where $d_N=\det(V_NS)$ and $*$ is an entry which we shall not specify further. Now use again the formulas for $CE^\times S$, $E^\times S$, $S^{-1}P^\times B$ and $S^{-1}(I-P^\times)B$. One finds that

$$T_N^{-1}=[\Phi_{i-j}^\times+K_{ij}^N]_{i,j=0}^N,$$

where the $\Phi_k^\times$ are given by (10.8) and

$$\begin{aligned}K_{ij}^N &= -\frac{1}{10}(d_N)^{-1}(-1)^i\left(\frac{1}{2}\right)^{i+j}\begin{bmatrix}-3&2\\-18&12\end{bmatrix}\\&\quad-\frac{3}{10}\left(\frac{1}{2}\right)^{N-i}\left(-\frac{1}{2}\right)^{N-j}\begin{bmatrix}4&-1\\4&-1\end{bmatrix},\qquad i,j=0,1,2,\dots.\end{aligned}$$

Note that $d_N\to-3$, and hence for each i and j

$$K_{ij}^N\to K_{ij}\qquad(N\to\infty),$$

where K_{ij} is given by (10.11). This corresponds to the fact that our function Φ also admits a left canonical factorization. To see this note that

$$S^{-1}[P^{\times}P+(I-P^{\times})(I-P)]=\frac{1}{5}\begin{bmatrix}0 & 0 & 3\\ 1 & 2 & 0\\ 0 & \frac{5}{2} & 0\end{bmatrix},$$

and use the remark at the end of Section 5.

REFERENCES

1. Bart, H., Gohberg, I. and Kaashoek, M.A.: Minimal factorization of matrix and operator functions. Operator Theory: Advances and Applications, Vol. 1, Birkhäuser Verlag, Basel, 1979.
2. Bart, H., Gohberg, I. and Kaashoek, M.A.: Wiener-Hopf integral equations, Toeplitz matrices and linear systems. In: Toeplitz Centennial (Ed. I. Gohberg), Operator Theory: Advances and Applications, Vol. 4, Birkhäuser Verlag, Basel, 1982, pp. 85–135.
3. Bart, H., Gohberg, I. and Kaashoek, M.A.: Convolution equations and linear systems. Integral Equations and Operator Theory 5 (1982), 283–340.
4. Bart, H., Gohberg, I. and Kaashoek, M.A.: The coupling method for solving integral equations. In: Topics in operator theory, systems and networks (Eds. H. Dym and I. Gohberg). Operator Theory: Advances and Applications, Vol. 12, Birkhäuser Verlag, 1983, pp. 39–73.
5. Cohen, N.: On spectral analysis and factorization of rational matrix functions. Ph.D. Thesis, Weizmann Institute of Science, Rehovot, Israel, August 1984.
6. Gohberg, I.C. and Feldman, I.A.: Convolution equations and projection methods for their solution. Transl. Math. Monographs, Vol. 41, Amer. Math. Soc., Providence RI, 1974.
7. Gohberg, I.C. and Krein, M.G.: Systems of integral equations on a half line with kernels depending on the difference of arguments. Uspehi Mat. Nauk 13 (1958), no. 2 (80), 3–72 [Russian] = Amer. Math. Soc. Transl. (2) 14 (1960), 217–287.
8. Nikouklah, N.: System theory for two point boundary value descriptor systems, Ph.D. Thesis, Laboratory for Information and Decision Systems, LIDS-TH-1559, MIT, Cambridge MA, 1986.
9. Stummel, F.: Diskrete Konvergenz linearer Operatoren. II, Math. Z. 120 (1971), 231–264.
10. Verghese, G.C., Lévy, B.C. and Kailath, T.: A generalized state space for singular systems. IEEE Trans. Aut. Control, Vol. AC-26 (1981), 811–831.

I. Gohberg
Raymond and Beverly Sackler
Faculty of Exact Sciences
School of Mathematical Sciences
Tel-Aviv University
Ramat-Aviv, Israel

M.A. Kaashoek
Department of Mathematics and Computer Science
Vrije Universiteit
Amsterdam, The Netherlands

Operator Theory:
Advances and Applications, Vol. 35

FINITE REPRESENTATIONS OF BLOCK HANKEL OPERATORS AND BALANCED REALIZATIONS

K.D. Gregson [1] and N.J. Young

The block Hankel operator Γ_g corresponding to a rational matrix function g, analytic in $\mathbb{D}$ and of McMillan degree d, has rank d. Its non-trivial part, acting from $(\text{Ker } \Gamma_g)^{\perp}$ to Range Γ_g, can therefore in principle be represented by a $d \times d$ matrix with respect to a pair of orthonormal bases. We show how to obtain such a representation using polynomial methods: that is, we work with the coefficients of the numerator and denominator polynomials and do not require the solution of any polynomial equations. We use this representation to derive an algorithm for the construction of balanced realizations of rational transfer functions.

1. INTRODUCTION

Block Hankel operators play an important role in the solution of certain interpolation and approximation problems for analytic matrix functions [1]. Such problems have found a recent application in the area of "robust control": that is, designing control systems in such a way as to take account of inaccuracies in the modelling process [4,5,16]. There is consequently a call for the numerical solution of such problems, and hence for the numerical representation of block Hankel operators. A satisfactory representation using the ideas of state space realizations of analytic matrix functions is one of the main constituents of Glover's solution of the model reduction and model matching problems [7], and several authors report successful implementation of his algorithm [3,15]. There remains nevertheless an interest in solving these problems directly from the given matrix function, without first passing to a state space realization [11,12,14,19]. Starting from a rational matrix function one may express it as a matrix polynomial multiplied by the inverse of another: a method of calculating directly from the coefficients of these matrix polynomials is customarily called a "polynomial method". We shall describe a polynomial

1) This work was supported by the Science and Engineering Research Council.

method for the analysis of block Hankel operators.

One traditionally thinks of the matrix of a Hankel operator as being an infinite matrix with the familiar Hankel pattern (constancy on cross-diagonals). This matrix representation could be regarded as a polynomial method of a sort, but the disadvantages of infinite matrices for computational work are obvious. In the case of true Hankel operators (in which the blocks are of type 1 by 1), correspondimg to approximation problems for scalar functions or to compensator design for SISO systems, there do indeed exist effective polynomial methods using finite matrices. These have been implemented and tested successfully [2,20]. It is natural to ask whether such methods can be extended to matrix-valued functions. We show here that they can, but that there are significant new complications, to such an extent that much of the computational advantage of the method in the scalar case does not survive. There is more than one way of carrying out the extension: we take care to derive a matrix representation which is not only finite, but even minimal, in the sense that if a block Hankel operator has rank d then we represent it by a $d \times d$ matrix with respect to orthonormal bases in its cokernel and range. We do not require spectral data (such as the poles of the symbol) and so do not need to solve any polynomial equations, and we use real arithmetic throughout when the given function is real rational (real on the real axis). We do however need a substantial amount of computation, including either the spectral factorization of a positive definite matrix-valued function on the unit circle or the evaluation of $O(d^2)$ integrals round the unit circle.

There are numerous computational problems to which our representation of block Hankel operators could be applied. We have chosen to use it for the construction of balanced realizations of given stable rational transfer function matrices. We take a particular minimal realization (the restricted shift realization) for which the observability Gramian is the identity and the reachability operator is a block Hankel operator Γ. To balance this realization we need to compute $(\Gamma\Gamma^*)^{\frac{1}{4}}$, which entails carrying out a singular value decomposition of Γ. For ease of reference we give low level descriptions of the algorithms for minimal and balanced realization in Sections 2 and 3. In Section 4 we describe the restricted shift realization. The major technical facts on which our representation of block Hankel operators is based are presented in Sections 5 and 7. Both the cokernel and the range of a block Hankel operator are subspaces of Hardy H^2 spaces invariant under the backward shift operator, and we introduce in Section 5 a certain natural basis for such spaces, which we call the *expedient basis*. This basis is typically not orthogonal, but it can be orthogonalized by the Gram-Schmidt process. In the scalar case this can be achieved surprisingly efficiently by means of a simple closed form expression for the Gram matrix of the basis. In the present approach to the matrix case using the analogue of this formula entails performing a spectral factorization, and it is no longer clear that any advantage is gained over the straightforward numerical evaluation of inner products. Nevertheless the formula has theoretical interest and so we present it in Section 7. In Section 8 we show how to compute the matrix of a block Hankel operator with respect to the relevant expedient bases. Sections 6 and 9 apply these results to the minimal and balanced realization problems, thereby justifying the algorithms given in Sections 2 and 3.

F.B. Yeh and co-workers [17,18] give an alternative way of extending the scalar methods of [2,20] to the matrix case. They also obtain a finite matrix representation of a block Hankel operator with rational symbol, using related bases and Gram matrix formula. However, they do not aim at minimality: they work with superspaces of the cokernel and range, possibly of quite large dimension, and they use a different method for obtaining the matrix of the block Hankel operator. Their algorithm is comparatively extravagant of storage, but avoids some of the computational steps needed here, so we make no claim as to the general superiority of either.

We write L_n^2 for the space of square-integrable Lebesgue measurable $\mathbb{C}^n$-valued functions on the unit circle $\partial\mathbb{D}$, modulo equality almost everywhere, with the inner product

$$(x,y)_{L_n^2} = \frac{1}{2\pi i} \int_{\partial\mathbb{D}} (x(z),\ y(z))_{\mathbb{C}^n} \frac{dz}{z} .$$

H_n^2 denotes the subspace of L_n^2 comprising the functions whose negative Fourier coefficients vanish. Elements of H_n^2 extend to analytic functions in the open unit disc $\mathbb{D}$: see [9] for details. For any essentially bounded m x n matrix-valued function g on $\partial\mathbb{D}$ we define the block Hankel operator Γ_g to be the operator from H_n^2 to H_m^2 given by

$$\Gamma_g x = P_+(gJx)$$

when $J : H_n^2 \to L_n^2$ is defined by

$$(Jx)(z) = x(\bar{z}), \qquad z\epsilon\partial\mathbb{D}$$

and $P_+ : L_m^2 \to H_m^2$ is orthogonal projection. If g has Fourier series

$$g(z) \sim \sum_{j=-\infty}^{\infty} g_j z^j$$

then, with respect to the obvious identification of H_n^2 with the orthogonal direct sum of countably many copies of $\mathbb{C}^n$, Γ_g is represented by the infinite block Hankel matrix $[g_{i+j}]_{i,j=0}^{\infty}$.

Let G be an $m \times n$ matrix-valued function meromorphic in the plane and vanishing at ∞. An *operator realization* of G consists of a vector space H and linear mappings $A : H \to H$, $B : \mathbb{C}^n \to H$, $C : H \to \mathbb{C}^m$ such that, for every regular point z of G, the matrix of the linear operator

$$C(zI - A)^{-1}B : \mathbb{C}^n \to \mathbb{C}^m$$

with respect to the standard bases of $\mathbb{C}^n$, $\mathbb{C}^m$ is $G(z)$. A *matrix realization* is defined similarly, except that the entities A, B, C are matrices rather than operators. Operator realizations, being co-ordinate free, are useful for theoretical development, but for practical purposes one needs matrix realizations. Passing from operators to matrices involves making a convenient choice of bases, and this paper is largely about how to make such a choice effectively. A matrix realization is *balanced* if its controllability and observability Gramians RR^* and $\mathcal{O}^*\mathcal{O}$ are equal and diagonal (the reachability and observability operators R and are defined in Section 4). A reference for basic realization theory is [10]: we shall also recall some terminology relating to matrix polynomials from this source. The *degree* of the jth column of a matrix polynomial $P(z)$ is defined to be the degree of the highest power of z occurring in the jth column of $P(z)$ with non-zero coefficient. If $P(z)$ is an $n \times n$ matrix polynomial and its jth column has degree d_j, $1 \leq j \leq n$, then the *leading column coefficient matrix* of $P(z)$ is defined to be the constant $n \times n$ matrix whose (i,j) entry is the coefficient of z^{d_j} in the (i,j) entry of $P(z)$. P is said to be *column reduced* if its leading column coefficient matrix is non-singular. P is *row reduced* if P^T is column reduced. Finally, the notation $H \ominus K$ means the orthogonal complement in the Hilbert space H of the subset K of H.

2. ALGORITHM 1: MINIMAL REALIZATION

All algorithms for constructing a balanced realization of a transfer function matrix G proceed by first finding a minimal realization of G and then performing a similarity transformation to achieve balance. Our approach to the minimal realization problem essentially coincides with the use of Nerode equivalence [see 10, Section 6.6], and so at the first stage we arrive at a standard realization (the observer form). We describe it here in a way suited to incorporation into our balancing technique, to be presented as Algorithm 2.

1. Read positive integers m, n and the strictly proper rational matrix function G of type $m \times n$.

2. Find a matrix fractional description

$$G = U^{-1}V \tag{2.1}$$

where U, V are left coprime polynomial matrices (of types $m \times m$, $m \times n$ respectively) and U is row reduced.

3. Let z^{d_i} be the highest power of z occurring in the ith row of $U(z)$, $1 \leqslant i \leqslant m$, and let $k = \max_i d_i$.

4. Let F be the $m \times m$ matrix polynomial

$$F(z) = z^k \operatorname{diag} \{z^{-d_1}, \ldots, z^{-d_m}\} \, U(z) \tag{2.2}$$

and let C_F be the mk-square block companion matrix of F. That is, if

$$F(z) = F_0 + F_1 z + \ldots + F_k z^k \tag{2.3}$$

then

$$C_F = \begin{bmatrix} -F_{k-1}F_k^{-1} & I_m & 0 & \ldots & 0 \\ -F_{k-2}F_k^{-1} & 0 & I_m & \ldots & 0 \\ \cdot & \cdot & \cdot & \ldots & \cdot \\ -F_1F_k^{-1} & 0 & 0 & \ldots & I_m \\ -F_0F_k^{-1} & 0 & 0 & \ldots & 0 \end{bmatrix} \tag{2.4}$$

(The fact that U is row reduced ensures that F_k is non-singular).

5. Let $\tilde{A}$ be the principal submatrix of C_F obtained as follows:

for $q = 0, 1, 2, \ldots, k-1$ do

for $r = 1, 2, \ldots, m$ do

if $q \geqslant d_r$ then delete both the row and column of C_F numbered $qm+r$ (in other words, the rth row/columnn in the qth block row/column of C_F).

6. Define constant matrices $B_o, \ldots, B_{k-1}$ of type $m \times n$ by

$$z^{-1} \operatorname{diag} \left\{z^{d_1}, \ldots, z^{d_m}\right\} V(1/z) = B_0 + B_1 z + \ldots + B_{k-1} z^{k-1}. \tag{2.5}$$

7. For $j = 0, 1, \ldots, k-1$ let m_j be the number of indices i ($1 \leqslant i \leqslant m$) such that $d_i > j$.

8. For $j = 0, 1, \ldots, k-1$ let b_j be obtained by deleting row i of B_j

whenever $d_i < j$, $1 < i < m$.

9. Let

$$\tilde{B} = \begin{bmatrix} b_o \\ b_1 \\ \cdot \\ \cdot \\ \cdot \\ b_{k-1} \end{bmatrix} \qquad (2.6)$$

10. Let $\tilde{c}$ be the $m \times m_o$ submatrix of F_k^{-1} obtained by deleting column j of F_k^{-1} whenever $d_j = 0$, $1 < j < m$.

11. Let

$$\tilde{C} = [\tilde{c} \quad 0] \qquad (2.7)$$

of type $m \times \sum_1^m d_i$.

12. Print the triple $(\tilde{A}, \tilde{B}, \tilde{C})$ of matrices, which is a minimal matrix realization of G.

We have aimed at ease of understanding rather than economy in presenting the algorithm: naturally, in an implementation one would not store the full block companion matrix (2.4), but would go directly to the principal submatrix indicated in step 5. Nor need the quantities $m_1, \ldots, m_{k-1}$ appear explicitly.

3. ALGORITHM 2: BALANCED REALIZATION

1. Read positive integers m,n and the strictly proper rational matrix function G of type $m \times n$.

2. Perform Algorithm 1 to obtain a minimal matrix realization $(\tilde{A}, \tilde{B}, \tilde{C})$ of G; retain also the polynomial matrices U,V calculated in step 2 of Algorithm 1, and the row degrees d_i from step 3. Let $d = \sum_i d_i$ (the McMillan degree of G).

3. Find right coprime polynomial matrices V_r, U_r of types $m \times n$, $n \times n$ respectively such that U_r is column reduced and

$$G = V_r U_r^{-1}.$$

4. Let z^{c_j} be the highest power of z occurring in the jth column of $U_r(z)$, $1 < j < n$, and let $\ell = \max_j c_j$. (Note that $\sum_j c_j = d$, the McMillan degree of G).

5. Find left coprime polynomial matrices L,K of types $m \times m$, $m \times n$ respectively such that

$$L^{-1}K = V\hat{U}_r^{-1}$$

where $\hat{U}_r$ is the polynomial matrix given by

$$\hat{U}_r(z) = \text{diag}\left\{z^{c_1}, \ldots, z^{c_n}\right\} U_r(z)^*, \; z \in \partial\mathbb{D}$$

6. Find polynomial matrices $\tilde{U}$, $\tilde{L}$ of type $m \times m$ such that $\tilde{U}$ is row reduced,

$$L U = \tilde{U}\tilde{L}$$

and the zeros of det $\tilde{U}$, det $\tilde{L}$ lie in $\mathbb{D}$, $\mathbb{C} \setminus$ clos $\mathbb{D}$ respectively.

7. Find polynomial matrices $\tilde{q}$, $\tilde{r}$ of type $m \times n$ such that

$$K = \tilde{U}\tilde{q} + \tilde{r}$$

and $\tilde{U}^{-1}\tilde{r}$ is strictly proper.

8. For j = 0 to $\ell-1$ find polynomial matrices Q_j, r_j of type $m \times m$ such that

$$z^j L = \tilde{U}Q_j + r_j$$

and $\tilde{U}^{-1} r_j$ is strictly proper.

9. For $p = 1$ to n do

let y_{ij}, $1 \leqslant i \leqslant m$, $0 \leqslant j < d_i$, be the solution of the system of linear equations

$$\sum_{i=1}^{m} \sum_{j=0}^{d_i-1} r_{i,d_i-j-1} y_{ij} = r^{(p)},$$

where $r^{(p)}$ is the pth column of $\tilde{r}$ and r_{ij} is the ith column of r_j;

let Y_p be the constant $d \times 1$ matrix $[y_{10} \; y_{20} \; \ldots \; y_{m0} \; y_{21} \; \ldots]^T$ containing the y_{ij}, $1 \leqslant i \leqslant m$, $0 \leqslant j < d_i$.

10. Let n_j, $0 \leqslant j \leqslant \ell$, be the number of indices i such that

$$j < c_i, \; 1 \leqslant i \leqslant n.$$

11. For $j = 0$ to ℓ let R_j be the constant matrix of type $d \times n_j$ obtained from the matrix

$$\tilde{A}^j [Y_1 \; Y_2 \; \ldots \; Y_n]$$

by deleting the pth column if $j \geqslant c_p$.

12. Let $\tilde{R}$ be the constant matrix

$$[R_0 \;\; R_1 \;\; R_2 \; \ldots \; R_\ell]$$

of type $d \times d$.

13. Find an outer matrix polynomial D_r of type $n \times n$ such that

$$D_r(z)^* D_r(z) = U_r(z)^* U_r(z), \; z \in \partial\mathbb{D}.$$

14. Define constant $n \times n$ matrices U_j, D_j, $0 \leqslant j \leqslant \ell$, by

$$U_r(z) = (U_0 + U_1 z^{-1} + \ldots + U_\ell z^{-\ell}) \text{ diag } \{z^{c_1}, \ldots, z^{c_n}\},$$
$$D_r(z) = (D_0 + D_1 z^{-1} + \ldots + D_\ell z^{-\ell}) \text{ diag } \{z^{c_1}, \ldots, z^{c_n}\}$$

for $z \in \mathbb{D}$.

15. Let X,Y be the matrices of type $d \times n\ell$ obtained from the block Toeplitz matrices

$$\begin{bmatrix} U_0^* & 0 & \cdots & 0 \\ U_1^* & U_0^* & \cdots & 0 \\ \cdot & \cdot & \cdots & \cdot \\ U_{\ell-1}^* & U_{\ell-2}^* & \cdots & U_0^* \end{bmatrix}, \quad \begin{bmatrix} D_0^* & 0 & \cdots & 0 \\ D_1^* & D_0^* & \cdots & 0 \\ \cdot & \cdot & \cdots & \cdot \\ D_{\ell-1}^* & D_{\ell-2}^* & \cdots & D_0^* \end{bmatrix}$$

respectively by deleting the ith row in block row number j, $1 \leq i \leq m$, $0 \leq j < \ell$, whenever $j \geq c_i$.

16. Let γ_r be the $d \times d$ constant matrix

$$\gamma_r = XX^* - YY^*.$$

17. Find an outer matrix polynomial D of type $m \times m$ such that

$$D(z)^* \, D(z) = U(\bar{z}) \, U(\bar{z})^*, \; z \in \partial\mathbb{D}.$$

18. Define constant $m \times n$ matrices U_j, D_j, $0 \leq j \leq k$, by

$$U(\bar{z})^* = (U_0 + U_1 z^{-1} + \ldots + U_k z^{-k}) \text{ diag } \{z^{d_1}, \ldots, z^{d_m}\},$$

$$D(z) = (D_0 + D_1 z^{-1} + \ldots + D_k z^{-k}) \text{ diag } \{z^{d_1}, \ldots, z^{d_m}\}.$$

19. Repeat step 15 with n,ℓ replaced by m,k respectively.

20. Let γ be the $d \times d$ constant matrix

$$\gamma = XX^* - YY^*.$$

21. If γ_r is not positive definite print "G has a pole outside the unit circle" and stop; otherwise, find a $d \times d$ constant matrix T_r such that $T_r T_r^* = \gamma_r$.

22. Find a $d \times d$ constant matrix T such that $TT^* = \gamma$.

23. Find the singlar values $\sigma_1, \ldots, \sigma_d$ and corresponding orthonormal right singular vectors $w_1, \ldots, w_d$ of the matrix $T_r^* \, \tilde{R}^* \, T^{-*}$.

24. Let

$$\Sigma = \text{diag } \{\sigma_1, \ldots, \sigma_d\},$$

$$P = T[w_1 \; \ldots \; w_d],$$

$$\hat{A} = \Sigma^{-\frac{1}{2}} \, P^{-1} \, \tilde{A} \, P\Sigma^{\frac{1}{2}},$$

$$\hat{B} = \Sigma^{-\frac{1}{2}} \, P^{-1} \, \tilde{B},$$

$$\hat{C} = \tilde{C} \, P \, \Sigma^{\frac{1}{2}}.$$

25. Print the balanced realization $(\hat{A}, \hat{B}, \hat{C})$ of G and its controllability/observability Gramian Σ.

4. THE RESTRICTED SHIFT REALIZATION

The *shift operator* S on H_m^2 is the operation of multiplication by the independent variable,

$$Sx(z) = zx(z), \qquad x \in H_m^2,\ z \in \mathbb{D},$$

and the adjoint S^* of S is the *backward shift operator*, given by

$$(S^*x)\ (z) = \begin{cases} \frac{1}{z}\,(x(z) - x(0)), & z \in \mathbb{D} \setminus \{0\}, \\ x'(0), & z = 0. \end{cases}$$

The idea of constructing a realization by taking a subspace of H_m^2 as a state space and a suitable restriction of S^* as evolution operator is due independently to P. A. Fuhrmann [6] and J. W. Helton [8]. It is based on the following formula: for any $x \in H_m^2$, $\lambda,\ z \in \mathbb{D}$, $z \neq \lambda$,

$$((I - \lambda S^*)^{-1}x)(z) = \frac{zx(z) - \lambda x(\lambda)}{z - \lambda}\ . \tag{4.1}$$

To see this, note that S is clearly an isometry on H_m^2, so that

$$\|S^*\| = \|S\| = 1.$$

Hence $I - \lambda S^*$ is invertible for any $\lambda \in \mathbb{D}$. Equation (4.1) is thus equivalent to

$$x = (I - \lambda S^*)y$$

where

$$y(z) = \frac{zx(z) - \lambda x(\lambda)}{z - \lambda}\ .$$

This is a matter of simple verification. It follows from (4.1) that if

$$C : H_m^2 \to \mathbb{C}^m$$

is defined by

$$Cx = x(0),$$

then, for any $x \in H_m^2$ and $\lambda \in \mathbb{D}$,

$$C(I - \lambda S^*)^{-1}x = x(\lambda). \tag{4.2}$$

Thus, if g is an analytic matrix function with each entry in H^2 and

$$B : \mathbb{C}^n \to H_m^2$$

is defined by

$$(Bu)(z) = g(z)u, \qquad u \in \mathbb{C}^n,\ z \in \mathbb{D}, \tag{4.3}$$

then

$$C(I - \lambda S^*)^{-1}Bu = g(\lambda)u. \tag{4.4}$$

A realization is visible here, but its state space H_m^2 is too large. We cut down to the smallest subspace H of H_m^2 for which the construction works. In order for the definition (4.3) of B to make sense we require that H contain the columns of g, while, for the evolution operator S^* to act on H, H must be S^*-invariant ($S^*H \subseteq H$). This brings us to the restricted shift realization *RS* described below.

4.1 THEOREM *Let G be an $m \times n$ matrix valued function, analytic in the complement of the closed unit disc and vanishing at infinity, and let*

$$g(z) = \frac{1}{z} G\left[\frac{1}{z}\right], \qquad z \in \mathbb{D}. \tag{4.5}$$

Suppose that each entry of g belongs to H^2. Then there is a controllable and observable realization RS of G defined as follows. Let H be the closed linear span in H_m^2 of the functions

$$\{S^{*j}g(.)u \; : \; u \in \mathbb{C}^n\}$$

and let

$$A = S^*|H : H \to H, \tag{4.6a}$$

$$B : \mathbb{C}^n \to H : u \to g(.)u, \tag{4.6b}$$

$$C : H \to \mathbb{C}^m : x \to x(0). \tag{4.6c}$$

RS is the realization (A, B, C) of G on the state space H. The observability operator $\mathcal{O}$ of RS is the injection mapping of H into H_m^2, and the reachability operator R of RS is the Hankel operator

$$\Gamma_g \; : \; H_n^2 \to H_m^2 \; : \; x \to P_+(gJx)$$

with codomain restricted to $H \subseteq H_m^2$.

PROOF When $|z| > 1$ we may put $\lambda = z^{-1}$ in (4.4) to obtain

$$C(I - z^{-1}S^*)^{-1}B = g(z^{-1}).$$

Multiply through by z^{-1}:

$$C(zI - S^*)^{-1}B = z^{-1}g(z^{-1}) = G(z).$$

Thus (A, B, C) is indeed a realization of G on the state space H.

The observability operator is defined to be the operator with matrix

$$\begin{bmatrix} C \\ CA \\ CA^2 \\ \vdots \end{bmatrix}$$

mapping H to sequences of outputs. If we make the customary identification of square summable sequences of vectors in $\mathbb{C}^m$ with elements of H_m^2, by

$$(y_j)_0^\infty \leftrightarrow \sum_0^\infty y_j z^j,$$

then it is easy to check that $\mathcal{O}$ is just the injection $H \to H_m^2$. Hence RS is observable. Similarly we identify the space of square-summable sequences of inputs with H_n^2. Then $R : H_n^2 \to H$ has operator matrix

$$[B \; AB \; A^2B \; \dots],$$

so that for any polynomial $\mathbf{u} = \sum_0^N u_j z^j \in H_n^2$, we have

$$\begin{aligned} R\mathbf{u} &= \sum_0^N A^j B u_j = \sum_0^N S^{*j} g(.) u_j \\ &= P_+ \sum_0^N g(.) \bar{z}^j u_j \\ &= P_+ g(z)\, \mathbf{u}(\bar{z}) = P_+(gJ\mathbf{u}) \\ &= \Gamma_g \mathbf{u}. \end{aligned}$$

Thus R is a restriction of Γ_g, as stated. Note also that this calculation shows that $S^{*j}g(.)u$ is the image under R of the polynomial $uz^j \in H_n^2$. Since H is defined to be the closed linear span of such vectors, it follows that the range of R is dense in H. That is, RS is controllable. □

We shall need a description of the state space H of RS in polynomial terms. It depends only on the denominator of G.

4.2 THEOREM *Let G be an $m \times n$ rational matrix function which is analytic in the complement of $\mathbb{D}$ and vanishes at infinity. Let*

$$G^{\vee}(z) = G(\bar{z})^*, \qquad z \notin \mathbb{D}, \tag{4.7}$$

and suppose that $G^{\vee}$ has the matrix fractional description

$$G^{\vee} = MN^{-1},$$

where M, N are right coprime polynomial matrices of types $n \times m$, $m \times m$ respectively. Then the state space of the restricted shift realization RS of G is $H_m^2 \ominus NH_m^2$.

PROOF We saw in Theorem 4.1 that the state space H is the closure of Range Γ_g in H_m^2. Hence

$$H^{\perp} = (\text{Range } \Gamma_g)^{\perp} = \text{Ker } \Gamma_g^*.$$

Now, for $y \in H_m^2$,

$$\begin{aligned} y \in \text{Ker } \Gamma_g^* &\Leftrightarrow (\Gamma_g^* y, uz^j) = 0, \quad \text{all } j \geqslant 0,\ u \in \mathbb{C}^n \\ &\Leftrightarrow (y, \Gamma_g(uz^j)) = 0, \quad \text{all } j \geqslant 0,\ u \in \mathbb{C}^n, \\ &\Leftrightarrow \int_{\partial\mathbb{D}} (y(z), g(z)\bar{z}^j u)\, dz/z = 0 \\ &\Leftrightarrow \int (g(z)^* y(z), \bar{z}^j u)\, dz/z = 0 \\ &\Leftrightarrow g^* y \perp z^{-j} u, \quad \text{all } j \geqslant 0,\ u \in \mathbb{C}^n \end{aligned}$$

$$\Leftrightarrow \quad g^* y \in zH_n^2$$
$$\Leftrightarrow \quad (\bar{z}G(\bar{z}))^* y \in zH_n^2$$
$$\Leftrightarrow \quad G^{\mathrm{v}} y \in H_n^2$$
$$\Leftrightarrow \quad MN^{-1} y \in H_n^2. \tag{4.8}$$

Clearly if $y \in NH_m^2$ then $MN^{-1}y \in H_n^2$ and so $y \in \operatorname{Ker} \Gamma_g^*$. Conversely, suppose $MN^{-1}y \in H_n^2$. Pick polynomial matrices X, Y of types $m \times n$, $m \times m$ respectively such that

$$XM + YN = I_m.$$

Then

$$\begin{aligned} N^{-1}y &= (XM + YN)N^{-1}y \\ &= XMN^{-1}y + Yy \in H_m^2. \end{aligned}$$

Thus $y \in NH_m^2$. Hence

$$H^{\perp} = \operatorname{Ker} \Gamma_g^2 = NH_m^2,$$

and so

$$H = H_m^2 \ominus NH_m^2. \qquad \square$$

5. A BASIS FOR A SPACE OF RATIONAL VECTOR FUNCTIONS

To convert the restricted shift realization to a matrix realization of G we must find a basis in the state space H which will enable us to compute the matrices of the operators A, B and C. Accordingly we consider (as in Theorem 4.2) an $m \times m$ matrix polynomial N. We shall suppose that N is column reduced, and that all the zeros of det $N(z)$ lie in $\mathbb{D}$. We seek a manageable basis for $H_m^2 \ominus NH_m^2$.

Let d_j be the highest power of z occurring in the jth column of $N(z)$ and let

$$\Delta(z) = \operatorname{diag} \{z^{d_1}, z^{d_2}, \ldots, z^{d_m}\}. \tag{5.1}$$

Then we can write

$$N(z) = (N_0 + N_1 z^{-1} + \ldots + N_k z^{-k})\Delta(z), \tag{5.2}$$

where $N_0, \ldots, N_k$ are constant $m \times m$ matrices and k is the highest power of z occurring in $N(z)$ (so that $k = \max_j d_j$). For example, if

$$N(z) = \begin{bmatrix} z^2+\alpha & z+\beta \\ z^2+\alpha & -z-\beta \end{bmatrix} \tag{5.3}$$

then we have

$$N(z) = \left[\begin{bmatrix}1 & 1\\ 1 & -1\end{bmatrix} + \begin{bmatrix}0 & \beta\\ 0 & -\beta\end{bmatrix} z^{-1} + \begin{bmatrix}\alpha & 0\\ \alpha & 0\end{bmatrix} z^{-2}\right] \begin{bmatrix}z^2 & 0\\ 0 & z\end{bmatrix}.$$

The assumption that N is column reduced means exactly that N_0 is non-singular. Let

$$\hat{N}(z) = N_0^* + N_1^* z + \ldots + N_k^* z^k. \tag{5.4}$$

Thus, in the example (5.3)

$$\hat{N}(z) = \begin{bmatrix}1+\bar{\alpha}z^2 & 1+\bar{\alpha}z^2\\ 1+\bar{\beta}z & -1-\bar{\beta}z\end{bmatrix}.$$

We claim that $\hat{N}^{-1} \in H^\infty_{m\times m}$. Since $\hat{N}^{-1}$ is analytic at all points of $\mathbb{C}$ except those at which det $\hat{N}(z)$ vanishes, it suffices to show that det $\hat{N} \neq 0$ for $z \in$ clos $\mathbb{D}$. We have, from (5.2)

$$\begin{aligned} N(1/z)^* &= ((N_0 + N_1 z + \ldots + N_k z^k)\ \Delta(1/z))^* \\ &= \Delta(1/\bar{z})\ \hat{N}(\bar{z}), \end{aligned}$$

and so

$$\begin{aligned} \hat{N}(z) &= \Delta(1/z)^{-1}\ N(1/\bar{z})^* \qquad (5.5)\\ &= \Delta(z)\ N(1/\bar{z})^*, \qquad z \neq 0. \end{aligned}$$

Now

$$\det \hat{N}(0) = \det N_0^* \neq 0,$$

while, if $z \neq 0$,

$$\begin{aligned} \det \hat{N}(z) &= \det \Delta(z)(\det N(1/\bar{z}))^- \\ &= z^d(\det N(1/\bar{z}))^-, \end{aligned}$$

where $d = d_1 + \ldots + d_m$, so that the zeros of det $\hat{N}(z)$ are the conjugates with respect to the unit circle of the zeros of det $N(z)$. The latter all lie in $\mathbb{D}$, and so the zeros of det $\hat{N}(z)$ lie in the complement of clos $\mathbb{D}$. Thus $\hat{N}^{-1} \in H^\infty_{m\times m}$.

With the aid of $\hat{N}$ and Δ we can give a concise concrete description of the state space $H = H^2_m \ominus NH^2_m$. Take adjoints in (5.5) to get

$$N(1/\bar{z}) = \hat{N}(z)^*\ \Delta(1/z)^*.$$

Thus, regarding N, $\hat{N}$ and Δ as functions on the unit circle $z\bar{z} = 1$, we have

$$N = \hat{N}^*\Delta. \tag{5.6}$$

Consequently, for $f \in H^2_m$,

$$\begin{aligned} f \perp NH^2_m &\iff f \perp \hat{N}^*\Delta H^2_m \\ &\iff \hat{N}f \perp \Delta H^2_m. \end{aligned}$$

Since $\hat{N}^{-1} \in H^\infty_{m\times m}$, if $\hat{N}f \in H^2_m$ then $f \in H^2_m$. We have shown the following.

5.1 THEOREM *Let N be a column-reduced $m \times m$ matrix polynomial such that all the zeros of* det $N(z)$ *lie in* $\mathbb{D}$. *Let Δ and $\hat{N}$ be as in (5.1) and (5.4) Then*

$$H^2_m \ominus NH^2_m = \hat{N}^{-1}(H^2_m \ominus H^2_m). \qquad \square$$

The point of this theorem is that the space

$$W \stackrel{\text{def}}{=} H^2_m \ominus \Delta H^2_m$$

is very easy to visualise. Note that in the scalar case ($m = 1$), $H^2 \ominus z^d H^2$ simply consists of the space of polynomials of degree less than d ($d \geqslant 1$). More generally, for the diagonal matrix Δ given by (5.1) W consists of all polynomial vectors

$$h = [h^1 \; h^2 \; \dots \; h^m]^T$$

where h^j is a scalar polynomial of degree less than d_j. In other words, the general element $h \in W$ has the form

$$h(z) = \begin{bmatrix} h^1_0 + h^1_1 z + \dots + h^1_{d_1-1} z^{d_1-1} \\ \cdot \quad \cdot \quad \cdot \quad \cdots \quad \cdot \quad \cdot \quad \cdot \\ h^m_0 + h^m_1 z + \dots + h^1_{d_m-1} z^{d_m-1} \end{bmatrix}.$$

There is an obvious basis for W: vectors having a power of z in one component and zeros in the others. Let us denote by $e_i \otimes z^j$ ($1 \leqslant i \leqslant m$, $j = 0, 1, 2, \dots$) the vector having z^j as its ith component and all other components zero:

$$(e_i \otimes z^j)(z) = [0 \; \dots \; 0 \; z^j \; 0 \; \dots \; 0]^T,$$

the non-zero entry being in the ith component, $1 \leqslant i \leqslant m$. Multiplication by $\hat{N}^{-1}$ is clearly a linear bijection of H^2_m onto itself, and Theorem 5.1 shows that it maps W onto $H^2_m \ominus NH^2_m$. The $e_i \otimes z^j$ form a basis for W, and so $\hat{N}^{-1}(e_i \otimes z^j)$ constitutes a basis for $H^2_m \ominus NH^2_m$.

5.2 DEFINITION Let N be an $m \times m$ matrix polynomial as in Theorem 5.1, and let z^{d_j} be the highest power of z occurring in the jth column of $N(z)$. Let $\hat{N}$ be defined by (5.4). The basis

$$\hat{N}^{-1}(e_i \otimes z^j), \quad 1 \leqslant i \leqslant m, \; 0 \leqslant j \leqslant d_i$$

of $H^2_m \ominus NH^2_m$ will be called the *expedient* basis of $H^2_m \ominus NH^2_m$. $\square$

This basis appears to be well suited to the representation within the context of polynomial methods of operators related to rational functions. There are four reasons for this.

1. It requires knowledge only of the coefficients occurring in $N(z)$.

Some bases which have been proposed or which are used in theoretical studies assume also spectral data for $N(z)$ - e.g. the zeros of det $N(z)$ and a basis for Ker $N(z)$ at each zero.

2. It allows easy computation of the restricted backward shift operator. As we saw in §4, $S^*|H_m^2 \ominus NH_m^2$ is the evolution operator in the restricted shift realization. This operator also plays a central role in numerous other system-theoretic problems (e.g. the operator-theoretic approach to the model matching problem [4]). We show in §6 that the matrix of $S^*|H_m^2 \ominus NH_m^2$ with respect to the expedient basis is a principal submatrix of a block companion matrix.

3. It uses real arithmetic. In applications the coefficients occurring in $N(z)$ will practically always be real numbers, and in this case calculations using the expedient basis can be carried out in the real field. Such is not the case with bases expressed in terms of spectral data: det $N(z)$ will usually have some non-real zeros.

4. Although the expedient basis is not orthonormal, it can be orthonormalised relatively easy. Orthonormalising any basis corresponds to transforming matrices by a similarity using a Cholesky factor of the Gram matrix of the basis: in this instance there is a closed form expression for the inverse of the Gram matrix (Theorem 7.1 below). In the scalar case this formula allows one to write down the inverse Gram matrix with virtually no computation, making it a valuable practical tool. In the vector case, however, its use appears to require a spectral factorization, and it is possible that for computation it may be better to calculate the entries of the Gram matrix directly by the evaluation of integrals round the unit circle. In rival approaches to balanced realization (e.g. [7]) one typically solves two Lyapunov equations to obtain the observability and controllability Gramians of a minimal realization. The expedient basis gives us these by an alternative route.

Definition 5.2 specifies the elements but not the ordering of the expedient basis: we must rectify this so that the matrices of operators with respect to the basis will be uniquely determined. There are two equally natural orderings of the expedient basis vectors $\hat{N}^{-1}(e_i \otimes z^j)$: we shall select the one in which the row index i varies faster than the "power index" j. In the notation of Definition 5.2, an ordered list of the expedient basis vectors may be obtained as follows. Write down the $m(\max_j d_j)$ functions

$$\hat{N}^{-1}(e_1 \otimes z^0),\ \hat{N}^{-1}(e_2 \otimes z^0),\ \ldots,\ \hat{N}^{-1}(e_m \otimes z^0),$$
$$\hat{N}^{-1}(e_1 \otimes z^1),\ \hat{N}^{-1}(e_2 \otimes z^1),\ \ldots,\ \hat{N}^{-1}(e_m \otimes z^1),$$
$$\hat{N}^{-1}(e_1 \otimes z^2),\ \ldots,\ \hat{N}^{-1}(e_m \otimes z^k),$$

where $k = \max_j d_j$. Then from this list strike out all functions $\hat{N}^{-1}(e_i \otimes z^j)$ such that $j \geq d_i$. We shall often think of the basis as being arranged in k blocks, the elements in the jth block being the functions $\hat{N}^{-1}(e_i \otimes z^j)$, $1 \leq i \leq m$, for which $j < d_i$.

W itself (cf (5.7)) has an expedient basis: if we take $N = \Delta$ then $\hat{N} = I$ and so the expedient basis of W is just the obvious basis $\{e_i \otimes z^j\}$ used above, with the ordering

$$e_1 \otimes z^0,\ e_2 \otimes z^0,\ \ldots,\ e_m \otimes z^{d_m - 1}.$$

Specialising still further, the space K of vector polynomials of degree less than k can be expressed as $H_m^2 \ominus z^k H_m^2$ and so is obtained by taking $N(z) = \Delta(z) = z^k I_m$. In this case the expedient basis is the natural basis

$$e_1 \otimes z^0,\ e_2 \otimes z^0,\ \ldots,\ e_m \otimes z^0,\ \ldots,\ e_m \otimes z^{k-1}.$$

For W and K, the expedient basis *is* orthonormal.

6. JUSTIFICATION OF ALGORITHM 1

To convert the restricted shift realization RS to a matrix realization of G we need to compute the matrices of the operators A, B and C of (4.6) with respect to suitable bases. We shall use the expedient basis in the state space

$$H = H_m^2 \ominus NH_m^2$$

of RS, and we begin with the evolution operator $A = S^*|H$. By Theorem 5.1 we can write a typical element of H in the form $\hat{N}^{-1}h$ where

$$h(z) = h_0 + h_1 z + \ldots + h_{k-1} z^{k-1}$$

is an element of W. Here each $h_j \in \mathbb{C}^m$. Then

$$\begin{aligned}(S^*\hat{N}^{-1}h)(z) &= z^{-1}[\hat{N}(z)^{-1}h(z) - \hat{N}(0)^{-1}h(0)] \\ &= z^{-1}\hat{N}(z)^{-1}[h(z) - \hat{N}(z)N_0^{-*}h_0].\end{aligned}$$

Now

$$\begin{aligned}h(z) - \hat{N}(z)N_0 h_0^{-*} &= h_0 + h_1 z + \ldots + h_{k-1}z^{k-1} \\ &\quad - (N_0^* + N_1^* z + \ldots + N_k^* z^k)N_0^{-*}h_0 \\ &= (-N_1^* N_0^{-*}h_0 + h_1)z + (-N_2^* N_0^{-*}h_0 + h_2)z^2 \\ &\quad + \ldots + (-N_{k-1}^* N_0^{-*}h_0 + h_{k-1})z^{k-1} - N_k^* N_0^{-*}h_0 z^k.\end{aligned}$$

Hence

$$S^*\hat{N}^{-1}h = \hat{N}^{-1}w \qquad (6.1)$$

where $w \in W$ is given by

$$w(z) = \sum_{j=0}^{k-2} (- N_{j+1}^{*} N_0^{-*} h_0 + h_{j+1}) z^j - N_k^{*} N_0^{-*} h_0 z^{k-1}. \qquad (6.2)$$

This relation enables us to write down the matrix of $S^*|H$. If all the d_j are equal, so that $W = H_m^2 \ominus z^k H_m^2$, which we can identify in an obvious way with $(\mathbb{C}^m)^k$, then we can infer that the matrix of $S^*|H$ with respect to the expedient basis is the block companion matrix

$$Co = \begin{bmatrix} -N_1^{*} N_0^{-*} & I_m & 0 & \dots & 0 \\ -N_2^{*} N_0^{-*} & 0 & I_m & \dots & 0 \\ \cdot & \cdot & \cdot & \dots & \cdot \\ -N_{k-1}^{*} N_0^{-*} & 0 & 0 & \dots & I_m \\ -N_k^{*} N_0^{-*} & 0 & 0 & \dots & 0 \end{bmatrix} \qquad (6.3)$$

In the case of unequal d_j the matrix will be of type $d \times d$ where $d = \Sigma_j d_j < mk$. Let us consider the example (5.3) again by way of illustration. Here

$$W = H_2^2 \ominus \begin{bmatrix} z^2 & 0 \\ 0 & z \end{bmatrix} H_2^2 = \begin{bmatrix} H^2 \ominus z^2 H^2 \\ H^2 \ominus zH^2 \end{bmatrix},$$

in a self-explanatory notation. W has dimension 3, and a basis for W is

$$\hat{N}^{-1} \begin{bmatrix} 1 \\ 0 \end{bmatrix}, \quad \hat{N}^{-1} \begin{bmatrix} 0 \\ 1 \end{bmatrix}, \quad \hat{N}^{-1} \begin{bmatrix} z \\ 0 \end{bmatrix}, \qquad (6.4)$$

or, in the notation of Definition 5.2,

$$\hat{N}^{-1}(e_1 \otimes z^0),\ \hat{N}^{-1}(e_2 \otimes z^0),\ \hat{N}^{-1}(e_1 \otimes z^1).$$

For $h_0 \in H_2^2 \ominus zH_2^2$ equations (6.1) and (6.2) give

$$S^* \hat{N}^{-1} h_0 = \hat{N}^{-1} [-N_1^{*} N_0^{-*} h_0 - N_2^{*} N_0^{-*} h_0 z]$$

$$= \hat{N}^{-1} \left[\begin{bmatrix} 0 & 0 \\ 0 & -\bar{\beta} \end{bmatrix} h_0 + \begin{bmatrix} -\bar{\alpha} & 0 \\ 0 & 0 \end{bmatrix} h_0 z \right].$$

Similarly,

$$S^* \hat{N}^{-1} \begin{bmatrix} z \\ 0 \end{bmatrix} = \hat{N}^{-1} \begin{bmatrix} 1 \\ 0 \end{bmatrix}.$$

Thus, with respect to the expedient basis of H, $S^*|H$ has matrix

$$\begin{bmatrix} 0 & 0 & 1 \\ 0 & -\bar{\beta} & 0 \\ -\bar{\alpha} & 0 & 0 \end{bmatrix}.$$

This is a submatrix of the block companion matrix *Co*. It is obtained simply by deleting the row and column corresponding to the basis vector $e_2 \otimes z^1$ of $H_2^2 \ominus z^2H_2^2$ which does not belong to W.

6.1 THEOREM *Let N be a matrix polynomial as in Theorem 5.1 and let $\Delta\ \hat{N}$ be given by (5.1 and (5.4). Let $H = H_m^2 \ominus NH_m^2$. With respect to the expedient basis of H in its conventional ordering, the matrix of $S^*|H$ is the principal submatrix of the block companion matrix Co in* (6.2) *obtained by retaining the rows and columns corresponding to the basis vectors $e_i \otimes z^j$ of $H_m^2 \ominus z^kH_m^2$ which belong to W and discarding the others.*

Observe that the row or column of *Co* numbered $qm + r$, where $0 \leq q \leq k-1$, $1 \leq r \leq m$, corresponds to the basis vector $e_r \otimes z^q$ of $H_m^2 \ominus z^kH_m^2$. It is thus retained if $q < d_r$ and deleted otherwise in the calculation of the matrix of $S^*|H$.

PROOF. The mapping, T say, from h to w given by equation (6.2) is well defined on all of $H_m^2 \ominus z^kH_m^2$. The matrix of this extended transformation with respect to the basis $e_i \otimes z^j$, $1 \leq i \leq m$, $0 \leq j < k$, with the ordering

$$e_1 \otimes z^0,\ e_2 \otimes z^0,\ \ldots,\ e_m \otimes z^0,\ e_1 \otimes z^1,\ \ldots,\ e_m \otimes z^{k-1},$$

is *Co*. To get the matrix of the restriction to W, which is spanned by the basis vectors $e_i \otimes z^j$ with $j < d_i$, we simply delete the columns corresponding to those basis vectors not in W. The result is the matrix of the mapping $h \to w$, acting on W, that is, of

$$T|W : W \to H_m^2 \ominus z^kH_m^2.$$

Since $H_m^2 \ominus NH_m^2$ is invariant under S^*, T maps W into itself. In other words, the rows of the matrix of $T|W$ which correspond to basis vectors $e_i \otimes z^j$ not in W are all zero. On suppressing these zero rows we obtain the desired matrix of $S^*|H$. □

Next we calculate the matrix of

$$B : \mathbb{C}^n \to H : u \to g(.)u$$

with respect to the standard basis of $\mathbb{C}^n$ and the expedient basis of H. To this end we wish to express g in terms of $\hat{N}$, Δ and M, all of which we are regarding as functions on the unit circle. We thus have, from (4.5)

$$g(z) = \bar{z}G(\bar{z}),$$

and hence, from (4.7)

$$G^\vee(z) = G(\bar{z})^* = \bar{z}g(z)^*.$$

Thus

$$g^* = zG^\vee = zMN^{-1},$$

while, from (5.6),

$$N = \hat{N}^*\Delta.$$

Hence

$$g^* = zM\Delta^{-1}\hat{N}^{-*},$$

and so

$$g = \hat{N}^{-1}\bar{z}\Delta^{-1*}M^* = \hat{N}^{-1}\bar{z}\Delta M^*.$$

It follows that, for $u \in \mathbb{C}^n$

$$Bu = \hat{N}^{-1}\bar{z}\Delta M^* u. \qquad (6.5)$$

To illustrate what this means for the matrix of B let us consider the example

$$G^\vee = MN^{-1}$$

where N is as in (5.3) and

$$M(z) = \begin{bmatrix} z & 1 \\ 0 & 2 \end{bmatrix}.$$

This corresponds to taking

$$G(z) = \tfrac{1}{2}\begin{bmatrix} \dfrac{2z^2+\bar{\beta}z+\bar{\alpha}}{(z^2+\bar{\alpha})(z+\bar{\beta})} & \dfrac{2}{z+\bar{\beta}} \\ \dfrac{\bar{\beta}z - \bar{\alpha}}{(z^2+\bar{\alpha})(z+\bar{\beta})} & -\dfrac{2}{z+\bar{\beta}} \end{bmatrix}.$$

As before, $\Delta(z) = \operatorname{diag}\{z^2, z\}$, and so (6.5) gives

$$Bu = \hat{N}(z)^{-1}\begin{bmatrix} z & 0 \\ 0 & 1 \end{bmatrix}\begin{bmatrix} \bar{z} & 0 \\ 1 & 2 \end{bmatrix}u$$

$$= \hat{N}(z)^{-1}\begin{bmatrix} 1 & 0 \\ 1 & 2 \end{bmatrix}u.$$

Thus, with respect to the standard basis of $\mathbb{C}^2$ and the basis (6.4) of H, the matrix of B is

$$\begin{bmatrix} 1 & 0 \\ 1 & 2 \\ 0 & 0 \end{bmatrix}.$$

6.2 THEOREM *Let G be a strictly proper rational* m x n *matrix function analytic on the complement of the open unit disc. Suppose that*

$$G(\bar{z})^* = M(z)N(z)^{-1},$$

where M, N are right comprime polynomial matrices of types n × m, m × m *respectively and N is column reduced. Let $g(z) = z^{-1}G(z^{-1})$. The operator B is defined by*

$$Bu(z) = g(z)u$$

maps $\mathbb{C}^n$ into $H^2_m \ominus NH^2_m$. With respect to the standard basis of $\mathbb{C}^n$ and the expedient basis of the codomain, the matrix $\mathfrak{B}$ of B is obtained as follows.

Let z^{d_i} be the highest power of z occurring in the ith column of N,

$1 \leqslant i \leqslant m$, and let

$$\Delta(z) = \operatorname{diag}\{z^{d_1}, \ldots, z^{d_m}\}.$$

Define constant matrices $B_0, \ldots, B_{k-1}$ of type $m \times n$, where $k = \max_i d_i$,

$$\bar{z}\Delta(z)M(z)^* = B_0 + B_1 z + \ldots + B_{k-1} z^{k-1}, \tag{6.6}$$

and let b_r, $0 \leqslant r \leqslant k-1$, be the matrix obtained from B_r by deleting row i, $1 \leqslant i \leqslant m$, whenever $d_i \leqslant r$. Then

$$\tilde{B} = \begin{bmatrix} b_0 \\ b_1 \\ \vdots \\ b_{k-1} \end{bmatrix}.$$

Here b_r is of type $m_r \times n$ where m_r is the number of indices i such that $d_i > r$.

PROOF That B maps $\mathbb{C}^n$ into $H_m^2 \ominus NH_m^2$ is contained in Theorems 4.1–4.2.

Let e_j denote the jth standard basis vector of $\mathbb{C}^m$. To find the jth column of $\tilde{B}$ we consider Be_j, which, by (6.5) and (6.6), satisfies

$$\begin{aligned} Be_j(z) &= \hat{N}^{-1}\bar{z}\Delta M^* e_j \\ &= \hat{N}^{-1}(B_0 + B_1 z + \ldots + B_{k-1} z^{k-1})e_j. \\ &= \hat{N}^{-1} \sum_{r=0}^{k-1} \sum_{i=1}^{m} (B_r)_{ij}\; e_i \otimes z^r. \end{aligned}$$

Now the function on the right hand side belongs to $H_m^2 \ominus NH_m^2$, which is the linear span of the functions $\hat{N}^{-1}(e_i \otimes z^r)$ with $1 \leqslant i \leqslant m$, $0 \leqslant r < d_i$. Hence

$$Be_j(z) = \sum_{r=0}^{k-1} \sum_{d_i > r} (B_r)_{ij}\; \hat{N}^{-1}(e_i \otimes z^r). \tag{6.7}$$

We can think of the expedient basis, in its conventional ordering, as consisting of k blocks, the rth block (where $0 \leqslant r < k$) comprising those of the functions

$$\hat{N}^{-1}(e_1 \otimes z^r),\ \hat{N}^{-1}(e_2 \otimes z^r),\ \ldots,\ \hat{N}^{-1}(e_m \otimes z^r)$$

for which $r < d_i$. The matrix $\tilde{B}$ of B will then be expressible as a $k \times 1$ block matrix, and in these terms (6.7) means precisely that the rth block is obtained from B_r by deleting its ith row whenever $d_i \leqslant r$. □

6.3 THEOREM *Let G, N and $d_1, \ldots, d_m$ be as in Theorem 6.2 and let*

$$C : H_m^2 \ominus NH_m^2 \to \mathbb{C}^m$$

be defined by $Cx = x(0)$. Let N_0 be as in (5.2). The matrix $\tilde{C}$ of C with respect to the expedient basis of $H_m^2 \ominus NH_m^2$ and the standard basis of $\mathbb{C}^m$ is *obtained as follows.*

Let m_0 denote the number of positive d_i's, $1 \leq i \leq m$, and let c be the $m \times m$ matrix obtained from $\bar{N}_0^{*}$ by deleting the jth column whenever $d_j = 0$, $1 \leq j \leq m$. Then $\tilde{C}$ is the block matrix

$$\tilde{C} = [c \quad 0],$$

where the zero block is of type

$$m \times \left[\left[\sum_1^m d_i\right] - m_0\right].$$

PROOF. The first block in the basis consists of the m_0 functions $\hat{N}^{-1}(e_j \otimes z^0)$ with $d_j > 0$, $1 \leq j \leq d_m$. For such j,

$$C\hat{N}^{-1}(e_j \otimes z^0) = \hat{N}(0)^{-1} e_j = \bar{N}_0^{*} e_j$$

and the right hand side is the jth column of $\bar{N}_0^{*}$. Thus the first m_0 columns of $\tilde{C}$ make up the $m \times m_0$ matric $\tilde{c}$ as stated. The remaining basis vectors are of the form $\hat{N}^{-1}(e_j \otimes z^r)$ with $r > 0$, and these are clearly annihilated by C. Hence the rest of the columns of $\tilde{C}$ are zero.

6.4 THEOREM *Let G be a non-zero strictly proper rational matrix function, and let $(\tilde{A}, \tilde{B}, \tilde{C})$ be the triple of matrices constructed from G according to Algorithm 1. Then $(\tilde{A}, \tilde{B}, \tilde{C})$ is a minimal realization of G.*

PROOF. Suppose to begin with that G is stable (i.e. all poles of G have modulus less than 1). Then by Theorem 4.1 RS is a minimal operator realization of G. It follows that a minimal matrix realization is obtained, corresponding to any choice of basis in the state space H of RS, by taking the matrices of the operators A, B, C occurring in RS. We select the expedient basis of H: Theorems 6.1 - 6.3 tell us the corresponding matrices $\tilde{A}$, $\tilde{B}$, $\tilde{C}$. We need to check that these are in agreement with the matrices generated by Algorithm 1.

Let G be of type $m \times n$ and suppose U, V are matrix polynomials as in step 2 of the algorithm. Then

$$G = U^{-1}V$$

and so

$$G^{\vee} = V^{\vee}(U^{\vee})^{-1},$$

and $V^{\vee}$, $U^{\vee}$ are right comprime matrix polynomials, $U^{\vee}$ being column reduced. We may therefore take $M = V^{\vee}$, $N = U^{\vee}$ in Theorems 6.1 - 6.3. Note that the highest power of z in the ith row of $U(z)$ is the same as the highest power of z in the ith column of $N(z)$, so that the d_i's occurring in §6 are the same as those in Algorithm 1. The $\hat{N}$ of §6, according to (5.5), satisfies

$$\begin{aligned}\hat{N}(z) &= \Delta(z)N(1/\bar{z})^* \\ &= \Delta(z)U^{\vee}(1/\bar{z})^* \\ &= \Delta(z)U(1/z).\end{aligned}$$

By (2.2), the polynomial matrix $F(z)$ satisfies

$$F(z) = z^k\Delta(1/z)U(z),$$

and so F and $\hat{N}$ are related by

$$F(z) = z^k\hat{N}(1/z);$$

that is,

$$F_0 + F_1 z + \ldots + F_k z^k = N_k^* + N_{k-1}^* z + \ldots + N_0^* z^k.$$

Thus

$$F_r = N_{k-r}^*, \qquad 0 \leqslant r \leqslant k.$$

The block companion matrix C_F in (2.4) is thus the same as Co in (6.3). The prescriptions for obtaining $\tilde{A}$ as a submatrix of C_F given in step 5 and Theorem 6.1 clearly agree.

To justify steps 6 - 9 of the algorithm we need to check that the B_r defined by (2.5) coincide with the B_r in (6.6). Since $M = V^{\vee}$, $M(z)^* = V(\bar{z})$ and so

$$\begin{aligned}\bar{z}\Delta(z)M(z)^* &= \bar{z}\Delta(z)V(\bar{z}) \\ &= z^{-1}\operatorname{diag}\{z^{d_1}, \ldots, z^{d_m}\}\, V(1/z),\end{aligned}$$

so that the left hand sides of (6.6) and (2.5) are equal. It follows from Theorem 6.2 that $\tilde{B}$ in step 9 is the desired matrix of B. In similar fashion Theorem 6.3 shows that $\tilde{C}$ in step 11 is the matrix of $C : H \to \mathbb{C}^m$.

We have established the validity of Algorithm 1 for the case of stable G: however, since the realization problem and the description of the algorithm are independent of the location of the poles of G, it is to be expected that the algorithm will be valid generally. We can show that this is so by analytic or algebraic continuation.

Fix m, $n \in \mathbb{N}$ and let

$$\mathbf{d} = (d_1, \ldots, d_m)$$

be a vector of non-negative integers. Let $\sum(\mathbf{d})$ be the set of pairs (U, V) of polynomial matrices of types $m \times m$, $m \times n$ respectively such that

(a) U is row reduced,

(b) $U^{-1}V$ is strictly proper,

(c) U, V are right coprime,

(d) the ith row of U has highest degree z^{d_i}.

Now the $m \times m$ matrix polynomials U satisfying (a) and (d) can be written

$$U(z) = \begin{bmatrix} u_1(z) \\ \vdots \\ u_m(z) \end{bmatrix}$$

where

$$u_i(z) = u_i^0 + u_i^1 z + \ldots + u_i^{d_i} z^{d_i},$$

$$u_i^j \in \mathbb{C}^{1\times m}, \quad u_i^{d_i} \neq 0, \quad 1 \leq i \leq m, \text{ and}$$

$$\det \begin{bmatrix} u_1^{d_1} \\ \vdots \\ u_m^{d_m} \end{bmatrix} \neq 0.$$

The set of such U's can thus be identified in a natural way with an open subset of $\mathbb{C}^M$, $M = m\sum_i (d_i + 1)$. If U is row reduced, a polynomial matrix V satisfies (b) if and only if the row degrees of V are less than the corresponding row degrees of U [10, Lemma 6.3-11], so that the general V satisfying (b) can be written

$$V = \begin{bmatrix} v_1 \\ \vdots \\ v_m \end{bmatrix}$$

where

$$v_i(z) = v_i^0 + v_i^1 z + \ldots + v_i^{d_i - 1} z^{d_i - 1},$$

$$v_i^j \in \mathbb{C}^{1\times n}, \ 1 \leq i \leq m, \ 0 \leq j < d_i.$$

Such V's can be identified in an obvious way with points of $\mathbb{C}^N$, $N = n\sum_i d_i$. Hence the set of pairs (U, V) satisfying (a), (b) and (d) can be identified with an open subset of $\mathbb{C}^{M+N}$,

$$M + N = m^2 + (m+n)\sum_{i=1}^{m} d_i.$$

The condition that U and V be right coprime can be expressed as the nonvanishing of a certain polynomial in the entries of U and V (cf. [10, Exercise 6.3-19]). Hence $\sum(\mathbf{d})$ can be identified with an open subset of $\mathbb{C}^{M+N}$.

Consider the relation

$$U(z)^{-1}V(z) = \tilde{C}(zI - \tilde{A})^{-1}\tilde{B}, \tag{6.8}$$

where $\tilde{A}$, $\tilde{B}$, $\tilde{C}$ are derived from U, V by Algorithm 1. Note that both sides of (6.8) are rational functions of z and of the entries of (U, V), for all $(U, V) \in \sum(\mathbf{d})$. Furthermore, we have proved that these rational functions coincide on the subset Ω of $\sum(\mathbf{d})$ consisting of the pairs (U, V) such that

$U^{-1}V$ is stable - i.e. U is an invertible element in the Banach algebra of bounded analytic $m \times m$ matrix-valued functions in $\{z: |z| > 1\}$. Since the set of invertible elements in a Banach algebra is open, it follows that Ω is open in $\sum(\mathbf{d})$. Two rational functions on $\sum(\mathbf{d})$ which agree on an open set $\Omega \subset \sum(\mathbf{d})$ must coincide, up to cancellations. Thus (6.9) holds on $\sum(\mathbf{d})$, i.e. $(\tilde{A}, \tilde{B}, \tilde{C})$ is a realization of $U^{-1}V$. □

7. THE GRAM MATRIX

Finding a minimal realization for a given transfer function is a linear problem: no inner products in the state space are involved, and the basis of the state space may be changed at will. As soon as we introduce conditions on the controllability and observability gramians of the system, however, we bring in the adjoint operation and hence an inner product in the state space. Consequently, if we have an operator realization with some desired properties, then in order to obtain a matrix realization with the same properties we must take matrices with respect to an *orthonormal* basis in the state space. Otherwise, taking conjugate transposes of matrices will not correspond to taking adjoints of operators. The expedient basis used in §6 is not orthonormal, and so to use it for computing balanced realizations we must first orthonormalize it by means of the Gram-Schmidt process. This entails knowing the inner product of any pair of expedient basis vectors, or equivalently, of knowing the Gram matrix of the expedient basis (the Gram matrix of a basis $x_1, \ldots, x_n$ of an n-dimensional inner product space is defined to be the $n \times n$ matrix whose (i,j) - entry is the inner product (x_j, x_i)). In §5 we promised a formula for the Gram matrix of the expedient basis. In the scalar (or SISO) case a related formula for a slightly different basis was used by Allison and Young [2] and Young [20]. For the case of matrix-valued $N(z)$, but with the additional restriction that the leading coefficient of N is non-singular, a generalization of the formula in [2] was established by F. B. Yeh [17]. Here we allow a general $N(z)$ in the class arising in the restricted shift realization (cf Theorem 4.2). However, the formula we obtain differs in an important respect from the scalar one: finding the polynomial D below requires no computation at all, whereas for matrix polynomials it is a substantial step.

7.1 THEOREM *Let N be a column-reduced $m \times m$ matrix polynomial and suppose all zeros of* $\det N(z)$ *lie in* $\mathbb{D}$. *The Gram matrix Gr of the expedient basis of $H^2_m \ominus NH^2_m$ can be obtained as follows.*

Let Δ, $\hat{N}$ *be the matrix polynomials defined by* (5.1), (5.4) *respectively. Let*

$$N(z) = \Theta(z)\, D(z) \qquad (7.1)$$

be an inner-outer factorization of N, *so that* Θ *is an* m x m *inner function and* D *is an outer matrix polynomial. Let*

$$\hat{D}(z) = \Delta(z)\, D(1/z)^*, \; z \in \mathbb{C} \setminus \{0\}. \qquad (7.2)$$

Then $\hat{D}$ *is a matrix polynomial. Write*

$$\hat{D}(z) = D_o{}^* + D_1{}^*z + D_2{}^*z^2 + \ldots$$

Then

$$(Gr)^{-1} = XX^* - YY^* \qquad (7.3)$$

where X, Y *are the matrices of type* $(\sum_i d_i)$ x mk *obtained from the block Toeplitz matrices*

$$\begin{bmatrix} N_o{}^* & 0 & \ldots & 0 \\ N_1{}^* & N_o{}^* & \ldots & 0 \\ \cdot & \cdot & \ldots & \cdot \\ N_{k-1}{}^* & N_{k-2}{}^* & \ldots & N_o{}^* \end{bmatrix}, \quad \begin{bmatrix} D_o{}^* & 0 & \ldots & 0 \\ D_1{}^* & D_o{}^* & \ldots & 0 \\ \cdot & \cdot & \ldots & \cdot \\ D_{k-1}{}^* & D_{k-2}{}^* & \ldots & D_o{}^* \end{bmatrix}$$

respectively by deleting the ith row in block row number j, $1 \leqslant i \leqslant m$, $0 \leqslant j \leqslant k-1$, *whenever* $j \geqslant d_i$.

Before proving the theorem let us use it to calculate the Gram matrix for the expedient basis corresponding to the example of N in (5.3). Here, for some α, $\beta \in \mathbb{D}$,

$$N(z) = \begin{bmatrix} z^2+\alpha & z+\beta \\ z^2+\alpha & -z-\beta \end{bmatrix} = \begin{bmatrix} 1 & 1 \\ 1 & -1 \end{bmatrix} \begin{bmatrix} z^2+\alpha & 0 \\ 0 & z+\beta \end{bmatrix}, \qquad (7.4)$$

$$\Delta(z) = \text{diag}\, \{z^2, z\}, \qquad (7.5)$$

$$\hat{N}(z) = \begin{bmatrix} 1+\bar{\alpha}z^2 & 1+\bar{\alpha}z^2 \\ 1+\bar{\beta}z & -1-\bar{\beta}z \end{bmatrix}.$$

To get $D(z)$ we need an inner-outer factorization of $N(z)$. It is clear from (7.4) that

$$N(z) = \frac{1}{\sqrt{2}} \begin{bmatrix} 1 & 1 \\ 1 & -1 \end{bmatrix} \text{diag} \left\{ \frac{z^2+\alpha}{1+\bar{\alpha}z^2}, \frac{z+\beta}{1+\bar{\beta}z} \right\} \sqrt{2} \begin{bmatrix} 1+\bar{\alpha}z^2 & 0 \\ 0 & 1+\bar{\beta}z \end{bmatrix}.$$

Hence we may write $N = \Theta D$ where Θ is inner and

$$D(z) = \sqrt{2}\ \text{diag}\left\{1+\bar{\alpha}z^2,\ 1+\bar{\beta}z\right\}$$

is outer. Then

$$\hat{D}(z) = \Delta(z)\ D(1/\bar{z})^* = \sqrt{2}\begin{bmatrix} z^2+\alpha & 0 \\ 0 & z+\beta \end{bmatrix},$$

so that

$$D_o{}^* = \sqrt{2}\begin{bmatrix} \alpha & 0 \\ 0 & \beta \end{bmatrix},\quad D_1{}^* = \sqrt{2}\begin{bmatrix} 0 & 0 \\ 0 & 1 \end{bmatrix}.$$

To obtain Y from the block Toeplitz matrix

$$\begin{bmatrix} D_o{}^* & 0 \\ D_1{}^* & D_o{}^* \end{bmatrix}$$

we must delete the second row in block row number 1 (i.e. the second block row) since $d_2 = 1$ (cf.(7.5)). This gives

$$Y = \sqrt{2}\ \begin{bmatrix} \alpha & 0 & 0 & 0 \\ 0 & \beta & 0 & 0 \\ 0 & 0 & \alpha & 0 \end{bmatrix}.$$

Similarly

$$X = \begin{bmatrix} 1 & 1 & 0 & 0 \\ 1 & -1 & 0 & 0 \\ 0 & 0 & 1 & 1 \end{bmatrix}.$$

Hence

$$(Gr)^{-1} = XX^* - YY^* = 2\ \text{diag}\left\{1-|\alpha|^2,\ 1-|\beta|^2,\ 1-|\alpha|^2\right\}.$$

Theorem 7.1 will follow from some simple manipulations of multiplication, injection and projection operators. Let H^∞_{mxm} denote the space of m x m matrix-valued functions which are bounded and analytic in $\mathbb{D}$. For $F \in H^\infty_{mxm}$ we denote by M_F the operation of multiplication by F acting on H^2_m:

$$M_F : H^2_m \to H^2_m:\ x \to Fx,$$

so that

$$(M_F x)(z) = F(z)x(z).$$

The adjoint operator $M_F{}^*$ maps $x \in H^2_m$ to the orthogonal projection on H^2_m of the L^2_m-function F^*x. We shall require compressions of multiplication operators. If K is a closed subspace of H^2_m then the compression of $T \in (H^2_m)$ to K is obtained by restricting T to K and following by the orthogonal projection onto K. Let us denote by

$$P_K : H^2_m \to K$$

the operation of orthogonal projection onto K. The adjoint

$$P_K{}^* : K \to H^2_m$$

is the injection operator, so that the compression of T to K is

$$P_K T P_K{}^* : K \to K.$$

In the case that K is the space $H^2_m \ominus z^k H^2_m$ of polynomial vectors of degree less than k there is a well known (and easily verified) expression for the matrix of the compression of M_F.

7.2 LEMMA *Let $F \in H^\infty_{m\mathrm{x}m}$ have Fourier series*

$$F(z) \sim F_o + F_1 z + F_2 z^2 + \dots$$

The matrix of the compression of M_F to

$$K = H^2_m \ominus z^k H^2_m$$

with respect to the expedient basis of K is the block Toeplitz matrix

$$\begin{bmatrix} F_o & 0 & \dots & 0 \\ F_1 & F_o & \dots & 0 \\ \cdot & \cdot & \dots & \cdot \\ F_{k-1} & F_{k-2} & \dots & F_o \end{bmatrix}. \qquad (7.6)$$

□

7.3 COROLLARY *Let Δ be as in (5.1), let $k = \max_i d_i$ and let F,K be as in Lemma 7.2. Let $W = H^2_m \ominus \Delta H^2_m$. The matrix of*

$$P_W M_F P_K{}^* : K \to W$$

with respect to the expedient bases of K and W is the submatrix of the block Toeplitz matrix (7.6) obtained by deleting the ith row in block row number j, $1 \leq i \leq m$, $0 \leq j \leq k-1$, whenever $j \geq d_i$.

PROOF Since W is a subspace of K, $P_W M_F P_K{}^*$ can be obtained by compressing M_F to K and following by the projection from K to W: in symbols,

$$P_W M_F P_K{}^* = (P_W P_K{}^*)\,(P_K M_F P_K{}^*).$$

The matrix of the projection operator

$$P_W P_K{}^* : K \to W$$

consists of the rows of the identity matrix corresponding to those expedient basis vectors $e_i \otimes z^j$ of K which belong to W. The result now follows from Lemma 7.2 since $P_K M_F P_K{}^*$ is the compression of M_F to K, and the ith row in block row number j of (7.6) corresponds to the basis vector $e_i \otimes z^j$ of K, which belongs to W if and only if $j < d_i$.

Note that, for any closed subspace K of H^2_m, $P_K{}^* P_K \in \quad (H^2_m)$ is the Hermitian projection with range K. In the case that K is the state space $H = H^2_m \ominus N H^2_m$ there is an expression for this projection in terms of multiplication operators.

7.4 LEMMA *Let Θ be the* m x m *inner matrix function defined by (7.1). The Hermitian projection on H^2_m with range H is given by*

$$P_H{}^*P_H = I - M_\Theta M_\Theta{}^*.$$

PROOF Since Θ is inner, M_Θ is an isometry on H_m^2, so that

$$M_\Theta{}^*M_\Theta = I.$$

It follows that $M_\Theta M_\Theta{}^*$ is idempotent, and hence is a Hermitian projection. Furthermore

$$\text{Ker } M_\Theta M_\Theta{}^* = \text{Ker } M_\Theta{}^* = (\text{Range } M_\Theta)^\perp = H_m^2 \ominus \Theta H_m^2.$$

Thus $M_\Theta M_\Theta{}^*$ is the Hermitian projection with range ΘH_m^2, and $I - M_\Theta M_\Theta{}^*$ is the Hermitian projection with range $H_m^2 \ominus \Theta H_m^2$. Since D in (7.1) is an outer polynomial matrix, DH_m^2 is dense in H_m^2 and hence ΘDH_m^2 is dense in ΘH_m^2. By (7.1) $\Theta D = N$, and so ΘH_m^2, NH_m^2 have the same orthogonal complement. Thus $H_m^2 \ominus \Theta H_m^2 = H$, and the range of the Hermitian projection $I - M_\Theta M_\Theta{}^*$ is H. □

PROOF OF THEOREM 7.1 We shall prove an identity for operators and deduce the desired formula for $(Gr)^{-1}$ by taking matrices. Define the linear operator

$$\tau : W = H_m^2 \ominus \Delta H_m^2 \to H = H_m^2 \ominus NH_m^2$$

by

$$(\tau w)(z) = \hat{N}(z)^{-1}w(z), \qquad z \in \mathbb{D}, \; w \in W. \tag{7.7}$$

By Theorem 5.1, τ is a bijection between W and H. As in §5 we pick the expedient basis

$$\left\{e_i \otimes z^j : 1 \leqslant i \leqslant m, \; 0 \leqslant j < d_i\right\}$$

for W, so that the expedient basis in H comprises the vectors $\tau(e_i \otimes z^j)$. Let us temporarily denote these bases in W and H by $x_1, x_2, \ldots$ and $y_1, y_2, \ldots$, so that $y_j = \tau x_j$. Then the desired matrix Gr satisfies

$$Gr = [(y_j, y_i)] = [(\tau x_j, \tau x_i)] = [(\tau^*\tau x_j, x_i)],$$

which is to say that Gr is the matrix of $\tau^*\tau$ with respect to the chosen basis of W. We shall get the desired formula for $(Gr)^{-1}$ by proving an identity for the operator $(\tau^*\tau)^{-1}$ on W and taking matrices with respect to the basis $e_i \otimes z^j$.

Let us show that $\hat{D}$ defined by (7.2) is a polynomial. It is immediate from (7.2) that $\hat{D}$ is a rational function and that its only possible pole is at $z = 0$. Recall from (5.5) that

$$\hat{N} = \Delta N^* \text{ on } \partial\mathbb{D}.$$

Take adjoints in (7.1) and use the fact that Θ is inner to obtain

$$N^*\Theta = D^* \quad \text{on } \partial\mathbb{D},$$

and multiply by Δ to get

$$\hat{N}\Theta = \Delta N^*\Theta = \Delta D^* = \hat{D} \tag{7.8}$$

as functions on $\partial\mathbb{D}$. This shows that $\hat{D}$ is analytic at 0 (since $\hat{N}$ and Θ are), and so $\hat{D}$ is a polynomial.

It is clear from the definition of τ in (7.7) that, for $h \in H$,

$$(\tau^{-1}h)(z) = \hat{N}(z)h(z).$$

This can be written

$$\tau^{-1} = P_W\, M_{\hat{N}}\, P_H^*,$$

whence

$$\tau^{-*} = P_H\, M_{\hat{N}}^*\, P_W^*.$$

Thus

$$(\tau^*\tau)^{-1} = \tau^{-1}\tau^{-*} = P_W\, M_{\hat{N}}\, P_H^*\, P_H\, M_{\hat{N}}^*\, P_W^*.$$

Hence, by Lemma 7.4,

$$\begin{aligned}(\tau^*\tau)^{-1} &= P_W\, M_{\hat{N}}\,(I - M_\Theta M_\Theta^*)\, M_{\hat{N}}^*\, P_W^* \\ &= P_W\,(M_{\hat{N}}\, M_{\hat{N}}^* - M_{\hat{N}\,\Theta}\, M_{\hat{N}\,\Theta}^*)\, P_W^* .\end{aligned}$$

By virtue of (7.8)

$$M_{\hat{N}\Theta} = M_{\hat{D}}$$

and so

$$(\tau^*\tau)^{-1} = P_W(M_{\hat{N}}\, M_{\hat{N}}^* - M_{\hat{D}}\, M_{\hat{D}}^*)P_W^* . \tag{7.9}$$

This simple but (we believe) non-intuitive operator identity will give us the desired matrix formula, but as it stands at present it suffers the disadvantage that $P_W\, M_{\hat{N}}$ and $P_W\, M_{\hat{D}}$ have infinite-dimensional domains. To remedy this we introduce the space

$$K = H_m^2 \ominus z^k H_m^2,$$

with $k = \max_i d_i$, so that $W \subseteq K$. For any matrix polynomial F we have

$$M_F(z^k H_m^2) \subseteq z^k H_m^2$$

and hence, by orthogonal complementation,

$$M_F^*\, K \subseteq K.$$

This is expressible in operator notation by

$$P_K^*\, P_K\, M_F^*\, P_K^* = M_F^*\, P_K^*.$$

Hence (7.9) yields

$$\begin{aligned}(\tau^*\tau)^{-1} &= P_W\, M_{\hat{N}}\, P_K^*\, P_K\, M_{\hat{N}}^*\, P_W^* - P_W\, M_{\hat{D}}\, P_K^*\, P_K\, M_{\hat{D}}^*\, P_W^* \\ &= \tilde{X}\tilde{X}^* - \tilde{Y}\tilde{Y}^*\end{aligned}$$

where

$$\tilde{X} = P_W\, M_{\hat{N}}\, P_K^*, \qquad \tilde{Y} = P_W\, M_{\hat{D}}\, P_K^* : K \to W.$$

Taking matrices with respect to the expedient basis in W we obtain

$$(Gr)^{-1} = XX^* - YY^*$$

where X, Y are the matrices of $\tilde{X}, \tilde{Y}$ with respect to the expedient bases in K and W. Corollary 7.3 shows that X and Y are indeed the submatrices of block Toeplitz matrices described in Theorem 7.1. □

The matrix polynomial $\hat{D}$ occurring in Theorem 7.1 is in fact of degree at most k. In the relation

$$N = \Theta D$$

N, D are matrix polynomials and Θ is a rational inner function, and one can show that this implies that the degree of the jth column of D is no greater than the degree of the jth column of N, which is d_j. Hence we can write

$$D(z) = (D_o + D_1 z^{-1} + \ldots + D_k z^{-k})\ \Delta(z),$$

so that

$$\hat{D}(z) = D_o{}^* + D_1{}^* z + \ldots + D_k{}^* z^k$$

(compare (5.2) and (5.4)).

8. BLOCK HANKEL OPERATORS AND EXPEDIENT BASES

In principle it is a straightforward matter to convert an arbitrary minimal realization into a balanced one by means of a change of variable in the state space [13]. It is particularly simple for the restricted shift realization *RS*, since *RS* is "output normal", which is to say that its observability Gramian is the identity:

$$\mathcal{O}^* \mathcal{O} = I_H.$$

This is immediate from Theorem 4.1, which tells us that $\mathcal{O}$ is the injection operator from H to H^2_m, and hence is an isometry.

Let (A, B, C) be the restricted shift realization of G. For any invertible linear transformation T of the state space H,

$$(A_T, B_T, C_T) = (TAT^{-1}, TB, CT^{-1})$$

is also a minimal realization of G. Its reachability and controllability operators are

$$R_T = TR : H^2_n \to H, \quad {}_T = \quad T^{-1} : H \to H^2_m,$$

and so the corresponding Gramians are

$$R_T R_T{}^* = TRR^* T^*,$$
$$\mathcal{O}_T{}^* \mathcal{O}_T = T^{-*} \mathcal{O}^* \mathcal{O} T^{-1} = (TT^*)^{-1}.$$

Hence, if we take

$$T = (RR^*)^{-\frac{1}{4}}$$

we have

$$R_T R_T{}^* = (RR^*)^{\frac{1}{2}} = \mathcal{O}_T{}^* \mathcal{O}_T.$$

If we now take matrices with respect to an orthonormal basis of H consisting of eigenvectors of RR^* then the observability and controllability Gramian matrices will be diagonal as well as equal. We have shown:

8.1 THEOREM *Let (A, B, C) be the restricted shift realization of G and let $\hat{A}$, $\hat{B}$, $\hat{C}$ be the matrices of the operators*

$$(RR^*)^{-\frac{1}{4}} A(RR^*)^{\frac{1}{4}}, \ (RR^*)^{-\frac{1}{4}}B, \ C(RR^*)^{\frac{1}{4}}$$

respectively with respect to an orthonormal basis of eigenvectors of RR^*, where R is the reachability operator of (A, B, C). Then $(\hat{A}, \hat{B}, \hat{C})$ is a balanced realization of G. □

To find the eigenvectors of RR^* we need the matrix of R with respect to *orthonormal* bases in H_n^2 and H. We know from Theorem 4.1 that R is a block Hankel operator: if we use the standard z^n bases in H_n^2 and the superspace H_m^2 of H we should obtain an *infinite* block Hankel matrix as the matrix of R. Naturally we prefer finite matrices where possible, and so our strategy is to use expedient bases, orthonormalized with the aid of the Gram matrix formula in Theorem 7.1.

8.2 LEMMA *Let G be as in Theorem 4.1 and let*

$$G = V_r U_r^{-1}$$

where U_r, V_r are coprime polynomial matrices of types m x n, n x n *respectively. Then the kernel of the reachability operator* R *of the restricted shift realization of G is $U_r H_n^2$.*

PROOF By Theorem 4.1,

$$Rx = P_+(gJx), \qquad x \in H_n^2.$$

Hence

$$\begin{aligned} Rx = 0 &\Leftrightarrow gJx \perp H_m^2 \\ &\Leftrightarrow \bar{z}\, G(\bar{z})\, x(\bar{z}) \in \bar{z}(H_m^2) \\ &\Leftrightarrow Gx \in H_m^2 \\ &\Leftrightarrow V_r\, U_r^{-1}\, x \in H_m^2. \end{aligned}$$

This is equivalent to $x \in U_r H_n^2$ (cf.equation (4.8)). □

In view of the lemma, for the purpose of finding the eigenvectors of RR^* we may regard R as acting between finite-dimensional spaces,

$$R : H_n^2 \ominus U_r H_n^2 \rightarrow H_m^2 \ominus NH_m^2,$$

both of which have expedient bases.

The following observation enables us to reduce the amount of computation needed to find the matrix of R.

8.3 LEMMA *For any $x \in H_n^2$,*

$$R(zx) = S^* Rx$$

where S^* denotes the backward shift operator (restricted to $H^2_m \ominus NH^2_m$).

PROOF This is just an operator-theoretic description of the familiar pattern of block Hankel matrices. We have

$$R(zx) = P_+(gJzx) = P_+(\bar{z}gJx),$$

while, for any $f \in L^2_n$,

$$P_+(\bar{z}f) = S^*P_+f,$$

as is immediate from consideration of Fourier series. Thus

$$R(zx) = S^*P_+(gJx) = S^*Rx. \qquad \square$$

The image of the expedient basis vector $\hat{U}_r^{-1}(e_i \otimes z^1)$ thus satisfies

$$R\,\hat{U}_r^{-1}\,(e_i \otimes z^1) = S^*\,R\hat{U}_r^{-1}(e_i \otimes z^0).$$

Now the matrix of $S^*|H$ with respect to the expedient basis of H is already known (cf. Theorem 6.1): it is computed in Step 5 of Algorithm 1. It follows that when we have obtained the columns in the first block column of the matrix of R (with respect to the two expedient bases in question), we can obtain the remaining columns by successive multiplications by the matrix $\tilde{A}$ of Algorithm 1.

We now address the problem of finding the first block column of the matrix of R: that is, of finding the components with respect to the expedient bases $(\hat{N}^{-1}(e_i \otimes z^j))$ of H of the images $R\hat{U}_r^{-1}(e_i \otimes z^0)$.

8.4 LEMMA *For $x \in H^2_n$ and $y \in H^2_m \ominus \Delta H^2_m$,*

$$Rx = \hat{N}^{-1}y \tag{8.1}$$

if and only if

$$Gx - U^{-1}\bar{z}\Delta Jy \in H^2_n.$$

PROOF We know from Theorems 4.1, 4.2 and 5.1 that, for given $x \in H^2_n$, (8.1) holds for a unique $y \in H^2_n$, and this y is in $H^2_n \ominus \Delta H^2_n$. Furthermore,

$$\begin{aligned} Rx = \hat{N}^{-1}y &\Leftrightarrow P_+(gJx) = \hat{N}^{-1}y \\ &\Leftrightarrow P_+(JzGx) = N^{-*}\Delta^*y \\ &\Leftrightarrow JzGx - N^{-*}\Delta^*y \perp H^2_m \\ &\Leftrightarrow zGx - N^{-\vee}\Delta Jy \in J(H^{2\perp}_m) = zH^2_m \\ &\Leftrightarrow Gx - U^{-1}\bar{z}\Delta Jy \in H^2_m \qquad \square \end{aligned}$$

Since $G = U^{-1}V$, the lemma shows that the image under R of a typical element $\hat{U}_r^{-1}\xi$, $\xi \in H^2_n \ominus \Delta_r H^2_n$, of H^2_n is $\hat{N}^{-1}y$ where

$$U^{-1}(V\hat{U}_r^{-1}\xi - \eta) \in H^2_m \tag{8.2}$$

and

$$\eta = \bar{z}\Delta Jy \in H^2_m \ominus \Delta H^2_m \tag{8.3}$$

Here

$$\hat{U}_r = \Delta_r U_r^*, \tag{8.4}$$

$$\Delta_r = \text{diag}\left\{z^{c_1}, \ \ldots, \ z^{c_n}\right\} \tag{8.5}$$

where c_j is the degree of the jth column of U_r. From these relations η and y can be found (in principle) by purely rational operations.

Let us first consider the scalar case ($m = n = 1$), as this is a good deal more straightforward. Multiply through by $\hat{U}_r$ in (8.2) to obtain the equivalent condition

$$U^{-1}(V\xi - \hat{U}_r\eta) \in \hat{U}_r H^2.$$

Since $\hat{U}_r$ is an outer polynomial $\hat{U}_r H^2 = H^2$, and so (8.2) is equivalent to

$$U^{-1}(V\xi - \hat{U}_r\eta) \in H^2. \tag{8.6}$$

By the division algorithm for polynomials we may write

$$V\xi = Uq_1 + r_1, \quad \hat{U}_r\eta = Uq_2 + r_2$$

where r_1, r_2, q_1, q_2 are polynomials and r_1, r_2 are of smaller degree that U. Since, in (8.6), η is what we are trying to calculate, r_1 is a uniquely determined polynomial while r_2 is a polynomial whose coefficients depend linearly on the unknown vector η. From (8.6) we have

$$U^{-1}(Uq_1 + r_1 - Uq_2 - r_2) \in H^2,$$

and hence

$$U^{-1}(r_1 - r_2) \in H^2.$$

Now $r_1 - r_2$ is a polynomial of smaller degree than U, and U is a polynomial all of whose zeros lie in D (recall the analyticity hypothesis on $G = U^{-1}V$). The quotient $U^{-1}(r_1 - r_2)$ can thus be analytic in D only if it is zero: i.e.

$$r_1 = r_2.$$

This is a set of linear equations for η, and since it is equivalent to the relation $R\hat{U}_r^{-1}\xi = \hat{N}^{-1}y$, it must have a unique solution for η.

Return now to the solution of (8.2) for η in the case of general m, $n \in \mathbb{N}$. We should still like to eliminate the factor $\hat{U}_r^{-1}$, which is the inverse of an outer polynomial, but we must first manoeuvre it to the beginning of the expression. Since $\hat{U}_r$ is an outer polynomial and is non-singular on the unit circle, there exist polynomial matrices K, L such that

$$V\hat{U}_r^{-1} = L^{-1}K \tag{8.7}$$

with L^{-1} bounded on $\mathbb{C} \setminus \mathbb{D}$. Then (8.2) is equivalent to

$$U^{-1} \ L^{-1}(K\xi - L\eta) \in H^2_m. \tag{8.8}$$

Now let $\tilde{U}$, $\tilde{L}$ be matrix polynomials of type m x m such that

$$LU = \tilde{U}\tilde{L}$$

where the zeros of $\tilde{U}$, $\tilde{L}$ lie in $\mathbb{D}$, $\mathbb{C} \setminus \text{clos } \mathbb{D}$ respectively. Then (8.8) and hence (8.2) are equivalent to

$$\tilde{U}^{-1}(K\xi - L\eta) \in \tilde{L}H_m^2 = H_m^2 \tag{8.9}$$

By the division algorithm for polynomials (cf.[10]) we can write

$$K\xi = \tilde{U}q + r$$

where r, q are $m \times 1$ polynomial vectors and $\tilde{U}^{-1}r$ is strictly proper. Likewise we can write

$$L(e_i \otimes z^j) = \tilde{U}q_{ij} + r_{ij}$$

where q_{ij}, r_{ij} are polynomials and $\tilde{U}^{-1}r_{ij}$ is strictly proper. Then (8.9) is equivalent to

$$\tilde{U}^{-1}(r - \Sigma_{ij}\ \eta_{ij}\ r_{ij}) \in H_m^2$$

where $\eta_{ij} \in \mathbb{C}$ are the components of η:

$$\eta = \Sigma_{ij}\ \eta_{ij}\ e_i \otimes z^j.$$

A strictly proper rational vector whose denominator has zeros only in $\mathbb{D}$ cannot belong to H_m^2 unless it is zero. It follows that (8.9) is equivalent to

$$\Sigma_{ij}\ \eta_{ij}\ r_{ij} = r.$$

Here

$$\eta = \bar{z}\Delta y \in H_m^2 \ominus \Delta H_m^2, \tag{8.10}$$

so the range of summation is $1 \leq i \leq m$, $0 \leq j < d_i$. Let us summarize.

8.5 THEOREM *Let G be an $m \times n$ rational matrix as in Theorem 4.1 and let $\Gamma : H_n^2 \to H_n^2$ be the block Hankel operator.*

$$\Gamma x = P_+ (JzGx),$$

where

$$Jx(z) = x(\bar{z}),\ x \in L_m^2.$$

Let

$$G = U^{-1}V = V_r U_r^{-1} \tag{8.11}$$

where U, V, U_r and V_r are polynomial matrices, U and V are left coprime, U_r and V_r are right coprime, U is row reduced and U_r is column reduced. Then

$$\text{Range } \Gamma \subseteq H_n^2 \ominus U^\vee H_n^2, \qquad (\text{Ker } \Gamma)^\perp \subseteq H_m^2 \ominus U_r H_m^2$$

and the matrix of the restriction

$$R : H_m^2 \ominus U_r H_m^2 \to H_n^2 \ominus U^\vee H_m^2$$

of Γ (with respect to the expedient bases of these two spaces) can be obtained as follows.

Let L, K be polynomial matrices of types m x m, m x n *respectively* *such that*

$$V\hat{U}_r^{-1} = L^{-1}K, \tag{8.12}$$

where $\hat{U}_r$ *is the outer polynomial matrix defined by (8.4) and the zeros of* det L *lie in* $\mathbb{D}$. *Let* $\tilde{U}$, $\tilde{L}$ *be polynomial matrices of type* m x m *such that*

$$LU = \tilde{U}\tilde{L} \tag{8.13}$$

and the zeros of det $\tilde{U}$, det $\tilde{L}$ *lie in* $\mathbb{D}$, $\mathbb{C} \setminus$ clos $\mathbb{D}$ *respectively.*

Let $c_1, \ldots, c_n$ *be as in (8.5) and let* n_o *be the number of indices* j *such that* $c_j > 0$, *so that the first block column of the matrix of* R *contains* n_o *columns. Let* E *be the* $n \times n_o$ *matrix obtained from the identity matrix* I_n *by deleting the* j*th column wherever* $c_j = 0$. *Let* Q, r *be polynomial matrices of type* $m \times n_o$ *such that*

$$KE = \tilde{U}Q + r \tag{8.14}$$

and $\tilde{U}^{-1}r$ *is strictly proper. For* $1 \leq i \leq m$, $0 \leq j < d_i$, *let* q_{ij}, r_{ij} *be polynomial matrices of type* $m \times 1$ *such that*

$$L(e_i \otimes z^j) = \tilde{U}q_{ij} + r_{ij} \tag{8.15}$$

and $\tilde{U}^{-1}r_{ij}$ *is strictly proper. Then the components* y_{ij}, $1 \leq i \leq m$, $0 \leq j < d_i$, *in the* p*th column of the first block column of the matrix of* R *are the unique solutions of the linear equations*

$$\sum_{i=1}^{m} \sum_{j=0}^{d_i-1} y_{i,\, d_i-j-1} = r^{(p)}, \tag{8.16}$$

where $r^{(p)}$ *denotes the* p*th column of* r, $1 \leq p \leq n_o$.

The columns in the remaining block columns of the matrix of R *are obtained as follows. If* c *is the column corresponding to the expedient basisvector* $\hat{U}_r^{-1}\, e_i \otimes z^o$, *then the column corresponding to* $\hat{U}_r^{-1}\, e_i \otimes z^j$ *is* $\tilde{A}^j c$, $0 \leq j < d_i$, *where* $\tilde{A}$ *is the matrix defined in Algorithm* 1.

PROOF The n_o columns in the first block column of the matrix of R correspond to the expedient basis vectors $\hat{U}_r^{-1}\, e_i \otimes z^o$, $1 \leq i \leq m$, $c_i > 0$, and so can be found by taking $\xi = e_i \otimes z^o$ in (8.2) for each of these values of i. These ξ can be regarded as the columns of the matrix E described in the theorem. The foregoing discussion then shows that η in (8.2) corresponding to the pth column of E is given by the system

$$\sum_{i=1}^{m} \sum_{j=0}^{d_i-1} \eta_{ij}\, r_{ij} = r^{(p)}.$$

However, the connection (8.10) between η and y implies that

$$\eta_{ij} = y_{i,d_i-j-1}, \quad 0 \leqslant j < d_i,$$

which establishes (8.16) □

To carry out the procedure described in the theorem we need "MFD" algorithms to find the matrix polynomials in (8.11) and (8.12), the division algorithm for (8.14) and (8.15) and some standard linear equation routine for solving the system (8.16). We also need some way of finding $\tilde{U}$ and $\tilde{L}$ in (8.13). This can be done in a purely rational way: there is no minimality requirement in (8.12) so that we can take L in (8.12) to be a scalar (replace L, K by det L and (adj L)K if necessary). Then we may take $\tilde{L} = L$, $\tilde{U} = U$. However, one might wish to avoid the use of polynomials of unnecessarily high degree, and other ways are possible. One can choose L and K in (8.12) to be left coprime and obtain $\tilde{U}$ and $\tilde{L}$ by spectral factorization; alternatively, one can reduce to the case of upper triangular L and U by performing elementary row operations on L and column operations on U.

9. JUSTIFICATION OF ALGORITHM 2

The high level structure of Algorithm 2 is as follows

I. Read the transfer function matrix G.

II. Calculate the matrices ($\tilde{A}$, $\tilde{B}$, $\tilde{C}$) of the operators (A, B, C) in the restricted shift realization RS of G, using the expedient basis of the state space H.

III. Calculate the matrix $\tilde{R}$ of the reachability operator R of RS (restricted to (Ker $R)^{\perp}$) using the expedient bases in (Ker $R)^{\perp}$ and H.

IV. Calculate the inverses γ_r, γ of the Gram matrices of the expedient bases of (Ker $R)^{\perp}$, H respectively.

V. Find the eigenvalues and eigenvectors of RR^* using $\tilde{R}$, γ_r and γ.

VI. Compute the matrices of the balanced operator realization

$$BR : ((RR^*)^{-\frac{1}{4}} A(RR^*)^{\frac{1}{4}}, \quad (RR^*)^{-\frac{1}{4}}B, \quad C(RR^*)^{\frac{1}{4}})$$

with respect to an orthonormal basis of H consisting of eigenvectors of RR^*.

Theorems 4.1 and 8.1 assure us that BR is a balanced realization of G, and consequently that the matrices we obtain will constitute a balanced matrix realization of G. Our task is to show that the matrix computations of Algorithm 2 do indeed correspond to the above operations.

Step II is just Algorithm 1, so I and II are effected by Steps 1 and 2 of Algorithm 2. Steps 3–12 implement III: this is the assertion of Theorem 8.5. In Steps 13-16 we compute γ_r, the inverse of the Gram matrix of the expedient basis of $H_n^2 \ominus U_r H_n^2$ using the formula in Theorem 7.1. By Lemma 8.2,

$$H_n^2 \ominus U_r H_n^2 = (\mathrm{Ker}\ R)^\perp,$$

Likewise, Steps 17–20 produce the matrix γ which is the inverse of the Gram matrix of the expedient basis of the state space

$$H = H_m^2 \ominus NH_m^2 = H_m^2 \ominus U^\vee H_m^2.$$

Thus Steps 13–20 correspond to IV.

V requires us to solve the eigenvalue problem for the positive definite operator RR^*. At our disposal are the matrix $\tilde{R}$ of R with respect to bases in the domain and codomain – say $e_1, \ldots, e_d$ and $f_1, \ldots, f_d$ – and the inverses γ_r, γ of the Gram matrices of these bases.

9.1 LEMMA *The matrix of the operator R^* with respect to the expedient bases in H, $(\mathrm{Ker}\ R)^\perp$ is $\gamma_r \tilde{R}\ \gamma^{-1}$ where $\tilde{R}^*$ denotes the conjugate transpose of the matrix $\tilde{R}$.*

PROOF Let $\tilde{R} = [r_{ij}]$ and let the matrix of R^* be $[s_{ij}]$: that is,

$$Re_j = r_{ij}\, f_i, \quad R^*f_k = s_{\ell k}\, e_\ell.$$

The relation

$$(Re_j,\ f_k) = (e_j,\ R^*f_k)$$

yields

$$r_{ij}(f_i,\ f_k) = \bar{s}_{\ell k}\ (e_j,\ e_\ell),$$

that is,

$$\gamma^{-1}\tilde{R} = [s_{k\ell}]^*\gamma_r^{-1}.$$

Thus, taking conjugate transposes, we have

$$R^* \sim [s_{ij}] = \gamma_r\tilde{R}^*\gamma^{-1}. \qquad \square$$

It follows that the matrix of RR^* with respect to the expedient basis of H is

$$RR^* \sim \tilde{R}\gamma_r\tilde{R}^*\gamma^{-1}.$$

By the spectral theorem there is an orthonormal basis $x_1, \ldots, x_d$ of H consisting of eigenvectors of the positive operator RR^*: say

$$RR^*x_i = \sigma_i^2 x_i, \qquad 1 \leqslant i \leqslant d,$$

with $\sigma_i > 0$. Let $v_i \in \mathbb{C}^d$ be the column vector containing the components of x_i with respect to the expedient basis of H. Then $v_1, \ldots, v_d$ are linearly independent solutions of the problem

$$(\tilde{R}\gamma_r\tilde{R}^*\gamma^{-1} - \lambda I)v = 0, \qquad (9.1a)$$

and the orthonormality of the x_i's corresponds to the condition

$$v_j^*\gamma^{-1}v_i = \delta_{ij}, \qquad (9.1b)$$

where δ_{ij} is the Kronecker symbol.

Choose $d \times d$ matrices T_r, T such that

$$T_r T_r^* = \gamma_r, \ TT^* = \gamma.$$

Equations (9.1) can be written

$$(T^{-1}\tilde{R}T_r T_r^* \tilde{R}^* T^{-*} - \lambda I)T^{-1} v = 0,$$

$$(T^{-1} v_j)^* (T^{-1} v_i) = \delta_{ij}.$$

In other words, $T^{-1}v_1, \ldots, T^{-1}v_d$ constitute an orthonormal set of right singular vectors of the matrix $T_r^* \tilde{R}^* T^{-*}$. Hence V is accomplished by Steps 22 and 23 in the sense that Tw_j is the column vector containing the components with respect to the expedient basis of H of the jth member of an orthonormal system $x_1, \ldots, x_d$ of eigenvectors of RR^*.

The final section (VI) is to compute the matrices of the operator realization BR with respect to the orthonormal basis $x_1, \ldots, x_d$ of H. In view of the preceding paragraph the matrix

$$P = [Tw_1 \ Tw_2 \ \ldots \ Tw_d]$$

of step 24 can be regarded as the matrix of the identity operator from H with basis $x_1, \ldots, x_d$ to H with the expedient basis. It follows that the matrix of A with respect to $x_1, \ldots, x_d$ is $P^{-1}\tilde{A}P$. Since the matrix of $(RR^*)^{\frac{1}{2}}$ with respect to $x_1, \ldots, x_d$ is

$$\Sigma = \text{diag} \ \{\sigma_1, \ \ldots, \ \sigma_d\},$$

the matrix of $(RR^*)^{-\frac{1}{4}} A (RR^*)^{\frac{1}{4}}$ is

$$\hat{A} = \Sigma^{-\frac{1}{2}} P^{-1} \ \tilde{A} \ P\Sigma^{\frac{1}{2}}$$

Similar reasoning justifies the formulae for $\hat{B}$, $\hat{C}$ in Step 24.

We plan to report on the performance of our implementation of the algorithm in a future paper.

REFERENCES

1. V. M. Adamyan, D. Z. Arov and M. G. Krein, Infinite Hankel block matrices and related extension problems, *Izv. Akad. Nauk Armyan. SSR Ser. Mat.* 6 (1971), 87–112; *Amer. Math. Soc. Transl. (2)* 111 (1978), 133–156.

2. A. C. Allison and N. J. Young, Numerical algorithms for the Nevanlinna-Pick problem, *Numer. Math.* 42 (1983) 125–145.

3. J. C. Doyle, Advances in multivariable control, ONR/Honeywell workshop, Minneapolis, 1984.

4. B. A. Francis, "A Course in H^∞ Control Theory", Lecture Notes in Control and Information Sciences 88 Springer Verlag, Berlin, 1986.

5. B. A. Francis and J. C. Doyle, Linear control theory with an H^∞ optimality criterion, *SIAM J. Control and Optimisation*, to appear.

6. P. A. Fuhrmann, Realization theory in Hilbert space for a class of transfer functions, *J. Functional Analysis* 18 (338-349) 1975.

7. K. Glover, All optimal Hankel-norm approximations of linear multivariable systems and their L^∞-error bounds, *Int. J. Control* 39 (1984), 1115-1193.

8. J. W. Helton, Discrete time systems, operator models and scattering theory, *J. Functional Analysis* 16 (1974) 15-38.

9. K. Hoffman, "Banach Spaces of Analytic Functions", Prentice Hall, New Jersey, 1962.

10. T. Kailath, "Linear Systems", Prentice Hall, N. J., 1980.

11. H. Kwakernaak, A polynomial approach to H^∞-optimization of control systems, in "Modelling, Robustness and Sensitivity Reduction in Control Systems", ed. R. F. Curtain, Springer Verlag, Heidelberg, 1987, 83-94.

12. S. Kung and D. W. Lin, Optimal Hankel norm model reductions: multivariable systems, *I.E.E.E. Trans. Automatic Control* 26 (1981), 832-852.

13. B. C. Moore, Principal component analysis in linear systems: controllability, observability and model reduction, *IEEE Trans. Automatic Control* 26 (1981) 17-32.

14. L. Pernebo and L. M. Silverman, Model reduction via balanced state space representation, *IEEE Trans. Automatic Control* 27 (1982) 382-387.

15. I. Postlethwaite, D. W. Gu, S. D. O'Young and M. S. Tombs, An application of H^∞-design and some computational improvements, in "Modelling, Robustness and Sensitivity Reduction in Control Systems", ed. R. F. Curtain, Springer Verlag, Heidelberg, 1987, 305-322.

16. M. Vidyasagar, "Control System Synthesis: a Factorization Approach", MIT Press, Cambridge, MA, 1985.

17. F. B. Yeh, Numerical solution of matrix interpolation problems, Ph. D. Thesis, Glasgow University, 1983.

18. F. B. Yeh and C. D. Yang, An efficient algorithm for H^∞-optimal sensitivity problems, preprint, Institute of Aeronautics and Astronautics, National Chen Kung University, Tainan, Taiwan.

19. N. J. Young, Interpolation by analytic matrix fuctions, in "Operators and Function Theory", Proceedings of NATO ASI, edited by S. C. Power, D. Reidel Publishing Co. 1985, 351-383.

20. N. J. Young, The singular value decomposition of an infinite Hankel matrix, *Linear Algebra and its Applications* 50 (1983) 639-656.

University of Glasgow
Mathematics Department
University Gardens
Glasgow G128QW

Operator Theory:
Advances and Applications, Vol. 35

NEARLY INVARIANT SUBSPACES OF THE BACKWARD SHIFT

Donald Sarason

A theorem of D. Hitt describing certain subspaces of H^2 that miss by one dimension being invariant under the backward shift operator is given a new approach and extended.

1. INTRODUCTION

Let S denote the unilateral shift operator on the Hardy space H^2 of the unit disk, D. A subspace M of H^2 will be called nearly invariant under S^* if it is S^*-invariant modulo the one-dimensional subspace of constant functions, that is, if S^*h is in M whenever h is and $h(0) = 0$. These subspaces arose in the work of and were characterized by D. Hitt [4] (who called them weakly invariant rather than nearly invariant).

In order to describe Hitt's result we note that, if the subspace M is nearly S^*-invariant and nontrivial, then M cannot be contained in H_0^2, so that $M \cap H_0^2$ has unit codimension in M. There exists therefore a unique function g in M that is orthogonal to $M \cap H_0^2$, has unit norm, and is positive at the origin. Hitt's theorem then states that if h is any function in M, the quotient h/g is in H^2 and has the same norm as does h; moreover, the subspace M' consisting of all such quotients is S^*-invariant. Thus, the Toeplitz operator T_g, the operator on H^2 of multiplication by g, maps the S^*-invariant subspace M' isometrically onto the given nearly S^*-invariant subspace M. From the famous theorem of A. Beurling and subsequent work of many others, one has a good picture of the structure of the S^*-invariant subspaces. Hitt's theorem thus refocuses that picture so as to provide a picture of the nearly S^*-invariant subspaces. One detail remains murky, however: the latter theorem leaves mysterious the relation between the function g and the subspace M'. Given a function g of unit norm in H^2, what are the S^*-invariant subspaces M' that can arise along with g in Hitt's theorem?

The purpose of this note is to offer an approach to Hitt's theorem that clarifies the last point. Section 4 contains a proof of the theorem that, while substantially the same as Hitt's in its initial stages, by-passes the most complicated part of his argument by exploiting a certain rank-one perturbation of S^*, which arises through the following observation. If M and g are as above then, as one easily verifies, the equality $\langle h,g\rangle = h(0)/g(0)$ holds for all h in M. From this it follows that M is an invariant subspace of the operator $R_g = S^*(1-g\otimes g)$, a perturbation of S^* which, it turns out, can be coisometrically intertwined with the restriction of S^* to a certain Hilbert space contained contractively in H^2. The intertwining is described in Section 3 and used there to derive the key property that $R_g^n \to 0$ strongly as $n \to \infty$. The map that implements the intertwining also provides the key to answering the question raised above. The answer is given in Section 4.

The Hilbert space in which R_g will be represented belongs to a class of spaces introduced and studied by L. de Branges and J. Rovnyak [1], and more recently studied by the present author [5], [6]. The required properties of these spaces are presented in Section 2.

Nearly S^*-invariant subspaces arise, in particular, as the kernels of Toeplitz operators, and this special case of Hitt's theorem was independently discovered, and established through different methods, by E. Hayashi [2]. Hayashi's result will be briefly discussed in the concluding Section 5.

As we shall have to deal below with certain unbounded Toeplitz operators, the sense in which those operators are to be interpreted will be clarified here. If x is any function in L^2 of the unit circle, then by T_x we shall understand the operator on H^2 that sends the function h to the function

$$(T_x h)(z) = \frac{1}{2\pi}\int_{-\pi}^{\pi} \frac{x(e^{i\theta})h(e^{i\theta})}{1 - ze^{-i\theta}}\, d\theta \qquad (|z| < 1) ;$$

in other words, $T_x h$ is the standard Fourier projection of the L^1 function xh. The preceding definition clearly reduces to the usual one when x is bounded. In the general case, the range of T_x is just a certain space of holomorphic functions in D; it is contained in H^p for $p < 1$, but that inclusion will have no bearing here. It does make sense, though, to follow T_x by an analytic Toeplitz operator, with a bounded symbol, say. Such products will arise below, and the ones of interest turn out to be bounded operators on H^2.

2. THE SPACES $\mathcal{H}(b)$

If B is a bounded operator acting in H^2 then, following L. de Branges, we define $\mathcal{M}(B)$ to be the space BH^2 with the Hilbert space structure that makes B into a coisometry of H^2 onto $\mathcal{M}(B)$. Thus, for example, if the function h in H^2 is orthogonal to $\ker B$, then the norm of Bh in $\mathcal{M}(B)$ equals $\|h\|_2$, the norm of h in H^2. The space $\mathcal{M}(B)$ does not determine B, but a simple argument shows that two such spaces, say $\mathcal{M}(B)$ and $\mathcal{M}(B_1)$, are identical as Hilbert spaces if and only if $BB^* = B_1B_1^*$. If B is a contraction operator then $\mathcal{H}(B)$, the so-called complementary space of $\mathcal{M}(B)$, is defined to be $\mathcal{M}((1 - BB^*)^{\frac{1}{2}})$.

Of chief concern here is the case $B = T_b$, where b is a function in the unit ball of H^∞. The corresponding spaces $\mathcal{M}(T_b)$ and $\mathcal{H}(T_b)$ will be denoted by $\mathcal{M}(b)$ and $\mathcal{H}(b)$. The norm in $\mathcal{H}(b)$ will be denoted by $\|\cdot\|_b$.

The kernel function in H^2 for the point w of D will be denoted by k_w ($k_w(z) = (1 - \bar{w}z)^{-1}$). A simple argument [1],[5] shows that the kernel function in $\mathcal{H}(b)$ for the point w is the function $k_w^b = (1-\overline{b(w)}b)k_w$.

The space $\mathcal{H}(b)$ is invariant under S^* and S^* acts as a contraction in it [1],[5]. The restriction operator $S^*|\mathcal{H}(b)$ will be denoted by X_b.

Two special cases will be of particular interest below.

The first is where b is an inner function. Then $\mathcal{M}(b)$ is just the S-invariant subspace bH^2, and $\mathcal{H}(b)$ is its ordinary orthogonal complement, an S*-invariant subspace (the most general proper one, by Beurling's theorem). The other is where b is not an extreme point of the unit ball of H^∞. In that case, as was proved in [5], the kernel functions k_w belong to $\mathcal{H}(b)$ and, as was proved in [6], actually span $\mathcal{H}(b)$.

3. AN INTERTWINING

Let g be a function of unit norm in H^2, and let f be the outer factor of g, normalized (for definiteness) by the condition $f(0) > 0$. Let F be the Herglotz integral of $|f|^2$:

$$F(z) = \frac{1}{2\pi}\int_{-\pi}^{\pi} \frac{e^{i\theta}+z}{e^{i\theta}-z} |f(e^{i\theta})|^2 \, d\theta \qquad (|z|<1) .$$

We note that $F(0) = 1$ and define the functions b and a by

$$b = \frac{F-1}{F+1} , \qquad a = \frac{2f}{F+1} .$$

Then $b(0) = 0$ and, as the function F has a positive real part, the function b is in the unit ball of H^∞. The function a is an outer function, being the quotient of two outer functions, and almost everywhere on ∂D we have

$$|a|^2 + |b|^2 = \frac{4|f|^2 + |F-1|^2}{|F+1|^2} = \frac{4\,\mathrm{Re}\,F + |F-1|^2}{|F+1|^2} = 1 .$$

Thus a is also in the unit ball of H^∞, and because $1-|b|^2 = |a|^2$ on ∂D, we see that $\log(1-|b|^2)$ is integrable, so that b is not an extreme point of the unit ball of H^∞.

LEMMA 1. *For* z *and* w *in* D,

$$\langle fk_w, fk_z \rangle = (1-b(z))^{-1}(1-\overline{b(w)})^{-1} k_w^b(z) .$$

This is just a computation. The inner product on the

left side equals

$$\frac{1}{2\pi}\int_{-\pi}^{\pi}\frac{|f(e^{i\theta})|^2}{(1-\bar{w}e^{i\theta})(1-ze^{-i\theta})}\,d\theta \quad ,$$

which can be rewritten as

$$\frac{1}{2\pi(1-\bar{w}z)}\int_{-\pi}^{\pi}\tfrac{1}{2}\left[\frac{e^{-i\theta}+\bar{w}}{e^{-i\theta}-\bar{w}}+\frac{e^{i\theta}+z}{e^{i\theta}-z}\right]|f(e^{i\theta})|^2\,d\theta \quad ,$$

in other words, as

$$\frac{F(z)+\overline{F(w)}}{2(1-\bar{w}z)} \quad ,$$

an expression that is easily reduced to the right side.

LEMMA 2. *The operator* $T_{1-b}T_{\bar{f}}$ *is bounded and is in fact an isometry of* H^2 *onto* $\mathcal{H}(b)$. *Hence, the operator* $T_{1-b}T_{\bar{g}}$ *is a coisometry of* H^2 *onto* $\mathcal{H}(b)$; *its null space equals* $\mathcal{H}(v)$, *where* v *is the inner factor of* g.

The second statement follows immediately from the first one. To establish the first statement we note that, because f is an outer function, the functions fk_w, with w in D, span H^2. From Lemma 1 it follows that $T_{1-b}T_{\bar{f}}$ sends fk_w to $(1-b(w))^{-1}k_w^b$. Lemma 1 also implies that the inner product of the two functions fk_w and fk_z in H^2 equals the inner product of their images in $\mathcal{H}(b)$. Hence $T_{1-b}T_{\bar{f}}$ maps a dense linear manifold in H^2 isometrically onto a dense linear manifold in $\mathcal{H}(b)$. A straightforward limit argument now completes the proof.

COROLLARY. $(T_{1-b}T_{\bar{g}})(T_{1-b}T_{\bar{g}})^* = 1 - T_bT_{\bar{b}}$.

The adjoint referred to here is the adjoint of $T_{1-b}T_{\bar{g}}$ as an operator of H^2 into itself. The equality follows from the identity of the two spaces $\mathcal{M}(T_{1-b}T_{\bar{g}})$ and $\mathcal{M}((1-T_bT_{\bar{b}})^{\frac{1}{2}})$, as explained in Section 2. We note here the equality $(T_{1-b}T_{\bar{g}})^* =$

$T_g T_{1-\bar{b}}$, which is needed in Section 4 and valid even when g is unbounded, as a simple argument shows.

LEMMA 3. $T_{1-b}T_{\bar{g}}S^*g = S^*b$.

In fact, we have seen in the proof of Lemma 2 that $T_{1-b}T_{\bar{f}}$ maps f to the constant function 1 (i.e., the function $(1-\overline{b(0)})^{-1}k_0^b$); hence also $T_{1-b}T_{\bar{g}}g = 1$. Thus, because $T_{\bar{g}}$ and S^* commute,

$$\begin{aligned} T_{1-b}T_{\bar{g}}S^*g &= T_{1-b}S^*T_{\bar{g}}g \\ &= S^*T_{1-b}T_{\bar{g}}g + (S^*T_{b-1} - T_{b-1}S^*)T_{\bar{g}}g \\ &= (S^*T_{b-1} - T_{b-1}S^*)T_{\bar{g}}g \quad . \end{aligned}$$

As $S^*T_{b-1} - T_{b-1}S^*$ equals the rank-one operator $S^*b \otimes 1$, one easily verifies that $(S^*T_{b-1} - T_{b-1}S^*)T_{\bar{g}}$ is the bounded operator $S^*b \otimes g$, and the desired equality follows.

Recall that R_g denotes the operator $S^*(1 - g \otimes g)$.

LEMMA 4. *The operator* $T_{1-b}T_{\bar{g}}$ *intertwines the operator* R_g *with the operator* X_b: $T_{1-b}T_{\bar{g}}R_g = X_bT_{1-b}T_{\bar{g}}$.

Letting v, as before, denote the inner factor of g, we note that $T_{\bar{g}}$ annihilates the subspace $\mathcal{H}(v)$. So does $g \otimes g$, so that R_g coincides with S^* in $\mathcal{H}(v)$, implying that $\mathcal{H}(v)$ is R_g-invariant. The desired equality thus holds in $\mathcal{H}(v)$, and it only remains to show that it holds in $\mathcal{M}(v)$. For that it will suffice to show that it holds for the functions vk_w with w in D. We have

$$\begin{aligned} R_g vk_w &= S^*vk_w - \langle vk_w, g\rangle S^*g \\ &= \bar{w}vk_w + S^*v - \overline{f(w)}S^*g \quad . \end{aligned}$$

As $T_{\bar{g}}$ annihilates S^*v we obtain, using Lemma 3,

$$
\begin{aligned}
T_{1-b}T_{\bar g}R_g v k_w &= \bar w T_{1-b}T_{\bar g} v k_w - \overline{f(w)}T_{1-b}T_{\bar g}S^*g \\
&= \bar w T_{1-b}T_{\bar f}k_w - \overline{f(w)}S^*b \\
&= \bar w \overline{f(w)}(1-b)k_w - \overline{f(w)}S^*b \\
&= \overline{f(w)}S^*((1-b)k_w) \\
&= S^*T_{1-b}T_{\bar f}k_w = X_b T_{1-b}T_{\bar g} v k_w ,
\end{aligned}
$$

as desired.

LEMMA 5. $R_g^n \to 0$ *strongly as* $n \to \infty$.

We note first that $X_b^n \to 0$ strongly as $n \to \infty$. In fact, for w in D we have $X_b k_w = \bar w k_w$, implying that $X_b^n k_w \to 0$ as $n \to \infty$. Because, as was mentioned in Section 2, the functions k_w span $\mathcal{H}(b)$, the desired conclusion follows.

We continue to let v denote the inner factor of g. Let h be any function in H^2, and fix a positive number ε. By the preceding observation, there is a positive integer m such that $\|X_b^m T_{1-b}T_{\bar g}h\|_b < \varepsilon$. Let h_0 and h_1 be the components of $R_g^m h$ in $\mathcal{H}(v)$ and $\mathcal{M}(v)$, respectively. By Lemmas 1 and 4, $\|h_1\|_2 = \|X_b^m T_{1-b}T_{\bar g}h\|_b < \varepsilon$. Since R_g coincides with S^* in $\mathcal{H}(v)$ we obtain, for any positive integer n,

$$
\begin{aligned}
\|R_g^{m+n}h\|_2 &\leq \|R_g^n h_0\|_2 + \|R_g^n h_1\|_2 \\
&\leqq \|S^{*n}h_0\|_2 + \|R_g^n\|\ \|h_1\|_2 \\
&< \|S^{*n}h_0\|_2 + \varepsilon .
\end{aligned}
$$

As $S^{*n} \to 0$ strongly we conclude that $\limsup\|R_g^n h\|_2 < \varepsilon$, and as ε is arbitrary, the proof is complete.

4. HITT'S THEOREM

THEOREM 1. *Let* M *be a nontrivial nearly invariant subspace of* S^*, *and let* g *be the function of unit norm in* M *that is orthogonal to* $M \cap H_0^2$ *and positive at the origin. Then*

$M = T_g M'$, *where* M' *is an* S^**-invariant subspace on which* T_g *acts isometrically.*

As mentioned in the Introduction, the proof of the theorem to be given here will begin in the same way as did Hitt's, except that Hitt's reasoning will be translated into a language that enables one to take advantage of the operator R_g, which leaves M invariant. Let h be any function in M, and let $c_0 = \langle h, g\rangle$. Then $R_g h = S^*(h - c_0 g)$, which implies that

$$h = c_0 g + SR_g h \quad ,$$

because $h - c_0 g$ vanishes at the origin. The function $SR_g h$ is thus in M, and as it is also in H_0^2 it is orthogonal to g, implying that

$$\|h\|_2^2 = |c_0|^2 \|g\|_2^2 + \|SR_g h\|_2^2 = |c_0|^2 + \|R_g h\|_2^2$$

Similarly, for any positive integer n,

$$R_g^n h = c_n g + SR_g^{n+1} h \quad ,$$

where $c_n = \langle R_g^n h, g\rangle$, and

$$\|R_g^n h\|_2^2 = |c_n|^2 + \|R_g^{n+1} h\|_2^2 \quad .$$

We can thus iterate to obtain

$$h = (c_0 + c_1 S + \ldots + c_n S^n) g + S^{n+1} R_g^{n+1} h$$

for any positive integer n, with

$$\|h\|_2^2 = |c_0|^2 + |c_1|^2 + \ldots + |c_n|^2 + \|R_g^{n+1} h\|_2^2 \quad .$$

Departing now from Hitt's line of reasoning, we let $n \to \infty$ and use Lemma 5; our conclusion is that h has the factorization gq where the H^2 function $q(z) = \Sigma_0^\infty c_n z^n$ has the same norm as does h. We have thus shown that $M' = \{h/g : h \in M\}$ is a subspace of H^2

and that T_g maps M' isometrically onto M. Moreover, with h, c_0 and q as above, we have $c_0 = q(0)$, and accordingly,

$$\begin{aligned} R_g h &= S^*(gq) - q(0)S^*g \\ &= gS^*q + q(0)S^*g - q(0)S^*g = gS^*q , \end{aligned}$$

showing that M' is S^*-invariant and completing the proof of the theorem.

One can distinguish two disparate cases of Hitt's theorem. If M' is all of H^2, then g obviously must be an inner function, and M is just the S-invariant subspace $\mathcal{M}(g)$. In the more interesting case M' is proper and so equals $\mathcal{H}(u)$ for some inner function u, which must vanish at the origin because M' clearly contains the constant function 1. The following result clarifies the isometric action of T_g in this case.

THEOREM 2. *Let* g *be a function of unit norm in* H^2 *and let* b *be as defined in Section 3. Let* u *be an inner function with* $u(0) = 0$. *The following conditions are equivalent:*

(i) T_g *acts isometrically on* $\mathcal{H}(u)$

(ii) u *divides* b

(iii) $\mathcal{H}(u)$ *is contained isometrically in* $\mathcal{H}(b)$.

The divisibility meant in condition (ii) is divisibility in the algebra H^∞. To say that u divides b is the same as saying that u divides the inner factor of b. The equivalence of conditions (ii) and (iii) can be found in [1] but will be proved here for completeness.

(ii) $\Longrightarrow$ (i). Assume u divides b, and let h be any function in $\mathcal{H}(u)$. Then $T_{\bar{b}}h = 0$, so, by the corollary to Lemma 2,

$$\begin{aligned} \|T_g h\|_2^2 &= \|T_g T_{1-\bar{b}} h\|_2^2 = \langle (T_{1-b}T_{\bar{g}})(T_{1-b}T_{\bar{g}})^* h,\ h \rangle \\ &= \langle (1 - T_b T_{\bar{b}})h,\ h \rangle = \langle h,h \rangle = \|h\|_2^2 , \end{aligned}$$

as desired.

(i) $\Longrightarrow$ (ii). Assume T_g acts isometrically on $\mathcal{H}(u)$, and let h be any function in $\mathcal{H}(u)$. Because $\mathcal{H}(u)$ is invariant under $T_{\bar{b}}$ we obtain, using Lemma 2 and its corollary,

$$\|T_{1-\bar{b}}h\|_2 = \|T_g T_{1-\bar{b}}h\|_2 = \|T_{1-b}T_{\bar{g}}T_g T_{1-\bar{b}}h\|_b$$
$$= \|(1 - T_b T_{\bar{b}})h\|_b = \|(1 - T_b T_{\bar{b}})^{\frac{1}{2}}h\|_2 ,$$

in other words,

$$\langle T_{1-b}T_{1-\bar{b}}h, h\rangle = \langle (1 - T_b T_{\bar{b}})h, h\rangle ,$$

which can be rewritten

$$2\|T_{\bar{b}}h\|_2^2 = \langle h, T_{\bar{b}}h\rangle + \langle T_{\bar{b}}h, h\rangle .$$

Since $u(0) = 0$ the space $\mathcal{H}(u)$ contains the constant functions, and since $b(0) = 0$ the operator $T_{\bar{b}}$ annihilates the constant functions. We can therefore replace h in the last equality by $h+c$, where c is any constant, obtaining

$$2\|T_{\bar{b}}h\|_2^2 = 2\,\mathrm{Re}\,\bar{c}(T_{\bar{b}}h)(0) + \langle h, T_{\bar{b}}h\rangle + \langle T_{\bar{b}}h, h\rangle .$$

This cannot possibly be true for all constants c unless $(T_{\bar{b}}h)(0) = 0$. But the last equality for all h in $\mathcal{H}(u)$ implies $T_{\bar{b}}h = 0$ for all h in $\mathcal{H}(u)$ (since $\mathcal{H}(u)$ is S^*-invariant). Thus $T_{\bar{b}}$ annihilates $\mathcal{H}(u)$, which implies that u divides b.

(ii) $\Longrightarrow$ (iii). If u divides b and h is in $\mathcal{H}(u)$, then $T_{\bar{b}}h = 0$, which implies that $(1 - T_b T_{\bar{b}})^{\frac{1}{2}}h = h$ and hence that h is in $\mathcal{H}(b)$ with

$$\|h\|_b = \|(1 - T_b T_{\bar{b}})^{\frac{1}{2}}h\|_b = \|h\|_2 .$$

(iii) $\Longrightarrow$ (ii). If $\mathcal{H}(u)$ is contained isometrically in $\mathcal{H}(b)$ and h is in $\mathcal{H}(u)$, then $h = (1 - T_b T_{\bar{b}})^{\frac{1}{2}}h_1$ for some h_1 in H^2, and

$$\|h_1\|_2 = \|h\|_b = \|h\|_2 = \|(1 - T_b T_{\bar{b}})^{\frac{1}{2}}h_1\|_2 .$$

The last equality implies $(1 - T_b T_{\bar{b}})^{\frac{1}{2}}h_1 = h_1$ (since $(1 - T_b T_{\bar{b}})^{\frac{1}{2}}$

is a positive contraction), which means that $h_1 = h$ and so $(1 - T_b T_{\bar{b}})h = h$, in other words, $T_{\bar{b}}h = 0$. That means $T_{\bar{b}}$ annihilates $\mathcal{H}(u)$, so that u divides b.

The hypothesis $u(0) = 0$ in Theorem 2 was used only for the implication (i) $\Longrightarrow$ (ii), and that implication can fail in its absence. For example, suppose u is the Blaschke factor $(z-w)/(1-\bar{w}z)$, where w is in D and $w \neq 0$. Then $\mathcal{H}(u)$ is spanned by the kernel function k_w. One easily checks that $\|gk_w\|_2 = \|k_w\|_2$ if and only if $\mathrm{Re}\, F(w) = 1$ (where F is as defined in Section 3), but that u divides b if and only if $F(w) = 1$.

In [6] it is shown that, for b as in Theorem 2, the proper invariant subspaces of the operator X_b are the subspaces $\mathcal{H}(u) \cap \mathcal{H}(b)$ with u an inner function. As the operator $T_{1-b}T_{\bar{f}}$ (where f is the outer factor of g) implements a unitary equivalence between the operators R_f and X_b, the proper invariant subspaces of R_f are the inverse images under $T_{1-b}T_{\bar{f}}$ of the subspaces $\mathcal{H}(u) \cap \mathcal{H}(b)$. In case u divides b, Theorem 2 says that $\mathcal{H}(u)$ sits isometrically in $\mathcal{H}(b)$ and so is by itself an invariant subspace of X_b. Then, as one would expect, the inverse image of $\mathcal{H}(u)$ under $T_{1-b}T_{\bar{f}}$ is just the nearly S^*-invariant subspace $T_f\mathcal{H}(u)$ of Hitt. In fact, denoting $T_f\mathcal{H}(u)$ by M and using the corollary to Lemma 2 plus the inclusion $\mathcal{H}(u) \subset \ker T_{\bar{b}}$, we obtain

$$\begin{aligned} T_{1-b}T_{\bar{f}}M &= T_{1-b}T_{\bar{f}}T_f T_{1-\bar{b}}\mathcal{H}(u) \\ &= (1 - T_b T_{\bar{b}})\mathcal{H}(u) = \mathcal{H}(u) \quad . \end{aligned}$$

We see from this that $T_{1-b}T_{\bar{f}}$ agrees on M with $T_{1/f}$.

5. KERNELS OF TOEPLITZ OPERATORS

Suppose x is a function in L^∞, not identically zero, such that the operator T_x has a nontrivial kernel. Then $\ker T_x$ is a nontrivial nearly S^*-invariant subspace so, according to Theorem 1, it equals $T_g M'$, where g has unit norm in H^2 and M' is an S^*-invariant subspace, containing the constant functions, on which T_g acts isometrically. Since $\ker T_x$ clearly contains the outer factor of each of its members, the function g must be an outer function. The case $M' = H^2$ is thus excluded by the assumption that x is not identically 0, implying that $M' = \mathcal{H}(u)$ for an inner function u that vanishes at the origin; thus $\ker T_x = T_g\mathcal{H}(u)$. As noted in the Introduction, the preceding description of the kernel of a Toeplitz operator is due to E. Hayashi [2], who used different methods (deriving from prediction theory). Hayashi in fact proved more, namely, he showed that g^2 is an exposed point of the unit ball of H^1 [3]. His argument could be incorporated without alterations into the present treatment of his result.

Because the function x multiplies a nonzero function in H^2 into $\bar{H}_0^2$, it must be log-integrable, so it can be written as $\bar{x}_1 y$, where y is unimodular and x_1 is the outer function with modulus $|x|$. Then $T_x = T_{\bar{x}_1}T_y$, and as $T_{\bar{x}_1}$ has a trivial kernel, the kernel of T_y coincides with that of T_x. In fact, $y = \overline{ug}/g$. This equality from [2] and [3] can be established as follows. Because the function g is in $\ker T_y$, the product yg is in $\bar{H}_0^2$, so (since g is outer) it can be written as $\bar{u}_1\bar{g}$ where u_1 is an inner function that vanishes at the origin. Thus $y = \bar{u}_1\bar{g}/g$. Suppose h is any function in $\mathcal{H}(u)$. Then gh is in $\ker T_y$, implying that $\bar{u}_1\bar{g}h$ is in $\bar{H}_0^2$. Since g is outer it follows that $\bar{u}_1 h$ is in $\bar{H}_0^2$, which shows that $T_{\bar{u}_1}$ annihilates $\mathcal{H}(u)$ and hence that u divides u_1. Suppose, on the other hand, that h is a bounded function in $\mathcal{H}(u_1)$. Then $ygh = \overline{gu_1}h$, a function in $\bar{H}_0^2$, implying that gh is in $\ker T_y$, that is, in $T_g\mathcal{H}(u)$, and hence h is in $\mathcal{H}(u)$. As $\mathcal{H}(u_1)$ is spanned by its bounded functions (for example, by its kernel functions), we can conclude that $\mathcal{H}(u_1) \subset \mathcal{H}(u)$, so that u_1 divides u. Therefore u_1 is a constant multiple of u, the desired conclusion.

From the results of Hayashi and those in Section 4 one sees that the Toeplitz operator with unimodular symbol y has a nontrivial kernel if and only if y has the form $\overline{ug}/g$, where g^2 is an exposed point of the unit ball of H^1, and u is an inner function that vanishes at the origin and divides the function b associated with g in the way specified in Section 3. The question arises whether, if y has the preceding form, the kernel of T_y actually equals $T_g\mathscr{H}(u)$. It is obvious that $\ker T_y$ contains $T_g\mathscr{H}(u)$, but the reverse inclusion seems elusive. Put differently, is every subspace of H^2 that is eligible according to Hayashi's results and Theorem 2 to be the kernel of a Toeplitz operator actually equal to such a kernel? The answer will probably await a better understanding than now exists of the exposed points of the unit ball of H^1.

REFERENCES

1. de Branges, L. and Rovnyak, J.: Square Summable Power Series (Holt, Rinehart & Winston, New York, 1966).

2. Hayashi, E.: The kernel of a Toeplitz operator, Integral Equations and Operator Theory 9 (1986), 588-591.

3. Hayashi, E.: The solution sets of extremal problems in H^1, Proceedings of the AMS 93 (1985), 690-696.

4. Hitt, D.: Invariant subspaces of H^2 of an annulus, forthcoming.

5. Sarason, D.: Shift-invariant spaces from the Brangesian point of view, Proceedings of the Conference on the Occasion of the Proof of the Bierberbach Conjecture, Mathematical Surveys, (AMS, Providence, 1986), 153-166.

6. Sarason, D.: Doubly shift-invariant spaces in H^2, Journal of Operator Theory 16 (1986), 75-97.

Department of Mathematics
University of California
Berkeley, California 94720 USA

Operator Theory:
Advances and Applications, Vol. 35

THE HEAT EXPANSION FOR SYSTEMS OF INTEGRAL EQUATIONS

Harold Widom*

In this paper we derive an analogue for integral operators of the well-known heat expansion for the Laplacian or other operators of positive order. Previous work established a partial expansion of $n+1$ terms for a single integral operator in n dimensions. This is here extended to systems of operators.

INTRODUCTION

In this paper we extend to systems of integral operators (more precisely, to pseudodifferential operators of negative order with matrix-valued symbol) a partial heat expansion derived in [5] for single operators (with scalar symbol).

Let A be a self-adjoint pseudodifferential operator of negative order $-r$ on R^n whose matrix symbol $\sigma(x,\xi)$ has an asymptotic expansion

$$\sigma(x,\xi) \sim \sum_{k=0}^{\infty} \sigma_k(x,\xi) \tag{1}$$

as $|\xi| \to \infty$, where σ_k is homogeneous of degree $-r-k$ in ξ and σ_0 is a positive definite matrix function. For a compact subset Ω of R^n with smooth boundary we denote by A_Ω the operator A restricted to $L_2(\Omega)$. (Take a function in $L_2(\Omega)$, extend it by zero to all of R^n, apply A, and restrict the result to Ω.) The operator A_Ω is compact and self-adjoint with a sequence of eigenvalues $\lambda_i \to 0$. The quantity in question is

$$\sum_i e^{-t/\lambda_i} \tag{2}$$

which may also be thought of as the trace of $e^{-tA_\Omega^{-1}}$ (this operator being defined by the spectral theorem) or as the integral over the diagonal of the heat kernel associated with A_Ω^{-1}.

Of course heat expansions for operators of positive order (especially differential operators) have been much studied. We mention in particular the work of Grubb [3] who obtained a partial heat expansion for boundary problems associated with positive

* Research sponsored in part by NSF Grant DMS-8601605.

order pseudodifferential operators satisfying the transmission condition. (This guarantees that if a function f is smooth in Ω up to the boundary then so is $A_\Omega f$.) The analysis in [5] was quite different: There were no boundary conditions, which of course simplified matters. But the transmission condition was not assumed and, further, negative order operators are in a way trickier than positive order operators because the resolvent for the former becomes worse as $\lambda \to 0$ along rays in the complex plane (the limit of interest in that case) while for the latter the resolvent becomes better as $\lambda \to \infty$ (the limit of interest for them).

Getting back to (2) we mention that its first order asymptotics as $t \to 0+$ are equivalent (via Abelian and Tauberian theorems) to the first order asymptotics of the λ_i as $i \to \infty$. These are well-known, even under very weak conditions on σ [1]. In [5] a formal partial expansion of $n+1$ terms

$$\sum_{k=0}^{n} a_k t^{(k-n)/r} \tag{3}$$

was derived for (2) where the a_k were determined by the σ_i appearing in (1). Each a_k was a sum $b_k + c_k$ where b_k was an integral over $\Omega \times R^n$ of an expression involving the σ_i and c_k was an integral over the cotangent bundle $T^*\partial\Omega$ of an expression involving Wiener-Hopf operators associated with these symbols. (The c_k with $k \geq 2$ involved also the second fundamental form of $\partial\Omega$.) For scalar symbols there were more concrete formulas for these coefficients in terms of the σ_i directly.

What was actually proved in [5], among other things, is that (3) is a correct $(n+1)$-term expansion for (2), in that the difference between (2) and (3) is $O(t^\delta)$, for some $\delta > 0$, as $t \to 0+$ under the following two extra assumptions.

(a) The symbol of A is scalar-valued.

(b) The null space of A_Ω, considered as acting on $\overset{o}{H}_{-r/2}(\Omega)$ (the distributions belonging to the Sobolev space $H_{-r/2}(R^n)$ which are supported in Ω), is trivial.

Without condition (b) the expansion (3) may be incorrect, as was shown by examples. What we shall show here is that condition (a) may be dropped.

The proof made heavy use of the Wiener-Hopf factorization of $\sigma - \lambda$ where σ now denotes a positive principal symbol of A and λ is a parameter lying in a region

$$\Lambda_\varepsilon = \{\lambda : \varepsilon < arg\lambda < 2\pi - \varepsilon\}.$$

For λ nonzero $\sigma - \lambda$ is an elliptic symbol of order 0 and its factorization, even in the matrix case, presents no difficulty. For $\lambda = 0$ it is an elliptic symbol of negative order which again has a nice factorization. What we needed was a certain result (Lemma 8.9 of [5], which we state later) about the behavior of the factors of $\sigma - \lambda$ as $|\lambda| \to 0$. We were able to prove it in the scalar case because then there are explicit integral formulas for the factors. We shall prove it here in the matrix case by exploiting the connection between factorization and inversion of Wiener-Hopf operators. It was pointed out in [5] (and we hope the reader accepts its truth) that it was only a lack of proof of the lemma that prevented everything from going through in the matrix case. This is fortunate since giving the entire proof of the heat expansion here would be a burden for both the author and the reader.

In the next section we describe the coefficients in more detail, and give the formulas for a_0 and a_1. In the third section we state the main result of this paper and prove some lemmas about elliptic factorization which will be needed for its proof. We shall actually have to develop the theory of symbol factorization more or less from scratch. The reason is that results in the literature deal with symbols whose behavior is very regular as $\xi \to \infty$ whereas we shall be dealing with symbols whose behavior is not so regular, at least not regular uniformly in λ. The fourth section contains the proof of the main result.

A final remark. One might wonder whether (3) can be extended to a complete asymptotic expansion. We conjecture that it can, that terms involving positive integral powers of t times powers of $\log t$ also appear, but that no coefficient beyond those appearing in (3) is determined by the σ_i alone.

THE COEFFICIENTS

The formulas for the coefficients involve a kind of higher derivative of the mapping $\sigma \to f(\sigma)$, where $f \in C^\infty(R)$ and σ runs through the hermitian elements of a Banach algebra $\mathcal{A}$. For a Schwartz function f and for $\tau_1, \dots, \tau_k \in \mathcal{A}$ we define

$$f^{(k)}(\sigma; \tau_1, \dots, \tau_k) = \frac{k!}{2\pi} \int_{-\infty}^{\infty} (it)^k \hat{f}(t)\, dt \int e^{is_o t\sigma} \tau_1 e^{is_1 t\sigma} \tau_2 \dots \tau_k e^{is_k t\sigma} ds \tag{4}$$

where the circumflex denotes Fourier transform and ds denotes the measure $ds_1 \dots ds_k$ on the simplex

$$\{(s_0, \dots, s_k) \in R^{k+1} : s_i \geq 0, \Sigma s_i = 1\}.$$

This integral depends only on the values of f on a neighborhood of $sp(\sigma)$ [5, Prop. 4.2] and so there is a natural extension of the definition to all $f \in C^\infty(R)$. If all the τ_i commute with σ then the Fourier inversion theorem gives

$$f^{(k)}(\sigma; \tau_1, \dots, \tau_k) = f^{(k)}(\sigma)\tau_1 \dots \tau_k. \tag{5}$$

In the general case the k-th Fréchet derivative at σ of the mapping $\sigma \to f(\sigma)$ is a symmetric k-linear function whose value at $\tau_1,\ldots,\tau_k$ equals the symmetrization over the τ_i of $f^{(k)}(\sigma;\tau_i)$.

In the case at hand we take $f(\lambda)=g(\lambda/t)$ where g is a C^∞ function equal to $e^{-\lambda^{-1}}$ on a sufficiently large interval in R^+. The algebra $\mathcal{A}$ is either the algebra of $m\times m$ matrices (in which our matrix symbols take their values) or else the algebra of bounded operators on the space $L_2(R^+)$ of square-integrable C^m-valued functions on R^+.

Here now are the formulas for the first two coefficients as derived in Chapter III of [5]. If we write the coefficients as $a_k=b_k+c_k$ then $c_0=0$ and

$$a_0=b_0=(2\pi)^{-n}r^{-1}\Gamma(n/r)\int_\Omega\int_{S^{n-1}} tr\sigma_0(x,\omega)^{n/r}d\omega dx$$

where $d\omega$ denotes surface measure on the unit sphere S^{n-1}.

The formula for b_1 is

$$b_1=(2\pi)^{-n}\int_\Omega\int_{R^n} tr[g^{(1)}(\sigma_0;\sigma_1)-i\Sigma_j g^{(2)}(\sigma_0;\partial\sigma_0/\partial\xi_j,\partial\sigma_0/\partial x_j)]d\xi dx. \tag{6}$$

The contribution of the first term on the right can be written more concretely since it follows easily from (4) that

$$trg^{(1)}(\sigma;\tau)=tr\tfrac{1}{2\pi}\int(it)\hat{g}(t)e^{it\sigma}\tau dt=trg'(\sigma)\tau=tr\sigma^{-2}e^{-\sigma^{-1}}\tau.$$

Using this and the homogeneity of σ_0 and σ_1 we can write the contribution of the first part of (6) as

$$(2\pi)^{-n}r^{-1}\Gamma(\tfrac{n+r-1}{r})\int_\Omega\int_{S^{n-1}} tr\sigma_0(x,\omega)^{(n-r-1)/r}\sigma_1(x,\omega)d\omega dx. \tag{7}$$

We leave this computation to the reader. Unfortunately it seems that nothing much can be done with the second part of (6) unless, for example, σ_0 is independent of x or the values of σ_0 mutually commute. In the latter case (5) shows that the contribution of this second part is purely imaginary and so (since σ_1 must be real and, as we shall soon see, c_1 is real so that b_1 is also real) b_1 is equal to the real part of (7).

More interesting is the first "boundary coefficient" c_1. For its representation we introduce some notation. Let $X=(x,\eta)$ be a cotangent vector to $\partial\Omega$. This means that $x\in\partial\Omega$ and η is a vector orthogonal to n_x, the inner unit normal to $\partial\Omega$ at x. For such an X define

$$\sigma_X(\xi)=\sigma_0(x,\eta+\xi n_x) \qquad (\xi\in R).$$

For $\eta\neq 0$ this is a one-dimensional symbol of order $-r$ which is independent of x. (In one dimension there is a singularity at $\xi=0$, which causes some awkwardness.) The formula for c_1 in dimension $n > 1$ is

$$c_1 = (2\pi)^{1-n} \int\limits_{T^*\partial\Omega} tr[e^{-W(\sigma_X)^{-1}} - W(e^{-\sigma_X^{-1}})]dX. \tag{8}$$

Let us explain the ingredients of this: dX denotes the measure $d\eta dx$ where $d\eta$ is Lebesque measure on $n_x^\perp$ and dx is surface measure on $\partial\Omega$. In general $W(\tau)$, where τ is a one-dimensional symbol independent of x, denotes the Wiener-Hopf operator associated with τ, convolution by the inverse Fourier transform of τ on $L_2(R^+)$. The operator

$$e^{-W(\sigma_X)^{-1}}$$

is defined, via the spectral theorem, as $g(W(\sigma_X))$ with g as before. Since σ_X is positive matrix-valued the trace appearing in (8) is real and therefore so is c_1 as was claimed above.

In general this formula also cannot be much simplified. However in the scalar case, or more generally when the values of the symbol mutually commute, there are formulas for traces such as appear in the integrand in (8). If the matrix symbol $\sigma_0(x,\omega)$ is independent of ω, say equal to $s_0(x)$, then

$$\sigma_X(\xi) = (|\eta|^2 + \xi^2)^{-r/2} s_0(x)$$

and so for each X the values of σ_X clearly commute. The computations on pp. 62-63 of [5] then give in this case

$$c_1 = 2^{-n}\pi^{-(n+2)/2}(n-1)\Gamma(\tfrac{n-1}{r})\Gamma(\tfrac{n}{2}+1)^{-1} \int\limits_{\partial\Omega} tr s_0(x)^{(n-1)/r} dx$$

$$\cdot \int_0^1 \tfrac{1-u^{n-r-1}}{1-u^{-r}}\, {}_2F_1(\tfrac{1}{2}, \tfrac{n+1}{2}; \tfrac{n}{2}+1; u^2) du$$

where ${}_2F_1$ denotes the hypergeometric function.

For $n = 1$ the symbols σ_X are singular at $\xi = 0$ and the formula (8) must be modified by first rounding off σ_0 at zero, applying (8) to the modified symbol, and then taking the limit as the round-off disappears. In the case when $\sigma_0(x,\omega)$ is independent of $\omega = \pm 1$ the computation was made in [5] (p.64) for scalar symbols and the result was

$$c_1 = \tfrac{r}{8}|\partial\Omega|$$

independently of σ_0. For $m \times m$ matrix-valued symbols this must be multiplied by m.

THE FACTORS

By an *elliptic factorization* of a one-dimensional matrix-valued elliptic symbol $\tau(\xi)$ of order s we shall mean a representation

$$\tau(\xi) = \tau_-(\xi)\tau_+(\xi)$$

where τ_- and τ_+ extend analytically to the upper and lower halves respectively of the complex ξ-plane and satisfy there estimates

$$|\tau_\pm(\xi)\,| \le C\langle\xi\rangle^{s/2}$$
$$|\tau_\pm(\xi)^{-1}\,| \le C\langle\xi\rangle^{-s/2}$$

where as usual $\langle\xi\rangle$ denotes $(1+|\xi|^2)^{1/2}$. The inverse Fourier transforms of $(\tau_-)^{\pm 1}$ and $(\tau_+)^{\pm 1}$ are then supported on $\overline{R^-}$, $\overline{R^+}$ respectively. (The reason the upper half-plane corresponds to R^- and the lower to R^+, and not the other way around, is that in the definition of the Fourier transform used in [5] the factor $-i$ appeared in the exponent rather than i.) The factorization, if it exists at all, is unique up to constant (matrix) factors. If τ depends on parameters then so of course will the factors and their dependence on the parameters will be important. For example, we think of an n-dimensional symbol

$$\tau(x,\xi',\xi) \qquad (x\in R^n, \xi' \in R^{n-1}, \xi\in R) \tag{9}$$

as a one-dimensional symbol with parameters x, ξ'.

We are interested in a positive definite matrix-valued elliptic symbol $\sigma(x,\xi',\xi)$ of order $-r$, where x belongs to a compact subset of R^n, a parameter λ belonging to the region

$$\Lambda_\varepsilon = \{\lambda : \varepsilon < arg\lambda < 2\pi - \varepsilon\},$$

and the factorization

$$\sigma(x,\xi',\xi) - \lambda = \sigma^-(x,\xi',\xi,\lambda)\ \sigma^+(x,\xi',\xi,\lambda). \tag{10}$$

We shall assume also that at least one term of expansion (1) is valid. More precisely that there is a function $\sigma_0(x,\xi',\xi)$ which is homogeneous of degree $-r$ in (ξ',ξ) such that for any functions $\varphi(\xi',\xi)\in C^\infty$ satisfying

$$\varphi(\xi',\xi) = 0 \text{ for } |(\xi',\xi)| \text{ small}, \ \varphi(\xi',\xi) = 1 \text{ for } |(\xi',\xi)| \text{ large}$$

the symbol

$$\sigma(x,\xi',\xi) - \varphi(\xi',\xi)\sigma_0(x,\xi',\xi) \tag{11}$$

is of order $-r-1$. Notice that for fixed $\lambda \ne 0$ the symbol $\sigma - \lambda$ is elliptic of order 0. It will be seen that an elliptic factorization exists and is uniquely determined by the requirement

$$\lim_{|\xi|\to\infty} \sigma^{\pm}(x,\xi',\xi,\lambda) = (-\lambda)^{1/2}.$$

(We take that branch of square root which is positive for λ negative.) What we are interested in is the behavior of the factors as λ ranges over Λ_ε. (And, of course, as ξ' ranges over R^{n-1}. The x-dependence will be harmless.)

Recall that an n-dimensional symbol $\tau(x,\xi)$ belongs to the symbol space S^s if for all multi-indices α,β

$$sup_{x,\xi}\, \langle \xi \rangle^{-s+|\beta|} \mid \partial_x^\alpha \partial_\xi^\beta \tau(x,\xi) \mid < \infty$$

and τ is called ***elliptic*** of order s if $\tau \in S^s$ and $\tau^{-1} \in S^{-s}$. (This is stronger than the more usual definition where the latter condition is required only for large (ξ',ξ).) These are the spaces we refer to when we speak of a symbol of some order. We shall also consider the spaces $\tilde{S}^s$ of symbols of the form (9) which satisfy for all multi-indices α,β and nonnegative integers k

(12) $$sup_{\xi,\xi',\xi}\langle(\xi',\xi)\rangle^{-s+k}\langle\xi'\rangle^{|\beta|} \mid \partial_x^\alpha \partial_{\xi'}^\beta \partial_\xi^k \tau(x,\xi',\xi) \mid < \infty.$$

Thus each ξ-differentiation reduces the order in (ξ',ξ) whereas each ξ'-differentiation only reduces the order in ξ'. These will be the symbol classes in which elliptic factors will generally lie. We also define the classes

$$S^{s+} = \bigcap_{t>0} S^{s+t}, \quad \tilde{S}^{s+} = \bigcap_{t>0} \tilde{S}^{s+t}.$$

MAIN RESULT : *For each* $\delta \in [0,1]$ *the factors* $\sigma^{\pm}$ *in* (10) *satisfy*

(13) $$(\sigma^{\pm})^{-1} \in |\lambda|^{-\delta/2}\tilde{S}^{\frac{1}{2}(1-\delta)r+}$$

uniformly for $\lambda \in \Lambda_\varepsilon$.

What this means, more precisely, is that each of the seminorms given by the left side of (12), with τ replaced by $(\sigma^{\pm})^{-1}$ and with s replaced by $\frac{1}{2}(1-\delta)r+t$ $(t>0$ fixed but arbitrary), is bounded by a constant times $|\lambda|^{-\delta/2}$ for all $\lambda \in \Lambda_\varepsilon$.

In rough outline the proof in one dimension goes as follows: First we factor σ as $\sigma_-\sigma_+$. This causes no problem since it is a nice elliptic symbol independent of λ. If we write $\tau = \sigma_-^{-1}\sigma_+^{-1}$ we are then left with $1-\lambda\tau(\xi)$. Since τ is close to homogeneous of order r (a consequence of our extra assumption on σ) this is approximately equal to

$$1 - sgn\lambda\ \tau(|\lambda|^{1/r}\xi)$$

The factorization for this is derived from that of $1-sgn\lambda\,\tau(\xi)$ which is a nicely behaved elliptic symbol of order r, uniformly for $\lambda \in \Lambda_\varepsilon$. But the error caused by the approximation leaves us with an elliptic symbol of order zero whose awkward dependence on λ is the main difficulty.

Lemma 1 will tell us about order zero elliptic factorization in nice and not-so-nice cases. The nice case is not far from what can be found in the literature. (For example [2], in particular sections 14 and 17. We have drawn heavily on the ideas presented there.) The not-so-nice case, the peculiar part of the lemma, is what makes everything work. First, some notation and terminology.

A family of operators on a Banach space is called *uniformly invertible* if the operators are invertible and the norms of their inverses are uniformly bounded.

We denote by P the projection from L_2 to $L_2(R^+)\hat{}$:

$$P\tau(\xi) = \tfrac{1}{2}\tau(\xi) + \tfrac{i}{2\pi} \int_{-\infty}^{\infty} \tfrac{\tau(\eta)}{\eta-\xi} d\eta. \tag{14}$$

The Wiener-Hopf operator $W(\tau)$ on $L_2(R^+)$ is unitarily equivalent to the operator $PM(\tau)P$ thought of as acting on $L_2(R^+)\hat{} = PL_2$ where $M(\tau)$ denotes multiplication by τ. For this reason we shall write, for convenience,

$$W(\tau)\hat{} = PM(\tau)P.$$

For a matrix-valued function τ we define $\tau^\dagger$ by

$$\tau^\dagger(\xi) = \text{transpose of } \tau(\xi)^{-1}.$$

A *derivation* on a set of symbols will mean a linear mapping which commutes with multiplication by any function of ξ and with any ξ-dilation (a mapping $\tau(\xi) \to \tau(a\xi)$) and which satisfies the product rule.

$$D(\tau_1\tau_2) = (D\tau_1)\tau_2 + \tau_1(D\tau_2).$$

In practice τ will be a one-dimensional symbol depending on a parameter and D will be a scaled derivative with respect to that parameter.

LEMMA 1. *Suppose the matrix-valued symbol $\tau(\xi), \xi \in R$, satisfies the conditions*

(i) $1 - \tau \in S^{-1}$ and $\tau^{-1} \in S^0$,

(ii) $W(\tau)$ and $W(\tau^\dagger)$ are invertible operators on $L_2(R^+)$.

Then there is an order zero elliptic factorization $\tau = \tau_-\tau_+$, which is uniquely determined by the conditions

$$\lim_{|\xi|\to\infty} \tau_\pm(\xi) = 1. \tag{15}$$

Moreover :

(a) Suppose we have a family of symbols for which conditions (i) and (ii) hold uniformly. Then the factors $\tau_\pm$ and their inverses belong to S^0 uniformly. If $D_1, \ldots, D_k$ are derivations on this family such that each $D_{i_1} \ldots D_{i_j}\tau$ (with $i_1 < \cdots < i_j$) belongs uniformly to S^{-1} then $D_1 \cdots D_k\tau_\pm \in S^0$ uniformly.

(b) Suppose we have a family of symbols each of which satisfies conditions (i) and (ii) and the conditions $\tau \in S^0, \tau^{-1} \in S^0$ hold uniformly. Suppose further that for each τ there is a Banach algebra B_τ contained in $L_\infty \cap L_2$ such that

(iv) the mappings $i : B_\tau \to L_\infty$ and $P : B_\tau \to B_\tau$ are uniformly bounded,
(v) $1 - \tau^{\pm 1} \in B_\tau$ and the norms $||1 - \tau^{\pm 1}||_{B_\tau}$ are uniformly bounded,
(vi) the operators $W(\tau)\hat{}$ on PB_τ are uniformly invertible,
(vii) for each $k = 1, 2, \ldots$ and each $\delta > 0$

$$\partial_\xi^k \tfrac{\tau(\xi)^{-1} - \tau(\eta)^{-1}}{\xi - \eta}$$

is the kernel of a bounded operator from B_τ to $\langle \xi \rangle^{-k+\delta} L_\infty$ (that is, L_∞ with weight function $\langle \xi \rangle^{k-\delta}$), the norms of these operators being uniformly bounded.

Suppose finally that the symbols $\tau^\dagger$ have analogous properties. Then the factors $\tau_\pm$ and their inverses belong uniformly to S^{0+}. If $D_1, \ldots, D_k$ are derivations such that each $D_{i_1} \cdots D_{i_j} \tau \in S^0 \cap B_\tau$ uniformly then also $D_1 \cdots D_k \tau_\pm \in S^{0+}$ uniformly.

PROOF: We have $P(1 - \tau) \in PL_2$. Set

$$\rho_+ = (W(\tau)\hat{})^{-1} P(1 - \tau).$$

(Eventually τ_+ will be $(1 + \rho_+)^{-1}$.) Of course $\rho_+ \in PL_2$, but we shall show that moreover $\rho_+ \in S^{-1+}$. Write the last relation as

$$PM(\tau)\rho_+ = P(1 - \tau) \tag{16}$$

and apply $PM(\tau^{-1})$ to both sides, writing the result as

$$\rho_+ - PM(\tau^{-1})(I - P)M(\tau)\rho_+ = PM(\tau^{-1})P(1 - \tau). \tag{17}$$

Since P takes the symbol class S^{-1+} to itself [5, Lemma 8.8] and since $\tau^{-1} \in S^0$, $1 - \tau \in S^{-1+}$, we have

$$PM(\tau^{-1})P(1 - \tau) \in S^{-1+}.$$

As for the term $-PM(\tau^{-1})(I - P)M(\tau)\rho_+$, we can write it as

$$[P, M(\tau^{-1})][P, M(\tau)]\rho_+ \tag{18}$$

where the brackets here denote commutators as usual. Now it follows from (14) that $[P, M(\tau)]$ is an integral operator whose kernel is a constant times

$$\tfrac{\tau(\xi) - \tau(\eta)}{\xi - \eta}.$$

Of course in this expression τ can be replaced by $\tau - 1$ which belongs to S^{-1}. Because of this there are estimates.

$$|\partial_\xi^k \tfrac{\tau(\xi)-\tau(\eta)}{\xi-\eta}| \le C\langle\xi\rangle^{-k-1}\langle\eta\rangle^{-1} \qquad (k=0,1,\ldots) \tag{19}$$

(different C's for each k): If

$$|\xi-\eta| \le \tfrac{1}{2}|\xi| \text{ or } |\xi-\eta| \le \tfrac{1}{2}|\eta|$$

we use the identity

$$\partial_\xi^k \tfrac{\tau(\xi)-\tau(\eta)}{\xi-\eta} = \int_0^1 t^k \tau^{(k+1)}(t\xi+(1-t)\eta)dt \tag{20}$$

and the fact $\tau^{(k+1)} \in S^{-k-2}$ to obtain the estimate; if neither inequality holds it is obtained more directly.

It follows from (19) applied to τ^{-1} and the fact

$$[P, M(\tau)]\rho_+ \in L_2$$

that there are estimates

$$|\partial_\xi^k [P, M(\tau^{-1})][P, M(\tau)]\rho_+| \le C\langle\xi\rangle^{-k-1}.$$

In other words, that $[P, M(\tau^{-1})][P, M(\tau)]\rho_+ \in S^{-1}$. Thus both the right side and second term on the left in (17) belong to S^{-1+}. Hence so does ρ_+.

If we define ρ_- by

$$\tau(1+\rho_+) = 1+\rho_- \tag{21}$$

then it follows from (16) that

$$\rho_- = (I-P)(1-\tau) + (I-P)\tau\rho_+$$

and so $\rho_- \in PL_2 \cap S^{-1+}$.

Let us now repeat everything for the symbol $\tau^\dagger$ and take the transpose of both sides of the identity (21) for it. We obtain one of the form

$$(1+\tilde\rho_+)\tau^{-1} = 1+\tilde\rho_- \tag{22}$$

where $\tilde\rho_\pm \in PL_2 \cap S^{-1+}$. Combining (21) and (22) gives

$$(1+\rho_+)(1+\tilde\rho_+) = (1+\rho_-)(1+\tilde\rho_-)$$

and a standard argument tells us that both sides equal 1. If we set

$$\tau_+ = (1+\rho_+)^{-1} = (1+\tilde\rho_+), \quad \tau_- = (1+\rho_-) = (1+\tilde\rho_-)^{-1}$$

then we have our factorization $\tau = \tau_-\tau_+$ with $\tau_\pm \in S^0$, $\tau_\pm^{-1} \in S^0$. (In fact these symbols differ from 1 by a symbol in S^{-1+}.) That the factors $\tau_\pm$ and their inverses have bounded analytic extensions into their respective half-planes follows by standard argument.

PROOF OF (a): All estimates in the argument just given are uniform for any family of symbols satisfying (i) and (ii) uniformly. For the statement concerning derivations, let D be one such that $D\tau \in S^{-1}$ uniformly. Applying D to both sides of (16) gives

$$PM(\tau)D\rho_+ = -PD\tau - PM(D\tau)\rho_+. \tag{23}$$

The right side belongs uniformly to S^{-1+}. The argument we gave above really showed that if the right side of (16) belonged to S^{-1+} then so did the solution ρ_+. Applying this to (23) shows that $D\rho_+ \in S^{-1+}$. Thus also $D\tau_+^{-1} \in S^{-1+}$ and so

$$D\tau_+ = -\tau_+(D\tau_+^{-1})\tau_+ \in S^{-1+}$$

and

$$D\tau_- = (D\tau)\tau_+^{-1} + \tau(D\tau_+^{-1}) \in S^{-1+}.$$

We leave to the reader the inductive proof of the assertion for a product of derivations.

PROOF OF (b): Because of (iv) and (v) the right side of (16) belongs to B_τ (with uniformly bounded norms; we shall no longer keep adding such phrases). Hence, because of (vi), so does ρ_+.

Next we claim that if we have a family of symbols σ, each of negative order and belonging to S^{0+} uniformly, and for which $P\sigma \in L_\infty$ uniformly, then $P\tau \in S^{0+}$ uniformly. For, since P commutes with differentiation we have

$$(P\sigma)' = P\sigma' \in S^{-1+}$$

uniformly. We have used once again the fact that P takes S^{-1+} to itself. Integrating from 0 to ξ and using the uniform boundedness of $P\sigma(0)$ establishes the claim.

If we use this fact twice, together with both parts of (iv) and with (v), we see that the right side of (17) belongs to S^{0+}. We turn to the second term on the left and the representation (19) for it. Of course

$$[P, M(\tau)]\rho_+ \in B_\tau, \quad [P, M(\tau^{-1})][P, M(\tau)]\rho_+ \in B_\tau \subset L_\infty.$$

But then assumption (vii), which is a substitute for estimates (19) in this part, tells us that for $k \geq 1$

$$\partial_\xi^k [P, M(\tau^{-1})][P, M(\tau)]\rho_+ \in \langle\xi\rangle^{-k+\delta} L_\infty$$

for each $\delta > 0$. And this shows

$$[P, M(\tau^{-1})][P, M(\tau)]\rho_+ \in S^{0+}.$$

Hence $\rho_+ \in S^{0+}$. By applying everything to $\tau^\dagger$ and proceeding as we did earlier we deduce $\tau_\pm^{-1}, \tau_\pm \in S^{0+}$. And the statement involving derivations is proved just as in part (a), using (23) for one derivation and applying an inductive argument for the product of several. This completes the proof of the lemma.

Remark: Lemma 1(a) will not be quite good enough when it comes to the case $r \le 1$. We would like to have the following improvement of it.

For any $\theta \in (0,1)$ the symbol class S^{-1} in the statement of Lemma 1(a) may be broadened to $S^{-\theta}$ and the condition (15) strengthened to

$$\tau_\pm(\xi) - 1 \in S^{-\theta}.$$

That this is so for any $\theta > \frac{1}{2}$ is easily seen by checking the proof. We have $PS^{-\theta} \subset S^{-\theta}$, $1-\tau \in L_2$ and the estimate (19) is good enough. The only problem with $\theta \le 1/2$ is that we no longer have $1-\tau \in L_2$, and that is definitely a problem. However we do know that $1-\tau$ belongs to any weighted L_2 space

$$L_{2,\nu} = \{\tau : \langle\xi\rangle^{-\nu}\tau(\xi) \in L_2\}$$

with $\theta + \nu > 1/2$. If $\nu < 1/2$ then P is bounded in this space (this is well known - see [2, Lemma 5.3] for example) and therefore $W(\tau)\hat{}$ is a bounded operator on $PL_{2,\nu}$. And we leave it to the reader to check that the above-stated improvement of Lemma 1(a) holds for $\theta \le 1/2$ if assumption (ii) is replaced by the following.

The operators $W(\tau)\hat{}$ and $W(\tau^\dagger)\hat{}$ are invertible on $PL_{2,\nu}$ for some ν satisfying $\theta + \nu > 1/2$ $(\nu < 1/2)$.

Next we consider the factorization of other nice symbols, ones that need not have the same limiting behavior at $\pm\infty$ and ones that need not have order zero.

Given two positive definite matrices a_- and a_+ let $\varphi(a_-, a_+, \xi)$ be any C^∞ positive definite matrix-valued function equal to a_- for $\xi \le -1$ and to a_+ for $\xi \ge 1$. Such a function is easy to find. The matrix

$$a_+^{1/2}\ a_-^{-1}\ a_+^{1/2}$$

is positive and so has a self-adjoint logarithm. Write

$$b = \tfrac{1}{2\pi i} \log a_+^{1/2}\ a_-^{-1}\ a_+^{1/2} \tag{24}$$

and consider the matrix-valued function

$$(\xi + i)^b = exp\{b \log\langle\xi\rangle + ib\ arg(\xi + i)\}$$

where we take $0 < arg(\xi + i) < \pi$. Because ib is self-adjoint this function is bounded, indeed it belongs to S^0. It also belongs to H_∞^-, the functions on R extending to bounded analytic functions in the upper half-plane. The same statements held for the inverse of this function, and analogously

$$(\xi - i)^{\pm b} \in S^0 \cap H_\infty^+$$

where we take $-\pi < arg(\xi - i) < 0$.

LEMMA 2. *Suppose $\tau \in S^s$ is elliptic, the operators $W(\langle\xi\rangle^{-s}\tau)$ and $W(\langle\xi\rangle^{s}\tau^\dagger)$ are invertible on $L_2(R^+)$, and there are complex numbers μ with $|\mu| = 1, \mu \neq -1$ and positive definite matrices $a_\pm$ such that*

$$\langle\xi\rangle^{-s}\tau(\xi) - \mu\varphi(a_-, a_+, \xi) \in S^{-1}. \tag{25}$$

Then there is an elliptic factorization $\tau = \tau_-\tau_+$ which can be uniquely determined by the condition

$$\tau_+(\xi) \sim \mu^{1/2}\xi^{b+s/2}a_+^{1/2} \qquad (\xi \to +\infty) \tag{26}$$

where b is given by (24) and $\mu^{1/2}$ is determined by $|arg\mu| < \pi$. The conclusion holds uniformly for any family of symbols satisfying the assumptions uniformly. For any derivations $D_1, \ldots, D_k$ satisfying the conditions

$$D_{i_1}\cdots D_{i_j}(\langle\xi\rangle^{-s}\tau(\xi) - \mu\varphi(a_-, a_\tau\xi)) \in S^{-1}$$

uniformly the symbols $D_1\cdots D_k\tau_\pm$ lie in $S^{s/2}$ uniformly.

PROOF: Assume first that $s = 0$ and consider the function

$$(\xi + i)^b\varphi(a_-, a_+, \xi)a_+^{-1/2}(\xi - i)^{-b}$$

$$= (\xi + i)^b[\varphi(a_-, a_+, \xi)a_+^{-1/2}(\tfrac{\xi+i}{\xi-i})^b](\xi + i)^{-b}. \tag{27}$$

The factor $[(\xi + i)/(\xi - i)]^b$ is a symbol of order zero which for positive ξ belongs to $1 + S^{-1}$ (that is, the symbol minus 1 satisfies for $\xi > 0$ the estimates for the class S^{-1}) and for negative ξ belongs to $a_+^{1/2}a_-^{-1}a_+^{1/2} + S^{-1}$. It follows that the expression in brackets on the right side of (27) belongs to $a_+^{1/2} + S^{-1}$, and therefore so also does the right side itself.

It follows from what we have just shown, and our assumption on τ, that

$$\mu^{-1}(\xi + i)^b\tau(\xi)a_+^{-1/2}(\xi - i)^{-b} = a_+^{1/2}\tilde{\tau}(\xi)$$

where $\tilde{\tau} \in 1 + S^{-1}$. Of course $\tilde{\tau}^{-1} \in S^0$ since τ is elliptic. To apply Lemma 1(a) to $\tilde{\tau}$ we have to show that $W(\tilde{\tau})$ and $W(\tilde{\tau}^\dagger)$ are invertible operators on $L_2(R^+)$. For this we shall use the well-known fact that invertibility is not affected by left (resp. right) multiplication by a function which together with its inverse belongs to H_∞^- (resp. H_∞^+). Of course the factors $a_+^{\pm 1/2}$ are irrelevant. Hence the invertibility of $W(\tilde{\tau})$ is equivalent to the assumed invertibility of $W(\tau)$. Similarly the invertibility of $W(\tilde{\tau}^\dagger)$ follows from that of $W(\tau^\dagger)$. The elliptic factorization $\tilde{\tau} = \tilde{\tau}_-\ \tilde{\tau}_+$ assured by Lemma 1(a) yields the desired factorization of τ, with factors

$$\tau_-(\xi) = \mu^{1/2}(\xi+i)^{-b}a_+^{1/2}\tilde{\tau}_-(\xi)$$
$$\tau_+(\xi) = \mu^{1/2}\tilde{\tau}_+(\xi)(\xi-i)^{b}a_+^{1/2}.$$

For the statement concerning derivations we observe that our assumption implies that $\tilde{\tau}$ satisfies the analogous requirement in the statement of Lemma 1(a) that guarantees $D_1 \dots D_k\tilde{\tau} \in S^0$, and this implies $D_1 \dots D_k\tau_\pm \in S^0$.

This concludes the proof in the case $s = 0$. For general s the minus factor τ_- is simply $(\xi+i)^{s/2}$ times the minus factor of $\langle\xi\rangle^{-s}\tau(\xi)$ while τ_+ is $(\xi-i)^{s/2}$ times the plus factor of $\langle\xi\rangle^{-s}\tau(\xi)$.

Remark: In analogy with the remark following the proof of Lemma 1(a) we have the following:

For any $\theta \in (0,1)$ the symbol class S^{-1} in (25) may be broadened to $S^{-\theta}$ and the normalization (26) strengthened to

$$\tau_+(\xi) \in \mu^{1/2}\ \xi^{b+s/2}(a_+^{1/2} + S^{-\theta}) \qquad (\xi > 0)$$

if, for $\theta \le 1/2$, the invertibility condition on the Wiener-Hopf operators is taken to refer to the space $PL_{2,\nu}$ for some ν satisfying $\theta + \nu > 1/2 \quad (\nu < 1/2)$.

PROOF OF THE MAIN RESULT

We shall prove it first in the one-dimensional case, but with parameters. This will enable us easily to extend it to higher dimensions. We begin with a criterion for invertibility of Weiner-Hopf operators on weighted L_2 spaces. It generalizes the criterion for ordinary L_2 that the numerical ranges of the symbol values lie in a compact convex set not containing zero.

LEMMA 3. *Suppose $\tau \in L_\infty$ and the numerical ranges of all the matrices $\tau(\xi)$ lie in a region*

$$\gamma_1 \le arg\ z \le \gamma_2, \qquad |z| \ge \delta$$

where

$$2\pi\nu + \gamma_2 - \gamma_1 < \pi. \tag{28}$$

Then $W(\tau)\hat{}$ is an invertible operator on $PL_{2,\nu}$ and the norm of its inverse is bounded by a constant depending only on δ and $\gamma_2 - \gamma_1$.

PROOF: We may clearly replace our wedge by

$$-\gamma - \pi\nu \leq arg\ z \leq \gamma - \pi\nu \tag{29}$$

where $2\gamma = \gamma_2 - \gamma_1$. We shall prove an estimate

$$\|\langle\xi\rangle^{-\nu} P\tau f\|_2 \geq \delta_1 \|\langle\xi\rangle^{-\nu} f\|_2 \tag{30}$$

for all $f \in PL_{2,\nu}$. Since

$$PL_{2,\nu} = (\xi - i)^{\nu} PL_2$$

we can rewrite (30) equivalently as

$$\|(\xi + i)^{-\nu} P(\xi - i)^{\nu}\tau f\|_2 \geq \delta_1 \|f\|_2 \qquad (f \in PL_2).$$

Assume $\|f\|_2 = 1$. Then

$$\begin{aligned}\|(\xi + i)^{-\nu} P(\xi - i)^{\nu}\tau f\|_2 &\geq Re\ ((\xi + i)^{-\nu} P(\xi - i)^{\nu}\tau f, f) \\ &= Re(P(\xi - i)^{\nu}\tau f, (\xi - i)^{-\nu} f).\end{aligned}$$

Now we may have assumed that actually $(\xi - i)^{\nu} f \in L_2$ since such f's form a dense subspace of PL_2. Since

$$(I - P)(\xi - i)^{\nu}\tau f$$

belongs to $(PL_2)^{\perp}$ we can drop the P in the last expression and so find that

$$\|(\xi + i)^{-\nu} P(\xi - i)^{\nu}\tau f\|_2 \geq Re \int_{-\infty}^{\infty} (\tfrac{\xi - i}{\xi + i})^{\nu} (\tau(\xi) f(\xi), f(\xi)) d\xi.$$

Now the function $[(\xi - i)/(\xi + i)]^{\nu}$ has absolute value 1 and its argument lies in the interval $(0, 2\pi\nu)$. It follows from this and (29) that the numerical range of this function times $\tau(\xi)$ lies in the region

$$-\gamma - \pi\nu \leq arg\ z \leq \gamma + \pi\nu, \qquad |z| \geq \delta.$$

It follows that the right side of the above inequality is at least

$$\delta \cos(\gamma + \pi\nu)$$

and this is our δ_1 in (30). Note that the assumption (28) implies $\gamma + \pi\nu < \pi/2$.

To finish the proof of invertibility (with the norm of the inverse bounded by δ_1) we have to show that $W(\tau)^{\wedge}$ has dense range. Now each linear functional L on

$PL_{2,\nu}$ is obtained from a function $f \in PL_2$ by setting

$$Lh = ((\xi - i)^{-\nu} f, h).$$

If L annihilates the range of $W(\tau)\hat{}$ then we have for all $g \in PL_2$

$$0 = ((\xi - i)^{-\nu} f,\ P\tau(\xi - i)^{\nu} g),$$

since $PL_{2,\nu} = (\xi - i)^{\nu} PL_2$. But the right side of this with $g = f$ is equal to

$$((\xi - i)^{-\nu} f, \tau(\xi - i)^{\nu} f)$$

which we have already shown to be nonzero if $f \neq 0$. Hence $L = 0$ and $W(\tau)\hat{}$ has dense range, as desired.

We can now prove the one-dimensional version of the main result, with parameters.

LEMMA 4. *Assume $\sigma \in S^{-r}$ is elliptic and positive definite matrix-valued and there are matrices $a_\pm$ such that*

$$\langle\xi\rangle^r \sigma - \varphi(a_-, a_+, \xi) \in S^{-1}.$$

Then for each $\lambda \notin \overline{R^+}$ there is an order zero elliptic factorization.

$$\sigma - \lambda = \sigma^- \sigma^+ \tag{31}$$

uniquely determined by the normalizations

$$\lim_{\xi \to \pm\infty} \sigma^\pm = (-\lambda)^{1/2}.$$

For each $\varepsilon > 0$ and each $\delta \in [0,1]$ the factors satisfy

$$(\sigma^\pm)^{-1} \in |\lambda|^{-\delta/2} S^{\frac{1}{2}(1-\delta)r+} \tag{32}$$

uniformly for $\lambda \in \Lambda_\varepsilon$. If we have a family of symbols for which the assumptions hold uniformly then so does the conclusion. If $D_1, \ldots, D_k$ are derivations (which may include $\lambda\partial_\lambda$) such that each

$$D_{i_1} \ldots D_{i_j}(\langle\xi\rangle^r \sigma - \varphi(a_-, a_+, \xi)) \in S^{-1}$$

uniformly then the analogue of (32) holds for $D_1 \ldots D_k(\sigma^\pm)^{-1}$.

PROOF: First we note that nothing changes in hypothesis or conclusion if we multiply σ by a positive constant. At one point in the proof (in handling the case $r \leq 1/2$) we shall say that we could have begun by multiplying σ by a small positive constant. How small depends on σ itself and r.

Next we show that the assertions of the lemma hold when λ is bounded away from zero. This is very easy, and indeed much more is true. The reason is that we can apply Lemma 1(a) to the symbol family $1 - \lambda^{-1}\sigma$. The only assumption that is not obvious is the one concerning Wiener-Hopf invertibility. But notice that for each λ the essential ranges of the matrices $1 - \lambda^{-1}\sigma(\xi)$ lie in $1 - \lambda^{-1}R^+$ and the distance from 0 to the convex hull of this is bounded below by a constant depending only on ε and $inf|\lambda|$. So condition (ii) is satisfied and Lemma 1(a) gives us an elliptic factorization of $1-\lambda^{-1}\sigma$, normalized so the factors have limit 1 at $\pm\infty$, which for families with derivations (including $\lambda\partial_\lambda$) has the properties stated there. Our factors $\sigma^\pm$ are $(-\lambda)^{1/2}$ times the factors for $1 - \lambda^{-1}\sigma$. So we find that in fact for λ bounded away from zero

$$(\sigma^\pm)^{-1} \in |\lambda|^{-1/2} S^0$$

with the same conclusion for any $D_1 \dots D_k(\sigma^\pm)^{-1}$. This is of course stronger than (32).

So we may assume that $|\lambda|$ is arbitrarily small and begin with the order $-r$ elliptic factorization

$$\sigma = \sigma_- \sigma_+$$

given by Lemma 2. The Weiner-Hopf invertibility conditions are satisfied because the relevant essential ranges lie in a compact subset of $(0, \infty)$. Because σ is self-adjoint we must have, by a familiar argument,

$$\sigma_- = \sigma_+^* c$$

for some constant matrix c. But as $\xi \to +\infty$ we have, according to the normalization (26),

$$\sigma_+(\xi) \sim \xi^{b-r/2} a_+^{1/2} \tag{33}$$

and so

$$\sigma_-(\xi) = \sigma(\xi)\sigma_+(\xi)^{-1} \sim a_+^{1/2} \xi^{-b-r/2}. \tag{34}$$

Since ib is self-adjoint (33) gives

$$\sigma_+(\xi)^* \sim a_+^{1/2} \xi^{-b-r/2}.$$

Comparing these last two relations shows that c must be the identity matrix and so σ_- and σ_+ are mutual adjoints.

Next, we write

$$\tau(\xi) = \sigma_-(\xi)^{-1}\sigma_+(\xi)^{-1}.$$

This is a positive definite matrix-valued elliptic symbol of order r and we consider the factorization of

$$1 - sgn\lambda\ \tau(\xi).$$

For the behavior of this symbol at $\pm\infty$ observe that, by the remark following the proof of Lemma 2, we can strengthen (33) to

$$\sigma_+(\xi) \in \xi^{b-r/2}a_+^{1/2}(1+S^{-\theta}) \qquad (\xi > 0)$$

for any $\theta \in (0,1)$. It follows that

$$\sigma_-(\xi) \in \xi^{-b-r/2}a_+^{1/2}(1+S^{-\theta}) \qquad (\xi > 0)$$

and so

$$\tau(\xi) \in \xi^{r}a_+^{-1}(1+S^{-\theta}) \qquad (\xi > 0).$$

Similarly $\tau(\xi) \in |\xi|^{r/2}a_-^{-1}(1+S^{-\theta})$ for $\xi < 0$ and we can conclude that

$$\langle\xi\rangle^{-r}(1 - sgn\lambda\ \tau(\xi)) + sgn\lambda\ \varphi(a_-^{-1}, a_+^{-1}, \xi) \in S^{-\theta}$$

for any θ satisfying

$$0 < \theta < 1, \quad \theta \le r. \tag{35}$$

We want to apply Lemma 2, as modified in the remark following its proof, to $1 - sgn\lambda\ \tau(\xi)$. Now the numerical ranges of the matrices

$$\langle\xi\rangle^{-r}(1 - sgn\lambda\ \tau(\xi))$$

lie in a compact subset of $R^+ - sgn\lambda\ R^+$ and so are bounded away from zero. They also lie in the wedge

$$arg\ z \text{ between } 0 \text{ and } arg(-\lambda)$$

which has opening at most $\pi - \varepsilon$. So the Wiener-Hopf operators are invertible on PL_2 and we have our nice order r elliptic factorization when $r > 1/2$, because then we can find $\theta > 1/2$ satisfying (35). For $r \le 1/2$ choose any ν satisfying

$$\tfrac{1}{2} - r < \nu < \tfrac{1}{2}$$

and then any θ satisfying $1/2 - \nu < \theta \le r$. To be sure the Wiener-Hopf operators are invertible on the spaces $PL_{2,\nu}$ we apply Lemma 3. The numerical ranges are bounded away from zero, as we have seen, so it is a question of the angle of the smallest wedge with vertex 0 which contains the numerical range of $1 - sgn\lambda\ \tau(\xi)$. And it is here that we use the observation made at the very beginning of this proof that we could have begun by multiplying σ by a small positive constant. For the numerical ranges of the values of the τ corresponding to σ lie in some interval $[\delta, \infty]$ with $\delta > 0$. The numerical ranges of the values of the τ corresponding to $c\sigma$ lie in $(c^{-1}\delta, \infty)$ and so the numerical ranges of the values of the $1 - sgn\lambda\ \tau$ corresponding to $c\sigma$ lie in the set

$$1 - sgn\lambda\,[c^{-1}\delta, \infty)$$

and this set is contained in a wedge around $arg\ z = arg(-\lambda)$ of opening which can be made arbitrarily small by taking c small enough. If this opening is small enough then (28) is satisfied. A similar argument applies to $(1 - sgn\ \lambda\ \tau(\xi))^\dagger$ and we have our order r elliptic factorization

$$1 - sgn\lambda\ \tau(\xi) = \tau_-(\xi)\tau_+(\xi).$$

Notice that the b for $1 - \lambda\tau$ is $-b$ and so the normalization (26) is

$$\tau_+(\xi) \sim \xi^{-b+r/2} a_+^{-1/2}(-sgn\lambda)^{1/2}.$$

What we have done so far gives

$$\begin{aligned}\sigma(\xi) - \lambda &= \sigma_-(\xi)[1 - \lambda\ \tau(\xi)]\sigma_+(\xi)\\ &= \sigma_-(\xi)\tau_-(|\lambda|^{1/r}\xi)\alpha(\xi)\tau_+(|\lambda|^{1/r}\xi)\sigma_+(\xi)\end{aligned}$$

where we have set

$$\alpha(\xi) = \tau_-(|\lambda|^{1/r}\xi)^{-1}[1 - \lambda\ \tau(\xi)]\ \tau_+(|\lambda|^{1/r}\xi)^{-1}. \tag{36}$$

This α is the not-so-nice family of symbols whose factorization will be handled by Lemma 1(b). The family of Banach spaces B_τ, which we shall write B_λ since they depend only on λ, are the $|\lambda|^{1/r}$-dilations of the space $L_2 \cap \text{Lip}\ \theta$ where now θ denotes any number in the interval

$$(0, \min(1, r)). \tag{37}$$

Recall that $L_2 \cap \text{Lip}\ \theta$ is the Banach space with norm

$$\|f\|_2 + sup_{|\xi-\eta|\le 1}|f(\xi) - f(\eta)|^\theta. \tag{38}$$

It is continuously embedded in L_∞ and is a Banach algebra if the norm is taken to be some sufficiently large multiple of (38). These things are easy to check. Our space B_λ

consists of those functions $f(\xi)$ such that the function $f(|\lambda|^{-1/r}\xi)$ belongs to $L_2 \cap \mathrm{Lip}\,\theta$, and we define

$$\|f\|_{B_\lambda} = \|f(|\lambda|^{-1/r}\xi)\|_{L_2\cap \mathrm{Lip}\,\theta}.$$

(Of course the set B_λ is the same as the set $L_2 \cap \mathrm{Lip}\,\theta$, but the norms are different.) Conditions (iv) of Lemma 1(b) hold for these spaces by the remarks just made, the invariance of $\|\ \|_\infty$ under dilation, the fact that P commutes with dilation, and familiar boundedness properties of P on L_2 and Lipθ spaces [4, Theorem 106]. We shall verify first that $\alpha(\xi)$ satisfies conditions (v) and (vi), then that $\alpha, \alpha^{-1} \in S^0$ uniformly, and finally that $\alpha(\xi)$ satisfies condition (vii).

Condition (v): Write

$$\beta(\xi) = \alpha(|\lambda|^{-1/r}\xi) = \tau_-(\xi)^{-1}[1 - \lambda\,\tau(|\lambda|^{-1/r}\xi)]\tau_+(\xi)^{-1}. \tag{39}$$

For $\xi \geq 1$ we have $\tau(\xi) = a_+^{-1}\ \xi^r + O(\xi^{r-1})$ and so for $\xi \geq |\lambda|^{1/r}$ we have

$$1 - \lambda\tau(|\lambda|)^{-1/r}\xi) = 1 - sgn\lambda\, a_+^{-1}\ \xi^r + O(|\lambda|^{1/r}|\xi|^{r-1}).$$

If $r \geq 1$ the error estimate is $O(|\lambda|^{1/r}\langle\xi\rangle^{r-1})$ but for $r \leq 1$ we have to take into account the possibility that $|\xi|$ is small. In fact if $r \leq 1$ the inequality $|\xi| \geq |\lambda|^{1/r}$ shows that the error is $O(|\lambda|^{1/r}$. Hence in any case we can write

$$1 - \lambda\tau(|\lambda|^{-1/r}\xi) = sgn\lambda\, a_+^{-1}\xi^r + O(|\lambda|^{\min(1,1/r)}\langle\xi\rangle^{r-1}) \tag{40}$$

for $\xi \geq |\lambda|^{1/r}$. The same estimate clearly holds for $0 \leq \xi \leq |\lambda|^{1/r}$ and a similar relation holds for $\xi \leq 0$.

We deduce in particular from (40) that

$$1 - \lambda\tau(|\lambda|^{-1/r}\xi) = 1 - sgn\lambda\,\tau(\xi) + O(\langle\xi\rangle^{r-1}).$$

Since $\tau_\pm(\xi)^{-1}$ are symbols of order $-r/2$ satisfying

$$\tau_-(\xi)^{-1}[1 - sgn\lambda\,\tau(\xi)]\tau_+(\xi)^{-1} = 1$$

we have

$$\beta(\xi) = 1 + O(\langle\xi\rangle^{-1}). \tag{41}$$

In particular we have $1 - \beta \in L_2$ (uniformly, of course, in λ).

To show $\beta \in \mathrm{Lip}\theta$ we shall estimate $\beta'(\xi)$. But first, let us estimate $\beta(\xi)$ itself in the most trivial way. The product $\tau_-(\xi)^{-1}\tau_+(\xi)^{-1}$ is of course $O(\langle\xi\rangle^{-r})$ while the rest of the right side of (39) has the estimate

$$O(|\lambda|\langle\xi\rangle^{-r}\langle|\lambda|^{-1/r}\xi\rangle^r).$$

And this is seen to be $O(1)$ by checking, as usual, the two cases $|\xi| \leq |\lambda|^{1/r}$ and $|\xi| \geq |\lambda|^{1/r}$. We bound $\beta'(\xi)$ by applying the product rule and estimating in the same simple way. Differentiating one of the factors $\tau_\pm(\xi)^{-1}$ in (39) yields an extra factor $\langle\xi\rangle^{-1}$ (since the factor belongs to the symbol space $S^{-r/2}$) while differentiating the inner factor gives a term

$$O(|\lambda|^{1-\frac{1}{r}}\langle\xi\rangle^{-r}\langle|\lambda|^{-1/r}\xi\rangle^{r-1}).$$

If $|\xi|\le|\lambda|^{1/r}$ this is $O(|\lambda|^{1-\frac{1}{r}})$ while if $|\xi|\ge|\lambda|^{1/r}$ it is $O(\langle\xi\rangle^{-r}|\xi|^{r-1})$. So if $r\ge 1$ this is bounded. If $r\le 1$ it is bounded for $|\xi|\ge 1$ and $O(|\xi|^{r-1})$ for $|\xi|\le 1$. Thus

$$\beta'(\xi)=O(1+|\xi|^{\min(0,r-1)}) \tag{42}$$

uniformly in λ. And it follows from this, in a straightforward way that, $\beta\in\text{Lip}\ \theta$ for any θ in the interval (37).

So we have shown that $\|1-\beta\|_{L_2\cap\text{Lip}\ \theta}$ is uniformly bounded in λ. The analogous statement for $1-\beta^{-1}$ will follow from (41) and our estimate for $\beta'(\xi)$ if we can show that the norms $\|\beta^{-1}\|_{L_\infty}$ are uniformly bounded. However, it follows from (40) and its analogue for $\xi\le 0$ that

$$\lim_{|\lambda|\to 0}\beta(\xi)=\tau_-(\xi)^{-1}(1-sgn\lambda\, a_\pm|\xi|^r)\tau_+(\xi)^{-1} \tag{43}$$

in the space $L_2\cap L_\infty$ where $a_\pm$ denotes a_+ for $\xi>0$ and a_- for $\xi<0$. This function is clearly bounded away from zero so we do have the desired estimate on the norms $\|\beta^{-1}\|_{L_\infty}$, at least for sufficiently small $|\lambda|$. Thus, the conditions (v) for α, and similarly the conditions for $\alpha^\dagger$, are satisfied for sufficiently small λ.

Condition (vi): To establish this we shall use the following criterion for convergence in $L_2\cap\text{Lip}\ \theta$.

(*) Suppose $f_n\to f$ in $L_2\cap L_\infty$ and for some $\theta'>\theta$ we have

$$|f_n'(\xi)|=O(1+|\xi|^{\theta'-1}) \tag{44}$$

uniformly in n. Then $f_n\to f$ in $L_2\cap\text{Lip}\ \theta$.

To prove this we may assume without loss of generality that $f=0$. The conclusion will follow if we can show that

$$\lim|\xi_n-\eta_n|^{-\theta}[f_n(\xi_n)-f_n(\eta_n)]\to 0 \tag{45}$$

for any sequences $\{\xi_n\},\{\eta_n\}$ satisfying $|\xi_n-\eta_n|\le 1$. This assertion in general will follow if we can prove it in the two special cases

(*a*) $|\xi_n-\eta_n|$ bounded away from 0;

(*b*) $|\xi_n-\eta_n|\to 0$.

In case (a), (45) holds because $f_n\to 0$ in L_∞. In case (b), we use Hölder's inequality where, in the standard notation for it, p is chosen so that

(46) $$p^{-1} > \theta, \quad q^{-1} > 1 - \theta'.$$

Application of the inequality gives

$$|\xi_n - \eta_n|^{-\theta} |f_n(\xi_n) - f_n(\eta_n)| \le |\xi_n - \eta_n|^{p^{-1}-\theta} \{ \int_{\eta_n}^{\xi_n} |f_n'(t)|^q \}^{1/q}.$$

By (b) and the first part of (46) the first factor tends to zero. By (44) and the second part of (46) the second factor is bounded. This establishes (45).

We shall now show that $W(\alpha)^\wedge$ is invertible on PB_λ uniformly for sufficiently small $|\lambda|$. It suffices to establish the uniform invertibility of $W(\beta)^\wedge$ on $H_2 \cap \mathrm{Lip}\ \theta$ where we have written $H_2 = PL_2$ as usual. Denote the right side of (43) by β_0. We have already seen that $\beta \to \beta_0$ in $L_2 \cap L_\infty$ as $|\lambda| \to \infty$. The estimate (42) and criterion (*) show that we have convergence in $L_2 \cap \mathrm{Lip}\ \theta$. Hence, the uniform invertibility of $W(\beta)^\wedge$ for small $|\lambda|$ would be a consequence of the invertibility of $W(\beta_0)^\wedge$. The first step in establishing this is to show that $W(\beta_0)$ is Fredholm.

The operator $I - W(\beta_0)^\wedge W(\beta_0^{-1})^\wedge$ equals the product

$$[P, M(\beta_0)][P, M(\beta_0^{-1})].$$

The right factor is bounded from $H_2 \cap \mathrm{Lip}\ \theta$ to $L_2 \cap \mathrm{Lip}\ \theta$ and the left has kernel a constant times

$$\frac{\beta_0(\xi) - \beta_0(\eta)}{\xi - \eta}.$$

If $1 - \beta_0$ belonged to C_c^∞ this could easily be shown to be the kernel of a compact operator on $L_2 \cap \mathrm{Lip}\ \theta$. However β_0 does satisfy

$$\beta_0'(\xi) = \begin{cases} O(|\xi|^{\min(0, r-1)}), & |\xi| \le 1 \\ O(|\xi|^{-1}), & |\xi| \ge 1. \end{cases}$$

(In fact for ξ bounded away from zero β_0 satisfies the estimates for a symbol of negative order.) Using this and criterion (*) we can see that convolving β_0 in the usual way by an approximate identity of functions in C_c^∞ yields a sequence of C_c^∞ functions converging to β_0 in $L_2 \cap \mathrm{Lip}\ \theta$. Thus $[P, M(\beta_0)]$ is compact and $W(\beta_0)^\wedge$ is Fredholm as claimed.

The next step is to show that $W(\beta_0)^\wedge$ has index zero and for this we consider the family of functions

$$\gamma_t(\xi) = \tau_-(\xi)^{-1}[1 - sgn\lambda\, ((1-t)a_\pm |\xi|^r + t\, \tau(\xi))] \tau_+(\xi)^{-1} \quad (0 \le t \le 1).$$

Using criterion (*) shows that this is a continuous family in $L_2 \cap \mathrm{Lip}\ \theta$. Each is Fredholm, by the argument given above. And we have $\gamma_0(\xi) = \beta_0(\xi)$ and

$$\gamma_1(\xi) = \tau_-(\xi)^{-1}[1 - sgn\lambda\, \tau(\xi)]\tau_+(\xi)^{-1} = 1.$$

Thus $\mathrm{ind}\ W(\beta_0)^\wedge = \mathrm{ind}\ W(1)^\wedge = 0$.

Much more easily, of course, we see that $W(\beta_0)\hat{}$, as an operator on H_2, is Fredholm of index zero. Thus to show invertibility on $H_2 \cap \text{Lip}\ \theta$, it suffices to show invertibility on H_2. Write $\beta_0(\xi)$ as

$$\tau_-(\xi)^{-1}(\xi+i)^{r/2}[\langle\xi\rangle^r(1-sgn\lambda\, a_\pm|\xi|^r)](\xi-i)^{r/2}\tau_+(\xi)^{-1}.$$

The outer factors together with their inverses belong to $H_\infty^\pm$ and so, as already mentioned, have no effect on invertibility. The middle factor has numerical range lying in a compact subset of $R^+ - sgn\lambda\, R^+$ (bounded away from zero) and so the corresponding Wiener-Hopf operator is invertible on H_2.

So the operators $W(\alpha)\hat{}$ are indeed uniformly invertible on PB_λ for $|\lambda|$ sufficiently small. An analogous argument holds for $W(\alpha^\dagger)$ and so condition (vi) is established.

$\alpha(\xi)$ and $\alpha(\xi)^{-1}$ belong to S^0 uniformly: if we apply the product formula to (36) to evaluate $\alpha^{(k)}(\xi)$ we find that it is bounded by a constant times

$$|\lambda|^{k/r}\langle|\lambda|^{1/r}\xi\rangle^{-r-k}+\sum_{j=1}^{k}|\lambda|^{1+(k-j)/r}\langle|\lambda|\xi\rangle^{-r-k+j}\langle\xi\rangle^{r-j}.$$

The first term arises when all k derivatives are applied to the outer factors in (36); the others when $k-j$ derivatives are applied to the outer factors and j to the inner. This expression is bounded by a constant times

$$\text{(47)}\qquad \begin{cases} |\lambda|^{k-r}+\sum_{j=1}^{k}|\lambda|^{1+(k-j)/r}\langle\xi\rangle^{r-j}, & \text{if } |\xi|\le|\lambda|^{-1/r} \\ \langle\xi\rangle^{-k}, & \text{if } |\xi|\ge|\lambda|^{-1/r}. \end{cases}$$

In particular, it is bounded by a constant times $\langle\xi\rangle^{-k}$ uniformly in λ. Of course, the boundedness of $\alpha(\xi)$ has already been established (See (41).) Thus $\alpha\in S^0$. That also $\alpha^{-1}\in S^0$ follows from this and the boundedness of $\|\alpha^{-1}\|_\infty=\|\beta^{-1}\|_\infty$.

Condition (vii). For convenience of notation, we shall replace α^{-1} by α and show that for $k\ge1$

$$\rho(\xi,\eta)=\partial_\xi^k\frac{\alpha(\xi)-\alpha(\eta)}{\xi-\eta}$$

is the kernel of a bounded operator from B_λ to $\langle\xi\rangle^{k+\delta}L_\infty$ for each $\delta>0$. Identity (20) can be applied once again to show that if

$$\text{(48)}\qquad |\xi-\eta|\le\tfrac{1}{2}|\xi| \text{ or } |\xi-\eta|\le\tfrac{1}{2}|\eta|$$

then $\rho(\xi,\eta)$ is bounded by a constant times

$$\text{(49)}\qquad \min(\langle\xi\rangle^{-k-1},\langle\eta\rangle^{-k-1}).$$

We have used, of course, the fact $\alpha^{(k+1)}(\xi)=O(\langle\xi\rangle^{-k-1})$. If neither inequality holds, then the product formula once again shows that $\rho(\xi,\eta)$ is bounded by a constant times

$$(50)\qquad \langle\eta\rangle^{-1}|\alpha^{(k)}(\xi)| + \langle\eta\rangle^{-1-\delta}\langle\xi\rangle^{-k+\delta} + \sum_{j=1}^{k-1}\langle\eta\rangle^{-1-\delta}\langle\xi\rangle^{-j+\delta}|\alpha^{(k-j)}(\xi)|.$$

The first term arises when $\alpha(\xi)-\alpha(\eta)$ is differentiated k times and the second when it is not differentiated at all. Of course we also used the negation of (48).

Now B_λ is embedded (with uniformly bounded norm) in L_∞ and (49) is clearly the kernel of a bounded operator from L_∞ to $\langle\xi\rangle^{-k}L_\infty$. Similarly all terms in (50) but the first are bounded from L_∞ to $\langle\xi\rangle^{-k+\delta}L_\infty$. As for the first, take $f\in B_\lambda$. Then

$$\int\langle\eta\rangle^{-1}|f(\eta)|d\eta \le 2\|f\|_\infty + \int_{|\eta|\ge 1}|\eta|^{-1}|f(\eta)|d\eta$$

and the second integral is at most a constant times

$$\int_{|\eta|\le|\lambda|^{1/r}}|\eta|^{-1}|f(|\lambda|^{-1/r}\eta)|d\eta.$$

The integral over $|\eta|\ge 1$ here is bounded by a constant times

$$\|f(|\lambda|^{-1/r}\eta)\|_2$$

whereas the second is bounded by $\|f\|_\infty$ times $\log|\lambda|^{-1}$. In any case we have

$$\int\langle\eta\rangle^{-1}|f(\eta|d\eta \le C\log|\lambda|^{-1}\|f\|_{B_\lambda}.$$

So it suffices to show that for some C

$$(51)\qquad \langle\xi\rangle^{k-\delta}|\alpha^{(k)}(\xi)|\log|\lambda|^{-1}\le C$$

and we use the estimates (47) for $\alpha^{(k)}(\xi)$. In the case $|\xi|\ge|\lambda|^{-1/r}$ (51) is immediate. In one of the terms appearing in the bound when $|\xi|\le|\lambda|^{-1/r}$ one considers separately the cases $k-\delta+r-j\ge 0$ and <0 and the same estimate follows. Thus condition (vii) is established.

Having shown that $\alpha(\xi)$ satisfies all the conditions stated in Lemma 1(b) we apply that lemma and so obtain a factorization $\alpha=\alpha_-\alpha_+$ with $(\alpha_\pm)^{\pm 1}\in S^{0+}$ uniformly in λ. And so we have the factorization

$$\sigma(\xi)-\lambda=\sigma_-(\xi)\tau_-(|\lambda|^{-1/r}\xi)\alpha_-(\xi)\alpha_+(\xi)\tau_+(|\lambda|^{-1/r}\xi)\sigma_+(\xi).$$

To compare this with (10) we check the normalizations. We have as $\xi\to+\infty$ (see (33) and the displayed formula two before (36))

$$\alpha_+(\xi) \to 1$$

$$\sigma_+(\xi) \sim \xi^{b-\frac{r}{2}} a_+^{1/2}$$

$$\tau_+(|\lambda|^{-1/r}\xi) \sim (|\lambda|^{-1/r}\xi)^{-b+\frac{r}{2}} a_+^{-1/2}(-sgn\lambda)^{1/2} = |\lambda|^{-b/r}(-\lambda)^{1/2}\xi^{-b+\frac{r}{2}} a_+^{-1/2}$$

and so the product of the "plus" factors is $\sim |\lambda|^{-b/r}$. (Note that a_+ commutes with b and so with ξ^b.) Hence the plus factor in (10) is given by

$$\sigma^+(\xi) = |\lambda|^{b/r}\alpha_+(\xi)\tau_+(|\lambda|^{1/r}\xi)\sigma_+(\xi).$$

(Recall that the plus factor is determined by a constant matrix factor on the left.) Similarly we find

$$\sigma^-(\xi) = \sigma_-(\xi)\tau_-(|\lambda|^{1/r}\xi)\alpha_+(\xi)|\lambda|^{-b/r}.$$

We have, uniformly for small $|\lambda|$,

(52) $$|\lambda|^{-b/r} \in L_\infty, \quad \sigma_+(\xi)^{-1} \in S^{r/2}, \quad \alpha_+(\xi)^{-1} \in S^{0+}, \quad \tau_+(\xi)^{-1} \in S^{-r/2},$$

all uniformly for small $|\lambda|$. From the last it is easy to check that for all $\delta \in [0,1]$

(53) $$\tau_+(|\lambda|^{1/r}\xi)^{-1} \in |\lambda|^{-\delta/2} S^{-\delta r/2}$$

and so $(\sigma^+)^{-1} \in |\lambda|^{-\delta/2} S^{\frac{1}{2}(1-\delta)r+}$ as required, and similarly for $(\sigma^-)^{-1}$.

We pass to consideration of the derivations and only outline the argument here. Notice that since our factors are analytic in λ (it is clear from the proof of Lemma 1(a) that if the symbol depends analytically on a parameter then so do the factors) we may replace the derivation $\lambda\partial_\lambda$ by $|\lambda|\partial_{|\lambda|}$. The first term in (52) is affected only by this derivation and behaves well under it. The second and fourth terms are not affected by $|\lambda|\partial_{|\lambda|}$ and behave well under the others, by the last assertion of Lemma 1(a). From this it follows easily that

$$D_1 \cdots D_k \tau_+(|\lambda|^{1/r}\xi)^{-1} \in |\lambda|^{-\delta/2} S^{-\delta r/2}$$

even if one of the derivations here is $|\lambda|\partial_{|\lambda|}$. For the final term $\alpha_+(\xi)^{-1}$, it is a matter of checking that $\alpha(\xi)$ verifies the conditions of the last part of Lemma 1(b). The verification that

$$D_{i_1} \cdots D_{i_j}\alpha \in S^0$$

involves estimates no different from those leading to (47). For the verification that this belongs to B_λ we use the fact that the D's commute with dilations to reduce this to the question of whether

$$D_{i_1}\cdots D_{i_j}\beta \in L_2 \cap \text{Lip }\theta.$$

Of course

$$1-\beta(\xi) = \tau_-(\xi)^{-1}[\lambda\tau(|\lambda|^{1/r}\xi) - sgn\lambda\,\tau(\xi)]\tau_+(\xi)^{-1}$$

and the proof that $D_{i_1}\cdots D_{i_j}$ of this belongs to $L_2 \cap \text{Lip }\theta$ follows the same lines as the proof that $1-\beta \in L_2 \cap \text{Lip }\theta$. This completes the proof of the lemma.

PROOF OF THE MAIN RESULT: We may assume $|\xi'| \geq 1$ since otherwise we may treat ξ' as a harmless C^∞-parameter and apply Lemma 3 to $\sigma(\xi', \xi)$. (We may always treat x as a harmless C^∞-parameter and so we ignore its presence.) For $|\xi'| \geq 1$ we write

$$\sigma(\xi', \xi) = \sigma_0(\xi', \xi) + \sigma_1(\xi', \xi)$$

where (see (11)) σ_0 is homogenous of degree $-r$ and $\sigma_1 \in S^{-r-1}$. Thus

$$|\xi'|^{-r}\sigma(\xi', |\xi'|\xi) = \sigma_0(\omega', \xi) + |\xi'|^{-r}\sigma_1(\xi', |\xi'|\xi)$$

where we have set $\omega' = \xi'/|\xi'|$, and we shall apply Lemma 4 to this family of symbols depending on the parameter ξ' in $|\xi'| \geq 1$. We leave to the reader the easy verification of the hypotheses of that lemma, where

$$a_\pm = \lim_{\xi\to\pm\infty} \sigma_0(\omega', \xi)$$

(these are independent of ω') and the derivations are taken to be the scaled derivatives $|\xi'|\partial/\partial\xi'_i$. So (changing notation) we have a factorization

$$|\xi'|^{-r}\sigma(\xi', |\xi'|\xi) - \lambda = \tilde{\sigma}^-(\xi', \xi, \lambda)\tilde{\sigma}^+(\xi', \xi, \lambda)$$

with the factors $\tilde{\sigma}^\pm$ satisfying (32) uniformly for all $\lambda \in \Lambda_\varepsilon$, even after applying a product of derivations $|\xi'|\partial/\partial\xi'_i$ or $\lambda\ \partial/\partial\lambda$. The factors in (10) are given in terms of these by

$$\sigma^\pm(\xi', \xi, \lambda) = |\xi'|^{r/2}\tilde{\sigma}^\pm(\xi, \xi/|\xi'|, \lambda/|\xi'|^r).$$

The estimates needed to establish (13) follow routinely from the stated properties of $\tilde{\sigma}^\pm$. Just to give an idea of what happens, let us consider the estimation of a derivative $\partial(\sigma^\pm)^{-1}/\partial\xi'_i$. Use of the product and chain rules lead to four expressions. Let's look at the one involving $\partial_\lambda(\tilde{\sigma}^{\pm 1})$. It follows from the stated effect of the derivation $\lambda\partial_\lambda$ that this term is the product of one having the same bounds as $\tilde{\sigma}^{\pm 1}$ and one bounded by a constant times

$$(|\lambda|/|\xi'|^r)^{-1}(|\lambda|/|\xi'|^{r+1}) = |\xi'|^{-1}.$$

All the other estimates are established similarly.

REFERENCES

1. S. Birman and M.Z. Solomjak, Asymptotic behavior of the spectrum of weakly polar integral operators, Math. USSR-Izvestija, 4 (1970) 1151–1168.

2. G.I. Eskin, Boundary value problems for elliptic pseudo-differential equations, Amer. Math. Soc. Transl. of Math. Monographs, 52 (1981).

3. G. Grubb, The heat equation associated with a pseudo-differential boundary problem, Copenhagen Univ. Math. Inst. (preprint), 2 (1982).

4. E.C. Titchmarsh, Introduction to the theory of Fourier integrals, Oxford, 1948.

5. H. Widom, Asymptotic expansions for pseudo-differential operators on bounded domains, Springer Lecture Notes in Math, 1152 (1986).

Department of Mathematics,
University of California,
Santa Cruz, CA 95064

LIST OF PARTICIPANTS

J. Agler	Department of Mathematics, UCSD, La Jolla, CA 92093
H. Atkinson	Department of Mathematics, University of Windsor, Windsor, Canada N9B3P4
F. Al-Musallam	Department of Mathematics, Arizona State University, Tempe, AZ 85287
S. Axler	Department of Mathematics, Michigan State University, E. Lansing, MI 48824
J. A. Ball	Department of Mathematics, Virginia Polytechnic Institute and State University, Blacksburg, VA 24061
E. Basor	Department of Mathematics, California Poly, San Luis Obispo, CA 93407
C. Berger	Department of Mathematics, CUNY, Lehman College, New York, NY 10468
J. Bunce	Department of Mathematics, University of Kansas, Lawrence, KS 66045
K. Clancey	Department of Mathematics, University of Georgia, Athens, GA 30602
L. Coburn	Department of Mathematics, SUNY, Buffalo, NY 14214
N. Cohen	Department of Mathematics, Michigan State University, East Lansing, MI 48824
G. Cole	Department of Mathematics, Arizona State University, Tempe, AZ 85287
J. Conway	Department of Mathematics, Indiana University, Bloomington, IN 47405
C. Cowen	Department of Mathematics, Purdue University, West Lafayette, IN 47907
R. Curto	Department of Mathematics, University of Iowa, Iowa City, IA 52242
J. Daughtry	Department of Mathematics, East Carolina University, Greenville, NC 27834
H.V.S. de Snoo	University of Groningen, Math Inst., Postbus 800 (9700 AV) Groningen, THE NETHERLANDS
J. Doyle	Electrical Engineering Department, Caltech, Pasadena, CA 91125

H. Dym — Department of Mathematics, Weizmann Institute of Science, Rehovot (76100) ISRAEL

L. Fialkow — Department of Mathematics, SUNY, New Paltz, New Paltz, NY 12561

B. A. Francis — Electrical Engineering Department, University of Toronto, Toronto, M5S1A4, Ontario, CANADA

T. Georgiou — Electrical Engineering Department, Iowa State University, Ames, Iowa 50010

I. Gohberg — School of Mathematics, Tel Aviv University, Ramat Aviv, Tel Aviv, 69978, ISRAEL

J. W. Helton — Department of Mathematics, University of California at San Diego, La Jolla, CA 92093

D. A. Herrero — Department of Mathematics, Arizona State University, Tempe, AZ 85287

A. Hopenwasser — Department of Mathematics, University of Alabama, Tuscallossa, AL 35487

S. Hui — Department of Mathematics, Purdue University, West Lafayette, IN 47907

L. Jodar — Department of Applied Mathematics, Polytechnical University of Valencia, P. O. Box 22.012, Valencia, SPAIN

T. Kailath — Department of Mathematics, Stanford University, Stanford, CA 94305

D. Khavinson — Department of Mathematics, University of Alabama, Tuscaloosa, AL 35487-1416

G. Knowles — Department of Electrical Engineering, Texas Tech. University, Lubbock, TX 79409

P. Lancaster — Department of Mathematics, University of Calgary, Calgary T2N1N4, CANADA

P. Lang — Department of Mathematics, Idaho State University, Pocatello, Idaho 83209

D. Larson — Department of Mathematics, Texas A&M University, College Station, TX 77843-3368

K. Lewis — Department of Mathematics, University of Michigan, Ann Arbor, MI 48109

C. Libis	Department of Mathematics, Arizona State University, Tempe, AZ 85287
M. Marsalli	Department of Mathematics, Arizona State University, Tempe, AZ 85287
D. Marshall	Department of Mathematics, University of Washington, Seattle, WA 98195.
S. McCullough	Department of Mathematics, University of California, San Diego, La Jolla, CA 92093
J. N. McDonald	Department of Mathematics, Arizona State University, Tempe, AZ 85287
P. McGuire	Department of Mathematics, Bucknell University, Lewisburg, PA 17837
O. Merino	Department of Mathematics, University of California, San Diego, La Jolla, CA 92093
B. Morrel	Department of Mathematics, Indiana University - Purdue University at Indianapolis, Indianapolis, IN 46223
P. Muhly	Department of Mathematics, University of Iowa, Iowa City, IA 52242
R. Olin	Department of Mathematics, Virginia Polytechnic Institute and State University, Blacksburg, VA 24061
V. Paulsen	Department of Mathematics, University of Houston-University Park, Houston, TX 77004
S. Pedersen	Department of Mathematics, University of Iowa, Iowa City, IA 52242
S. Pinzoni	Department of Electrical and Computer Engineering, Arizona State University, Tempe, AZ 85287
G. Picci	Department of Electrical & Computer Engineering, Arizona State University, Tempe, AZ 85287
C. Prather	Department of Mathematics, Virginia Polytechnic Institute and State University, Blacksburg, VA 24061
J. Quigg	Department of Mathematics, Arizona State University, Tempe, AZ 85287
A.C.M. Ran	Vrije University, Subfaculteit Wiskunde en Informatica, 1007 MC Amsterdam, THE NETHERLANDS
R. Redheffer	Department of Mathematics, UCLA, Los Angeles, CA 90024

R. Rochberg	Department of Mathematics, Washington University, St. Louis, MO 63130
L. Rodman	Department of Mathematics, Arizona State University, Tempe, AZ 85287
J. Rovnyak	Department of Mathematics, University of Virginia, Charlottesville, VA 22903
L. Rubel	Department of Mathematics, University of Illinois, Urbana-Champaign, IL 61801
R. E. Saeks	Department of Electrical & Computer Engineering, Arizona State University, Tempe, AZ 85287
D. Sarason	Department of Mathematics, University of California at Berkeley, Berkeley, CA 94720
A. Sourour	Department of Mathematics, University of Victoria, Victoria V8W2Y2, CANADA
R. Smith	Department of Mathematics, Mississippi State University, Mississippi State, MS 39762
J. Stampfli	Department of Mathematics, Indiana University, Bloomington, IN 47405
W. Szymanski	Department of Mathematics, West Chester University, West Chester, PA 19383
A. Tannenbaum	Department of Electrical Engineering, University of Minnesota, Minneapolis, MN 55455
T. Taylor	Department of Mathematics, Arizona State University, Tempe, AZ 85287
T. Trent	Department of Mathematics, University of Alabama, Tuscaloosa, AL 35487-1416
A. Wang	Department of Mathematics, Arizona State University, Tempe, AZ 85287
J. L-M Wang	Department of Mathematics, University of Alabama, Tuscaloosa, AL 35487-1416
Z. Wang	Department of Mathematics, Arizona State University, Tempe, AZ 85287
D. Westwood	Department of Mathematics, Wright State University, Dayton, OH 45435

H. Widom — Department of Mathematics, University of California, Santa Cruz, CA 95064

H. Woerdeman — Department of Mathematics & Computer Science, Vrije Universiteit, De Boelelaan 1081 (1081HV) Amsterdam, THE NETHERLANDS

W. R. Wogen — Department of Mathematics, University of North Carolina, Chapel Hill, NC 27514

D. Xia — Department of Mathematics, Vanderbilt University, Nashville, TN 37235

J. Xia — Department of Mathematics, Indiana University-Purdue University, Indianapolis, IN 46202

R. Zhang — Department of Mathematics, Arizona State University, Tempe, AZ 85287

X. Zhu — Department of Mathematics, Arizona State University, Tempe, AZ 85287

LIST OF SPEAKERS

J. Agler	Interpolation in several variables and a theorem of Lempert.
S. Axler	Toeplitz and Hankel operators on Berman spaces.
J. A. Ball	A nonlinear Beurlig-Lax theorem with applications to nonlinear inner-outer factorization and interpolation.
C. Berger	Operator geometric techniques in the functional analysis of the bounded symmetric domains.
K. Clancey	Toeplitz operators on multiple connected domains and Theta-functions.
L. A. Coburn	Operator theory and functions of bounded mean oscillation in several complex variables.
J. B. Conway	A functional calculus for subnormal tuples and approximation in several complex variables.
C. Cowen	Subnormality and composition operators on H^2.
R. Curto	Hyponormal pairs of commuting operators.
J. Daughtry	Invariance of projections in the diagonal of a CSL algebra.
H. de Snoo	Spectral theory for canonical systems.
J. Doyle	Operator theoretic problems in control.
H. Dym	Maximum entropy principles.
L. Fialkow	Majorization and factorization in C*-algebras.
I. Gohberg	Inversion of Toeplitz matrices with rational symbols.
J. W. Helton	Positive definite matrices with given sparsity pattern.
D. A. Herrero	An essay on quasitriangularity.
A. Hopenwasser	Hilbert-Schmidt interpolation in CSL algebras.
L. Jodar	Explicit solution for the operator differential equation $Z^{(n)} + A_{n-1} Z^{(n-1)} + \ldots + A_0 Z = 0$ without increasing the dimension of the problem.

D. Khavinson	Duality and uniform approximation by solutions of elliptic equations.
G. Knowles	Hankel operators, strict cyclicity and co-prime factorizations.
P. Lancaster	Parallel algorithms for integral equations with displacement kernels.
P. Lang	Denseness of generalized eigenvectors of Hilbert-Schmidt discrete operators.
D. Larson	Some topics on reflexivity.
C. Libis	Continued fractions, Jacobi matrices and orthogonal polynomials.
M. Marsalli	A classification of operator algebras.
D. Marshall	Unzipping plane domains.
S. McCullough	3-isometries and periodic disconjugacy.
J. N. McDonald	A sequence of extremal problems for trigonometric polynomials.
P. McGuire	On the spectral picture of an irreducible subnormal operator.
B. Morrel	Similarity invariant sets of operators.
P. Muhly	Random Toeplitz and Hankel operators.
R. Olin	A characterization of cyclic subnormal operators without nontrivial disjoint invariant subspaces.
S. Pedersen	Harmonic analysis on tori.
V. Paulsen	Schur products and matrix completions.
G. Picci	Hamiltonian realization of stationary processes.
S. Pinzoni	Factor analysis models for multivariable stationary processes.
A.C.M. Ran	Hankel norm approximation of infinite dimensional systems and Wiener-Hopf factorization.
R. Redheffer	The star product in scattering and transfer.

R. Rochberg	Singular value estimates for singular integral operators.
J. Rovnyak	Vector extensions of subordination theorems for solutions of Loewner's differential equation.
L. Rubel	An application of inner-outer factorization to differential algebra.
D. Sarason	Nearly invariant subspaces of the backward shift.
J. Stampfli	Recent results on spectral sets.
W. Szymanski	Liftings in the dilation theory.
A. Tannenbaum	On the spectra of a certain class of operators appearing in control theory.
A. Tannenbaum	Local nonlinear Beurling-Lax-Halmos theorem and the linearization of manifolds in Hilbert space.
T. Taylor	A topological nonlinear stochastic realization result.
T. Trent	A Carleson measure inequality on weighted Bergman spaces.
H. Woerdeman	Minimal rank extensions of lower triangular operators: The unique case.
A. Wang	Solutions for non-stationary transfer equation.
J. L-M Wang	Approximation by rational modules.
H. Widom	The heat expansion for a system of integral operators.
W. Wogen	Smooth maps which preserve the Hardy space of the ball.
D. Xia	Analytic theory of subnormal operators.
J. Xia	On the classification of commutator ideals.
X. Zhu	A cristallographic approach to spectrum unmixing.

Integral Equations and Operator Theory

The journal is devoted to the publication of current research in integral equations, operator theory and related topics, with emphasis on the linear aspects of the theory. The very active and critical editorial board takes a broad view of the subject and puts a particularly strong emphasis on applications. The journal contains two sections, the main body consisting of refereed papers, and the second part containing short announcements of important results, open problems, information, etc. Manuscripts are reproduced directly by a photographic process, permitting rapid publication.

Subscription Information
1988 subscription
Volume 11 (6 issues)
ISSN 0378-620X

Published bimonthly
Language: English

1/88